INTERVIEWING
AND
INVESTIGATING

INTERVIEWING
AND
INVESTIGATING

ESSENTIAL SKILLS FOR THE
LEGAL PROFESSIONAL

Fifth Edition

STEPHEN P. PARSONS, J.D.

Wolters Kluwer
Law & Business

Copyright © 2013 CCH Incorporated.

Published by Wolters Kluwer Law & Business in New York.

Wolters Kluwer Law & Business serves customers worldwide with CCH, Aspen Publishers, and Kluwer Law International products. (www.wolterskluwerlb.com)

No part of this publication may be reproduced or transmitted in any form or by any means, electronic or mechanical, including photocopy, recording, or utilized by any information storage or retrieval system, without written permission from the publisher. For information about permissions or to request permissions online, visit us at www.wolterskluwerlb.com, or a written request may be faxed to our permissions department at 212-771-0803.

To contact Customer Service, e-mail customer.service@wolterskluwer.com, call 1-800-234-1660, fax 1-800-901-9075, or mail correspondence to:

Wolters Kluwer Law & Business
Attn: Order Department
PO Box 990
Frederick, MD 21705

Printed in the United States of America.

1 2 3 4 5 6 7 8 9 0

ISBN 9781454818137

Library of Congress Cataloging-in-Publication Data

Parsons, Stephen P., 1949-
    Interviewing & investigating : essential skills for the legal professional / Stephen P. Parsons, J.D. — Fifth Edition.
        pages cm. — (Aspen college series)
    Includes index.
        ISBN 978-1-4548-1813-7 — ISBN 1-4548-1813-1 1. Attorney and client—United States. 2. Interviewing in law practice—United States. 3. Investigations. 4. Evidence (Law)—United States. 5. Attorney and client—United States. 6. Legal assistants—Legal status, laws, etc.—United States. I. Title. II. Title: Interviewing and investigating.

    KF311.P373 2012
    340.023'73—dc23
                                                        2012042113

About Wolters Kluwer Law & Business

Wolters Kluwer Law & Business is a leading global provider of intelligent information and digital solutions for legal and business professionals in key specialty areas, and respected educational resources for professors and law students. Wolters Kluwer Law & Business connects legal and business professionals as well as those in the education market with timely, specialized authoritative content and information-enabled solutions to support success through productivity, accuracy and mobility.

Serving customers worldwide, Wolters Kluwer Law & Business products include those under the Aspen Publishers, CCH, Kluwer Law International, Loislaw, Best Case, ftwilliam.com and MediRegs family of products.

CCH products have been a trusted resource since 1913, and are highly regarded resources for legal, securities, antitrust and trade regulation, government contracting, banking, pension, payroll, employment and labor, and healthcare reimbursement and compliance professionals.

Aspen Publishers products provide essential information to attorneys, business professionals and law students. Written by preeminent authorities, the product line offers analytical and practical information in a range of specialty practice areas from securities law and intellectual property to mergers and acquisitions and pension/benefits. Aspen's trusted legal education resources provide professors and students with high-quality, up-to-date and effective resources for successful instruction and study in all areas of the law.

Kluwer Law International products provide the global business community with reliable international legal information in English. Legal practitioners, corporate counsel and business executives around the world rely on Kluwer Law journals, looseleafs, books, and electronic products for comprehensive information in many areas of international legal practice.

Loislaw is a comprehensive online legal research product providing legal content to law firm practitioners of various specializations. Loislaw provides attorneys with the ability to quickly and efficiently find the necessary legal information they need, when and where they need it, by facilitating access to primary law as well as state-specific law, records, forms and treatises.

Best Case Solutions is the leading bankruptcy software product to the bankruptcy industry. It provides software and workflow tools to flawlessly streamline petition preparation and the electronic filing process, while timely incorporating ever-changing court requirements.

ftwilliam.com offers employee benefits professionals the highest quality plan documents (retirement, welfare and non-qualified) and government forms (5500/PBGC, 1099 and IRS) software at highly competitive prices.

MediRegs products provide integrated health care compliance content and software solutions for professionals in healthcare, higher education and life sciences, including professionals in accounting, law and consulting.

Wolters Kluwer Law & Business, a division of Wolters Kluwer, is headquartered in New York. Wolters Kluwer is a market-leading global information services company focused on professionals.

To Marcia, Andrew, and Emily Grayce:

abeatus ter

(I am thrice blessed)

Summary of Contents

Contents

Chapter 6: Rules of Evidence for the Investigator—Part 1   175

List of Illustrations

Preface

Approach

One underlying premise to this text is that interviewing and investigating are *skills* to be mastered, rather than a unit of information to be memorized. A second is that interviewing and investigating are *essential* skills for both the lawyer and the paralegal assisting the lawyer, every bit as critical as legal research skills.

Consequently, the approach taken in the text is twofold. First, textual discussion of the subject matter is joined with hands-on learning activities in the Learn by Doing (LBD) exercises. Like any skill, interviewing and investigating can be learned effectively only by practice. Second, varied and realistic legal scenarios are provided in which the student applies the principles studied. With that in mind, the Illustrations, Examples, Hypotheticals, LBD, and Sleuth on the Loose exercises used throughout the book, as well as the Case Studies provided in Appendix A, present a variety of both civil and criminal and litigation and non-litigation scenarios.

A multi-layered approach is utilized in each chapter of this book. First, numerous brief Examples are sprinkled through the text along with frequent Illustrations. Then lengthier Hypotheticals, typically three to six, are positioned at key points throughout each chapter. The Hypotheticals present a specific factual and legal context, complete with characters, in which the student can see the application—or misapplication—of the concepts being studied. Discussion Questions accompany the Hypotheticals rather than being collected at the end of the chapter so the student, or the class as a whole, can engage in immediate analysis to reinforce the lessons taught by the Hypotheticals.

In most chapters, the Hypotheticals are serial in nature. They follow the exploits of a single new lawyer or paralegal working on a particular case. This allows the students to see how an investigation progresses over time in a real case. It also allows them to see the various types of responsibilities imposed on the lawyer or paralegal involved in investigation. And it allows them to see the consequences of decisions made and actions taken—for good or ill—as a legal matter moves along.

At the end of each chapter, numerous LBDs are presented, designed to be selectively assigned by the instructor. The LBDs require the student to close the book, go out, and engage in some hands-on learning activity related to the subject covered in the chapter. The LBD activities range from having the student determine a state's requirements for becoming a licensed private investigator (LBD 1-2); to interviewing an experienced trial attorney or litigation paralegal concerning the importance of using verbal and nonverbal communication skills to evaluate clients, witnesses, jurors, judges, and opposing counsel (LBD 8-4); locating and evaluating actual experts in various disciplines who live in the student's area (LBD 15-2); touring the local or regional office of a federal or state agency to learn, among other things, how the agency collects and maintains records and how it handles requests for information (LBD 16-3 and 17-5); and performing a factual investigation of a large local business using the Internet and other resources (LBD 18-4). Although the LBDs are collected at the end of each chapter, references to them are made at relevant points throughout the text.

Additionally, the text provides four detailed Case Studies (Appendix A), complete with characters, designed to be assigned to the students individually or in small groups. The Case Studies present realistic scenarios (a murder case, a personal injury case, a domestic relations case, and a real estate development project) and provide a vehicle for the student to put into practice the skills being learned. As the student moves through the text with an assigned Case Study, the LBDs at the end of chapters are keyed to each of the Case Studies and require the student to identify and evaluate evidentiary questions based on the facts in the case (Chapter 7); prepare a complete investigation plan for the case (Chapter 9); schedule, prepare for, and conduct the interview of a person role-playing as the client in the Case Study (Chapters 10 and 11); schedule, prepare for, and conduct the interview of a person role-playing as a witness in the case (Chapters 12 and 13); prepare investigation reports, authorizations, witness statements, and correspondence related to the case (Chapters 10–13); identify potential witnesses and plan how to locate missing witnesses in the case (Chapter 14); locate and evaluate qualified experts who might be needed in the case (Chapter 15); and determine how they would go about seeking relevant factual information in the case from federal, state, and local government sources and private sources (Chapters 16–18). In short, to learn by doing.

Great emphasis is placed in this text on resources available to the investigator, particularly Internet resources. Appendix B, Resources for the Investigator, provides a rich, diverse source of investigative tools along with information on how to locate and access them. In Appendix B, the student will find online and other resources for locating experts; online resources and an extensive bibliography on alternative dispute resolution; extensive reading lists for developing good communication skills in verbal, nonverbal, and written communication; online sources for accessing information from state and local governments and all three branches of the federal government; written and online resources for utilizing the Freedom of Information and Privacy Acts; citations to the open records acts of all fifty states; people-locating resources, from online people-search services to genealogical resources; extensive lists of records-search companies and online database vendors; and even a comprehensive section on resources for and about private investigators. References to Appendix B are made at relevant places throughout the text and a number of LBDs require the student to utilize the resources found there.

Organization of the Book

The text is divided into two parts:

- **Part 1:** Foundations for Interviewing and Investigating (Chapters 1–8)
- **Part 2:** Formulating and Executing a Plan of Investigation (Chapters 9–18)

Part 1 introduces the student to the legal contexts in which interviewing and investigating skills are utilized by attorneys and paralegals assisting them. Based on 30 years of experience as a trial attorney, the author firmly believes that in order to be effective in any understand the type of contested matter both attorneys and paralegals must:

1. understand the critical connection between law and fact;
2. be able to engage in effective factual analysis;
3. have well-developed communication skills;
4. be knowledgeable and committed to the highest standards of legal ethics; and
5. be well grounded in the adversarial system, the formal discovery rules in civil and criminal cases, the distinctions between formal and informal investigation, and the basic rules of evidence.

Accordingly, those subjects are covered in Part 1 of the book. They are studied from the viewpoint of the investigating lawyer or paralegal, with emphasis on practical application in real-life scenarios reinforced by the LBD exercises.

Part 2 of the book walks the student step by step through an investigation. We begin with how to plan an investigation and how to properly handle documents and physical evidence uncovered in an investigation (Chapter 9). Then we consider how to schedule, prepare for, and conduct a client interview (Chapters 10 and 11), and a fact witness interview (Chapters 12 and 13). Next we learn how to identify potential witnesses and how to locate the missing witness (Chapter 14). Chapter 15 is devoted to the important topic of locating, evaluating, and working with expert witnesses. The text concludes with three chapters devoted to the myriad sources of information available to the investigator, including information available from the federal government (Chapter 16), information available from state and local governments (Chapter 17), and private sources of information (Chapter 18).

Because of its emphasis in Part 1 on the legal context in which the interviewing and investigating is done, including the emphasis on the adversarial system, civil and criminal procedure, formal discovery, and the supporting Case Studies, this work can be used as a text for a litigation course as well as an investigation course. The Instructor's Manual provides a sample syllabus and suggested chapter sequencing for teaching the course over one or two academic terms, and for using the text for either a comprehensive litigation course, or a more narrowly focused interviewing/investigation or clinical practice course.

Key Features

Among the many learning tools which distinguish this book are those multi-layered features discussed above:

- Brief Examples
- Illustrations
- Hypotheticals
- Discussion Questions following the Hypotheticals
- Key Words and Phrases
- Learn by Doing exercises
- Sleuth on the Loose
- Case Studies
- Comprehensive glossary

In addition, the text contains occasional Ethical Notes and Career Tips for the student.

The text is designed for use by both law students and paralegal students. Thus the Examples, Hypotheticals, etc. refer interchangeably to lawyers or paralegals. Of course, it should be understood that unless a particular Example or Hypothetical is role-specific, it can and does apply to either category of future legal professional.

The Instructor's Manual for the text contains detailed Character Descriptions for each of the clients and witnesses mentioned in the Case Studies, Instructions for persons role-playing as clients or witnesses, and an Evaluation Form for those persons to complete for each interviewer and return to the instructor. The Instructor's Manual also contains suggested procedures for videotaping and critiquing student interviews, model syllabi, comprehensive examination questions covering all of the chapters with answer keys, and a comprehensive section containing suggested approaches to teaching with the text, including testing and grading, how to use the LBDs in each chapter, how to use Appendix B effectively, and how best to utilize the Hypotheticals, Examples, and Illustrations in each chapter. The complete texts of the Privacy Act and the Freedom of Information Act are also set out in the Instructor's Manual.

Finally, a word about the alliterative and other fictitious names used in the Hypotheticals. These names are not used simply to be clever. The author has developed these materials over fifteen years of teaching an interviewing and investigating course for paralegal students, as well as trial preparation courses for law students, and there are calculated pedagogical goals involved in the name selections. Some Hypotheticals use names keyed to the factual context. For example, in Chapter 6 we learn the importance of knowing the basic rules of evidence by following a dispute between professional golfer, Snap Hook, and his caddy, Teed Off, over an alleged promise to share the winnings in a major golf tournament. In Chapter 7, we review the specific rules of evidence by focusing on a fraud allegation made by Gulli Bull against Smooth Talker. In Chapter 9 we learn how to prepare a plan of investigation by working on an automobile accident case involving Speed Freak and Granny Puttalong. And in Chapter 14 we learn how to identify witnesses and locate missing witnesses when Turnme Loose dumps her boyfriend, Getta Life, and then turns up dead.

Other Hypotheticals use names keyed to the lesson to be learned. For example, in Chapter 2 paralegal Sally Oops teaches us the consequences of mishandling client funds, even inadvertently. The experiences of paralegal Ned Newatit demonstrate why new paralegals and the attorneys supervising them need to be familiar with the dangers of unauthorized practice of law (UPL), and why both need to be aware of the danger of disclosing client confidences. In Chapter 8, paralegal Dis Tracted illustrates the perils of not using good communication skills with co-workers. In Chapter 12, Dee Termined demonstrates how to handle the hostile witness and the skeptical witness. And in Chapters 10–13, Paul Perfect just does a, well, perfect job of preparing for and conducting client and witness interviews.

Thus, the names serve not only to catch and hold the *attention* of the student but also to constantly *remind* the student of what the Hypothetical is about and to *reinforce* the concept being taught. Of course, the names might also make the learning experience a little more enjoyable for the students and even for the instructor.

To keep the dates used in Illustrations, Examples, and Case Studies current, this fifth edition continues to use the flexible year notation system in which YR00 is always the present year. Previous years are designated as YR-1, YR-2, YR-3, etc. Future years are designated YR+1, YR+2, YR+3, etc. The instructor can choose to have students use this year designation system in documents they are assigned to prepare or have them convert the year designations in the materials to the actual year of use.

New for the Fifth Edition

For this fifth edition, all Web sites have been updated and references to many new Web sites and more than a dozen new cases are included. A number of fresh new LBD and Sleuth on the Loose features have been added throughout the text. All references to the Federal Rules of Civil Procedure in Chapters 3 and 4 have been brought into compliance with the Federal Courts Jurisdiction and Venue Clarification Act of 2011. Likewise, all references to the Federal Rules of Criminal Procedure in Chapter 4 and to the Federal Rules of Evidence in Chapters 5 and 6 are updated to the latest amendments approved by Congress.

Significantly, the material in Part 1 of the text dealing with the Foundations for Interviewing and Investigating has been expanded to make it more comprehensive. Subjects such as personal and subject matter jurisdiction in civil cases, venue, and alternative dispute resolution in Chapter 3 are dealt with in more detail than ever before, and a number of new Examples and Illustrations added. The continuing impact of the Supreme Court's adoption of the plausibility standard in civil pleadings in *Iqbal* and *Twombley* is dealt with, as well as that Court's dramatic revision of the notion of corporate citizenship for purposes of diversity of citizenship in *Hertz Corp. v. Friend*. The material on discovery from an opponent's expert witnesses in Chapter 4 has been revised to reflect recent changes to the wording of FRCP 26 and expanded with new Examples. The discussion of e-discovery in Chapter 4 has been reorganized as well as updated in order to make it clearer. The coverage of the Federal Rules of Evidence in Chapter 7 has also been significantly expanded and new Examples added, particularly in connection with the hearsay rule and its exceptions.

Both Parts 1 and 2 of the text have been updated as appropriate to reflect continuing changes in communication technology. Thus the topics of e-discovery in Chapter 4, identifying and locating witnesses in Chapter 14, and the identification of private, non-governmental sources of information from individuals and entities in Chapter 18, all include discussions of the latest developments in online social networking and technology. In Chapter 13, paralegal Paul Perfect now records his interview with Bee Mufriend using his new smart phone rather than a tape recorder, takes a photo using his phone, dictates a memorandum using the word recognition software on the phone, and e-mails all three digital files from the phone to an e-mail address so the files can be downloaded onto other computers. He even Tweets about his career satisfaction. The fifth edition floats in the e-cloud.

The material treating public records held by state and local governments in Chapter 17 and particularly the explanation of what state public records acts cover and how they are used procedurally has been significantly expanded with new Illustrations and Examples.

Previous editions of the text included three appendices containing selected sections of the federal rules of civil and criminal procedure and evidence. That was never ideal since the rules are amended annually in December in small or large ways, and thus the printed excerpts were quickly out of date. Given that drawback, the easy accessibility of current versions of the rules online, and the near ubiquitous online savvy of today's college students, those appendices are deleted for this fifth edition. Instead, in the chapters dealing with those rules (Chapters 3–7) the text provides students with one or more online sites where versions of the rules being studied are always current and encourages the student to access and reference those rules as the relevant chapters are studied. The instructor is encouraged to remind students to access the current rules online as they study those chapters of the text and to use online technology in the classroom to display the current rule as it is being considered in class discussion.

With the elimination of those three old appendices, the Resources for the Investigator material now is found in Appendix B rather than Appendix E as it was in earlier editions. But have no fear—that material has been freshened and expanded to be more comprehensive and practical than ever before.

Textbook Resources

The companion Web site for Stephen P. Parsons's *Interviewing and Investigating: Essential Skills for the Legal Professional*, Fifth edition, at www.aspenparalegaled.com/books/parsons_investigating/default.asp includes additional resources for students and instructors, including:

- Study aids to help students master the key concepts for this course. Visit the site to access interactive StudyMate exercises such as flash cards, matching, fill-in-the-blank, and crosswords. These activities are also available for download to an iPod or other handheld device.
- Instructor resources to accompany the text.
- Links to helpful websites and updates.

Instructor resources to accompany this text include a comprehensive Instructor's Manual, Test Bank, and PowerPoint slides. All of these materials are available for download from our companion Web site.

In Appreciation

For this fifth edition the author has again had the good fortune to be ably assisted by a number of people at Wolters Kluwer Law & Business. Special mention goes to Appalachian School of Law students Joseph McAfee and Kyle Moore who assisted so ably with research for the last two editions. And a very special thanks to all of my paralegal students at Walters State Community College and law students at Appalachian School of Law, who are the continuing inspiration for this project and who for years have served as its willing crash dummies. Thanks guys, and bless your hearts.

February 2013   Stephen P. Parsons

Acknowledgments

The author is grateful to copyright holders and others for providing permission and assistance in using the following materials:

American Arbitration Association, Submission to Resolution Services, Form SRS 605.

Johnny Hart and Creators Syndicate, Inc., Wizard of Id cartoon dated 9-2-96. Copyright © 1996, Creators Syndicate, Inc.

Lyndon Baines Johnson Library, Austin, Texas, for assistance in locating and using the LBJ/Abe Fortas photograph. From the LBJ Library collection. Photographed by Yoichi R. Okamoto.

Phillip Margolin, excerpt from *The Last Innocent Man*. Copyright © 1995 by Phillip Margolin.

American Bar Association, references to the *ABA Model Rules of Professional Conduct*, 2009 Edition. Copyright ©2009 by the American Bar Association. Copies of the *ABA Model Rules of Professional Conduct*, 2008 Edition are available from Service Center, American Bar Association, 321 North Clark Street, Chicago, IL 60654, 1-800-285-2221.

INTERVIEWING
AND
INVESTIGATING

PART ONE

FOUNDATIONS FOR INTERVIEWING
AND INVESTIGATING

PART OUTLINE

Chapter 1

Introduction to Interviewing and Investigating

CHAPTER OBJECTIVES

In this introductory chapter you will learn:

- Why lawyers do interviewing and investigating work
  and need new associates and paralegals skilled at
  these tasks.
- Why it is important for the legal professional to also be
  skilled at legal research and writing and to know the
  rules of evidence and procedure, basic substantive
  law, and principles of legal ethics and
  professionalism.
- The role of the legal professional in interviewing and
  investigating.

A. Why These Skills Are Important to the Lawyer

"You ever play any sports in high school or college?"

David shrugged.

"I ran a little track in college and wrestled some."

"Okay. Why don't you tell me how trying a case compares to the feeling you get just before a sporting event. How's that?"

David thought for a few minutes before answering.

"I don't think they're that similar," David said. "Winning or losing at sports depends on your performance during the sporting event, but a lawyer can't win a case at trial. Or, anyway, not usually."

"What do you mean?"

"Well, the facts of each case are determined by the time the case gets to you. All the facts might not be revealed, but they're there. So a lawyer wins his case before trial by finding out, through investigation, what the facts are. A lawyer can't change the facts, but once he knows what the facts are, he can deal with them. Try to get the jury to look at them in a certain way. And there is usually more than one way to look at the facts.

"A few years back I represented a man who tried to hold up a mini-mart. He walked in with a shotgun and told the manager to give him the money or he would kill him. The manager was a feisty little guy, and he whipped out a handgun and shot my client through the neck. When the police arrived, my man was lying in a pool of blood holding the gun, and there were five eyewitnesses who swore that he tried to rob the place. The DA charged my client with armed robbery. Those were the facts I started with. Want to guess the verdict?"

Gault smiled.

"It has to be not guilty, but how did you do it?"

"There were other facts we didn't know about when we started. When they took the defendant to the hospital for surgery, they took a blood sample. One of the routine checks the hospital makes before performing surgery is to find out how much alcohol a person has in his system. My man was loaded. He had consumed so much alcohol that I was able to get two prominent psychiatrists to testify that a person in his condition would not be able to form the intent to commit the crime, and the district attorney must prove intent as one of the elements of the crime of armed robbery.

"The next step was to find out why my client drank like that. It turned out that his wife had died and he had gone to pieces. When I got him, he was already an alcoholic.

"Finally, we had to figure out why he had been at the minimart in the first place. My investigator asked around, and it turned out that our boy had been blotto that day. Two of his buddies had planned the robbery and sent him inside. He was so drunk, he didn't know what he was doing. In fact, he doesn't remember what happened to this day.

"When we presented all the facts to the jury, they acquitted. It wasn't what we did at trial, but the investigation before trial, that mattered. Getting the facts, then presenting them in a favorable light at trial."

—Excerpt from *The Last Innocent Man*,
Copyright © 1981, 1995 by Phillip Margolin.

Investigation is the process by which attorneys and those assisting them gather relevant information from a variety of public and private sources in order to successfully represent the interests of their client. The ability to effectively interview clients, potential witnesses, and other persons who may have helpful information is a critical part of the investigation process. These skills are essential in criminal and civil litigation matters and in all other types of legal representation as well.

1. The relationship between law and fact

The law does not exist in a vacuum. In every matter that a lawyer handles for a client the **facts** that are discovered will determine what **law** controls. Even a slight change in the facts can result in a change in the controlling law. When facts are disputed as between parties to a lawsuit, that dispute will give rise to competing arguments by the attorneys for those parties as to which facts are more believable and, consequently, as to what law should control the dispute. And if the dispute is litigated in a civil or criminal lawsuit, the judge or the jury, sitting as finder(s) of fact, will have to make a decision as to what the actual facts are before applying the applicable law to those facts to reach a decision. **Interviewing** and **investigating** are the means by which lawyers identify and gather the facts that will control the law of the case.

HYPOTHETICAL 1-1

Assume that in your state the criminal homicide statutes permit the state to charge and convict a person for first degree murder based on proof of the willful, deliberate, and premeditated taking of a human life; for second degree murder based on proof of the willful taking of human life but without deliberation or premeditation; for manslaughter based on proof of reckless behavior (including sudden passion) that forseeably results in the taking of a human life; and for negligent homicide based on proof of negligent behavior that forseeably results in the taking of a human life. The use of reasonable force in self-defense or in defense of a third party is recognized in your state. This is the law of the case. The attorney you work for is representing Quick Temper, who is charged with first degree murder in the shooting death of his neighbor, Hi Fi. The indictment alleges that Quick Temper told a friend the day before the killing that he hated Hi Fi because he played loud music all night long, that Quick Temper purchased a rifle the day of the murder, that he laid in wait in the darkness outside Hi Fi's door, and that he shot Hi Fi as the victim entered his apartment.

What difference might it make to the outcome of this case if your investigation turns up the following facts?

1. Quick Temper had abandoned his plan to kill Hi Fi but dropped the rifle on the ground as he was leaving the scene. The gun discharged, and the bullet struck and killed Hi Fi.
2. Quick Temper had been adjudicated mentally incompetent a week before the shooting.
3. The neighbor living on the other side of Hi Fi also hated him and had fired a rifle at him at the same time as Quick Temper.
4. Quick Temper fired the shot that killed Hi Fi but was actually trying to hit the neighbor who was aiming her gun at Hi Fi.
5. Quick Temper had fired at Hi Fi only when he saw Hi Fi kissing his (Quick Temper's) wife.
6. Hi Fi had threatened to kill Quick Temper and in fact had a gun in his hand at the time of the shooting. (But what if it was a sling shot and not a gun?)
7. Quick Temper thought the gun was not loaded and only intended to scare Hi Fi.
8. The rifle discharged not because Quick Temper pulled the trigger but because of a defect in the firing mechanism.
9. Although the bullet fired by Quick Temper did strike Hi Fi, the actual cause of death was a massive heart attack that occurred immediately before the shot was fired.
10. Quick Temper did tell the friend of his hatred for Hi Fi but said this five years before the shooting.

What other facts can you hypothesize that, if discovered, would change the application of the law to Quick Temper's situation?

None of the facts in Hypothetical 1-1 change the law. But they do dramatically change the application of the law to the case and thus the potential outcome of the case. Factual investigation is an essential skill for those involved in the legal system.

2. Factual analysis

Think for a moment about the process your mind went through as you considered whether and how each of the facts given to you in Hypothetical 1-1 impacted on the legal issue of whether Quick Temper should be charged or convicted under any of the criminal homicide statutes. We call this process **factual analysis.** Factual analysis is a **critical thinking** skill. It is the process of taking information, making sure that you understand it, evaluating it in order to determine if it is reliable, and then applying it to determine the impact or difference it makes on your legal question. From that definition, we can see that there are three steps involved in the process of factual analysis:

- *Comprehension*   of the law and of the facts discovered;
- *Evaluation*   of the facts discovered to see if they are reliable; and
- *Application*   of the facts to the legal issues.

Let's consider each of these three steps in turn.

a. Comprehension

You must **comprehend** or understand the law you are dealing with in a given case and the facts that you discover in the investigation. For example, if the investigator does not understand that in order to convict Quick Temper of first degree murder the state must prove that he took the life of Hi Fi willfully, deliberately, and with premeditation, then the investigator will be unable to see the relevance of fact no. 1 in Hypothetical 1-1—that Quick Temper had abandoned his plan to kill Hi Fi, but dropped his rifle on the ground with the result that it fired and killed Hi Fi anyway.

Once we do understand the law—that *willfully* means that Quick Temper must have intended Hi Fi's death when he dropped the rifle; that *deliberately* means he must have acted with the purpose of taking Hi Fi's life when he dropped the rifle; and that *premeditation* means that he must have acted with forethought in taking Hi Fi's life—then and only then are we able to recognize that this fact, if true, means that Quick Temper did not take Hi Fi's life willfully, deliberately, or with premeditation.

Unless the legal professional investigating a case has a basic understanding of the law at issue in a client's case, she will be unable to do effective investigation. She won't know what factual information to look for and she won't recognize relevant information even if she stumbles over it!

And, of course, the investigator must be able to understand the factual information she discovers as well. That may sound simple enough when we are talking about someone who tells us they accidentally dropped a rifle. But factual information sometimes comes in such great volume that it is difficult to assess. And factual information also comes to us in more complex forms, such as the financial statements of a corporation that we must be able to read with comprehension. And often factual information comes to us in technical jargon that we must be able to interpret, such as when a computer expert throws out terms like *URL, HTML, digital subscriber loop,* or *arithmetic logic unit,* and expects the interviewer to understand them.

b. Evaluation

By **evaluation of information** we mean that every piece of information discovered in a legal investigation has to be examined carefully. We have to test it and compare it to other information we have, in order to determine whether and to what extent it is *reliable.*

The first commandment in interviewing and investigating work is: **DON'T ASSUME ANYTHING.** In particular, don't assume that everything you are told by a client or witness or everything you read in a document is automatically true, accurate, complete, or trustworthy.

SLEUTH ON THE LOOSE

Do you Google, Yahoo, or Bing? Of the three most popular search engines, Google (www.google.com) accounts for 64% of all searches, Yahoo (www.yahoo.com) for 20%, and Microsoft's new Bing (www.bing.com) for 18%. Conduct a search using all three of these search engines by entering the name of someone you want to know more about. See what different information each search engine locates. Do the same for yourself by entering your name, or the name of someone in your family.

- Sometimes people lie.
- Sometimes people tell half-truths.
- Sometimes people are mistaken in what they thought they heard or saw.
- Sometimes people guess but don't tell you they're guessing.
- Sometimes people forget or misremember what they heard or saw in the past.
- Sometimes people make unwarranted assumptions and pass those assumptions off as fact.
- Sometimes people speak in conclusions that are not supported by fact.
- Sometimes people allow their prejudices to color what they "know."
- Sometimes people have only second- or third-hand information rather than first-hand information but leave it to the interviewer to figure that out.
- Sometimes people confuse their opinions with facts.
- Sometimes people are reluctant to tell what they know.
- Sometimes two people can hear or see the same event and each describe it differently from the other while both swear they are telling the truth.
- Sometimes the same types of inaccuracies and falsehoods get included in documents.

Welcome to the real world! We assume nothing in legal investigation. Instead, we follow the second commandment of interviewing and investigating, which is: **VERIFY EVERYTHING.** That means we evaluate information that comes to us by testing it. We take it apart and put it back together. We sift it and shake it and turn it on its head until we can reach a conclusion regarding its accuracy and reliability. More specifically:

- We attempt to determine if the source of the information is competent, honest, reliable, and objective.
- We try to filter out opinions, assumptions, and statements of prejudice to get to the real, provable facts.

- We distinguish between first-hand information and second- or third-hand information.
- We work to verify the information by seeking corroboration (information that tends to confirm or verify other information).
- We seek details and leads to other sources of information.
- We seek clarification of confusing or incomplete information.
- We compare the information to other information we have found and see how the different pieces of information fit together.
- We look for contradictions and inconsistencies.
- We look for gaps in information and seek to fill them in.
- We draw reasonable inferences from the information we locate but seek confirmation nonetheless.
- We resist the urge to draw unwarranted conclusions from information and look for hard evidence.

This is factual evaluation and it is at the heart of the interviewing and investigating process.

EXAMPLE

Assume that our source for the information that Quick Temper abandoned his plan to shoot and kill Hi Fi but dropped the gun as he was leaving is Quick Temper himself. How reliable is that source? Not very reliable, is it? Why? Because Quick Temper has a strong motive to lie—to save himself! But what if the source of that information is a bystander who says she was there and saw Quick Temper walk away from Hi Fi's house and drop the gun? More reliable? Yes, but remember the first commandment—don't assume anything. If the prosecutor's paralegal investigator follows that commandment, he may discover that the bystander is actually Quick Temper's sister, or is legally blind, or was actually driving by in a car at 90 mph at the time, or is mentally insane, or has a history of telling lies to the police to get attention. Attorneys, and those who assist them, are constantly searching for new factual information relevant to the legal issues in the client's case. And they are constantly evaluating and testing the facts discovered to determine their accuracy and reliability.

c. Application

The final step in factual analysis is the determination of whether the information we locate, regardless of its reliability, is **legally relevant.** By that we mean, does the information matter? Does it arguably impact or make a difference on the legal issues we are considering? Could it be significant in any way for the legal problem we are handling for the client?

EXAMPLE

Assume that in the course of your investigation you discover that Quick Temper is 45 years old and still lives with his mother. You may be able to verify that information as absolutely true. But so what? Are those facts relevant to whether Quick Temper violated any one of the homicide statutes? They don't appear to be. So what will we do with these facts? We will categorize them as irrelevant to any legal issue we have and set them aside—at least for now.

This **categorizing of information** is an important part of the factual analysis process. It is the ability to look at information from all different sides and angles and to recognize what information is relevant—is significant and makes a difference—and what information is not. If information is not relevant to any legal issue before us, we cull it out.

We not only categorize factual information according to whether it is legally relevant but we also consider which legal issue(s) it is relevant to.

EXAMPLE

> The information contained in fact no. 4 of Hypothetical 1-1, that Quick Temper fired his rifle not at Hi Fi but at a neighbor who was aiming a gun at Hi Fi, is not legally relevant to the question of whether Quick Temper "willfully" took a human life—he admits he shot to kill. But it is relevant to the legal defense he will assert—using reasonable force to defend the life of a third person. The investigator must be able to categorize information in order to understand why it is relevant and where it fits in among all the legal issues and other facts.

Not only is the information we gather in a factual investigation usually relevant to different legal issues, sometimes the information appears to be irrelevant to any issue, then later becomes relevant because a new issue arises.

EXAMPLE

> Remember those facts we established, that Quick Temper is 45 years old and still lives with his mother? Not significant, until his mother testifies that her son couldn't have killed Hi Fi because at the time of the shooting he was with her at the mall! Now those facts become very relevant. The prosecution will bring those facts out in order to show that the mother is close to the son and thus is biased in his favor and has a strong motive to lie for him.

Go through the factual statements set out in Hypothetical 1-1. For each fact given, identify every legal issue, if any, to which you think that fact is legally relevant. Be prepared to explain why you think that fact is (or isn't) relevant to that issue.

Factual analysis is central to the interviewing and investigating tasks. It is a learned art. It takes work and practice. The legal professional gets better at it with practice, and we will attempt to give you plenty of practice in succeeding chapters.

3. The role of factual investigation in civil litigation

a. By the attorney for the plaintiff

In **civil litigation** (the distinction between civil and criminal law is discussed in detail in Chapter 3), the attorney who is retained by the potential plaintiff will engage in factual investigation *before* filing a complaint initiating the lawsuit. This **pre-filing investigation** is done in order to determine:

- if the client has a valid **cause of action** on any legal theory;
- if the client has a timely cause of action in light of the controlling statute(s) of limitation and repose;
- the likelihood that the client will be able to prevail if suit is brought;
- the existence and relative strength of any defenses that may limit or defeat the client's recovery;
- the identity and availability of all potential defendants;
- the likelihood of a counterclaim being filed against the plaintiff;
- the solvency of potential defendants and the existence of insurance or indemnity agreements as sources to satisfy a judgment;
- the identity, availability, and value of potential witnesses; and
- the existence and value of all documentation and physical proof that may tend to support or defeat the client's claim.

All of this will go into the decision to file the lawsuit and, if so, against whom and on what theories.

b. By the attorney for the defendant

The attorney retained to represent the defendant in a civil suit will need to do investigation prior to filing an answer or other response to the complaint in order to determine:

- whether to admit or deny the allegations in the complaint;
- whether any factual or affirmative defenses are available;
- whether a motion to dismiss or for summary judgment is advisable;
- whether a counterclaim against the plaintiff exists on behalf of his client;
- whether a cross-claim against a third party exists on behalf of his client; and
- how to evaluate the case for his client, i.e., the likelihood and cost of winning or losing and thus the advisability of attempting to settle out of court and, if so, on what terms.

HYPOTHETICAL 1-2

Assume you work in a law office specializing in plaintiff's personal injury work. A potential new client, Road Rage, meets with you and tells you he was involved in a car accident when another driver, Lead Foot, ran a red light at an intersection and collided with his car.

Also assume that in your state, to recover on a theory of negligence a plaintiff must allege and prove that the defendant owed a duty of care to the plaintiff; that the defendant breached that duty; that the injuries of plaintiff were in fact and foreseeably caused by that breach of duty; and that the plaintiff was in fact injured. Your state is a pure comparative fault jurisdiction, which means the plaintiff's ultimate recovery will be reduced by any percentage of fault the jury attributes to him rather than the defendant. The statute of limitations for filing a personal injury action is one year. This is the law of the case.

What factual investigation will you probably want to do before recommending that your office file suit on behalf of Road Rage? What kind of questions will you ask Road Rage? Who else do you want to interview? What documents or physical evidence do you want to locate and view? Consider how what you find out in your investigation will affect the decision to take this case.

If you work in the law office representing Lead Foot when Road Rage files suit, what factual investigation will you want to do before drafting a response to the complaint filed by Road Rage?

4. The role of factual investigation in criminal litigation

In **criminal litigation** (the distinction between civil and criminal law is discussed in detail in Chapter 3), the prosecution will engage in pre-filing investigation for the same reasons that the civil plaintiff's attorney does, except that the legal theories explored will be criminal rather than civil. Likewise, the criminal defense attorney will engage in investigation in order to:

- evaluate the government's charges against his client;
- advise his client how to plead and whether to defend the charges or plea bargain; and
- prepare the defense for trial.

HYPOTHETICAL 1-3

Using the facts set out in Hypothetical 1-1 involving Quick Temper and the death of Hi-Fi, assume you work for the state prosecutor. What, if any, homicide crime would you recommend Quick Temper be charged with in connection with each of the assumptions set out in Hypothetical 1-1?

If you worked for counsel defending Quick Temper on a first degree murder charge, what recommendation would you make regarding a plea bargain versus trying the case in connection with each of the assumptions set out in Hypothetical 1-1?

And, as with civil litigation, factual investigation continues in a criminal case after the case is commenced up until the time of trial.

5. The role of factual investigation in other legal representation

Interviewing and investigating skills are also vital to the lawyer engaged in representing a client in a non-litigation matter. In any commercial, corporate, or private legal matter the lawyer must determine:

- what options are available to the client based on the available facts;
- what risks and rewards there are for the client with regard to each such option;

- the advisability of pursuing one available option over another; and
- how best to put together the information necessary to accomplish the goals selected.

HYPOTHETICAL 1-4

Assume that you work for a law firm specializing in business and commercial law. A husband and wife and their two adult children come to see your supervising attorney and tell him that they have come up with a sensational recipe for cinnamon rolls. They have been selling their rolls (which they call Sinfully Cinnamon Sensations) in their neighborhood with great success. The feedback has been so positive and the demand so great that the four have decided to quit their other jobs and go into business full time producing the cinnamon rolls and distributing them regionally at first and then perhaps nationally.

During the conference you hear your supervising lawyer tell the clients that, from a legal standpoint, they will have to make initial decisions regarding securing product and name protection; whether to do business as a corporation, partnership, or limited liability company, including tax considerations; how to raise necessary financing; whether and when to franchise or license the product to others; where and how to initially market their product; compliance with federal, state, and local regulations or ordinances governing food production, packaging and distribution; distribution agreements; and liability insurance.

What questions would you want to ask these clients or others on each of these topics?

B. ► Other Skills and Areas of Knowledge Related to Interviewing and Investigating

Interviewing and investigating are not isolated skills. Legal professionals undertake these activities for specific reasons and with particular goals in mind. And the legal professional who wishes to be successful at interviewing and investigating must have a number of related skills and be knowledgeable in other areas related to the law.

1. Substantive law

It is critical that the legal professional engaging in interviewing and investigating have a firm foundation in various areas of **substantive law**. Substantive law is the law that defines the rights and duties of persons with respect to each other, as opposed to **procedural law,** which defines the manner in which those rights and duties may be enforced. Examples of substantive law include constitutional law, contract law, the law of business associations, tort law, criminal law, real property law, and so on. Knowledge of substantive law is essential in order for the paralegal to:

- understand why and for what purposes the investigation is being done in a particular case;

- plan a successful investigation; and
- identify all sources of information available regarding a particular legal matter.

EXAMPLE

If the legal professional is asked to investigate a corporation as a potential defendant in a civil lawsuit, it will be critical for the investigator to understand how corporations are created under the law, how they function, how they are organized, the records they must keep or usually keep, the sources of public and private information about corporations, etc. Without such knowledge no plan of investigation will be successful.

2. Legal research and writing

Interviewing and investigating are sister skills to legal research and writing. Facts that are gathered in the investigation must be fitted into civil causes of action and defenses, criminal charges and defenses, legal business arrangements, or whatever the subject matter of the representation is. The legal professional must have the ability to locate and understand the law and the ability to apply the facts discovered to the law involved in the representation.

Using the situations described in Hypotheticals 1-1, 1-2, and 1-4, what legal issues might you want to research? Other than your research memorandum, what legal documents might you need to draft in those various hypothetical situations?

3. Rules of evidence

In litigation matters, the legal investigator must have a knowledge of the fundamental rules of evidence that will govern in the trial of the matter, whether civil or criminal. (See Chapters 6 and 7.) Such knowledge not only has an impact on the decision of what evidence to pursue, but the form in which evidence must be obtained in order to be admissible in a court of law, as well as the importance of properly storing and preserving evidence in such a way as to prevent attack on its authenticity or reliability.

EXAMPLE

If the state charges Quick Temper with first degree murder as suggested in Hypothetical 1-1, there may be evidentiary questions of relevance and hearsay raised at trial regarding the statement of Quick Temper to the friend concerning his hatred of Hi Fi, and questions of authenticity and hearsay regarding the sales receipt for the rifle. What other evidentiary questions can you foresee based on the various factual findings set out in Hypothetical 1-1?

4. The adversarial system and rules of procedure

In litigation matters, the legal investigator must have an understanding of the adversarial system, knowledge of various statutes of limitation and repose (see Chapter 3), and knowledge of the rules of civil or criminal procedure that will govern the proceeding (see Chapters 4 and 5). This will determine the form and the timing of the investigation, as well as the procedures that must be followed in order to accomplish **formal discovery**.

EXAMPLE

> We have already seen in Hypothetical 1-2 that the date of an event needs to be factually determined as early as possible to determine if the client can now bring an otherwise valid cause of action.

5. Ethics and professional responsibility

The legal investigator must be knowledgeable of and comply with all ethical obligations (see Chapter 2). Both the attorney engaging in investigative work and the paralegal assisting the attorney either as an employee or contract agent of the attorney must know and comply with the ethical rules that govern that attorney. In particular, the ethical rules governing client confidentiality, conflicts of interest, the unauthorized practice of law, how to contact a party already represented by counsel, the duty of competence, and the handling of client funds and other property should be well known and observed.

Keep in mind too that ethical and legal requirements frequently overlap. Behavior that is unethical may also be criminal. The unauthorized practice of law is a good example. It is not only unethical for an unlicensed person to engage in the practice of law, it is likely to be a crime as well. And a lawyer that allows an unlicensed person such as a paralegal to engage in the practice of law may have committed a crime. Another example is the mishandling of client funds. There are not only strict ethical rules governing this but, in addition, to mishandle those funds may constitute a theft crime or some type of criminal fraud. Unethical behavior may also give rise to civil causes of action against the offending legal professional. To the extent that a client's interests are damaged, the client may have a cause of action to recover those damages under breach of contract, breach of fiduciary duty, or tort theory.

C. The Lawyer's Use of Paralegals in Interviewing and Investigating

1. Lawyers using paralegals

In the last generation paralegals have become a fixture in the practice of law. Private law firms, whether large, medium, or small, have found paralegals to be an efficient, economic way to deliver quality legal services to clients. Federal, state, and local agencies have made increasing use of trained legal assistants, and the legal and other departments of numerous corporations depend on them. Many paralegals now specialize in certain areas of the law just like the lawyers who supervise them. (See LBD 1-7.)

Across the country, hundreds of colleges and universities have established degree and certificate programs in paralegal studies, and there are a number of non-degree private training programs available as well. The American Bar Association has established guidelines for the operation of paralegal training programs and a rigorous inspection/approval process for programs that wish to present themselves as operating in compliance with ABA guidelines. Nationwide, more than 200 paralegal programs have received ABA approval, and hundreds more operate excellent programs without seeking ABA approval. (See LBD 1-8.)

Today it is as crucial for attorneys to understand the proper role and function of a paralegal as it is for them to know how to use Westlaw or Lexis. In addition to performing legal research and drafting legal documents, attorneys use paralegals to interview clients and witnesses, conduct informal factual investigation, and assist in formal discovery. Thus the following information regarding how attorneys use paralegals in interviewing and investigating is as important for attorneys to know as it is for paralegals.

2. Definition of a paralegal

The widely accepted definition of a **paralegal** is the one developed by the American Bar Association's Committee on Ethics and Responsibility:

> A person qualified by education, training or work experience who is employed or retained by a lawyer, law office, corporation, governmental agency or other entity and who performs specifically delegated substantive legal work for which a lawyer is responsible.

In most jurisdictions, and for our purposes in this text, the terms **paralegal** and **legal assistant** are used interchangeably. (See LBD 1-9.)

3. The paralegal as an agent of the attorney

In the eyes of the law, a paralegal working with an attorney is an **agent** of that attorney and a **subagent** of the attorney's client. That has many ramifications, including:

a. *The actions of the paralegal may be legally binding on the attorney and the client*

EXAMPLE

Assume a paralegal is authorized by her supervising attorney to set up a deposition for the client. The paralegal is told to set up the deposition for a time *after* the opposing party is deposed. If the paralegal ignores or forgets those instructions and agrees for the client to be deposed before the opposing party, that agreement may be enforced against the supervising attorney by the court under principles of **agency** law.

b. The attorney may be liable for damages caused to another by the paralegal

Under the doctrine of *respondeat superior* (Latin for "let the master respond"), also called **vicarious liability** (when legal responsibility is placed on one for the acts of another), the attorney who employs and supervises the paralegal may be liable along with the paralegal herself for damages incurred by the client or others due to the negligent and sometimes even the fraudulent or intentional acts of the paralegal.

c. The attorney may be sanctioned for actions of the paralegal

The attorney employer of the paralegal who engages in unethical or unprofessional conduct while acting for the attorney may receive sanctions from the state body that regulates attorney behavior. These sanctions are enforced as if the attorney himself had engaged in the behavior or for the attorney's failure to properly supervise the paralegal.

4. Paralegals as licensed private investigators

Attorneys and paralegals should check the **private investigators** licensing statute in the state(s) where they practice (see LBD 1-1, 1-2, 1-3, and 1-6). The wording of these statutes as to what constitutes engaging in private investigating (and thus requires a license from the state for that purpose) varies widely, as does the wording of exceptions to the licensing requirement. For example, under some statutes, one engaging in this work on behalf of an attorney need not secure a private investigator's license but must be careful not to identify themselves or hold themselves out as a private investigator.

Some attorneys may prefer that paralegals engaging in investigation who work on their behalf on a regular basis obtain a private investigator's license. The procedure for that is also controlled by state law, but is typically not difficult or expensive.

5. What attorneys expect from paralegals

Though specific expectations and ways of doing things will vary from attorney to attorney, it is safe to say that attorneys utilizing paralegals to engage in interviewing and investigating work will expect the paralegal to have, in addition to the related skills discussed in this chapter, a professional attitude, good people skills, and highly developed investigative skills. More specifically that means:

a. The willingness to work under the supervision of the attorney

It is one thing to understand that a paralegal is defined as one who performs certain tasks under the supervision of an attorney. But it is another to *accept* that limitation and be willing to abide by it every day in the law office.

CAREER TIP

Obtaining one's private investigator's license may also be a smart career move for a paralegal. It may make your credentials more appealing to a hiring attorney and may qualify you to work for an experienced private investigator as an alternative career. It is also a step toward working for yourself if you truly enjoy this kind of work.

b. The initiative to clarify assignments

Sometimes the assignment the paralegal receives will be unclear in scope or purpose. It is critical in those situations for the paralegal to know that she should go back to the supervising attorney and clarify the assignment rather than making a guess and proceeding on it.

c. Good judgment

For example, you need the judgment to know when to use your own initiative to complete an assignment already given, and when to come back to the attorney for further authority—not always easy. Good judgment comes from experience in doing this kind of work, experience in working with a particular attorney, and common sense. A good rule of thumb here for the paralegal is *better safe than sorry!*

d. The discipline to keep the supervising attorney well advised

In investigating, it is critical for the paralegal to report back promptly to the supervising attorney, to keep him thoroughly and regularly advised regarding the status of the investigation. Keep in mind that the attorney's ethical responsibility is to supervise the paralegal's work and it is the attorney who maintains the direct relationship with the client. The attorney must be kept advised to fulfill both these responsibilities.

e. The ability to work well under pressure

There is tremendous pressure in a law office. Heavy workloads, pressing time deadlines, and demanding clients are the stuff our days are made of. But the work is challenging and rewarding—for those who can handle the pressure.

f. Good communication and people skills

Communication skills are essential to the paralegal to work effectively with the assigning attorney, other staff in the office, opposing counsel and her staff, the client, witnesses, and other information sources (see Chapter 8).

g. Objectivity

It is easy for the attorney or the paralegal to identify emotionally with the problems or position of a client or witness (or in some instances, the position of an adverse party). That is a very human instinct that you do not want to extinguish. However, part of being a professional is the ability to set those feelings aside and *do your job*.

The affirmative ethical obligation of the attorney (and her agents) to represent the interests of a client demands objectivity. This may mean asking tough questions to someone obviously upset by them. It may mean digging up and reporting negative information about likeable or pitiable people. It may also mean resisting the urge to sugarcoat your analysis of the damage that a witness is going to do to the position of a client you like very much. The possibilities are endless. The paralegal, like the lawyer, must learn to set certain feelings aside and do the job.

SLEUTH ON THE LOOSE

Identify an attorney or law firm you would like to know more about then access the Martindale-Hubbell Law Directory at www.martindale.com and see what information you can locate concerning that attorney or firm. Then try it using the "Find a Lawyer" feature at www.FindLaw.com, or at www. LegalMatch.com.

h. Thoroughness

Unlike the preparation of a document that the attorney will review and correct after the paralegal has drafted it, when the paralegal investigator interviews a potential witness and reports back that the witness has no helpful information, the attorney may rely on that report and make no further contact with the witness. Or if the investigator is assigned to locate factual information the attorney may rely on the accuracy of the information produced by the paralegal. The nature of interviewing and investigating work is such that the paralegal is often the only person to make certain inquiries, and the supervising attorney and ultimately the client depend on the work to be done thoroughly.

EXAMPLE

A paralegal is asked by his supervising attorney to contact the secretary of state's office to obtain the name and address of the registered agent for service of process for a corporation that is a potential defendant in a civil suit. The clerk in the secretary of state's office supplies the paralegal with that information but the paralegal neglects to confirm that the corporation is in good standing with the state. In fact, it is not and its charter has been revoked by the state. Only after the supervising attorney files suit against the corporation for her client does she learn that the corporation is defunct.

i. Creativity

There is no substitute for an investigator who can think through a problem, overcome obstacles, and find a way to get the job done. Nowhere is there more opportunity for creative thinking than in legal investigation. Information that we thought would be available from one source isn't, so we have to think of another place to find it. A critical witness we thought would cooperate won't, so we have to find a way to convince him to talk with us. A witness we expected to say one thing says another during a taped interview and we have to revise our planned questions on the spot. The creative juices have to be constantly flowing to excel at this work. But that's what makes it challenging and fun.

j. Sound interviewing and investigating skills

It is difficult to overstate the importance of the paralegal engaged in interviewing and investigating work for an attorney KNOWING HOW TO DO IT AND DOING IT WELL. The paralegal who can competently prepare for and conduct the interview of a client or witness, who knows how to locate witnesses and factual information, who knows how to preserve evidence, who is honest and ethical, who is resourceful and dogged, will find herself indispensable to the attorney for whom she works. And it is not going too far to say that the interviewing and investigating skills of the paralegal can make all the difference in a case won or a case lost for the client.

Chapter Summary and Conclusion

Every lawyer engages in interviewing and fact investigation. Consequently, interviewing and investigating constitute basic skills for the legal professional, closely related to other skills and knowledge the legal professional must possess. The legal professional must understand the relationship between law and facts and engage in factual analysis utilizing critical thinking skills. The paralegal or associate attorney assisting a supervising attorney is an agent of that supervising attorney and there are significant legal consequences that flow from that relationship. The attorney supervising the work of an assisting paralegal or associate lawyer has high expectations of that assistant. The assistant must always be mindful of those expectations and aspire to meet them.

A supervising attorney has no expectation of an assisting legal professional that is more important than her legal ethics and professionalism. We will consider that topic next, in Chapter 2.

Review Questions

1. Explain the relationship between law and fact in a lawyer's work.
2. What are the three steps in the critical thinking process?
3. The two commandments in interviewing and investigating are _____ nothing and _____ everything.
4. What do we mean by saying that information discovered in an investigation is or is not "legally relevant"?
5. Why will a plaintiff's lawyer in a civil case engage in a pre-filing investigation? List as many reasons as you can.
6. Why will a defense lawyer in a civil case engage in a factual investigation prior to responding to a complaint? List as many reasons as you can.
7. Why does the legal investigator need to be familiar with the rules of evidence?
8. Why is the unauthorized practice of law a danger for a lawyer supervising a paralegal and not just for the paralegal herself?
9. A paralegal is a person qualified by _____, _____, or _____ experience who is _____ or _____ by a lawyer, law office, _____, _____ agency or other entity and who performs specifically _____ substantive legal work for which a _____ is _____.
10. What traits do lawyers expect in well-trained paralegals? List as many traits as you can think of.

KEY WORDS AND PHRASES TO REMEMBER

abuse of process
agency
application of information
categorizing of information

cause of action
civil litigation
comprehension of information
criminal litigation

critical thinking
evaluation of information
facts
factual analysis
formal discovery
informal discovery
informal investigation
investigation
law
legal assistant
legal professional

legally relevant information
malicious prosecution
paralegal
pre-filing investigation
private investigator
procedural law
respondeat superior
subagent
substantive law
vicarious liability

LEARN BY DOING

LBD 1-1. Locate the statute(s) in your state setting forth the definition of a private investigator. Prepare a memorandum summarizing whether, and under what circumstances, a paralegal performing interviewing and investigating work for an attorney, as an employee or on a case-by-case basis, will need to obtain a private investigator's license.

LBD 1-2. Locate the statute(s) in your state setting forth the requirements for obtaining a private investigator's license. Contact the agency or administrative board that regulates issuance of the license in your state and obtain an application and other relevant information.

LBD 1-3. Arrange and conduct an interview with a licensed private investigator in your area who works frequently with attorneys on civil and/or criminal cases. Your questions should focus on:

- the process of becoming a licensed private detective;
- the skills and procedures routinely used by private detectives;
- the role of ethics in the profession; and
- the importance to the private detective of understanding litigation procedure, the rules of evidence, legal ethics, and any other areas indicated by your instructor. Prepare a memorandum summarizing your interview.

LBD 1-4. Locate the most recent case(s) decided by the highest court in your state setting forth the elements of an action for malicious prosecution and abuse of process. Prepare a short memorandum distinguishing the two causes of action in your jurisdiction.

LBD 1-5. Determine whether your state has adopted any formal guidelines for attorneys licensed in the state governing their supervision of paralegals. (Such guidelines may have been adopted by statute, court rule, case law, or by the state bar association.) Prepare a memorandum summarizing how those guidelines apply to a paralegal involved in interviewing and investigating work under the supervision of an attorney.

LBDs 1-6 through 1-9 are accessible on the Author Updates link to the text website at www.aspenparalegaled.com/books/parsons_investigating/default.asp.

Chapter 2

Ethical and Professional Responsibilities for Legal Professionals Engaged in Interviewing and Investigating

CHAPTER OBJECTIVES

This chapter introduces you to the important ethical and professional responsibilities that rest on one involved in legal interviewing and investigating. You will learn:

- The various ethical rules and guidelines that have been promulgated by the American Bar Association for attorneys, and by the ABA, NALA, and NFPA for paralegals.
- The various civil, criminal, and career-ending consequences that may be suffered by attorneys and paralegals who engage in unethical or unprofessional conduct while engaged in interviewing and investigating work.
- The specific ethical and professional concerns that arise regularly in interviewing and investigating work including unauthorized practice of law (UPL), maintaining client confidences, conflicts of interest, and improper communications.

A. Sources of Ethical and Professional Responsibility

The various ethical and professional obligations imposed on the legal professional engaged in investigation work arise from a number of sources.

1. State statutes which prohibit the unauthorized practice of law (UPL)

Attorneys are licensed to practice law by the states. Engaging in the practice of law without a license is known as the **unauthorized practice of law,** or **UPL,** and most states have statutes in effect that make it a **misdemeanor** (a crime punishable by up to a year in jail). Some of the UPL statutes purport to define what constitutes the practice of law in that state but, surprisingly, many do not, leaving it to court decisions to flesh out. It is important for both the attorney and the paralegal to become familiar with the existing UPL statute in the state(s) where they practice, and to be familiar as well with court decisions that may have construed and applied the statute to particular factual situations. The paralegal must do so in order to avoid engaging in UPL. The attorney must do so in order to ensure that any paralegal she supervises does not engage in UPL. Not only is UPL itself commonly a misdemeanor but under state law, enabling, assisting, or conspiring with another to engage in UPL may be as well. (See LBD 2-1.) As we will see, there may be ethical consequences for both the paralegal and the supervising attorney when the paralegal engages in UPL.

2. Mandatory ethical rules governing attorneys

In each of the 50 states the governing body for attorneys has adopted ethical rules that are binding on attorneys licensed to practice in that state. (Links to the ethical and professional conduct rules of each state can be found at www.americanbar.org/groups/professional_responsibility/resources/links_of_interest.html.) These ethical rules carry the force of law for attorneys bound by them, which means that the failure of an attorney to comply with them can result in a variety of **penalties** or **sanctions** including the revocation of his license to practice law in that state. Forty-nine states, all but California, as well as the District of Columbia, have adopted some form of the **ABA Model Rules of Professional Conduct** (ABA Model Rules, accessible online at www.americanbar.org/groups/professional_responsibility/publications/model_rules_of_professional_conduct/model_rules_of_professional_conduct_table_of_contents.html) to govern attorneys.

It goes without saying that the attorney must know and comply with the ethical and professional rules that govern her, but it is important for the paralegal being supervised by the attorney to know and comply with them as well. As discussed in Chapter 1, the paralegal is considered the agent of the supervising attorney and there are serious consequences for the supervising attorney when the paralegal violates an ethical or professional rule governing the attorney. Consequently, part of the attorney's responsibility is to make sure any paralegal knows and complies with those rules.

3. Ethical rules promulgated for the paralegal

Both the **National Association of Legal Assistants (NALA)** and the **National Federation of Paralegal Associations (NFPA)** have promulgated ethical codes purporting to define the ethical responsibilities of paralegals. NALA has its **Code of Ethics and Professional Responsibility** (NALA Code of Ethics, accessible online at www.nala.org/code.aspx), which consists of the different canons, and NFPA has its **Model Code of Ethics and Professional Responsibility and Guidelines for Enforcement** (NFPA Model Code, accessible online at www.paralegals.org/associations/2270/files/Model_Code_of_Ethics_09_06.pdf), which consists of eight different canons, each followed by more specific Ethical Considerations (ECs) (see LBD 2-9). The ethical rules of these organizations do not currently carry the force of law in any jurisdiction. However, members of each organization pledge to comply with the respective ethical rules adopted by the organization and both of these ethical codes have come to be recognized by attorneys as setting the standard for expected professional conduct by paralegals. Both the paralegal and the attorney supervising the paralegal should be familiar with all ethical and professional guidelines governing the paralegal. The supervising attorney should require that the paralegal comply with them.

4. Guidelines for attorneys and paralegals working together in the law office

In 1984 NALA promulgated its **Model Standards and Guidelines for Utilization of Paralegals** (NALA Guidelines, accessible online at www.nala.org/model.aspx), which summarize the specific types of activities that a paralegal can (and cannot) engage in legally and ethically. In 1991 the ABA adopted its **Model Guidelines for the Utilization of Paralegal Services** (ABA Guidelines, , accessible online at http://apps.americanbar.org/legalservices/paralegals/downloads/modelguidelines.pdf), which set forth ten specific guidelines for attorneys utilizing paralegals each followed by a lengthy comment concerning the origin, scope, and application of the guideline. The bar associations or highest appellate courts in a number of states have adopted their own guidelines based on the NALA or ABA Guidelines. Both the paralegal and the supervising attorney should determine whether the state in which they work has adopted such guidelines and become familiar with them (see LBD 2-2).

5. Advisory ethical opinions

For many years the ABA has issued **advisory ethical opinions** on a large range of topics. The bar associations or the highest appellate courts of most states, and some local bar associations, have a procedure in place to issue advisory opinions as well. These opinions do not typically purport to establish new ethical requirements but, as the word "advisory" suggests, attempt instead to clarify questions that arise regarding the application of established ethical principles to specific fact situations or to provide guidance on the propriety of some anticipated course of conduct. In addition, the NFPA's Ethics Board issues advisory opinions on a broad range of topics related to paralegals (See NFPA Guidelines for Rendering Ethics and Disciplinary Opinions at www.paralegals.org/default.asp?page=69.) (See LBD 2-10.)

It is the obligation of the paralegal engaged in interviewing and investigating work not only to know and comply with existing ethical requirements, but to stay updated on changes in such requirements. This can be done by regularly reading professional journals for both paralegals and attorneys, reading advance sheets containing new court opinions and new advisory opinions, and by attending seminars providing ethics updates. The attorney supervising the paralegal needs to stay abreast of significant developments in the paralegal field herself. Just as a paralegal advises the supervising attorney of all developments in a case on which the paralegal is working, so should the paralegal pass along significant developments in the paralegal field, including developments in the area of ethics and professionalism.

B.   Consequences of Unethical Conduct

1. To the lawyer

a. *The lawyer may be fired by the client*

The lawyer/client relationship is a contractual one in which the lawyer acts as the agent of the client. The relationship is a terminable one. An unethical act by the lawyer or the paralegal working for the lawyer in the course of the representation of a client may well be deemed by the client a reason to terminate the relationship.

b. *The lawyer may be sued by the client damaged by the unethical behavior*

Because the attorney is a licensed professional and the client must rely on the attorney's training and expertise, and because the client entrusts the attorney with his confidences and, in many cases, his property as well, the law imposes on the attorney a **fiduciary duty.** Not only must the attorney use reasonable care in handling the client matter, she must be scrupulously honest and loyal to the client in all matters related to the representation and must keep the client fully advised regarding developments in the matters being handled.

If the unethical behavior of the lawyer or the paralegal working for the lawyer in the course of the representation causes harm to the client, the client may sue the attorney for breach of this fiduciary duty. Such a suit against an attorney is referred to as a suit for **legal** or **professional malpractice.** As discussed in Chapter 1, the paralegal should never forget that he acts as the agent of the supervising attorney and the law may impose vicarious liability on the attorney for the paralegal's wrongful acts that result in harm to the client.

c. The lawyer may be sanctioned

The lawyer may be subject to an investigation by the state authority charged with the regulation of legal ethics. Depending on state law, the **sanctions** may range from private or public reprimand to temporary license suspension to license revocation. (See LBD 2-3.)

d. The lawyer may face criminal prosecution

If the unethical act involved fraud or the misappropriation of client funds or other property, the attorney may face criminal fraud or theft charges. And, as already noted, in some states it is not only a crime for an unlicensed person to engage in the practice of law, it is also a crime for anyone—including an attorney—to enable, aid, or conspire with another to engage in UPL.

e. The lawyer's reputation may be damaged

To the extent that an ethical violation is known to others, it typically damages the reputation of the lawyer among his peers, with other clients, and with the public. This could lead directly to a loss of existing clients and future business for the attorney.

HYPOTHETICAL 2-1

Assume that Johnny Go-Gettum is a prominent plaintiff's personal injury lawyer in your area. Last year he obtained the highest jury verdict in the history of your state and now has all the lucrative plaintiff's work he could desire. Every week he turns down cases, which other lawyers would consider the case of a lifetime. Then Johnny hires Sally Oops as his new paralegal.

One of Sally's responsibilities is to handle the funds that come into the office on settlements and collected judgments. Since Johnny Go-Gettum handles almost all his plaintiffs' cases on a contingency basis, his office processes a lot of settlement funds. When a settlement check is received, Sally's job is to deposit the check in Johnny's **trust account**, wait for the check to clear, and prepare a final bill to the client showing the gross settlement amount received, the deduction of Johnny's contingency fee amount, the deduction of Johnny's out-of-pocket expense charges, and the net amount payable to the client.

Unfortunately, Sally Oops concentrated more on her law classes in paralegal school than she did on her math and accounting courses and she regularly makes errors in the calculations contained in the final bills she prepares. She also has a lazy streak, which causes her to regularly put off preparing the final bill and pay-out until weeks after the settlement checks are received and deposited.

One client, Phil Finicky, already upset by the delay in distribution of his settlement funds, looks over Johnny's final bill very thoroughly, finds an error in the bill that resulted in his receiving $200 less than he should have, and calls the state body charged with disciplining attorneys. In the ensuing investigation, it is discovered that Sally Oops has made errors resulting in underpayments to more than 100 clients and that she has regularly held client funds too long, depriving them of interest they could have been earning.

Do you think the authorities who enforce the ethical standards for attorneys in your state will find that Johnny Go-Gettum was ethically and professionally responsible for Sally's mishandling of the funds? What specific provisions of your state's ethical code for attorneys might he have violated?

List all the negative consequences that could reasonably occur to Johnny Go-Gettum as a result of this situation. (Hint: The last we heard of Johnny, he was operating a hot dog stand across from the court house.)

What do you suppose may have happened to Sally Oops?

2. To the paralegal

a. The paralegal may lose her job

Few attorneys would consider keeping an employee who committed a serious ethical breach or a series of minor ones. The risk to the attorney is too great, as is the potential damage to clients.

b. The paralegal may lose her certification

If the paralegal is certified by the NALA or NFPA, or by a state certification authority, that certification may be suspended or lost.

c. The paralegal may lose her right to appear before administrative agencies

If the paralegal is authorized to appear before a state or federal governmental agency on behalf of claimants (see the extended discussion of the unauthorized practice of law below), that authorization may be revoked as a result of unethical conduct.

d. The paralegal may be sued by the client damaged by the unethical action

Paralegals can be named as defendants in **legal malpractice** suits growing out of unethical conduct, and plaintiffs also will seek to impose vicarious liability on the attorney under principles of agency.

e. The paralegal may be subject to criminal prosecution

If the unethical conduct involves the practice of law, the paralegal may be subject to criminal prosecution under the state UPL law. (See LBD 2-1.) If it involves the mishandling of money or other property belonging to another, she may face a more serious charge of theft or criminal fraud.

f. The paralegal's reputation may be tarnished

To the extent that an ethical violation is known to others, it may damage the reputation of a paralegal both among her peers, in the community at large, and with other prospective employers.

> **HYPOTHETICAL 2-2**
>
> Here's what happened to Sally Oops following the disclosure of her mishandling of client funds. Johnny Go-Gettum fired her immediately. No one else in town would hire her. Phil Finicky named her as a defendant in the class action suit he initiated on behalf of all of Johnny's clients. And her CLA certification was suspended by the NALA. (The last we heard of Sally, she had gone into politics.)
>
> What specific provisions of the NALA Code of Ethics and the NFPA Model Code did Sally Oops violate?
>
> As a client, would you hire an attorney who had Sally working for her?

C. Specific Ethical and Professional Concerns for Legal Professionals Engaged in Interviewing and Investigating

1. The unauthorized practice of law

We have considered the possible consequences to both the paralegal and the supervising attorney if the paralegal engages in UPL. Now let's consider what UPL is in more detail.

Reference should be made to the UPL statute in the state(s) where the attorney and paralegal practice, and other related state materials for the prevailing definition and interpretations. But, in general, the following often-quoted definition of the practice of law stated in *Davies v. Unauthorized Practice Committee of State Bar of Texas*, 431 S.W.2d 590 (Tex. Civ. App. 1968) is helpful:

> According to the generally understood definition of the practice of law, it embraces the preparation of pleadings and other papers incident to actions of special proceedings, and the management of such actions and proceedings on behalf of clients before judges in courts. However, the practice of law is not confined to cases conducted in court. In fact, the major portion of the practice of any capable lawyer consists of work done outside of the courts. The practice of law involves not only appearance in court in connection with litigation, but also services rendered out of court, and includes the giving of advice or the rendering of any service requiring the use of legal skill or knowledge, such as preparing a will, contract or other instrument, the legal effect of which under the facts and conclusions involved must be carefully determined.

431 S.W.2d at 593.

It is fairly well settled that *only* licensed attorneys can perform the following acts and, consequently, that they *cannot be properly delegated* to others by the attorney:

a. Establishing an attorney-client relationship

This means that the paralegal cannot say or do anything in dealing with a potential client that amounts to reaching an agreement for the attorney to undertake the representation of that potential client. It also means that the paralegal cannot say or do anything in dealing with an existing client that amounts to an agreement for the attorney to undertake a different or additional representation for that client.

Paralegals involved in interviewing and investigating will work closely with potential and existing clients of the attorney. They will frequently develop familiar and even friendly relationships with these persons and may feel strongly about helping them. Nonetheless, this important decision must be left to the attorney. The paralegal must not create expectations or assumptions concerning representation in the mind of the existing or potential client and the supervising attorney must not allow her to do so.

b. Setting legal fees

Clients often ask many questions of the paralegal regarding charges and billing procedures. Some attorneys have established fixed fee schedules and billing and payment procedures for many legal services, and those attorneys may authorize their assistants to communicate these scheduled amounts and procedures to inquiring persons. That appears to be permissible so long as the paralegal limits the communication to decisions the attorney has made and authorized her to communicate. But even here the paralegal and attorney must exercise caution because the discussion of established charges may be construed by the lay person as an acceptance of their representation. For that reason, many lawyers have established procedures in their office that preclude nonlawyers from discussing fees at all.

c. Giving legal opinions or legal advice

These activities are at the heart of the practice of law and cannot be performed by unlicensed persons. Nor can the authority to perform these functions be delegated by the attorney to the paralegal. See NALA Guideline IV. Problems in this area typically arise in four different contexts for the paralegal engaged in interviewing and investigating work:

1. **When interviewing a prospective client.** Paralegals frequently screen calls or visits from potential clients when the attorney is unavailable. These persons are typically quite anxious to get quick answers to their legal questions and will assume the paralegal must know the answer because she works in a law office. And frequently the paralegal may know (or think she knows!) the answer to the legal question being asked. In those situations, and especially when the paralegal identifies closely with the anxiety of the potential client, the paralegal must resist the temptation to answer the legal questions being asked.

   Paralegals must remember, and supervising attorneys must remind them, that in the law what appear to be simple questions may not be so simple at all. While compassion for a troubled and anxious person is understandable and even appropriate, a professional detachment must be maintained.

2. **When interviewing witnesses.** During interviews with witnesses and other information sources, the paralegal will frequently be

asked questions about the case at hand or about other legal matters of interest to the witness or source. Again, the paralegal may think she knows the answer and reason, "What's the harm?" She may also feel pressured to help in order to ensure the cooperation of the witness or source. Such temptations must be resisted.

3. **When dealing with clients in the course of a case.** The paralegal will often become the primary contact person for the client. Trust, familiarity, and even friendship may develop between the paralegal and the client. But the legal questions must still be deferred to the busy or absent attorney.

HYPOTHETICAL 2-3

Assume that Ned Newatit has just finished his formal paralegal training. He lands his first paralegal job with a two-lawyer firm specializing in domestic relations work. The firm has an established fee schedule for certain kinds of legal work including separation agreements ($500), uncontested divorces ($750), and name changes ($250).

Sue Debum, who is not currently a client of the firm, calls to speak with a lawyer, and since both lawyers are in court (aren't they always?) the call is referred to Ned. Sue says she and her husband Iam Debum are getting a divorce and she wants to know how much it will cost if the firm handles it. Is it okay for Ned to tell Sue that the firm will charge $750 if the divorce is uncontested? What should he tell her about how much it will cost in legal fees if the divorce is contested?

During the conversation, Sue says that she is not sure if her husband will agree to a divorce but she wants to go ahead and file anyway. Can Ned tell her that the firm will "probably" handle the case since that is the kind of work it does? Can Ned go ahead and set up an appointment for Sue Debum to come in and meet with a lawyer to discuss the case? If he does the latter, what explanation, if any, do you recommend he give Sue about the firm's representing her?

During the conversation, Sue tells Ned that her husband is still in the town where they have been living for the past five years, but he may be moving to another state soon. She asks if the divorce suit can still be filed against him in this state even if he moves before it is filed. Ned knows the answer to this question. He made the high grade in his domestic relations course in paralegal school. He has also heard the attorneys he works for answer this question dozens of times. Under those circumstances, can he answer Sue's question?

4. **When family or friends ask for help.** Everyone knows that lay persons share legal opinions and give each other advice regarding legal matters all the time, especially in friendship and family contexts. Why does it become inappropriate for a paralegal to do that? Because with greater knowledge comes greater responsibility.

When a friend or family member knows that you have received legal training and work with an attorney, they may well rely on that training and experience, trusting your advice and judgment. And that is the essence of legal practice. It is never easy, but in those situations the paralegal must explain to friends and family members that she cannot offer legal advice or opinions. The only recommendation that should be made to avoid the danger of UPL is to advise the person to speak with an attorney.

HYPOTHETICAL 2-4

Assume that all of the family of Ned Newatit has come into town to attend his graduation. Afterward his tightwad grandfather even springs for lunch for everybody at the most expensive restaurant in town. Ned is enjoying himself until his grandfather sidles up to him and says in a low voice:

> Say Ned, you may know the answer to this. My neighbor planted some trees along our property line a few years ago and I didn't like it but I hated to say anything to him. You know how it is. But now the trees are getting bigger and the branches have grown over onto my side of the property line. Seems like after every storm I'm finding limbs I've got to pick up and in the fall the leaves blow onto my side. What do you think I should do? I'm probably never going to do anything anyway but I'd just like to know what my rights are. And I hate to take a little ol' piddling thing like this to an expensive lawyer.

What ethical danger(s) are presented to Ned by this development? What harm could occur if he answers his grandfather's questions? How would you suggest that Ned respond to his grandfather (and get his grandfather to go ahead and pay the lunch bill!)?

d. Representing a client before a court or tribunal

This is forbidden to the unlicensed person unless such representation is expressly authorized by the rules of that court or tribunal. Reference should be made to the local rules of some state courts, which allow non-licensed persons to appear in court on behalf of a client for very limited reasons, for example, to set a hearing date. In addition, increasing numbers of federal and state administrative agencies (e.g., the United States Social Security Administration and many state welfare agencies) are allowing paralegals to appear and represent the interests of claimants. This may be a growing trend reflecting both the increased professionalism of paralegals and the higher standard to which they will consequently be held. But the supervising attorney and paralegal should be careful to check the rules and regulations of the court or tribunal before sending a paralegal there on behalf of a client.

e. Negotiating a legal matter on behalf of a client

Closely related to the concepts of giving legal advice and representing a client before a court or tribunal is negotiating legal matters on behalf of a client. Since this would amount to the exercise of legal judgment on behalf of a client, it is also prohibited to the unlicensed person.

f. Delegable tasks and the attorney's responsibility to avoid an agent's UPL

Attorneys must ensure that proper training and procedures are in place in their offices to avoid the occurrence of UPL. Ethically, lawyers are specifically obligated to avoid aiding another to engage in UPL. See ABA Model Rule 5.5(b). This ethical obligation is in addition to the potential criminal liability some states impose on lawyers who enable, assist, or conspire with another to engage in UPL.

Both attorneys and paralegals should be familiar with the ethical rules regarding the proper delegation of tasks by the attorney to the paralegal and the adequate supervision of that work to avoid committing UPL. In general, other than the five matters mentioned above, the paralegal may perform any task that would otherwise constitute the practice of law so long as certain conditions are satisfied. See Rule 5.3 of the ABA Model Rules. Generally, those conditions are:

- The attorney must properly supervise the paralegal's work.
- The attorney must maintain a direct relationship with the client.
- The attorney must assume full responsibility for the paralegal's work product.

Assuming those conditions are satisfied, the paralegal can:

- interview clients and witnesses,
- conduct factual investigations,
- draft contracts, pleadings, memoranda, discovery documents, and other legal documents for the attorney's review and signature,
- prepare correspondence,
- conduct legal research into a client's legal issues,
- assist the attorney in depositions, document production, and in the courtroom, and
- perform many other related tasks that would otherwise constitute the practice of law.

2. Maintaining client confidences and secrets

The basic ethical obligation imposed on lawyers and paralegals to maintain client information as confidential is the evidentiary privilege commonly known as the **attorney-client privilege.** But the ethical duty of maintaining client confidentiality is much broader than the evidentiary privilege.

a. The attorney-client privilege

This is an **evidentiary privilege** (a privilege relating to what information can be offered and received in evidence in a court of law, see Chapter 6), which applies to communications in any form (oral, written, electronic, body signal, etc.) between an attorney and her client that are deemed confidential in nature and that relate to the subject matter of the representation. Such information is privileged from discovery or involuntary disclosure in a trial or other proceeding. In other words, the client cannot be compelled even under oath to disclose the confidential communication and can also prevent the attorney from disclosing it without the client's consent. All 50 states recognize the attorney-client privilege by **statute** (act of the legislature), **court rule** (rule of procedure or practice adopted by a court), or **common law** (court decision in a contested case).

Confidential communications that occur between a client and agents of the attorney, such as paralegals, are protected, as are communications between the client and the attorney with those agents present (see LBD 2-6). Communications made by the client in the presence of persons not working as employees or agents of the attorney may *not* be deemed privileged even though the attorney or the paralegal is present as well.

The attorney-client privilege belongs to the client, not the lawyer, and it is up to the client to waive it. The privilege, if not waived by the client, lasts indefinitely, which means that it survives the end of the attorney-client relationship and usually even the death of the client.

The attorney-client privilege is generally construed very broadly by the courts to protect confidential communications from disclosure. For example, confidences disclosed in consultations between a lawyer and a prospective client are protected by the privilege even when the lawyer does not undertake the representation.

Some types of information divulged to the attorney by the client are generally not protected by the privilege including, for example, the identity of the client or his whereabouts or the fee arrangement. The privilege cannot be properly asserted to conceal physical evidence of the client's crime from the authorities.

Moreover, there are various exceptions to the **attorney-client privilege,** the most notable of which for our purposes is that the privilege is deemed **waived** if the confidential communication is disclosed to others by the client or by the client's representatives, including his attorney or the paralegal working for the attorney. Some courts have held that even inadvertent disclosure of confidential information by the client or the client's representatives waives the privilege (see LBD 2-6). The danger of waiver of the privilege in the context of the discovery of **electronically stored information (ESI)** is discussed in Chapter 4.

b. The broader ethical duty of confidentiality

To be distinguished from the evidentiary rule of attorney-client privilege is the broader ethical obligation imposed on attorneys and their assistants to keep confidential *any and all information* they have obtained from or about a client. Indeed, there is no rule of attorney-client relations older or more sacred than the duty imposed on the attorney to maintain the **confidences and secrets** of the client. Traditionally, **confidences** of a client refers to information protected by the attorney-client privilege. **Secrets** of a client refers to other information gained in the professional relationship that the client has requested to be held inviolate or the disclosure of which would be embarrassing or would likely be detrimental to the client. Rule 1.6 of the ABA Model Rules contains a more expansive definition of the obligation of confidentiality. It prohibits attorneys from disclosing "information relating to representation of a client."

Thus the ethical obligation to maintain the confidences and secrets of a client is much broader than the evidentiary rule surrounding the attorney-client privilege. Information obtained by the attorney or her assistants from or about a client must not be disclosed without the client's knowledge and consent even though it does not rise to the level of a confidential communication protected by the attorney-client privilege.

The duty to protect client information from disclosure is imposed on the attorney, the paralegal, and anyone else working with or for them on client matters. Canon 7 of the NALA Code of Ethics and EC 1.5 of the NFPA Model Code both require the paralegal to preserve and protect client confidences.

Legal professionals must exercise reasonable care to ensure that they do not disclose or use **client confidences and secrets**. Rule 5.3 of the ABA Model Rules and the Comment to it impose on attorneys the duty to supervise their legal assistants and other employees to ensure their compliance with the lawyer's ethical obligations, "particularly regarding the obligation not to disclose information relating to representation of the client." Moreover, Guideline 6 of the ABA Model Guidelines provides: "It is the responsibility of a lawyer to take reasonable measures to ensure that all client confidences are preserved by a legal assistant."

c. *Protecting client information from disclosure*

The broad scope of the duty to maintain all client information as confidential, the ease with which confidential communications can lose their privileged evidentiary status if made in the presence of unauthorized persons, and the fact that even privileged information can be waived inadvertently has a number of practical implications for the legal professional engaged in interviewing and investigating.:

1. **When speaking on the phone.** Care must be taken when speaking with the client (or other privileged agent) about client matters in person or by phone. Always be sure no third person is present or can overhear verbal communications. Close the door to your office when you are on the phone regarding client matters. Ask the party to whom you are speaking if they are alone.

   Speaker phones pose special problems on either end of a conversation because another person may be in or near the room and able to hear. So, on your end of the conversation, close the door and turn the volume down so it can't be heard outside the door. Then ask the person(s) on the other end to do the same.

   Calls made via **cellular phones** are susceptible to interception. It is better to avoid making calls regarding client matters by cellular phone unless you have no alternative. Get direction from your supervising attorney before using a cellular phone for those calls.

2. **When sending letters.** When corresponding by mail with a client or with an expert or private investigator working with you on a client matter, it is good practice to place the words *Confidential* or *Personal* on the letter and the envelope in a prominent place (see Illustration 8-4). Remember that many people do not open their own mail. We must endeavor to prevent unauthorized persons from opening or seeing confidential communications.

3. **When sending communications by FAX.** Care must be taken in sending written communications by facsimile (FAX) to ensure that no unauthorized person receives or handles the FAX message.

4. **When sending e-mail or text messages.** Communications sent or received by electronic modem (e-mail or texting) are not secure, privacy cannot be assured, and communications sent that way may not be impressed with confidentiality at all. E-communications appear on a computer tape and can be shared on a network, copied, stored, or forwarded to others. Currently, the only way to assure a measure of privacy in e-communications is to send encrypted (coded) messages (see LBD 2-11).

5. **When interviewing a witness.** Neither the attorney nor the paralegal, as legal professionals engaged in informal investigating, can disclose client confidences in the process of explaining to a witness why information is being sought (see Chapters 12 and 13).

6. **In the office.** Confidential client information must be kept in a safe and organized fashion in the office so that it isn't lost or inadvertently seen by visitors. In many law offices, the policy is to prevent even other office employees without a need to know from seeing confidential client information. Attorneys and those working for them should show zeal in protecting client information. It is a mark of professionalism and an expression of genuine client concern that can increase the public's respect for the legal profession.

7. **At home and online.** Outside the office the legal professional must avoid discussing specific client matters with family, friends, or others. That caution applies as well to online social networking via Facebook, MySpace, Twitter, etc.

8. **In working with opposing counsel and paralegals.** Over the course of a case, the legal professional will have numerous occasions to speak with personnel from the offices of opposing attorneys. The professional must exercise discretion in what information she discloses about the client and the case and in what she allows those persons to see.

9. **In responding to formal discovery requests.** Care must be taken too in answering formal discovery requests such as interrogatories and document requests (see Chapters 4 and 5) not to disclose confidential information that is not discoverable.

HYPOTHETICAL 2-5

Assume that during the course of the phone conversation between Ned Newatit and Sue Debum mentioned in Hypothetical 2-3, Sue mentions the following things to Ned in no particular order:

- She is 35 years old and her husband, Iam Debum, is 36.
- She is a wonderful cook.
- Her husband has been guilty of numerous extramarital affairs.
- She is a registered Democrat who sometimes votes Republican.
- She wants to keep the marital home after the divorce.
- Her father killed Jimmy Hoffa and she helped him dispose of the body.
- Her sister is coming to stay with her this week.

Assume further that Ned makes an appointment for Sue Debum to come in and meet with an attorney but she fails to keep the appointment and he never hears from her again.

> Which item(s) of information that Sue gave Ned qualify as "confidences" and which as "secrets" within the meaning of the ABA Model Code? Which items would be subject to the confidentiality provisions of the ABA Model Rules?
>
> Under the ethical rule governing attorneys in your state, *must* or *may* Ned or the attorneys he works for disclose the information regarding the crime(s) related to the murder of Jimmy Hoffa to the authorities?
>
> If Ned were called to testify at some later time in a criminal proceeding against Sue Debum and her father in connection with the death of Jimmy Hoffa, could Sue successfully assert her attorney-client privilege to keep him from testifying to her statements on that subject?

3. Competence

For attorneys, Rule 1.1 of the ABA Mode Rules provides:

> A lawyer shall provide competent representation to a client. Competent representation requires the legal knowledge, skill, thoroughness and preparation reasonably necessary for the representation.

The paralegal, too, has an affirmative ethical duty to seek and maintain what Canon 6 of the NALA Code of Ethics calls "a high degree of competency" (see also EC 1.1 of the NFPA Model Code). The supervising attorney should demand a high degree of competence from those assisting him just as he does for himself. Attorneys should encourage paralegals to think of themselves as professionals and to be proud of that standing. Because of the agency relationship that exists between the supervising attorney and the paralegal and the consequences of that relationship for both legal professionals, each has a vested interest in furthering the competence of the other.

For the practicing or aspiring paralegal, achieving a high degree of competence means:

a. Seek good education and training

One seeking a career as a paralegal should seek the best education and training available and do her best while pursuing that education.

SL EUTH ON THE LOOSE

Access www.tile.net/ lists and look over the various listservs that you can sign up for. Choose three you think might be useful to you as an investigating legal professional.

b. Seek certification

The paralegal should make it a professional goal to seek and obtain the highest level of certification available to her in her field by private paralegal organizations or the state(s) in which she practices.

c. Stay informed concerning changes in the law and the profession

The paralegal should conscientiously and regularly read professional journals, case summaries, and other legal publications to keep abreast of changes and developments in the law and the paralegal profession. Attending seminars and workshops in substantive law areas and professional skill areas is another means of keeping up with changes and developments.

d. Stay on the cutting edge of technological advancements

But that is the world in which we live and no professional can afford to be behind the curve technologically. Twenty-five years ago it was the facsimile machine that revolutionized communications in law offices. Today, FAX machines are taken for granted and we are now challenged to learn to utilize computers, the Internet, e-mail, and distance communication tools. This is not easy in a world where such advances are coming with mind-boggling speed.

e. Commit yourself to excellence

The paralegal should dedicate herself to achieving the best possible result in every single client matter on which she is called to work. Competence is not just having knowledge and skills, it is applying them on a daily basis in each individual case. This is where competence becomes professionalism. Thoroughness, consistency, perseverance, and hard work on every single file—this is the stuff of which competence is made.

4. Integrity

The legal field is like most others in that the persons who achieve the highest level of respect from their peers and who enjoy the greatest success professionally and monetarily are those who are known for their integrity. But beyond this truism, both lawyers and paralegals are required by their governing codes of ethics and professionalism to practice integrity.

For lawyers, ABA Model Rule 8.4 provides:

> It is professional misconduct for a lawyer to:
>
> (a) violate or attempt to violate the Rules of Professional Conduct, knowingly assist or induce another to do so, or do so through the acts of another;
>
> (b) commit a criminal act that reflects adversely on the lawyer's honesty, trustworthiness or fitness as a lawyer in other respects;
>
> (c) engage in conduct involving dishonesty, fraud, deceit or misrepresentation;
>
> (d) engage in conduct that is prejudicial to the administration of justice;
>
> (e) state or imply an ability to influence improperly a government agency or official or to achieve results by means that violate the Rules of Professional Conduct or other law; or
>
> (f) knowingly assist a judge or judicial officer in conduct that is a violation of applicable rules of judicial conduct or other law.

Canon 6 of the NALA Code of Ethics provides that, "A paralegal must strive to maintain integrity." EC 1.2 of the NFPA Model Code says that, "A paralegal shall achieve and maintain a high level of personal and professional integrity."

Let's consider some specifics of what integrity means for the lawyer and the paralegal in the context of doing interviewing and investigating work.

a. Truthfulness in dealing with clients, co-workers, and others

In the course of his work, the legal professional will work with many different kinds of people every day, including clients, co-workers, witnesses, other attorneys and their staff, and court personnel. The legal professional should never use deception or misstatement in his work.

EXAMPLE

Never tell a client you haven't received something on their case when you have it but it's still sitting in your in-box waiting for you to get around to it. Never tell a court clerk you need something immediately if you don't. Never tell a senior attorney desiring to assign you work that you are too swamped to take it on if you aren't. Never promise a witness you will take only a few moments of their time for an interview if you know it's going to take longer.

b. Fidelity in handling client funds and other property

The legal professional must be familiar with the specific ethical rules and office policies regarding the handling, depositing, and accounting for funds and other property that pass through a law office. For example, it is fundamental that monetary funds that come into the possession of the law office for use in client transactions must be placed in **trust accounts** separate from the lawyer's accounts and strictly accounted for. See Rule 1.15 of the ABA Model Rules.

In Chapter 9 we will consider in detail the procedures that should be in place and followed when documents and other material come into the custody of the investigating legal professional. The law office will obtain custody of client materials and things that belong to third parties. There is an ethical obligation to preserve and care for those custodial items and to return them when a case is closed. That obligation involves both competence and integrity.

The legal professional should also be familiar with the specific ethical rules and office policies regarding the recording of billable time, the charging of expenses, and collection practices, all of which have obvious implications for the ethical obligation to practice integrity.

c. Loyalty

A key ingredient of integrity is loyalty. That includes loyalty to the firm, loyalty to the supervising attorney, loyalty to the client, and loyalty to the legal profession.

5. Diligence and communication with the client

In most states, the most frequent ethical complaint made against attorneys is the failure to adequately communicate with a client regarding the status of their case. In client relations, there is simply no substitute for regular, thorough communication with clients (see Chapter 8). Attorneys and paralegals are required to be zealous in their representation of client interests.

For lawyers, ABA Model Rule 1.3 provides that, "A lawyer shall act with reasonable diligence and promptness in representing a client." Regarding communication with a client, ABA Model Rule 1.4(a) provides:

A lawyer shall:

(1) promptly inform the client of any decision or circumstance with respect to which the client's informed consent, as defined in Rule 1.0(e), is required by these Rules;

(2) reasonably consult with the client about the means by which the client's objectives are to be accomplished;

(3) keep the client reasonably informed about the status of the matter;

(4) promptly comply with reasonable requests for information.

For paralegals, Canon 10 of the NALA Code of Ethics is relevant here as it provides that a paralegal's conduct is to be guided by relevant provisions of the ABA Model Code and ABA Model Rules. In addition, EC 1.1(c) of the NFPA Model Code provides that, "A paralegal shall perform all assignments promptly and efficiently" (see Rule 1.3(e)).

Keeping every client file current, responding to client inquiries promptly, and keeping the client fully informed regarding the status of their case is the essence of diligence.

6. Conflicts of interest

A **conflict of interest** is anything that compromises or which could reasonably appear to compromise the loyalty of the attorney or paralegal to the client. One important aspect of conflicts of interest is that they need not be *actual conflicts* in order to cause problems. Even a *potential conflict* of interest must be identified, disclosed, and dealt with. In this area, as in all areas of ethical concern, it is uniformly held that attorneys must avoid even the **appearance of impropriety**. Similarly, EC 1.3(b) of the NFPA Model Code states that, "A paralegal shall avoid impropriety and the appearance of impropriety," and Canon 9 of the NALA Code of Ethics exhorts paralegals to do "all things incidental, necessary, or expedient for the attainment of ethics." EC 1.6 of the NFPA Model Code states, "A paralegal shall avoid conflicts of interest and shall disclose any possible conflict of interest to the employer or client, as well as to prospective employers and clients."

For the legal professional, conflicts can arise in a number of ways.

a. Simultaneous representation

This occurs when the attorney represents the interests of two or more clients simultaneously in the same transaction or case. The inherent danger is that at some point in the representation the attorney may feel compelled to take some position or action for the benefit of one client that will work to the detriment of the other. It is not always easy at the outset of a representation, when the interests of the multiple clients seem identical and feelings are amicable, to anticipate future events that may make the clients' interests diverge and feelings between them grow hostile, leaving the attorney in a compromised position.

Most attorneys try to avoid placing themselves in this position by declining **simultaneous representation** when there is any possibility of such a conflict developing. And many jurisdictions have local rules that prohibit simultaneous representation in certain areas fraught with likely conflicts, such as divorce proceedings. However, where it is not barred by such rule, simultaneous representation can be undertaken by the attorney who concludes it will not prejudice the interests of either client, but only if potential conflicts are fully disclosed to both clients and the consent of both is obtained.

Associate attorneys and paralegals working in the interviewing and investigating area need to be especially sensitive to this rule when the supervising attorney is representing more than one client in a single matter. The legal professional will frequently be the one having the most contact with those clients and should immediately communicate to the supervising attorney all evidence of hostility or disparate interests reflected by the clients. And, in gathering information related to the case, the legal professional should be aware of the implications of any discovered information that creates or could create a real or potential conflict and report that possibility to the supervising attorney immediately.

b. Representing an interest adverse to a former client

Rule 1.9 of the ABA Model Rules states "[a] lawyer who has formerly represented a client in a matter shall not thereafter represent another person in the same or substantially related matter in which that person's interests are materially adverse to the interests of the former client unless the former client consents after consultation." This ethical concern arises out of the obligation to preserve the confidences of a client and the climate of trust that is critical to the attorney-client relationship. Confidences of a client must remain confidences even after the attorney-client relationship has ended or otherwise no client can have trust in the attorney-client relationship at all. There are a number of times and situations when this conflict can arise:

(1) Before accepting representation

Before agreeing to represent a new client or to take on a new matter for an existing client, there should be a procedure in place within the law office to check for potential conflicts. The parties adverse or potentially adverse to the client may be former or current clients or be employed by or otherwise related to former or current clients. The attorney and the paralegal should make sure that a thorough conflicts check is done before the attorney accepts the new client or matter.

(2) After representation has begun

Conflicts of interest with important consequences can arise throughout the representation. Sometimes all potential adverse parties have not been identified when a case is accepted by a lawyer and it is left to the investigation process to identify such additional adverse parties. And sometimes the employment or other relationship of known adverse parties to other persons or entities that can create a conflict are not known until some point in the investigation process. Consequently, the legal professional involved in the investigation must always be alert to potential conflicts and report them to the supervising attorney immediately upon their discovery.

EXAMPLE

Suppose you are working for a plaintiff's personal injury firm and get a much better offer to work for an insurance defense firm. You accept the offer but then remember that your new employer is defending one or more cases brought by plaintiffs represented by your old employer. And you were working on those cases when you switched jobs. As you might expect, the clients of your former employer may be quite upset that you have "gone over to the enemy camp," taking with you knowledge about their case. Obviously, anyone working in the legal field (attorney, paralegal, and possibly the legal secretary or office manager) who changes employment cannot ethically work on behalf of the new employer against the interests of the former client. But should you be prevented from changing jobs due to the potential conflict?

(3) Job changes

The typical solution in these situations is for the new employer to implement policies that effectively screen or wall off the new employee from having anything to do with cases in which there might be a conflict. (Thus this arrangement is sometimes called an *invisible wall* or an *ethical wall*.) For example, the paralegal or associate attorney working under such an arrangement in the Example would not have access to any files involving those cases or be routed any memos dealing with them or be involved in the billing of such work. If computers in the new office are networked it typically is necessary to flag screened files with warning messages.

Note that everyone involved in this potential conflict has a real motivation to ensure that the interests of the clients of the former employer are protected. Both the employee who has made the move and the former employer may be sued by a client if in fact client confidences are compromised, resulting in harm to the client. The employee and the new employer may face an ethical complaint if they fail to establish and implement appropriate screening procedures.

(4) Personal relationships

Canon 8 of the NALA Code of Ethics provides that, "A paralegal must disclose to his or her employer any pre-existing client or personal relationship that may conflict with the interests of the employer or prospective employer and/or their clients." (See also Canon 6 of the NFPA Model Code.)

EXAMPLE

> Suppose you are working for that same plaintiff's personal injury firm mentioned above and you plan to marry (or just become involved in a dating relationship with) that cute paralegal working for the defense firm that just happens to be defending one or more cases brought by your firm. Might the clients of both your firms be a little curious about what you two lovebirds discuss at dinner?

One option, of course, is lifelong celibacy. But a more practical solution is full and prompt disclosure of the relationship by both persons involved to their respective supervising attorneys. The attorneys will then disclose the relationship to their respective clients and either obtain the clients' consent (preferably written) for the paralegals to continue working on the case (with appropriate assurances of client confidentiality being preserved) or remove them from working on those cases.

(5) Recognizing potential conflicts

SLEUTH ON THE LOOSE

Identify a well-known corporation or corporate executive, then access the Business page of www.internet-news.com and see if you can locate stories concerning that company or executive.

Anything that does or could reasonably be seen as affecting your impartiality and loyalty to a client is a conflict of interest. It may be discovering that a witness in a case is a friend of yours. If the statement that witness/friend gives you about the case later comes under attack by the opposing party, that friendship may be the basis on which the other side attempts to undermine its integrity, by showing either that the witness was biased because of the friendship or that you unfairly traded on the friendship to obtain a favorable statement.

The possibilities are endless. If at any time during investigating or interviewing the legal professional becomes aware of a real or potential conflict of interest involving the financial, business, property, or other personal interest of themselves or anyone else involved in representing the client, that conflict should be immediately reported to the supervising attorney.

HYPOTHETICAL 2-6

> Assume that a year after his conversation with Sue Debum outlined in Hypotheticals 2-3 and 2-5, Ned Newatit leaves the domestic relations firm and goes to work for a larger firm specializing in defending employers against employment discrimination charges. On his first day at work with the new firm, Ned is called into a new client conference and there sits Sue Debum, who is telling one of the lawyers that she was fired from her job due to unlawful age discrimination and that she is 45 years old. Ned recognizes Sue's voice from their prior conversation and recalls that she told him then that she was 35 years old. Ned realizes that if Sue is under 40 years of age she has no standing to bring an age discrimination complaint under federal or state law. What, if anything, should Ned do with his information and why?
>
> Assume instead that when Ned enters the conference room at the new firm for the new client conference, he is introduced to Iam Debum who wishes to engage the firm to defend a lawsuit recently filed against his company by a former employee who also happens to be his former wife, Sue Debum. What should Ned do and why?
>
> Assume that Iam Debum wants to retain Ned's new firm to represent his company in an employment suit brought by someone other than Sue Debum. Should Ned disclose anything about his earlier contact with Sue Debum and why?

7. Disclosure of status in verbal and written communications

Paralegals are required to disclose their status as a paralegal in all verbal and written communications (see Canon 5 of the NALA Code of Ethics). That means, in phone conversations, introducing yourself by both name and paralegal status. That means, in written correspondence, making sure your signature is followed by the designation of paralegal or legal assistant. In jurisdictions that allow paralegals to have business cards or to have their name appear on firm stationery, it means being sure that the title appears with your name. One major reason for these requirements is the need to avoid UPL since, unless the paralegal status is properly disclosed, lay persons may assume they are dealing with an attorney.

Attorneys should also disclose their status in verbal and written correspondence. In interviewing and investigating work it can be tempting to mislead an information source into believing you are someone you are not (or that you are not someone you are, namely, a lawyer), in order to obtain information from them. This is inherently dishonest. Rule 4.1(a) of the ABA Model Rules provides that, "In the course of representing a client a lawyer shall not knowingly make a false statement of material fact or law to a third person."

8. Improper communications

SLEUTH ON THE LOOSE

Find the link to your state's health department at www.cdc.gov/nchs/about/major/natality/sites.htm, then see what information is made available there regarding health professionals (doctors, dentists, nurses, etc.) including license verification, disciplinary actions, suspensions for failure to pay child support, or other reasons. Choose one or more local health professionals and see what information you can locate about him/her.

Both attorneys and paralegals are prohibited from communicating or causing another to communicate with persons known to be represented by counsel about matters related to the representation (see Rule 4.2 of the ABA Model Rules and EC 1-2(b) of the NFPA Model Code). All communications, in that event, must be with the attorney for that person unless the attorney for that person consents to direct communication. Legal professionals involved in interviewing and investigating work will frequently have reason to inquire of potential witnesses whether they are represented by counsel and must be careful to comply with this rule.

9. Discovery of client misconduct

The legal professional involved in investigating work will typically have considerable client contact or will be gathering considerable information regarding the client. There are several categories of **client misconduct** that have ethical consequences and should be reported immediately to the supervising attorney.

a. Intent of the client to commit a criminal act

This is a grounds for the attorney to withdraw from representing a client. And if the criminal act threatened is one the attorney believes could result in imminent death or substantial bodily harm, the attorney-client privilege does not prevent the attorney from disclosing it to proper authorities. See Rule 1.6 of the ABA Model Rules.

b. Fraudulent claim or malicious harassment

If the client is making a false, fraudulent, or frivolous claim or is undertaking litigation against another merely to harass or maliciously injure another, the attorney must decline employment or must withdraw from employment if it has already been undertaken. See Rule 3.1 of the ABA Model Rules. For the attorney to undertake or continue in such representation may cause the attorney to run afoul of Rule 11 of the Federal Rules of Civil Procedure or corresponding state rule and subject both the client and the attorney to potential tort liability for malicious prosecution.

c. Commission of fraud on the court or perjury

An attorney cannot knowingly use perjured testimony in a trial or proceeding. In some cases, the attorney may have a duty to disclose the use or intended use of perjured testimony or the perpetration of a fraud on the court to the court or tribunal. See Rule 3.3 of the ABA Model Rules.

Chapter Summary and Conclusion

Ethical and professional rules for lawyers and paralegals arise primarily from state law. Organizations such as the ABA, NALA, and NFPA also promulgate ethical rules and opinions. There are serious legal and professional consequences for both lawyers and paralegals that will result from the violation of controlling ethical and professional rules. Every state limits the right of a non-lawyer to practice law, and the paralegal as well as her supervising attorney must understand and observe the limits imposed by UPL. Both the lawyer and the paralegal must maintain client confidences and secrets and guard against improper disclosure or waiver of the evidentiary privilege. Competence, integrity, and diligence are basic ethical obligations of the legal professional. The scenarios in which a conflict of interest can arise when representing a client are endless. The law office must have procedures in place to identify real and potential conflicts and deal effectively with them. Legal professionals must always disclose their status in communications with third persons regarding their representation, must avoid direct contact with those represented by counsel, and must be alert to client misconduct and their duties upon its discovery.

In chapter 3, we will consider the American adversarial system and the distinction between pre-filing investigation and formal post-filing discovery.

Review Questions

1. The organization that has formulated proposed ethical and professional rules for attorneys across the country and guidelines for attorneys who utilize paralegals is the _____.
2. List five negative consequences to the lawyer for engaging in unethical conduct.

3. List six negative consequences to the paralegal for engaging in unethical conduct.
4. List five law-related activities paralegals cannot engage in, even if delegated to them by a supervising lawyer, because they constitute the practice of law.
5. What three conditions must be satisfied before a lawyer can delegate tasks to a paralegal?
6. Assuming those three conditions are satisfied, name six law-related tasks that a lawyer can delegate to a paralegal.
7. Explain the difference between the attorney-client evidentiary privilege and the broader duty of client confidentiality.
8. Name five things a paralegal can do to attain and maintain the professional goal of competence.
9. Why is it essential that a paralegal disclose his status as a paralegal in all communications with those outside the office?
10. What should a paralegal do when learning, upon calling a witness to set up an interview, that the witness is represented by counsel in connection with the matter?

KEY WORDS AND PHRASES TO REMEMBER

ABA Model Guidelines for the Utilization of Paralegal Services
ABA Model Rules of Professional Conduct
adverse interest
advisory ethical opinion
American Bar Association
appearance of impropriety
attorney-client privilege
client confidences and secrets
client misconduct
common law
conflict of interest
court rule
Disciplinary Rule
electronically stored information (ESI)
Ethical Canon
evidentiary privilege
fiduciary duty
improper communications
legal malpractice
misdemeanor
National Association of Legal Assistants (NALA)
NALA Code of Ethics and Professional Responsibility
NALA Model Standards and Guidelines for the Utilization of Paralegals
National Federation of Paralegal Associations (NFPA)
NFPA Model Code of Ethics and Professional Responsibility and Guidelines for Enforcement
penalties
professional malpractice
sanctions
simultaneous representation
statutory law
trust account
unauthorized practice of law (UPL)

LEARN BY DOING

LBD 2-1. Locate the statute(s) in your state governing the unauthorized practice of law and prepare a memorandum summarizing how your state has defined the practice of law and the penalties for engaging in the unauthorized practice of law.

LBD 2-2. Determine if the authority that governs attorneys licensed in your state(s) has adopted guidelines for attorney utilization of paralegals, or if the ethical code for attorneys in your state(s) addresses that topic and, if so, prepare a memorandum comparing such guidelines or code provisions to the NALA and ABA Guidelines. If your state has not adopted any such guidelines, review those adopted by the state of Colorado at www.cobar.org/index.cfm/ID/106/subID/23108/CLAS// and compare those to the NALA and ABA Guidelines.

LBD 2-3. Locate the rules regarding authorized disciplinary measures, both public and private, that may be taken against attorneys in your state(s) for unethical conduct. Prepare a memorandum summarizing those measures and the existing procedure for imposition of such measures.

LBD 2-4. We have been asked to render an ethical opinion based on the following facts. Please review the facts of the case, research the governing ethical rules in your state, and draft an opinion letter with your conclusions for your instructor's review.

Mary Bryant was employed as a legal assistant by the law firm of Rock, Roll, and Remember. Ms. Bryant had a friend, Ruth Jones, who wanted to divorce her husband, Ralph Jones. Ms. Jones, however, did not feel she could afford to hire an attorney. Knowing that Ms. Bryant's law firm did divorce work, she asked Ms. Bryant for assistance in filing her divorce suit. Ms. Bryant explained to her friend that she was not a lawyer and could not represent her. However, Ms. Bryant did agree to copy certain forms in her employer's office and provide them to Ms. Jones so Ms. Jones could fill them out and file them *pro se* with the appropriate court. Ms. Bryant proceeded to do this without the knowledge of her employer. She provided the papers to Ms. Jones and explained to her how to fill them out and that was the extent of the assistance she rendered to her friend. However, to her surprise, Ralph Jones retained Rock, Roll, and Remember to represent him in the divorce action filed by Ms. Jones. Ms. Bryant did not work on the case and decided to say nothing about her assistance to Ms. Jones. This all came to light in the course of Ms. Jones's discovery deposition. The law firm was fired by Mr. Jones. Ms. Bryant was fired by the law firm. An ethical complaint has now been filed against the law firm by Mr. Jones. Ms. Bryant has filed for unemployment compensation which is being opposed by the firm on the grounds that she was fired for cause.

Please address the following questions in your draft opinion letter:

a. Did Ms. Bryant violate any legal or ethical rules by assisting Ms. Jones in the way that she did?

b. Did Ms. Bryant violate any ethical rules by remaining silent when her employer agreed to represent Mr. Jones in the divorce?

c. Can the law firm be held responsible for any ethical violation or liable for any tortious conduct committed by Ms. Bryant in this matter?

      d. What kind of punishment or sanction can the law firm expect to receive if it is found to be responsible for unethical conduct with respect to Mr. Jones?

LBD 2-5. Read, then prepare a memorandum summarizing one or more of the following articles regarding tort liability of paralegals and attorneys who use them: Christine B. Lissitzyn, *What's in a Name? Should Paralegals be Liable for Legal Malpractice?*, 15 No. 4 Prof. Law. 2 (2005); Jeffrey A. Thaler, *An Attorney's Professional Responsibility for Non-Lawyer Staff and Consultants: Beware!*, 17 Me. B.J. 106 (2002); Frances P. Kao, *No, a Paralegal Is Not a Lawyer*, 16-Feb BUSLT 11 (Jan./Feb. 2007); John W. Wade, *Tort Liability of Paralegals and Attorneys Who Use Their Services*, 24 Vand. L. Rev. 1133 (1971). Then read and brief one or more of the following cases: *Lockney v. Vroom*, 61 Va. Cir. 359 (2003) (compare *Musselman v. Willoughby Corp.*, 230 Va. 337, 337 S.E.2d 724 (1985)); *People v. Smith*, 74 P.3d 566 (Colo. 2003); *Fla. Bar v. Abrams*, 919 So.2d 425 (Fla. 2006) (compare *Florida Bar v. Lawless*, 640 So. 2d 1098 (Fla. 1994)).

LBDs 2-6 through 2-12 are accessible on the Author Updates link to the text Web site at www.aspenparalegaled.com/books/parsons_investigating/default.asp.

Chapter 3

The Adversarial System, ADR, and Pre-filing Investigation

CHAPTER OBJECTIVES

This chapter provides an overview of the adversarial system in our country, including:

- The civil and criminal court process
- Federal and state court systems
- The role of the rules of procedure and evidence in that adversarial system
- The role of informal investigation in civil and criminal cases
- Specific reasons that lawyers engage in pre-filing investigation in civil and criminal litigation

This chapter also provides an overview of administrative procedures and various forms of **alternative dispute resolution (ADR)** and considers the role of the legal professional in those areas. Finally, the chapter discusses the specific goals of pre-filing investigation.

A. The Adversarial System

In the United States, we have an **adversarial system** of justice. This means that when disputing parties are unable to resolve the dispute themselves there is a system in which those parties can present their dispute as adversaries before a court or tribunal empowered to resolve the dispute for them. The parties to the lawsuit present, or *plead*, their side of the case to the judge or jury. They also attack the opponent's presentation with a view toward convincing the judge or jury to decide in their favor rather than the opponent's. The courtroom becomes a legal battlefield bounded by well-defined rules of procedure and proof in which both sides seek to win and cause the other side to lose. The process is sometimes referred to as *civilized warfare*.

1. Civil and criminal law

In the adversarial system, cases are broadly classified as either civil or criminal. **Criminal law** involves a prosecution by the government, either federal or state, which seeks to punish by fine or imprisonment, or both, one accused of violating societal laws as codified in criminal statutes passed by the U.S. Congress or a state legislature. Criminal laws are typically classified as crimes against the person, crimes against property, or crimes against the public.

Civil law involves the determination and enforcement of all private or public rights—essentially all law that does not involve a criminal matter. Civil disputes involve claims between persons, that one party has engaged in conduct injurious to the person, property, or personal rights of the other. Examples of civil areas of the law include torts, contracts, business associations, estate planning and administration, and domestic relations.

2. The court systems

In the United States, because of the doctrine of **federalism** (the division of power between the U.S. government and the various state governments), we have a two-tiered court system—a single federal court system for the entire country and 50 separate state court systems. Illustration 3-1 charts the U.S. government court system.

The court systems of the various states are diverse but most are modeled on the federal system with one or more trial courts, one intermediate appellate court, and a supreme appellate court. Illustration 3-2 charts a typical state trial court system. The legal professional should be thoroughly familiar with the federal court system and the state court system for the state(s) in which she practices. (See LBD 3-1.)

Illustration 3-1   THE UNITED STATES COURT SYSTEM

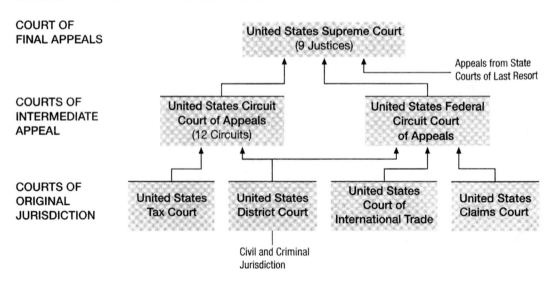

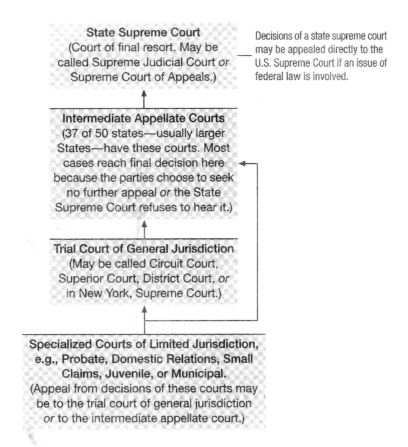

Illustration 3-2
A TYPICAL STATE
COURT SYSTEM

State Supreme Court
(Court of final resort. May be
called Supreme Judicial Court *or*
Supreme Court of Appeals.)

Decisions of a state supreme court
may be appealed directly to the
U.S. Supreme Court if an issue of
federal law is involved.

Intermediate Appellate Courts
(37 of 50 states—usually larger
States—have these courts. Most
cases reach final decision here
because the parties choose to seek
no further appeal *or* the State
Supreme Court refuses to hear it.)

Trial Court of General Jurisdiction
(May be called Circuit Court,
Superior Court, District Court, *or*
in New York, Supreme Court.)

Specialized Courts of Limited Jurisdiction,
e.g., Probate, Domestic Relations, Small
Claims, Juvenile, or Municipal.
(Appeal from decisions of these courts may
be to the trial court of general jurisdiction
or to the intermediate appellate court.)

3. Rules of procedure

An adversarial system that encourages hostility to an opposing position is bounded by many rules. The rules that govern the adversarial process in our courts are called the **rules of procedure.** In civil cases, these rules are called **rules of civil procedure.** In criminal cases, these rules are called **rules of criminal procedure.**

Because of the two-tiered court system, there are different rules of procedure governing the proceedings in the different courts. The **Federal Rules of Civil Procedure** (FRCP) govern civil proceedings in all federal district courts across the country (see Chapter 4). The **Federal Rules of Criminal Procedure** (FRCrP) govern criminal proceedings in all federal district courts (see Chapter 5). Each state will have rules of procedure that govern civil and criminal proceedings in that state's courts, and these rules of procedure may be quite different from the federal rules and from the rules of other states. Current versions of the FRCP and FRCrP can be accessed online at www.law. cornell.edu/rules/frcp/ and www.law.cornell.edu/rules/frcrmp/, respectively.

For appellate proceedings in both the federal and state court systems, there are separate rules of procedure. In the federal system, the **Federal Rules of Appellate Procedure** (FRAP), accessible online at www.law.cornell.edu/ rules/frap) will govern, and each state will have its own rules of appellate procedure to govern proceedings in its courts. For our purposes, we will concentrate on the federal rules of civil, criminal, and appellate procedure.

Illustration 3-3 STAGES OF A CIVIL LAWSUIT

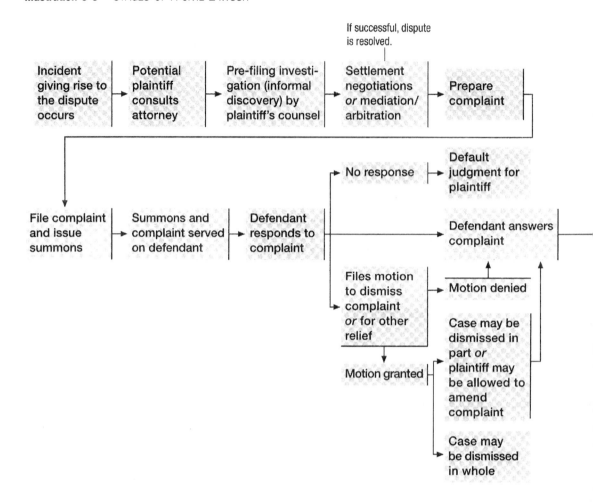

Illustration 3-3 demonstrates the stages of a civil lawsuit as it moves from the time of the incident giving rise to the dispute through trial. Illustration 3-4 demonstrates the stages of a criminal lawsuit from the time of the crime giving rise to the prosecution of the accused through trial.

As was discussed in Chapter 1, to be effective at investigation, the legal professional must be thoroughly familiar with the basic rules of procedure in the civil and/or criminal cases that his law office handles and with the trial process.

4. Rules of evidence

In the actual trial of a civil or criminal case there are also rules that strictly govern what evidence the judge or jury may hear and consider in order to make a decision in a case. These are known as the **rules of evidence** and, again, due to our two-tiered court system, the legal professional must become familiar with the **Federal Rules of Evidence** (FRE) (see Chapters 6 and 7) and the rules of evidence that govern in the state

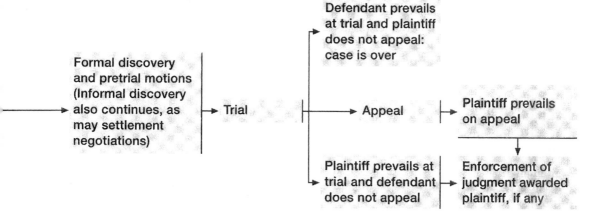

courts of the state(s) where the legal professional works. (The current version of the FRE is accessible online at www.law.cornell.edu/rules/fre/.)

5. Court rules

In addition to the rules of procedure and evidence, each individual court typically will have adopted its own **local court rules** governing certain procedures in that particular court. Local rules may cover matters such as particular days when the court hears argument on various kinds of motions, whether a legal brief must be submitted along with a motion, how long before trial subpoenas must be served on witnesses, and so forth. These rules are typically available from the clerk of the court that propounds them. The legal professional must be familiar with local rules of every court in which clients have cases pending. (See LBD 3-16.)

6. The cause of action

a. In a civil suit

In the adversarial system, parties cannot make any allegation they wish against another in court and expect to be heard by a judge or jury. Our laws

Illustration 3-4   STAGES OF A CRIMINAL PROSECUTION

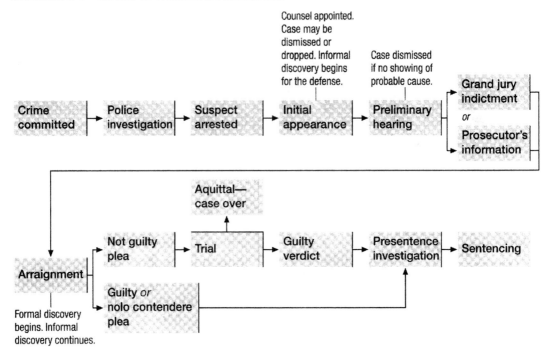

have developed in such a way that, in civil law, we identify certain theories or **causes of action** that a private party may bring against another and that the courts will entertain. Some of these causes of action have been developed by court decisions (**common law**) and others have been enacted by legislation passed by Congress at the federal level or state legislatures at the state level (**statutory law**). Still other causes of action arise from the United States Constitution or a state constitution (**constitutional law**).

A recognized **cause of action** is made up of certain **elements** or parts that must be pled and proven by the party making the allegation.

EXAMPLE

If one wishes to sue another for **breach of contract**, the elements of that cause of action will typically be:

- the existence of a valid contract;
- the material breach of that contract by the defendant; and
- provable damages sustained by the plaintiff because of the breach.

If one seeks to allege a cause of action in **negligence** against another, the elements of that cause of action will typically be:

- a duty of care owed by defendant to plaintiff;
- a breach of that duty by defendant;
- damages sustained by plaintiff; and
- legal and proximate causation between the breach of duty by defendant and the damage sustained by the plaintiff.

Unless every required element of a cause of action is proven by the **plaintiff** in a civil suit, the case will be dismissed by the judge on motion of the **defendant** (see Chapter 4). And, of course, what lawyers use to prove the cause of action for their client is **facts**, gathered through interviewing and investigating.

In federal court the pleading of sufficient facts to support a civil cause of action has become more critical in light of two recent decisions of the U.S. Supreme Court. FRCP 8(a)(2) requires that, to be sufficient, a pleading stating a claim for relief need only contain, "a short and plain statement of the claim showing that the pleader is entitled to relief." In *Conley v. Gibson*, 355 U.S. 41 (1957), the U.S. Supreme Court interpreted this rule to mean that, in order to be sufficient, a pleading need contain only enough information to fairly put the opposing party on notice of the particular claim being made or the particular defense being raised. This minimal requirement, which came to be known as notice pleading, was a radical change from the highly complex and formalized requirements of common law pleading that preceded the adoption of the FRCP. Under notice pleading, a complaint or answer cannot be devoid of any factual allegations, but need only contain sufficient minimal facts to alert the other party to the nature of the claim or defense in order to survive a motion to dismiss. If that minimal standard is met, the case then proceeds to the **formal discovery** stage (see Illustration 3-3), where the parties flesh out additional facts before testing the sufficiency of the factual allegations to go to trial. Under the notice pleading standard, a cause of action set forth in a complaint or a defense raised in an answer is not to be dismissed prior to trial unless it appears beyond doubt to the trial judge that the pleader can prove no set of facts at trial to support the claim or defense. See *Conley*, 355 U.S. at 45-46. And this determination is not normally made until the pleading party has had opportunity to engage in formal discovery to develop its factual contentions. In subsequent years, most states came to model their rules of civil procedure after the FRCP and adopted the liberal notice pleading of *Conley* for those state rules.

But all that changed with the Supreme Court's decisions in *Bell Atlantic Corp. v. Twombly*, 550 U.S. 544 (2007) and *Ashcroft v. Iqbal*, 556 U.S. 662 (2009), which reconstrued FRCP 8 to mean that plaintiffs in civil cases can no longer overcome a pre-trial or even a pre-discovery motion to dismiss for failure to state a claim for relief with a bare bones, conclusory pleading, even if such pleading clearly indicate what the cause of action or defense is. Instead, pleaders must state enough facts (as distinguished from legal conclusions) to immediately demonstrate to the trial judge deciding the motion that a claim for relief or defense is "plausible" and beyond a "speculative level." This new **plausibility pleading standard** for civil lawsuits in federal courts is highly controversial since it radically alters 70 years of consistent construction of the federal rule with no corresponding change in the wording of the rule itself by Congress (see LBD 3-11). The standard makes it very difficult for a plaintiff who can allege some facts to support a claim but needs to gather additional facts during formal discovery in order to demonstrate plausibility of the claim to survive an early motion to dismiss and raises serious questions of fundamental fairness. Nonetheless, the Supreme Court has spoken, and plausibility is now the pleading standard for civil cases in federal court. It remains to be seen whether those states whose civil pleading rule is modeled on FRCP 8(a)(2) will abandon notice pleading for plausibility pleading for civil actions filed in their state courts in light of *Twombly* and *Iqbal* (see LBDs 3-12 and 3-13).

b. In a criminal prosecution

Neither the federal government nor state governments can prosecute a person criminally for just anything. The government must prosecute for a crime already recognized by the state or federal government. And the alleged criminal act will also have elements that the government must allege and prove to the requisite degree (usually beyond a reasonable doubt—see Chapter 6) to prevail.

EXAMPLE

> Take a look back at Hypothetical 1-1 and note the various elements of each of the homicide crimes mentioned there.

In both civil and criminal cases, the legal investigator must be able to determine and understand the elements of the cause of action involved in the client's representation in order to know what factual information to seek. (See the discussion of factual analysis in Chapter 1.)

7. Remedies

a. In a civil suit

In a civil suit, the plaintiff will seek some type of **remedy** from the defendant(s). Most often the remedy sought is **money damages.** Money damages sought may be either compensatory or punitive. **Compensatory damages** are money damages that *compensate* the plaintiff or make the plaintiff whole. Compensatory damages may be **general** (compensation for pain and suffering) or **specific** (out-of-pocket expenses such as medical bills, lost wages, etc.). (Lawyers sometimes refer to specific compensatory damages as the *specials* in a case, as in "What are his specials?".)

EXAMPLE

> If Road Rage sues Lead Foot for negligence in causing the automobile accident described in Hypothetical 1-2, Road Rage, as plaintiff, may seek compensatory damages for his past and future pain and suffering, permanent disability, loss of enjoyment of life, past and future medical expenses, past and future lost income, and travel expenses to and from the doctor. All of these would be considered compensatory damages. Which would fall into the category of general compensatory damages and which into the category of specials?

Punitive damages, sometimes called **exemplary damages**, are damages which are meant to punish or make an example of the wrongdoer for his conduct. In most states, such damages can only be recovered against a defendant whose actions are proven to have been willful, reckless, or malicious (see LBD 3-14).

EXAMPLE

> If Road Rage can prove that Lead Foot deliberately (willfully) ran the red light in order to strike his vehicle, he may be awarded some amount of money as punitive damages in addition to his compensatory damages.

In some types of civil actions, **equitable relief** may be sought instead of or as an alternative to money damages. There are a number of different kinds of equitable relief but two of the most common forms are **injunctive relief** and **declaratory relief.** An **injunction** is an order by the court directing a party to do or refrain from doing something.

EXAMPLE

> If Road Rage is able to show that Lead Foot is stalking him by car and attempts to cause a collision with him every time Road Rage takes to the streets, Road Rage may be able to secure an injunction from the court enjoining Lead Foot from coming around or about him in a vehicle.

Declaratory relief is a remedy sought when the plaintiff is uncertain of what action is proper to take and seeks the court's "declaration" of what is proper.

EXAMPLE

> If Road Rage was killed in the car accident with Lead Foot and had a life insurance policy covering his life at the time of his death, the life insurance company will want to pay the proceeds of the policy to the beneficiary. If both the wife and adult child of Road Rage each claim to be the sole beneficiary and the insurance policy is unclear, the insurance company may file a lawsuit seeking a declaration from the court as to which of the claimants is the proper beneficiary.

And, of course, the remedies available in a civil suit depend on the **facts** gathered through interviewing and investigating.

b. In a criminal prosecution

In criminal proceedings, the government usually seeks the incarceration of the criminal defendant or a monetary fine or both. A crime may be a **misdemeanor,** which is punishable by incarceration for up to one year, or a **felony,** which is punishable by incarceration for more than one year.

Civil law and criminal law sometimes overlap. Criminal charges may be filed by the state for actions that also give rise to a civil suit by the victim for money damages.

EXAMPLE

> If it is shown that Lead Foot did in fact run the stop sign and strike the car driven by Road Rage, Lead Foot may not only be sued for damages in a civil action for damages by Road Rage, he may also be prosecuted for the misdemeanor of reckless driving. If Road Rage is killed in the accident, Lead Foot may be prosecuted for a homicide offense.

In both civil and criminal cases a major focus of factual investigation is on matters relating to the remedies sought. The legal investigator must be able to determine and understand the law regarding remedies in a particular case.

8. Defenses

a. In a civil suit

For every civil cause of action that may be alleged, the defendant may merely **deny** the allegations and force the plaintiff to carry his **burden of proof** on all the elements of the cause of action (see discussion of the burden and degree of proof below). But in addition, the defendant may allege **affirmative defenses** which, if proved, will defeat plaintiff's right to recover in whole or part even if the plaintiff does prove all the elements of his cause of action (see extended discussion in Chapter 4). For these affirmative defenses, there are recognized elements that must be properly pled and proven by the defendant who asserts them.

EXAMPLE

> If the defendant in the negligence action wants to raise the affirmative defense of **assumption of risk**, he will have to allege and prove:
>
> - that the plaintiff was injured while voluntarily engaging in risky behavior;
> - that the plaintiff knew and appreciated the risk of the behavior;
> - that the plaintiff's undertaking of the risky behavior was unreasonable; and
> - that the injuries sustained by plaintiff were caused by his voluntary and unreasonable undertaking of the known risk.

b. In a criminal prosecution

To every crime with which one may be charged, there are recognized **defenses** that may be available to the criminal defendant beyond a simple denial of guilt. These defenses, like the alleged crimes themselves, will have elements which the criminal defendant will typically have the burden of alleging and proving (see Chapter 5).

EXAMPLE

> If Quick Temper from Hypothetical 1-1, is charged under one of the homicide statutes for killing Hi Fi, it may be a defense to him if he can show he fired at Hi Fi because he thought Hi Fi was about to shoot him. Depending on the laws of the state, to make out a case of self-defense, Quick Temper might have to show:

- that he reasonably believed himself to be in mortal danger from Hi Fi;
- that the mortal danger he perceived was imminent; and
- that he used reasonable force under the circumstances to protect himself.

In both civil and criminal cases a major focus of **factual investigation** is on matters relating to the defenses that are or might be raised.

9. The burden and degree of proof

a. In a civil suit

In a civil case, the burden of proof is initially on the plaintiff to prove all the elements of her cause of action. The **degree of proof** required in civil cases is typically by a **preponderance of the evidence.** This means the plaintiff, in order to prevail, must convince the trier of fact that it is *more likely than not* that her allegations regarding the elements of her action are true and that she is entitled to prevail. If the defendant in a civil action asserts an affirmative defense, the defendant will have the burden of proving all the elements of that defense, typically by a preponderance.

In some civil actions, the degree of proof required may be slightly higher than the preponderance. For example, in some states, civil fraud must be proven by **clear and convincing evidence,** not by a mere preponderance.

b. In a criminal prosecution

In a criminal case, the burden is on the prosecution to prove all the elements of the crime alleged. The degree of proof required in a criminal case is greater than in a civil case, for the government must prove its case **beyond a reasonable doubt.**

In both civil and criminal cases, where the burden of proof lies and what the degree of proof is both have significant impact on the factual investigation that must be done to carry the burden of proof by the requisite degree.

10. Means of proof

As is discussed in more detail in Chapters 6 and 7, in both civil and criminal cases, the proof of facts relevant to the issues is controlled by the rules of evidence. Evidence may be presented to the court in several different ways:

- **Testimonial evidence** is evidence received from the sworn testimony of witnesses.
- **Documentary evidence** is evidence received from properly admitted documents or other data compilations (e.g. electronically stored information).
- **Real or physical evidence** is evidence in the form of properly admitted objects (e.g., the weapon in a murder case or the defective machine in a products liability case).

- **Demonstrative evidence** is evidence that has been prepared for trial by the litigants, usually in the form of pictures, videos, charts, graphs, diagrams, computer simulations, etc., which portray or illustrate something relevant to the case.

Understanding the rules that govern the kinds of evidence that can be received in court is critical to the legal investigator who seeks that kind of information.

11. Statutes of limitation and repose

SLEUTH ON THE LOOSE

Identify a prescription medication you or someone you know has taken recently, then access the Web site of the American Society of Health Systems Pharmacists at www.safe-medication.com to learn more about that medication including its chemical makeup, side effects, and contra-indications.

The rules of procedure and local rules of court mentioned above contain many time limitations and deadlines with which the legal professional must become familiar. In addition, state and federal statutes and regulations set forth time periods in which a civil cause of action or criminal prosecution can be brought. These are referred to as statutes of limitation or statutes of repose. If the civil case or criminal prosecution is not instigated within the designated time, it is typically barred forever.

A **statute of limitation** states the time in which a lawsuit must be commenced against a defendant. The time limitation varies depending on the cause of action and typically begins to run from the date the particular cause of action arose. For example, in many states a lawsuit seeking damages for personal injury based on a **negligence** cause of action must be commenced within a year from the date the cause of action arose, which usually will be the date of the negligent act itself.

A **statute of repose** places an absolute limit on the time in which a lawsuit must be commenced without regard to when the cause of action arose. For example, some states have statutes providing that a suit alleging an injury due to a defect in a product be commenced within some number of years from the date the product was first offered for sale regardless of when the defect was discovered or when the injury occurred.

HYPOTHETICAL 3-1

Assume that in your state the statute of limitations for commencing a personal injury action in negligence is one year from the date the cause of action arose. For causes of action in strict liability, the statute is three years from the date the cause of action arose. And for causes of action in breach of warranty, the statute is four years from the date of purchase of the product. Your state also has a ten-year statute of repose for products liability actions, which commences on the date the product was first offered for sale to the public.

Today a new client comes into the law office where you work and you are assigned to interview her. The facts you elicit in the initial interview are that two months ago the client was badly injured when the riding lawn mower she was using to mow her lawn failed to slow down when she engaged the clutch, causing the mower to go over a steep slope. She also says she bought the mower two years ago from a dealer specializing in reconditioned yard equipment. Later, in consultation with the partner responsible for the case, it is decided that the client may have a valid cause of action in negligence, strict liability, and breach of warranty. You are assigned the factual investigation.

Your investigation confirms that the mishap and injury occurred two months ago and that she bought the mower a little over a year ago, but you also learn that this particular mower was first sold and put in service 11 years ago. Absent other facts, what should this client be advised regarding her potential causes of action?

Assume your investigation reveals that the product was first sold and put in service five years ago, but that the accident and injury actually occurred 14 months ago. What should this client be advised regarding her potential causes of action?

The failure of lawyers to initiate actions within a statute of limitation or repose may constitute legal malpractice. And in most jurisdictions there are many different statutes of limitation and repose for the various causes of action that may be brought. (See LBD 3-2.)

There are statutes of limitation limiting the time for the federal and state governments to initiate criminal prosecutions as well. Almost all crimes carry statutes of limitation with the universal exception of homicide. In some states, other more serious crimes are declared exempt from any limitation period (e.g., arson, rape, child molestation, and some drug offenses). At the federal level, there is no statute of limitation for treason or acts of terrorism and at the international level none for genocide, crimes against humanity, or war crimes.

In either the civil or criminal context, a statute of limitations may be deemed **tolled** (i.e, stayed or frozen) for various reasons. In civil cases where the cause of action lies with an injured or aggrieved plaintiff, the statute may be tolled while the plaintiff is a minor or under some physical or mental disability rendering the plaintiff unable to take action (See LBD 3-2).

EXAMPLE

Assume a 14-year-old minor is injured in a car accident due to the negligence of the driver, and the jurisdiction imposes a two-year statute of limitations for bringing tort actions for personal injury. If the age of minority in the jurisdiction is 18, the statute will be tolled for this plaintiff until she reaches the age of majority. She will have two years following her 18th birthday to file the lawsuit. She need not wait, of course. The lawsuit can be filed immediately on her behalf by a parent or legal guardian.

In both civil and criminal cases the action may be tolled by reason of the fraudulent concealment of the bad act by the defendant (e.g., a doctor who commits malpractice but defrauds the patient into believing there was no malpractice). And a bad act can be deemed continuing in nature so that the applicable statute of limitations does not begin to run until the end of the continuing bad act (e.g., a civil fraud that continues for ten years—the statute of limitations will only begin to run at the end of the ten years; same result with an embezzlement that goes on for ten years). See a good discussion of the **continuing violations doctrine** in *Treanor v. MCI Telecommunications, Inc.*, 200 F.3d 570 (7 Cir. 1999) (see LBD 3-2).

B. ▷ Administrative Procedures

Because of the plethora of **administrative agencies** (governmental bodies charged with administering legislation in specific areas) at both the state and federal levels, much litigation today occurs in the administrative context rather than in a civil or criminal lawsuit. Governmental agencies are actively engaged in interviewing and investigating in the furtherance of their responsibilities regarding rule making, enforcement, and adjudication. Both federal and state agencies employ many attorneys and paralegals who are expected to have adequate interviewing and investigating skills.

Whenever an agency action is to be challenged or appealed, it is necessary for the legal professional to be familiar with:

- the **enabling legislation** (the statute that created and controls the agency);
- the **rules and regulations** promulgated by the agency that define the perimeters of its authority and the procedures by which it acts; and
- the **Administrative Procedures Act,** which, in most cases, governs the procedures by which agency action may be challenged or appealed.

Generally, no suit may be brought in a court of law challenging agency action until the required administrative procedures have been exhausted (called the **exhaustion of remedies**). Illustration 3-5 sets out the procedural steps involved in an administrative adjudication.

Interviewing and investigating skills are just as important in an administrative proceeding as in traditional civil and criminal litigation. Differences will arise in the procedure and, sometimes, in the form in which factual information must be placed for evidentiary purposes.

Illustration 3-5
PROCEDURAL STEPS IN AN ADMINISTRATIVE ADJUDICATION

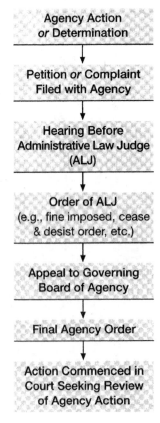

Agency Action *or* Determination

↓

Petition *or* Complaint Filed with Agency

↓

Hearing Before Administrative Law Judge (ALJ)

↓

Order of ALJ (e.g., fine imposed, cease & desist order, etc.)

↓

Appeal to Governing Board of Agency

↓

Final Agency Order

↓

Action Commenced in Court Seeking Review of Agency Action

C. ▶ Alternative Dispute Resolution (ADR)

Because of the growing expense of litigation, the crowded court dockets, the time it takes to move a suit through the court system, growing disenchantment with the hostile nature of the adversarial process, and the problem of attorney abuse of the adversarial system, there has been a growing interest in providing disputing parties an alternative means of resolving their dispute. The most common methods of ADR are as follows:

1. Negotiation

Negotiation is the process by which the adverse parties, either before or during the litigation process, talk informally, usually through their attorneys, to try and work out a compromise settlement of the dispute. Today, more than 90 percent of all civil suits settle out of court before trial by negotiation and the vast majority of criminal cases are plea bargained the same way.

The great weakness of negotiation, however, is that it usually does not take place until the parties have retained attorneys, suit has been filed, much formal discovery has taken place, and pretrial motions have been filed and ruled on with the attendant expense and delay. Many conscientious attorneys attempt to resolve disputes prior to filing a lawsuit. Too often, however, time does not permit this because a statute of limitations is about to run, or the opposing party decides to engage in discovery in order to determine the merits of the claim prior to negotiating. In addition, some less scrupulous attorneys still avoid or delay negotiations to give themselves an opportunity to *churn the file* and earn more fees.

Judges will frequently inquire of the parties to a pending suit whether settlement negotiations have taken place and encourage the parties to attempt them. Of course, the judge cannot order parties to settle. However, FRCP 26(f) now authorizes the U.S. district courts to require the parties to meet and discuss a number of things about the case including "the possibilities for promptly settling or resolving the case." This procedure is frequently used in the federal courts.

An interesting new online negotiation service, Cybersettle (www. cybersettle.com/pub/), may be the wave of the future. Disputing parties who utilize Cybersettle use no mediator or other human facilitator. Instead the parties submit blind offers and counteroffers until they hit each other's settlement range and then average or split the difference (see LBD 3-25).

2. Mediation

A **mediator** is a neutral third party who seeks to facilitate a voluntary settlement between disputing parties. The mediator will listen to both sides, serve as a communication link between the disputing parties, and will encourage both sides to be reasonable and move toward a realistic settlement. The mediator has no authority to compel a settlement or to make any ruling in the favor of either party, nor does the mediator report the content of the discussions to the judge.

In the past generation, mediation has become a popular and successful ADR tool, and now states are adopting rules giving trial judges the authority to mandate mediation and to select the mediator from a list of **court approved mediators** (see Career Tip and see LBDs 3-9, 3-10). Many federal district courts have adopted similar procedures by local rule, and some state appellate courts and federal circuit courts of appeals have mediation procedures for cases on appeal (see, e.g., **mediation conference** procedures for the Sixth Circuit at www.ca6.uscourts.gov/internet/mediation/aboutmediationconferences.htm and see LBD 3-21). (See the various resources on ADR available in Appendix B, Resources for the Investigator.)

The rise in mandated mediation, the activist role of trial judges in facilitating mediation and settlement, and the evolving mindset that all cases should settle and not go to trial, are all factors that have contributed to a startling decline in the number of civil cases actually decided by trial by jury or by judge (the bench trial). A recent study for the Roscoe Pound Civil Justice Institute (see LBD 3-22) announced that between 1962 and 2010 the percentage of civil cases in federal courts decided by trial dropped from about 12% per year to about 1% per year. A similar though less drastic trend has been documented in the state courts. The pendulum has swung so far toward presumption that all civil cases should settle that there is now a backlash, questioning whether this presumption is actually in the best interest of all clients or in the best interest of the common public good, especially when so many private settlements involve a continuing denial of culpability by a defendant who pays a settlement and a confidentiality clause in the settlement agreement that protects the defendant from any public disclosure of the terms of settlement. Many are questioning whether lawyers and clients are being pressured into unwise settlements not in a client's best interest and whether more high profile or otherwise significant lawsuits *ought to be* tried in public in order to (1) expose reckless or even corrupt business practices so the wider public will know; (2) motivate voluntary change in reckless or corrupt business practices by non-defendants who fear being held accountable in a similar fashion; and (3) influence state legislatures and/or Congress to regulate in the interest of consumers when they otherwise would not due to lack of information or the influence of corporate money on that branch of government (see LBD 3-23).

3. Arbitration

In **arbitration** the parties agree to submit their dispute to a disinterested person (or panel of persons) other than a judge or jury. The arbitrator(s) will listen to both sides and then render a decision. That decision may be binding or non-binding, depending on the nature of the dispute and the terms of any agreement between the parties. Disputing parties may voluntarily agree to arbitrate after a dispute arises (*voluntary arbitration*). Or contracting parties may agree at the time the contract is entered into that in the event of a dispute they will submit it to arbitration rather than litigating (*mandatory arbitration*). Many contracts today routinely contain clauses requiring arbitration in the event of a dispute and designating it as *binding* or *non-binding*. The decision of the arbitrator in binding arbitration may not be set aside by a court unless it is determined that the arbitration award was not made in good faith or that the arbitrator was guilty of misconduct.

The federal government and a number of state governments favor arbitration over litigation. The Federal Arbitration Act of 1925 (FAA), 9 U.S.C. §§1-15, provides that courts must give deference to all arbitration provisions agreed to in contracts involving transactions that impact on interstate commerce, even where such contracts are governed by state law. See *Southland Corp. v. Keating*, 465 U.S. 1 (1984). Controversially, the U.S. Supreme Court has interpreted the FAA to require enforcement of a contractual arbitration provision even in situations where state contract law or equitable principles would strike down such provision as unconscionable or as violative of state public policy or state consumer protection laws or state deceptive advertising laws. See *AT&T Mobility v Concepcion*, 131 S. Ct. 1740 (2011) (see LBD 3-15). In addition, the court has stricken provisions in such agreements that purport to give the courts more power to review an arbitration decision than is granted in the FAA. See *Hall Street Associates, LLC v. Mattel, Inc.*, 552, U.S. 577 (2008). The growing utilization of contracts containing mandatory arbitration clauses, especially in employment and consumer contracts, is another significant factor in the drop in number of civil cases decided by trial.

Procedures in an arbitration often are governed by the Uniform Arbitration Act (UAA) formulated by the National Conference of Commissioners on Uniform State Laws in 1955 and adopted by 34 states and the District of Columbia.

Arbitration services are available from numerous private organizations and from various government agencies. The American Arbitration Association (AAA) (online at www.adr.org), a non-profit corporation, and one of the oldest and largest provider of arbitration services, assists in locating qualified arbitrators. AAA suggests appropriate language for an arbitration agreement and provides helpful forms and a set of procedures for the arbitration process. Illustration 3-6 sets out the AAA form for submission of a commercial dispute to arbitration resolution. (See Appendix B for additional resources on arbitration. See LBDs 3-10 and 3-24.)

D. Distinguishing Between Formal Discovery and Informal Investigation

The distinction between formal and informal discovery is important and should always be kept in mind when planning and undertaking investigation.

1. Formal discovery

Formal discovery is that discovery governed by rules 26 through 37 of the rules of civil procedure or by applicable rules of criminal procedure (see Chapters 4 and 5). Such discovery, with very limited exceptions, occurs *after* a civil lawsuit has been filed or a formal criminal prosecution has begun and requires notice to and the right to participation by all parties to the lawsuit or their legal representatives.

Often it is necessary to do investigation through the formal rules of discovery. For example, the only way to compel an opposing party to give a statement or provide documents in a civil case may be by formal deposition and document requests submitted after a lawsuit is started. Likewise, an uncooperative witness sometimes may be compelled to talk only by subpoenaing that witness to a deposition after the lawsuit has been filed.

2. Informal investigation

Informal investigation is private investigation that may be undertaken by an attorney on behalf of a client either before (**pre-filing investigation**) or after a lawsuit is commenced and which need not follow the formal rules set forth in the rules of civil or criminal procedure. There is no legal or ethical prohibition on continuing to engage in informal investigation after a lawsuit has been commenced. Illustration 3-7 highlights the important distinction between formal discovery and informal investigation.

3. The advantages of informal investigation

Where possible, it is usually preferable to engage in informal investigation before beginning formal discovery and to do so as early in the representation as possible. There are several reasons why this is true.

a. Early investigation produces more information

Documents do get changed, lost, or destroyed. Witnesses move, die, forget. Accident scenes change. Physical evidence can change form or disappear.

b. Information located early is more reliable

Statements of witnesses taken a week after an accident are likely to be more reliable than statements taken nine months later.

c. Information sought informally is more easily obtained

Many witnesses tend to be less cooperative if they know a lawsuit is pending. Many information sources tend to want to share the information with the other side to be "fair" if they know a lawsuit is pending.

Illustration 3-6   AMERICAN ARBITRATION ASSOCIATION FORM FOR SUBMISSION
OF DISPUTE TO RESOLUTION

American Arbitration Association
Dispute Resolution Services Worldwide

Please visit our website at www.adr.org if you
would like to file this case online.   **SUBMISSION TO DISPUTE RESOLUTION**
AAA Customer Service can be reached at 800-778-7879

The named parties hereby submit the following dispute for resolution, under the rules of the American Arbitration Association.
To be completed and signed by all parties (attach additional sheets if necessary).

Rules Selected: ☐Commercial ☐Construction ☐Employment ☐Other (please specify) _____

Procedure Selected: ☐Binding Arbitration ☐Mediation ☐Other (please specify)_____ .

NATURE OF DISPUTE:

Dollar Amount of Claim $	Other Relief Sought: ☐ Attorneys Fees ☐ Interest
	☐Arbitration Costs ☐Punitive/ Exemplary ☐ Other _____

PLEASE DESCRIBE APPROPRIATE QUALIFICATIONS FOR ARBITRATOR(S) TO BE APPOINTED TO HEAR THIS DISPUTE:

Amount Enclosed $_____   In accordance with Fee Schedule: ☐Flexible Fee Schedule   ☐Standard Fee Schedule

HEARING LOCALE REQUESTED: _____	Estimated time needed for hearings overall: _____ hours or _____ days

We agree that, if arbitration is selected, we will abide by and perform any award rendered hereunder and that a judgment may be entered on the award.

Name of Party	Name of Party
Address:	Address:
City: State Zip Code	City: State Zip Code
Phone No. Fax No.	Phone No. Fax No.
Email Address:	Email Address:
Signature (required): Date:	Signature (required): Date:
Name of Representative:	Name of Representative:
Name of Firm (if applicable)	Name of Firm (if applicable)
Address (to be used in connection with this case)	Address (to be used in connection with this case)
City: State Zip Code	City: State Zip Code
Phone No. Fax No.	Phone No. Fax No.
Email Address:	Email Address:

To begin proceedings, please send a copy of this Demand and the Arbitration Agreement, along with the filing fee as provided for in the Rules, to: American Arbitration Association, Case Filing Services, 1101 Laurel Oak Road, Suite 100 Voorhees, NJ 08043. Send the original Demand to the Respondent.

Illustration 3-7
COMPARING FORMAL
DISCOVERY AND
INFORMAL
INVESTIGATION

Event giving rise to the suit	Lawsuit is filed	Trial *or* Settlement

Formal Discovery*

Informal Investigation**

* Must follow formal procedural rules of notice to and participation by all parties.
** Need not follow procedural rules. No notice to or participation by other parties.

d. Information sought informally is less expensive

The formal discovery process can be quite expensive. Informal investigation need not be. For example, taking a witness's statement informally will take less time and involve a lot less expense than waiting for a formal deposition after a suit is filed.

e. No opposing party is present for informal investigation

Formal discovery requires notice to all other parties and they have the right to be present and participate in the discovery event. In contrast, when the investigator undertakes informal investigation, no notice need be given to adverse parties of informal investigation and they have no right to be present or participate.

f. The first side to locate relevant information gains advantages in litigation

This is true for all the reasons considered in *a* through *e* above. The side obtaining relevant information first can better evaluate the case, plan strategy, and seize the initiative.

g. Prompt investigation enhances settlement prospects

Litigation is expensive and time consuming. There also is emotional stress for the parties involved in a lawsuit. Early settlement of a dispute avoids these problems for the client and prompt investigation leads to early settlement.

Informal investigation is limited only by:

- the parameters of what is legal;
- the ethical rules that govern lawyers and those that work with them;
- the scope of authority given to the investigator by the client; and
- the investigator's imagination and industriousness.

HYPOTHETICAL 3-2

Assume the legal office where you work undertakes representation of Road Rage from Hypothetical 1-2. You learn that the accident occurred only last week and because there is a one-year statute of limitations, your office has nearly a year to prepare and file the suit for Road Rage against Lead Foot. Road Rage says that not only did Lead Foot run the red light, but the brakes on Road Rage's car failed to work when he braked. The supervising partner says this is worth investigating since it could produce a second defendant. Road Rage also tells you that he thinks Lead Foot will claim that he (Road Rage) actually ran the red light rather than Lead Foot but that there were two other witnesses to the accident whose names are on the accident report who should confirm his version of the incident.

You are assigned the task of interviewing the two known witnesses to the accident and of taking your consulting expert out to inspect the brakes on Road Rage's car which was totaled in the accident and is now stored at Biff's Garage. Your supervising attorney hopes that your investigation can confirm Road Rage's allegations and lead to a settlement without even having to file suit.

Since you have plenty of time on this file you let it slip to the bottom of your work pile and don't get around to it for six months. When you finally contact witness number one to set up an interview you learn that the witness was an elderly man who died two months after the accident. His widow says somebody from an insurance company did interview him before he died though. You conclude this must have been the insurance adjuster from Lead Foot's insurance company. When you contact the second witness she grants you an interview but says the cars were both blue and she can no longer recollect which car ran the red light. When you call Biff's to set up a time for you and the expert to inspect Road Rage's car you learn that the insurance company has already authorized it to be sold as junk and it's gone. When you get back to the office you learn that Road Rage has just been sued for negligence by Lead Foot who is alleging that Road Rage ran the red light.

You decide to go home and update your resume on the assumption you may soon be in the market for a new job! Before you leave for good though, you might want to suggest to your supervising partner that he notify the firm's professional liability carrier of a potential malpractice claim!

Identify each of the reasons for doing informal investigation early, as listed in 3(a) through (g) above, that you have ignored. What could you have done differently and what difference might it have made to Road Rage, your attorney, and to you?

E. ▶ Pre-Filing Procedures

1. The mandate for pre-filing investigation

The days when a competent lawyer would file a lawsuit and then begin to look into the real merits of it are long gone. Today, for several reasons, the attorney must do a legitimate and adequate investigation prior to filing the lawsuit to determine that it has merit. The consequences of failing to do so can be quite serious.

- The mandates of FRCP 11 and similar state rules may be violated, resulting in fines and penalties assessed against the client and the lawyer. (See Chapter 1.)
- Filing a frivolous or insupportable suit may result in ethical sanctions against the attorney. (See Chapter 2.)

- Filing a frivolous or insupportable suit may result in the client and the lawyer both being sued by the adverse party for malicious prosecution or abuse of process. (See Chapter 1.)
- Doing an inadequate or untimely pre-filing investigation, or filing a frivolous or insupportable suit may result in the attorney being sued for legal malpractice by the client for whom he filed the suit. (See Chapter 2.)

2. Objectives of pre-filing investigation

a. To determine if there are facts sufficient to state one or more causes of action

It is the responsibility of the attorney representing a potential plaintiff in a civil case to determine what, if any, valid causes of action may exist on behalf of the client. Making that determination almost always requires the attorney to conduct or supervise an associate attorney or paralegal in conducting an investigation to verify facts and information provided by the client and to locate additional facts and information to support the potential causes of action. The state or federal prosecutor has a similar responsibility in identifying and developing proof regarding all alleged crimes a defendant may have committed.

It is critical that the legal investigator have a sufficient understanding of the elements of the different causes of action or criminal charges being considered in order to plan and execute an investigation seeking legally relevant information (see Chapter 9). Only then will the investigator recognize the relevance and value of information she obtains in her investigation. Only then will the investigator know what leads to follow to locate more helpful information. The investigator should also be able to recognize potential causes of action or criminal charges not yet under consideration but which may be supportable by new information that is discovered in the investigation.

Identifying provable causes of action or criminal charges in pre-filing investigation is critical too because of the various statutes of limitation and repose that may be running on each. Woe to the lawyer in a civil case who fails to identify a cause of action which could have been identified in pre-filing investigation and files the lawsuit without alleging that cause of action and discovers its existence only later. Subject to the rules on amending pleadings contained in the rules of civil procedure (and the tender mercies of the presiding judge), the attorney may have committed malpractice by this inadequate pre-filing investigation. And woe to the prosecuting attorney who fails to identify and charge a defendant with provable crimes. The people's interests have not been competently represented, and justice has not been done.

b. To determine provable damages

Closely related to the decision on what causes of action are available to a client in a civil case is the decision on what damages may be successfully recovered in a given action. Plaintiffs' attorneys learn quickly that a case may be a good one on liability but not be worth filing because of little or no provable damages, as shown in Hypothetical 3-3.

HYPOTHETICAL 3-3

Assume that Clum Zee works as a clerk in a discount retail store. One busy Saturday, while stocking shampoo on the shelves of the store, Clum Zee drops a bottle on the floor and sees it burst, spreading a slick white puddle across the white tiled floor in the aisle. Clum Zee goes off to get a mop to clean up the spill but he does not place any warning sign or barrier at the spot of the spill. Clum Zee intends to come right back and clean the spill, but when he gets to the back of the store he finds some of his friends on break watching a soccer match on TV and decides to join them. Thirty minutes later, a customer in the store, Born Toshop, is walking down the aisle where the spilled shampoo is with her hands full of merchandise. She would have used a shopping cart or a hand shopping basket but there were none at the front of the store. Born Toshop does not see the spill, steps in it and slips, falling on her backside and spilling the merchandise she was holding. Just as Born Toshop sits up, Clum Zee returns to the aisle and says, "Oh my gosh, I knew I should have gotten back here sooner. This is all my fault." Two other shoppers hear him say this and provide Born Toshop with their names and addresses. One of them retrieves a video camera from her car and videotapes the spill with Clum Zee standing proudly beside it with his mop explaining how and when he had caused the spill, apologizing to Born Toshop, and saying repeatedly that it was his fault.

Born Toshop contacts an attorney the next week, thinking she has hit the jackpot and can now put her daughter through college. She relates the facts to the attorney and his paralegal, both of whom try to keep from salivating on the table while they watch the videotape of Clum Zee. When it is over, the attorney, giddy with anticipation, tells Born Toshop he will take her case. The paralegal, slightly more in control of his emotions, whispers to the attorney, "Don't you want to ask her if she was hurt?" The attorney nods and asks Born Toshop how she was injured in the fall. "Oh, that's the most amazing thing about all this," she replies. "I wasn't hurt a bit. In fact it was really sort of fun. I almost felt like I was snow-boarding down that aisle. And no one saw me fall so it wasn't even that embarrassing. How much do you think we can get?"

Do you think the attorney might change his mind about taking Born Toshop's case? Why?

c. To determine if there are facts sufficient to assert a valid defense

On the defense side of a civil or criminal action, once the plaintiff or prosecutor has filed the initial pleading containing the allegations, an investigation must occur prior to filing an answer or responsive motion. Remember that the dictates of Rule 11 and the relevant ethical rules apply not only to complaints that initiate civil lawsuits, but to all pleadings, motions, and discovery papers filed in a civil or criminal action by any party.

The initial investigation done by the defense counsel will not only enable counsel to decide whether and what to plead in the client's defense but will assist in making other critical recommendations to the client regarding, for example, whether to seek an early settlement in a civil case or to plea bargain in a criminal case.

d. To satisfy special pleading requirements

In addition to the plausibility pleading requirement imposed in federal civil litigation under FRCP 8(a)(2) as construed by *Twombly* and *Iqbal*, the FRCP (accessible online at www.law.cornell.edu/rules/frcp/) contain other special pleading requirements that must be met by plaintiffs and defendants in civil litigation. FRCP 9 requires that the facts supporting some types of allegations, such as fraud, be pled *with particularity*; general allegations will not suffice. Unless pled with sufficient particularity, such allegations will be dismissed by the court or the plaintiff's lawyer will be unable to prove them at trial. And FRCP 8(c) mandates that affirmative defenses asserted by the defendant in a civil case, such as the running of the statute of limitations, release, satisfaction, etc., be set forth affirmatively in the responsive pleading. The consequence of failing to do so may be the permanent **waiver** of such defenses that could have been discovered in pre-filing investigation. The lawyer for a defendant cannot put on proof of such defenses at trial if they have not been included in the answer filed on behalf of the defendant.

State rules of civil procedure typically contain similar special pleading requirements. (See LBD 3-17.)

As we will see in more detail in Chapter 5, in criminal prosecutions there are strict pleading requirements in place for the prosecution in the drafting of an indictment or information (the formal charging documents in a criminal prosecution). Unless every element of an alleged crime is carefully pled, the charging document may be quashed and the prosecution dismissed. And like a defendant in a civil case, the criminal defendant must give timely written notice to the prosecution of affirmative defenses to be raised to the charges brought (e.g., insanity, diminished capacity, alibis, justification, etc.). As in civil cases, if proper and timely notice is not given, the defense cannot rely on such affirmative defenses at trial.

e. To identify all potential defendants

Frequently the client in a civil case may be able to identify only one potential defendant in a case. That known defendant may be **judgment proof** (having insufficient assets to pay any judgment rendered). It will be up to the plaintiff's attorney, in pre-filing investigation, to identify other defendants. In fact, it is part of the attorney's duty to the client to identify all potential defendants. Defendants considering a counterclaim or third-party claim in response to a suit filed against them will also look for potential defendants to such claims.

Identifying potential defendants frequently requires an understanding of various other areas of the law that render persons other than the wrongful actor liable for the consequences of the wrong. The investigating legal professional must understand and be able to see the potential application of:

1. **The law of agency and principle of** *respondeat superior.* In the law of torts, one who commits a wrongful act that injures another while acting as the **authorized agent** of another may not only be liable himself to the injured party, but may render the principal for whom he was acting liable as well.

2. **The principle of indemnity.** Sometimes the law recognizes that a party is legally responsible for an obligation, but the party liable is able to place the obligation on another. This is the concept of **indemnity.** It is common in the business world for one person or entity to agree to be liable for the debts or obligations of another. This is **contractual indemnity.** The policy of liability insurance that you (hopefully) carry on your automobile is an example of contractual indemnity. If you operate your vehicle in a negligent manner and cause the injury of another, your liability carrier agrees by contract to indemnify you for the liability up to the limits of the policy.

Sometimes the law implies the existence of indemnity (**implied indemnity**) without regard to the existence of a contract. Usually this has to do with the relationship or dealings between two parties. The first party may commit the wrongful act but have been so controlled or directed by the second party that the law implies that the second party is liable for the harm done by the first party. It is a well-established principle of agency law, for example, that the principal must indemnify the agent for liability imposed on the agent for torts committed by the agent in the course and scope of the agency and for liability on contracts entered into by the agent on the principal's behalf.

Another frequent application of implied indemnity is seen in the products liability area when suppliers of defective products may be found strictly liable to persons harmed by the defective product even when the defect is attributable to the design or manufacture of the product by a party other than the supplier. In those cases the supplier, though properly found liable to the injured party, may obtain indemnity against the party who had the higher duty and greater responsibility for causing the defect. This branch of the implied indemnity doctrine is sometimes called *active-passive indemnity.*

In criminal prosecutions the search for potential defendants is similarly urgent. Federal and state prosecutors and their investigators will seek not only the known perpetrators of a crime, but also co-conspirators, facilitators, aiders and abettors.

SLEUTH ON THE LOOSE

For current business information and economic statistics check the Stat-USA Service of the Department of Commerce at www.stat-usa.gov.

3. **The law of business organizations.** The way that people organize themselves to carry on business can have significant consequences on their legal liability. The legal professional involved in pre-filing investigation must have a fundamental understanding of the various business organizations and the rules of liability that apply to a particular business entity, its owners, employees, and other representatives. And the legal professional must know where and how to locate information on such business organizations (see Chapters 16 through 18).

HYPOTHETICAL 3-4

Assume that the law office where you have just been hired represents Ben Runover, who was badly injured one morning last month when a truck driven by Needa Floorit crossed lanes and struck Ben Runover's new Cadillac head-on. Runover's injuries from the collision were worsened by the fact that the air bag in the steering column of the Cadillac failed to deploy until seconds after the collision. It also didn't help that the city-licensed ambulance crew transporting Runover to the hospital following the accident stopped for pizza on the way because it was nearly lunch time. You have been assigned to investigate the facts and identify all potential defendants.

Ben Runover has told you that he purchased the Cadillac brand-new two months ago from a local Cadillac dealer here in town. The local dealer had custom-ordered the car for Runover from the manufacturer.

According to the accident report and your interview with the investigating officer, Needa Floorit said she was making deliveries for Funny Bread at the time of the accident and the truck she was driving is titled jointly in the names of Funny Bread, Inc. and a Mr. Big Hurry. Needa Floorit also told the officer that her boss, whom she referred to as Mr. Hurry, had told her to finish her deliveries by noon that day or she would be fired.

Based on these facts, what potential defendants can you identify for Ben Runover's personal injury suit?

Based on what you know so far, what additional information do you want to obtain to possibly identify other defendants?

If Ben Runover sues the local Cadillac dealer and obtains a judgment against it, could that local dealer seek indemnity against anyone else? Who and on what basis?

Assume it is learned that the contract between the local Cadillac dealer and the manufacturer contains an indemnity provision pursuant to which the local dealer agrees to indemnify and hold harmless the manufacturer from all claims and awards related to vehicles provided to the dealer by the manufacturer. Will this provision prevent Ben Runover from suing the local dealer? Will it prevent Ben Runover from suing the manufacturer? Both of them? What other effect(s) might it have?

Assuming that your investigation determines that Funny Bread Inc. is a corporation organized and existing under the laws of your state and that Big Hurry is the sole shareholder and director as well as president of the corporation, can he be sued by Ben Runover based on the facts you have so far?

Assume that your investigation determines that all of the potential defendants identified so far are insolvent and have no insurance. In desperation, your supervising partner tells you to take a close look at the pizza place where the ambulance crew stopped for pizza on the way to the hospital. (Or did you already think of it?) This sounds like a long shot to you but you begin to think of questions you could ask to determine if the pizza place might actually be a potential defendant in this suit. What are your questions?

f. To determine the assets of identified defendants

It does a plaintiff no particular good to identify numerous potential defendants if none of them have sufficient assets to pay any judgment that may be rendered against them. Such a defendant is judgment proof. Pre-filing investigation may involve determining the existence of policies of insurance, their coverage and limits, and checking a number of public records to determine assets, the equity in assets, and any recent transfer of assets held by potential defendants. (See Chapters 16 through 18.)

g. To determine questions of personal jurisdiction

The legal professional engaged in pre-filing investigation must understand the requirements of **personal jurisdiction** (also called *in personam* jurisdiction) in civil cases. It does little good to locate potential solvent defendants if they are not subject to the jurisdiction of the court in which the attorney wants to bring the action. Personal jurisdiction concerns the power of a court to enter an order binding on a defendant. Essentially, we ask when is it fair for the courts of a state in which a lawsuit is filed (the **forum state**) to assert jurisdiction over a particular defendant in a civil case? The fairness requirement derives from the **Due Process Clauses** found in the Fifth and Fourteenth Amendments to the U.S. Constitution, which prohibit the federal and state governments, respectively, from depriving "any person of life, liberty, or property without due process of law."

EXAMPLE

Assume you are involved in a car accident in the city where you live. The other driver is a citizen of another state where you have never visited and have had no business or other connections whatsoever. If the other driver sues you for negligence in the state courts of your state or in a federal court in your state (based on diversity of citizenship), is it fair for either of those courts to assert jurisdiction over you? Sure, because you live in that state. If you sued the other driver in one of those courts alleging he was negligent in causing the accident, is it fair for those courts to assert jurisdiction over him even though he does not reside there? Sure, because he was present in the state when he committed the negligent act. But what if the other driver goes home to his state and sues you there in his state or federal court? Is it fair for you to be subject to the power of a court in a state where you do not reside, have never visited, committed no negligent act, and have no business or other interests at all? Probably not. Do you see why a lawsuit seeking money damages filed against a defendant in a state or federal court is a utilization of state or federal power to take his property, thus triggering the Due Process Clause protection?

In a long line of cases beginning with the seminal case of *International Shoe Co. v. State of Washington*, 326 U.S. 310 (1945), the Supreme Court has interpreted the due process requirement in the personal jurisdiction context to mean that in order to assert personal jurisdiction over a defendant a state court or federal court sitting in that state must be satisfied that the defendant has "minimum contacts with [the forum state] such that maintenance of the suit does not offend traditional notions of fair play and substantial justice." Apply the **minimum contacts rule** to the facts in the last example. Do you see why, using that rule, the other driver could be held to account in the courts of your state but you likely could not be held to account in the courts of his state? It is always fair for a court in a state to assert jurisdiction over current residents of that state including both individuals and businesses located within the state. And a non-resident can choose to consent to personal jurisdiction rather than challenge it. But beyond that, the certainties are few. What about a former resident of the state? What about a part-time resident? What about a

Illustration 3-8 TYPICAL STATE LONG-ARM STATUTE

Long-arm statute: personal service; unavailability; jurisdiction

(a) Persons who are nonresidents of this state and residents of this state who are outside the state and cannot be personally served with process within the state are subject to the jurisdiction of the courts of this state as to any action or claim for relief arising from:

    (1) The transaction of any business within the state;
    (2) Any tortious act or omission within this state;
    (3) The ownership or possession of any interest in property located within this state;
    (4) Entering into any contract of insurance, indemnity, or guaranty covering any person, property, or risk located within this state at the time of contracting;
    (5) Entering into a contract for services to be rendered or for materials to be furnished in this state;
    (6) Any basis not inconsistent with the constitution of this state or of the United States;
    (7) Any action of divorce, annulment or separate maintenance where the parties lived in the marital relationship within this state, notwithstanding one party's subsequent departure from this state, as to all obligations arising for alimony, custody, child support, or marital dissolution agreement, if the other party to the marital relationship continues to reside in this state.

(b) "Person," as used herein, includes corporations and all other entities which would be subject to service of process if present in this state.
(c) Any such person shall be deemed to have submitted to the jurisdiction of this state who acts in the manner above described through an agent or personal representative.

---

business that sells a product in one state that a buyer takes to the forum state where it hurts or kills someone? What about a business that is not located in the forum state but advertises there, or sends communications there, or negotiates a contract there? What about an Internet company that uses a server in one state but is sued in another by someone who accessed the Web site in the other state? As you can see, all kinds of issues can arise in a defendant's challenge to personal jurisdiction under the minimum contacts analysis. These can be explored further in LBD 3-18. But suffice it to say that making a determination regarding whether a particular defendant is or may be subject to the personal jurisdiction of a court requires a combination of fact investigation and legal research.

States have **long-arm statutes** that set forth the factual criteria for determining when a non-resident defendant has sufficient contacts with a forum state to satisfy due process and justify the assertion of jurisdiction, e.g., using the roadways of the state, entering into contracts to be performed in the state, etc. Illustration 3-8 shows a typical state long-arm statute. A factual investigation must be made using those criteria and the attorney will make a determination regarding the likely outcome of a challenge to jurisdiction if suit is brought in that state. (See LBD 3-3.)

h. To determine questions of subject matter jurisdiction

Subject matter jurisdiction concerns the power of a court to hear a particular kind of case. Questions of subject matter jurisdiction are fact-sensitive. In other words, the decision regarding which court may have jurisdiction to determine a particular dispute has to do with facts regarding the identity of the parties, their residence, and the causes of action to be alleged, all factual matters to be determined in pre-filing investigation.

All states have one or more trial courts of **general jurisdiction,** authorized to hear most kinds of civil lawsuits. But all states also have specialized courts of **limited jurisdiction** in which matters of a particular kind of dispute or matters involving a particular sum of money can or must be brought. A simple example is what many states call their small claims court, or municipal court, or justice of the peace court. These courts typically have subject matter jurisdiction over some kinds of civil and criminal cases but not all. They may, for example, be able to hear civil disputes involving relatively small sums at issue, say $25,000 or less, or disputes involving contracts but not personal injuries, and so forth.

Of course, most states have specialized courts in which certain types of suits *must* be brought. For example, in some states, all matters regarding wills, administration of estates, and guardianship of minors must be brought in probate court. In some states, all divorce actions must be filed in domestic relations court. The legal professional must be familiar with the court system of the state(s) in which she practices to understand the significance of the pre-filing investigation that she is involved in and how it affects the choice of forum. (See LBD 3-5.)

Federal court jurisdiction is uniform across the country and more limited than state court jurisdiction. The basic concepts of federal court jurisdiction with which the legal professional engaged in pre-filing investigation must be familiar are:

1. **Federal question jurisdiction.** 28 U.S.C. §1331 allows U.S. district courts to have original jurisdiction of civil actions arising under the Constitution, statutes, regulations, or treaties of the United States.
2. **Diversity jurisdiction.** 28 U.S.C. §1332 allows U.S. district courts to have original jurisdiction of civil cases between citizens of different states where the amount in controversy exceeds $75,000, exclusive of interest and costs.

EXAMPLE

Assume that a resident of St. Paul, Minnesota, is involved in a car accident with a resident of California on the streets of St. Paul. If either driver concludes that the other was negligent in causing the accident, negligence will be a state law theory of liability, not a federal question. However, since the plaintiff and defendant are residents of different states, that negligence lawsuit could be filed in U.S. District Court based on diversity jurisdiction so long as the amount in controversy exceeds $75,000.

In order for diversity jurisdiction to accord the federal courts subject matter jurisdiction, there must be **complete diversity** between plaintiffs and defendants; that is, all plaintiffs must be residents of different states from all defendants.

EXAMPLE

If Sally and John, residents of Arizona, file suit against Andrea and Carl, that suit can be placed in federal court based on diversity of citizenship jurisdiction if both Andrea and Carl are residents of states other than

> Arizona. But if either of them are Arizona residents, there is no complete diversity, and the case will have to be filed in state court (unless it involves a federal question, of course).

A special problem in diversity cases (also an issue in venue determination, discussed below) is presented by corporations. What state is a corporation a citizen of if it is incorporated under the laws of one state but doing business in another? That is especially confusing where the corporation is incorporated in one state but has its headquarters in another state. And what if a corporation has more than one headquarters? Should a corporation be considered the resident of the state where it is incorporated, the state where it has its headquarters, and all states where it has offices? In *Hertz Corp. v. Friend*, 130 S. Ct. 1181 (2010), the United States Supreme Court finally clarified these questions by construing corporate citizenship for purposes of 28 U.S.C. §1332 to mean that a corporation is a resident *only* of the state where it has its principal place of business, its "nerve center," the state in which its high-level officers control and coordinate its activities. One important result of *Hertz* is that it is now easier to see a corporation in federal court based on diversity jurisdiction since the corporate defendant will not be deemed a resident of any state except the one in which it has its headquarters.

EXAMPLE

> Wal-Mart Stores, Inc. is incorporated in the state of Delaware, has its headquarters in Bentonville, Arkansas, but has stores and other facilities in all 50 states. Under *Hertz*, it will be deemed a resident of Arkansas only. If Wal-Mart is sued in any state other than Arkansas, a resident of the forum state can place the lawsuit in federal court based on diversity of citizenship, and that includes someone suing Wal-Mart in Delaware, the state of its incorporation.

3. **Supplemental pendent jurisdiction**. 28 U.S.C. §1367 allows U.S. district courts to have jurisdiction over both pendent and ancillary claims. A pendent claim arises where a plaintiff has a claim with federal question or diversity jurisdiction but wants to assert a second claim in the same lawsuit when the second claim by itself would not trigger federal jurisdiction by itself. Under supplemental pendent jurisdiction, the plaintiff may litigate both claims in the federal action if the second claim arises out of "the same case or controversy" as the first claim. Or as the U.S. Supreme Court phrased it in *United Mine Workers of America v. Gibbs*, 383 U.S. 71 (1966), where pendent jurisdiction was first recognized, the second claim can be asserted in the federal action if it "derives from a common nucleus of operative fact" with the first claim.

EXAMPLE

> Assume that a woman who is a resident of Virginia sues her employer, also a resident of Virginia, in federal court. Her first cause of action is for employment discrimination in violation of Title VII of the Civil Rights Act of

1964, a federal statute. That claim has federal question jurisdiction. But her complaint alleges a second cause of action based on the alleged assault of the woman by her immediate supervisor. If the alleged assault is part and parcel of the employment discrimination claim, if the two claims arise out of that common nucleus of operative fact, the assault claim, normally a state law cause of action, can be maintained in the federal action based on supplementary pendent jurisdiction. If, however, the second cause of action alleges a breach of contract by the employer having nothing to do with the alleged employment discrimination, the court will not recognize pendent jurisdiction for that contract claim. It will be dismissed from the federal lawsuit and will have to be brought in state court. Of course, if the employer of the Virginia plaintiff was a resident of Pennsylvania, then the second claim could be maintained in federal court based on diversity of citizenship.

4. **Supplemental ancillary jurisdiction**. 28 U.S.C. §1367 also allows a party other than the plaintiff, in a case properly filed in federal court, to file a counterclaim, cross-claim, or third-party complaint even though the latter claim does not have an independent jurisdictional basis that would have allowed it to be initiated in federal court. The counterclaim, etc., must arise out of the same case or controversy as the plaintiff's claim. Or as the U.S. Supreme Court phrased it in *Owen Equipment Co. v. Kroeger*, 437 U.S. 365 (1978), where supplemental ancillary jurisdiction was first recognized, the ancillary claim will be allowed where there is a "logical basis" that it and the plaintiff's original claim does have independent jurisdiction.

EXAMPLE

Assume our Virginia plaintiff sues her Virginia employer in federal court for violation of Title VII, and the employer counterclaims alleging breach of contract by the plaintiff. The breach of contract claim will only be heard by the federal court if it is related in some logical way to the plaintiff's claim of employment discrimination. Otherwise it lacks independent federal jurisdiction, will be dismissed from the federal lawsuit, and must be litigated in state court.

5. **Removal jurisdiction.** 28 U.S.C. §§1441-1452 set forth a procedure where a case filed in a state court may be removed by the defendant to federal court if the case is one which could have been brought originally in federal court and if notice of removal is filed by the defendant within 30 days of the receipt by the defendant of a copy of the initial pleading. In the case of multiple defendants, all of them must consent to the removal to federal court.

The *Hertz* decision has major ramifications in removal jurisdiction. Since a corporation is only deemed a resident of the state where its headquarters is located, a corporate defendant is more likely to be able to remove a case filed against it in state court based on diversity.

EXAMPLE

> Since Wal-Mart has its headquarters in Arkansas, a lawsuit filed against it in the state courts of any other state, including Delaware, the state of its incorporation, will be removable by Wal-Mart to federal court based on diversity of citizenship. Of course, if the plaintiff happens to be a resident of Arkansas, that won't work because there would not be complete diversity of citizenship between plaintiff and defendant. Same result occurs if Wal-Mart is sued in state court along with a co-defendant who is a resident of the forum state—there is no complete diversity. And there is the same result if a non-resident co-defendant will not consent to removal.

i. To determine the proper venue for a case

Unlike subject matter jurisdiction, which has to do with the power of a court to hear a particular kind of case, **venue** has to do with the most appropriate geographic location for the case to be heard. For example, the general trial court of a state clearly may have subject matter jurisdiction of the controversy, but there still may be a question regarding in which county of the state the case should heard. Or a case may clearly have federal jurisdiction, but a question may remain regarding in which federal district the case should be heard.

Like jurisdictional questions, venue issues are fact-sensitive. In most states, venue is properly laid in the county in which (1) the cause of action arose (e.g., in a car accident case, the county where the accident occurred); or (2) the defendant resides; or (3) the property in dispute is located (e.g., a dispute over title to land can be brought in the county where the land is located).

EXAMPLE

> If a contract is negotiated between parties in two different counties, signed in a third, and performance undertaken in several counties, when breach is alleged, where did the cause of action arise?
>
> Or, if a defective product is advertised across the state, sold in one county, and hurts the consumer in another, where did that cause of action arise? To resolve such questions, reference must be made to the venue statutes of the particular state but the decision regarding venue begins with pre-filing factual investigation.

All states have special venue statutes for particular kinds of actions. Divorce cases (venue in county of separation or in county where plaintiff resides if defendant has left the state) and suits brought against the state government or its agencies (venue in county of state capital) are examples of kinds of cases that may have specialized venue requirements. (See LBD 3-6.)

In federal court suits, the general venue statute is 28 U.S.C. §1391, which utilizes the same three- pronged approach to venue as state statutes summarized above. However, more than 200 federal laws contain specialized venue provisions that will take precedence over the general rules of §1391 (e.g., suits against federal agencies may have to be brought in the District of Columbia depending on the nature of the claim and the agency involved).

Since venue questions can turn on the residence of a defendant, the residence of a corporation for purposes of venue can present problems. For example, if a corporation having its headquarters in Dallas, Texas, can be sued in a federal court, can the plaintiff file the lawsuit in the Eastern District of Texas, which may be a remote or unfamiliar venue to the corporation, rather than in the Northern District of Texas, which includes Dallas? Historically, such forum shopping against corporate defendants has been a common plaintiff's lawyer tactic to put the corporation in unfamiliar territory or before a jury more likely to be pro-plaintiff. By enacting the **Federal Courts Jurisdiction and Venue Clarification Act of 2011,** which became effective in January 2012, Congress made such forum shopping much more difficult. New 28 U.S.C. §1391(d) provides that for venue purposes (not subject matter jurisdiction purposes—don't confuse them) a corporation is a resident of a district in which it would be subject to personal jurisdiction if that district were a separate state. In other words, it's not enough that our Dallas-based corporation can be sued in a federal court in Texas. For venue to be proper, plaintiff must show that the defendant corporation does enough business or otherwise has enough contact with the judicial district chosen to satisfy due process (fairness).

j. To determine questions regarding governmental immunity

Any time the state or federal government or one of their agencies is a potential defendant in an action, consideration must be given to **governmental immunity** (also called **sovereign immunity**). Historically, the sovereign cannot be sued unless it consents and waives its immunity. In such cases, reference must be made to federal or state statutes in which the government has consented to be sued in particular matters to determine if the facts of the case satisfy the statutory waiver of immunity.

There are a number of federal statutes pursuant to which the U.S. government has waived immunity in certain matters. The three most commonly used statutes are:

- The Federal Tort Claims Act, 28 U.S.C. §1346(b);
- The Court of Claims Act, 28 U.S.C. §1491; and
- The Tucker Act, 28 U.S.C. §1346(a).

Similarly, every state will have statutes providing for waiver of its immunity from suit in limited areas. Such statutes not only define the scope of the waiver but set forth the procedures for bringing such a claim. (See LBD 3-7.)

k. To accomplish required service of process

A civil lawsuit begins when the plaintiff files the lawsuit in the court chosen for the litigation. See FRCP 3. But due process, discussed above in another context, requires that all named defendants be formally notified of the filing of the lawsuit and receive a copy of the complaint filed against them, together with instructions on how and when to respond to the complaint to avoid a default judgment being entered against them. This formal notification is accomplished by what we call **service of process** and involves delivery to the defendant of a copy of the complaint together with either a **summons** from the court or a request for waiver of service of summons.

A summons is court document issued signed and issued by the clerk of the court in which the complaint is filed. The clerk will accept the original complaint for filing, assign a docket number to the newly filed case, sign and issue one summons for each named defendant, then give the summonses to the plaintiff's lawyer. Per FRCP 4(c), it is the responsibility of the attorney for plaintiff to properly serve a copy of the summons together with a copy of the complaint on each defendant. Whoever serves the summons on a defendant must execute an **affidavit proving service** per FRCP 4(l) and file that affidavit with the clerk of the court. That way the court knows that service has been accomplished and when, how, and by whom. The timing of the service is important because a defendant's time to respond to a complaint runs from the date he or she is served with process. A copy of the standard Summons in a Civil Action used in federal courts can be seen in Illustration 3-9.

FRCP 4(e)-(j) details the various ways that process (the complaint and summons) may be served on an individual or entity defendant. Where the defendant is an individual, service is most commonly made by delivering the complaint and summons to the individual or his or her designated agent personally, or by leaving the documents at the individual's home "with a person of suitable age". Many state rules of procedure allow service on a defendant by certified mailing of the documents to the defendant at the person's home or place of business, and in those states FRCP 4(e)(1) authorizes such service in a federal case filed in that state.

Where the defendant is a corporation or partnership, service is most commonly made by delivering the process to an officer, manager, or general agent per FRCP4(h), though, again, service may be by mail if state rules allow. There are many specialized methods of service dealt with in FRCP 4 (e.g., service on non-resident defendants, on minors or incompetent adults, on state or federal agencies, etc.) with which the legal professional assisting in service of process must be familiar.

When a case is filed in state court, the state rules of procedure regarding service of process will control, but the methods authorized in FRCP 4 are typical of those found in state rules. (See LBD 3-19.)

A defendant served with a summons normally has 21 days from the date of service to file a response to the complaint per FRCP 12(a)(1)(A)(1). If he or she fails to file a response in that time frame, the plaintiff may move for default judgment against the defendant per FRCP 55. For lawsuits pending in state court, the time frame for response by a defendant and procedure for default judgment will be governed by state procedural rules (see LBD 3-20).

According to FRCP 4(d), in lieu of having a summons issued by the clerk, serving it, and making the affidavit proving service, a plaintiff may now provide each defendant with a copy of the complaint and a **notice of lawsuit and request for waiver of service of summons** (see Illustration 3-10). The complaint and request must be accompanied by two copies of a form waiver of service of summons (see Illustration 3-11) and a self-addressed stamped envelope for its return.

Illustration 3-9   SUMMONS IN A CIVIL ACTION FORM (FEDERAL)

AO 440 (Rev. 06/12) Summons in a Civil Action

UNITED STATES DISTRICT COURT
for the

	)	
	)	
	)	
	)	
Plaintiff(s)	)	
v.	)	Civil Action No.
	)	
	)	
	)	
	)	
Defendant(s)	)	

SUMMONS IN A CIVIL ACTION

To: *(Defendant's name and address)*

A lawsuit has been filed against you.

Within 21 days after service of this summons on you (not counting the day you received it) — or 60 days if you are the United States or a United States agency, or an officer or employee of the United States described in Fed. R. Civ. P. 12 (a)(2) or (3) — you must serve on the plaintiff an answer to the attached complaint or a motion under Rule 12 of the Federal Rules of Civil Procedure. The answer or motion must be served on the plaintiff or plaintiff's attorney, whose name and address are:

If you fail to respond, judgment by default will be entered against you for the relief demanded in the complaint. You also must file your answer or motion with the court.

CLERK OF COURT

Date: _____   _____
                                                  Signature of Clerk or Deputy Clerk

Illustration 3-9   SUMMONS IN A CIVIL ACTION FORM (FEDERAL) *(continued)*

AO 440 (Rev. 06/12) Summons in a Civil Action (Page 2)

Civil Action No.

PROOF OF SERVICE
(This section should not be filed with the court unless required by Fed. R. Civ. P. 4 (l))

This summons for *(name of individual and title, if any)*

was received by me on *(date)*   .

☐ I personally served the summons on the individual at *(place)*

on *(date)*   ; or

☐ I left the summons at the individual's residence or usual place of abode with *(name)*

, a person of suitable age and discretion who resides there,

on *(date)*   , and mailed a copy to the individual's last known address; or

☐ I served the summons on *(name of individual)*   , who is

designated by law to accept service of process on behalf of *(name of organization)*

on *(date)*   ; or

☐ I returned the summons unexecuted because   ; or

☐ Other *(specify):*

My fees are $ for travel and $ for services, for a total of $ 0.00   .

I declare under penalty of perjury that this information is true.

Date:

_____
Server's signature

_____
Printed name and title

_____
Server's address

Additional information regarding attempted service, etc:

Illustration 3-10   NOTICE OF LAWSUIT AND REQUEST FOR WAIVER OF SERVICE OF SUMMONS (FEDERAL)

AO 398 (Rev. 01/09) Notice of a Lawsuit and Request to Waive Service of a Summons

UNITED STATES DISTRICT COURT
for the

_____	)
Plaintiff	)
v.	) Civil Action No. _____
_____	)
Defendant	)

NOTICE OF A LAWSUIT AND REQUEST TO WAIVE SERVICE OF A SUMMONS

To: _____

(Name of the defendant or - if the defendant is a corporation, partnership, or association - an officer or agent authorized to receive service)

Why are you getting this?

A lawsuit has been filed against you, or the entity you represent, in this court under the number shown above. A copy of the complaint is attached.

This is not a summons, or an official notice from the court. It is a request that, to avoid expenses, you waive formal service of a summons by signing and returning the enclosed waiver. To avoid these expenses, you must return the signed waiver within _____ days *(give at least 30 days, or at least 60 days if the defendant is outside any judicial district of the United States)* from the date shown below, which is the date this notice was sent. Two copies of the waiver form are enclosed, along with a stamped, self-addressed envelope or other prepaid means for returning one copy. You may keep the other copy.

What happens next?

If you return the signed waiver, I will file it with the court. The action will then proceed as if you had been served on the date the waiver is filed, but no summons will be served on you and you will have 60 days from the date this notice is sent (see the date below) to answer the complaint (or 90 days if this notice is sent to you outside any judicial district of the United States).

If you do not return the signed waiver within the time indicated, I will arrange to have the summons and complaint served on you. And I will ask the court to require you, or the entity you represent, to pay the expenses of making service.

Please read the enclosed statement about the duty to avoid unnecessary expenses.

I certify that this request is being sent to you on the date below.

Date: _____

_____
Signature of the attorney or unrepresented party

_____
Printed name

_____
Address

_____
E-mail address

_____
Telephone number

Illustration 3-11   WAIVER OF SERVICE OF SUMMONS (FEDERAL)

AO 399 (01/09) Waiver of the Service of Summons

UNITED STATES DISTRICT COURT
for the

_____	)	
Plaintiff	)	
v.	)	Civil Action No.
	)	
_____	)	
Defendant	)	

WAIVER OF THE SERVICE OF SUMMONS

To: _____

 (Name of the plaintiff's attorney or unrepresented plaintiff)

I have received your request to waive service of a summons in this action along with a copy of the complaint, two copies of this waiver form, and a prepaid means of returning one signed copy of the form to you.

I, or the entity I represent, agree to save the expense of serving a summons and complaint in this case.

I understand that I, or the entity I represent, will keep all defenses or objections to the lawsuit, the court's jurisdiction, and the venue of the action, but that I waive any objections to the absence of a summons or of service.

I also understand that I, or the entity I represent, must file and serve an answer or a motion under Rule 12 within 60 days from _____, the date when this request was sent (or 90 days if it was sent outside the United States). If I fail to do so, a default judgment will be entered against me or the entity I represent.

Date: _____

_____   _____
                                              Signature of the attorney or unrepresented party

_____   _____
Printed name of party waiving service of summons   *Printed name*

                                                _____
                                                Address

                                                _____
                                                E-mail address

                                                _____
                                                Telephone number

Duty to Avoid Unnecessary Expenses of Serving a Summons

Rule 4 of the Federal Rules of Civil Procedure requires certain defendants to cooperate in saving unnecessary expenses of serving a summons and complaint. A defendant who is located in the United States and who fails to return a signed waiver of service requested by a plaintiff located in the United States will be required to pay the expenses of service, unless the defendant shows good cause for the failure.

"Good cause" does *not* include a belief that the lawsuit is groundless, or that it has been brought in an improper venue, or that the court has no jurisdiction over this matter or over the defendant or the defendant's property.

If the waiver is signed and returned, you can still make these and all other defenses and objections, but you cannot object to the absence of a summons or of service.

If you waive service, then you must, within the time specified on the waiver form, serve an answer or a motion under Rule 12 on the plaintiff and file a copy with the court. By signing and returning the waiver form, you are allowed more time to respond than if a summons had been served.

Illustration 3-12 RESPONSIBILITIES OF AN ASSISTING LEGAL PROFESSIONAL IN CONNECTION WITH FILING AND SERVICE OF A COMPLAINT

- Preparing the proper number of copies of the complaint for filing with the court or, if electronic filing is used, put complaint in proper format for e-filing
- Preparing the summons or request for waiver of service of summons for each named defendant
- Arranging for the issuance of a check to cover the required filing fee
- Taking the complaint, summons, or request for waiver of service of summons to the court clerk and having it properly filed and stamped with the filing date, time, and the assigned docket number or e-file complaint
- Arranging for service of process on each named defendant and seeing to it that the affidavit of service or waiver of service of summons is properly returned to and filed with the court
- Calendaring relevant dates of service and due dates for responses from defendants

A signed and returned waiver of service is filed with the clerk by plaintiff's lawyer and accomplishes service of process for that defendant. If the defendant does sign and return the waiver of service of summons within 30 days after it was sent to him, the individual is rewarded by being given 60 days (90 if defendant is outside the judicial district) rather than 21 when served by summons to file a response to the complaint measured from the date the request to waive was sent to him. If that defendant refuses to waive service of summons and is later served with a summons, the defendant can be punished by being ordered to reimburse plaintiff the costs of service by summons plus attorneys fees related to that service per FRCP 4(d)(2). Many states have now adopted the request for waiver of service of summons procedure for civil suits in their state courts (see LBD 3-20).

Although service of process is performed after the lawsuit is filed, part of pretrial investigation is determining how service will be accomplished on each defendant once the suit is filed. Per FRCP 4(m), once the complaint is filed, service by summons or waiver of summons must be accomplished within 120 days or the lawsuit will be dismissed unless plaintiff can show good cause for extending the time for service. Thus, the legal professional assisting plaintiff's lawyer who is charged with accomplishing service of process must be prepared to promptly accomplish service as soon as the complaint is filed. There are other matters to consider in the filing of a civil lawsuit. In federal court and some state courts, a civil cover sheet must be prepared and filed with the complaint (see the federal civil cover sheet form at www.flnd.uscourts.gov/forms/Attorney/civilCoverSheet.PDF). Unless the filing is by plaintiff's pauper's oath, a filing fee must be paid to the clerk when the complaint is filed. A sufficient number of copies of the complaint must be made and so forth. Illustration 3-12 contains a list of responsibilities the legal professional assisting plaintiff's lawyer may have in connection with filing and service of the complaint.

Chapter Summary and Conclusion

The United States utilizes an adversarial system of justice that resolves both civil and criminal disputes, is administered by the state and federal courts, and is governed by applicable rules of procedure and evidence, as well as by statutes of limitation and repose. In both criminal prosecutions and civil actions a cause of action must be alleged by the plaintiff and all elements of the cause of action proven by the applicable degree of proof. The defendant may raise various defenses upon which he will have the burden of proof. In lieu of trial the parties may negotiate a settlement directly, or with the aid of mediation, or they may submit their dispute to binding arbitration. Formal lawsuits are preceded by informal investigation which is a critical period for investigation in both criminal and civil suits.

Once a civil lawsuit is filed, the rules of formal discovery may be utilized for factual investigation and evaluation together with continuing informal investigation. Chapter 4 focuses on the means of formal discovery in a civil suit.

Review Questions

1. Why is the American system of justice properly described as "adversarial"?
2. Distinguish civil law from criminal law.
3. What is the difference between common law and statutory law?
4. How do actual damages differ from compensatory damages?
5. What is the degree of proof normally required for a plaintiff to prevail in a civil suit? For the prosecution to prevail in a criminal case?
6. What are the four categories or kinds of evidence that may be presented at trial?
7. Explain the difference between a statute of limitation and a statute of repose.
8. Name five advantages of informal investigation over formal discovery.
9. Explain the difference between mediation and arbitration.
10. Explain the difference between personal jurisdiction and subject matter jurisdiction.

KEY WORDS AND PHRASES TO REMEMBER

administrative agencies
Administrative Procedures Act
adversarial system
affidavit proving service
affirmative defense
alternative dispute resolution
   (ADR)

arbitration
assumption of risk
authorized agent
beyond a reasonable doubt
breach of contract
burden of proof
cause of action

civil law

clear and convincing evidence

common law

compensatory damages (general, specific)

complete diversity

consequential damages

constitutional law

continuing violations doctrine

contractual indemnity

court approved mediators

court-annexed ADR

criminal law

declaratory relief

defendant

defense's degree of proof

defenses

degree of proof

demonstrative evidence

diversity jurisdiction

documentary evidence

Due Process Clause

elements of a cause of action

enabling legislation

equitable relief

exemplary damages

exhaustion of remedies

facts

factual investigation

Federal Courts Jurisdiction and Venue Clarification Act of 2011

federal question jurisdiction

Federal Rules of Appellate Procedure

Federal Rules of Civil Procedure

Federal Rules of Criminal Procedure

Federal Rules of Evidence

federalism

felony

formal discovery

forum state

general damages

general jurisdiction

implied indemnity

in personam jurisdiction

informal investigation

injunction

injunctive relief

judgment proof

law of agency

limited jurisdiction

local rules of court

long-arm statutes

mediation

mediation conference

mediator

mini-trial

minimum contacts rule

misdemeanor

money damages

negligence

negotiation

notice of lawsuit and request for waiver of service of summons

notice pleading standard

pendent jurisdiction

personal jurisdiction

plaintiff

plausibility pleading standard

pre-filing investigation

preponderance of the evidence

punitive damages

real evidence

remedy

removal jurisdiction

respondeat superior

rules and regulations

rules of civil procedure

rules of criminal procedure

rules of evidence

rules of procedure

service of process

sovereign immunity

special damages

statute of limitation

statute of repose

statutory law

subject matter jurisdiction

summons

supplemental ancillary jurisdiction

supplemental pendent jurisdiction

testimonial evidence

tolled

venue

waiver

LEARN BY DOING

LBD 3-1. Prepare a diagram of the court system in your state and summarize the subject matter jurisdiction of each court.

LBD 3-2. Locate the statutes of limitation in your state for the following civil causes of actions and prepare a memo summarizing them and your sources of authority. Also indicate if there is a statute of repose which relates to any of these.

negligent personal injury
medical malpractice
negligent injury to personal property
legal malpractice
outrageous conduct
slander
libel
fraud
products liability
assault

LBD 3-3. Assume your client was injured by a product she ordered from a shop-at-home catalog distributed by a company in a distant state. Your client did not receive the catalog directly from the company but borrowed it from a friend who also lives in another state. You wish to file a product liability suit in the state where your client resides and was injured by a defect in the product purchased out of the catalog. Locate your state's long-arm statute and prepare a memorandum stating an opinion as to whether the civil trial court(s) of your state courts will be able to assert personal jurisdiction over the non-resident catalog company. Include in your memo other facts that you might want to determine in order to form a better opinion.

LBD 3-4. Determine whether your state has a rule with language similar to FRCP 11. If so, research the decisions of your state courts regarding what constitutes a "reasonable inquiry" sufficient to satisfy the rule's requirements and prepare a memorandum summarizing your findings. Or, locate and read one of the following: Philip Talmadge, Emmelyn Hart-Biberfeld, and Peter Lohnes, *When Counsel Screws Up: The Imposition and Calculation of Attorney Fees as Sanctions*, 33 Seattle U. L. Rev. 437 (2010) (viewable at http://digitalcommons.law.seattleu.edu/cgi/viewcontent.cgi?article=1982&context=sulr), or Jerold S. Solovy, et al., *Sanctions Under Federal Rule of Civil Procedure Rule 11*, 583 Practicing Law Institute: Litigation 105 (April 1998) (viewable at http://digitalcommons.lmu.edu/cgi/viewcontent.cgi?article=2417&context=llr). Then prepare a memorandum summarizing the various sanctions that different courts have imposed for Rule 11 violations.

LBD 3-5. We wish to file a lawsuit in state court alleging breach of contract and fraud in connection with a land sale transaction. We wish to demand a jury and will also be seeking immediate injunctive relief in the complaint because we have information that the defendant is removing assets from the state for the purpose of defeating our client's ability to satisfy any judgment that may be awarded. Locate the following information and prepare a memorandum summarizing what you find:

a. Which trial court(s) in your state will have subject matter jurisdiction to hear this suit?
b. What rules govern proper preparation of the complaint for filing in that court and its service on the defendant?
c. Does that court have any local rules that pertain to the proper preparation of the complaint or its service?
d. Are there any special rules or statutes that come into play since we will be seeking injunctive relief in the complaint?
e. What rules govern how quickly we can get a hearing on our request for injunctive relief after we file the complaint?
f. Do the rules of procedure or the local rules of the court tell us when the court conducts hearings on motions for injunctive relief and whether a legal brief is required in support of the motion?

LBDs 3-6 through 3-25 are accessible on the Author Updates link to the text Web site at www.aspenparalegaled.com/books/parsons_investigating/default.asp.

Chapter 4
Formal Discovery in Civil Litigation

CHAPTER OBJECTIVES

In this chapter you will learn:

- The procedural rules that govern formal discovery in a civil case.
- The kinds of information that is discoverable in civil litigation.
- The various methods of formal discovery including depositions, interrogatories, document requests, requests for physical or mental examination, and requests for admission.
- The order in which formal discovery ought to be conducted.
- The role of the investigating legal professional in each method of formal discovery.
- How to draft the various kinds of discovery documents and related motions.
- How to index or summarize a deposition.

A. Introduction

Once the pre-filing investigation has been completed and decisions made concerning appropriate causes of action, defendants, forum, defenses, etc., the lawsuit will be initiated and the issues joined in accordance with Rules 2 through 25 of the FRCP or applicable state rules of procedure. Keep in mind that informal investigation does not end with the institution of formal litigation. It may continue throughout trial preparation and even during the time of trial (see Illustration 3-7). Institution of formal litigation does, however, bring into play the formal rules of discovery available under the governing rules of procedure. The attorney will continue with informal investigation while initiating formal discovery.

New associate attorneys as well as paralegals may be heavily involved in assisting the senior attorney in planning and implementing discovery accomplished through the formal rules and must be well acquainted with those rules and skilled in their use. In this chapter we will summarize the discovery rules under FRCP 26 through 37. Remember, there may be important differences between the discovery rules under the FRCP and applicable state rules of civil procedure.

The current version of the FRCP is easily accessible online at www.law.cornell.edu/rules/frcp/ or as a link from the Federal Judiciary Homepage at www.uscourts.gov/Home.aspx. The student should locate and consult the current version of the rules while reading this chapter.

B. The Scope and Purposes of Formal Discovery in a Civil Case

FRCP 26(b)(1) provides in pertinent part:

> Parties may obtain discovery regarding any nonprivileged matter that is relevant to any party's claim or defense—including the existence, description, nature, custody, condition, and location of any documents or other tangible things and the identity and location of persons who know of any discoverable matter. . . . Relevant information need not be admissible at the trial if the discovery appears reasonably calculated to lead to the discovery of admissible evidence. . . .

The **scope of permissible discovery** is thus quite broad. This is consistent with the overall purposes of the federal discovery rules—to facilitate the flow of information between the parties, to avoid trial by surprise, and to encourage settlement.

1. The relationship between the scope of formal discovery and the rules of evidence

Rule 26(b) says that the information sought in discovery need not be admissible at trial. Information is discoverable even though inadmissible at trial if it appears to be reasonably calculated to lead to the discovery of admissible evidence. Thus the discovery permitted under the rules of civil procedure is not governed by the evidentiary rules (see Chapters 6 and 7), which strictly limit and control what can be testified to or presented at trial. Another way to say this is that the discovery rules permit broader factual inquiry before trial than do the evidentiary rules at trial.

HYPOTHETICAL 4-1

Assume that you are working for the law office representing Ben Runover from Hypothetical 3-4. A suit has been filed on behalf of Runover against Needa Floorit and her employer, Funny Bread, Inc. In her FRCP 30 deposition, Needa Floorit has denied that she was speeding and lost control of her truck at the time of the collision with Ben Runover. The partner responsible for Runover's case deposes the investigating officer and asks her if she has any reason to believe that the Funny Bread truck had been speeding. The officer responds that she has no information of her own but that one bystander told her after the accident that he "saw the truck flying down the road like a bat out of hell before it crossed the median and hit the Cadillac." The attorney for Funny Bread, Inc., makes no objection to this question or the answer.

After the officer's deposition you excitedly ask the supervising partner if the statement by the bystander witness won't help win the case for Runover. He replies that unless you can locate this bystander to testify, the statement of the officer will do Ben Runover no good. He tells you that the statement of the officer about what the bystander witness said is probably inadmissible at trial because it is hearsay. You reply, "But if it's inadmissible hearsay, why didn't the Funny Bread lawyer object during the deposition?"

Why is your supervising lawyer giving you a disgusted look?

Could the attorney for Funny Bread, Inc., have properly objected to the question asked of the investigating officer at the deposition on the grounds that it was not reasonably calculated to lead to the discovery of admissible evidence? Could he have properly objected to the answer given?

2. Privileged materials not discoverable

Though the scope of permissible discovery is broad, it is not unlimited. **Privileged material** such as attorney-client correspondence and attorney work product (see full discussion in Chapter 6) is rarely discoverable.

3. Discovery of experts

Rule 26(a)(2) requires the disclosure to opposing parties of the identity of persons who may provide **expert testimony** at trial (**testifying experts**), and Rule 26(b)(4)(A) allows discovery to be had of such experts by way of deposition. New Rule 26(b)(4)(C) now prohibits the discovery by an opponent of correspondence between a testifying expert and the attorney who retained the expert unless that correspondence relates to:

- Compensation paid to the expert
- Facts and data supplied to the expert by the attorney that were considered by the expert in forming opinions to be expressed
- Assumptions provided by the attorney on which the expert has relied in forming opinions to be expressed

That Rule also prohibits discovery of draft reports (as opposed to the final report) prepared by the testifying expert, a topic addressed later in the chapter.

Discovery of experts retained by parties for consultation only and not for testimony (**consulting experts**) is strictly limited by Rule 26(b)(4)(D) and usually cannot be had except on a showing of exceptional circumstances under which it is impracticable for the party seeking the discovery to obtain facts or opinions on the same subject by other means.

HYPOTHETICAL 4-2

Assume that you are working for the law office representing Ben Run-over from Hypothetical 3-4. As part of the pre-filing investigation, you take your consulting expert to inspect the wrecked Cadillac. The expert identifies the air bag in the car as a Safe Bag 1000 designed and manufactured by a company called Soft Landing, Inc. The expert also takes notes, draws diagrams, and snaps some pictures of the car and the air bag apparatus, then tells you and your supervising attorney verbally that in his opinion the air bag installed in Ben Runover's Cadillac did in fact malfunction due to a design defect.

Three months later your firm files suit on behalf of Runover against Soft Landing, Inc. The partner who will try the case does not intend to use the expert who inspected the car with you as a testifying expert because he is vacillating and does not handle the pressure of cross-examination well. After the suit is commenced, Soft Landing files a FRCP 34 request to inspect the Cadillac. However, you learn that the car has been sold for scrap since the inspection by you and your expert and is no longer available.

Might Soft Landing prevail on a request to the court to obtain discovery from your consulting expert under FRCP 26(b)(4)(D)?

What arguments could you suggest to the supervising partner to prevent such discovery on these facts?

4. Required voluntary disclosures

FRCP 26(a) requires voluntary disclosures by the parties to each other without waiting for formal discovery requests. These disclosures include:

- the identity and location of persons likely to have discoverable information relevant to disputed facts;
- a copy or compilation of all documents, electronically stored information, and things relevant to the disputed facts;
- a computation of damages claimed and allowed inspection of supporting documents;
- the inspection and copying of any insurance agreement that may reflect that the insurer is liable for part or all of any judgment rendered; and
- a written report from each expert retained or specially employed to testify containing all opinions expected to be offered, and the basis for them (see LBD 4-10).

Per FRCP 26(a)(1)(C), these disclosures are to be made at or within 14 days following the parties' **Rule 26(f) conference**. The 26(f) conference is to be arranged by the parties themselves without court participation in contrast to a **scheduling conference,** which is a court-mandated meeting between the attorneys and the judge or judge's clerk authorized by FRCP 16(b). Federal trial judges and many state trial judges routinely order a scheduling conference shortly after the commencement of a civil action, usually within 90 days in civil suits per FRCP 16(b)(2). At the scheduling conference, a trial date will be set if possible and deadlines imposed for amending pleadings, completing discovery, filing dispositive motions, exchanging exhibits and witness lists, etc. (An increasingly important topic addressed at the scheduling conference and often by standing local rule is how to regulate discovery of **electronically stored information (ESI)**, a topic addressed in more detail in Section F of this chapter.) All decisions made at the conference will be reduced to a formal **scheduling order** which will be signed by the judge and filed in the record of the case. (A scheduling order entered in the *Runover v. Soft Landing, Inc.* case might look like what you see in Illustration 4-1).

Some trial judges do not conduct a formal 16(b) scheduling conference but instead instruct the attorneys to meet in their Rule 26(f) conference and produce an agreed **discovery plan** or an entire agreed scheduling order for filing with the court. In either event, per FRCP 26(f)(1), the parties' 26(f) conference is to be held at least 21 days before any 16(b) scheduling conference or the due date of a mandated scheduling order.

Illustration 4-1   SCHEDULING ORDER

IN THE UNITED STATES DISTRICT COURT
FOR THE EASTERN DISTRICT OF YOURSTATE
NORTHERN DIVISION

BEN RUNOVER,	)	
Plaintiff	)	
v.	)	DOCKET NO. YR00-00001
SOFT LANDING, INC.,	)	
Defendant	)	

SCHEDULING ORDER

Pursuant to FRCP 16(b), the parties in this case are ORDERED to proceed with discovery and other pre-trial preparation according to the following schedule:

a) This cause is set for trial by jury on March 10, YR+1, at 9 a.m.;

b) The parties shall exchange their FRCP 26(a)(1) disclosures on or before August 1, YR00;

c) Plaintiff shall provide defense counsel with the written report for all experts expected to testify at trial for plaintiff on or before November 30, YR00 and defendant shall provide plaintiffs' counsel with the written report for all experts expected to testify at trial for defendants one week after receipt of the report for plaintiffs' expert(s);

d) The parties shall conclude formal discovery on or before January 10, YR+1 including the deposition of experts and any deposition to be taken for proof;

e) Any motions for summary judgment or other dispositive motions as to any or all causes of action or defenses in the case shall be filed with the court on or before February 1, YR+1 and shall be accompanied by a memorandum or law;

f) The parties shall exchange witness lists and proposed trial exhibits no later than February 10, YR+1;

g) All motions in limine shall be filed with the court on or before March 3, YR+1;

h) All proposed jury instructions shall be filed with the court on or before March 3, YR+1.

ENTER:

_____
U.S. District Judge

At the 26(f) conference, the parties are required to consult in good faith and to:

- consider the nature and basis of their claims and defenses and the possibilities for promptly settling or resolving the case
- make or arrange for making the Rule 26(a)(1) disclosures
- discuss any issues about preserving discoverable information, and develop a proposed discovery plan that is to be filed with the court within 14 days following the conference

In addition to the required voluntary disclosures of FRCP 26(a)(1), at least 30 days before trial or as set by local court rule, FRCP 26(a)(3) requires the parties to disclose:

- the identity and location of all anticipated witnesses;
- the designation of witnesses whose testimony is to be presented by deposition; and
- a listing of anticipated documents and other exhibits.

Moroever, FRCP 26(a)(2) requires the parties to voluntarily disclose to the opposition no later than 90 days before trial the identities of experts they expect to call as witnesses at trial together with a report for each such expert. We will consider the contents of that report later in the chapter.

As you can see, the required voluntary disclosure scheme outlined in the federal rules is extensive. A number of states have adopted the voluntary disclosure scheme for their state procedural rules in hopes of reducing discovery disputes and expediting the adversarial process. (See LBD 4-1)

C. ▶ Methods of Formal Discovery in a Civil Case

1. Depositions (FRCP 27 through 32)

In a **deposition**, a lawyer asks questions of a party or witness (the **deponent**) who answers under oath. Depositions are typically oral inter-rogations, although FRCP 31 does provide a procedure for depositions by written questions. The questions, answers, and objections that occur during the deposition are transcribed by a **court reporter** and, on request of the lawyer taking the deposition, are typed up by the court reporter into a **transcript.**

a. Why lawyers take depositions

Lawyers take depositions for four primary reasons:

1. To discover prior to trial what knowledge and information the deponent has.
2. To observe the deponent and make a decision regarding his effective-ness as a witness at trial.
3. To get the witness to commit under oath to a version of recollected events prior to trial so that the witness can be impeached at trial with

the deposition testimony if he deviates from that deposition in trial testimony. See FRCP 32(a)(2).

4. To preserve and present the deposition testimony of a witness at trial when that witness cannot be present at trial. See FRCP 32(a)(4).

b. Lawyers using assisting legal professionals in depositions

Though only a licensed attorney can take a deposition since it is the practice of law (see Chapter 2), the paralegal may be given various responsibilities in securing deposition testimony. (See LBD 4-3.) Associate attorneys assisting the supervising attorney who will try the case may be given these responsibilities as well.

1. **To help identify potential deponents.** The assisting legal professional may be asked to help identify potential deponents in a case and gather pertinent background information on them.

2. **To help prepare questions.** The assisting legal professional may be asked to help formulate suggested questions to be used by the attorney at the deposition, or questions it is anticipated opposing counsel may ask.

3. **To arrange the time and place of the deposition.** If the deposition is taken by agreement with opposing counsel, the assisting legal professional may be the one who arranges the time and place of such depositions. In that event, the one assisting should be careful to confirm arrangements made orally in a prompt letter to all concerned parties. As with all correspondence the legal professional generates on a matter, the supervising attorney, other office personnel working on the matter, and the file should receive a copy of the correspondence. (See Illustration 4-2.)

4. **To arrange for the court reporter.** The assisting legal professional may be responsible for arranging for the court reporter to handle the deposition. The court reporter should be contacted as soon as the depositions are scheduled and such arrangements confirmed by a letter to the court reporter with copies to all concerned parties. (See Illustration 4-3.)

5. **To calendar the deposition dates.** The assisting legal professional may be responsible for calendaring the deposition in her office and making sure the dates are properly recorded in the office's **docket control system.**

6. **To prepare and file the notice of deposition.** The assisting legal professional may be asked to draft the required **notice of deposition** in compliance with FRCP 30(b). As with all other court filings after the original complaint, a copy of the notice of deposition must be served on every other party to the lawsuit because all parties and their counsel have a right to be present and participate in questioning the deponent. (See Illustration 4-4.)

7. **To prepare necessary subpoenas.** If a **subpoena** (a document issued by the court clerk ordering a person to appear at a deposition or trial) is necessary to secure the presence of a witness at the deposition, the assisting legal professional may be responsible for preparing

SLEUTH ON
THE LOOSE

Identify a nearby nursing home then access *www.medicare.gov* and see what information you can find about the nursing home, including whether it has been cited for any violations of state or federal regulations.

Illustration 4-2   LETTER TO OPPOSING COUNSEL CONFIRMING DEPOSITION BY AGREEMENT

May 3, YR00

Hard Case, Esq.
Duck, Dodge & Deny
(Address)

Re: Runover v. Soft Landing, Inc.

Dear Mr. Case:

This will confirm our telephone conversation of today's date to the effect that we have agreed to schedule the deposition of Dr. Bright Idea, Chief Engineer for the Design/Build Division of Soft Landing, Inc., for May 24, YR00, to begin at 10:00 a.m. in our offices. You have also agreed to accept service of the deposition subpoena duces tecum for Dr. Bright, which I will deliver to you this week.

We will make arrangements for the court reporter.

Thank you for your courtesies.

Sincerely,

Dee Pendable
Paralegal

cc: Mellow Fellow, Esq.*
    Mr. Ben Runover

(*In some offices it may be the practice to not show copies on the original. The file copy of the letter will show the copies as blind copies, abbreviated "bcc.")

the subpoena, having the clerk of the court issue it, and arranging for its service and return in compliance with FRCP 45 and 30(a)(1).

A subpoena that not only compels the presence of a witness but directs that witness to bring documents or things with him to the deposition is called a **subpoena *duces tecum.*** FRCP 30(b)(2). (See Illustration 4-5.)

The subpoena must be served on the named person as provided in FRCP 45(b) and the server of the subpoena (often an associate or paralegal in the firm) must complete a certified **proof of service** (sometimes called a *return of service*) and file it with the clerk of the court that issued the subpoena. A typical proof of service form is shown in Illustration 4-6.

Some U.S. district courts require the use of Administrative Office (AO) Form 88A, a copy of which is set out in Illustration 4-7, for deposition subpoenas in civil cases. Many state courts will have their own forms for the subpoena and subpoena duces tecum and may require their use. (See LBD 4-15.)

8. **To help prepare the deponent.** The assisting legal professional may be asked to help prepare a client or friendly witness for a deposition by communicating the supervising attorney's explanation of

Illustration 4-3 LETTER TO COURT REPORTER CONFIRMING ENGAGEMENT

May 3, YR00

Ms. Listen Close
Close Court Reporting Service
(Address)

Re: Ben Runover v. Soft Landing, Inc.

Dear Ms. Close:

This will confirm that you will be handling the court reporting duties for the audio-visual deposition of Dr. Bright Idea, Chief Engineer for the Design/Build Division of Soft Landing, Inc., which is scheduled for May 24, YR00, to begin at 10:00 a.m. in our offices.

Please let me know if you have any questions.

Sincerely,

Dee Pendable
Paralegal

cc: Hard Case, Esq.
     Mellow Fellow, Esq.
     Mr. Ben Runover

---

deposition procedure and areas of expected examination, or by participating in a mock examination.

9. **To copy and arrange exhibits.** The assisting legal professional may be asked to make a sufficient number of copies and organize documents the lawyer expects to use in the deposition.

10. **To assist at the deposition.** If the assisting legal professional attends the deposition, she may be expected to keep the documents used as exhibits organized and furnish them to the supervising attorney at the appropriate time; to take extensive notes on the deposition; to make discreet, written suggestions to the supervising attorney for additional or forgotten areas of inquiry; to observe, record, and advise the supervising attorney at the appropriate time of the demeanor of deponents and parties present during the deposition.

11. **To arrange for the preparation of the transcript.** The assisting legal professional may have the responsibility of ordering the deposition transcript from the court reporter. She will then be expected to stay in touch with the court reporter regarding prompt preparation and delivery of the transcript, particularly if the depositions are taken close to a trial or hearing where the transcript will be needed.

12. **To help a client review the transcript.** If signature by the deponent was not waived at the deposition, it may be the responsibility of the assisting legal professional to be sure the transcript is

Illustration 4-4   NOTICE OF DEPOSITION

IN THE UNITED STATES DISTRICT COURT
FOR THE EASTERN DISTRICT OF YOURSTATE
NORTHERN DIVISION

BEN RUNOVER,
  Plaintiff
 	
  v.
SOFT LANDING, INC.,
  Defendant
	)
	)
	) DOCKET NO. YR00-00001
	)
	)
	)

NOTICE OF DEPOSITION

To: Soft Landing, Inc.
     c/o Hard Case, Esq.
     (Address)

Plaintiff, Ben Runover, pursuant to Rule 30(b) of the Federal Rules of Civil Procedure, hereby gives notice that counsel for plaintiff will take the audio-visual deposition of Dr. Bright Idea, Chief Engineer for the Design/Build Division of defendant Soft Landing, Inc., on May 24, YR00, at 100 South Main St., Capital City, Yourstate, beginning at 10:00 a.m. (EDST), before an officer duly authorized to administer oaths. A stenographic record of the deposition will also be made. This deposition may be adjourned from day to day until completed.

_____
Mellow Fellow
Counsel for plaintiff Ben Runover
(Address)

CERTIFICATE OF SERVICE

The undersigned hereby certifies that a copy of the foregoing notice of deposition was served upon the following counsel of record by placing a copy in the United States mail, postage prepaid, addressed as follows:

Hard Case, Esq.
(Address)

This _____ day of May, YR00.

_____
Mellow Fellow

reviewed by the deponent, a **statement of changes** made, signed, and returned to the court reporter as required by FRCP 30(e).

13. **To file the transcript with the court.** Under FRCP 30(f)(1) and in many state jurisdictions, the court reporter does not file the deposition transcript, but only certifies it and delivers the original to the attorney who requested it. It is then up to that attorney to preserve the transcript and to give notice to all parties if and when it is filed with the clerk of the court. The assisting legal professional may be charged with taking care of a delivered transcript, filing it when instructed to do so, and giving proper FRCP 30(f)(4) notice of that filing.

Illustration 4-5 DEPOSITION SUBPOENA DUCES TECUM

IN THE UNITED STATES DISTRICT COURT
FOR THE EASTERN DISTRICT OF YOURSTATE
NORTHERN DIVISION

BEN RUNOVER,	)	
Plaintiff	)	
	)	DOCKET NO. YR00-00001
v.	)	
SOFT LANDING, INC.,	)	
Defendant	)	

DEPOSITION SUBPOENA DUCES TECUM

To: Dr. Bright Idea, Chief Engineer
Design/Build Division
Soft Landing, Inc.
c/o Hard Case, Esq.
(Address)

YOU ARE HEREBY COMMANDED to appear and give testimony under oath at the law offices of Shake, Rattle & Roll, 100 South Main Street, Capital City, Yourstate on May 24, YR00, beginning at 10:00 a.m. (EDST).

YOU ARE FURTHER COMMANDED to bring the following with you:

All written, recorded or graphic matter, however produced or stored, and specifically including copies of data stored on computer disk or by other electronic means, which refer or relate in any way to the development, testing, design, manufacture, production and/or distribution of the Safe Bag 1000 system including, but not limited to correspondence, notes, memoranda, interoffice communications, studies, analysis, reports, reviews, proposals, contracts, working papers, statistical reports, blue prints, sketches, drawings, drafts, or documents similar to any of the foregoing, however denominated.

Dated: May 3, YR00

_____
Clerk of the Court

14. **To review the deposition transcript for leads.** The assisting legal professional may be asked to review deposition notes and/or transcripts for leads to additional information and witnesses.

15. **To prepare a summary or index of the deposition.** The **deposition summary** or **index** is prepared from the transcript. There are four different types of deposition summaries typically used by attorneys:

> the **chronological summary**
> the **subject matter summary**
> the **topical summary**
> the **narrative summary**

The four types of deposition summaries are shown in Illustration 4-8. Such summaries enable attorneys to use depositions effectively at trial for the impeachment of a witness or for the rehabilitation of an impeached

Illustration 4-6 PROOF OF SERVICE OF SUBPOENA

IN THE UNITED STATES DISTRICT
COURT FOR THE EASTERN DISTRICT OF YOURSTATE
NORTHERN DIVISION

BEN RUNOVER,   )
    Plaintiff   )
)   DOCKET NO. YR00-00001
    v.   )
SOFT LANDING, INC.,   )
    Defendant   )

PROOF OF SERVICE OF DEPOSITION SUBPOENA DUCES TECUM

I, Patsy Paralegal, hereby declare under penalty of perjury under the laws of the United States of America that:

1. I am over eighteen (18) years of age.
2. On May 5, YR00, I served a copy of the attached subpoena duces tecum on Dr. Bright Idea, Chief Engineer of the Design/Build Division of Soft Landing, Inc., by hand delivering a copy thereof, by agreement, to Mr. Hard Case, attorney for Soft Landing, Inc., at 123 North Tulip Street in Capital City, Yourstate.

Executed this 5th of May, YR00.

_____
                                      Patsy Paralegal

witness. They are especially important when the depositions taken in a case have been lengthy and/or numerous. When asked by an attorney to prepare a **deposition index**, the assisting legal professional should be sure to ask which type the supervising lawyer prefers.

2. Interrogatories (FRCP 33)

Interrogatories are written questions submitted by one party to another, which must be answered in writing and under oath by the party being interrogated. Interrogatories have been the subject of much abuse by attorneys because they can be extremely time consuming and expensive to have to answer numerous written questions. Consequently, FRCP 33(a) now limits parties to 25 interrogatories, including subparts, subject to the discretion of the trial court to limit or increase that amount by order or local rule. Many states have begun imposing similar restrictions by rule of civil procedure or by local court rule and care should be taken to consult such rules before posing or answering interrogatories. (See LBD 4-15.)

a. Information to be sought by interrogatories

Interrogatories are primarily used to obtain basic background information from the opposing party; information that can provide leads for further informal investigation or provide the basis for more detailed deposition questions. Though the specific questions to be posed in interrogatories will vary depending on the facts and law of a particular case, there are some general areas of inquiry that should typically be covered:

Illustration 4-7   AO FORM 88A: DEPOSITION SUBPOENA FOR CIVIL CASES USED IN FEDERAL COURT

AO 88A (Rev. 06/09) Subpoena to Testify at a Deposition in a Civil Action

UNITED STATES DISTRICT COURT
for the

_____	)
Plaintiff	)
v.	) Civil Action No.
	)
_____	) (If the action is pending in another district, state where:
Defendant	))

SUBPOENA TO TESTIFY AT A DEPOSITION IN A CIVIL ACTION

To:

❏ *Testimony:* **YOU ARE COMMANDED** to appear at the time, date, and place set forth below to testify at a deposition to be taken in this civil action. If you are an organization that is *not* a party in this case, you must designate one or more officers, directors, or managing agents, or designate other persons who consent to testify on your behalf about the following matters, or those set forth in an attachment:

Place:	Date and Time:

The deposition will be recorded by this method: _____

❏ *Production:* You, or your representatives, must also bring with you to the deposition the following documents, electronically stored information, or objects, and permit their inspection, copying, testing, or sampling of the material:

The provisions of Fed. R. Civ. P. 45(c), relating to your protection as a person subject to a subpoena, and Rule 45 (d) and (e), relating to your duty to respond to this subpoena and the potential consequences of not doing so, are attached.

Date: _____

CLERK OF COURT	
OR	
_____	_____
Signature of Clerk or Deputy Clerk	*Attorney's signature*

The name, address, e-mail, and telephone number of the attorney representing *(name of party)* _____
_____ , who issues or requests this subpoena, are:

Illustration 4-7 AO FORM 88A: DEPOSITION SUBPOENA FOR CIVIL CASES USED IN FEDERAL COURT *(continued)*

AO 88A (Rev. 06/09) Subpoena to Testify at a Deposition in a Civil Action (Page 2)

Civil Action No.

PROOF OF SERVICE
(This section should not be filed with the court unless required by Fed. R. Civ. P. 45.)

This subpoena for *(name of individual and title, if any)* _____

was received by me on *(date)* _____

☐ I served the subpoena by delivering a copy to the named individual as follows: _____

_____ on *(date)* _____ ; or

☐ I returned the subpoena unexecuted because: _____

Unless the subpoena was issued on behalf of the United States, or one of its officers or agents, I have also tendered to the witness fees for one day's attendance, and the mileage allowed by law, in the amount of

$ _____ .

My fees are $ _____ for travel and $ _____ for services, for a total of $ 0.00 .

I declare under penalty of perjury that this information is true.

Date: _____

_____
Server's signature

_____
Printed name and title

_____
Server's address

Additional information regarding attempted service, etc:

---

1. **The identity and relationship of parties.** Frequently there is a question regarding the correct identity and legal relationship of parties, potential parties, related parties, agents, and employees. We cannot always determine in pre-filing informal investigation all that we need to know about the organization of business entities and the relationships between such entities and their owners and agents. As we have seen, it is vital to be able to identify all potential parties before applicable statutes of limitation expire.

Illustration 4-8 DEPOSITION SUMMARIES

---

(1) The chronological summary digests the deposition in the order in which topics appear. A chronological summary might look like this:

| Biographical Info. | Born 8-1-52 in Dodge City, KS. Through high school there. BA from U. |
| P1-P4 L.12 | Kansas, in Lawrence. Married '74. No children. |

| Employment His. | P-T for father's drug store in H.S. Artist for Hallmark Cards 72-83. |
| P4 L.13-P.6 L.2 | Self-employed commercial artist since. |

(2) The subject matter summary organizes the deposition into subjects without regard to where in the deposition they may appear. That might look like this:

Negotiations re contract
P17, L.1-16	John Brown, Hallmark manager in June '01
P22, L.4-11	John Brown again in Dec. '01
P23, L.16-24	Carl Able, Co. president in Jan. '05

(3) The topical summary is identical to the subject matter summary except that it only covers selected topics in the deposition and is not comprehensive. The attorney will typically identify which topics he needs summarized from the deposition.

(4) The narrative summary is a condensed version of the deposition put in memorandum form. It is useful to give to the client and to help identify areas of additional investigation. A narrative summary might begin like this:

Peter Jesse James was born 8-1-52 in Dodge City, KS. He lived there through high school with his parents Paul and Peggy James and his younger brother Perry James. During high school Peter worked as a waiter at the Red Robin Cafe in Dodge City. . . .

---

2. **The identity and location of witnesses.** Although FRCP 26(a)(1)(A)(i) compels parties in civil litigation to voluntarily disclose information regarding persons likely to have knowledge of disputed facts, this **interrogatory** should still be posed. In state court actions, the governing rules of procedure may not have a voluntary disclosure requirement. And, even in federal litigation, there still are counsel who honor neither the letter nor the spirit of that rule and will not comply with it.

HYPOTHETICAL 4-3

Assume that our pre-filing investigation on behalf of Ben Runover raises a serious question as to whether Soft Landing, Inc., is judgment proof. However, your attorney learns in the deposition of Dr. Bright Idea that at the time Dr. Idea tested and developed the Safe Bag 1000 system he was employed not by Soft Landing, Inc., but by a large conglomerate known as World Wide Discoveries (WWD). Dr. Idea thinks WWD created or spun-off Soft Landing, Inc., to market the Safe Bag 1000.

Draft no more than two interrogatories that might be posed to defendant Soft Landing, Inc., to determine the details of this relationship.

3. **Information regarding documents and things.** Interrogatories are ideal to learn the identity, location, and custodian of documents and things related to the case, including computerized files and electronic messages. (See Section F below.) Everything said of the voluntary disclosure required by FRCP 26(a)(1)(A)(i) also applies to that required by FRCP 26(a)(1)(A)(ii). Why is it important to know where documents and things are and who is the custodian of them? (See Chapters 6 and 7.)

4. **Medical history and damages information.** In any personal injury case it is important to obtain the plaintiff's complete medical history as well as information regarding the treatment of alleged injury as early as possible and, in any case, well before the deposition of the plaintiff. Asking for this in an interrogatory served early in the case gives the defendant time to do informal discovery into the medical history and current condition of the plaintiff to enable the attorney to thoroughly cover those areas in the deposition. FRCP 26(a)(1)(A)(iii) requires a plaintiff seeking damages to voluntarily disclose categories of damage and supporting documentation, but a zealous and thorough defense counsel will want more (see Illustration 4-9).

   Interrogatories posed by Soft Landing, Inc., to Ben Runover regarding his medical history might read as those in Illustration 4-9.

5. **Defendant's ability to satisfy a judgment.** It is important for case evaluation and possible settlement purposes for the plaintiff to determine early on as much as possible about the financial condition of each defendant. In many instances, informal investigation into public records can produce much helpful information regarding this matter. (See Chapters 17 and 18.) However, it will frequently be necessary to determine additional or more definite information through formal discovery.

   FRCP 26(a)(1)(A)(iv) requires the voluntary production of insurance policies that may be available to satisfy judgments. However, many states do not have a voluntary disclosure rule. In addition, some states will not require production of insurance information even upon request, considering it an improper violation of a defendant's privacy prior to a judgment being entered. (See LBD 4-5.)

   In cases where the issues make the current financial condition of the defendant a relevant topic of inquiry, that information should be requested as well. In most states, such information is discoverable only in special situations, as where punitive damages are sought. (See LBD 4-5.)

6. **Details as to events and transactions.** Asking an opposing party by interrogatory to explain an event or series of events in detail prior to their deposition can help the attorney prepare better deposition questions. It also provides time for informal discovery to test the credibility of the details provided. It is also permissible to ask a party by

Illustration 4-9   INTERROGATORIES REGARDING MEDICAL CONDITION AND TREATMENT

IN THE UNITED STATES DISTRICT COURT
FOR THE EASTERN DISTRICT OF YOURSTATE
NORTHERN DIVISION

BEN RUNOVER,
            Plaintiff
 	
    v.
SOFT LANDING, INC.,
        Defendant
	)
	)
	) DOCKET NO. YR00-00001
	)
	)
	)

DEFENDANT'S FIRST INTERROGATORIES TO PLAINTIFF

Defendant, Soft Landing, Inc., pursuant to FRCP 33, requests that plaintiff answer the following interrogatories under oath within thirty (30) days of service upon counsel for plaintiff.

Interrogatories

1. Identify each and every physician, osteopath, chiropractor or other health care provider or medical personnel of any kind who has treated or consulted with you as a result of the injuries alleged in your complaint and for each one identified state:

    a. the date(s) of such treatment or consultation;
    b. the medical or other condition for which the treatment or consultation was rendered;
    c. the diagnosis made and treatment rendered, including medication(s) and physical therapy;
    d. the amount charged for such treatment or consultation and whether such charges have been paid.

2. Identify each and every hospital, clinic or other health care facility of any kind where you have received treatment as an in-patient or out-patient for the injuries alleged in your complaint and for each one identified state:

    e. the date(s) of such treatment, including dates of admission and discharge;
    f. the medical or other condition for which the treatment was rendered;
    g. the treatment rendered, including medical procedures performed, medication(s) and physical therapy;
    h. the amount charged and whether such charges have been paid.

3. Identify each and every physician, osteopath, chiropractor or other health care provider or medical personnel of any kind who has treated or consulted with you as a patient during the last ten years other than those identified in response to No.1 and for each one identified state:

    i. the date(s) of such treatment or consultation;
    j. the medical or other condition for which the treatment or consultation was rendered;
    k. the diagnosis made and treatment rendered, including medication(s) and physical therapy.

4. Identify each and every hospital, clinic or other health care facility of any kind where you have received treatment as an in-patient or out-patient during the last ten years other than those identified in response to No. 2 and for each one identified state:

    l. the date(s) of such treatment, including dates of admission and discharge;
    m. the medical or other condition for which the treatment was rendered;
    n. the treatment rendered, including procedures performed, medication(s) and physical therapy.

In any suit for damages, details should be obtained by interrogatory regarding the factual basis and means of calculating such damages. In a federal court suit, do not rely exclusively on the voluntary disclosure requirement for this information.

interrogatory what the factual basis is for a legal position taken in a pleading.

EXAMPLE

If the plaintiff sues alleging the defendant breached a contract, the interrogatory may ask the plaintiff:

State in detail each and every action or inaction by defendant which plaintiff contends constitutes a breach of the contract at issue.

7. **Information regarding experts.** FRCP 26(a)(2) now requires parties to civil litigation in federal court to disclose the identities of experts they expect to testify at trial (testifying experts). For experts who are "retained or specially employed to provide expert testimony in the case or one whose duties as the party's employee regularly involve giving expert testimony," 26(a)(2)(B) requires that such disclosure be accompanied by a **written expert report** containing:

- a complete statement of all opinions the expert will offer and the basis for each such opinion
- all facts and data considered in reaching such opinions
- copies of exhibits the expert will use to support such opinions
- the expert's qualifications, including all publications within the last ten years
- a list of all cases in which the expert has testified as an expert within the last four years
- a statement of compensation the expert has or will receive

Experts who must provide the written expert report under the rules are referred to as **retained experts**. But what about a witness who will provide expert opinion but is neither retained or specially employed to do so nor an employee regularly involved in doing so? Often fact witnesses who are not retained and paid by either party will be qualified to give expert opinion on a matter, and many employees of parties testify who, in addition to being fact witnesses, may be qualified to offer relevant opinions but do not regularly do so. For these **non-retained experts**, FRCP 26(a)(2)(C) requires only that the disclosure also contain 1) a summary of the subject matter on which they are expected to opine as an expert and 2) a summary of the facts and opinions which they are expected to provide. (See LBD 4-16.)

Many states have adopted the mandatory disclosure scheme of the federal rules in their state procedures (see LBD 4-15). One drawback to the 26(a)(2) mandatory expert disclosure is that per FRCP 26(a)(2)(D) such disclosure need not be made until 90 days before the scheduled trial date, much later than the other mandatory disclosures required under FRCP 26(a)(1). Consequently, many lawyers in federal civil litigation will seek information regarding an opponent's experts via interrogatories and do so early in discovery. And lawyers handling cases in state courts where there is no mandatory disclosure requirement will routinely use interrogatories to discover the identity, etc. of an opponent's experts as early as possible. Discovering an opponent's experts early allows the inquiring attorney time to prepare to depose the opponent's experts and may well impact the attorney's own choice of experts.

EXAMPLE

An **expert witness** interrogatory might read like this:

1. Identify each and every expert witness you expect to testify at trial and for each one identified state:

a) all opinions the expert will offer;
b) the factual basis for each such opinion; and
c) all data or other information considered by the expert in reaching each such opinion.

2. For each expert identified in response to No. 1, identify and describe in detail each and every communication whether verbal, written or electronic between said expert and counsel for plaintiff or any agent acting on behalf of counsel for plaintiff in which:

a) relates to compensation to be paid to the expert for a report or for testimony;
b) identifies facts or data supplied to the expert and which the expert considered in forming opinions to be expressed; or
c) identifies assumptions supplied to the expert and which the expert relied upon in forming opinions to be expressed.

b. Lawyers using assisting legal professionals in discovery by interrogatories

The assisting legal professional's duties with respect to discovery by interrogatories (see LBD 4-4), include the following:

1. **Drafting interrogatories for the opposing party.** (See the drafting guidelines below.)
2. **Helping the client compile information to answer interrogatories.** Note that FRCP 33(d) allows a party answering interrogatories to do so by producing **business records**, including electronically stored information, that contain the information requested.
3. **Drafting responses for the client's review.** The wording of such responses can be just as important as the wording of the interrogatories themselves.
4. **Suggesting possible objections to the lawyer.** If an interrogatory is so **vague** that it cannot be reasonably understood or requires guessing, or if it is so **over broad** that it requires an unreasonable amount of time and expense to answer, or if it inquires into privileged areas, or is outside the permissive scope of discovery, or is otherwise objectionable, the **objection** must be stated in writing in the response to the interrogatories. Since the assisting legal professional will frequently

take the lead in reviewing and preparing responses to interrogatories, the attorney will expect him to identify objectionable questions and draft or suggest objections for her review.

EXAMPLE

If defendant Soft Landing, Inc., were to pose an improper interrogatory to plaintiff Ben Runover regarding his financial condition, the question and response might look like this:

15. State your current net worth.

Response: Plaintiff objects to answering this interrogatory on the grounds that the information sought is not relevant to any issue in the case and the question is not reasonably calculated to lead to the discovery of admissible evidence.

5. **Drafting a motion for protective order.** As defined in FRCP 7(b), a **motion** is an oral or written application made by the attorney to the court asking for an order of some kind. **Motion practice** is an important part of the litigation process including in formal discovery. In the event an objectionable question is asked in an interrogatory or a deposition, FRCP 26(c) permits the party to whom the discovery is directed to file a motion with the court for a **protective order** with regard to that discovery. FRCP 26(c) requires a certification that prior to filing a motion for protective order the moving party conferred or attempted in good faith to confer with the opposing side to work out the objection. The assisting legal professional may be involved in this attempt to resolve conflicts or may be asked to draft letters for the attorney reflecting his attempts to work them out.

   If counsel for plaintiff Ben Runover decides to object to interrogatories nos. 3 and 4 served by Soft Landing, Inc., in Illustration 4-9 because they ask about Runover's medical history unrelated to the injuries he is suing for in the present case, the FRCP 26(c) motion for protective order might look like Illustration 4-10.

6. **Drafting a motion to compel discovery.** In the event an opposing party does not properly or timely comply with interrogatories posed (or other discovery as well), FRCP 37 authorizes a **motion to compel discovery** and, in certain circumstances, **sanctions** to be imposed on the other side. The assisting legal professional may be asked to draft such motion and may be directly involved in the required pre-motion effort to resolve the conflict. In the event that Dr. Bright Idea refuses at his May 24, YR00 deposition to produce memorandum he sent to the legal department of Soft Landing, Inc., regarding the design of the Safe Bag 1000 System (see Illustration 4-5), counsel for Ben Runover might file a FRCP 37 motion similar to that in Illustration 4-11.

7. **Monitoring time deadlines associated with answering interrogatories.** FRCP 33 imposes certain timing requirements regarding answering interrogatories. If the assisting legal professional works with the attorney who has posed the interrogatories, this means calendaring the date when answers from the other side are due. If

Illustration 4-10   FRCP 26 MOTION FOR PROTECTIVE ORDER

IN THE UNITED STATES DISTRICT COURT
FOR THE EASTERN DISTRICT OF YOURSTATE
NORTHERN DIVISION

BEN RUNOVER, 　　Plaintiff 　　v. SOFT LANDING, INC., 　　Defendant	))))　　　DOCKET NO. YR00-00001)))

MOTION FOR PROTECTIVE ORDER AND CERTIFICATION
OF GOOD FAITH EFFORT TO RESOLVE DISPUTE

Motion

Plaintiff, Ben Runover, pursuant to FRCP 26(c), moves the court for an order providing that he not be required to answer interrogatories 3 and 4 from Defendant's First Interrogatories to Plaintiff served on counsel for plaintiff on May 10, YR00. The interrogatories objected to are as follows:

3. Identify each and every physician, osteopath, chiropractor or other health care provider or medical personnel of any kind who has treated or consulted with you as a patient during the last ten years other than those identified in response to No.1 and for each one identified state:

　　a. the date(s) of such treatment or consultation;
　　b. the medical or other condition for which the treatment or consultation was rendered;
　　c. the diagnosis made and treatment rendered, including medication(s) and physical therapy.

4. Identify each and every hospital, clinic or other health care facility of any kind where you have received treatment as an in-patient or out-patient during the last ten years other than those identified in response to No. 2 and for each one identified state:

　　d. the date(s) of such treatment, including dates of admission and discharge;
　　e. the medical or other condition for which the treatment was rendered;
　　f. the treatment rendered, including procedures performed, medication(s) and physical therapy.

Plaintiff objects to answering these interrogatories on the grounds that they are overly broad and burdensome and request information regarding medical treatment received by plaintiff unrelated to the injuries received by plaintiff in the instant suit.

Certification

Counsel for plaintiff, Mellow Fellow, hereby certifies that he has made a good faith effort to resolve this discovery dispute by placing a telephone call to Mr. Hard Case, counsel for defendant, on May 17, YR00. In that phone conversation Mellow Fellow explained to Mr. Case his objections to answering interrogatories 3 and 4. Notwithstanding that explanation, Mr. Case advised that he would take the position that the interrogatories must be answered.

　　　　　　　　　　　　　　　　　　　　　_____
　　　　　　　　　　　　　　　　　　　　　Mellow Fellow
　　　　　　　　　　　　　　　　　　　　　Attorney for plaintiff Ben
　　　　　　　　　　　　　　　　　　　　　Runover
　　　　　　　　　　　　　　　　　　　　　(Address)

　　　　　　　　　　　　(Certificate of Service omitted)

Illustration 4-11   FRCP 37 MOTION TO COMPEL DISCOVERY

IN THE UNITED STATES DISTRICT COURT
FOR THE EASTERN DISTRICT OF YOURSTATE
NORTHERN DIVISION

BEN RUNOVER,   )
    Plaintiff   )
)   DOCKET NO. YR00-00001
    v.   )
SOFT LANDING, INC.,   )
    Defendant   )

MOTION TO COMPEL DISCOVERY AND FOR SANCTIONS WITH CERTIFICATION
OF GOOD FAITH EFFORT TO RESOLVE DISPUTE

Motion

Plaintiff, Ben Runover, pursuant to FRCP 37(a), moves the court for an order compelling defendant Soft Landing, Inc., and Dr. Bright Idea, Chief Engineer of the Design/Build Division of Soft Landing, Inc., to produce for inspection all memorandum delivered by Dr. Idea to the legal department of Soft Landing, Inc., that discuss the Safe Bag 1000 System and to answer questions regarding those memoranda in his deposition which began on May 24, YR00, and has been continued by plaintiff pending the resolution of this motion.

Plaintiff further moves the court, pursuant to FRCP 37(a)(4), for an order directing defendant and/or defendant's counsel to reimburse plaintiff for the attorney's fees incurred by plaintiff for the preparation, filing, and hearing on this motion and for the additional *per diem* court reporter expense to be incurred in the continuation of the deposition of Dr. Idea.

In support of this motion, plaintiff would show that at his May 24, YR00 deposition, Dr. Idea, on advice of counsel for Soft Landing, Inc., refused to produce those memoranda or to answer questions concerning them. Plaintiff would also show that Dr. Idea was lawfully subpoenaed to the May 24, YR00 deposition and ordered to bring those documents with him. A copy of the subpoena *duces tecum* served on Dr. Idea on May 5, YR00, is attached hereto as Exhibit 1. A copy of the Return of Service executed by Patty Paralegal on May 5, YR00 showing service of the subpoena *duces tecum* on May 5, YR00, is attached hereto as Exhibit 2.

Certification

Counsel for plaintiff, Mellow Fellow, hereby certifies that he has made a good faith effort to resolve this discovery dispute by placing a telephone call to Mr. Hard Case, counsel for defendant, on May 25, YR00. In that phone conversation Mellow Fellow explained to Mr. Case the relevance of the subpoenaed documents and the inadequacy of the claimed attorney-client privilege. Notwithstanding that explanation, Mr. Case advised that he would take the position that the memoranda were protected by attorney-client privilege and that any questions put to Dr. Idea regarding the memoranda would be improper as infringing on that privilege.

                                                             Mellow Fellow
                                                             Attorney for plaintiff Ben
                                                             Runover
                                                               (Address)

                           (Certificate of Service omitted)

the assisting legal professional works with the attorney who has received the interrogatories, this means calendaring the date when answers from the client are due. It can be severely damaging to the interests of the client to fail to meet a deadline for answering an interrogatory, and may constitute malpractice as well.

3. Requests for production of documents and things (FRCP 34)

Rule 34 permits a written request to be served on any other party to the lawsuit requesting documents or electronically stored information for inspection and copying; tangible things for inspection, copying or testing; and the entry on land or property for inspection and testing. Responses to these requests must be in writing but are *not* made under oath as with interrogatory answers. The attorney for the party served with the document request will sign the response but the client need not.

To obtain documents, electronically stored information, and things from persons who are not parties to the litigation, FRCP 34(c) permits the use of the subpoena power of FRCP 45. (See the subpoena *duces tecum* to Dr. Bright Idea in Illustration 4-5.)

The role of the assisting legal professional in connection with document requests and the guidelines for drafting requests and responses is essentially the same as with interrogatories. However, there are some special considerations for document requests:

a. Serving document requests and interrogatories together

Document requests are frequently served along with interrogatories. It is good practice to have only one set of definitions or instructions (see detailed discussion in the section on drafting guidelines below) that are worded to apply to both interrogatories and document requests. That way they need not be repeated in the two documents. Thus the definition section of a document request may read, "The definitions and instructions contained in plaintiff's first set of interrogatories served on defendant are incorporated herein by reference." (See Illustration 4-12.)

Also, identify interrogatories and document requests as sequential sets—for example, *Plaintiff's First Set of Interrogatories and First Request for Production of Documents to Defendant.* In the course of extended litigation the parties may eventually serve two or more sets of interrogatories or document requests on each other. The identification of them as the first or second set, etc., helps avoid confusion, and things such as definitions used in the first set can be incorporated by reference in subsequent sets without having to be repeated. (See Illustration 4-12.)

As a time and space-saving technique, have the document requests and interrogatories refer to each other by number.

EXAMPLE

> If interrogatory number 5 asked the plaintiff to itemize all damages she is claiming to have sustained due to the accident, document request number 3 might simply ask for her to "produce all documents that refer or relate in any way to your response to interrogatory number 5 in Defendant's First Set of Interrogatories to Plaintiff." (See Illustration 4-12.)

b. Assisting the client to locate and review documents

When the client is served with document requests, it may be the assisting legal professional's job to help the client locate, assemble, and prepare the documents for inspection by the opposing party. In performing this task, special considerations must be kept in mind:

Illustration 4-12   REQUEST FOR PRODUCTION OF DOCUMENTS

IN THE UNITED STATES DISTRICT COURT
FOR THE EASTERN DISTRICT OF YOURSTATE
NORTHERN DIVISION

BEN RUNOVER,	)	
Plaintiff	)	
	)	DOCKET NO. YR00-00001
v.	)	
SOFT LANDING, INC.,	)	
Defendant	)	

DEFENDANT'S FIRST REQUEST FOR PRODUCTION OF DOCUMENTS TO PLAINTIFF

Defendant, Soft Landing, Inc., pursuant to Rule 34 of the Federal Rules of Civil Procedure, requests that plaintiff, Ben Runover, produce the following documents for inspection and/or copying at 10:00 a.m. on June 7, YR00, at the offices of Duck, Dodge & Deny, 123 Tulip Street, Capital City, Yourstate or at such other place and time as the parties, through counsel, may agree.

Definitions

The definitions contained in Defendant's First Interrogatories to Plaintiff are incorporated herein by reference.

Requests

1. All medical reports, records, charts, x-ray reports, and all records regarding any and all medical examinations and/or treatment received by plaintiff as a result of the injuries alleged in the complaint.

2. All documents which refer or relate in any way to plaintiff's response to interrogatory no. 15 in Defendant's First Interrogatories to Plaintiff.

3. All documents which refer or relate to the service and/or repair history of the Cadillac.

4. All federal, state and/or local income tax returns filed by plaintiff for all tax years since YR-3.

Hard Case, Esq.
Attorney for Soft Landing
Inc.
(Address)

(Certificate of Service omitted)

---

1. **Review documents carefully before production.** Caution must be taken to review every one of the documents your client has *before* they are inspected by the other side to ensure that they are properly to be produced. Remember that your client does not know the rules surrounding formal discovery and probably does not understand the concept of privileged documents. It will be up to you to identify documents that are outside the scope of the request, or privileged from being disclosed, or the request for which is otherwise objectionable. This can be a time-consuming and challenging responsibility, particularly when the documents to be reviewed are numerous or detailed.

2. **Start early to comply with a document request.** Because of the time involved in reviewing documents to be produced and the number

of documents involved in many cases, you need to start early. The assisting legal professional must work closely with the client to be sure the documents are located and assembled for review in ample time to allow the one assisting and the supervising lawyer to inspect them closely. This may mean making numerous reminder calls to a busy or procrastinating client.

3. **Sometimes parts of documents are discoverable and other parts are not.** Sometimes the non-discoverable parts of a document must be blacked out on a copy before they are produced for inspection. A document produced for inspection by an opposing party which has non-discoverable information deleted from it might look like that in Illustration 4-13.

4. **Make sure the supervising attorney reviews documents to be produced.** The ultimate decision as to what documents to produce or withhold from production lies with the supervising attorney as lead counsel. As the one assisting, your review of the client's documents should always be reported to the supervising attorney. And your suggestions with regard to which documents to withhold or object to producing should be made known to her in plenty of time to allow the attorney's own review of them.

5. **Arrange the time and place for the document production.** Frequently this job will fall to the assisting legal professional. Depending on the number of documents, their sensitivity and the feelings of the client, the inspection may be allowed in your office or that of opposing counsel. You should discourage the idea of allowing a document inspection in your client's office since it encourages the other attorney to ask for more documents, which may be nearby.

6. **Remain present during the inspection.** The assisting legal professional should remain present at all times that the opposing side is inspecting her client's documents and things. Though in the vast majority of cases trustworthiness can be assumed, your client may not share that view and even honest mistakes (lost documents, documents placed out of order, documents with new markings on them) can be made to look devious later. Better to be present at all times and watch after your client's documents and things.

7. **Keep a record of documents produced and withheld.** Litigation drags on and, as it heats up, disputes can arise between attorneys as to what was or was not produced on a given day months or years ago. When the opposing party produces documents for you, keep a record of what was produced and copied by you. Keep a copy and a record of what your side produced or withheld from production to the opponent.

8. **Reviewing documents produced by the opponent.** The assisting legal professional may be asked to review documents produced by the opponent. If that responsibility falls to you, your review should be careful and thorough. Report to the supervising lawyer deleted pages or blacked out portions of documents or anything else that appears unusual or inappropriate.

Illustration 4-13 DOCUMENT MODIFIED FOR PRODUCTION AND INSPECTION

MEMORANDUM

FROM: Dr. Bright Idea, Chief Engineer Design/Build Division

TO: Legal Department

DATE: September 6, YR-3

RE: Safe Bag 1000 System

I have just been advised by Maka Quickbuck, head of the Production, that a decision has been made by the board to suspend testing of the new Safe Bag 1000 Air Bag System effective September 12. It is my strong opinion that this decision is ███████████ ██ ██████████████████. There are at least three reasons for this opinion as I have discussed with ████████████████ at least three times:

1. In today's litigious climate it is important that our products be as fully tested as possible.

2. ██

3. ██

I am urging your department to take a similar position to that outlined here. If you would like to meet regarding this, I am available at your request.

4. Requests for physical or mental examination (FRCP 35)

This rule allows the examination of a person to be ordered by the court upon motion and a showing of good cause. In a personal injury case, particularly one involving a soft tissue injury, the defendant may want to have the plaintiff examined by a physician of the defendant's choosing. This is called an **independent medical examination** (IME) and usually will be agreed to by the plaintiff. The assisting legal professional's role in arranging such an IME may be in locating or suggesting a qualified physician or psychologist to conduct the examination.

5. Request for admissions (FRCP 36)

Rule 36 permits parties to ask opponents in writing before trial to admit the truthfulness of facts or of the genuineness of documents or things related to the case. Responses must be submitted in writing and must fairly and in good faith respond to the substance of the request. For example, the answering party cannot simply give lack of knowledge or information as a reason for failing to admit unless they have conducted a reasonable inquiry into it. Failure of a party to respond to the requests to admit in a timely fashion or giving an insufficient reason for failing to admit the matter requested may result in the matter being deemed admitted against them. And if the answering party refuses to admit the matter requested and the asking party proves that matter as true at trial, the court has the discretion to impose the costs the asking party incurred in proving the matter on the answering party even if the answering party prevails at trial.

FRCP 36 is a useful tool to cut down on what has to be proven at trial. Getting the opposing side to admit what is undisputed means it need not be proven at trial, reducing the time and expense of the trial. It is also a useful tactical tool, causing a party confronted with a request to admit on an issue on which they are likely to lose at trial to run the risk of costs being imposed on them if they fail to admit prior to trial.

The role of the assisting legal professional in connection with this Rule includes identifying factual and other matters that can be the subject of a request to admit, recommending its use to the supervising attorney, and then drafting the request. As with all discovery documents, careful, concise drafting of the requests to admit is critical to their successful use. (See Illustration 4-14.)

D. ▶ Drafting Guidelines for Discovery Documents

One of the most important skills that a legal professional can possess is the ability to draft legal documents well. Nowhere is this more important than in drafting discovery documents such as interrogatories, document requests, and related discovery motions. It is a skill that is developed over time from practice. Here are some general drafting guidelines in the discovery area. Keep in mind that these guidelines apply to the drafting of all kinds of legal documents.

1. Identify and organize the topics to be addressed

Start by brainstorming a list of the areas of inquiry and then rework that list into carefully worded questions placed in a logical order—what should be asked first, second, etc. By doing this you will eliminate duplicative questions that need not be asked in an interrogatory. (See LBD 4-5.)

Illustration 4-14 REQUEST FOR ADMISSIONS

IN THE UNITED STATES DISTRICT COURT
FOR THE EASTERN DISTRICT OF YOURSTATE
NORTHERN DIVISION

BEN RUNOVER,
    Plaintiff
 	
    v.
SOFT LANDING, INC., AND
WORLD WIDE INDUSTRIES, INC.
    Defendant
	)
	)
	)
	) DOCKET NO. YR00-00001
	)
	)
	)
	)

PLAINTIFF'S FIRST REQUEST FOR ADMISSIONS FROM DEFENDANTS

Plaintiff, Ben Runover, pursuant to Rule 36 of the Federal Rules of Civil Procedure, hereby requests that defendants Soft Landing, Inc., and World Wide Industries, Inc., admit the following facts and genuineness of documents.

1. The Safe Bag 1000 car air bag system was designed by defendant World Wide Industries, Inc., between YR-5 and YR-3.

2. In YR-4 defendant World Wide Industries, Inc., caused defendant Soft Landing, Inc., to be incorporated under the laws of the state of Delaware.

3. Defendant Soft Landing, Inc., was incorporated for the purpose of marketing the Safe Bag 1000 car air bag system to the American automobile industry.

4. At all times since its incorporation, all outstanding shares of stock in defendant Soft Landing, Inc., have been owned by defendant World Wide Industries, Inc.

5. The letter attached as *Exhibit 1* to this request for admissions is a true, genuine, and authentic copy of a memorandum dated September 6, YR-3 from Dr. Bright Idea, Chief Engineer of the Design/Build Division of Soft Landing, Inc., to the Legal Department of Soft Landing, Inc.

6. The letter attached as *Exhibit 2* to this request for admissions is a true, genuine, and authentic copy of a letter dated September 13, YR-3 from Marcus Jawosky, President of defendant Soft Landing, Inc., to John Brown, President of defendant World Wide Industries, Inc.

7. The letter attached as *Exhibit 2* to this request for admissions was written in response to the memorandum attached as *Exhibit 1* to this request for admissions.

                                            Mellow Fellow
                                            Attorney for plaintiff Ben Runover
                                            (Address)

(Certificate of Service omitted)

2. Use clear and concise language

Avoid vague, unclear, or ambiguous terms or phrases. Remember our system is an adversarial one. That means the opposing party that receives your attorney's interrogatories will be scrutinizing them carefully to avoid answering any more than the interrogatory calls for—as your side will do for interrogatories served on your client. If a question contains a word or phrase that is vague or ambiguous, it may be objected to on that grounds rather than answered. Though you may eventually clear up the objection through negotiation or court order, the consequence is delay and additional time and expense that could have been avoided.

It may take several rounds of editing to make your interrogatories clear and concise but it is worth the effort. Read over your draft of interrogatories and ask yourself, "What am I really asking for here? Is it clear to me? Will it be clear to the one receiving it? Will they be able to object to it in good faith? Can I say this any better?"

HYPOTHETICAL 4-4

> Assume that the attorney you work for has filed suit on behalf of Ben Runover against Needa Floorit and Funny Bread, Inc., alleging negligence by Needa Floorit in operating the truck on behalf of Funny Bread. The attorney for defendant Needa Floorit serves a set of interrogatories on Ben Runover, which you are assigned to review. The following questions are included in the interrogatories you are reviewing.
>
> 1. What were you doing before the accident happened?
> 2. State whether you have been injured and, if so, how.
> 3. List all medications you were taking prior to this accident.
> 4. Explain in detail how you can't do anything now that you could do before the accident.
> 5. List everybody who saw your car or might have seen it before or after the accident.
> 6. List all medical problems you had before this accident and the names of everybody who helped you with them and when.
> 7. Were you alone or by yourself when the accident happened and if you weren't who was with you?
> 8. List everybody you talked to after the accident.
> 9. List all your bills and how much they are.
> 10. Explain in your own words how this accident could have been avoided.
>
> What, if any, objection would you suggest your supervising attorney make to each of these questions?
>
> How would you word the objections if your supervising attorney asks you to prepare a draft response?
>
> Try your hand at rewriting each question to make it clearer.

3. Be thorough

Be sure your questions cover all the areas you intended. And be sure they are worded well enough to cover all the information you want to obtain. Don't leave loopholes in your questions. The other side will find them.

4. Don't be wordy

Generally, the fewer and simpler words you use in your interrogatories, the clearer and more concise they will be. It is a real art to achieve the goals of clarity, conciseness, and thoroughness using the simplest words possible. Remember, practice makes perfect.

5. Use subparts carefully

In general, subparts should be used in a question only if the subparts are substantially related to the main question. The expert witness interrogatory is a good example:

Identify every expert witness that you expect to use at trial and for each one identified state:

1. all opinions they will offer;
2. the factual or other basis for each such opinion; and
3. all data or other information considered by the expert in reaching each such opinion.

Remember you are allowed only a limited number of interrogatories. Poorly worded subparts may be considered more than one question.

6. Use definitions

Good interrogatories contain definitions of words and phrases unique to the case or that might be objected to otherwise as vague or over broad. For example, in the Ben Runover case, you will be asking many questions about the accident. To avoid confusion over which accident or an objection for vagueness if you simply refer to it in your questions as "the accident," and to avoid needless repetition, define the phrase "the accident" before you ask any questions using it. (See Illustration 4-15.)

If you are going to ask the opposing party to "identify" witnesses or documents, which is regularly done in interrogatories, define that word before you use it in questions. What it means to you might not be how the opposing party chooses to interpret it. (See Illustration 4-15.) Other similar words and phrases that are often defined in interrogatories include **plaintiff, defendant, document(s)**, and **person(s)**.

Once you have defined a word or phrase, you need only use the word or phrase in succeeding questions and not the entire definition. For example, if you have defined "identify" when used in reference to a person to mean to state his or her entire name, current or last known home and business addresses, current or last known home and business phone numbers, etc., you don't have to repeat that entire definition in every interrogatory in which you ask the opposing party to identify someone.

In fact, once you have defined a word or phrase, you should be sure to use the word or phrase throughout the interrogatories. It may be confusing and possibly objectionable to fail to use the defined term.

EXAMPLE

In the Ben Runover case, if you have defined "Cadillac" to mean the car operated by plaintiff at the time of the accident, don't refer to it in the interrogatories as "the Cadillac automobile" or "plaintiff's car."

Illustration 4-15 DEFINITIONS IN INTERROGATORIES

For purposes of these interrogatories the following definitions shall apply:

1. The word "plaintiff" shall mean plaintiff Ben Runover.

2. The word "Floorit" shall mean defendant Needa Floorit.

3. The letters "FBI" shall mean defendant Funny Bread, Inc.

4. The phrase, "the accident" shall mean that collision between the automobile operated by plaintiff Ben Runover and the truck operated by defendant Needa Floorit which occurred on December 1, 2006 at the intersection of Fifth Street and Vine in Harmony City, Yourstate and which is referenced in the original complaint filed in this cause.

5. The word "Cadillac" shall mean that automobile operated by plaintiff at the time of the accident.

6. The word "truck" shall mean that truck operated by Floorit at the time of the accident.

7. The word "person" shall mean all natural persons and entities, including, without limitation, all sole proprietorships, associations, companies, corporations, partnerships, joint venturers, limited liability companies, trusts, estates, agencies, licensing arrangements, franchise arrangements, and any other business arrangement.

8. The word "document(s)" shall mean all written, recorded or graphic matter, however produced, reproduced or stored, including, but not limited to, photographs, audio or video tapes, transcripts, data stored on computer disk or by other electronic means, correspondence, notes, memoranda, interoffice communications, studies, analysis, reports, reviews, proposals, contracts, working papers, statistical reports, blue prints, sketches, drawings, drafts, computer data, calendars, diaries, books of account, inventories, business records, financial records, or documents similar to any of the foregoing, however denominated.

9. The phrase "electronically stored information" shall mean all information stored on the defendant's computers, laptops, scanners, fax machines, personal digital assistants, pagers, cell phones, storage discs, backup tapes, and CDs, or on the same or similar equipment of current or former owners, officers, managers, or employees of the defendant and shall include metadata on programs, network data, and deleted data.

10. The word "identify" when used with respect to a person(s) shall mean to:

   a. state the fullest known name, present or last known address(es), designating which, and telephone number(s) of such person;
   b. provide the name and address of the present or last known employer(s), place of employment, and job title of such person; and
   c. if such person was affiliated at any time with a party to this litigation by employment or otherwise, to state the nature (including job title, if any) and dates of such affiliation.

11. The word "identify" when used with respect to a document or electronically stored information shall mean to:

   a. specify the nature of the document or information (such as, for example, letter, memorandum, e-mail message, etc.);
   b. state the date, if any, appearing on the document or information, or, if none, the date upon which the document or information was prepared;
   c. identify each person who wrote, signed, dictated, or otherwise participated in the preparation of the document or information; and
   d. identify each person, if any, who was an addressee or recipient of the document or information.

7. Use instructions with caution

Some attorneys like to use general instructions along with definitions in interrogatories. For example, there may be a general instruction that says: "For each answer provided, state the identity of each person known to have personal knowledge of the answer."

Instructions should be used with caution. First, there are already extensive rules regarding the answering of interrogatories set forth in the rules of procedure and it may be onerous and objectionable to attempt to add to those obligations with instructions.

Second, many instructions tend to be duplicative of requirements already set out in the rules of procedure and thus needlessly redundant. This is especially true of instructions which purport to require the other party to supplement their responses at a later date if they discover additional information pertinent to an answer given earlier or if they discover their original answer was incorrect. FRCP 26(e) imposes an obligation on all parties responding to discovery requests to supplement their responses under certain circumstances. An instruction to do so is needlessly repetitive. And, if the instruction purports to impose an obligation on the other party in excess of that imposed by Rule 26(e), it will likely draw an objection.

Third, instructions tend to add to the complexity and difficulty of answering interrogatories, which are already burdensome enough. Thus, instructions should typically be used only in highly technical or complex cases when there is good reason to do so.

8. Avoid abusing discovery

Interrogatories historically have been the most misused discovery method. They are too often used merely to harass another party by keeping them busy, to increase the other lawyer's time spent on the case, or to run up the opposing client's bill. The wording of interrogatories can make them tricky, burdensome, or needlessly complex. Never do this on purpose. That is **sharp practice** (behavior that is on the fine line of being dishonest) at best and often unethical.

The courts generally do not favor interrogatories because they are subject to abuse and may accordingly be sympathetic to a motion for protective order and sanctions. Also, remember that what goes around comes around, and the law office that files needlessly lengthy, poorly worded, tricky, or burdensome interrogatories may see the same instructions coming back at them. Just try objecting to them then!

9. Before responding to discovery requests review them carefully for objections

The assisting legal professional should always advise the supervising attorney as to suggestions. See the discussion of objections above.

10. In responding to discovery requests, answer only what is fairly asked

It is a cardinal rule in responding to all formal discovery not to volunteer information. In answering interrogatories, help the client draft a truthful response, but one which gives no more information than is asked. And with document requests, produce the documents that fairly correspond to the request but nothing more.

11. Comply with all rules of procedure and local rules of court regarding discovery

It is common for both state and federal courts to adopt local rules directing that interrogatories, document requests, etc., not be filed with the clerk, but only the responses thereto or motions relating to discovery disputes. Increasingly, federal and state courts are ordering the **electronic** (paperless) **filing** of discovery materials and pleadings by local rule (see LBD 4-7).

E.   The Order of Discovery

The rules of formal discovery in civil litigation provide for broad, comprehensive discovery from opposing parties and witnesses. To maximize their effectiveness and avoid wasted or duplicative effort and expense, the side seeking discovery should carefully plan in what order the formal discovery tools will be utilized in a particular case. Every case will call for its own analysis but generally the formal discovery in a civil case should proceed in this order:

1. Interrogatories and document requests

Interrogatories and document requests should be utilized first, and simultaneously. If well planned and carefully worded, they will obtain the broad general information and documents needed to plan more detailed and specific formal and informal discovery.

2. Depositions

The depositions of parties and witnesses are taken after interrogatories have been answered and documents produced for inspection. The oral examination of a party will be much more comprehensive and effective if the attorney has background information from interrogatory answers and responses to document requests.

3. Requests for physical or mental examination

Requests for physical or mental exams can occur at any time during a civil case, but typically occur after the plaintiff's medical condition and history has been discovered and the plaintiff deposed.

4. Requests for admissions

This discovery tool can be used early on to clarify exactly what has to be proven and what doesn't. But generally it is used near the time of trial after other discovery has been completed. Or, it can be used to lay the groundwork for a dispositive pretrial motion such as a Rule 56 motion for summary judgment, to demonstrate conclusively that there is no genuine issue of any material fact.

F. Discovery of Electronically Stored Information (E-discovery)

1. The explosion in electronically stored information (ESI)

SLEUTH ON THE LOOSE

Visit Kroll Ontrack (*www.krollontrack. com*) and Trial Solutions (*www.trialgraphic.com*), two litigation support companies offering attorneys assistance with e-discovery. Look for forms or articles containing comprehensive definitions of what is considered electronic evidence that you might use in drafting your next discovery documents.

As a result of the explosive growth in electronic communications and electronic record-keeping by individuals, professionals, and businesses, "the universe of discoverable material has expanded exponentially," as the court noted in *Zubulake v. UBS Warburg LLC*, 217 F.R.D. 309, 311 (S.D.N.Y. 2003) (now known as *Zubulake I*). Worldwide, approximately 30 billion **e-mail messages** are sent each day (excluding spam messages, which would raise the total to about 300 billion) by approximately 2 billion different e-mail users. ABI Research (www.abiresearch.com/home.jsp) estimates that 7 trillion **short message service (SMS)** messages, referred to commonly as **text messages**, were sent in 2011 from a variety of mobile devices. The average business person sends and receives between 50 and 150 e-mail or text messages each day. Those messages may contain text and digital images. Goods and services are now routinely sold via **electronic commerce (eCommerce)**. Forrester Research, Inc. (www.forrester.com/) reports that in 2012 retail eCommerce sales topped $225 billion in the United States alone. Worldwide products of all kinds are advertised, bought, and sold 24-7 from Web sites of manufacturers and distributors and are resold constantly on popular sites like **eBay**, **CraigsList**, and many others. **Electronic funds transfers (EFT)** continue to replace the exchange of cash and processing of paper checks. People, businesses, and other organizations are engaging in an explosion of **online social networking** via **blogs**, **Twitter**, **LinkedIn**, **Flickr**, **Facebook** and **Google+**. Each day, thousands of photos, videos, and other images are being posted on sites like **YouTube** and **PhotoBucket**. People are searching for companions on **Match.com** and **eHarmony**. Both professionals and amateurs are contributing to **collaborative journalism** sites like **WikiNews** and CNN's **iReport**. Everywhere you look, individuals and businesses are utilizing desktops, laptops, notebooks, tablets, PDAs (personal digital assistants), cell phones, smart phones, and even pagers with texting software to communicate electronically.

And it's not just communications and transactions in goods and services. Individuals as well as businesses, professions, financial institutions and governments are creating and storing more and more records electronically. More than 90 percent of all documents produced worldwide are created in digital form. Many businesses have multiple network servers to handle the flood of data being created, stored, and transmitted. Computer systems typically have backup tapes to insure against the loss of data and from which most deleted data can be recovered.

As a result of this revolution in communications and information storage, trial lawyers have become very aggressive in seeking comprehensive discovery of all types of electronically stored information (ESI) including e-mails, text messages, software files, computerized records, or other computerized data compilations. Discovery requests are often prepared with the assistance of computer experts who understand the difference between electronic **data** (information) and **metadata** (data that describes other data including formatting information and edited content), who know the capacity of computers and software programs to retain traces of data even after it has been "deleted," and who comprehend the nature of networks and information processing systems and so can trace electronic communications and files.

Most people by now know that deleting an e-mail or text message from your account does not mean that the message is permanently extinguished. It may be recovered either from the computer or cell phone from which it was sent or from the **internet service provider (ISP)**.

EXAMPLE

In March 2004, SCO Group, owner of the UNIX operating system, filed suit against Daimler-Chrysler for violations of a software agreement. The complaint was prepared using Microsoft Word and filed electronically. Metadata viewable in the electronic document revealed that in earlier drafts of the complaint, SCO had named Bank of America as the defendant instead of Daimler-Chrysler and asked for slightly different relief than did the complaint ultimately filed. The metadata not only revealed changes made to the document but comments made electronically in the margin of the document during the editing process. Read the article at http://news.cnet.com/2100-7344_3-5170073.html. Pretty embarrassing.

EXAMPLE

John sends his girlfriend, Mary, a number of suggestive text messages from his Verizon cell phone. The messages are received on Mary's AT&T cell phone and she forwards them to her Hotmail e-mail account, which she normally accesses on her home desktop computer. Sally, John's wife, sues for divorce and wants to discover those messages. If John and Mary think that they have prevented that discovery by deleting the messages on their cell phones and her home computer, they may have a nasty surprise coming. The messages may still be stored on either cell phone or on Mary's computer hard drive. Failing that, Verizon, AT&T, and/or Hotmail may have those messages stored on their servers and be ordered to produce them in response to a discovery or trial subpoena.

2. ESI as potentially relevant evidence

Recall from FRCP 26(b)(1) that the scope of permissible discovery in a civil case is "any nonprivileged matter that is relevant to any party's claim or defense—including the existence, description, nature, custody, condition, and location of any documents or other tangible things and the identity and location of persons who know of any discoverable matter." Thus any **potentially relevant evidence** that is not privileged (a concept we will visit in Chapter 6) is fair game for discovery.

3. The litigation hold and dangers of spoliation of evidence

As you consider the ramifications of all this ESI being potentially discoverable in a civil suit, add to the equation the legal rule that once a party is or should be aware that litigation is possible, a **litigation hold** is placed on all reasonably accessible potential evidence, and you begin to see the perimeters of the problem. Not only is potentially relevant ESI under the control of litigating parties subject to possible discovery by an opponent, the litigation hold rule means that as soon as either or both of those parties is aware or reasonably should be aware that litigation could arise they are under a duty to not change or discard such material. The ramifications of this rule as applied to ESI are terrifying to litigants that routinely generate large quantities of ESI and just as routinely alter and discard it. Such entities live under a continuing cloud of uncertainty regarding what they can alter or discard at any given moment. After all, exactly at what point should you be aware that a dispute with another party could result in litigation? Every time a customer complains? Every time there is a dispute over a contract provision? Every time a negotiation falls through?

The seminal case of *Zubulake v. UBS Warburg LLC*, 217 F.R.D. 309, 311 (S.D.N.Y. 2003) (*Zubulake I*) and its prodigy (*Zubulake II-V* and *Zubulake Revisited Six Years Later*, see LBD 4-11) confirms that the **litigation hold** rule is alive and well in the context of potentially relevant ESI—once a party is or should reasonably be aware that a dispute may be litigated, no reasonably accessible evidence of any kind, including ESI that may be relevant to the issues in the dispute, can be altered, discarded, or destroyed. Instead, it must be preserved for the potential litigation. No formal notice of litigation is required to trigger the litigation hold, and disputes can arise over whether a party had sufficient notice (see LBD 4-20). Given the inherent uncertainty of exactly when a party is or should be aware of potential litigation, it has become common practice for attorneys to issue a formal **preservation letter** to advise a potential adverse party that litigation is possible and that all records in whatever format should be preserved from that point onward. Illustration 4-16 contains a preservation letter that might have been written to potential defendants prior to the filing of suit in the Ben Runover case.

The party who has custody of or control over the information subject to the litigation hold now has a duty to suspend any routine retention/destruction policy and to not destroy, dispose of, or alter the information subject to the litigation hold. To do so is **spoliation of evidence** and can result in monetary and other sanctions on the party who engages in the spoliation intentionally, and under some circumstances, even negligently (see discussion in *Zubulake V* cited in LBD 4-11, and see LBD 4-20). There is no question now that the duty to preserve evidence extends to ESI that a party knows or should know is relevant to any present or future litigation (see, e.g., *John B. v. Goetz*, 531 F.3d 448, 459 (6th Cir.2008)). In *Link v. Wabash R. Co.*, 370 U.S. 626 (1962), the Supreme Court recognized that when a trial judge is presented with a case of spoliation of evidence by a party, the judge is not limited to imposing sanctions based on statue or rule such as those set forth in FRCP 37 (which must involve violation of a court order). Instead the judge, empowered by "the court's inherent authority to control the judicial process," may fashion an appropriate sanction "to achieve the orderly and expeditious disposition of cases" (370 U.S. at 630-31).

Such **spoliation sanctions** may include ordering the offending party to pay the opponent's attorney's fees (see, e.g., *Leon v. IDX Sys. Corp.*, 464 F.3d 951 (9th Cir. 2006) or to bear the costs of the other party attempting to locate the lost or altered data from another source (see, e.g., *Nacco Materials Handling Group, Inc. v. Lilly Co.*, 278 F.R.D. 395 (W.D. Tenn. 2007)). Such sanctions may also include the dreaded **adverse interest jury instruction** pursuant to which a jury in the case is instructed that the jury is free to conclude that evidence that was wrongfully destroyed, disposed of, changed, or otherwise withheld from the party seeking discovery would have been unfavorable to the party guilty of the spoliation (see, e.g., *Mosaid v. Samsung*, 348 F. Supp. 2d 322 (D.N.J. 2004) and *Pension Comm. of the Univ. of Montreal Pension Plan v. Banc of Am. Secs., LLC*, 685 F.Supp.2d 456 (S.D.N.Y.2010). In extreme cases where spoliation is intentional or done in bad faith, the trial court may even grant default judgment against the party guilty of spoliation of ESI, as happened in *Gutman v. Klein*, 2008 WL 4682208 (E.D.N.Y.) and in *Metropolitan Opera Ass'n., Inc., v. Local 100, Hotel Employees*, 212 F.R.D. 178 (S.D.N.Y. 2003) (see LBD 4-12). It is clear that the obligations regarding ESI subject to a litigation hold apply to all litigants, whether corporate or individual. See, e.g., *Teague v. Target Corp.*, 2007 WL 1041191 (W.D.N.C.) (individual plaintiff sanctioned with adverse interest jury instruction for failing to preserve laptop). (See LBD 4-21 and 4-22.)

Significantly, once a party is aware of a litigation hold on potential evidence, including electronic data, *Zubulake* imposes a duty on the attorney for the party having custody or control of such evidence to oversee the client's compliance with the litigation hold and monitor the client's efforts to retain and produce the evidence pursuant to the discovery rules. To fulfill that duty, counsel is expected to become familiar with the client's data retention policies as well as its data production/retention systems. Counsel is expected to communicate as needed with the client's information technology personnel and other key players involved in data production/retention to ensure compliance with the litigation hold and to instruct that copies be routinely made of current active electronic files relevant to the dispute. Attorneys failing to comply with this duty may face sanctions themselves. See, e.g., *Phoenix Four, Inc. v. Strategic*

Illustration 4-16   SAMPLE PRESERVATION LETTER

Date

Ms. Gladys Z. Boss, President
Soft Landing, Inc.
1977 West Main St.
Technology City, Nextstate 55505

Mr. Gother Instyle, President,
Capital City Cadillac
144 Cardealer Lane
Capitol City, Yourstate 44404

Re: Data preservation in potential claim of Ben Runover

Dear Ms. Boss and Mr. Instyle:

This office represents Ben Runover, a resident of Capital City, Yourstate, who sustained serious injuries last month in an automobile accident in which the SafeBag 1000 air bag designed and manufactured by Soft Landing, Inc. and installed in the Cadillac operated by Mr. Runover, which had been sold to him by Capital City Cadillac, unexpectedly failed to properly deploy. This letter is to formally advise you that 1) litigation by Mr. Runover against either or both Soft Landing, Inc. and Capital City Cadillac may be forthcoming in connection with this automobile accident and the failure of the Safe Bag 1000 air bag system, and 2) certain evidence relevant to the claims of Mr. Runover in this potential litigation should be preserved.

More specifically, the claims of Mr. Runover against you require the preservation of all information from your computer systems, removable electronic media, and other locations relating to the design, testing, manufacture, installation, operation, and performance of the SafeBag 1000 air bag system or this accident. This includes, but is not limited to, word processing documents, spreadsheets, databases, calendars, e-mail, and other electronic communications, telephone logs, contact manager information, Internet usage files, and network access information.

Soft Landing, Inc. and Capital City Cadillac should preserve the following platforms in the possession of either company or any third party under the control of or affiliated with either company (such as employees, independent contractors, parent, subsidiary or sister companies, divisions, partners, or joint venturers): databases, networks, computer systems including legacy systems (hardware and software), servers, archives, backup or disaster recovery systems, tapes, discs, drives, cartridges and other storage media, laptops, personal computers, Internet data, personal digital assistants, handheld wireless devices, mobile telephones, paging devices, and audio systems including voicemail.

Please let me know if anything in this letter is unclear or if you have other questions.

Sincerely,

Mellow Fellow, Esq.

cc: Mr. Ben Runover

Resources Corp., 2006 WL 1409413 (S.D.N.Y.) (imposing sanctions, including attorney's fees and costs on a party and its counsel, where counsel acted with gross negligence for failing to conduct a thorough search for ESI sources).

4. Undue hardship issues in e-discovery

Issues of **undue hardship** routinely arise when discovery into ESI is sought particularly in **class actions** and other **complex litigation** where so much of it is likely to exist and be potentially relevant. When a party receives a document request seeking years of ESI in the form of records or communications or when interrogatories require the answering party to review years of such records in order to answer in good faith, the time and labor demands placed on the answering party can be crushing. Often the production of requested e-data will involve expensive and time consuming review of back-up disks, or even the expensive tracing or recreation of files by computer experts. What business has the time or resources to spend weeks or months reviewing old ESI to determine what might be relevant to the request or what might be privileged?

EXAMPLE

A single computer with a 200-gigabyte hard drive can store the equivalent of 150 million pages of text. If the computer system of the party subject to interrogatories or a document request consists of multiple computers or several network servers as well as laptops, personal digital assistants, desktops, etc., the amount of data that potentially must be reviewed in order to comply with the discovery requests becomes almost incomprehensible. The time and expense of completing even a cursory review may be staggering.

These problems have given rise to the increasing use of specialized software for search of ESI rather than depending on time-intensive people searches. **Text analysis software** designed for use in potential or actual litigation and featuring **predictive coding** (essentially a key word/phrase diagnostic empowered to identify records containing not just those actual words/phrases but records having a similar meaning) is now available from any number of technology companies. Illustration 4-17 lists a number of the leading ESI technology companies.

HYPOTHETICAL 4-5

An interesting case involving a request to respond to ESI discovery using text analysis software was presented in *Da Silva Moore v. Publicis Groupe*, 2012 U.S. Dist. LEXIS 23350 (S.D.N.Y. Feb. 24, 2012) summarized at www.applieddiscovery.com/ws_display.asp?filter=Case%20Summaries %20Detail&item_id=%7BBBCA82492-A46B-49F0-8780-C7E72A54F5F3%7D. How many documents did the defendant need to review in that case? On what basis did the trial judge approve defendant's request to utilize text analysis software to search that database? Did the judge find that such software is always sufficiently reliable to supplant an old-fashioned search done by people?

The undue hardship often present in responding to ESI production requests has also given rise to increasing requests made by the responding party that the party seeking the discovery compensate the responding

Illustration 4-17   POPULAR E-DISCOVERY TECHNOLOGY COMPANIES

---

1. Aderant (www.aderant.com/)

2. Applied Discovery (www.applieddiscovery.com/)

3. Esentio Technologies (www.esentio.com/)

4. InData (http://indatacorp.com/Products/eDiscovery/services.aspx)

5. IntApp (www.intapp.com/)

6. Integreon (www.integreon.com/)

7. MindSHIFT Technologies (www.integreon.com/)

8. Profiscience Partners (www.profiscience.com/)

9. TDC Global Enterprises (www.tdcge.com/Home.html)

10. TechLaw Solutions (www.techlawsolutions.com/index.asp)

---

party for all or part of the costs involved in the search and response (**cost shifting**).

Addressing the undue hardship problem in ESI production, *Zubulake I* established a seven-factor balancing test to be applied by trial courts to determine when the cost of e-discovery should be shifted in whole or part from the producing party to the requesting party. The seven-factor *Zubulake* test is set forth in Illustration 4-18.

5. ESI production and waiver of attorney-client or work product privilege

A vexatious problem regarding discovery of ESI has been the possible **waiver** of attorney-client privilege or the attorney's work product privilege when ESI that is produced for inspection inadvertently contains such privileged material. Such **inadvertent disclosure** (sometimes called **inadvertent production**) often occurs as a result of the difficulty of closely reviewing the voluminous materials to be provided.

HYPOTHETICAL 4-6

Assume a law firm complying with an extensive ESI request inadvertently provides opposing counsel with a trial strategy memorandum prepared by the firm and subject to the attorney work product privilege. Has the work product privilege been waived by the inadvertent disclosure? If opposing counsel reads the memorandum before realizing what it is, should opposing counsel be disqualified from further representation of its client? Can opposing counsel retain the memorandum, or must they advise the firm that inadvertently provided the memorandum of their error and return it? Whether they return it or not, if they are not disqualified, can they use the information contained in the memorandum? On the issue of disqualification, see how one court handled this situation in *Rico v. Mitsubishi Motors Corp.*, 171 P.3d 1092 (Cal. 2007). On the issue of whether the privilege has been waived, courts have taken three different approaches: 1) a strict "if you provided it you waived the privilege" approach; 2) a "simple negligence will not waive a privilege but gross negligence will" approach; and 3) a middle-of-the-road "it depends on a balancing of factors including the reasonableness of precautions taken to avoid disclosure to how quickly the disclosure was discovered and action to rectify taken" approach. See a discussion of all three approaches in *Hopson v. Baltimore*, 232 F.R.D. 238 (Md. 2005). Which approach do you favor?

FRCP 26(f)(3)(D) instructs the parties conducting their Rule 26(f) conference to include views on claims of privilege or protection of trial preparation materials in their discovery plan. The Advisory Committee Notes encourages them to agree to what is called a "**nonwaiver agreement**" (also referred to as a "**quick peek**," as in "You can take a quick peek at something privileged I send you by mistake, but then you'll send it back and not use it") or "**clawback**" (as in "If I send you something privileged by mistake I can later claw it back") agreement. A nonwaiver agreement is one where the parties agree that in the event of inadvertent disclosure of privileged material, the receiving party can read the privileged material in order to determine that it is privileged, but will then advise the providing party of the error, return the privileged material, make no use of it, and claim no waiver of privilege. However, not all courts will enforce nonwaiver agreements, especially where the producing party makes no effort to screen documents before producing them, relying instead on the nonwaiver agreement to save them from a waiver claim (see the cases collected in *In re Columbia/HCA Healthcare Corp. Billing Practices Litig.*, 293 F.3d 289 (6th Cir. 2002)). Where courts are willing to endorse such agreements disputes will still arise as to whether a particular alleged waiver comes within the terms of the agreement (see the three approaches in *Hopson* cited in Hypothetical 4-6). Moreover, agreements between parties in one case, even if incorporated into a court order, will not typically be binding on third parties or litigants in

Illustration 4-18   SEVEN-FACTOR ZUBULAKE TEST FOR APPORTIONING COSTS IN E-DISCOVERY

1. The extent to which the request is specifically tailored to discover relevant information;

2. The availability of such information from other sources;

3. The total cost of production, compared to the amount in controversy;

4. The total cost of production, compared to the resources available to each party;

5. The relative ability of each party to control costs and its incentive to do so;

6. The importance of the issues at stake in the litigation; and

7. The relative benefits to the parties of obtaining the information.

other cases. New Federal Rule of Evidence (FRE) 502, effective in December 2008, should help alleviate this problem in federal actions and related state proceedings. FRE 502 essentially adopts the middle-of-the-road view from *Hopson* for inadvertent production so that a disclosure made in a federal proceeding will not waive privilege for the purposes of federal or related state proceedings, provided the privilege holder took reasonable precautions to prevent disclosure and reasonably prompt measures to rectify the error when it came to light. The new rule of evidence also provides that nonwaiver agreements incorporated into a federal court order will bind third parties in all state or federal proceedings

Inadvertent disclosure of privileged material can also result from **data mining**, the discovery of metadata within ESI. ESI can contain hidden "fingerprints" related to the observable information, buried away in a properties folder, edit file, or folder index. Someone who knows how to access these "buried treasures" within the ESI may be able to determine who drafted the document, edited it, or read it. Original language prior to changes and insertions can be determined; deleted data can be recovered; and files attached to produced e-mails thought deleted prior to production can be read.

HYPOTHETICAL 4-7

Assume that a lawyer responding to an ESI request determines she should produce a memorandum prepared by her client that contains both discoverable information and privileged statements made by the attorney to her client. The lawyer deletes or blocks out the privileged portions of the memorandum and, thus redacted, supplies it to opposing counsel. Opposing counsel's IT person is able to read and disclose the deleted or blocked statements of counsel appearing in the memorandum. Is the attorney client privilege waived? Has opposing counsel committed an ethical violation by mining the memorandum? Can opposing counsel use the mined information or must they advise of the disclosure and ignore the information? Does it matter whether opposing counsel knows or should know that the privileged material was supplied inadvertently? If the case was in federal court and the parties had entered into a nonwaiver agreement, how might a claim of waiver be decided under new FRE 502? If the case was in state court and there was no nonwaiver agreement, how would Rule 9 of the NCCUSL's proposed Uniform Rules Relating to Discovery of ESI (viewable at www.law.upenn.edu/bll/archives/ulc/udoera/2007am_final.pdf) decide these questions?

ABA Formal Ethical Opinion 06-442 issued in August 2006 provides that the Model Rules of Professional Conduct do not prohibit a party from finding and reviewing metadata in ESI produced by an opponent, but does recommend that parties complying with ESI requests first utilize software that will **scrub** the electronic information being sent to remove metadata (not always possible or effective) (see LBD 4-14) or create an alternative version of the information for production that does not include the metadata (could be prohibitively expensive and subject to objections for not producing originals). On the other hand, some state ethical committees have declared data mining to be unethical and sanctionable. See, e.g., N.Y.S.P.A. Comm. Prof. Eth. Op. 749 (25-001) (Dec. 14, 2001), and Fla. B.A. Eth. Comm. Op. 06-02 (Sep. 15, 2006). One opinion suggested that a receiving attorney should not review metadata if he has actual knowledge that it was sent inadvertently. See D.C. Bar Comm. Eth. Op. 341 (Sep. 2007). Another opinion found there was no duty on the recipient to determine whether the metadata was sent inadvertently. See Md. B.A. Comm. Eth. 2007-092 (Oct. 16, 2006).

It is this ominous five-way intersection of concerns about e-discovery—ESI being so voluminous in the modern world, the generous standard of permissible discovery (potentially relevant evidence), the demands of the litigation hold, the potentially crushing burden of filtering through ESI to comply with discovery requests, and the constant dangers of inadvertent production and waiver or privilege—that have combined to make ESI the hottest topic in modern civil discovery. Small wonder that so many **litigation support companies** now offer attorneys assistance with electronic discovery. Leaders in e-discovery support include Fios (www.fiosinc.com/default.aspx), Kroll Ontrack (www.krollontrack.com), and Trial Solutions (www.trialgraphic.com). An excellent e-discovery blog for legal professionals is available from DiscoveryResources.org (www.discoveryresources.org/technology-counsel/sound-evidence/). (See Appendix B for more e-discovery resources.)

6. Recent E-discovery amendments to the Federal Rules of Civil Procedure

Because of the dramatic growth in e-discovery and the challenges presented, a number of the discovery rules were amended beginning in 2006 to provide some guidelines in this turbulent area. (See LBD 4-19.) The voluntary disclosure obligations of FRCP 26(a) now specifically include ESI relevant to the issues (see FRCP 26(a)(1)(A)(ii)). FRCP 34(a) now specifically provides that document requests can include ESI. Rule 45(a)(1)(A)(iii) now authorizes subpoenas duces tecum to non-party witnesses to compel the production of ESI. Pursuant to FRCP 26(f)(3)(C) and (D), the discovery plan that the parties are to develop at their Rule 26(f) conference, discussed earlier, is to include a discussion of "issues about disclosure or discovery of electronically stored information, including the form or forms in which it should be produced" and "claims of privilege or of protection as trial preparation material" that may arise before or after production.

The new amendments also attempt to bring balance to the undue hardship aspect of e-discovery. Pursuant to FRCP 33(d), interrogatories may now be answered by providing electronically stored business records that contain the information requested. Although FRCP 34(b)(2)(E)(ii) provides that ESI is to be produced for inspection in the "form or forms in which it is ordinarily maintained or in a reasonably usable form or forms," Rule 34(b)(2)(D) authorizes the producing party to object to producing the ESI in the form in which it is ordinarily maintained or in a specifically requested form. The basis of such objection is that producing the data in the form in which it is ordinarily maintained may be too burdensome or may endanger confidential or privileged materials. When such objection is made, the court will conduct a hearing where both sides are heard in full on the matter, then make a ruling. Rule 34(b)(2)(E)(iii) protects the producing party from having to produce ESI in more than one form since ESI is often duplicated and appears in many different locations in a company's records. Rule 45(d) provides similar protections for a non-party responding to a subpoena seeking ESI.

Most significantly, FRCP 26(b)(2)(B) now allows a party to object to producing ESI on the grounds that it is "not reasonably accessible because of undue burden or cost."

EXAMPLE

Assume a relatively small company is served with a set of interrogatories and document requests in a lawsuit. The owners of the company explain to their attorney that answering the interrogatories will require review of at least ten years of records and correspondence, all electronically stored on retired disks. Complying with the document requests will require a careful review and selection of documents from the same store of information. They estimate 500 worker hours to do the search or the purchase of customized software that will cost them $10,000. Either way, they can't afford it. Complying in good faith with the discovery requests could well put them out of business.

If a **motion to compel production** is made under FRCP 37 by the party requesting discovery and the responding party raises Rule 26(b)(2)(B) as a defense, or if the responding party files a FRCP 26 motion for protective order based on 26(b)(2)(B), the rule puts the burden on the party responding to the discovery request (the party objecting to production) to show that production would be unduly burdensome or costly. Even if the party succeeds with that showing, if the requesting party can show a good faith need for the ESI, the trial judge is given the discretion to order all or some of the ESI to be produced. The trial judge in effect can modify the discovery request to try and provide the requesting party with most of what it needs while alleviating the burden on the producing party. The trial judge is specifically directed to use the factors set out in FRCP 26(b)(2)(C) in making that decision:

- Can the discovery sought be obtained from some other source or in some less burdensome format?
- Is the discovery sought duplicative or cumulative?
- Has the requesting party sought the information in a timely fashion?
- All things considered, does the burden on the producing party outweigh the likely benefit to the requesting party of discovering the information?

FRCP 45 (d)(1)(D) provides a non-party with the right to voice a similar objection in connection with ESI sought by subpoena.

Finally, dealing in part with the dangers posed by the litigation hold and allegations of spoliation, FRCP 37(f) now provides that a court cannot normally impose sanctions on a party "for failing to provide electronically stored information lost as a result of routine, good-faith operation of an electronic information system."

7. Organizational recommendations, local court rules, and guidelines addressing ESI issues

The ABA recently amended its Civil Discovery Standards to include guidelines relating to e-discovery (see LBD 4-13). In 2007 the National Conference of Commissioners on Uniform State Laws proposed Uniform Rules Relating to Discovery of ESI for states to consider adopting (viewable at www.law.upenn.edu/bll/archives/ulc/udoera/2007am_final.pdf). In 2006 the Conference of Chief Justices issued its Guidelines for State Trial Courts Regarding Discovery of ESI (reviewable at www.ncsconline.org/images/EDiscCCJGuidelinesFinal.pdf). In late 2009, an new professional entity, the **Organization of Legal Professionals (OLP)** (www.theolp.org/), was created, dedicated to establishing uniform standards for all professionals involved with e-data, including lawyers, paralegals, litigation support staff, technical support staff, vendors, and the judiciary. In furtherance of that goal, OLP has created a **E-discovery Certification Exam** (see LBD 4-18). Those who successfully complete the exam are designated a **Certified e-Discovery Professional (CeDP)** Many individual law firms are adopting formal **metadata policies** to deal with the multiple challenges and potential hazards of e-discovery (see LBD 4-14).

There is a growing body of case law beyond the *Zubulake* family of decisions dealing with the various issues raised by e-discovery. One thing that is clear is that judges expect counsel to cooperate in good faith with each other and with the court itself in resolving those issues. See, e.g., *William A. Gross Consr. Assocs., Inc. v. Am. Mfrs. Mutual Ins. Co.*, 256 F.R.D. 134 (S.D.N.Y. 2009) and *Mancia v. Mayflower Textiles Servs. Co.*, 253 F.R.D. 354 (D. Md. 2008). (See LBD 4-17.)

A number of state and federal courts around the country have addressed e-discovery issues via local rule, adopted guidelines, or model orders. Currently, there is a wide variety of approaches reflected in these efforts to address issues such as early consultation on e-discovery, automatic discovery limits, factors to use in balancing claims of need for ESI versus undue hardship in production, inadvertent disclosure issues, and cost shifting. Illustration 4-19 lists some of the most often referenced court rules and guidelines on e-discovery.

We live in a rapidly changing information age. Legal professionals must keep abreast of changes in technology and the law in drafting and complying with discovery requests, in planning and executing investigations, and in interviewing clients and witnesses. Many law offices are adopting formal metadata policies to deal with the multiple challenges and potential hazards of e-discovery (see LBD 4-14).

Illustration 4-19   OFTEN REFERENCED LOCAL COURT RULES, GUIDELINES, AND
MODEL ORDERS ON E-DISCOVERY

1. U.S. District of Delaware Default Standard for Discovery of Electronic Documents: www.ded.uscourts.gov/court-info/local-rules-and-orders/guidelines

2. Northern District of Illinois Proposed Case Management Order: www.ilnd.uscourts.gov/legal/wdadr/pdf/newcmo.pdf

3. U.S. District of Maryland Protocol for Discovery of ESI: www.mdd.uscourts.gov/news/news/ESIProtocol.pdf

4. U.S. District of Mississippi Uniform Local Rules: www.mssd.uscourts.gov/rules/Rules%20v%202004.pdf

5. U.S. District Court for the Middle District of Pennsylvania: www.pamd.uscourts.gov/docs/LR120110.pdf

Chapter Summary and Conclusion

There are five methods of formal discovery in a civil lawsuit. The scope of formal pre-trial discovery is broader than the admissibility of evidence at trial, but even in formal discovery, privileged materials and attorney work product are normally off limits, as are the opinions of experts who advise a party but do not testify. The FRCP and some state rules of procedure also mandate certain voluntary disclosures by the parties. Lawyers take depositions in civil suits for a number of reasons and the legal professional assisting with depositions may play an important role in them, including preparing a summary or index of the deposition. The assisting legal professional must also be able to draft effective interrogatories and document requests and to draft an appropriate response to the same when directed to the client. A special concern today is the discovery of electronic evidence. The legal professional must be knowledgeable concerning the kinds of e-data that may be available for discovery, and the importance of preserving such evidence when a dispute has arisen or is imminent.

There are a number of methods of formal discovery permitted in a criminal case as well. Those are the topic of Chapter 5.

Review Questions

1. Explain how the scope of discovery in a civil case is broader than the scope of evidence allowed at trial. Why?
2. List four types of information that a party in a civil case in federal court must disclose voluntarily to other parties.
3. Name the five methods of formal discovery allowed in a civil case.
4. List the five methods of formal discovery in a civil case in the order in which they are normally used.
5. Identify which of the five methods of formal discovery allowed in a civil case that involves answers given under oath.
6. List at least five ways that supervising lawyers use assisting legal professionals in discovery depositions.

7. List at least five ways that supervising lawyers use assisting legal professionals in discovery by interrogatories.
8. Why is it often helpful to use definitions in interrogatories and document requests?
9. What is sharp practice?
10. Explain what a "litigation hold" is, the purpose of a "preservation letter," and the consequences of a party engaging in the "spoilation" of evidence.

KEY WORDS AND PHRASES TO REMEMBER

adverse interest jury instruction
business records
Certified e-Discovery Professional (CeDP)
class actions
clawback
collaborative journalism
complex litigation
consulting experts
cost shifting
CraigsList
data mining
deponent
deposition
deposition index
deposition summary
discovery plan
docket control
document request
ebay
e-discovery
E-discovery Certification Exam
e-mail
electronic filing
electronically stored information (ESI)
expert witness
inadvertent disclosure
inadvertent production
independent medical exam
interrogatory
iReport
LinkedIn
litigation support companies
metadata policies
motion to compel discovery
non-retained experts

nonwaiver agreement
notice of deposition
objection
online social networking
Organization of Legal Professionals (OLP)
over broad
preservation letter
proof of service
protective order
quick peek
request for admissions
request for physical or mental examination
request for production of documents and things
retained expert
Rule 26(f) conference
sanctions
scheduling conference
scope of discovery
scrub software
sharp practice
short message service (SMS)
spoliation of evidence
spoliation sanctions
statement of changes
subpoena
subpoena *duces tecum*
testifying experts
text message
transcript
undue hardship
vague
waiver
WikiNews
written expert report

LEARN BY DOING

LBD 4-1. Determine whether the rules of procedure governing civil actions in the state courts of your state or the local rules of your state trial court(s) contain a voluntary disclosure rule similar to FRCP 26(a) or the discovery of 1) the existence and provisions of liability insurance agreements as is permitted by FRCP 26(a); and 2) the financial condition of a defendant. If so, prepare a memorandum comparing any differences in the state and federal rules.

LBD 4-2. Your instructor will provide you with the transcript of a deposition. Prepare a chronological index of the deposition, then a subject matter index, and finally a narrative summary of the deposition.

LBD 4-3. Arrange and conduct the interview of an experienced trial attorney or a litigation paralegal regarding the importance of the paralegal or new associate being familiar with the adversarial system and the rules of civil and/or criminal procedure including, in particular, the discovery rules, to effectively assist the trial lawyer in pre-filing investigation, formal discovery, trial preparation, and trial.

LBD 4-4. Assume you are asked by your supervising attorney to work on a case involving the following facts. Your client, Big John, broke his leg while working for his employer Slim Jim, Inc., on a construction site. Big John's doctor, Dr. Jack, set the leg and sent him to Big Bargain Home Health Care, Inc. ("BBHHC"), to rent a crutch, instructing Big John to use it for two weeks before returning to see him. Big John, who is 6'3" and weighs 240 lbs., went to BBHHC and was fitted for a crutch by Sally Slack, a new, part-time employee of BBHHC. Ms. Slack had the owner of BBHHC, Little Jake, check the fitting of the crutch before Big John left the premises. Two days later the crutch gave way as Big John was coming down a set of stairs and he fell, breaking his other leg. The crutch has a sticker on it saying it was made by B & J, Inc., a corporation in your state. Suit will be filed by your supervising lawyer on behalf of Big John in the general trial court of your state. The theories of liability will include negligence and strict liability due to an inherently dangerous and defective crutch. Do the following:

a. List prospective defendants in this suit.

b. List prospective witnesses to be deposed in this suit.

c. Select one of the prospective witnesses you listed in (b) and do the following:

1. Outline the questions your lawyer should ask that witness.
2. List the documents, if any, that should be requested or subpoenaed to the deposition of that witness, including electronically stored documents.
3. Prepare an appropriate notice of deposition to be served on opposing counsel in connection with the deposition of that witness.
4. Prepare an appropriate deposition subpoena for that witness.
5. Assuming suit has been filed, draft a letter to the opposing counsel confirming the agreed-upon date for the deposition and enclosing the notice.

6. Assuming suit has been filed, draft a letter to the court reporter confirming the arrangements for the deposition.

LBD 4-5. Assume the same facts as in LBD 4-4 and assume further that suit is filed on behalf of Big John against defendants including BBHHC. Draft a set of interrogatories and document requests on behalf of Big John to this defendant.

LBD 4-6 through 4-22 are accessible on the Author Updates link to the text Web site at www.aspenparalegaled.com/books/parsons_investigating/default.asp.

Chapter 5

Formal Discovery in Criminal Litigation

CHAPTER OUTLINE

A. The Scope of Formal Discovery in Criminal Litigation
B. Means of Formal Discovery Available to the Defense in Criminal Litigation
C. Means of Formal Discovery Available to the Prosecution in Criminal Litigation
D. The Resolution of Discovery Disputes in Criminal Litigation
E. The Role of the Legal Professional in Formal Criminal Discovery

---

CHAPTER OBJECTIVES

In this chapter you will learn:

• The procedural rules that govern formal discovery in a criminal case.
• The kinds of information discoverable by the defense and by the prosecution in criminal litigation.
• The role of pretrial hearings in discovery in a criminal case.
• The use of motions in a criminal case to aid in discovery.
• The role of the legal professional in formal discovery in a criminal case.

A. The Scope of Formal Discovery in Criminal Litigation

At both the state and federal levels, formal discovery in criminal litigation is more limited than in civil litigation. Consequently, for both the prosecution and the defense, great reliance must be placed on informal investigation. Otherwise, **trial by ambush** is a possibility.

Still, there are a number of formal procedures in the criminal process that provide discovery opportunities. (It may be helpful at this time to review the stages of a criminal case as set forth in Illustration 3-4.) At the federal level, the scope and means of formal discovery in criminal cases is controlled by the Federal Rules of Criminal Procedure (FRCrP) and by certain constitutional rights as determined by the U.S. Supreme Court.

Many states have modeled their rules of criminal procedure after the FRCrP, but the legal professional who works in the criminal area for either the prosecutor or defense attorney should be familiar with both the federal and state rules. (See LBD 5-1 and 5-2.)

Under the FRCrP and the procedure of most states, the scope and means of formal discovery available to the defense are different from those available to the prosecution. We will therefore address the discovery available to the defense and prosecution separately.

The current version of the FRCrP is easily accessible online at either www.law.cornell.edu/rules/frcrmp/ or as a link from the Federal Judiciary home page at www.uscourts.gov/Home.aspx. The student should locate and consult the current version of the rules while reading this chapter. (See Appendix B, Resources for the Investigator, for additional resource material related to criminal law.)

B. Means of Formal Discovery Available to the Defense in Criminal Litigation

HYPOTHETICAL 5-1

Aluh Bye is assisting attorney Plea Bargain who specializes in criminal defense. Plea Bargain has been retained to defend Yugotta Bekiddin, a 30-year-old man who has been arrested and charged by the state with aggravated robbery. Bekiddin called Plea Bargain from jail following his arrest on the morning of January 11, YR00, and asked Plea Bargain to be present on his behalf later that day at the initial appearance.

The story the client tells is that on January 10 he took his girlfriend out to a fancy dinner at Gino's Italian Restaurant in Capital City. He planned to propose marriage to her during the dinner. Last Christmas Yugotta had been given a gift certificate by his mother, good for a dinner for two at Gino's. He presented the gift certificate to the hostess when he and his girlfriend arrived and they were seated at a private table in a quiet corner of the restaurant. They both ordered the house specialty, spaghetti with meatballs. Everything was fine until the couple began to try to eat the spaghetti. The noodles were tough as leather and the meatballs hard as rocks. The sauce had the consistency of motor oil. Yugotta says it was impossible to eat.

Frustrated, Yugotta called the waiter over and told him they could not eat the spaghetti. He requested that they be served something else. The waiter said that was fine and brought them both a seafood pasta that was delicious. Just as the couple was finishing their pasta and Yugotta was reaching into his pocket for the engagement ring, the waiter approached the table, presented a bill in the amount of $68.92, and asked if Yugotta would be paying with cash or credit card. Yugotta reminded the waiter about the gift certificate. The waiter responded by saying he knew about the gift certificate, but it only covered the spaghetti dinners, not the seafood pasta. Yugotta said that he was broke and asked to see the owner.

Shortly thereafter, another man came to the table who identified himself as Gino Maretti, owner of the restaurant. He asked what the problem was. Yugotta says he again explained that the spaghetti was inedible and that he and his girlfriend had asked to be served something else in its place and assumed the seafood pasta dinners would be covered by the gift certificate. Maretti replied that he was sorry for the apparent misunderstanding, but that the gift certificate would only cover the spaghetti dinners, not the seafood pasta and the bill for $68.92 would have to be paid.

Yugotta Bekiddin says that he told Maretti, "You gotta be kiddin me," but Maretti said he was entirely serious. Yugotta then told Maretti he refused to pay for the seafood pasta. His girlfriend intervened at that point and paid the bill in cash, saying she didn't want a nasty scene.

Everything would have been all right except that as Yugotta and his girlfriend were leaving the restaurant, Maretti spoke to his girlfriend and said, "You and Mr. Big Spender have a nice evening." Yugotta says he lost it at that point. He went back to the table where the cold spaghetti was still sitting, dumped a plate of it into a cloth napkin, twisted the ends of the napkin into a handle and came back to the cash register. He demanded the refund of the $68.92 and when Maretti refused, he banged the napkin with the spaghetti and meatballs inside against the counter several times, causing Maretti to back away. Yugotta says he didn't mean to frighten Maretti with the spaghetti, didn't ever strike him, and thinks Maretti only backed away so the spaghetti sauce wouldn't splatter on him. Yugotta told Maretti he wasn't leaving until the money was refunded, at which point Maretti opened the cash register and handed his girlfriend $68.92. Yugotta's girlfriend backs him up on his story.

Yugotta had no idea anything was wrong until he was arrested early in the morning of January 11 at his house. The arresting officer told him he was under arrest for aggravated robbery.

1. Review of the criminal complaint

Under FRCrP 4 the **criminal complaint** may be used to obtain either an **arrest warrant** for a defendant or a **summons** ordering the defendant to appear before a magistrate. The criminal complaint is the initial charging instrument in a criminal case. FRCrP 3 defines the criminal complaint as follows:

> The complaint is a written statement of the essential facts constituting the offense charged. It must be made under oath before a magistrate judge or, if none is reasonably available, before a state or local judicial officer.

Pursuant to FRCrP 4(a), the complaint must establish "probable cause that an offense has been committed and that the defendant committed it." In 2011 FRCrP 4.1 was added, authorizing a magistrate to consider information communicated "by telephone or other reliable electronic means" when reviewing a criminal complaint and deciding whether to approve a warrant or summons (see LBD 5-7). If the accused is arrested without a warrant, FRCrP 5(a) requires that a criminal complaint satisfying the probable cause requirements of FRCrP 4(a) "shall be promptly filed." The criminal complaint may also be used by the prosecution to establish probable cause at the preliminary examination under FRCrP 5.1.

Illustration 5-1 sets forth the form of the criminal complaint used in the federal courts. Illustration 5-2 sets forth the form of the summons in a criminal case used in the federal courts.

SLEUTH ON THE LOOSE

Check the Bureau of Justice Statistics site at *www.ojp.usdoj.gov/bjs* and see if you can locate crime statistics for your area.

Illustration 5-1
CRIMINAL
COMPLAINT FORM
USED IN FEDERAL
COURT

AO 91 (Rev. 11/11) Criminal Complaint

UNITED STATES DISTRICT COURT
for the

United States of America	)	
v.	)	
	)	Case No.
	)	
	)	
	)	
Defendant(s)	)	

CRIMINAL COMPLAINT

I, the complainant in this case, state that the following is true to the best of my knowledge and belief.

On or about the date(s) of _____ in the county of _____ in the _____ District of _____ , the defendant(s) violated:

Code Section	*Offense Description*

This criminal complaint is based on these facts:

❒ Continued on the attached sheet.

_____
Complainant's signature

_____
Printed name and title

Sworn to before me and signed in my presence.

Date: _____

_____
Judge's signature

City and state: _____

_____
Printed name and title

Reviewing the criminal complaint in a case is the first means of formal discovery available to the attorney representing the criminal accused. FRCrP 4(b) provides that the criminal complaint need not be written upon personal knowledge and the officer executing the complaint can rely on hearsay and inference from circumstantial evidence. However, the criminal complaint must set forth the facts alleged by the prosecution constituting the offense, and it may be supported by **affidavits** (signed statements made under oath subject to penalties of perjury) of police officers, victims, or witnesses with personal knowledge of the facts. Thus, reviewing the criminal complaint may provide the defense team with important information about the prosecution's case against their client.

HYPOTHETICAL 5-2

Before going to the initial appearance for Yugotta Bekiddin, Plea Bargain has asked Aluh Bye to do some legal research and factual investigation into the charges against the client. Aluh Bye goes first to the law library to locate the aggravated robbery statute and to determine the penalty for conviction under the statute. The aggravated robbery statute located by Aluh Bye in the criminal code for Yourstate provides as follows:

YS. Crim. Code §39-13-402: Aggravated Robbery.

(a) Aggravated robbery is robbery as defined in §39-13-401:

(1) Accomplished with a deadly weapon or by display of any article used or fashioned to lead the victim to reasonably believe it to be a deadly weapon; or
(2) Where the victim suffers serious bodily injury.

(b) Aggravated robbery is a Class B felony.

Since the statute refers to the crime of robbery, Aluh Bye also locates the robbery statute, which reads as follows:

YS. Crim. Code §39-13-401: Robbery.

(a) Robbery is the intentional or knowing theft of property from the person of another by violence or putting the person in fear.
(b) Robbery is a Class C felony.

Aluh Bye also checks on the definition of a "deadly weapon" under the criminal code and finds the following:

YS. Crim. Code §39-11-106: Definitions

(a) The following definitions apply in this title: . . .

(5) "Deadly weapon" means:

(A) A firearm or anything manifestly designed, made or adapted for the purpose of inflicting death or serious bodily injury; or
(B) Anything that in the manner of its use or intended use is capable of causing death or serious bodily injury.

Aluh Bye also determines that a Class C felony is punishable by up to 15 years incarceration and a Class B felony by up to 25 years incarceration.

Next, Aluh Bye goes to the Criminal Court Clerk's office and obtains a copy of the criminal complaint filed against Yugotta Bekiddin. The criminal complaint against Yugotta Bekiddin is set forth in Illustration 5-3.

1. Note that the criminal complaint in Illustration 5-3 is not accompanied by an affidavit of any eyewitness to the alleged crime. Does that make it defective to support an arrest warrant?
2. Does the criminal complaint in Illustration 5-3 allege sufficient facts to establish probable cause that Yugotta Bekiddin committed the crime of aggravated robbery as it is defined in YS. Crim. Code §39-13-402?
3. How complete a picture of what happened at Gino's Italian Restaurant can we gather from the criminal complaint in this case?

Illustration 5-2
SUMMONS IN A
CRIMINAL CASE
FORM USED
IN FEDERAL
COURT

AO 83 (Rev. 06/09) Summons in a Criminal Case

UNITED STATES DISTRICT COURT
for the

United States of America
v.

)
)
)
)   Case No.
)
)
)

Defendant

SUMMONS IN A CRIMINAL CASE

YOU ARE SUMMONED to appear before the United States district court at the time, date, and place set forth below to answer to one or more offenses or violations based on the following document filed with the court:

☐ Indictment   ☐ Superseding Indictment   ☐ Information ☐ Superseding Information   ☐ Complaint
☐ Probation Violation Petition   ☐ Supervised Release Violation Petition ☐ Violation Notice   ☐ Order of Court

Place:

Courtroom No.:

Date and Time:

This offense is briefly described as follows:

Date:

Issuing officer's signature

Printed name and title

I declare under penalty of perjury that I have:

☐ Executed and returned this summons

☐ Returned this summons unexecuted

Date:

Server's signature

Printed name and title

2. The initial appearance

After an arrest, FRCrP 5(a) requires the accused be taken before a federal magistrate judge for an initial appearance, "without unnecessary delay." In most cases this **initial appearance** will be made within 24 hours of the arrest, unless the arrest is effected on a weekend in which case the initial appearance may be delayed to the following Monday. Little happens at the initial appearance that advances discovery. The judge will confirm the identity of the defendant as the one named in the criminal complaint, advise the defendant of his various rights and, if necessary, appoint counsel to defend the accused. The one exception involves the judge's decision on whether to grant a **pretrial release** to the defendant who is in custody (sometimes called the bail/bond hearing). The judge has the discretion to release a criminal defendant until trial on

Illustration 5-2
SUMMONS IN A
CRIMINAL CASE
FORM USED
IN FEDERAL
COURT
(continued)

AO 83 (Rev. 06/09) Summons in a Criminal Case (Page 2)

Case No.

**This second page contains personal identifiers and therefore should
not be filed in court with the summons unless under seal.**
(Not for Public Disclosure)

INFORMATION FOR SERVICE

Name of defendant/offender:

Last known residence:

Usual place of abode *(if different from residence address)*:

If the defendant is an organization, name(s) and address(es) of officer(s) or agent(s) legally authorized to receive service of process:

If the defendant is an organization, last known address within the district or principal place of business elsewhere in the United States:

PROOF OF SERVICE

This summons was received by me on *(date)*

❑ I personally served the summons on this defendant   at
(place)   on *(date)*   ; or

❑ On *(date)*   I left the summons at the individual's residence or usual place of abode
with *(name)*   , a person of suitable age and discretion who resides
there, and I mailed a copy to the individual's last known address; or

❑ I delivered a copy of the summons to *(name of individual)*
who is authorized to receive service of process on behalf of *(name of organization)*
                                                on *(date)*   and I mailed a copy to
the organizations's last known address within the district or to its principal place of business elsewhere in the
United States; or

❑ The summons was returned unexecuted because:

I declare under penalty of perjury that this information is true.

Date returned:

_____
Server's signature

_____
Printed name and title

Remarks:

his **personal recognizance**, impose **conditional release** (e.g., ankle monitor, house detention), or upon posting cash **bail, surety bond** (where a third person such as a **bail bondsman** guarantees payment for nonappearance), or **property bond** in an amount set by the court. The **Eighth Amendment** to the United States Constitution prohibits the imposition of "excessive bail." (See LBD 5-8.)

The purpose of the bail/bond requirement is to ensure that the defendant will appear at trial—the defendant who does not appear forfeits the bail or bond posted. Under the federal **Bail Reform Act of 1984** (18 U.S.C. §§3141-3150), the judge has the discretion to deny bail or bond and order the defendant held until trial (**pretrial detention**) if there is good reason to believe the defendant will flee before trial or that he poses a threat to persons in the community. State procedure on granting pretrial release or detention vary widely, with some following the federal model and some presumptively

The prosecution, if it is arguing for no pretrial release or for the setting of a high bail figure, will have the burden of convincing the judge that there is good reason to believe that the defendant will flee or that he poses a risk to the community. There are some federal and state statutes which create a *presumption* of intent to flee or danger to the community. Serious drug charges may carry with them the former presumption and crimes of violence charged against someone with a prior conviction involving violence committed during a pretrial release often carry with them the latter presumption. In that case the burden will shift to the defense to rebut the presumption. To carry its burden on the bail issue, the prosecution may disclose information by way of oral argument or by calling witnesses. And that may provide the defendant more information about the case than appears in the criminal complaint. Thus the initial appearance may be a discovery opportunity for the defense.

At the initial appearance, the judge will also schedule the preliminary hearing, to be conducted not later than 14 days following the initial appearance if the defendant is in custody and 21 days if the defendant is not in custody.

Illustration 5-3   CRIMINAL COMPLAINT

IN THE CRIMINAL COURT
FOR HARMONY COUNTY, YOURSTATE

STATE OF YOURSTATE	)	CRIMINAL COMPLAINT
v.	)	
YUGOTTA BEKIDDIN	)	CASE NO. YR00-199CR

I, the undersigned complainant, being duly sworn according to law, state that the following is true and correct to the best of my knowledge and belief: On or about the 10th day of January, YR00, in Capital City, Harmony County, Yourstate, defendant did commit a robbery and accomplished same with a deadly weapon or by display of an article used or fashioned to lead the victim to reasonably believe it to be a deadly weapon in violation of YS. Crim. Code §39-13-402, Aggravated Robbery.

I further state that I am a Sergeant with the Capital City Police Department and that this complaint is based upon the following facts: At 9:15 p.m. on 1-10-YR00 my partner and I received a call to respond to an assault in progress at Gino's Italian Restaurant, 533 West Main Street in Capital City. Arriving at 9:18 p.m. I was informed by the proprietor of Gino's Italian Restaurant, Gino Maretti, that the defendant had robbed him of $68.92 by threatening to strike him about the head and shoulders with a club.

_____
Complainant

Sworn to before me and subscribed in my presence this _____ day of _____, YR00 at
_____.

_____
Name and Title of Judicial Officer

_____
Judicial Officer

3. The preliminary hearing

At the **preliminary hearing** (usually called a **preliminary examination** under state rules of criminal procedure) the judge hears proof to determine if there is **probable cause** to believe that the accused committed the crime alleged (FRCrP 5.1) (see LBD 5-9). If probable cause is found by the judge, the case is bound over to a grand jury or to trial. If probable cause is not found by the judge, the charges are dismissed and the defendant released.

The preliminary hearing is adversarial with witnesses called by both the prosecution and the defense if it chooses to do so, and the attorneys make arguments to the judge. Consequently, this hearing can be an important source of discovery for the defense in hearing at least part of the prosecution's case, and for the prosecution to the extent the defense calls witnesses or takes a position in legal argument. However, the preliminary hearing has limitations on its usefulness as a formal discovery technique.

a. Frequently, no preliminary hearing is held

There is no constitutional right to a preliminary hearing. *Gerstein v. Pugh*, 420 U.S. 103 (1975). A few states do not have a preliminary hearing procedure at all. In those that do, the prosecution can usually avoid the hearing by submitting the case directly to the grand jury for an indictment or by filing an information directly (see discussion below). In the federal system, if a grand jury indictment has been issued, the preliminary hearing can be dispensed with. 8 U.S.C. §3060(e). (See LBD 5-1.)

Grand jury proceedings are non-public, secret proceedings at both the federal and state levels, so they do not provide a discovery opportunity to the defense. Defendants can also waive their right to a preliminary hearing where such right exists.

b. There typically is little time to prepare for the preliminary hearing

Since, per FRCrP 5.1(c), the preliminary hearing must occur within 14 days of the initial appearance if the defendant is in custody and within 21 days if the defendant has been released, time to prepare is limited. Most states have similar time limitations for their preliminary examinations.

c. The prosecution need not present its entire case at the preliminary hearing

The only burden placed on the government at the preliminary hearing is to show probable cause that the offense occurred and that the defendant probably committed the offense. The probable cause threshold is far below the **beyond a reasonable doubt** burden that the government must meet to convict at trial (see LBD 5-9). Accordingly, and since the prosecution knows that the preliminary hearing often presents a discovery opportunity to the defense, the prosecution may not present its entire case or even its best proof. Instead it will usually rely on the same information set forth in the criminal complaint.

4. The information and the indictment

The **information** is the formal charging instrument filed by prosecutors. The **indictment** is the formal charge issued by the grand jury. The **grand jury** consists of 16 to 23 people selected from the community (the number may be different in state proceedings) to hear evidence of alleged criminal conduct, and it has the power to issue an indictment based on a finding of probable cause. Procedures before the grand jury are unique in our adversarial system for several reasons. First, grand juries are closed to the public; not even the defendant is entitled to attend. Second, only the prosecutor may present evidence to the grand jury; the defendant has no right to appear, testify, present proof, or cross examine prosecution witnesses. Third, the actions of the grand jury are secret; no one in attendance may disclose what transpired. Fourth, those who testify before the grand jury have no right to have an attorney present with them in the grand jury room. In most states, however, witnesses are permitted to leave the jury room to confer with their attorney before returning to answer.

The grand jury has the power to subpoena witnesses to appear, to subpoena the production of documents, records and things, to hold reluctant witnesses in contempt, and to grant immunity from prosecution. Illustration 5-4 shows the form of grand jury subpoena used in federal grand jury proceedings.

When an information is filed or an indictment issued, it will replace the criminal complaint as the formal charging document in the case. Note that the information and the indictment are *alternative* charging instruments. You would never have both issued in one case. The Fifth Amendment to the United States Constitution requires that all prosecutions for capital and infamous crimes be by indictment. The Supreme Court held long ago that "infamous" means crimes punishable by imprisonment for more than a year. *Ex parte Wilson*, 114 U.S. 417 (1884). Today, FRCrP 7(a)(1) provides:

> An offense (other than criminal contempt) must be prosecuted by an indictment if it is punishable:
>
> (A)   by death; or
> (B)   by imprisonment for more than one year.

A defendant may waive his right to grand jury review in all federal cases except those involving the **death penalty** (*capital cases*) and consent to be prosecuted by information. Illustration 5-5 sets forth the **waiver of indictment** form used in the federal courts.

The Supreme Court has never held that the Fifth Amendment right to grand jury review is a **fundamental right** or a right *essential to an ordered liberty* and therefore has never said that it is applicable to the states under the Fourteenth Amendment pursuant to the **selective incorporation doctrine**. (See *Hurtado v. California*, 110 U.S. 516 (1884).) However, many states have the grand jury system and require that serious charges be prosecuted by indictment. (See LBD 5-1.)

Illustration 5-4   FEDERAL GRAND JURY SUBPOENA FORM

AO 110 (Rev. 06/09) Subpoena to Testify Before a Grand Jury

UNITED STATES DISTRICT COURT
for the

SUBPOENA TO TESTIFY BEFORE A GRAND JURY

To:

YOU ARE COMMANDED to appear in this United States district court at the time, date, and place shown below to testify before the court's grand jury. When you arrive, you must remain at the court until the judge or a court officer allows you to leave.

Place:	Date and Time:

You must also bring with you the following documents, electronically stored information, or objects *(blank if not applicable)*:

Date: _____

CLERK OF COURT

_____

Signature of Clerk or Deputy Clerk

The name, address, e-mail, and telephone number of the United States attorney, or assistant United States attorney, who requests this subpoena, are:

FRCrP 7(c)(1) provides that: "The indictment or information must be a plain, concise and definite written statement of the essential facts constituting the offense charged." If more than one crime is charged, the

Illustration 5-4 FEDERAL GRAND JURY SUBPOENA FORM *(continued)*

AO 110 (Rev. 06/09) Subpoena to Testify Before Grand Jury (Page 2)

PROOF OF SERVICE

This subpoena for *(name of individual or organization)* _____

was received by me on *(date)* _____ .

☐ I served the subpoena by delivering a copy to the named person as follows: _____

_____ on *(date)* _____ ; or

☐ I returned the subpoena unexecuted because: _____

_____ .

I declare under penalty of perjury that this information is true.

Date: _____

_____
Server's signature

_____
Printed name and title

_____
Server's address

Additional information regarding attempted service, etc:

---

indictment or information must satisfy those requirements as to all crimes charged.

Reviewing the information or the indictment can provide necessary and important information to counsel for the criminal defendant. Significantly, however, there is no requirement that the government disclose its entire case in an indictment or information and the government frequently will try to avoid doing so in order to deprive the defense of this discovery opportunity. On the other hand, many states require by statute of court rule that the names of witnesses appearing before the grand jury be endorsed on the indictment.

Illustration 5-5   WAIVER OF INDICTMENT FORM USED IN FEDERAL COURT

AO 455 (Rev. 01/09) Waiver of an Indictment

UNITED STATES DISTRICT COURT
for the

United States of America   )
            v.   )   Case No.
)
)
_____   )
           Defendant   )

WAIVER OF AN INDICTMENT

I understand that I have been accused of one or more offenses punishable by imprisonment for more than one year. I was advised in open court of my rights and the nature of the proposed charges against me.

After receiving this advice, I waive my right to prosecution by indictment and consent to prosecution by information.

Date: _____

_____
Defendant's signature

_____
Signature of defendant's attorney

_____
Printed name of defendant's attorney

_____
Judge's signature

_____
Judge's printed name and title

HYPOTHETICAL 5-3

Assume that at the initial appearance of Yugotta Bekiddin, his bond was set at $10,000, which he was able to post with a surety bond. The prosecutor for the state, Hangem High, made little argument on the bond amount and no evidence was presented. When the judge dealt with setting the date for the preliminary hearing, Hangem High announced to the court that the state would submit the case directly to the grand jury, thereby bypassing the preliminary hearing. Plea Bargain tells Aluh Bye that he was hoping for a preliminary hearing so he could get a chance to cross examine the witnesses for the state because all he has heard is the client's version of what happened that night. Plea Bargain tells Aluh Bye they will just have to wait to see if the grand jury indicts Yugotta Bekiddin and see what the indictment says.

Within days, Yugotta Bekiddin is indicted by the grand jury for aggravated robbery. (When the client is told of the indictment, he says, "You gotta be kiddin me!") Plea Bargain tells Aluh Bye to get a copy of the indictment from the court. The front and back pages of the indictment issued by the grand jury against Yugotta Bekiddin are set out in Illustration 5-6.

1. What facts and leads can Aluh Bye obtain from the indictment that were not available from the criminal complaint?
2. Can Aluh Bye and Plea Bargain feel confident that Gino Maretti is the only witness besides Yugotta Bekiddin and his girlfriend with first-hand knowledge of the incident since he was the only witness to appear before the grand jury? Why?
3. Does the indictment in Illustration 5-6 appear to satisfy the requirement that an indictment contain a plain, concise, and definite written statement of the essential facts constituting the offense charged?

5. The bill of particulars

In the federal system and in most state systems, a criminal defendant may ask the court by motion to compel the prosecution to provide a **bill of particulars**, the purpose of which is to make general allegations contained in the indictment or information more specific. However, the defendant has no absolute right to a bill of particulars; it is in the judge's discretion to grant such a motion. FRCrP 7(f). The test is whether the defendant needs more details concerning the charges to avoid prejudicial surprise at trial. *United States v. Diecidue*, 603 F.2d 535 (5th Cir. 1979), *cert. denied*, 445 U.S. 946 (1979).

HYPOTHETICAL 5-4

Assume that Plea Bargain, frustrated at his lack of information regarding the specifics of the prosecution's case against Yugotta Bekiddin, instructs Aluh Bye to draft a motion for a bill of particulars for his review. Aluh Bye drafts the motion you see in Illustration 5-7.

1. Are there any additional requests you would add to this bill of particulars?
2. Do you think Plea Bargain has a good chance of convincing the judge to grant this motion under the standard set forth in *United States v. Diecidue*?
3. Assume the motion for bill of particulars as it appears in Illustration 5-7 is filed by Plea Bargain and the court grants his motion and orders the State to provide responses to all the information requested. The bill of particulars filed by the State can be seen in Illustration 5-8.

Although a motion for bill of particulars is not routinely granted, criminal defense lawyers utilize the motion regularly to fulfill their duty of zealous representation to the client. And in those cases where the motion is granted, the information provided can greatly advance defense counsel's knowledge of the prosecution's case.

Illustration 5-6   INDICTMENT

(front page)

IN THE CRIMINAL COURT
FOR HARMONY COUNTY, YOURSTATE

STATE OF YOURSTATE	)	INDICTMENT FOR
v.	)	AGGRAVATED ROBBERY
YUGOTTA BEKIDDIN,	)	
defendant	)	CASE NO. YR00-199CR

IN THE NAME OF AND BY THE AUTHORITY OF THE STATE OF YOURSTATE:

The Grand Jurors of the State of Yourstate, empaneled and sworn to inquire and true presentment made in and for the county of Harmony, upon their oaths, do present that

YUGOTTA BEKIDDIN

on the 5th day of January, YR00, in Gino's Italian Restaurant, 533 Main Street in Capital City, Harmony County, Yourstate, did then and there knowingly and intentionally steal and obtain property by theft from the person of Gino Maretti, by violence and threat of violence with a deadly weapon and the display of a deadly weapon used or fashioned to lead Gino Maretti to reasonably believe it to be a deadly weapon all with the intent to deprive said Gino Maretti of the property and without his effective consent, in violation of YS. Crim. Code §39-13-402, contrary to said statute and against the peace and dignity of the people of the State of Yourstate.

_____
Hangem High
District Attorney General

---

6. Rule 16 discovery

FRCrP 16 contains a laundry list of information discoverable by the defendant from the prosecution in a criminal case. The rules of criminal procedure in effect in most states track Rule 16. (An example of a discovery request made under a state rule that tracks FRCrP 16 may be seen in Illustration 5-9.)

a. Statements of the defendant

FRCrP 16(a)(1)(A) and (B) require the prosecution "upon a defendant's request" to allow the defense counsel to inspect and copy any relevant oral, written, or recorded statements made by the defendant which are in the possession, custody, or control of the prosecution or which the prosecution may discover through due diligence. This includes the defendant's testimony before the grand jury (though typically the defendant will not have been called by the prosecution to testify before the grand jury and, if called, will assert his **Fifth Amendment right against self-incrimination**). And, it includes all statements by the defendant relevant to the charges against him, not just the ones the prosecution intends to use at trial. Organizational defendants are accorded the same right under FRCrP 16(a)(1)(C) as to statements made by their agents.

Illustration 5-6 INDICTMENT *(continued)*

(back page)

TRUE BILL   NO. YR00-199CR   WITNESSES

                          INDICTMENT

1. *Edgar Boone*   THE STATE   1. Gino Maretti
2. *Wayne Mason*   V.
3. *John Hargis Sr.*   YUGOTTA BEKIDDIN
4. *Kenneth Sells*
5. *Billy Cochran*   Aggravated Robbery
6. *Ron Hansen*
7. *Ron Hansen*
8. *Sylvia Haff*
9. *Kathy Green*   Prosecutor: Hangem High
10. *Velma Wright*
11. *Debra Barnes*   Witnesses sworn by me in the
12. *Jim Moor*   presence of the Grand Jury
13. *Scott Hay*   *January 30,*   , YR00
                            Edgar Boone
                                    Foreman
                            Filed, **30** day of *Jan.*, YR00.
                            Karen Shipley   , Clerk

---

b. The criminal record of the defendant

FRCrP 16(a)(1)(D) requires the prosecution, upon request, to furnish to defense counsel copies of the prior criminal record of the defendant that the prosecution has or that can be discovered by the prosecution through due diligence.

c. Documents, electronically stored information, and things

FRCrP 16(a)(1)(E) requires the prosecution, upon request, to allow defense counsel to inspect and copy or photograph books, papers,

Illustration 5-7   MOTION FOR BILL OF PARTICULARS

IN THE CRIMINAL COURT
FOR HARMONY COUNTY, YOURSTATE

STATE OF YOURSTATE	)	
v.	)	CASE NO. YR00-199CR
YUGOTTA BEKIDDIN,	)	
Defendant	)	

MOTION FOR BILL OF PARTICULARS

The defendant, pursuant to Rule 7(f) of the Yourstate Rules of Criminal Procedure, moves the court for an Order directing the State to furnish a Bill of Particulars with reference to the indictment. The State should be compelled to provide the following particulars to counsel for defendant:

1. The exact nature and description of the "property" referred to in the indictment.

2. Whether Gino Maretti was the actual owner of the "property" referred to in the indictment.

3. The exact nature and description of each and every "deadly weapon" referred to in the indictment.

4. The exact manner and means by which the defendant is alleged to have used "violence" to obtain the "property" from the person of Gino Maretti.

5. The exact manner and means by which the defendant is alleged to have used "threat of violence" to obtain the "property" from the person of Gino Maretti.

_____
Plea Bargain
Attorney for Defendant

(Certificate of Service omitted)

documents, data, photographs, tangible objects, buildings or places that are within the possession, custody, or control of the prosecution and that are:

- material to preparing the defense; or
- to be used by the prosecution in its case-in-chief at trial (as opposed to being used as **rebuttal evidence**); or
- items which belong to or were obtained from the defendant.

The discovery of relevant unprivileged **electronically stored information (ESI)** is within the scope of "data" and is therefore as much a part of discovery in a criminal case as in a civil case. You may want to review the discussion of ESI discovery in Section F of Chapter 4.

Illustration 5-8 BILL OF PARTICULARS

IN THE CRIMINAL COURT
FOR HARMONY COUNTY, YOURSTATE

STATE OF YOURSTATE	)	
v.	)	CASE NO. YR00-199CR
YUGOTTA BEKIDDIN,	)	
Defendant	)	

BILL OF PARTICULARS

The State, pursuant to Order of the Court, hereby furnishes the following Bill of Particulars to defendant:

1. The exact nature and description of the "property" referred to in the indictment.

RESPONSE: The "property" referred to in the indictment is $68.92 in cash.

2. Whether Gino Maretti was the actual owner of the "property" referred to in the indictment.

RESPONSE: No. The actual owner of the property referred to in the indictment was Maretti Enterprises, Inc., a corporation wholly owned by Gino Maretti.

3. The exact nature and description of each and every "deadly weapon" referred to in the indictment.

RESPONSE: The "deadly weapon" referred to in the indictment was a large mound of hardened spaghetti noodles and meatballs encased in a cloth napkin which had been twisted to enclose the spaghetti and meatballs and which was wielded as a club by the defendant by holding the ends of the napkin together.

4. The exact manner and means by which the defendant is alleged to have used "violence" to obtain the "property" from the person of Gino Maretti.

RESPONSE: The defendant used violence by swinging the above referenced deadly weapon over his head while advancing in a threatening manner toward Gino Maretti and demanding that Mr. Maretti turn over the property to him. In addition, the defendant repeatedly slammed the deadly weapon on the counter within inches of Mr. Maretti demonstrating its capacity to cause death or severe bodily injury to Mr. Maretti.

5. The exact manner and means by which the defendant is alleged to have used "threat of violence" to obtain the "property" from the person of Gino Maretti.

RESPONSE: The defendant used threat of violence to obtain the property by swinging the above referenced deadly weapon over his head while advancing in a threatening manner toward Gino Maretti and demanding that Mr. Maretti turn over the property to him. In addition, the defendant repeatedly slammed the deadly weapon on the counter within inches of Mr. Maretti demonstrating its capacity to cause death or severe bodily injury to Mr. Maretti all the while demanding that Mr. Maretti turn the property over to him.

Hangem High
District Attorney General

(Certificate of Service omitted)

Illustration 5-9 DISCOVERY REQUEST

IN THE CRIMINAL COURT
FOR HARMONY COUNTY, YOURSTATE

STATE OF YOURSTATE   )
   v.   )   CASE NO. YR00-199CR
YUGOTTA BEKIDDIN,   )
   Defendant   )

REQUEST FOR DISCOVERY, INSPECTION, AND
NOTICE OF INTENT TO USE EVIDENCE

The defendant, through his counsel of record, requests that the District Attorney for the State of Yourstate provide certain information which the defendant contends is material to the preparation of his defense.

Definitions

For purposes of this request, the defendant defines the "State" to mean and include the District Attorney General for Harmony County, the Capital City Police Department, the Harmony County Sheriff's Office, the Yourstate Highway Patrol, the Yourstate Bureau of Investigation, any agents or employees of those offices, any other law enforcement department or agency of Yourstate, any other law enforcement officer, and any other person acting in conjunction with, or in behalf of, any such law enforcement agency, including without limitation, the Federal Bureau of Investigation.

The defendant defines each of the requests to include items currently within the actual or constructive possession, custody, control, or knowledge of the State, and items which may become known, identified, or available through the exercise of due diligence by the State.

Requests

1. To receive a list of the names and current addresses of all witnesses the State intends to call to testify, whether or not they are listed upon the indictment.

2. To be provided with any police reports and witness statements to the extent they contain the defendant's prior criminal record, his statement, or the results of any tests or examinations.

3. To be provided with the statements and reports of any witnesses after the witness testifies, said production to be made outside the presence of the jury.

4. To inspect and copy any written or recorded statement, confession, or admission against interest made by the defendant.

5. To be advised of the substance of any oral statement, confession, or admission against interest made by the defendant, whether before or after arrest, in response to any person then known to the defendant to be a law enforcement officer.

6. To receive a copy of the defendant's prior criminal record, if any.

7. To be allowed to inspect and copy all books, papers, documents, photographs, tangible objects, buildings, or places or copies or portions thereof, which are intended for use by the State as evidence-in-chief at trial of this cause.

8. To be allowed to inspect and copy all books, papers, documents, photographs, tangible objects, buildings, or places or copies or portions thereof, which are material to the preparation of the defense in this matter.

9. To be allowed to inspect and copy all books, papers, documents, photographs, tangible objects, buildings, or places or copies or portions thereof, which were obtained from or belong to the defendant.

Illustration 5-9 DISCOVERY REQUEST *(continued)*

10. To be allowed to inspect and copy any results of reports or physical or mental examinations, and of scientific tests or experiments, or copies thereof, which are material to the preparation of the defense.

11. To be allowed to inspect and copy any results of reports or physical or mental examinations, and of scientific tests or experiments, or copies thereof, which are intended for use by the State as evidence-in-chief at trial.

12. To be furnished the names and addresses of all persons known to the State to have been present at the time and place of the alleged offense.

13. Pursuant to *Brady v. Maryland*, 373 U.S. 83, 83 S. Ct. 1194, 10 L. Ed. 2d 215 (1963) and *United States v. Agurs*, 427 U.S. 97, 96 S. Ct. 2392, 49 L. Ed. 2d 342 (1976), to be advised of and allowed to inspect and copy or photograph any and all evidence that might be fairly termed "favorable" to the defense, whether that evidence be completely exculpatory in nature or simply tending to reduce the degree of the offense or punishment therefore, or whether that evidence might be termed "favorable" in the sense that it might be fairly used by the defendant to impeach the credibility of any witness the government intends to call in this matter including, but not limited to:

   a. The nature and substance of any agreement, immunity promise, or understanding, between the State or federal government or any agent thereof, and any witness, relating to the witness's expected testimony, including but not limited to, understandings or agreements relating to pending or potential prosecutions.

   b. The nature and substance of any preferential treatment given at any time by any state agent, whether or not in connection with this case, to any potential witness, including but not limited to letters from State Attorneys or other law enforcement personnel to federal or state agencies, creditors, etc., setting out that witness's cooperation or status with the state, and which letter or communication might fairly be said to have been an attempt to provide some benefit or help to the witness.

   c. Any money or other remuneration paid to any witness by the State, including but not limited to rewards, subsistence payments, expenses, or other payments made for specific information supplied to the State.

   d. Any and all information in the possession of the State regarding the mental condition of the state's witnesses which would reflect or bring into question the witnesses' credibility.

   e. The original statement and any amendment thereto, of any individuals who have provided the State with a statement inculpating the defendant, who later retracted all or any portion of that statement where such retraction would raise a conflict in the evidence which the State intends to prove.

   f. Any and all interview memoranda or reports which contain any information, whatever the source, which might fairly be said to contradict or be inconsistent with any evidence the State intends to adduce in this matter.

   g. The names and addresses of any witnesses whom the State believes would give testimony favorable to the defendant in regard to the matters alleged in the indictment, even though the State may not be in possession of a statement of this witness and regardless of whether the state intends to call this witness at trial.

   h. The results of any scientific tests or analysis done on any person or object in connection with this case where the result of that test or analysis did not implicate, or was neutral to the defendant.

   i. Any documentary evidence which contradicts or is inconsistent with any testimony the State intends to introduce in this case.

   j. The statement of any individual who has given a description to any person of an individual involved in the perpetration of the charged offense, which person the State alleges to be the defendant, where such description might fairly be said not to match the defendant in characteristics such as height, weight, body build, color of skin, color of hair, etc.

   k. The name and address of any individual who has been requested to make an identification of the defendant in connection with this case, and failed to make such identification.

Illustration 5-9 DISCOVERY REQUEST *(continued)*

WHEREFORE, defendant requests as follows:

a. That the State respond in writing to each and every request as soon as possible, but no later than fifteen (15) days prior to the scheduled trial of this case.

b. That should the State be of the opinion that any item of information requested herein is not discoverable, is privileged, or is not relevant to these proceedings, that the State, for each such item of information, acknowledge whether that item of information exists, cite the authorities the State relies upon to refuse the request for such item of information, and produce the item of information under seal to the Court for *in camera* inspection.

c. That the clerk of the court file this request within the record of these proceedings, but the defendant waives any present necessity for a hearing upon these issues until such time as a motion to compel production may be filed.

————————————————
Plea Bargain
Attorney for Defendant

(Certificate of Service omitted)

---

d. Reports of examinations and tests

FRCrP 16(a)(1)(F) requires the prosecution, upon request, to allow defense counsel to inspect and copy or photograph any results or reports of physical or mental exams, or scientific tests or experiments (autopsy, blood, fingerprint, drug, DNA, etc.) that are within the possession, custody, or control of the prosecution and that are material to the preparation of the defense or intended for use by the prosecution in its **case-in-chief** at trial.

e. Expert witnesses

FRCrP 16(a)(1)(G) requires the prosecution, upon request, to provide defense counsel with a written summary of expert witness testimony the prosecution intends to use in its case-in-chief at trial, including expert testimony the prosecution may offer to rebut the defendant's expert witnesses who testify regarding the defendant's mental state.

f. Procedure for conducting Rule 16 discovery

You may have noticed that the various forms of discovery allowed by Rule 16 are "upon request." Unlike the bill of particulars, which is sought by *motion*, **Rule 16 discovery**, like other means of discovery discussed below, is sought by *request*. See Illustration 5-9 for a typical **request for discovery** form under Rule 16.

7. Identity of witnesses

The Supreme Court has held that the defendant is entitled, upon request, to advance notice of the names of the witnesses to be called by the prosecution. See *United States v. Agurs*, 427 U.S. 97, 96 S. Ct. 2392, 49 L. Ed. 2d 342 (1976). This only applies to witnesses to be called by the government in its case-in-chief, not **rebuttal witnesses** (witnesses called to rebut the opposing party's proof). And, as discussed below, the right of the defendant to obtain pretrial statements of witnesses is very limited, as is its right to depose those witnesses prior to trial. Practically speaking, during the discovery phase of the criminal case, the defense team must attempt to obtain information from the government's witnesses by informal discovery, which usually means persuading those witnesses to consent to an interview (see Chapters 14 and 15 on interviewing witnesses).

8. Statements of witnesses

FRCrP 16(a)(2) states specifically that it does not authorize the discovery or inspection of statements made by prosecution witnesses or prospective witnesses except as authorized by 18 U.S.C. §3500. In the federal system and in most state systems, criminal defendants are not entitled to inspect or copy statements of witnesses the prosecution intends to call at trial. However, 18 U.S.C. §3500, commonly known as the **Jencks Act**, requires the prosecution to provide the defense, upon request, with prior written or recorded statements of witnesses *after* they have testified. This is an example of **trial discovery**, that is, discovery that can only be made at or during the trial.

Note that while witnesses' statements are not generally discoverable before trial under this rule, they must be disclosed pretrial to the extent they contain defendant's statement, his prior criminal record, or the results of tests related to the investigation.

The procedure for obtaining witnesses' statements is governed by FRCrP 26.2, which provides that following the direct testimony of the witness at trial, the party who did not call the witness may make a motion to be allowed to examine and use any statement of the witness in the possession of the prosecution that relates to the subject matter concerning which the witness has testified. The prior statements, or material portions of them, are then produced, and the moving party may apply for a recess to allow time to inspect the statements. The types of statements that must be produced pursuant to this procedure are defined in FRCrP 26.2(f) and include written statements of the witness, recorded or transcribed oral statements of the witness, and the statement or transcript of the witness's grand jury testimony.

9. Exculpatory material—the *Brady* doctrine

Under the decisions in *Brady v. Maryland*, 373 U.S. 83, 83 S. Ct. 1194, 10 L. Ed. 2d 215 (1963) and *United States v. Agurs*, 427 U.S. 97, 96 S. Ct. 2392, 49 L. Ed. 2d 342 (1976), the prosecution in both state and federal proceedings must provide to the defense all evidence in its possession, custody, or control that is **exculpatory**, that is, favorable to the defense in that it tends to prove the defendant not guilty. Note there is no obligation arising from *Brady* for the prosecution to reveal **incriminating evidence** to the defense before trial.

10. Depositions

The FRCrP and most state rules of criminal procedure allow very little use of **depositions** for pretrial discovery. FRCrP 15 allows depositions to be taken only when "exceptional circumstances" exist and then the court may order it and the deposition may be used at trial. Exceptional circumstances might include impending death or the necessary (and permitted) absence of a witness from trial.

HYPOTHETICAL 5-5

Assume that, following the arraignment of Yugotta Bekiddin (at which the defendant, when asked to enter a plea said, "You gotta be kiddin me," which the judge accepted as a not guilty plea), Plea Bargain instructs Aluh Bye to draft a standard discovery request in the case for his review. Illustration 5-9 sets forth the discovery request drafted by Aluh Bye. Illustrations 5-10 and 5-11 set forth the letters drafted by Aluh Bye for Plea Bargain's signature forwarding the discovery request to the court clerk and to the prosecution.

1. Are there other discovery requests you would include in Illustration 5-9?
2. Notice the definitions included in the discovery request preceding the requests themselves. What advantages can you see in using such definitions in a discovery request?

Illustration 5-10   LETTER COMMUNICATING DISCOVERY REQUEST TO THE COURT CLERK

Date

Harmony County Criminal Court Clerk
(address)

Re: State of Yourstate v. Yugotta Bekiddin (Case No. YR00-199CR)

Dear _____:

Find enclosed a copy of our request for discovery in the above styled case which has been delivered to the State as of this date. Please mark the document filed with the Court. It is not necessary that it be set on the Court's motion docket since we are not requesting that this matter be treated as a motion at this time. The request is being filed simply to preserve the fact that the request for discovery has been made.

Very truly yours,

_____

Plea Bargain
Attorney for Defendant

cc: Attorney General Hangem High

Illustration 5-11 LETTER COMMUNICATING DISCOVERY REQUEST TO THE PROSECUTION

Date

Attorney General Hangem High
(address)

Re: State of Yourstate v. Yugotta Bekiddin (Case No. YR00-199CR)

Dear General High:

Find enclosed our request for discovery in the above styled case. Please respond to the specific requests in writing. If there are physical items to be examined please let me know when it would be convenient to make the examinations.

Very truly yours,

_____
Plea Bargain
Attorney for Defendant

---

11. Documents, records, and things from non-parties

FRCrP 17(c)(1) authorizes a subpoena to be served on non-party witnesses ordering them to to "produce any books, papers, documents, data, or other objects the subpoena designates." The subpoena may instruct the witness to produce the items before or at trial, and they will be available for inspection by the parties prior to being offered in evidence. If a party wishes to depose the witness producing the subpoened items, FRCrP 15 will control the party's right to do that. As in other places in the FRCrP where the word "data" is used, that term includes ESI.

12. Motions as discovery devices

There are a number of **pretrial motions** that the defense may make in a criminal case. Although the primary purpose of such motions is not discovery, some of them may, in fact, aid defense counsel in learning more about the prosecution's case. Here are three such pretrial motions that may aid the defense in discovery.

a. The motion to dismiss

FRCrP 12 authorizes a pretrial **motion to dismiss** (sometimes referred to as a **motion to quash**) on various grounds. In fact, under FRCrP 12(b)(3) and some state rules, the motion to dismiss on some grounds *must* be filed before trial. The motion may be directed at some defect in the institution of the proceeds or at the indictment or information. Examples of theories advanced by the defense in a motion to dismiss are:

- The court lacks jurisdiction.
- The facts alleged do not constitute a crime.
- An essential element of the crime is not alleged.
- The defendant has a complete legal defense such as double jeopardy or running of the statute of limitations.

Depending on the nature of the motion, the court may conduct an **evidentiary hearing** (a hearing in which witnesses testify under oath and exhibits may be offered in evidence) in deciding the motion, which may provide the defense an important discovery opportunity.

b. The motion to suppress

FRCrP 12(b)(3)(C) authorizes the pretrial **motion to suppress evidence** (sometimes called a **motion to exclude evidence**). Like the motion to dismiss on various grounds, the motion to suppress *must* be filed before trial under the federal rules and some state rules. The motion to suppress is generally used by the defense to exclude unlawfully obtained evidence from trial. Examples of such unlawfully obtained evidence might include coerced confessions from the defendant or evidence seized in a warrantless search in violation of the Fourth Amendment.

When a motion to suppress is filed, the court will conduct an evidentiary hearing called a **suppression hearing** to decide on the motion, again allowing the defense a discovery opportunity. In particular, FRCrP 12(h) provides that Rule 26.2 applies in a hearing on a motion to suppress and that a law enforcement officer is deemed a government witness. This means that the defense may get an early, pretrial look at the statements of witnesses called at the suppression hearing, including law enforcement officers (e.g., investigation notes, police reports) who will later testify for the government at trial.

c. The motion in limine

The **motion *in limine*** is a request to the court prior to trial seeking to have the court order the other party not to question a witness about certain matters or not to allow a witness to mention certain inadmissible things while testifying. They may be used in civil or criminal litigation. For example, if the defense believes that the prosecution plans to call a witness who will be asked to testify concerning the defendant's character before the defense has put that at issue (see Chapter 7), a motion *in limine* may be appropriate.

Depending on the nature of the particular case, defense counsel may be able to use the motion *in limine* to discover in advance what the prosecution does or does not intend to try to prove with a particular witness.

13. The Freedom of Information Act and the Privacy Act

The **Freedom of Information Act (FOIA)**, 5 U.S.C. §552, is a federal statute allowing anyone to access certain files, documents, records, and other information in the possession of federal government agencies. **The Privacy Act**, 5 U.S.C. §552(a), allows an individual to obtain access to certain information maintained by federal agencies about themselves. Many states have their own **open records acts** allowing access to information held by state and local governments. (A full discussion of the scope and procedures for using the FOIA and Privacy Act is included in Chapter 16. A full discussion of state open records act is included in Chapter 17. A list of current citations to the state open records acts for all 50 states and the District of Columbia is provided in Appendix B, Resources for the Investigator, together with other resources related to the FOIA/PA.)

Not all information held by a federal agency is obtainable using the FOIA or Privacy Act. Both statutes contain exemptions which allow the government to withhold access to some information. For example, under the FOIA, there is an exemption for law enforcement records providing that they may be withheld from disclosure if they will:

- interfere with enforcement proceedings;
- deprive a person of a fair trial;
- constitute an unwarranted invasion into a person's privacy;
- disclose government investigative techniques and procedures; or
- endanger the life or safety of law enforcement personnel.

Similarly, not all information known to state and local governments is obtainable through a state open records act. But notwithstanding those limitations, there is a substantial amount of information about people, public and private organizations, and events that is obtainable through these statutes.

C.   Means of Formal Discovery Available to the Prosecution in Criminal Litigation

1. The initial appearance

Although there are no witnesses called at the initial appearance, it does provide the prosecution with what may be its first opportunity to observe the appearance and demeanor of the defendant.

2. The preliminary examination

The defense may call witnesses to testify at the preliminary hearing if it chooses, including the defendant. As a practical matter, the defendant rarely testifies at this hearing, choosing rather to rest on his Fifth Amendment privilege against self-incrimination. But if he does testify, or if the defense calls other witnesses, the hearing provides the prosecution an opportunity to discover information known to those witnesses and get an early look at defense strategies.

3. Grand jury testimony

The grand jury proceedings, discussed earlier, provide the prosecution with an unchallenged opportunity to discover information known to witnesses. Because it is a process controlled by the prosecution, closed to the defense, and because the grand jury has the power to subpoena any witness the prosecution wishes to hear from (see Illustration 5-4), the grand jury process gives the prosecution a clear advantage over the defense in pretrial discovery.

4. Rule 16 discovery

FRCrP 16(b) allows the prosecution to engage in some limited discovery from the defendant. However, the right of the prosecution to obtain Rule 16(b) discovery from the defendant is conditioned on the defense having requested discovery *and* the prosecution having complied with those requests. Subject to those conditions, the prosecution may engage in the following discovery under Rule 16(b):

a. Documents and objects

FRCrP 16(b)(1)(A) requires the defense, upon request, to allow the prosecution to inspect and copy or photograph books, papers, documents, data, photographs, tangible objects, buildings or places that are within the possession, custody, or control of the defendant and that the defendant intends to introduce as evidence in its case-in-chief at trial (as opposed to being used as rebuttal evidence). As previously noted, ESI within the possession, custody, or control of a defendant is subject to discovery under this rule.

b. Reports of examinations and tests

FRCrP 16(b)(1)(B) requires the defense, upon request, to allow the prosecution to inspect and copy or photograph any results or reports of physical or mental exams, or scientific tests or experiments (autopsy, blood, fingerprint, drug, DNA, etc.) that are within the possession, custody, or control of the defendant and that the defense intends to introduce as evidence in its case-in-chief at trial.

c. Expert witnesses

FRCrP 16(b)(1)(C) requires the defense, upon request, to provide the prosecution with a written summary of expert witness testimony the defense intends to use in its case-in-chief at trial, but only when the defense has either made a similar request under FRCrP 16(a)(1)(E) or given notice under FRCrP 12.2(b) of its intent to present expert testimony on the defendant's mental condition.

The procedure followed by the government to obtain Rule 16 discovery is to make request for the discovery, in the same form as the defense (see Illustrations 5-9, 5-10, and 5-11).

5. Statements of witnesses

The prosecution may obtain the prior statements of witnesses called by the defense under the procedure set forth in FRCrP 26.2 as discussed above. And if the defense files a motion to suppress evidence, the prosecution may benefit from FRCrP 12(h) allowing the production of defense witness statements at the suppression hearing.

6. Prior notice of affirmative defenses

The defendant in a criminal case need not put on any proof at trial. He may simply put the government to its proof and hope to persuade the jury that the government has failed to prove all elements of the alleged offense beyond a reasonable doubt.

The defendant may also raise **affirmative defenses** such as **insanity, diminished capacity, justification** or **excuse** in the form of **self-defense** or **defense of a third person, alibi**, etc. FRCrP 12 requires the defendant to give the prosecution pretrial notice of some of these affirmative defenses.

a. Alibi witnesses

FRCrP 12.1 allows the government to serve on the defendant a written demand for notice of an alibi defense. The defendant must respond within ten days with written notification to the government of its intent to rely on an alibi defense. The defendant's notice must state the specific place or places at which the defendant claims to have been at the time of the alleged offense and the names and addresses of witnesses on whom the defendant intends to rely to prove his alibi defense. The government then has ten days to supply the defense with a written notice stating the names and addresses of the witnesses it intends to rely upon to place the defendant at the scene of the crime or to otherwise rebut the defendant's alibi witnesses.

b. Insanity defense

FRCrP 12.2 requires the defendant to give the government written notice of its intent to rely upon the **defense of insanity** and/or its intent to call an expert witness at trial to testify regarding the defendant's mental condition. The written notice normally must be given by the defense before the deadline the court has established pursuant to FRCrP 12(c) for filing pretrial motions. Rule 12.2(c) then gives the government the right to ask the court for an order directing the defendant to submit to a mental examination.

c. Public authority defense

FRCrP 12.3 requires the defendant who intends to rely on the defense of having been acting with actual or believed **public authority** on behalf of a law enforcement or federal intelligence agency at the time of the alleged offense to give the prosecution written notice of that intended defense. The notice must identify the specific law enforcement or federal intelligence agency involved and the dates during which the defendant had actual or believed public authority to act. Within ten days, the government must respond in writing by admitting or denying the defendant's claim of public authority.

The government may then serve on defendant, no later than 20 days before trial, a written demand for the names and addresses of persons upon whom the defense intends to rely to prove its defense. The defendant must respond within seven days. The government then has seven days to supply the defense with its list of witnesses who will be called to rebut that defense.

D. ▶ The Resolution of Discovery Disputes in Criminal Litigation

FRCrP 16(d) authorizes either the prosecution or the defense to file an appropriate motion with the court seeking a protective order from inappropriate discovery requests or seeking to compel the opposing party to comply with discovery requests. The form of the **motion to compel** or the **motion for protective order** is similar to those used in civil litigation (see Chapter 4). The FRCrP do not currently contain any requirement that the parties seeking to compel discovery or obtain protection from it, certify to the court good-faith attempts to resolve the dispute prior to filing the Rule 16(d) motion.

E. ▶ Lawyers Using Assisting Legal Professionals in Formal Criminal Discovery

As discussed in Chapter 4, in civil litigation new associate attorneys and paralegals may be heavily involved in assisting the attorney responsible for a case, both in planning and implementing discovery accomplished through the formal rules in a criminal case. And though only a licensed attorney can take a deposition, sign a discovery document, or appear in court on behalf of a client, since those things amount to the practice of law (see Chapter 2), both the paralegal and the new associate attorney may be given various responsibilities in criminal litigation.

SL EUTH ON THE LOOSE

To learn more about the quantities of information now available online from the various agencies and departments of the federal government, access the government's most comprehensive Web site at www.usa.gov.

1. Attendance at pretrial proceedings

Assisting legal professionals for both the prosecution and defense may be asked to attend all pretrial proceedings including, in particular, the preliminary hearing. They may not only assist the supervising attorney as that attorney presents evidence, but may take exhaustive notes and observe the proceedings carefully to maximize the discovery opportunity.

2. Review and analysis of court filings

The assisting legal professional for the defense may be asked to obtain and perform the initial review of the criminal complaint or the indictment or information in order to determine the legal sufficiency of the charging documents and to glean from them all information that can be discovered regarding the prosecution's case.

3. Drafting discovery documents and related motions

The assisting legal professional for the prosecution may be involved in the initial drafting of the information or indictment. This is a critical step in the prosecution because, as we have seen, a defective indictment may result in a motion to dismiss or to quash. She may be asked to draft requests for discovery on behalf of the government or responses to discovery served on the government by the defense. She may be asked to draft or respond to the various motions commonly filed in a criminal case.

The assisting legal professional for defense counsel may be asked to draft the motion for bill of particulars, the defendant's request for discovery, responses to discovery requested by the prosecution, and the same types of motions as the assisting legal professional on the prosecution side.

Good writing skills are critical to the assisting legal professional working in the criminal law area. Careful, thorough drafting by the one assisting will help ensure that the supervising attorney is able to obtain all discoverable information from the opposing party. And when the one assisting is drafting a document responsive to a discovery request, careful drafting is important to ensure good-faith compliance with the request, while at the same time checking that no disclosure is made of unrequested, privileged, or other non-discoverable information. (See Chapter 4 for drafting guidelines and a discussion of inadvertent disclosure of privileged material.)

4. Familiarity with discovery procedures

It is precisely because the assisting legal professional in the criminal law area is involved in reviewing and analyzing court filings and in drafting all kinds of documents relevant to formal discovery that it is critical for that legal professional to be thoroughly familiar with the FRCrP and the rules of criminal procedure in the state(s) where she practices. In criminal law the scope of permitted discovery and the procedures for obtaining discovery vary widely among the states. In some states, criminal procedure to some extent is still based on case law, as well as on statutes or court rules.

The court, by standing rule or scheduling order made on a case-to-case basis, will establish time frames in which permitted formal discovery must be initiated and complied with. It will typically fall to the assisting legal professional to know these time frames, calendar them as they arise in the office, and make sure that her office complies with all discovery deadlines and that the supervising attorney is advised of the adversary's failure to comply with any discovery deadline.

5. Familiarity with forms

In both civil and criminal discovery, familiarity with forms plays a large part in the work of the assisting legal professional because she may be asked to prepare the initial draft of discovery documents. In using forms for discovery documents, the one assisting must be sure her forms are current, that is, that they comply with the requirements of the applicable rules of procedure. The assisting legal professional must also avoid the temptation to be too dependent on forms in drafting discovery documents for the attorney's review. Every case is different. And the forms we use for discovery requests or responses or motions must be customized to suit the particular case.

6. Reviewing documents, reports, and summaries

The assisting legal professional may be expected to review carefully all information produced by the opposing side by formal discovery, or pursuant to the Jencks Act or the *Brady* doctrine, to confirm that party's compliance with the discovery requests and to identify leads for additional formal discovery or informal investigation.

7. Assisting the client in responding to discovery requests

The assisting legal professional may be expected to review documents to see if they fall within the scope of requested discovery or are privileged, or to interview witnesses to see if they should be identified in response to discovery requests as having particular knowledge, or to assist in preparing the summary of an expert's opinions for production to the opposing party.

The ability to read and understand the scope of a discovery request, an understanding of the law of privileges (see Chapter 6), and the discipline to review numerous documents carefully are just some of the skills needed by the effective legal professional in this area.

HYPOTHETICAL 5-6

Assume the case of *State v. Yugotta Bekiddin* goes to trial.

1. What do you consider the defendant's best argument against conviction? What do you consider the State's best argument for conviction?
2. Based on the facts as you know them, what verdict do you think a jury would return on the charge of aggravated robbery? Why?
3. What witnesses do you think the prosecution would call at trial other than Gino Maretti?
4. What witnesses do you think the defense would call, if any?
5. Would you recommend that Yugotta Bekiddin testify at trial on his own behalf? What other information might you want to have before you make that decision?
6. If Yugotta was convicted, what do you think the first thing he said was?

Chapter Summary and Conclusion

Formal discovery is more limited in a criminal prosecution than in a civil case. There are, however, a number of means of discovery available to the criminal defendant, from the review of the formal charging documents, to questions asked at the preliminary hearing, to utilization of the discovery allowed by Rule 16 of the FRCrP. Decisions of the courts enable criminal defendants to obtain exculpatory material from the prosecution. The Jencks Act entitles them to receive statements of witnesses after they have testified for possible use as impeachment. Motions may also serve as discovery devices for criminal defendants. The prosecution in a criminal case may use the formal discovery devices and notice requirements imposed on the defense by Rule 12 of the FRCrP. The legal professional assisting an attorney representing the prosecuting governmental entity or the criminal defendant may have any number of drafting, review, or client/witness preparation responsibilities in a criminal case.

In either a civil or criminal case all pre-trial investigation and formal discovery must be undertaken in the shadow of the rules of evidence that will govern the admissibility at trial of the factual information gathered. In Chapter 6 we begin a detailed look at the rules of evidence.

Review Questions

1. Explain why "trial by ambush" is more likely in a criminal case than in a civil case.
2. The criminal complaint is a _____ statement of the essential _____ constituting the _____ charged. It must be made under _____ before a _____ _____ or, if none is reasonably available, before a state or local _____ officer.
3. What is the first formal hearing of a criminal accused before a judge called?
4. What is the difference between a surety bond and a property bond?
5. Who issues an indictment? Who issues an information?
6. How many people sit on a grand jury?
7. Explain the difference between a request for discovery and a motion for bill of particulars.
8. *U.S. v. Agurs* is the U.S. Supreme Court case that established the criminal defendant's right to receive what prior to trial?
9. What is the Jencks Act and what does it require the state to do in a criminal prosecution?
10. What is exculpatory evidence? What two U.S. Supreme Court cases established the defendant's right to obtain such evidence in the custody of the prosecution?

KEY WORDS AND PHRASES TO REMEMBER

affidavit

affirmative defenses

alibi

arrest warrant

bail

bail bondsman

Bail Reform Act of 1984

beyond a reasonable doubt

bill of particulars

Brady doctrine

case-in-chief

conditional release

criminal complaint

death penalty

defense of a third person

diminished capacity defense

Eighth Amendment

electronically stored information (ESI)

evidentiary hearing

exculpatory evidence

Fifth Amendment right against self-incrimination

Freedom of Information Act (FOIA)

fundamental right

grand jury

in camera

incriminating evidence

indictment

information

initial appearance

insanity defense

Jencks Act

justification defense

motion for protective order

motion *in limine*

motion to compel

motion to dismiss

motion to exclude evidence

motion to quash

motion to suppress evidence

open records acts

preliminary examination

preliminary hearing

pretrial detention

pretrial motions

pretrial release

probable cause

property bond

public authority defense

rebuttal evidence

rebuttal witnesses

request for discovery

Rule 16 discovery

self-defense

summons

suppression hearing

surety bond

trial by ambush

trial discovery

waiver of indictment

LEARN BY DOING

LBD 5-1. Locate the rules of criminal procedure for your state. Prepare a memorandum comparing the scope and procedures for discovery allowed under those rules with the scope and procedures allowed by the FRCrP.

LBD 5-2. Read *Brady v. Maryland*, 373 U.S. 83, 83 S. Ct. 1194, 10 L. Ed. 2d 215 (1963), and *United States v. Agurs*, 427 U.S. 97, 96 S. Ct. 2392, 49 L. Ed. 2d 342 (1976). Then research the case law of your state to see how your courts have construed and applied the *Brady* doctrine to specific discovery requests. Prepare a memorandum summarizing your findings.

LBD 5-3. Review the Jencks Act at 18 U.S.C. §3500. Prepare a memorandum discussing whether you agree or disagree with the limited procedures allowed there to obtain statements of witnesses and why. How, if at all, would you change that procedure?

LBD 5-4. Arrange and conduct the interview of an experienced attorney specializing in criminal defense work, or a prosecuting attorney or paralegal who works in that area of the law. In your interview, ask questions about the importance of formal pretrial discovery to their work, whether they think the rules favor the prosecution, the defense, or neither, and the role they believe the assisting legal professional can play in assisting with formal discovery. Prepare a memorandum summarizing your interview.

LBD 5-5. Assume that Rowdy Outlaw (Case Study No. 1 in Appendix A) is going to be charged with first degree murder under the homicide statutes of your state. Draft the indictment for that charge.

LBDs 5-6 through 5-9 are accessible on the Author Updates link to the text Web site at www.aspenparalegaled.com/books/parsons_investigating/default.asp.

Chapter 6

Rules of Evidence for the Investigator—Part 1

CHAPTER OUTLINE

A. Introduction to the Rules of Evidence
B. The Role of the Rules of Evidence in Interviewing
   and Investigating
C. The Doctrine of Privileges

CHAPTER OBJECTIVES

The rules of evidence control the proof that can be admitted in both civil and criminal trials. Knowledge of the basic rules of evidence is essential to the legal professional involved in interviewing and investigating work. In this chapter we will look at a number of reasons why this is true. Also in this chapter you will learn a number of the fundamental concepts that investigators need to know about evidence including:

- The difference between testimonial, real, documentary, and demonstrative evidence.
- The distinction between first-hand and second-hand knowledge and between direct and circumstantial evidence.
- The importance of being able to lay a proper foundation for certain kinds of evidence.
- The role of the burden of proof and the degree of proof required in civil and criminal cases.
- The various kinds of privileged information that cannot always be discovered, including trial preparation materials (the work product doctrine), the marital privilege, the spousal testimony privilege, the physician-patient privilege and the privilege against self-incrimination.

This chapter and the next deal with the basic **rules of evidence** that control the admissibility of facts, circumstances, and to some extent opinions, in contested civil and criminal cases. While some rules of evidence are still determined by case law (e.g., burdens of proof and privileges, both discussed in this chapter), most are now codified at the federal and state levels. We will use the **Federal Rules of Evidence** (**FRE**) in this chapter and the next to look at the codified rules, but it should be kept in mind that in state court proceedings, the rules of evidence for that state will control. State court rules of evidence—including both those established by case law and those that are codified—may differ significantly from the federal rules, and there is considerable variation from state to state as well (see LBD 6-7).

The current version of the FRE is easily accessible online at either www.law.cornell.edu/rules/fre/ or as a link from the Federal Judiciary homepage at www.uscourts.gov/Home.aspx. The student should locate and consult the current version of the rules while reading this chapter.

A. Introduction to the Rules of Evidence

1. What the rules of evidence do

The rules of evidence govern the information that may be heard and considered by the judge or jury in the course of a trial. These rules control in both civil and criminal trials. In our adversarial system, not just any fact, item of information, opinion, or exhibit can be offered as evidence at the whim of a party. The rules of evidence closely control what can be offered and received in evidence and thus what can be considered by the judge or jury in reaching a decision in a case. One fundamental rule in our system is that the **finder of fact** must decide contested issues based only on the evidence presented at trial. Consequently, most **objections** made at trial are evidentiary in nature—one party trying to limit or keep out some evidence tendered by the other side.

Observing a judge apply the rules of evidence to allow some evidence in and keep other evidence out is puzzling to the untrained observer. The ruling may appear illogical and arbitrary and the evidence disallowed may appear imminently relevant to the issue. And it may well be! But the various rules of evidence have been developed over a long period of time and, for the most part, are intended to ensure some level of genuineness and reliability before the proffered testimony or exhibit will be received.

SLEUTH ON THE LOOSE

Go to the Court Statistics Project at www.courtstatistics .org/ and see if you can determine the number of criminal cases initiated in the courts of your state in 2009 and the number of criminal cases disposed of in the courts of your state in the same year.

2. The burden of proof

a. In a civil case

The admissibility of evidence at trial is directly related to whether a party to the litigation can carry its burden of proof. In a civil case the **burden of proof** is initially on the plaintiff to prove all the elements of the cause of action. If the defendant **counterclaims** against the plaintiff, **cross-claims** against another defendant, or files a **third-party claim** against a new defendant (see Chapters 3 and 4), the defendant, as counter plaintiff, cross plaintiff, or third-party plaintiff, will have the burden of proof on all the elements of those claims. And if the defendant raises any **affirmative defenses** to the claims of the plaintiff against him, the defendant will have the burden of proof on all the elements of those defenses.

EXAMPLE

In a civil lawsuit in which the plaintiff is suing the defendant in negligence to recover for personal injuries, the plaintiff will have the burden of proving all the elements constituting his cause of action in negligence. If the plaintiff fails to carry that burden, his lawsuit will be dismissed by the judge, or the jury will find in favor of the defendant on that basis.

If the defendant in that civil suit raises affirmative defenses of contributory fault by the plaintiff or assumption of the risk by plaintiff, then the defendant will have the burden of proving all elements of those affirmative defenses. If the defendant in that civil suit counterclaims against the plaintiff alleging negligence, then the defendant, as counter plaintiff, has the burden of proof on those allegations.

b. In a criminal prosecution

In a criminal case the government, as plaintiff, will have the burden of proving all elements of the crime alleged to have been committed by the defendant. If it fails to do so, the charges will be dismissed against the defendant, or the jury will find the defendant not guilty on that basis. If the criminal defendant raises an affirmative defense such as insanity, entrapment, self-defense, or alibi, then the burden will shift to the criminal defendant to prove the necessary elements to establish those defenses (see LBD 6-1).

3. The standard or degree of proof

a. In a civil case

The admissibility of evidence at trial is also directly related to the **degree of proof** required of a party who has a burden of proof. In civil cases the required degree of proof is typically by a **preponderance of the evidence**, which means the plaintiff must convince the trier of fact that it is *more likely than not* that the allegations regarding the elements of the action are true. If the defendant in a civil action asserts an affirmative defense, the defendant will have the burden of proving all the elements of that defense and, again, the degree of proof required is typically by a preponderance.

In some civil actions the degree of proof required may be slightly higher than the preponderance. For example, in some states, civil fraud must be proven by **clear and convincing evidence**, not by a mere preponderance. (See LBD 6-2.)

b. In a criminal prosecution

In criminal cases the prosecution must prove the necessary elements of the crime alleged **beyond a reasonable doubt**. If the criminal defendant alleges affirmative defenses such as insanity, entrapment, or alibi, then in many states the burden of proof will rest on that defendant to prove all the elements of those defenses, usually by a preponderance. (See LBD 6-1.)

To do a thorough job of factual investigation, the legal professional must know and understand which party to the lawsuit has the burden of proof as to which issues and the standard or degree of proof to which each party will be held on each issue.

4. Means of proof

In both civil and criminal cases proof of facts and circumstances relevant to the issues is controlled by the rules of evidence. Evidence may be presented to the court in several different formats:

- **Testimonial evidence** is evidence received from the sworn testimony of witnesses.
- **Documentary evidence** is evidence received from properly admitted documents or other data compilations (e.g., electronically stored information).
- **Real or physical evidence** is evidence in the form of properly admitted objects (e.g., the weapon in a murder case; the defective product in a civil products liability case).
- **Demonstrative evidence** is evidence that has been prepared for trial by the litigants, usually in the form of pictures, videos, charts, graphs, diagrams, computer simulations, etc., that portray, illustrate, or demonstrate something relevant to the case.

5. First-hand and second-hand knowledge

Information that is obtained from witnesses may be first-hand or second-hand. **First-hand knowledge** is something known to a person because they perceived it through one of the senses. It is something the person saw, heard, smelled, tasted, or felt. **Second-hand knowledge** is something known to a person only because someone else told them about it or they read it somewhere.

As common sense might suggest, first-hand knowledge is more reliable and thus more valuable to attorneys than second-hand knowledge. Although relevant first-hand knowledge is not always admissible as evidence, it usually is, whereas relevant second-hand knowledge often is excluded from evidence due to the **hearsay rule** (discussed in detail in Chapter 7).

EXAMPLE

One witness to a murder says she saw the defendant point a gun at the victim, shoot the victim, and run. That is first-hand knowledge and almost certainly admissible as evidence at trial. A second witness says she saw and heard nothing but did hear the first witness say that she saw the defendant shoot the victim. That is second-hand knowledge and, if offered as evidence by the prosecution at trial, will likely be excluded as hearsay.

Legal professionals involved in investigating work must be able to distinguish between first-hand and second-hand knowledge. Attorneys always prefer first-hand knowledge of relevant facts.

6. Direct and circumstantial evidence

Evidence is frequently categorized as being either direct or circumstantial. **Direct evidence** is evidence that, if believed, establishes a relevant fact without the need for any inference (beyond the inference necessary in all proof that the source is accurate and truthful).

EXAMPLE

> A witness testifies that she saw the defendant point a gun at the victim, shoot the victim, and run. If believed, that is direct evidence that the defendant shot the victim.

Circumstantial evidence is indirect evidence that requires an inference (in addition to the accurate and truthful inferences) to prove a relevant fact.

EXAMPLE

> A second witness testifies that she heard a gunshot and turned to see the victim on the ground and the defendant running away with a gun in his hand. That would be circumstantial evidence that the defendant shot the victim, but not direct evidence of it.

Note that the circumstantial evidence offered by the second witness is first-hand knowledge. The second witness is testifying to what she saw and heard herself. But because she didn't actually see the defendant fire the gun at the victim, the jury will have to infer that he did from what the witness did see and hear.

Circumstantial evidence, if relevant to the issues, is usually admissible as evidence. But it isn't as reliable or convincing as direct evidence. Its **probative value** may not be as great as direct evidence. Or, as lawyers and judges sometimes say, it doesn't carry the **"weight"** of direct evidence. Judges will leave it to the jury to determine the weight of the relevant circumstantial evidence but will typically allow it to be heard.

Legal professionals involved in investigating work must be able to distinguish between direct and circumstantial evidence.

7. Laying the foundation

Many kinds of evidence are not admissible until a proper foundation has been established for them.

EXAMPLE

> An expert witness cannot offer opinions as an expert until his credentials as an expert have been established by testimony or stipulation of the parties and the trial judge finds he is indeed qualified as an expert in the field in which he will offer his opinions. A document cannot be received in evidence until it has first been properly authenticated, that is, established by some proof to genuinely be what it appears to be. In a murder trial, the murder weapon will not be allowed in evidence until an adequate **chain of custody** has first been established showing that it is in fact the weapon found at the crime scene. That chain of custody will include proof as to how the weapon has been stored and preserved and in whose custody it has been every moment since its discovery by the police.

We call the establishment of this basis for the admissibility of evidence **laying the foundation**. As you study the various specific rules of evidence in Chapter 7, watch for references to the need to establish the foundation before evidence can be admitted. Laying a proper foundation for evidence is every bit as critical as the evidence itself, since without a proper foundation the evidence either will not be admitted by the trial judge or, if admitted under a cloud of doubt, will lose some or all of its probative value. Laying a proper foundation can sometimes take as much or more time than offering the testimony itself.

8. Rulings on admissibility and offers of proof

Under FRE 104 and corresponding state rules of evidence, it is the presiding trial judge who makes the determination as to the admissibility of any offered evidence. It is the role of the jury to hear the factual evidence allowed in by the judge and to decide the factual issues before it based on that evidence. That is why the jury is called the finder of fact. But questions regarding the admissibility of evidence present issues of law to be decided by the judge, not the jury.

When an objection is made to offered evidence, the judge will either **sustain** the objection, which means the objection is valid and the evidence will be disallowed, or the judge will **overrule** the objection, which means the objection is not valid and the evidence is allowed in.

However, it is within the province of the jury to decide what **weight or credibility** (believability) to give to evidence that is allowed in by the judge. See FRE 104(e). Just because the judge allows the jury to hear particular testimony does not mean the jury must believe it or give it any credence. Those decisions are up to the jury in its deliberations.

Frequently, when it is a close legal decision as to whether evidence ought to be admitted or not, the judge will choose to allow it in, saying it is up to the jury to accept it or not. And in a **bench trial** (a trial conducted without a jury) where the trial judge is the finder of fact, most judges are more lenient in allowing disputed evidence to be heard than they would be in a jury trial. Most trial judges reason that in a bench trial they, with their experience in the adversarial process, will not be confused or misled as a jury might be and can reliably give the disputed testimony its proper weight.

A party dissatisfied with the ruling of the trial judge on admitting evidence can preserve the ruling as an issue of alleged **error for appeal**. The attorneys must be careful at trial, however, to preserve the right to appeal the judge's evidentiary ruling. Under FRE 103(a)(1), a party cannot appeal the judge's ruling allowing evidence in as error unless that party makes a timely objection to its admission at trial.

Under FRE 103(a)(2), a party cannot appeal a judge's ruling excluding tendered evidence unless the substance of what the evidence would have been is evident from the excluded question or the party makes an **offer of proof** at trial. An offer of proof is conducted out of the jury's hearing for the purpose of preserving it for the record. It may consist of the witness testifying out of the hearing of the jury or of the lawyer summarizing what the witness would have said if allowed to testify.

B. The Role of the Rules of Evidence in Interviewing and Investigating

Knowledge of the basic rules of evidence enables the legal professional involved in factual investigation in several ways.

1. Planning and carrying out effective informal investigations

Having some idea of what kinds of facts and information will or will not be admissible in court enables the legal professional to prioritize the investigation, to seek usable information, and to avoid wasting time pursuing dead ends.

HYPOTHETICAL 6-1

Assume that the law office you work for is representing Teed Off in a civil suit pending in the U.S. district court (where the FRE apply) against Snap Hook, a professional golfer who plays on the PGA tour. Teed Off alleges that he was the full-time caddie for Snap Hook last year and that at the beginning of the year Snap Hook verbally promised to pay Teed Off 10 percent of all his tournament winnings during the year plus a $200,000 cash bonus if Snap Hook won any one of the four major tournaments—the Masters, the U.S. Open, the British Open, or the PGA Tournament.

Snap Hook did win the PGA Tournament but has refused to pay Teed Off the bonus and denies that any such promise was made. The supervising attorney handling the case for Teed Off has told him that the case looks like a swearing match and the jury will just have to decide who to believe. Teed Off is, well, teed off!

In the course of your assigned investigation, you discover at the court house in the county where Snap Hook lives that he has a 20-year-old misdemeanor conviction for smoking marijuana (during a round of golf no less) and a 3-year-old misdemeanor conviction for shoplifting (golf balls at a Wal-Mart). Both convictions were based on guilty pleas and the sentences in both cases were satisfied by community service hours.

Which lead is more useful to Teed Off in his case against Snap Hook? Which lead deserves more of your attention in follow-up investigation? Read FRE 609(a) and 609(b) and articulate a response to those two questions.

Assume that Snap Hook has given a deposition in this case and has denied under oath that he has any criminal convictions in his past. Does that alter your conclusion about the usefulness of both of these convictions? Read FRE 613 and articulate a response to that question.

2. Putting discovered information in admissible form

A number of evidentiary rules go not just to the content of the information but to its form. Unless the evidence is offered in proper form or unless a proper foundation is laid, it will be inadmissible, regardless of how relevant or persuasive it is.

HYPOTHETICAL 6-2

Assume that you make the discovery of the prior convictions of Snap Hook mentioned in Hypothetical 6-1 the day before trial is set to begin and in a county more than 500 miles away from where the case is to be tried. You place a long-distance call to ask the supervising attorney how to proceed but he is not available to talk with you. As you hang up the phone, you look at the clock and realize that the clerk's office where you have found these records closes in ten minutes. You remember that Snap Hook denied in his deposition that he had any criminal convictions and that the case may be decided on the credibility of the two parties. A growing feeling of panic closes around your throat.

What can you do to make the information you have discovered admissible in court tomorrow? What form does it have to be in?

Fighting back the panic, you have the clerk of the court make you copies of the court records of the two convictions then head for your car to return home. But something keeps nagging at you, so you finally pull out your copy of the rules of evidence.

There it is, right there in FRE 901. How could you have forgotten? The records of these convictions, like all documents and things offered in evidence, must be properly authenticated (i.e., shown to be genuine) before they will be admitted in evidence. "I just need to arrange for an authenticating witness is all," you shout to yourself, delirious with relief. You bound back up the steps to the courthouse and slip your foot in the door of the clerk's office just as they are closing for the day. Putting on your best *you gotta love me* smile, you explain your dilemma to the clerk and ask if she will mind traveling out of town over night to appear in court 500 miles away tomorrow in order to authenticate these records.

You can tell from the look on her face that she's not going to agree. She asks if you have a subpoena for her and you admit that you do not. She silently takes your copy of the rules of evidence from your trembling hand, turns to FRE 902(4) and points at it.

Sheepishly, you read that a copy of a public record (like the court records of Snap Hook's criminal convictions) may be self-authenticating (no live witness is needed to authenticate) if it is certified by the custodian or other authorized person. All you ever had to do was get copies of the records of the convictions certified by the clerk of the court where they are of record. The clerk graciously agrees to certify the records for you even though it is now after hours. A few minutes later you are stuck in rush-hour traffic on your way home but feeling no pain.

Just then, out of the blue, panic strikes again. What about the hearsay rule? One knowledgeable of the rules of evidence knows that these copies of the convictions are hearsay—out-of-court statements offered to prove the truth of them. Will that keep them out of evidence tomorrow? Your whole poor, pathetic life passes before your eyes. You swerve over to the shoulder of the road and grab your copy of the rules of evidence again. Finally, FRE 803(8) jumps out at you and you breathe easy. The sky is blue and the birds are singing. Why? Because FRE 803(8) says that public records are not excluded by the hearsay rule.

You head home now, at peace, visualizing the well-deserved pat on the back the supervising attorney will give you. Maybe Teed Off will even give you some tips on getting rid of that nasty slice!

3. Drafting formal discovery requests and responses

As we saw in Chapter 4, the scope of permissible formal discovery under FRCP 26(b) is broader than the scope of what is admissible at trial under the rules of evidence. Still, under FRCP 26(b), information sought in formal discovery must be relevant to these issues, not privileged, and at least calculated to lead to the discovery of admissible evidence. Consequently, those involved in planning and drafting formal discovery requests must be familiar with what is—and isn't—admissible evidence.

HYPOTHETICAL 6-3

Assume that in the lawsuit between Teed Off and Snap Hook you locate a witness, Sand Trap, who was in the gallery at the PGA Tournament when Snap Hook made his winning putt on the last hole. Sand Trap tells you in an interview that he heard Snap Hook say something to himself as he stood over that last putt but couldn't understand what it was. He asked the man standing next to him what Snap Hook said and the man replied, "I think he said, 'This is a million for me and two hundred grand for my caddie.'"

The formal deposition of Sand Trap is scheduled. In the deposition the supervising lawyer handling the case for Teed Off asks him what the man standing next to him told him that Snap Hook said. The attorney for Snap Hook objects to the question on the grounds that it calls for a hearsay response. The supervising lawyer responds, "That might be a good objection at trial but not here in this deposition."

Assuming that the attorney for Snap Hook is correct that the question calls for a hearsay response (see Chapter 7), articulate a reason why the supervising attorney's response to the objection is correct under FRCP 26(b).

Assuming that Sand Trap is able to answer the question about what the man standing next to him in the gallery heard Snap Hook say, what will the next question to Sand Trap probably be?

For the same reasons, the rules of evidence may provide a basis to object to requested discovery if the asking party cannot demonstrate that the information sought is calculated to lead to the discovery of admissible evidence under FRCP 26.

HYPOTHETICAL 6-4

> Assume that the attorney for Snap Hook serves your office with interrogatories to be answered by Teed Off in the suit over the promised $200,000 bonus. Assume further that one of the interrogatories asks about Teed Off's medical history.
>
> Review the section of Chapter 7 dealing with relevant evidence and articulate a recommendation to the supervising attorney as to whether this question should be objected to and why.
>
> Based on what you know so far of the suit between Snap Hook and Teed Off, what, if any, argument might the attorney for Snap Hook make in defense of the propriety of his interrogatory to Teed Off?

4. Drafting affidavits or declarations for use in pretrial motions

Frequently when motions are made to the court prior to trial, particularly FRCP 56 **motions for summary judgment**, the motions will be supported or opposed by written statements of testimony called **affidavits** in some jurisdictions and **declarations** in others. These written statements are made under oath just like trial testimony and must comply with the rules of evidence. (See Illustrations 6-1 and 6-2.)

HYPOTHETICAL 6-5

> Assume that in the course of your investigation for Teed Off in his suit against Snap Hook you discover a letter written by Snap Hook to his mentor and coach, Double Eagle, prior to Snap Hook's winning the PGA Tournament. In the letter to Double Eagle, Snap Hook acknowledges the agreement to pay Teed Off the $200,000 bonus. Based on that letter, your supervising attorney may decide to file a Rule 56 motion for summary judgment on behalf of Teed Off on the grounds that there are no genuine issues of material fact and that Teed Off is entitled to judgment as a matter of law. The motion and supporting affidavit of Teed Off might look like Illustrations 6-1 and 6-2, respectively.
>
> If you assist in the preparation of the affidavit of Teed Off, you will have to be careful to ensure that all factual testimony given in the affidavit complies with the rules of evidence.
>
> Review the material in Chapter 7 on the authentication of documents and articulate an opinion as to whether paragraphs 5 and 6 of the Teed Off affidavit set out in Illustration 6-2 lay a sufficient foundation for the introduction of the letter of Snap Hook addressed to Double Eagle into evidence. What more, if anything, would you suggest to the supervising attorney might be needed to ensure the admission of that letter into evidence? To add to its credibility or weight?

5. Planning the evidence to be offered at trial

For every witness the trial attorney expects to call to testify at trial, his pretrial preparation will include a review of the projected

Illustration 6-1   MOTION FOR SUMMARY JUDGMENT

IN THE UNITED STATES DISTRICT COURT
FOR THE EASTERN DISTRICT OF YOURSTATE
NORTHERN DIVISION

TEED OFF, Plaintiff	)))	
v.	)	DOCKET NO. YR00-00002
SNAP HOOK, Defendant	)))	

PLAINTIFF'S MOTION FOR SUMMARY JUDGMENT

Plaintiff, Teed Off, pursuant to Rule 56 of the Federal Rules of Civil Procedure, moves the court for an order entering summary judgment in his favor as to all allegations contained in the complaint. Plaintiff alleges that there are no genuine issues as to any material fact in this case and that plaintiff is entitled to judgment as a matter of law.

In support of this motion, plaintiff relies on the following, all of which are submitted with this motion:

1. plaintiff's memorandum of law and fact;

2. excerpts from the pleadings;

3. excerpts from the depositions of plaintiff and defendant; and

4. the affidavit of plaintiff, Teed Off.

Wherefore, plaintiff asks the court to enter an order awarding judgment in his favor against defendant in the amount of $200,000 plus prejudgment interest on that amount as prayed for in the complaint.

Mellow Fellow
Attorney for Plaintiff Teed Off
(Address)

(Certificate of Service omitted)

SLEUTH ON THE LOOSE

Need to determine the value of a car totaled in an accident? Look it up on the Kelley Blue Book Web site at *www.kbb. com* or the National Automobile Dealers Association Web site at *www.nadaguides.com.* Try finding the current value of your own car there.

testimony to anticipate and prepare for possible objections from the other side. For every document or object the attorney intends to offer in evidence at trial he must anticipate and prepare for possible objections based on relevance, authentication, chain of custody, hearsay, or some other basis. The legal professional may be asked to assist the attorney in anticipating objections and preparing to overcome them.

And, of course, for every witness the opposing party plans to call and every document or object the opposing party intends to offer in evidence, the trial attorney's pretrial preparation will include a determination of whether a valid objection can be raised to the testimony or document.

Illustration 6-2 AFFIDAVIT IN SUPPORT OF MOTION FOR SUMMARY JUDGMENT

IN THE UNITED STATES DISTRICT COURT
FOR THE EASTERN DISTRICT OF YOURSTATE
NORTHERN DIVISION

TEED OFF,	)	
Plaintiff	)	
	)	DOCKET NO. YR00-00002
v.	)	
SNAP HOOK,	)	
Defendant	)	

<u>AFFIDAVIT OF PLAINTIFF TEED OFF</u>

STATE OF YOURSTATE)
COUNTY OF HARMONY)

Affiant, Teed Off, after first being duly sworn according to law, deposes and states as follows:

1. I am the plaintiff in this case.

2. I have personal knowledge of the matters contained in this affidavit. This affidavit is submitted in support of my motion for summary judgment.

3. I have been a caddie for professional golfers on the Professional Golfers Association (PGA) tour for approximately ten years. On or about January 5, YR-1, I was contacted by phone by the defendant Snap Hook, a professional golfer. In that conversation Snap Hook offered me the full-time position as his caddie for the upcoming YR-1 golfing season. In consideration for my agreement to be his full-time caddie during the YR-1 season, Snap Hook promised to pay me 10 percent of all his tournament winnings plus a cash bonus of $200,000 if he won any of the four major tournaments (including the Masters, the U.S. Open, the British Open, and the PGA Tournament) during the YR-1 season.

4. I did caddie for Snap Hook during the entire YR-1 golfing season as I had agreed to do. Snap Hook did pay me 10 percent of all of his tournament winnings for the YR-1 golfing season. However, in August YR-1, Snap Hook won the PGA tournament but he has failed and refused to pay me the $200,000 bonus.

5. Attached as Exhibit 1 to this affidavit is a copy of a handwritten letter dated September 4, YR-1 and addressed to Double Eagle. Double Eagle is known to me to be the mentor and golfing coach for Snap Hook.

6. I am familiar with the handwriting of Snap Hook. I saw him sign many autographs for fans during the YR-1 season. In those autographs he would sign his name and often write some personal message. Based on my knowledge of and familiarity with the handwriting of Snap Hook, I can state that the letter attached as Exhibit 1 to this affidavit was written by Snap Hook and that the signature on the letter is his.

FURTHER AFFIANT SAYETH NOT.

_____
                             TEED OFF

SWORN TO AND SUBSCRIBED BEFORE ME,
THE UNDERSIGNED NOTARY PUBLIC, THIS
_____ DAY OF MAY, YR00

_____

              notary public

my commission expires on _____.

6. Assisting the lawyer at trial

No matter how thorough the pretrial preparation, the unexpected always happens at trial. The opposing party offers evidence that was not anticipated. Or the opposing party makes an unexpected objection to your side's evidence. Evidentiary objections must be made or responded to immediately or it is too late.

One of the most important qualities of a good trial lawyer is to be able to think quickly in such situations. If a legal professional is assisting the trial lawyer in the courtroom or is back at the office waiting for an emergency phone call from the courthouse, she needs to be qualified to render quick, competent assistance in such situations.

C.   The Doctrine of Privileges

Closely related to evidentiary matters is the doctrine of privileges. The various privileges were developed through the **common law** (decisions of courts). Over the years, the courts determined that, due to various **public policy** concerns, certain information should not be subject to disclosure in informal investigation, formal discovery, or even in sworn testimony at trial. Consequently, if information can be fitted into one of the recognized privileges, it is excepted from discovery and need not be disclosed to anyone for any purpose. The one having the privilege is deemed immune from having to testify concerning the privileged information or otherwise disclose it. Accordingly, this area of the law is sometimes referred to as **privileges** and **immunities**.

In most states the recognized privileges have now been made **statutory** (i.e., enacted into law by the legislature of that state). Some, however, are still of common law authority only and you will need to check not only the statutes but the case law of your state to determine the exact privileges recognized in your jurisdiction. (See LBD 6-3 and 6-4.)

Not all states recognize the same privileges or apply them in the same way. Most states do recognize the **attorney-client privilege,** the **physician-patient privilege,** a **spousal confidential communications privilege,** and a **spousal testimony privilege.**

Furthermore, some privileges are **absolute** (meaning they apply in all circumstances), some are **qualified** (meaning that under certain circumstances the privilege may not apply), and any privilege may be **waived.** The following is a summary of the most widely recognized privileges other than the attorney-client privilege, which was discussed in detail in Chapter 2.

1. Trial preparation materials

Sometimes called the **work product rule**, this privilege has its origin in the seminal Supreme Court case of *Hickman v. Taylor*, 329 U.S. 495 (1947), and is now firmly embodied in federal law as Rule 26(b)(3) of the Federal Rules of Civil Procedure (www.law.cornell.edu/rules/frcp/). Most states have substantially the same language in their state court rules of procedure but the legal professional should check the rules of the jurisdiction in which she practices.

This rule recognizes an absolute privilege for any material containing the "mental impressions, conclusions, opinions, or legal theories of an attorney or other representative of a party concerning the litigation." Such material is sometimes referred to as *attorney work product*.

In many law offices there is a policy to stamp any notes, memoranda, or correspondence containing such material with the designation *work product* or *attorney work product*. Such a procedure will not guarantee that the court will protect such material from disclosure if it is challenged, but the designation, if used in good faith, is a helpful indication of intent.

FRCP 26(b)(3) recognizes a qualified privilege for documents and things prepared in anticipation of litigation or for trial by or for the party or by or for the party's representative (e.g., photographs, videos, witness statements, etc.). The opposing side in a lawsuit can compel the disclosure of those materials in formal discovery only upon a showing of **substantial need** in preparation of its case and the inability to obtain the substantial equivalent of the materials by other means.

2. The physician-patient privilege

This privilege applies to confidential information disclosed to a treating physician by or on behalf of a patient and related to treatment or diagnosis of the patient. The privilege belongs to the patient and only the patient can waive the privilege and permit disclosure, or assert the privilege and prevent disclosure.

HYPOTHETICAL 6-6

Assume that as part of your pre-filing investigation in connection with the suit of Teed Off against Snap Hook you interview Double Eagle and take extensive notes during the interview. Your notes not only indicate your questions and his answers, they also contain your impressions of Double Eagle as a credible witness. Shortly after your interview with Double Eagle, he dies in an accident.

Later, the supervising attorney files suit on behalf of Teed Off. The attorney for Snap Hook serves a document request on your office asking to see and copy the notes from your interview with Double Eagle.

1. Do these facts support an argument of "substantial need" under FRCP 26(b)(3)?
2. Will the attorneys for Snap Hook be able to obtain all your notes from the interview or only those portions containing the questions and answers? Why?
3. If Double Eagle were still alive and available to the attorneys for Snap Hook, what would be the appropriate response to this document request?

The most common example of waiver is seen when the patient puts her medical condition at issue, as by filing a personal injury lawsuit. The plaintiff's entire relevant medical history will then be discoverable.

3. The psychotherapist-patient privilege

Recognized by most states, the **psychotherapist-patient privilege** protects confidential communications related to the diagnosis or treatment of a mental or psychological condition. This privilege too is not absolute and is waived if the patient puts his mental or psychological condition at issue in a proceeding.

4. The spousal confidential communications privilege

This privilege, sometimes called the **marital privilege**, applies to confidential communications of all kinds between married persons. To be privileged, the communication must have been intended to be confidential when it occurred, and it must have occurred while the couple was married.

EXAMPLE

> If a married couple has a conversation within the hearing of a third person able to understand what they are saying, it will not be considered confidential. If an unmarried couple has a conversation between themselves only, that they do intend to be confidential, it will not be privileged even if they marry later.

This privilege belongs to both spouses and either of them may refuse to disclose the communication and prohibit the other spouse or any third person from disclosing it. Most states provide that the privilege survives divorce so long as the confidential communication was made while the marriage was still valid. In most states, this privilege is available in both civil and criminal cases. Note that that the confidential communication privilege is not a basis to refuse to testify; it is only a basis to refuse to testify or to prevent the other from testifying to the confidential communication.

Exceptions to the spousal confidential communications privilege are recognized in an action by one spouse against the other (e.g., divorce actions). In some states the privilege is not available to shield communications made in furtherance of a criminal act. And many states today are enacting statutes denying the privilege in criminal actions involving allegations of child or spousal abuse. (See LBD 6-4.)

5. The spousal testimony privilege

A related privilege recognized in many states is the spousal testimony privilege, which provides that one spouse cannot be compelled to give any testimony against the other spouse regardless of whether the testimony would involve the disclosure of confidential marital communications. This privilege can be asserted only at a time when the couple is married. It does not matter whether they were married when the conversation to be testified to occurred.

EXAMPLE

If an unmarried couple have a conversation, later marry, and then one spouse is called to testify against the other concerning that pre-marital conversation, the privilege can be asserted. Note that the spousal confidential communication privilege would not apply here because the couple was not married when the conversation in question occurred.

In most states the spousal testimonial privilege only applies in criminal cases and is held by the testifying spouse only, not the defendant spouse. In some states the testimonial privilege is held by both spouses, such that the defendant spouse could assert the privilege to prevent a spouse from testifying against him, even if she were willing and anxious to do so.

6. The privilege against self-incrimination

The Fifth Amendment to the United States Constitution provides that no person "shall be compelled in any criminal case to be a witness against himself." As interpreted by the courts, this means that persons cannot be compelled to disclose any information that would tend to incriminate themselves. And the privilege can be asserted in a civil proceeding as well as a criminal one because compelled disclosure of criminal conduct in a civil proceeding could lead to a criminal charge.

The privilege against **self-incrimination** is not absolute. The witness can be compelled to testify if the prosecution grants **transactional immunity,** which is full immunity from prosecution on all charges related to the witness's testimony. A witness granted transactional immunity cannot be prosecuted on any charge related to the witness's testimony even if the government obtains evidence of the crime independently of the testimony.

Or, the government may grant the witness **derivative use immunity,** commonly referred to only as **use immunity**. The granting of use immunity to a witness prohibits the government from using the witness's testimony or any evidence derived from it to prosecute the witness. However, any evidence the government obtains against the witness independent of the witness's testimony and not derived from it can still be used to prosecute the witness.

7. Miscellaneous privileges

There are a number of other types of privileges recognized by various states including **priest-penitent** and **accountant-client privileges**.

Whenever your case involves a state or federal statute, you should research the statute carefully to determine if it provides for any special privileges from disclosure in any lawsuit or administrative proceeding brought under the statute.

8. Procedural matters relating to privileges

A procedural question that often arises concerning cases pending in federal court is whether the privileges recognized by the law of the state in which the federal court sits will apply in the federal court proceeding. This is not always an easy question to answer, but primary guidance comes from FRE 501. That rule provides in essence that suits in federal court based on diversity jurisdiction (such suits are almost always controlled by state substantive law) will be governed by state immunity law. Cases in federal court on some other jurisdictional basis (usually federal question cases) will be governed by the privilege rules as developed by the federal courts.

Again, care should be taken to inform yourself regarding the various privileges recognized in the jurisdiction in which you practice, the recognized exceptions to them, and the interpretation of them by the state courts. (See LBD 6-3 and 6-4.)

Chapter Summary and Conclusion

The rules of evidence control what information is admissible in a civil or criminal trial. When the rules of evidence make information admissible, there are a number of means by which that information may be proven, from direct witness testimony, to statements contained in documents, to real or physical items of evidence, to demonstrative material prepared for trial. Proof allowed in under the rules of evidence may be direct or circumstantial with the difference going to persuasiveness. A foundation of authenticity must be laid for most kinds of evidence to be admissible. The trial judge is the gatekeeper as to admissible evidence, deciding what proffered evidence is admissible under the rules, and what is not. There are a number of types of information that are deemed privileged and consequently not admissible at trial under the rules of evidence, unless the privilege is waived or found inapplicable. The legal professional engaged in interviewing and investigating must be knowledgeable of the rules of evidence in order to plan and carry out an effective interview or factual investigation, and to adequately assist in formal discovery.

In Chapter 7 we will look at specific important rules of evidence.

Review Questions

1. Explain the role of the rules of evidence at trial.
2. In a trial, when is the burden of proof on the plaintiff? When is it on the defendant?
3. What is the difference between direct and circumstantial evidence?
4. What do we mean by "laying the foundation" for certain evidence? Can you think of examples?
5. List five reasons why the rules of evidence matter in interviewing and investigating.
6. Explain the difference between the spousal testimonial privilege and the spousal confidential communications privilege.
7. What is the attorney work product rule? Which U.S. Supreme Court case established it?

8. Name one situation in which the physician-patient privilege is deemed waived.
9. Name one privilege that derives from the U.S. Constitution.
10. What kind of case pending in federal court will nonetheless be governed by state privilege law?

KEY WORDS AND PHRASES TO REMEMBER

absolute privilege
accountant-client privilege
affidavit
affirmative defense
attorney-client privilege
bench trial
beyond a reasonable doubt
burden of proof
chain of custody
circumstantial evidence
clear and convincing evidence
common law
counterclaim
credibility
cross-claim
declaration
degree of proof
demonstrative evidence
direct evidence
documentary evidence
error for appeal
Federal Rules of Evidence
finder of fact
first-hand knowledge
immunity
laying the foundation
marital privilege
objection overruled

objection sustained
offer of proof
physician-patient privilege
preponderance of the evidence
priest-penitent privilege
privilege
probative value
psychotherapist-patient privilege
public policy
qualified privilege
real evidence
rules of evidence
second-hand knowledge
self-incrimination
spousal confidential communications privilege
spousal testimony privilege
statutory law
substantial need
sustain
testimonial evidence
third-party claim
transactional immunity
use immunity
weight of the evidence
work product rule

LEARN BY DOING

LBD 6-1. Determine which party (the prosecution or criminal defendant) has the respective burden(s) of proof to prove or refute on the issue of insanity in your jurisdiction when the defendant raises the insanity defense. Also determine what standard or degree of proof (preponderance, clear and convincing, beyond a reasonable doubt) is required for the party having the burden to prove/refute. Put your findings in the form of a research memorandum.

LBD 6-2. Determine what standard or degree of proof is required of a plaintiff to prevail in a case of civil fraud in your jurisdiction. How do the statutes or court decisions of your state distinguish between the "preponderance" standard and the "clear and convincing" standard? Put your findings in the form of a research memorandum.

LBD 6-3. List and summarize the various statutory and common law privileges currently recognized in your state.

LBD 6-4. Research and prepare a memorandum regarding the history, development, and current status of the spousal privileges in your state. Regarding the spousal testimonial privilege in your state, is it available to both spouses or to only the testifying spouse? Is it available only in criminal cases or both civil and criminal? Regarding the marital confidential communications privilege, is it available to both spouses? Is it available in both civil and criminal cases? What common law or statutory exceptions are recognized to these privileges?

LBD 6-5. Interview a government prosecutor and/or a criminal defense lawyer concerning their agreement or disagreement with the marital privilege, the spousal testimony privilege, and the Fifth Amendment privilege against self-incrimination. Prepare a memorandum comparing the two viewpoints expressed as well as your own opinions on those privileges.

LBDs 6-6 and 6-7 are accessible on the Author Updates link to the text Web site at www.aspenparalegaled.com/books/parsons_investigating/default.asp.

Chapter 7

Rules of Evidence for the Investigator—Part 2

CHAPTER OBJECTIVES

In this chapter you will learn the basic rules of evidence and how they apply in a practical way to interviewing and investigating work by the legal professional. We will consider the rules regarding:

- Relevant evidence
- Lay and expert witnesses
- Hearsay and its various exceptions
- Admissions by party opponent
- Character evidence
- Bias and interest
- Prior inconsistent statements
- Authentication of documents and things
- The best evidence rule
- The admissibility of evidence for alternative reasons

In this chapter we continue our study of the basic **rules of evidence** using the **Federal Rules of Evidence (FRE)** as our model. Remember that the current version of the FRE is easily accessible online at either www.law.cornell.edu/rules/fre/ or as a link from the Federal Judiciary homepage at www.uscourts.gov/Home.aspx. The student should locate and consult the current version of the rules while reading this chapter. Remember, too, that states have their own rules of evidence that control in their state courts, and those state rules of evidence may be very different from the FRE (see LBD 6-7).

A. ▶ Relevance

To be admissible, evidence must be **relevant** to the issues in the lawsuit. See FRE 402. FRE 401 provides that evidence is relevant if "it has any tendency to make a fact more or less probable than it would be without the evidence and the fact is of consequence in determining the action." There are two parts to this definition. Evidence must tend to prove something. And what it tends to prove must bear on the issues to be decided in the lawsuit. Evidence may be true, interesting, even shocking, but that doesn't mean it is relevant to the issues to be decided.

HYPOTHETICAL 7-1

Assume that you are assisting with a civil lawsuit involving an alleged trespass to land. The defendant is alleged to have poured a concrete driveway that lies, in part, on the property of his neighbor, the plaintiff. Assume that in your jurisdiction this is a type of strict liability tort. That is, it doesn't matter whether the defendant knew that he was pouring concrete over the property line, only whether he in fact did so without the consent of the plaintiff.

With the issue framed like that, which of the following facts do you think would be deemed relevant under FRE 401 and 402 and why?

1. That the defendant was born with two heads and had one removed?
2. That at the defendant's last residence he poured a concrete driveway that encroached on his neighbor's property?
3. That while the defendant was having the driveway poured the plaintiff watched but said nothing?
4. That defendant poured the concrete at night?
5. That defendant had a survey of the property line done before he poured the concrete?
6. That defendant is a member of a fringe religious group that worships concrete and believes that all the earth should be placed under at least three inches of concrete? (You guessed it, he's a real estate developer!)
7. That defendant had previously planted a hedge along the property line that encroached on the plaintiff's property and the plaintiff had cut it down?
8. That plaintiff does not actually own the property encroached upon but rents it from the owner, the defendant?
9. That plaintiff wrote his initials and the date in the concrete after it was poured?
10. That the morning after the concrete appeared, the defendant and plaintiff were leaving their houses at the same time and the defendant pointed at the concrete and said, "Well, who did that?"

Now assume that this is not a strict liability tort and that in order to recover the plaintiff must show that the defendant intentionally encroached on the property line. How does that change your decision regarding the relevance of the facts listed above?

Under FRE 403, even relevant evidence may be excluded if "its **probative value** is substantially outweighed" by a danger of unfair prejudice, confusion of the issues, misleading the jury, or by considerations of undue delay, waste of time, or needless presentation or cumulative evidence. The most common objection made to relevant evidence under FRE 403 is that the evidence, while relevant, is unfairly prejudicial.

EXAMPLE

Assume a man is being prosecuted for robbing a bank. The defendant denies having done so. To prove that defendant robbed the bank on the occasion alleged, the prosecution offers evidence that defendant has been convicted of bank robbery on three other occasions. Think how relevant that is, how probative. If he has been convicted of bank robbery three other times, that drastically increases the likelihood he did it again on this occasion. But that's just the problem with this evidence; it is likely too probative, unfairly so, and the judge will likely sustain an objection to it on that basis under 403. Why? Because the jury is likely to focus on the three prior convictions rather than the specific facts of this alleged robbery in deciding guilt. We want juries to focus on the facts of a given case to decide guilt or innocence.

Can you think of other examples where the 403 criteria might be asserted to block the admissibility of otherwise relevant evidence?

B. Lay Witnesses

All witnesses must be competent to testify (FRE 601). The non-expert witness, called a **lay witness** (as distinguished from the **expert witness**), must generally limit his testimony to matters of which he has **personal knowledge** (FRE 602). However, even the lay witness can offer an opinion based on rational perception if it is within the range of common experience and not dependent on scientific or technical expertise (FRE 701).

EXAMPLE

A lay witness might be able to testify that a reddish substance looked to her like blood. Or that the car appeared to be speeding. Or that the noise sounded like a gunshot. Or that someone's breath smelled of alcohol. Most of us have life experience perceiving such things and can form rational opinions based on those perceptions without the need for expertise.

C. Expert Witnesses

Witnesses qualified as **experts** (one qualified "by knowledge, skill, experience, training or education") can testify by opinion in the field of their expertise (FRE 702). It is up to the judge, not the jury, to decide if a witness is in fact qualified to testify as an expert. FRE 104(a). In two significant cases regarding the role of the trial judge in determining the admissibility of expert testimony, the U.S. Supreme Court described the role of the trial judge as that of a *gatekeeper* and gave the trial judge broad discretion to allow or disallow expert testimony by testing its relevance and reliability based on a number of factors. See *Kumho Tire Co. v. Carmichael*, 526 U.S. 137 (1999), and *Daubert v. Merrell Dow Pharmaceuticals, Inc.*, 509 U.S. 579 (1993). (See LBD 7-2.) Today it is routine for trial judges, exercising their gatekeeper status, to conduct pretrial hearings on the qualifications of experts or on the sufficiency of the opinions such experts intend to testify to at trial. Such a hearing is referred to by practitioners as a ***Daubert* hearing**.

Expert testimony is commonly used in all kinds of litigation today and it is critical for the legal professional to know how to locate, interview, do background checks on, communicate with, and otherwise work effectively with expert witnesses. We will consider this in detail in Chapter 15.

Under FRE 702, expert testimony may be used anytime such knowledge "will help the trier of fact to understand the evidence or to determine a fact in issue."

What kind of experts do you think might be called to testify in the suit between Teed Off and Snap Hook described in Hypotheticals 6-1 through 6-5? In the suit between the parties in Hypothetical 7-1?

Experts may even testify to the **ultimate** (i.e., determinative) **issue** in the case (FRE 704) except that they cannot testify as to the state of mind of a criminal defendant where that state of mind is an element of the crime alleged or a defense raised.

EXAMPLE

> In a case in which the plaintiff is alleging that the defendant was negligent for failing to stop his car in time to avoid rear-ending the plaintiff's car, the plaintiff may call an accident reconstruction expert to testify. The following question may be permissible even though it goes to the ultimate question that the jury has to decide as fact finders: "Professor Brown, do you have an opinion as to whether defendant Smith was negligent in failing to brake sooner?"

Under FRE 703, experts may base their opinions and inferences on facts or data made known to them at trial or before trial (which could include hearsay) and even on facts or data not admissible in court if they are of a type reasonably relied on by the expert in forming opinions on the subject.

The state evidentiary rules regarding expert witnesses may differ significantly from the federal rules and special care should be taken by the legal professional to note any differences. (See LBD 7-1.)

D. Examination of Witnesses

Both lay and expert witnesses testify by answering questions put to them by the attorneys (or by the judge). Questioning of a witness by the attorney who called the witness to testify is called **direct examination**. Following direct examination, every witness called to testify is subject to **cross-examination** by counsel for all other parties (FRE 614(a)). Generally, **leading questions** (questions that contain the answer and that call for a yes or no in response; see Chapter 10) cannot be asked of a witness on direct examination but only on cross-examination (FRE 611(c)).

The scope of cross-examination is limited to matters raised in the direct examination and to credibility of the witness (FRE 611(b)) (see discussion of credibility below). At the request of any party, witnesses who are not parties themselves or the designated representative of a business entity party (a corporation, partnership, etc.) will be **sequestered** (excluded from the courtroom) during the testimony of other witnesses (FRE 615).

<h1>E.   The Rule Against Hearsay</h1>

1. Hearsay defined

Hearsay is defined by FRE 801(c) as "a statement that the declarant [the one making the statement] does not make while testifying at the current trial or hearing [i.e., an out-of-court statement] and a party offers in evidence to prove the truth of the matter asserted in the statement."

Hearsay statements are not admissible in evidence. FRE 803. To determine whether offered testimony might run afoul of the hearsay rule, you must ask:

a. Is it a statement?

FRE 801(a) defines a statement for hearsay purposes as an oral or written assertion or conduct by a declarant that is intended as an assertion. Not every sound a person makes would be a statement for hearsay purposes if repeated in court because it may not be intended as a statement or assertion of anything. For example, testimony that a person was heard humming to themselves or was seen doodling cartoon faces on a sheet of paper would probably not be hearsay. Gestures or bodily motions can be statements too. For example, the head shake or nod, the thumbs-up sign, or rolling the eyes. But, again, such conduct must be intended as an assertion. Someone absentmindedly biting his or her nails is not likely to be an assertion while someone biting his or her nails in order to signal another person likely is.

Per FRE 801(b) a "declarant" who makes a statement must be a person. So statements made by machines (e.g. an alarm clock, honking horn, or speedometer reading) or by animals (e.g. barking dog or crowing rooster) are not subject to a hearsay objection because the one making such statements is not a declarant.

b. Is it a statement made out of court?

Note that a witness may be asked in court to repeat a statement that she made herself out of court. That will trigger the hearsay rule just as if the witness was asked to repeat in court a statement made by someone else.

HYPOTHETICAL 7-2

Assume that you are assisting at the trial of a civil fraud case. Your client is the plaintiff, Gulli Bull, who is alleging that the defendant, Smooth Talker, a used car salesman, sold him a car showing only 120,000 miles on the speedometer but that actually had more than 300,000 miles on it. Gulli Bull alleges that Smooth Talker knew that the mileage shown was incorrect but failed to disclose this information to him. Gulli Bull is suing for rescission of the contract to get his money back, for emotional distress, and for punitive damages.

You learned during your investigation that while Smooth Talker was trying to sell the car to Gulli Bull, another salesman, Honest John, whispered to Smooth Talker, boss, "that car has at least 300,000 miles on it." According to Honest John, Smooth Talker just shrugged when he told him that and said nothing to Gulli Bull about the mileage.

Now, at trial, the attorney trying the case for Gulli Bull, the plaintiff, has called Honest John to testify. The attorney asks Honest John to tell the judge what he said to Smooth Talker that day. The attorney for Smooth Talker objects to the question on the basis of hearsay.

1. Is what Honest John is being asked to say a statement or declaration within the meaning of FRE 801(a)?
2. Is what Honest John is being asked to say a statement made out of court? Does it matter that Honest John is being asked to repeat in court his own statement made out of court to Smooth Talker?
3. Assume the trial judge finds that what Honest John is being asked to say is a statement within FRE 801(a) and that it is an out-of-court statement. She then asks the attorney for Gulli Bull for what purpose he is asking Honest John this question. If the attorney says he is asking Honest John this question to prove that there were actually more than 300,000 miles on the car, how should the trial judge rule on the objection and why? If the attorney says he is asking Honest John this question only to prove that Smooth Talker had actual notice prior to the sale that the car had more than 120,000 miles on it, how should the trial judge rule on the objection and why?
4. If the attorney for Gulli Bull responds to the judge's question by saying that he is asking the question only to show that Smooth Talker had actual notice prior to the sale that the car had more than 120,000 miles on it, is that fact relevant to this lawsuit?

Assume the trial judge allows Honest John to answer the question about what he said to Smooth Talker concerning the mileage on the car. The attorney for Gulli Bull then asks Honest John how Smooth Talker responded to his statement. Before Honest John can answer that Smooth Talker just shrugged, the attorney for Smooth Talker again objects saying that this question also asks for a hearsay response.

1. Was the shrug of Smooth Talker conduct intended as an assertion under FRE 801(a)?
2. If so, what was Smooth Talker arguably asserting by his shrug?
3. If so, was the shrug of Smooth Talker an out-of-court assertion?
4. Assuming the trial judge finds that the shrug of Smooth Talker was intended as an assertion, what purpose could your supervising attorney have in asking that question other than to prove that assertion?
5. How do you think the trial judge should rule on the hearsay objection to this question to Honest John? (Hint: You may want to review the discussion of FRE 801(d)(2) below before you answer that question too definitely.)

c. Is it a statement offered to prove the truth of the matter asserted?

Frequently, statements are offered in testimony not to prove the truth of what was asserted but for some independent purpose, usually to prove that something was in fact said whether true or not.

FRE 613 presents a good example of this requirement in the context of a witness's **prior inconsistent statement**. Anytime a witness testifies, the individual may be impeached on cross-examination by being confronted by a statement the witness made verbally or in writing before trial that is inconsistent with what the witness is now saying at trial. But that prior inconsistent statement is a classic assertion made by the declarant out of court, so is it subject to a hearsay objection? Well, if the prior inconsistent statement is offered by the cross-examiner for its truth, then, yes, it is subject to a hearsay objection. But if the prior inconsistent statement is not offered for its truth but only to impeach the witness's credibility on the grounds that the person once said something different from what he or she is saying at trial, then the statement can be received in evidence over the hearsay objection; it is not being offered for its truth but for some other relevant reason, to impeach the credibility of the witness. Confusing, isn't it? And because that can be a very confusing distinction to the jury, the judge who decides to allow the prior inconsistent statement in evidence will deliver a FRE 105 **limiting instruction** to the jury that they are not to consider the statement for its truth but only for its impact in their judgment on the credibility of the witness.

EXAMPLE

Assume in a divorce case a witness for the wife testifies that she saw husband strike wife with his fist last New Year's Eve. On cross-examination, the witness is confronted with a letter she wrote to a friend a week later saying that she's never seen husband strike wife. Is the letter with that inconsistent statement admissible over a hearsay objection? Maybe not if it's offered to prove husband had never stricken wife since that is the truth asserted in the statement. But if it's offered not to prove the truth asserted but instead only to attack the witness's credibility because she has been caught saying something different from her present testimony, then it may be received over a hearsay objection pursuant to FRE 613 with a proper limiting instruction to the jury. If you were on that jury, could you make that distinction as instructed by the judge?

HYPOTHETICAL 7-3

Assume that you obtain a written statement from Honest John in which he discloses his conversation with Smooth Talker about the mileage on the car purchased by Gulli Bull. At trial, however, Honest John testifies that he did *not* have that conversation with Smooth Talker.

1. Can the written statement of Honest John be offered in evidence as a prior inconsistent statement in order to prove that the version of events stated in it is true?
2. Can it be offered to prove that the witness previously made a different statement from the one being made at trial and thus is discredited?

Hypothetical 7-3 illustrates an important point about evidentiary rules that should always be borne in mind by the investigating legal professional. Whether or not something is admissible in evidence may depend on the reason for which it is offered and against whom it is offered. Note that if we were talking about the unsworn statement of defendant Smooth Talker in Hypothetical 7-3, it would be admissible over a hearsay objection as an **admission by party opponent** under FRE 801(d)(2) as discussed below.

FRE 612, **writing to refresh a witness's recollection,** presents another example of a statement being used for a non-truthful purpose. Under that rule, if a testifying witness forgets something and cannot recall it from present recollection, the examining attorney can, with court permission, show the witness a writing and allow the witness to read it silently to see if the writing refreshes the recollection of the witness. If the writing shown to the witness refreshes the witness's recollection, the writing is removed from the witness's possession and the witness is allowed to testify from refreshed memory. There is no hearsay problem here because the writing itself is not being offered in evidence or read into the record. Counsel for the opposing party may use and refer to the writing on cross-examination to test the refreshed recollection of the witness—a question going to whether the witness was actually testifying from personal knowledge as required by FRE 602—but not to prove the truth of its contents. Thus there is no hearsay issue.

EXAMPLE

> Assume that prior to trial Honest John gave the attorney for Gulli Bull a written statement in which he described in detail his conversation with Smooth Talker on the day Gulli Bull bought the car, as related in Hypotheticals 7-1 and 7-2. At trial, however, Honest John freezes up and cannot even remember what day the sale occurred. The quick-thinking attorney may show Honest John his statement and ask questions that go like this:
>
> ATTY: Mr. John, let me show you a document and ask you to look at it and then tell us if you recognize the signature at the bottom?
> HJ: Uh, yes, sir. That's my signature.
> ATTY: And tell us whether or not that is a written statement that you made to a paralegal from my office concerning the facts in this case?
> HJ: It is, yes, sir.
> ATTY: And when you gave my paralegal that written statement, were the things you talk about in there fresh on your mind?
> HJ: Yes, sir, I could remember everything then (smiling and blushing), but I wasn't looking at a jury like I am now.
> ATTY: Well, sir, take a moment more and tell us if (laughing slightly) that statement you are holding refreshes your recollection of those events described.
> HJ: Yes, it does, sir. It certainly does.
> ATTY: Well, let me have the statement back then and let's proceed with our questions.

In addition to prior inconsistent statements offered to impeach a witness's credibility (and writings used to refresh the recollection of a forgetful witness though the writings themselves are not admissible), there are a number of other times when statements can be offered in evidence for a reason other than to prove their truth:

- A statement offered to infer the speaker's state of mind (e.g., offering statement of an elderly person, "I am a walrus," to infer not that

the speaker is actually a walrus, but that the individual may not be mentally competent)
- A statement offered to infer a hearer's state of mind (e.g., Peggy says she told John, "The guards at the bank don't have bullets in their guns," offered to infer not that the guards don't have bullets, but that John may have believed that and decided to rob the bank the next day)
- A statement offered to explain why a person acted as he or she did (e.g., police officer testifies that he heard dispatcher say, "The suspect has entered the residence at 211 Maple, armed and dangerous," not to prove that the suspect was armed and dangerous, but to explain why he, the police officer, drew his weapon before entering that residence.)
- A statement offered to demonstrate a person's capacity or lack thereof (e.g., Tomas testifies he heard Carlos say, "I like tomatoes," to prove not that Carlos likes tomatoes but that Carlos can speak English.)
- A statement to provide context and meaning for the finder of fact (e.g., a witness is prepared to testify that the defendant admitted committing the crime while they were fishing. He will probably be allowed to repeat the conversation they had the night before about going fishing merely to set up the context of the admission for the jury.)
- A statement that has **independent legal significance** (also called a **verbal act**) (e.g., on the issue of whether Jane made an agreement with Janet to sell her a car, witness will be allowed to testify she heard Jane offer to sell the car to Janet and heard Janet say, "I accept." The words, regardless of their truth, are verbal acts of offer and acceptance.)

Of course, for statements to be admissible for these reasons over a hearsay objection, the non-truthful purpose for which they are offered must be relevant to the lawsuit. And if the trial judge allows the statement to be used over a hearsay objection, a limiting instruction will be given to the jury to consider the statement only for the permissible, non-truthful reason.

d. Is there a recognized exemption or exception for the statement?

Over the years, because of the harsh results of the strict application of the hearsay rule, the courts have developed numerous exemptions and exceptions to it. When it is determined that testimony to be offered is or might be considered inadmissible hearsay, the next step is to look at the exemptions or exceptions to find one or more that may apply to allow the statement to be received in evidence over a hearsay objection.

Exemptions to the hearsay rule are collected in FRE 801(d) and identified simply as statements that are declared to be not hearsay. The numerous **exceptions to the hearsay rule** are set out in FRE 803 and 804. The difference between those two rules is that the exceptions recognized under FRE 803 apply without regard to whether the declarant (the person whose statement is being repeated in court) is available as a witness at trial. But the exceptions under FRE 804 apply only when the declarant is not available as a witness at trial.

Illustration 7-1 summarizes the hearsay rule and its primary exemptions and exceptions.

2. Admission by party opponent exemption

Under FRE 801(d)(2), any statement made by or on behalf of a party to the suit, or which has been adopted by the party as true, is admissible if offered against that party. Such statements are declared to be *not hearsay*.

This exemption allows in substantial amounts of evidence that would otherwise be inadmissible as hearsay. It allows in evidence all statements made by a party or the party's authorized representatives so long as the statements are offered by an opposing party, are relevant to an issue in the suit, and are not privileged.

HYPOTHETICAL 7-4

Remember Smooth Talker's shrug after Honest John told him the car had at least 300,000 miles on it, in Hypothetical 7-2? That shrug was quite likely an out-of-court, declarative statement, and testimony of it was probably offered to prove what it communicated to Honest John—Smooth Talker was in effect saying, "I don't care if the car has more than 300,000 miles on it." Classic hearsay. But is it admissible as non-hearsay under FRE 801(d)(2) if offered as evidence by Gulli Bull? Why would testimony of the shrug be inadmissible hearsay if offered by Smooth Talker?

Many states treat the party opponent statement as an exception, not an exemption, as the federal rules do. The effect is the same—the statement is received in evidence for its truth over a hearsay objection.

3. Prior inconsistent statement made under oath exemption.

Recall the last example using FRE 613 and a witness's prior inconsistent statement received in evidence not for its truth but to impeach the credibility of the witness. Now consider if the prior inconsistent statement of that witness had been made under oath subject to penalties of perjury at a prior trial or hearing or in a deposition. FRE 801(d)(1)(A) makes such prior inconsistent statements made under oath admissible not just to impeach, but for the truth of what the statement asserts. Thus in that last example, if our witness had said under oath in a deposition that she had never seen the husband strike the wife, that statement could be received in evidence at trial over a hearsay objection not only to impeach the credibility of the witness, but also to establish the truth of what it asserts.

This is one reason lawyers like to take pretrial depositions of witnesses to lock them into a version of their story. If witnesses deviate at trial from that deposition testimony, they can be impeached with the prior inconsistent statement, and if it was given under oath in a deposition, the inconsistent statement can also be received for its truth.

4. Prior consistent statement offered to rebut charge of recent fabrication exemption

Under 801(d)(1)(B), prior statements of a witness that are consistent with witness's trial testimony are declared not hearsay and may be admissible for its truth, but only if offered to rebut a prior inconsistent statement offered to impeach the witness or to rebut any other allegation that the witness has recently fabricated testimony, has an improper motive for testifying as he or she has, or has been improperly influenced to testify as he or she has.

5. Prior statement identifying a person perceived earlier exemption

FRE 801(d)(1)(C) declares non-hearsay statements made before trial that involved the identification of a person after perceiving that person.

EXAMPLE

Assume a defendant is charged with carjacking. The victim is called to testify at trial and identifies the defendant as the man who forced her out of her car and drove it away. But what if she had previously identified the defendant in a police lineup? Can she or a policeman who was present at the lineup testify that she pointed to defendant at the lineup (an assertive act) and said, "That's the man who stopped me and stole my car"? Under this rule, the victim or anyone who heard her say that at the lineup can so testify over a hearsay objection. The same would be true about an identification made at the scene of the crime or an identification from a photo array.

6. FRE 803 exceptions to the hearsay rule— availability of declarant immaterial

The most commonly used FRE 803 exceptions to the hearsay rule are discussed next.

a. Present sense impression (FRE 803(1))

Historically, the law has trusted the veracity of a statement explaining or describing an event or condition if the statement is made at the time the declarant is experiencing the event or condition or immediately after it. This trust is reflected in this old and venerable exception to the hearsay rule.

EXAMPLE

I smell smoke.
I'm not feeling so well.
This is exciting.
I'm sure having fun.
I really love this class.

But the statement must be essentially contemporaneous with or just immediately after the event experienced. If there is a delay sufficient to allow the declarant time to reflect and calculate what he or she wants to say, this exception will not apply.

b. Excited utterance (FRE 803(2))

Similarly, the law has historically trusted a statement made about a startling event or condition, but only if the statement is made while the declarant is still under the influence of the excitement.

EXAMPLE

Oh, _____, he just ran that light.
You scared me to death!
I think he might be dead!
I just can't get enough of this evidence stuff!

A commonly contested issue when a statement is offered under the **excited utterance** exception is how long would a person reasonably be under the influence of the startling event.

EXAMPLE

Assume you are eating in a restaurant and someone nearby drops a glass shattering it. Startling, yes, but if you quickly realize what happened, for how long are you likely to be excited about that? Compare that to being involved in a bad car accident. Do you think the lingering effect of the excitement from that will likely last longer than the excitement from the broken glass?

c. Current state of mind or condition (FRE 803(3))

In another venerable exception, the law trusts a statement of the declarant's then-existing mental, emotional, or physical condition. This includes the speaker's state of mind, motive, intent or plan as well as the speaker's mental or physical condition. The key to this exception is that the statement offered in evidence must be 1) the statement of the declarant's own state of mind or condition, not someone else's (e.g., "Maggie is angry" won't work here) and 2) it must be the declarant's then-existing (at the time the statement is made) state of mind. Thus, "I'm angry" will work because it describes the declarant's present state of mind, but "I was really angry at him for a long time," won't because it describes the declarant's past but not present state of mind. Here are some examples of statements that will fall within this exception.

EXAMPLE

I think I might just drive all night so I can be in Miami by daybreak.
I've decided to quit my job.
I want a divorce.
I love you.

> *I don't feel well.*
> *I'm worried that Tom will try to kill me.*
> *"I'm going to rob that bank someday."*

Do not confuse this exception to the hearsay rule with what we observed earlier about a statement being received in evidence not for its truth, but in order to infer the speaker's state of mind (e.g., the elderly person who is quoted as saying, "I am a walrus," to infer mental incompetence or a man asking, "What's for dinner" to infer that his condition at that moment was one of feeling hungry). The difference is that the 803(3) exception allows in evidence statements that involve the speaker expressing what is his then existing state of mind or condition ("I'm hungry" or "I'm mentally incompetent"). The not-for-its truth statement from which we are allowed to infer the speaker's state of mind ("What's for dinner" or "I'm a walrus") is one that does not express the speaker's then existing state of mind or condition itself. If you find that distinction difficult to grasp, welcome to the club. It takes a while to sink in.

d. Statements made for purposes of medical diagnosis or treatment (FRE 803(4))

In any case where medical diagnosis or treatment is relevant to the issues, as it would be in a personal injury suit, statements made by the patient or by third persons, to obtain a diagnosis or treatment for the patient, will be admissible over a hearsay objection.

HYPOTHETICAL 7-5

> Assume that as part of his claim of emotional distress against Smooth Talker, Gulli Bull testifies that he has been unable to sleep since he learned of the fraud and has had to see a doctor and rely on medication to rest. The doctor's records discovered by the attorney for Smooth Talker show that on the first visit of Gulli Bull to the doctor, Gulli Bull's wife accompanied him and told the nurse that her husband was having trouble sleeping because his business was struggling.
>
> At trial, will the attorney for Smooth Talker be able to have the doctor testify as to this statement by Mrs. Bull under FRE 803(4) notwithstanding a hearsay objection? What if Mrs. Bull had made the statement to a neighbor as she and her husband were leaving the house to go to the doctor's office?

e. Recorded recollection (FRE 803(5))

What happens if a witness forgets something that happened in the past? If there is some written record (a letter, diary entry, memorandum, computer file, or e-mail message, etc.) of the event, it may be possible to read it into evidence over a hearsay objection under this rule. A strict foundation must be laid, however, before the writing can be read in lieu of the testimony of the witness. It must be shown:

- that the writing was made or adopted by the forgetful witness;
- that the writing was made or adopted when the matter was fresh on the mind of the witness;

- that the writing reflects the witness's former knowledge of the matter accurately; and
- that the witness once had knowledge of the matter but now has insufficient recollection to testify.

The **recorded recollection** exception of FRE 803(5) should not be confused with the FRE 612 use of a writing to refresh a witness's recollection discussed earlier.

f. Business records (FRE 803(6) and (7))

The **business records exceptions** are very broadly construed by the courts to allow into evidence just about any type of relevant business record over a hearsay objection if the foundation is properly laid. To have documents or a data compilation containing what would otherwise be hearsay admitted in evidence, it must first be shown through the testimony of a custodian of the document or other qualified witness that:

- the document or compilation was created at or near the time of the events or transactions referenced in it;
- the document or compilation was created by a person with knowledge of the events or transactions referenced in it or from information transmitted by such a person;
- the document or compilation was kept in the course of a regularly conducted business activity; and
- it was the regular practice with regard to that business activity to make the document or compilation.

HYPOTHETICAL 7-6

Assume that as part of the pretrial investigation into the claim of Gulli Bull against Smooth Talker you are interviewing Honest John who is now a former employee of Smooth Talker. Honest John tells you about his conversation with Smooth Talker and you ask him how he knew the car had more than 300,000 miles on it. He responds that he had seen it in "the book." You ask him what book and he says:

> Well, there's this book we sorta kept around there where when we took a car in on a trade we wrote down whatever the owner told us about it. And I remember seeing something in there on that car that said, "Mileage reads 120k but closer to 350k." Or something like that.

Recognizing the potential importance of this information and with the business records exception to the hearsay rule in mind, what additional questions will you now ask Honest John during the interview?

g. Public records (FRE 803(8) and (10))

The records maintained by federal, state, local agencies, and departments are admissible over a hearsay objection. The law presumes that public officials charged with maintaining such records will perform their duty properly and that if called as witnesses are unlikely to have personal knowledge of any of the voluminous records they routinely keep. Chapters 16 and 17 will cover in detail the kinds of information available from public records at all levels of government. (See Hypothetical 6-2 in the last chapter for an example of a public record to be offered in evidence.)

7. FRE 804 exceptions to the hearsay rule—applicable where the declarant is unavailable to testify

In this section we will look at the most commonly used FRE 804 exceptions to the hearsay rule. They can be used only where the declarant whose statement is being offered in evidence is unavailable to testify at trial. For purposes of 804 the declarant is considered unavailable if he or she:

- is deceased or too disabled physically or mentally to appear
- is exempt from testifying due to a proper claim of privilege (e.g., asserting the Fifth Amendment privilege against self-incrimination)
- refuses to testify despite being ordered to do so
- testifies that he cannot remember the subject matter of the statement
- is outside the subpoena power of the court or has not been successfully subpoenaed to appear despite the proponent's efforts to do so

a. Former sworn testimony (FRE 804(b)(1))

If the unavailable declarant previously gave sworn testimony at a trial, hearing, or by deposition, FRE 804(b)(1) allows the use of that former testimony so long as the party against whom it is offered was present at the time the former testimony was given and had the opportunity and similar motive to cross-examine the declarant at that time.

HYPOTHETICAL 7-7

If you interview Honest John as in Hypothetical 7-6 but he dies in an accident before trial:

1. Could the attorney for Gulli Bull tender your notes of the interview as testimony under this exception?
2. If Honest John had given you a signed statement following your interview and then dies in an accident, could the attorney tender his statement as testimony at trial?
3. If Honest John was deposed in Gulli Bull's lawsuit against Smooth Talker under FRCP 30 and then dies in an accident, could the attorney tender the deposition transcript at trial?

In contrast, 801(d)(1)(A), treated by the FRE as non-hearsay rather than as an exception to the hearsay rule, makes admissible prior sworn testimony of one who is present and testifying at trial if the prior testimony is inconsistent with the witness's testimony at trial. Also in contrast, 801(d)(1)(B), also treated by the FRE as non-hearsay, allows in evidence prior testimony of a witness who is present and testifying at trial that is consistent with his trial testimony if offered to rebut a prior inconsistent statement of the witness or to rebut any other allegation that the witness recently fabricated their testimony, has an improper motive for testifying as he has, or has been improperly influenced to testify as he has.

b. Statement under belief of imminent death (FRE 804(b)(2))

Sometimes referred to as the **dying declaration**, the **statement made under belief of imminent death** is admissible under FRE 804(b)(2) if the declarant made the statement reasonably believing that death was imminent and the statement concerns the cause or circumstances of the imminently expected death. Under the federal version of the rule, the declarant need not actually die for the statement to be admissible, but must be unavailable at trial for one of the stated reasons. Some state versions of the rule require that the declarant actually have expired following the making of the statement.

c. Statement against interest (FRE 804(b)(3))

A statement made by the unavailable declarant at a time when it was against the declarant's pecuniary (money), proprietary (ownership), or culpability (civil or criminal) interests is admissible pursuant to FRE 804(b)(3).

HYPOTHETICAL 7-8

SLEUTH ON THE LOOSE

Trying to find that someone who ran a stop sign and smashed into your client's car? If you have a name, phone number, or e-mail address, you might be able to track her down at www.theultimates. com. Try using it to find an old friend that you haven't heard from in a while.

Assume that you interview Honest John as in Hypothetical 7-6 and he tells you about his conversation with Smooth Talker regarding the actual mileage on the car purchased by Gulli Bull and about the book, too. To save costs the attorney for Gulli Bull does not bother to depose Honest John before trial. Honest John is subpoenaed to appear and give testimony at trial, but he calls you the day before trial and says he won't repeat at trial what he told you in the interview because he is afraid of Smooth Talker. He will just say he can't remember. The attorney says that if Honest John does that then you will be called as a witness to testify to what Honest John told you in the interview! You say, "Won't that be inadmissible hearsay?" The supervising attorney says, "I think I can get it in under FRE 804(b)(3)."

List the arguments the lawyer for Gulli Bull should make under FRE 804(b)(3) to get your testimony in over a hearsay objection.

What are the ethical considerations in your being called as a witness in this situation?

If Honest John testified at trial and simply denied having the conversation with Smooth Talker that he told you about in the interview and denied the existence of the book, could the attorney for Gulli Bull then have you testify to his interview statements under FRE 804(b)(3)?

A recent amendment to 804(b)(3) allows the admissibility of a statement by an unavailable declarant under this exception that amounts to a confession of a crime only if the statement is corroborated by other proof.

EXAMPLE

> Assume Don is accused of burglary. His attorney calls Don's friend Dan to testify that he, Dan, heard a third person, Doug, who is not available to testify, admit to committing the burglary by himself. Technically, this statement of Doug, offered for its truth through Dan, is a statement against Doug's culpability interest since he is admitting to committing a crime and so would be admissible under 803(4) over a hearsay objection by the prosecution. But the rule now requires the defense to offer corroborating proof that the absent Doug actually said this before it can be admitted. What policy reasons do you think drove this amendment to 804(b)(3)?

d. Statement offered against or by one who caused or procured declarant's unavailability (804(a) and (b)(6))

If a party has wrongfully caused or acquiesced in causing a declarant to be unavailable and did so with the intent that the declarant be unavailable to testify, then any relevant statement of that unavailable declarant can be received in evidence against that party under FRE 804(b)(6).

On the other hand, per new language added recently at the end of FRE 804(a), none of the 804 exceptions can be relied upon by a party seeking to introduce statements made by an unavailable declarant whom that party caused to be unavailable.

EXAMPLE

> Jack and Janice have been living together. Janice knows that Jack is a drug dealer. After Jack and Janice split up, Jack is arrested for a drug offense and Janice is expected to be a prosecution witness against him. Jack has a friend threaten to kill Janice if she testifies against Jack, so Janice disappears and is unavailable to testify at Jack's trial. At trial the prosecution calls Jill, a friend of Janice's, to testify that Janice told her she had seen Jack sell drugs on many occasions. If the defense objects to Jill's testimony on the basis of hearsay, the FRE 804(b)(6) exception may be relied upon by the prosecution to overcome the objection. On the other hand, if Jack's lawyer has deposed Janice before she disappeared and offers certain sworn statements she made in the deposition in evidence under the sworn prior testimony exception of 804(b)(1), the prosecution may be able to block the defense from relying on that exception under the new language of 804(a).

8. The residual exception (FRE 807)

This **residual exception** to the hearsay rule arguably reflects growing dissatisfaction with the antiquated hearsay rule and the increased willingness to give trial judges the discretion to admit testimony that, though technically hearsay, appears trustworthy and should, in all fairness, be considered. This exception allows in evidence hearsay statements that do not fit into any of the recognized exceptions but which the trial judge finds 1) is offered as evidence of a material fact in the case; 2) is more probative on the point offered than other evidence the proponent can reasonably offer; and 3) the interests of justice will be best served by admitting the statement. (See LBD 7-4.)

Illustration 7-1   THE HEARSAY RULE: ITS PRIMARY EXEMPTIONS AND EXCEPTIONS UNDER THE FRE

THE RULE: Hearsay is a statement, other than one made by the declarant while testifying at trial, offered in evidence to prove the truth of the matter asserted. Hearsay evidence is inadmissible at trial.

THE EXEMPTIONS:

1. Admission by party opponent or his agent

2. Prior inconsistent statement made in prior testimony

3. Prior consistent statement offered to rebut charge of recent fabrication

4. Prior statement identifying a person after perceiving him or her

THE EXCEPTIONS:

1. Availability of declarant immaterial
    a. Present sense impression
    b. Excited utterance
    c. Current state of mind or condition
    d. Statement made for purpose of medical diagnosis or treatment
    e. Recorded recollection
    f. Business records
    g. Public records

2. Where the declarant is unavailable.
    a. Former sworn testimony
    b. Statement made under belief of imminent death
    c. Statement against interest
    d. Statement offered against or by one who has procured the absence of the declarant

---

Illustration 7-1 summarizes the hearsay rule and its exceptions and exclusions.

9. Character evidence

Under FRE 404(a)(1), **evidence of a person's character** (truthful or untruthful, reliable or unreliable, honest or dishonest, peaceful or violent, etc.) or evidence of crimes, wrongs, or acts of a person that illustrate his character, is generally not admissible for the purpose of proving that the person acted in conformity with that character trait on a particular occasion. Note that such evidence could arguably be quite relevant. And, in contrast, under FRE 406, evidence of a person's habit or routine practice is generally admissible in evidence to prove that the person acted in conformity with it on a particular occasion.

EXAMPLE

Where a man is charged with a violent assault on another it would be highly probative for the jury to hear that he has had a violent nature since childhood or that he has been previously convicted of a crime of violence. But unless one of the following exceptions is present, the jury will never hear that proof. On the other hand, if the crime occurred early in the morning and the defense offers proof that the defendant had a habit of sleeping until noon, that might be admissible.

There are a number of exceptions to the general ban on character evidence, which we consider next. Where character evidence is admissible, FRE 405(a) provides that such proof can be made only through an opinion or reputation witness. There can be no testimony regarding specific acts showing character except on cross-examination of the character or reputation witness. This important procedural point will be illustrated as we consider the exceptions to the general ban on character evidence.

a. The criminal accused

A criminal accused may put a pertinent trait of his own character in evidence, i.e., he may **open the door** to his character. This is called the "**mercy rule**." Once a criminal accused puts a pertinent trait of his character in evidence using the mercy rule, the prosecution may then offer character evidence to rebut it. See FRE 404(a)(2)(A).

EXAMPLE

> If Charlie is being tried for aggravated assault, he may call witnesses to testify that he is not a violent person. The prosecution may then call rebuttal witnesses to testify that the Charlie is in fact a violent person. The prosecution would not be allowed to do that if the defendant had not opened the door first by calling his character witnesses.

In cases not involving alleged sexual offenses, a criminal defendant may offer evidence of a pertinent trait of a victim's character per FRE 404(a)(2)(B) in which case the prosecution can 1) rebut that proof with its own proof of the victim's character and 2) offer evidence that the defendant has that same character trait even though the defendant has not put his own character at issue.

EXAMPLE

> If the victim of the assault with which Charlie in our last example has been charged is Bill, and Charlie's defense is that Bill assaulted him first and he was only defending himself, Charlie may open the door to Bill the victim's character by calling opinion or reputation witnesses to opine that Bill is a violent person. Once Charlie the defendant opens that door, the prosecution can not only call rebuttal witnesses to rehabilitate the character of Bill the victim as a peaceful person, they can now call witnesses to show that it is in fact Charlie who has the violent character.

FRE 412, sometimes referred to as the **rape shield law**, severely limits a criminal defendant's ability to attack the victim's character in a sexual offense case. The rule bars defendant from offering evidence of the victim's sexual history or sexual disposition unless the evidence demonstrates by specific instance that someone other than the defendant committed the offense or unless it is evidence of the victim's sexual history with the defendant and offered to show consent.

EXAMPLE

Assume Mark is being prosecuted for the alleged rape of Lucy. Mark admits sleeping with Lucy but says she consented. Mark will not be allowed to use 404(a)(2)(B) to offer witnesses giving the opinion or saying that Lucy has a reputation of sleeping around to suggest that she consented to sleeping with him. However, if he has specific evidence that she slept with him consensually on occasions preceding the alleged rape, he can prove those. Or if Lucy was physically injured the night he slept with her, he can offer specific evidence, if he has it, that she slept with someone else later that night and that second partner is the source of the injuries.

Per FRE 404(a)(2)(C), in a homicide case where the defendant claims self-defense, the prosecution can initiate proof that the deceased victim had a peaceful, non-violent character even though the defendant has not called witnesses to directly attack the character of the victim as having been violent.

FRE 405(a) requires that witnesses called by the defense or prosecution to prove character as allowed in any of the FRE 404(a)(2) circumstances must be opinion or reputation witnesses only (FRE 412 proof is not so limited). That means that on direct examination those witnesses can only testify to their opinion of the character trait of the defendant or victim or to the reputation of the defendant or victim for having that character trait. They cannot, on direct examination, relate specific acts by the person about whom they are opining showing the character trait testified to; they cannot give examples to illustrate the opinion or reputation testified to. However, on cross-examination, the cross-examiner can inquire into specific acts to test the opinion given or the reputation testified to.

EXAMPLE

Charlie is charged with a violent assault. He denies the charge. He opens the door to his character for violence by calling his friend Charlene who says that she has known Charlie for ten years and that in her opinion he is not a violent person. Defense counsel who called Charlene cannot ask her to give examples of specific acts of non-violence that support this opinion. However, on cross-examination the prosecutor can ask Charlene about specific acts of violence to test the opinion she has given. For example, the prosecutor might ask, "When you formed the opinion that he's not a violent person were you aware that he instigated a bar fight two years ago in which five people were sent to the hospital?"

FRE 413-415 allow the prosecution in a criminal case or plaintiff in a civil case involving sexual assault or child molestation to prove that the accused committed a similar act in the past whether or not it resulted in conviction or civil judgment.

b. Where character is an essential element of a claim or defense

Per FRE 405(b), character evidence is admissible when the character trait is an essential element of the claim or defense in the lawsuit.

EXAMPLE

If plaintiff sues defendant for libel because defendant said plaintiff was a dishonest person, evidence of the character of plaintiff for honesty or dishonesty is admissible by either party to prove that he is, or isn't, a dishonest person. After all, that is the essential issue raised in the lawsuit. In a custody dispute where one parent accuses the other of being an unfit parent, fitness and all that means to one's character is the issue to be decided so the door is open to all such proof.

And note that when character proof is offered for this reason, it need not be limited on direct examination to opinion and reputation; specific acts showing character are freely admissible here both on direct and cross.

c. Other crimes, wrongs, or acts

For limited purposes, evidence of other crimes, wrongs, or acts of a person may be admissible, not to show that the person acted in conformity with them on a particular occasion (character), but for other relevant purposes, such as to show motive, opportunity, intent, plan, capacity, knowledge, absence of mistake, etc. See FRE 404(b).

HYPOTHETICAL 7-9

Assume that Smooth Talker is arrested for breaking into the offices of the attorney for Gulli Bull the night before the civil trial is to begin and stealing the book containing the notation of Honest John regarding the true mileage on the car purchased by Gulli Bull. At the criminal trial, the prosecution wishes to present evidence of the civil fraud claim of Gulli Bull against Smooth Talker in order to prove that Smooth Talker is a dishonest person who again acted dishonestly when he broke into the attorney's office.

1. Under FRE 404(a), can the prosecution offer this evidence for this purpose?
2. Could this same evidence be admissible if offered under FRE 404(b) to show, not character, but motive for the break-in?

FRE 404(b) character-suggesting evidence offered for a relevant reason other than to prove character is most commonly offered by the prosecution in criminal cases. And such proof may be made by specific act on direct examination; no need to limit it to opinion or reputation.

EXAMPLE

Assume a defendant is prosecuted for money counterfeiting. The prosecution might be allowed to prove under 404(b) that he previously worked for a counterfeiting gang or that he spent two years in a jail cell with a convicted counterfeiter in order to show how he gained the knowledge or capacity to commit the crime he is now charged with. Assume a defendant is charged with robbing a bank and fleeing in a green Ford Mustang. The prosecution may be allowed to prove under 404(b) that the defendant stole the Mustang the day before the robbery he is charged with as part of the plan or scheme to accomplish the robbery. All these bad acts suggest something negative about the character of the defendants but will be received in evidence not to prove character but the other relevant matter—knowledge, capacity, plan, scheme, etc.

d. A witness's character for truthfulness

Under FRE 608(a), the credibility of any witness may be attacked (or supported after attack) by evidence in the form of an opinion or known reputation as to the witness's character for truthfulness or untruthfulness. Specific instances of conduct offered to attack or support the witness's character may not be proved by **extrinsic evidence** (testimony of witnesses or exhibits other than the witness being attacked or supported) but the witness himself may be asked about them per FRE 608(b). And as always, those opinion and reputation witnesses can be confronted with specific acts on cross-examination.

HYPOTHETICAL 7-10

Assume that Gulli Bull wins his civil fraud suit against Smooth Talker and is awarded rescission of the contract, return of the purchase price of the car plus interest, and $100,000 in punitive damages. Five years later Honest John is arrested and charged with forging the signature of another in order to cash a check and keep the proceeds. At the criminal trial of Honest John on the forgery charge, his defense attorney calls Smooth Talker as a witness for Honest John.

1. On cross-examination of Smooth Talker, can the prosecution ask him specific questions about the judgment taken against him in the civil fraud matter five years before?
2. If, after Smooth Talker testifies, can the prosecution call Gulli Bull as a witness to talk about the judgment he obtained against Smooth Talker five years before? What if Smooth Talker denied any knowledge of the civil fraud judgment on cross-examination?
3. After Smooth Talker testifies, can the prosecution call Gulli Bull as a witness to testify to Smooth Talker's reputation for honesty?
4. After Smooth Talker testifies, can the prosecution call Gulli Bull as a witness to testify to Honest John's reputation for honesty?

e. Character for truthfulness of a witness as evidenced by conviction of a felony or other crime involving dishonesty

Under FRE 609, the character for truthfulness of a witness may be attacked by showing that he was *convicted* (not just accused or arrested or tried unsuccessfully) of a felony or any crime involving dishonesty or false statement (e.g. embezzlement or cheating on taxes). However, if it has been more than ten years since the conviction or since the release of the witness from punishment imposed for the crime (whichever is later), such evidence is generally not admissible. See FRE 609(b). A pardon or annulment of the conviction may render it unusable (see FRE 609(c)), and a juvenile conviction is generally unusable. See FRE 609(d). (See Hypothetical 6-3.)

10. Impeaching a witness by showing bias or interest

The credibility of a witness may always be attacked under FRE 607. We call this **impeaching a witness.** And, under the federal rules, a witness can even be impeached by the attorney who called that witness to testify. Some state evidentiary rules follow the **voucher rule** whereby the party calling a witness is deemed to vouch for his credibility and may not impeach him unless he is affiliated with the opposing party or provides testimony hostile to the party that called him (see LBD 7-8).

In contrast to the limited right to impeach a witness by showing character for truthfulness or untruthfulness under FRE 608 or by prior conviction of certain crimes under FRE 609, a witness may *always* be impeached by showing **bias**. Bias constitutes any reason the witness might have to favor or disfavor one side or another in the dispute.

EXAMPLE

> The witness is a relative or friend of the one for whom he testifies; or the witness bears a grudge against the party against whom he testifies.

A witness can also be impeached by showing **interest.** Interest is any self-serving reason the witness might have to not be objective in her testimony.

EXAMPLE

> An employee testifies favorably for her employer—is she just trying to keep her superiors happy? A man testifies unfavorably against the former husband of his girlfriend—is he just trying to eliminate a potential rival?

In criminal proceedings the prosecution frequently allows one criminal to receive immunity from prosecution, plead to a lesser offense, or receive a reduced sentence in exchange for testifying for the prosecution against another criminal defendant. Counsel for the criminal defendant against whom such a witness testifies can always put the "deal" received by the witness in evidence, cross examine the witness on the terms of the deal, and use it to suggest that the witness has a self-serving motive to testify however the prosecution wishes. Most experienced criminal defense attorneys will tell you that they relish cross examining such government witnesses because of the ease of suggesting interest and because juries tend to be highly skeptical of the veracity of such witnesses.

Bias and interest can arise from innumerable relationships and factual contexts. Together, they can present a rich and important area for investigation by the assisting legal professional. Bias and interest can be shown by specific act or example on direct examination and are not limited to opinion or reputation proof by FRE 405(a). Nothing can be more important to the outcome of a lawsuit than to be able to discredit the critical witnesses of the other side by showing bias or interest.

HYPOTHETICAL 7-11

Assume that you are assisting the attorney defending Smooth Talker in the civil fraud case brought against him by Gulli Bull. The attorney learns of the devastating testimony that Honest John is going to give against Smooth Talker at trial and asks you to review the discovery done to date and to investigate Honest John to see if something can be found to discredit him. In the course of your investigation you come up with the facts listed below.

After reviewing the information below: (a) state whether each fact should be categorized as bias or interest or both or neither; (b) state whether you would recommend to the attorney for Smooth Talker that each of these be offered in evidence to impeach Honest John and why or why not; (c) consider how and where you might have located each item of information; and (d) in connection with each fact give thought to additional information you might want to seek to make the impeachment of Honest John more effective.

1. Smooth Talker and Honest John are actually half-brothers, having the same mother. The mother had Smooth Talker first and raised him but gave Honest John up for adoption when he was born two years after Smooth Talker.
2. Honest John twice tried to buy the used car business from Smooth Talker but did not succeed.
3. Honest John has told several people over the past year that he intends to set up his own used car business in town.
4. Smooth Talker is active in the Republican Party. Honest John is a committed Democrat.
5. Last year Smooth Talker was the coach of the little league baseball team on which Honest John's son plays. The boy got very little playing time leading to several chin-to-chin confrontations between coach and father.
6. Several years ago Smooth Talker and Honest John were partners in a kangaroo-meat taco venture that failed badly. Honest John had put up most of the money in the deal. Smooth Talker had contributed only a little cash but a lot of "expertise."
7. Last year Honest John went through a nasty divorce. His wife's attorney called Smooth Talker as a witness to testify to Honest John's compensation from the used car business. Smooth Talker agreed to testify without a subpoena and gave completely candid testimony, which cost Honest John a bundle.
8. Honest John has been Smooth Talker's best salesman for the last five years but has never received a raise or a bonus during that time, while other lower-producing salesmen have.
9. Smooth Talker's wife is divorcing him, though the divorce is not yet final. She and Honest John have been dating.
10. Honest John and Gulli Bull have recently formed a partnership in which they plan to revive the kangaroo-meat taco idea. They are currently trying to raise capital.

11. Authentication of documents and things

Any document or demonstrative item (e.g., photograph, video, diagram, model, map, or computer simulation) or any physical object (e.g., the weapon in a criminal case or the defective machine in a civil product liability case) must be properly **authenticated** before it is received in evidence. That means there must be adequate proof that the document or thing is in fact what the offering party claims it is. See FRE 901(a). Presenting that adequate proof as a condition precedent to the introduction of the item into evidence is called *laying the foundation*, discussed in Chapter 6.

a. Authenticating physical objects

The authentication of objects typically is done by means of one or more testifying witnesses who can establish: (a) that the item is in fact the actual object claimed; and (b) that it is in substantially the same condition now as it was at the time of the incident. This second element is sometimes referred to as the **chain of custody.** To eliminate the possibility that an object has been switched or altered in a way that would mislead the finder of fact, witnesses must show who has had custody of the object and how they took care of it at all times it was in their possession.

Legal professionals will frequently find themselves in custody and control of objects that will be offered as exhibits at trial, and it is critical that they know the importance of preserving and protecting physical evidence (see Chapter 9). Establishing the chain of custody of physical exhibits prior to their admission in evidence is also part of laying the foundation.

b. Authenticating demonstrative evidence

Demonstrative evidence such as pictures, video tapes, diagrams, or computer simulations is typically authenticated by means of one or more testifying witnesses who can establish (a) that the exhibit is a genuine representation of the item pictured or event demonstrated; and (b) that the exhibit is a reasonably accurate depiction of the item shown or event demonstrated.

c. Authenticating documents

Authenticating a document (other than one that is self-authenticating as discussed below) is typically done by means of one or more testifying witnesses who can establish (a) what the document is and (b) who wrote or signed it. This latter matter frequently involves authenticating the signature, handwriting, or other origin of a document. Authenticating a signature or handwriting can involve calling a witness who is familiar with the signature or handwriting of the author of the document. Or it can involve the testimony of an expert who arrives at a professional opinion based on a comparison of patterns or distinctive characteristics of a person's other writings. See FRE 901(2) through (4).

SLEUTH ON THE LOOSE

There are lots of medical diagnosis Web sites on the Internet, but how do you know they are reliable? Try Merck's new Web site at *www.merck.com/ pubs*, where you can access its well-recognized Merck Manual of Diagnosis and Therapy. Pick a disease or medical condition and try it out.

HYPOTHETICAL 7-12

> Assume that in your interview with Honest John as related in Hypothetical 7-6 he told you he was the one who made the entry in the book regarding the actual mileage of the car purchased by Gulli Bull. You are able to locate the book and have possession of it at trial. However, assume that Honest John was never deposed prior to trial and is deceased at the time of trial. List all the ways you can think of that the other attorney might be able to prove that the entry in the book is in the handwriting of Honest John.

FRE 902 simplifies the authentication process for a host of documents by declaring many categories of documents to be **self-authenticating.** Of particular importance are the following:

- Certified copies of public records. FRE 902(4). (See Hypothetical 6-4.)
- Books, pamphlets, and other publications purporting to be published by a public authority. FRE 902(5).
- Newspapers and periodicals. FRE 902(6).
- Acknowledged documents (i.e., sworn to and signed in the presence of a notary public). FRE 902(8).
- Commercial paper (promissory notes, drafts, etc.). FRE 902(9).

d. Authenticating voices

Voices that are identified in testimony must also be authenticated. Typically this is done by the testimony of the speaker himself or, if that is not possible, by another witness who is familiar with the speaker's voice and recognizes it.

EXAMPLE

> The plaintiff wants to offer in evidence a tape recorded threat from the defendant, Mr. Jones, that she found on her answering machine. Jones denies that it is his voice speaking. Plaintiff herself, if she is familiar with the defendant's voice from past dealings with him, may testify that it is the defendant's voice on the tape, but her identification of his voice may be challenged by defense counsel as not credible. What would be the basis of the defense lawyer's challenge to the plaintiff's authentication of defendant's voice? The plaintiff may prefer to call a non-party, disinterested witness who is familiar with defendant's voice to make the authentication. (See FRE 901(5).) Why?

Voice authentication can be difficult when a party or witness wants to testify to a telephone conversation with someone whose voice she has never heard before or since, and no one can be found to authenticate the voice. In those situations, FRE 901(6) raises some presumptions that help authenticate those discussions.

EXAMPLE

> If the witness or party offering the recorded message testifies that she called the number assigned in the phone book to Mr. Jones and spoke with someone who identified himself as Mr. Jones, that will sufficiently authenticate the voice with whom she spoke as that of Mr. Jones.

12. Best evidence rule

The original of a document, photo, or recording should be offered as the actual exhibit if it is available. However, the FRE are liberal in allowing copies to be offered so long as there is no issue regarding fairness or the authenticity of the original. See FRE 1002 and 1003. The best rule to follow is better safe than sorry: if you have the original, offer it as the exhibit unless the opposing side stipulates to the acceptability of a copy.

If neither the original nor a copy is available, verbal testimony of the document's contents is governed by FRE 1004 and will be admissible only if the proponent can show 1) the original has been lost or destroyed and not as a bad faith act by the proponent; 2) the original cannot be obtained by any available judicial process (e.g., subpoena); 3) the original is in the possession of an opposing party; or 4) the document relates to a collateral (not critically important) issue.

13. Generally prohibited matters

There are a number of rules generally barring the admissibility of certain types of evidence with which investigating legal professionals should be familiar. There are **public policy** reasons behind the various rules prohibiting the admissibility of some kinds of evidence—we don't want to discourage these practices so we won't allow evidence of them to be offered at trial.

a. Subsequent remedial measures

Evidence of **subsequent remedial measures** taken after an event that is the subject of the lawsuit and that might have prevented it cannot be shown in evidence to prove liability. FRE 407.

EXAMPLE

> A person falls down a flight of stairs because the handrail was loose and the owner of the stairs fixes the loose handrail the next day. It cannot be shown at trial that the owner had the handrail fixed the day after the accident if that proof is offered to show that the handrail was in fact loose.

Do you see the public policy reasoning at work in this example? If we allow the plaintiff in her suit against the owner of the handrail to offer evidence of his repairing it, he may be less motivated to repair it, and we want him to repair it. Do you agree with that rationale?

Under FRE 407, evidence of the subsequent remedial measure may be offered as evidence if it is offered for a reason other than to prove liability.

EXAMPLE

> If the owner of the stairs denies at trial that he is responsible for them, evidence of his having repaired them may be offered to prove that he does in fact act as if he is responsible for them.

b. Settlement discussions and offers

In almost every civil case there are settlement discussions and even settlement offers made that are not accepted. These negotiations and offers cannot be made known to the finder of fact because we want to encourage settlement negotiations. FRE 408.

c. Paying or offering to pay expenses

Paying or offering to pay expenses related to an injury (such as medical costs) cannot be offered in evidence in order to prove liability. FRE 409. Again, public policy dictates this rule—we don't want to discourage persons from making these offers. Do you agree that such evidence should not be admissible on liability?

d. Plea bargain discussions or a guilty plea later withdrawn

In almost every criminal case there are plea bargain negotiations and offers to plea bargain that are not accepted. And sometimes a criminal defendant will enter a guilty plea then later withdraw it. None of this may be offered as evidence in court in any civil or criminal proceeding involving the defendant. FRE 410.

e. Liability insurance

That a defendant in a civil suit had or did not have liability insurance cannot be shown for the purpose of proving culpability. FRE 411. Remember that under FRCP 26(a)(1)(D), the existence and terms of liability policies must be disclosed in discovery but this does not make them admissible in evidence. Why do you think the federal rules allow the discovery of liability insurance but not its admissibility at trial?

f. Religious beliefs

A witness's religious beliefs or opinions (no matter how wacky or mainstream) cannot be used to impair or enhance the witness's credibility. FRE 610. Of course, they may be shown if otherwise relevant to the case.

EXAMPLE

> In a dispute among church members over who owns the church property, a witness could certainly testify that he was a member of that church. An Orthodox Jew accused of committing a crime on the Sabbath Day could provide testimony as to his observance of the Sabbath as a religious belief to make it less likely he committed the crime. But a lawyer calling a witness could not establish that he is a Baptist deacon merely to enhance the witness's credibility with a religious jury.

F. ▶ Final Considerations Regarding Evidence

1. Admissibility for alternative reasons

As we have seen repeatedly in this review, evidence may be inadmissible for one reason but admissible for another. (Recall the discussions on hearsay, character evidence, prior inconsistent statements, and generally prohibited matters such as subsequent remedial measures.) FRE 105 expressly contemplates this possibility.

Experienced trial lawyers know that there are very few times when a reasonable, good-faith argument cannot be made for the introduction of evidence if it relates in some way to the case. But fashioning those arguments takes a solid knowledge of the rules of evidence and a willingness to plan the arguments for the admissibility (or inadmissibility) before the trial itself. (See LBD 7-3.) Flexible, creative thinking is essential to work in this important area.

2. Clearing all the hurdles

With many types of proof there are several evidentiary hurdles to be cleared before the proof will be received in evidence.

EXAMPLE

> If there is a document the trial lawyer wants to have admitted in evidence, she must be able to show that it is relevant to an issue in the case and she must be prepared to overcome an objection to the document based on hearsay as well. She must also be sure she can properly authenticate the document. And she might have to be concerned about the **best evidence rule** if she doesn't have the original. Failing to successfully clear any one of those hurdles may result in the document not being allowed in evidence.
>
> Conversely, if the other side has a document it wants in evidence and your side would like to keep it out, you may help your supervising attorney plan how best to oppose its admissibility. That may mean planning an attack at each hurdle.

Much of the pretrial preparation in which a trial lawyer and assisting staff engage has to do with evidentiary matters: planning how to get desirable testimony into evidence over anticipated objections and how to successfully object to evidence the other side is expected to offer.

▶ Chapter Summary and Conclusion

To be admissible at trial, evidence must be relevant to an issue in the case in the sense that it tends to make a fact of consequence to the action more or less probable. Generally a witness must testify from personal knowledge. Only experts can give opinions unless the opinion relates to a matter of common knowledge among lay persons. An expert must be shown to be qualified in the field of proffered expertise and the opinions she is to offer based on reliable principles and methods. Witnesses are examined on direct examination without leading questions, but may be examined with them on cross examination. The hearsay rule excludes in court testimony regarding statements made out of court if they are offered in court to prove their truth. There are a number of exceptions to the hearsay rule, two of the most important of which are statements of the party opponent and qualified business records. Generally, evidence of a person's character is not admissible to show that he acted consistent with that character on a relevant occasion, but there are exceptions, as when a criminal defendant puts his character at issue in the case. When character is provable, it is normally proven only by reputation or opinion, and not by specific acts. When a person testifies at trial, she may be impeached by prior inconsistent statements, or by prior conviction of a felony or a misdemeanor involving dishonesty. Evidence of the bias and interest of a witness are always admissible to impeach her credibility. Documents offered in evidence must be properly authenticated, as must other forms of evidence, including objects and voices. Generally the original of a document is preferred over a copy, though the copy may be admissible if the original is unavailable.

The legal professional engaged in interviewing and investigation work needs superior communication skills and the ability to hear and understand what is being communicated to her verbally and non-verbally. We will consider those communication skills in Chapter 8.

Review Questions

1. Under FRE 403, relevant evidence may be "_____ if its _____ value is _____ outweighed by the danger of unfair _____ prejudice, confusion of the _____, or misleading the _____ or due to considerations of undue _____, waste of _____, or needless presentation or _____ evidence."
2. When can a lay witness testify regarding an opinion? Can you think of an example?
3. Experts are witnesses qualified "by knowledge, _____, _____, training or _____."
4. Can experts testify as to the ultimate issue to be decided by a jury?
5. Why do we call the trial judge the "gatekeeper" in connection with expert testimony?
6. When can leading questions be used in examining a witness?
7. Hearsay is defined by FRE 801(c) as a _____, other than the one made by the _____ while _____ at the trial or hearing offered in evidence to prove the _____ of the matter asserted.
8. A hearsay objection will not exclude testimony of the relevant statement of a party _____.
9. What do we mean by a criminal defendant "opening the door" to his own character?
10. Under FRE 609 a witness can always be impeached by showing _____.

KEY WORDS AND PHRASES TO REMEMBER

admission by party opponent
authentication
best evidence rule
bias
business records exception
chain of custody
character evidence
cross-examination
Daubert hearing
direct examination
discretionary exceptions
dying declaration
exceptions to the hearsay rule
excited utterance
expert witness
extrinsic evidence
former testimony exception
habit witness
hearsay
impeaching a witness
independent legal significance
inference
interest
lay witness
leading questions
mercy rule

reputation witness
limiting instruction
opening the door
personal knowledge
present sense impression
prior inconsistent statement
probative value
public policy
public records exception
rape shield law
recorded recollection
relevant evidence
self-authenticating
sequestered
state of mind
statement against interest
statement under belief
  of imminent death
subsequent remedial measure
ultimate issue
verbal act
voucher rule
writing used to refresh recollection

LEARN BY DOING

LBD 7-1. Review FRE 701 through 704 regarding the use of expert testimony. Then research the rules regarding use of expert testimony in state court proceedings in your state. Prepare a memorandum comparing the differences between the federal rules and state rules.

LBD 7-2. Read the cases of *Kumho Tire Co. v. Carmichael*, 526 U.S. 137 (1999), and *Daubert v. Merrell Dow Pharmaceuticals, Inc.*, 509 U.S. 579 (1993). Prepare a memorandum summarizing the procedure and factors to be considered by a trial judge in deciding whether to admit expert testimony. Research the case law in your state or federal circuit since *Daubert* to see how those courts are applying these rulings of the Supreme Court. Include a summary of those findings in your memorandum.

LBD 7-3. Interview an experienced trial attorney who utilizes new associates or paralegals, or an experienced litigation paralegal concerning the importance of the assisting legal professional knowing the rules of evidence to effectively assist the attorney in pretrial investigation, formal discovery, trial preparation, and trial.

LBD 7-4. Research case decisions in your federal circuit or state courts or both regarding the discretionary hearsay exceptions found in FRE 803(24) and 804(b)(5). Prepare a memorandum summarizing your research. Discuss the kinds of evidence the appellate courts have allowed or disallowed under these exceptions. Do the courts seem to favor these exceptions by construing them broadly or disfavor them by construing them narrowly?

LBDs 7-5 through 7-8 are accessible on the Author Updates link to the text Web site at www.aspenparalegaled.com/books/parsons_investigating/default.asp.

Chapter 8

Communication Skills for the Investigator

CHAPTER OUTLINE

A. The Importance of Communication in the Work of Legal Professionals
B. Verbal Communication—More than Words
C. Nonverbal Communication—Body Language
D. Written Communication
E. Putting Communication Skills to Work in Interviewing and Investigating

CHAPTER OBJECTIVES

Communication skills are critical to successful interviewing and investigating. In this chapter you will learn:

- The three ways that all people communicate: verbally, nonverbally, and in writing.
- The role that verbal, nonverbal, and written communications play in the interviewing and investigating work of the attorney and the paralegal.
- How to use active listening skills to recognize the messages and signals others send us by body language.
- Practical guidelines for written communications in the law office.

By permission of Johnny Hart and Creators Syndicate, Inc.

A. ▶ The Importance of Communication in the Work of Legal Professionals

1. How we all communicate

In general, there are three ways in which we all communicate with each other:

a. Written communication

Written communication is communication in which we put our thoughts on paper or screen for electronic communication (e-mail).

b. Verbal communication

Verbal communication is the process of speaking to another either directly or through a mechanical device such as the telephone, dictating machine, tape recorder, video recorder, television, or computer.

c. Nonverbal communication

Nonverbal communication is the impression we convey to others by **body language,** which can include posture, gestures, facial expressions, eye contact, and even our clothes or our environment—the things with which we choose to surround ourselves.

2. The importance of written and verbal communication

Both written and verbal communication involve *words*. It is no exaggeration to say that words are the tools of the lawyer's trade. Like the hammer to the carpenter, like the brush to the painter, so words are to the lawyer. Lawyers are trained professionals not only in the law and in legal reasoning, but in the use of words as well.

Everything the lawyer does involves the spoken or written word. Consider the tasks that an attorney might perform on a typical day. She will engage in telephone or face-to-face conversations with clients, witnesses, office staff, other attorneys, court personnel, and others. If she goes to court, she will speak as an advocate to the court on behalf of her client. She will dictate correspondence of all kinds, draft contracts, and prepare pleadings, motions, or briefs for court filing. She may do legal research, draft memoranda, and spend time in continuing legal education by reading current developments in the law. The thing all these tasks have in common is words. In performing these tasks it is essential for the supervising attorney and the assisting legal professional to:

- appreciate the importance of words to her responsibilities;
- be competent in utilizing both the spoken and written word; and
- be constantly working to improve her verbal and writing skills.

Go to the Web site for the Dialect Survey performed by Dr. Bert Vaux of the University of Wisconsin in Milwaukee found at www4.uwm.edu/FLL/ linguistics/dialect/ maps.html and review the research done on the various dialects used in our country. See if you can figure out why people may look at you strangely if you pronounce "aunt" as "ahnt" anywhere outside New England; or "pajamas" to rhyme with "jam" outside the Upper Midwest; or if you ask for a "soda" in the South.

In verbal communication this means the legal professional must be concerned with **vocabulary, pronunciation, enunciation,** and **grammar.** In written communication this means the legal professional must be concerned with **vocabulary, grammar, spelling, punctuation, sentence** and **paragraph structure,** and **writing style.**

It is beyond the scope of this text to provide detailed instruction in grammar, vocabulary, and spelling. But later in this chapter we will consider some suggestions for effective writing as it relates to the investigating task. And, included in Appendix B, Resources for the Investigator, is a comprehensive list of written and online resources to assist the legal professional in increasing competence in grammar, vocabulary, spelling, and related areas. (See LBD 8-2.)

3. The importance of nonverbal communication

We are all constantly sending important messages to others with our body language. And we are constantly receiving those messages from others. If you are not aware of the nonverbal messages you are sending others and not attuned to the messages being sent by others, you cannot perform interviewing and investigating work effectively.

In this chapter we will consider all three means of communication as they relate to interviewing and investigating.

B. ▶ Verbal Communication—It's More Than the Words

We all know from our common experience of interacting with others that verbal communication consists of more than just the words used. It's not just *what* people say, but *how* they say it. It's not just what they *say*, it's what they *mean*. What makes the Wizard of Id cartoon at the beginning of this chapter humorous is that while the peasant understood what the King said, he misunderstood what the King meant! In interviewing and investigating we have to not only listen to what people say, but also **actively listen** for what they mean.

HYPOTHETICAL 8-1

Scenario A: Assume that Honey Dew sees her boyfriend, Honey Don't, watching TV on the couch. She comes up behind him and begins tickling him. He grabs his sides and says, "Stop it." Honey Dew doesn't stop tickling him and soon they both fall on the floor laughing.

Scenario B: Assume that Honey Dew sees her boyfriend, Honey Don't, watching TV on the couch. She comes up behind him and begins tickling him. He grabs his sides and says, "Stop it." Honey Dew doesn't stop tickling him and he slaps her hands away. They wind up angry at each other.

1. How do you think Honey Don't said, "Stop it" in Scenario A?
2. How do you think Honey Don't said, "Stop it" in Scenario B?

To understand both what a person says and what they mean in verbal communication, the interviewer and investigator has to be sensitive to the speaker's:

1. Tone of voice

In Hypothetical 8-1, the **tone of voice** used by Honey Don't probably made all the difference in whether the outcome of the tickle attack was Scenario A or B.

2. Volume

A raised voice in most circumstances might indicate excitement, anger, or stress. A low voice might indicate insecurity or a desire to not be overheard. Of course, a voice might be raised because the room is noisy or lowered because a baby is asleep nearby.

3. Rate of speaking

Some people just talk rapidly. It's normal for them. But for others speaking rapidly indicates some excitement, concern, or rush. Others speak slowly. It may be normal for them, but for others it may be an indication of nervousness or impairment.

4. Voice inflection

The words a speaker emphasizes in a sentence can make a significant difference in meaning.

HYPOTHETICAL 8-2

Assume you are interviewing a witness about a case in which a boy has allegedly been injured by an animal. An eyewitness makes the following statement to you: "The big red dog jumped over the fence and bit the boy."

Try saying this sentence several different times. Each time you repeat the sentence place the greatest emphasis on one of the following words: big, red, dog, jumped, fence, and bit.

1. If the word "big" is emphasized, doesn't that suggest to you that there might be two or more red dogs suspected in the attack?
2. If the word "red" is emphasized, doesn't that suggest to you that there might be dogs of different colors suspected in the attack?
3. If the word "dog" is emphasized, doesn't that suggest to you that the kind of animal that attacked the boy is at issue?
4. If the word "jumped" is emphasized, doesn't that suggest to you that how the dog got out of the fenced-in area may be in question?
5. If the word "fence" is emphasized, doesn't that suggest to you that the direction the dog came from may be in question?
6. If the word "bit" is emphasized, doesn't that suggest to you that the kind of injury inflicted on the boy might be in question?

Another aspect of **voice inflection** is its absence—the *monotone.* Some people speak in a monotone naturally. Interviewing such people at length can pose a special challenge for the interviewer—to stay focused (or maybe even to stay awake!). But if a person who normally does not speak in a monotone does so on a particular occasion, what might that tell you? Are they fatigued? Bored? On medication?

Or if a person speaks with more than normal inflection—they emphasize odd words or all their words—what does that suggest to you about them?

5. Enunciation

A person who enunciates well speaks clearly. And it matters. If you are interviewing a client who runs sentences together or slurs his speech, making it hard to understand, what might that tell you about how effective a witness he will be at trial?

Or if a person who normally speaks clearly speaks with a distinct slur on a particular occasion, what might that tell you? Has he been drinking? Is he ill? Fatigued?

6. Vocabulary

Vocabulary is closely tied to education and training. It has been estimated that the average high school graduate in the United States uses only about 700 different words in the course of normal conversation. That number rises to 1,200 for the college graduate.

In communicating with others during the course of an interviewing assignment, it is important that the legal professional take note of the vocabulary of others and adjust his own to communicate effectively with them.

EXAMPLE

If you are interviewing an adult, fifth-grade dropout you probably don't want to ask him, "Can you articulate a plausible explanation for the scenario just described?" Instead, you want to try something like, "Do you have any idea why that happened?" Notice the difference in the length and complexity of the words in the two sentences.

7. Grammar

Nothing is more immediately striking about a person's speech than the use of improper grammar. Some grammatical mistakes are minor and cause us to do little more than note the goof.

EXAMPLE

Recently at an awards show on television, a group of five persons accepted the award for best costuming. The spokesman for the group said, "This is a great honor for my team and I." Of course, he should have said, "my team and me," but minor slips like that are common and we don't make much of it.

On the other hand, if the spokesman had said, "We'uns is right proud of this here honor. We know'd we done good but we never seen this aco-min'," the audience would probably have gone into shock. What would be your impression of a person who spoke that way. Uneducated? Ignorant? Embarrassing himself and others? Fair or not, those are the opinions people form when they hear blatantly improper grammar used.

For the legal professional, there are several lessons to be learned about the impact of using improper grammar. The first and most important is the one stressed in the first section of this chapter—don't use improper grammar yourself!

But there are other important lessons. Take note of the grammar of clients and witnesses you interview and consider the impression it will make on others—particularly on a judge or jury if the person will be a witness at trial. Be sure to report your observations and impressions to the supervising attorney. Don't react in any noticeable way when a client or witness uses improper grammar in your presence. They may notice your reaction and feel insulted or resentful at what they see as your arrogance.

8. Slang, colloquialisms, idioms, and accents

a. Slang

Slang is words or phrases used to mean something other than their standard definition. Some slang is generally referred to today as **street talk.**

EXAMPLE

duh	postal
out of sight	hit the road
radical	redneck
space cadet	rocket science
cool it	wacko
slam dunk	geek
go for it	wonk
basket case	weasel out
big enchilada	wag
you go girl	bling
no problem	flash rave
chill out	smokin'
nothing but net	greased palm
all-nighter	bail
rip-off	hurl
shake a leg	peeps
icky	hit on
googled	hook up
inside job	cheesy

Is a client or witness using slang terms that you don't recognize? Go to www.peevish.co.uk/slang/introduction.htm and see if you can locate the term and its definition.

Slang varies among age groups, ethnic groups, trades and professions (e.g., *weasel words, rainmaker,* and *silk stocking firm* in legal slang), and also by region of the country (e.g., *high heels* for women in one place are *party pumps* in another; you order a *soft drink* in one place and a *pop* in another; in some places you say, "I'll drive you" to a person needing a lift while in others you say, "I'll carry you."). And our electronic communication age has given rise to a huge library of **Internet slang** (also called **netspeak** or **text slang**). See if there are any netspeak terms you *don't* recognize in the following example. If any stump you, try looking them up at www.noslang.com/dictionary/. (See LBD 8-6.)

EXAMPLE

lol	gbtw
btw	g8
a3	i <3 u
b4	IMHO
c2c	iyd
bbl	mb
cid	*s*
cu2nit	shut^
g1	w.b.s

b. Colloquialisms

Colloquialisms are words or phrases that are used incorrectly but that have gained widespread use in informal conversation.

EXAMPLE

"He is *about* eight years old" rather than, "He is approximately eight years old." "We couldn't *help but notice* the change" rather than, "We couldn't help noticing the change." "You *sure are* tall" rather than, "You are surely tall."

c. Idioms

An **idiom** is a phrase having a meaning different from the literal meaning of the words themselves. Idioms are established by common usage in a particular culture, region, profession, or business. We all use them, usually without thinking.

EXAMPLE

"This project will be a piece of cake."
"She got a taste of her own medicine."
"He's all hat and no cattle."
"This college education is costing me an arm and a leg."
"That actor was a flash in the pan."
"This city is going to hell in a handbasket."
"Just hold your horses."
"As soon as I finish this chapter I'm going to hit the hay."
"He works for a silk stocking firm in New York."
"Get out of that bed lazy, you're burning daylight!"

Are any of the idioms in that last example unfamiliar to you? Sooner rather than later in interviewing, you'll hear one that isn't. How about this one from a life-long railroad worker: "He's on a gravy train with biscuit wheels," describing a coworker with a cushy job? Ever heard of a California widow? That's an idiom from 19th century America describing a married woman whose husband has left her to go to West and find his fortune. Anybody play poker? If so, you probably know what's meant by the idiom, "I trust the river will deliver."

d. Accents

Although there has been a leavening of **accents** in our country due to national communications through television and radio, regional accents are still with us. How hard is it, after all, to pick out a New York City (*New Yawk*) or a Boston (*Haavud* is a school?) or a deep South (just try saying *you* or *hi* with two syllables, *y'all*) accent?

In interviewing and investigating work, the legal professional should be careful to note and report witnesses who use noticeable slang, colloquialisms, or street talk to communicate, or who have a noticeable accent.

EXAMPLE

> If an associate attorney or paralegal assisting with a case pending in a court in Birmingham, Alabama, interviews an important witness with a distinct New York accent or who uses, like, you know, like California Valley Girl slang, she had best report it to the supervising attorney. It is something the attorney will take into account in determining the impact, pro or con, of that witness on the judge and jury. And, of course, the same would be true if the case was pending in New York or Los Angeles and the witness was from Birmingham (or, as the witness might say, "Buminham").

To the extent possible, the investigating legal professional should also try to be familiar with slang, idioms and colloquialisms used in the area where she works in order to be able to communicate effectively with witnesses. And if a person being interviewed uses an unfamiliar one, ask them what it means.

C. Nonverbal Communication—Body Language

We all know from our common experience of interacting with others that nonverbal communication or **body language** can convey messages just as clearly—and sometimes more clearly—as any words. The science of non-verbal behavior or body language is called **kinesics**. Kinesics teaches that it is much easier to control *what* we say than *how* we say it, and even the person who deliberately lies has great difficulty preventing his body from manifesting tell-tale **deception stress** that can be picked up on by the observant interviewer (see LBD 8-5).

HYPOTHETICAL 8-3

Assume, following Scenario B in Hypothetical 8-1, that Honey Dew and Honey Don't not only argue, they break up, and Honey Don't sues Honey Dew for the tort of battery. When she receives the suit papers, Honey Dew calls the attorney for whom you work asking him to represent her in defending the case. That attorney asks you to meet with Honey Dew and interview her regarding the facts of the case.

Honey Dew comes to the office and meets with you in a small conference room where she sits immediately across the table from you. While you ask Honey Dew questions designed to obtain biographical and background information on herself, she seems relaxed and friendly. She sits forward in her chair with her hands clasped comfortably on the table in front of her. She smiles, laughs easily, and looks directly at you. She speaks at a normal pace, without any hesitation, and seems to express herself well.

Then you begin asking her questions about the day of the alleged battery. You notice a frown appear on her forehead and she sits back in her chair. She folds her arms across her chest. You ask her directly if she did in fact tickle Honey Don't without warning or consent as he has alleged. Her eyes look away from yours and begin to scan the ceiling. You hear her clear her throat. Finally she speaks, but slowly, softly, and hesitantly. She seems to stumble over her words. What she says is, "Well . . . not . . . I mean . . . no . . . I just . . . He . . . No, I didn't. He only . . . It's . . ."

"It's . . . He's making this up just to. . . . Because he wanted to . . . wants to break it off."

1. What did the nonverbal communication or body language of Honey Dew tell you before you got to questions about the day of the alleged battery?
2. List each way that the body language of Honey Dew changed during the interview?
3. What does each noted change in her body language communicate to you?
4. What changes did you note in Honey Dew's verbal communication style and what do those changes communicate to you?

Body language speaks volumes, doesn't it? In order to understand not only what a person says with words, but what they communicate with body language, the investigator has to be sensitive to the speaker's:

1. Body position

Body position includes both a person's posture and proximity. In Hypothetical 8-3, what did it communicate to you that at the beginning of the interview Honey Dew sat forward in her chair with her hands clasped comfortably in front of her on the table? That she was comfortable? Confident? Friendly? Candid? What did it mean when she later sat back in her chair and folded her arms across her chest? Defensive? Threatened? Uncertain?

Take a look at the picture of President Lyndon Johnson speaking to Supreme Court Justice Abe Fortas in Illustration 8-1. What does the body position of these two men suggest to you about their personalities? About their respective positions of authority? About their respect for other person's privacy? About their confidence?

As investigators, legal professionals must be diligent students and observers of body language—our own and others.

2. Facial expressions

Try the experiment set out in Hypothetical 8-4.

HYPOTHETICAL 8-4

> What kind of a mood are you in right now as you read this? No matter what mood it is, go to the nearest mirror and look at yourself. Does your face reflect your mood? Almost certainly it does. While you are in front of the mirror think of different moods than the one you are in now (happy, sad, amused, angry, confused, frightened, shocked, disapproving, disbelieving, frustrated, tired—oops, that's the one you were already in, right?). Try to adjust your face to reflect the different moods. Note two things when you do this: (1) your face *will* change with the different moods; and (2) it may be difficult to *make* your face change to reflect a mood you are not in presently.
>
> If someone else is there with you, try to observe them for a moment without being noticed. What kind of mood do you think that person is in based on his or her facial expression? Once you decide, and if you dare, ask them what mood they are in. How close did you come to being right?

The lessons to be learned from the experiment in Hypothetical 8-4 are that people's **facial expressions** communicate a lot about them, and most people are not good enough actors to conceal those messages.

In Hypothetical 8-3, what did it communicate to you at the beginning of the interview that Honey Dew smiled and laughed easily? That she was relaxed? Friendly? Straightforward? What did it communicate later in the interview that her face clouded with a frown? Worried? Anxious? Just a headache coming on?

Frowns, smiles, winks, excessive blinking, pursing the lips, licking the lips, biting the lips, raised eyebrows, nose squinched—all these facial expressions tell us something about the person and the circumstances, if we are *listening*.

Illustration 8-1
PHOTOGRAPH OF
PRESIDENT
JOHNSON
SPEAKING TO
ABE FORTAS*

Abe Fortas gets 'the Johnson Treatment'

*Yoichi R. Okamoto—LBJ Library Collection

3. Eye contact

Have you ever had the experience of speaking face to face with a person who sort of looks past you to something behind you? How did that make you feel? Ignored? Insulted? Unimportant?

On the other hand, have you ever had the experience of speaking face to face with a person whose eyes seem to bore a hole in you and never seem to blink? How did that make you feel? Uncomfortable? Threatened? Intimidated?

People communicate volumes of information to each other by **eye contact** or the lack of it. Normally, close, steady eye contact (but not the hole-boring kind) is a sign of interest in what the other person is saying and respect for the person. Refusal to make steady eye contact can mean shyness, insecurity, or lack of truthfulness. (And now you know why your mother, when she doubted your story about how her favorite glass dish got broken, said, "Look me in the eye and tell me that.")

When people who have been making eye contact with us suddenly break it, that sends a message as well. In Hypothetical 8-3, what did it communicate to you when Honey Dew broke eye contact with you and started searching the ceiling as you asked her about tickling Honey Don't?

4. Nervous signals

The body tends to give us away when we are **nervous** or feeling pressure. Think about yourself. What signals do you give when you are anxious? It may be that line of sweat over the upper lip, on the forehead, or under the arms. Or that frog in the throat. It may be the inability to sit still. It may be a slight tremor in the hands or the knees or the voice. It may be an elevation of the voice, by **volume** or pitch, or an accelerated **rate of speaking**. It may be a wringing of the hands, a yawn when you aren't sleepy, a giggle when nothing's funny, or a rubbing of the brow.

Of course there may be more than one explanation for any body language. A person may begin to perspire because the room is overheated or he is dressed too warmly. A frog in the throat can mean a voice that has been overexerted. A tremor in the hands can be a sign of aging or illness. Some people "talk with their hands," using many gestures as they speak. It is not necessarily a sign of nervousness unless the person normally doesn't use those gestures or unless they are excessive even for that person.

Another factor to keep in mind when interpreting what appear to be nervous signals, reluctance, or even disingenuousness in an interviewee, is a basic tenet of kinetics: the one being interviewed is studying the interviewer's verbal and non-verbal signals as intensely as the interviewer is the interviewee's. The interviewer has to consider whether her own nervousness or other signals may be triggering the response in the interviewee. Interviewing is not for the faint of heart or the unprepared. We have to use our common sense, instincts, and training in interpreting body language.

5. The sounds of silence

You've undoubtedly heard the phrase, "The silence was deafening." We understand that saying because we know that in certain situations a person's silence can be telling us something significant.

In Hypothetical 8-3, what did it communicate to you when Honey Dew paused before answering your question about whether she did in fact tickle Honey Don't? That's called the **pregnant pause** or the *telltale hesitation*. A pause can, of course, mean that the person simply didn't hear the question or that their mind was on something else. Again, we have to use our common sense and instincts to interpret body language.

6. Clothes and environment

Clothes do make a statement—and surroundings do too. We communicate messages to others by our choices regarding clothing and personal grooming styles, and by the way we maintain the space around us.

HYPOTHETICAL 8-5

Assume you are conducting the interview of Honey Dew as assigned in Hypothetical 8-3. You conduct the interview in the conference room of the law office where you work. Before she says a word, what would your initial impressions of Honey Dew be if she arrives for the interview:

1. Dressed in short shorts, a halter top, and sandals?
2. Dressed in a conservative navy blue suit with matching shoes and purse?
3. Dressed in a nurse's uniform?
4. Dressed in black leather pants, motorcycle jacket, and boots, with "Kiss This" written on the back side of her pants?
5. With her hair pulled back in a ponytail and tied with a pink bow that matches her dress?
6. With her hair spiked and colored half green and half orange?
7. Nicely dressed, but with her hair dirty and unkempt?

What might *her* impression of *you* be if you arrived at that interview dressed and groomed as mentioned above?

Assume you conduct the interview of Honey Dew at her office where she manages a temporary employment agency. You are escorted into her office, seated, and told she will be with you shortly. As you wait for Honey Dew, you look around her office. Having not yet spoken to or seen her, what would your initial impressions of her be if, as you look around the office, you notice:

1. An 18″ × 24″ portrait of Honey Dew immediately behind her chair?
2. A wall full of awards and pictures of Honey Dew with local and state politicians?
3. A mounted deer head on the wall?
4. Nothing on the walls?
5. Several pictures of Honey Dew with a man and two small children?
6. Several pictures of Honey Dew with different men?
7. A neat, orderly desk and light rock music playing softly in the background? (What if it was hard rock? Country? Rap? Big band? Blues? Golden oldies from the '50s and '60s?)
8. A messy, disorganized desk, files on the floor, and half of an obviously stale hamburger closer to your chair than you would like?
9. Childrens' crayon drawings taped to the side of her computer monitor?
10. An open bottle of Pepto Bismol on the desk beside several rolls of antacid tablets?

Assume an unexpected guest comes to your home at this moment. What impression would they probably form of you from the condition of . . . oh, okay, we won't pursue this one!

We are all experts

When it comes to interpreting the unspoken messages contained in verbal and nonverbal communication, we are all experts. Why? Because we are experienced social creatures. From the moment of birth we have been constantly interacting with others and honing these skills. Grammar, spelling, and punctuation are learned arts. Writing skills must be developed. But picking up on the nuances of verbal communication and interpreting body language come naturally to us all because we have been doing it all of our lives. In interviewing and investigating work we have to consciously and conscientiously exercise those skills to be effective.

D. ▶ Written (Including Electronic) Communication

Illustration 8-2 sets forth a list of the kinds of written communications legal professionals routinely produce. Increasingly, such written communication is done electronically rather than on paper.

In other chapters we consider each of these kinds of written communication in more detail. But here are some general suggestions applicable to all written communications whether produced electronically or via traditional paper document.

1. Be aware of grammar

SLEUTH ON THE LOOSE

Have a question about a sensitive subject relating to a client or witness? Wonder why people are different in ways related to age, gender, religion, or culture but embarrassed to ask? Take a look at www.yforum. com, a Web site created for you to ask that question and get an answer from people in the know.

Grammar matters—and spelling, punctuation, vocabulary, and sentence and paragraph structure do too.

2. Use tools for effective writing

Keep the necessary tools for effective writing close at hand. These include a good dictionary, legal dictionary, thesaurus, and grammar and style text. (See Appendix B, Resources for the Investigator, for suggestions regarding helpful grammar and style texts.)

3. Avoid slang and colloquialisms

Be familiar with slang and colloquialisms in order to communicate effectively when speaking with clients and witnesses. But unless you are quoting someone else or summarizing what another person said, never use them yourself in professional written communications.

4. Be precise

Say exactly what you mean. That may mean reworking phrases and sentences until you get them right. With experience you will need to do less rewriting. Be sure you know the meaning of every word you use. If you're not sure about meaning, spelling, punctuation, capitalization, etc., don't guess—look it up.

5. Be thorough but concise

Cover everything you need to in the document you write, but say it as briefly as possible. No one wants to read more than necessary, and learning to use words economically will prove a blessing to your reader.

Illustration 8-2   TYPES OF WRITTEN (INCLUDING ELECTRONIC) COMMUNICATION THAT LEGAL PROFES-
SIONALS ROUTINELY PRODUCE

---

1. correspondence to clients

2. correspondence to other law offices

3. correspondence to witnesses and non-witness information sources

4. correspondence to courts

5. internal case-file memoranda

6. internal legal research memoranda

7. internal investigation reports

8. draft pleadings

9. draft discovery documents (interrogatories, document requests, deposition notices, requests to admit)

10. draft motions

11. subpoenas and subpoenas *duces tecum*

12. proposed court orders

13. fee agreements

14. witness statements

15. records authorizations

---

6. Avoid repetition

Say it as well as you can the first time. And don't say it again!

7. Be consistent

Make sure your document is internally consistent. Nothing is more confusing than receiving a memo, letter, or other document that starts out saying one thing but then seems to say another.

8. Use shorter, simpler, non-technical words

Sometimes we must use technical words. If, in a letter you are drafting to a client, you need to tell him that the theory of *res ipsa loquitur* may be available in his case, you will use that Latin phrase, although you will have to explain what it means. But when technical words are not required, avoid them.

Always try to select shorter, simpler words and phrases over longer, more complex ones. The well-known acronym **KISS** stands for *Keep It Simple Stupid*—a good rule to remember in legal writing. Set out in Illustration 8-3 is a list of phrases commonly seen in legal writing. The use of these phrases almost always represents poor writing. Beside each phrase is a single word that could better express the same thought. Those phrases in the list with no word beside them could be deleted completely with no loss of meaning.

Illustration 8-3 COMMONLY USED PHRASES THAT COULD BE ELIMINATED

1. for the reasons stated	therefore
2. by virtue of the fact that	because
3. in the event that	if
4. due to the fact that	because
5. by means of	by
6. for the purposes of	for
7. comes the plaintiff (defendant)	plaintiff (defendant)
8. in order to	to
9. there can be no doubt that	doubtless
10. notwithstanding the fact that	regardless or although
11. at this time (or as of this moment)	presently
12. for all intents and purposes	
13. all things considered	
14. as far as we are concerned	
15. the fact is that	

9. Use paragraphs

Paragraphs are the way we address different topics in a written document. Organize them logically. Each should begin with a topic sentence and when the topic changes a new paragraph should begin. In general, when in doubt, begin a new paragraph. Shorter paragraphs are generally to be preferred over longer ones.

10. Use drafts and proof your work

You should make it a personal goal *never* to turn in a written document to your supervising attorney or send a professional communication to an attorney or client that contains a typographical error. In law offices, there is no margin for error in what we write because it is so critical to clients. Part of performing at a professional level is insisting on error-free documents—from yourself and others.

The only way to guarantee this level of writing is to *draft* documents and communications before putting them in final form. If time allows, your documents may go through several drafts. Every draft should be thoroughly proofed, not only for errors, but to improve word choice, sentence and paragraph structure, and writing style. If practical, have someone else in the office proof your work. We can look at our own documents so many times that we don't catch the mistakes. A person looking at your document for the first time will be more likely to catch them.

The challenge to draft and proof is perhaps most challenging in the context of electronic communications like text messaging and e-mail. It is so easy to type something quickly and send it, and most of us do that routinely in informal communication with family and friends. But in professional communications you must learn to proof that message before sending the Send button.

11. Protect confidentiality and privilege

It is always critical in drafting, finalizing, and distributing documents to protect client confidentiality and all applicable privileges. Documents you are working on in the office should be put away safely when you are not present—even for a short while. Work taken home should be carefully shielded from other eyes. Copies distributed in the office should be hand-delivered or sent in routing envelopes to prevent accidental reading by unauthorized persons.

Documents mailed should be carefully and properly addressed only to the person(s) authorized to receive them and care should be taken not to copy anyone with confidential correspondence who is not also privileged. Take care in addressing envelopes as well. Because we do not have control over who will actually handle the envelope at the receiving end (a child or spouse at home; a secretary or receptionist at the office), envelopes containing confidential or privileged material should be conspicuously marked *CONFIDENTIAL* or *PERSONAL* or both. See Illustration 8-4. See the discussion of confidentiality in electronic communications below.

12. Practice makes perfect—and reading helps too

Writing does not come easy to most people and no one is naturally perfect at it. Writing well is a learned art, so don't be discouraged if you have a long way to go. The more you write, and the more different things you write, the better you will become at it.

It also helps to read good writing by others. Read well-written books and articles of all kinds. Note the word choice, sentence, and paragraph structure in what you read.

13. Special considerations for electronic communications (netiquette)

Law office personnel, like people everywhere, are communicating electronically more than ever before: **e-mail**, **text messaging**, tweets on **Twitter**, short messages on **Flickr** or **LinkedIn**, etc. It is important to know and observe certain etiquette rules for job-related electronic communications. Many government agencies, businesses, and professional offices have adopted such rules, sometimes called **netiquette**. If your office hasn't done so, you should observe your own netiquette rules. Doing so will demonstrate professionalism, promote efficiency, protect client confidentiality, and prevent liability that can result from inappropriate communications. Here is a list of suggested netiquette rules:

- Do not use e-mail, texting, etc., for any client or other confidential communications without the prior consent of your supervising attorney and the client or other recipient.

Illustration 8-4   ENVELOPE CONTAINING CONFIDENTIAL OR PRIVILEGED MATERIAL

Smith, Jones & Greely
Attorneys at Law
114 Main Street
Harmony City, Yourstate 11212

Mr. Frank Childs
Childs Industries
911 Madison Street
Harmony City, Yourstate 11212

PERSONAL AND CONFIDENTIAL

- Always obtain prior authorization from your supervising attorney for an electronic communication regarding a client matter, just as you would for a letter.
- Use proper spelling, grammar, and punctuation.
- Use proper sentence and paragraph structure.
- Resist the urge to be flip or cute; be friendly but professional in tone.
- Proofread your message before sending it; use spell check.
- Think about your message before sending it; never send an electronic message when you are angry or otherwise emotional.
- Never send a message containing any libelous, defamatory, offensive, racist, profane, or obscene remarks.
- Do not overuse the *high priority* option.
- Do not hit the *reply to all* button unless you mean to do that.
- Do not forward chain letters, virus warnings, or political, religious, or social issue mass mailings.
- Do not reply to spam.
- Check your messages frequently and reply promptly if appropriate.
- Include a disclaimer on your electronic messages such as that seen in Illustration 8-5.

Illustration 8-5   DISCLAIMER LANGUAGE TO ACCOMPANY E-MAIL MESSAGES

This transmission, regardless of modality, may contain confidential information and may be subject to protection under the law. If you are not the intended recipient, or an authorized agent for the intended recipient, you are hereby notified that use, such as but not limited to disclosure, copying, or distribution, is prohibited. Please destroy any and all copies immediately and notify the sender of this erroneous receipt. We may monitor electronic communications to and from our network.

E. ▶ Putting Communication Skills to Work in Interviewing and Investigating

1. What are you communicating to others?

In interviewing and investigating work, the legal professional must be constantly aware of what he is communicating to others verbally and nonverbally. Illustration 8-6 lists the contexts in which the legal professional's own communication skills are critical to success.

In any business or profession, successful people are the ones with superior communication skills.

Illustration 8-6
CONTEXTS IN WHICH THE LEGAL PROFESSIONAL'S COMMUNICATION SKILLS ARE CRITICAL

- working with a supervising attorney(s)
- working with other attorneys and staff in the office
- working with attorneys and staff in other law offices
- working with clients
- working with witnesses
- working with non-witness information sources
- working with court personnel

HYPOTHETICAL 8-6

Assume that Dis Tracted works for attorney Good Guy. Over the weekend, with Christmas only a few days away, Dis Tracted broke up with her boyfriend and on Monday morning she is, shall we say, not in the best of moods. Nonetheless, she gets to work on time at 8:30 a.m., only to find a note on her desk telling her Good Guy needs her to cover an interview for him. Dis Tracted groans because she already has too much to do. But she takes her pen and legal pad and heads for Good Guy's office. On the way she passes the office runner, Eager One, in the hall. Eager One smiles and says hello pleasantly but Dis Tracted doesn't notice; she's wondering if the store will take back that sweater she bought for her ex-boyfriend. She doesn't see Eager One give her a puzzled look and then a frown after she passes by him.

Dis Tracted knocks on Good Guy's door and he tells her to come in. He greets her with a quick smile as he shuffles through a small mountain of papers on his desk, motions her to a chair in front of his desk, and without looking up at her says, "Hope you had a good weekend because we've got a lot to do."

Dis Tracted lays the legal pad and pen aside and says, "Thanks for asking. In fact I had a terrible weekend. I've been dating this guy Jack for six months and I thought everything was going okay. Then Saturday night we had this big fight and I hoped he would call me Sunday to apologize so I hung around the apartment. . . ."

Good Guy interrupts by clearing his throat and says, "Do you think we could talk about this later? We've got Sad Shape, that divorce client I took on last week, in the conference room and somebody needs to talk to her. I've got to leave for court right now so you'll need to cover it. Apparently her husband pulled some dumb stunt over the weekend and we may need to seek a restraining order against him. Go meet with her and find out what's going on and we'll talk when I get back from court, okay?" Without saying more, Good Guy grabs his coat and briefcase and is out the door.

Dis Tracted makes a few notes on her legal pad then walks back to her office. Her secretary, Teaor Coffee, is sitting at her desk outside Dis Tracted's office taking some aspirin with water. Dis Tracted says, "Teaor, get me the Sad Shape file from the file room," then goes into her office. After throwing her legal pad on the desk and muttering under her breath, Dis Tracted glances out the door to see Teaor Coffee putting the aspirin away in a desk drawer. Angrily, Dis Tracted says, "Teaor, I need that file, now," and watches as the secretary scurries away to get the file.

A few moments later, Dis Tracted enters the conference room and sees Sad Shape sitting at the long table, sobbing. Dis Tracted puts on the best smile she can manage and cheerily says, "Good morning, Mrs. Shape. Do you remember me? I'm Dis Tracted. I'm assisting Mr. Guy with your case." As Sad Shape tries unsuccessfully to control her tears, Dis Tracted takes a seat at the head of the conference room table, sighs audibly, looks at her watch, and asks, "What can we help you with today?"

Thirty minutes later the interview is over. Dis Tracted has the vague suspicion it didn't go as well as it could have but she attributes that feeling to it being Monday. She is surprised later in the week to learn that she is getting no year-end bonus and no raise for the new year. At home she tells her boyfriend (with whom she made up Tuesday night), "You know, Jack, no matter how hard you try, you just can't please some people."

1. How did Dis Tracted fail to communicate effectively with Eager One? What should she have done differently?
2. How did Dis Tracted fail to communicate effectively with Good Guy? What should she have done differently?
3. How did Dis Tracted fail to communicate effectively with Teaor Coffee? What should she have done differently?
4. How did Dis Tracted fail to communicate effectively with Sad Shape? What should she have done differently?

SLEUTH ON THE LOOSE

Access the Dictionary of American Regional English (DARE) at http://dare.wisc.edu/?q=node/1. Locate the Dare Map showing the geographical groupings in which DARE's language samplings were taken to see which group you are in. Then find the 100 sample entries displayed on the site and determine which of the following phrases is more likely to be heard in your geographical area: on the fritz, bear claw, mourner's bench, goozle, duck on a rock.

2. What are others communicating to you?

Communication is a two-way street. Just as it is critical to be aware of what we are communicating to others verbally and nonverbally, it is just as critical to be aware of what others are communicating to us.

Many of the mistakes Dis Tracted made in Hypothetical 8-6 were attributable to her failure to notice what others were communicating to her. If you didn't do so already in connection with Hypothetical 8-6, make a list of every verbal and nonverbal signal Dis Tracted missed in her communications with Eager One, Good Guy, Teaor Coffee, and Sad Shape.

3. Suggestions for phone communications

Legal professionals spend a lot of time on the telephone or cell phone—many investigations are accomplished primarily or completely over the phone. Here are some suggestions for communicating effectively over a **phone**.

a. Your voice is critical

Use a pleasant tone. Remember that in a phone conversation your voice is all the other person has to go by to determine if they like you and if they want to help you. If you are speaking to a stranger, that person will form an immediate first impression of you from your voice. In investigating work, we make phone calls hoping that the people to whom we speak will assist us in some way. Make sure your voice works for you to accomplish that purpose.

b. Identify yourself properly

Both attorneys and paralegals are required, ethically and professionally, to properly identify themselves in phone conversations. (E.g., "Hello, this is Martha King. I am a paralegal in the office of attorney Marvin Jones.") Avoid the temptation to play act or otherwise mislead the other person to obtain their assistance.

c. Return calls promptly

This is true of all calls, but especially calls from clients. You will recall that part of the ethical duty owed to clients is a duty to keep them reasonably informed regarding the matter of the representation (see Chapter 2). One of the most frequent ethical complaints made against attorneys is their (or their assistant's) failure to return calls. Don't just return calls—return them promptly.

d. Sound interested—even if you're not

We all know how to do this, don't we? A friend phones when we are really too busy to talk but we choose not to say so to avoid hurting their feelings. A spouse or companion can't wait to tell us about an exciting event we couldn't care less about. An in-law we have nothing in common with comes to visit . . . for a week.

e. Take notes while you talk

Never assume that you will recall all the details of even a brief phone conversation. Making contemporaneous notes of your conversation will help you recall it later, and the notes can be placed in the file for others working on the case to see and to support later billing.

f. Phone ego—"Please hold for Mr. Big"

Ever been on the receiving end of one of these calls? A secretary interrupts you with a call and then makes you wait while the caller moseys to the phone? First, don't do this to others. Second, if others do it to you, don't lose your cool. If it's a client, a supervising attorney, or someone else you cannot afford to offend, tolerate it. Third, if it's a client who does this to you, bill him for the waiting time!

g. Phone conversations with information sources

Here are six suggestions to follow when you place a call seeking information or cooperation. Call them the six Bs:

1. Be ready. Know exactly what you are going to ask before you get on the phone.
2. Be brief. Remember that everybody's time is important.
3. Be friendly. The sweet draws the flies, not the sour.
4. Be patient. It is usually rewarded.
5. Be polite. Using "please" and "thank you" will make people like you.
6. Be grateful. And say so; you may need this person again!

4. The investigator as a LOvER!

Simply stated, the legal professional cannot be successful at interviewing and investigating work unless she is constantly aware of what others, particularly clients and witnesses, are communicating to her both verbally and nonverbally. We can understand intellectually what communication involves, and we can acknowledge that we are all experts at comprehending the unspoken signals in verbal communication and in interpreting body language, but unless we consciously turn those systems on when we engage in interviewing and investigating tasks we are going to miss critical information. How do we turn those systems on? By being a **LOvER!** This means the investigator has to be:

- A Listener
- An Observer
- An Evaluator
- A Reporter

a. A Listener

We will not pick up on nuances and subtle signals sent to us in verbal communication unless we actively listen to others. Hearing and listening are not the same thing. In the Wizard of Id cartoon, the peasant *heard* the King clearly enough but he wasn't really *listening* so he didn't *understand!* **Active listening** is an activity of the mind as well as the ears; it is concentration on what is being said and how it is being said.

b. An Observer

We will not catch the important messages that body language and physical surroundings may be sending to us if we do not consciously observe what is going on with and around others. As listening is more than hearing, so observing is more than seeing; it is a concentrated mental activity.

c. An Evaluator

As was stressed in the discussion on aspects of verbal and nonverbal communication, the investigator must use instinct, experience, and common sense to interpret what is seen and heard. Remember Honey Dew from Hypothetical 8-3? When the frown crossed her face and she sat back in her chair and crossed her arms, was it because she felt threatened and defensive? Or could it have been a headache? Was she uncomfortable in the chair? Was it too cold in the room? We have to evaluate, reasonably and systematically, the verbal and nonverbal data we perceive in order to draw reliable conclusions.

d. A Reporter

In all interviewing and investigating work the paralegal is under an attorney's supervision. An associate attorney is working under the critical eye of a senior attorney. For either it is essential to report back to the supervising attorney in an effective way all that was heard and observed and an evaluation of that data given. The supervising attorney can then make his own analysis of the information and decide how best to use it for the benefit of the client.

Chapter Summary and Conclusion

We communicate with each other verbally, non-verbally, and in writing. The legal professional must develop the skill of active listening, especially when interviewing clients and witnesses. The legal professional must also be aware of what message body language is communicating, both that of his own and of others. There are numerous types of written communications the legal professional is called upon to produce. The basics of grammar, spelling, punctuation, vocabulary, as well as effective sentence and paragraph structure must be utilized. Phone communications are also a routine part of the legal professional's daily life, and the special rules for those communications must be remembered and used. The effective investigator is a listener, an observer, an evaluator, and a reporter.

With these basics we are ready to consider the formulation and execution of a plan of investigation, the subject of Part II of the text, which begins with Chapter 9.

Review Questions

1. What are the three ways we communicate with each other?
2. What are the different things that a raised volume of voice can indicate?
3. What is slang? Can you think of some examples?
4. What is a colloquialism? Can you think of some examples?
5. What are the different things that a person's failure to maintain eye contact with an interviewer might indicate?
6. What do we mean by "active listening"?
7. What do we mean by the "pregnant pause"?
8. What do we mean by saying we are all experts in interpreting unspoken messages in the words and body language of others?
9. What does KISS mean? How does it relate to professional writing skills?
10. What do we mean by saying that the good investigator is a LOvER?

KEY WORDS AND PHRASES TO REMEMBER

accent
active listening
body language
colloquialisms
deception stress
e-mail
enunciation
eye contact
facial expressions
Flickr
grammar
idioms
Internet slang
kinesics
KISS
LinkedIn
LOvER
nervous signals
netspeak
netiquette

nonverbal communication
paragraph structure
phone etiquette
pregnant pause
pronunciation
punctuation
rate of speaking
sentence structure
slang
spelling
street talk
text slang
tone of voice
Twitter
verbal communication
vocabulary
voice inflection
volume
writing style
written communication

LEARN BY DOING

LBD 8-1. Over the course of a week, maintain a journal documenting your observations of three different people with whom you come in regular contact. Note and record your impressions of their voices, body language, and facial expressions. Keep a running record of dates and times of observation, physical surroundings, and a description of your observations. Choose both people you know well and people you don't know well. Don't tell them what you are doing and make every effort to not be obvious or unduly obtrusive. Following each observation, interpret it—write down what you think you have observed tells you about that person. What were they consciously or unconsciously communicating to you at the time?

LBD 8-2. If you have access to the *Certified Paralegal Review Manual: A Practical Guide to CP Exam Preparation (Test Preparation)* by Virginia Koerselman Newman (3d ed., Delmar Cengage, 2010), study Chapter 1 on Communications and then complete the self-test included in the book. Repeat the test until you score at least a 90 percent on it.

LBD 8-3. Review the list of books pertaining to verbal and nonverbal communication skills in Appendix B, Resources for the Investigator. Select one of the books and prepare a book report briefly summarizing the main points of each chapter.

LBD 8-4. Arrange and conduct the interview of an experienced trial lawyer. In the interview focus on the lawyer's experience at using the verbal and nonverbal communication skills discussed in this chapter to evaluate clients, witnesses, juries, judges, and opposing counsel.

Let the interviewee know in advance that you will be focusing on this particular skill.

LBD 8-5. The term "kinesics" is believed to have been coined by dancer turned anthropologist, R.L. Birdwhitsell. His seminal work, *Introduction to Kinesics*, is listed in Appendix E along with a number of other resources dealing with verbal and non-verbal communication. See if you can locate a kinesics expert in your area and arrange an interview. Ask about the expert's experience and training in the field; any experience in consulting or testifying for attorneys; and what the expert considers the basic principles of reading body language.

LBDs 8-6 and 8-8 are accessible on the Author Updates link to the text Web site at www.aspenparalegaled.com/books/parsons_investigating/default.asp.

PART TWO

FORMULATING AND EXECUTING
A PLAN OF INVESTIGATION

PART OUTLINE

CHAPTER 9
Formulating a Plan of Investigation

CHAPTER 10
Preparing for a Client Interview

CHAPTER 11
Conducting a Client Interview

CHAPTER 12
Preparing for a Witness Interview

CHAPTER 13
Conducting a Witness Interview

CHAPTER 14
Identifying and Locating Fact Witnesses

CHAPTER 15
Working with Expert Witnesses

CHAPTER 16
Public Sources of Information—Federal

CHAPTER 17
Public Sources of Information—State and Local

CHAPTER 18
Private Sources of Information

Chapter 9
Formulating a Plan of Investigation

CHAPTER OBJECTIVES

In this chapter we consider what a plan of investigation is and how to formulate an effective and successful plan. You will learn:

- That an effective investigator has a number of distinguishing traits including persistence, creativity, flexibility, and skepticism.
- That having a carefully thought-out plan of investigation is essential to a successful investigation.
- That formulating a plan of investigation begins with what we know, is defined and guided by the law of the case, and is organized in steps to help us locate all information relevant to the client's case.
- That every plan of investigation has limits imposed by a number of factors including client resources, client authorization, and the value of the case.
- That every plan of investigation must be modified as it is executed.
- That the investigating legal professional is frequently the custodian of documents and physical evidence located in an investigation and must know how to label, secure, and document such items of evidence to comply with the rules of evidence.

A.   Introduction

Simply put, factual investigation in a law office is the process of locating, gathering, and verifying factual information related to the representation of a client. Historically, attorneys have received no real training in how to conduct factual investigations themselves and have had to learn the hard way—on the job. Because of their lack of training in this critical area and because of other factors (including their chronic lack of time), attorneys have relied on private investigators to conduct anything other than the simplest investigations.

Today that is changing rapidly. Well-trained paralegals are able to conduct effective, competent factual investigations for their supervising attorneys. It is one of the skills that makes them so valuable—and so marketable. Many senior lawyers now train and use new associate lawyers for these tasks as well, making interviewing and investigating another common skill of the lawyer and the paralegal.

B.   Traits of the Effective Investigator

Before considering the specifics of how to plan an effective investigation, it may be helpful to consider a number of traits that the legal professional who wishes to be an effective investigator should have. The adjectives in Illustration 9-1 describe some of these traits. Consider what you would add to that list.

1. The effective investigator is *knowledgeable*

SL EUTH ON THE LOOSE

Identify a small community in another part of your state and assume you are sent there on an investigation assignment. Access www.mapquest.com to get a detailed map showing how to get there from where you are.

- of the substantive law controlling the case (see Chapter 1);
- of the adversarial system and procedural law (see Chapters 3 through 5);
- of the rules of evidence (see Chapters 6 and 7); and
- of ethical rules and professional standards (see Chapter 2).

2. The effective investigator is *skilled*

- at factual analysis (see Chapter 1);
- at communicating with others (see Chapter 8);
- at interviewing clients and witnesses (see Chapters 10 through 13);
- at identifying potential witnesses, locating missing witnesses, and working with experts (see Chapters 14 and 15); and
- at locating information from public and private sources (see Chapters 16 through 18).

3. The effective investigator is *persistent*

Information does not always come easily in this line of work. Where to find what you need is not always obvious. Witnesses are missing, uncooperative, or even hostile. Documents are not where they should be and clients prove unhelpful. The investigator must learn to expect all this and resolve to keep digging.

Those who have done legal investigation for years know that **persistence** always pays. Persistent factual investigation always yields *something* of value—and frequently of great value—to the client's case.

Illustration 9-1
TRAITS OF THE
EFFECTIVE
INVESTIGATOR

The effective investigator must be:

knowledgeable	*perceptive*
skilled	*skeptical*
persistent	*flexible*
creative	

HYPOTHETICAL 9-1

Assume that Never Quit works for the attorney representing Speed Freak. Speed Freak has been sued by Granny Puttalong, a 70-year-old grandmother who was involved in an automobile accident with Speed Freak. Puttalong alleges in her complaint that she was putting along the road under the speed limit (as always) when Speed Freak came up behind her and proceeded to honk and ride her bumper. She panicked, lost control of her car, and hit a telephone pole. Speed Freak denies he was tailgaiting Puttalong. He contends he kept a safe distance from her but she stopped without warning. That's when he honked. He says she seemed to panic when he honked and swerved into the telephone pole.

Puttalong has sued Speed Freak for negligence and alleges permanent injury to her back. In her deposition, Granny Puttalong denied any prior problems with her back. In interrogatories served on Puttalong, the attorney for Speed Freak asked Puttalong to list all her doctors or other health care providers for the ten years preceding the accident. Those interrogatory answers have been received and the medical records from the identified physicians have been obtained and reviewed by Never Quit.

Assume Never Quit can find no reference in the medical records of Puttalong to any complaints of or treatment for back problems prior to the accident with Speed Freak. However, there are references in the medicals to three other doctors seen by Puttalong years before who were not identified in the interrogatory answers. All three of those doctors practice in a neighboring state. They are apparently doctors seen by Puttalong more than ten years preceding the accident. Should Never Quit do any more investigation into Puttalong's medical history or should Never Quit quit? Why?

Well, Never Quit never quits! Instead she uses the medical authorization obtained from Puttalong to obtain the medicals from the three newly discovered doctors. Medicals come to Never Quit from two of those doctors but are not helpful. The medical authorization from the third doctor, whose name is Nohome Visit, is returned to Never Quit with the handwritten message on it, "Doctor Visit is deceased." Should Never Quit do any more investigation into Puttalong's medical history or should she quit? Why?

Well, Never Quit never quits! Instead she locates and places a call to the agency that licenses medical doctors in the state where Nohome Visit practiced and makes inquiries regarding when Dr. Visit passed away. She is advised that Dr. Visit has been deceased for eight years. What else do you think Never Quit might want to ask? That's right! She asks about other physicians with whom Dr. Visit may have practiced or who may have taken over his practice following his death.

She learns that Dr. Visit's practice was taken over by his partner, Dr. Bedside Manner. Unfortunately, she learns that Dr. Manner is himself deceased as of three years ago and no other physician took over that practice. Should Never Quit do any more investigation into Puttalong's medical history or should she quit? Why?

Well, as you now know, Never Quit never quits! Instead she determines that Dr. Manner has a surviving widow who still lives in the same small community in which her husband and Dr. Visit practiced. Never Quit places a phone call to Mrs. Manner and learns that, yes, she does still have all of her late husband's old medical records and, yes, those records would probably include the old files of Dr. Visit. They're in her dusty old attic and Never Quit can come look for what she wants anytime.

1. How justifiable would it have been for Never Quit to quit earlier than this?
2. We still don't know if Dr. Visit's file on Granny Puttalong is in Mrs. Manner's attic or what it might contain. Who will have to decide whether to spend the extra time and money to make that search?
3. If it is decided to make that search, what are the different ways we might arrange to do it?
4. What does this Hypothetical say about the importance of an investigation plan being flexible?
5. Under the substantive law of negligence and damages in your state, what might be the legal significance of a factual determination that Granny Puttalong was in fact treated by Dr. Visit for chronic back problems 12 years before the accident? Does this help you understand why Never Quit would be so persistent in pursuing this information?

4. The effective investigator is *creative*

The imagery may be appropriately out of fashion these days, but the truth behind the old saying "there's more than one way to skin a cat" is still valid. Some investigative tasks are straightforward and routine (e.g., "Go over to the courthouse and get a copy of the divorce decree."). However, many assignments require the exercise of discretion and judgment. Decisions have to be made about how to go about the assignment economically and effectively. The investigator will hit roadblocks to finding what is needed and will have to think of other ways to get what is wanted. In investigation, there is no substitute for **creative thinking**.

HYPOTHETICAL 9-2

Assume that Never Quit is authorized to travel to the neighboring state where Mrs. Manner, the widow of Dr. Bedside Manner, resides to look through the records of Granny Puttalong. Never Quit travels to Mrs. Manner's house along with Better Idea who works for a local in-state law office which is assisting with this part of the investigation.

Unfortunately, when Never Quit and Better Idea arrive, Mrs. Manner gets nervous and balks at letting the two investigators look through her husband's records to locate Puttalong's old medical file. She says she knows it wouldn't be violating any laws or anything but it just makes her nervous. She says she should have thrown those old files out long ago and is going to do so soon.

Never Quit tries to think what to do. She can:

a. strong-arm her way past the frail widow and take the file by force;

b. wait until Mrs. Manner is out, then break in and steal the file; or
c. come back later disguised as a state investigator who needs to see the files for official purposes.

Fortunately, Never Quit quickly eliminates these possibilities and tells Better Idea they have no option but to recommend that the attorney for Speed Freak have Mrs. Manner subpoenaed to a deposition and require her to bring the file with her. They agree that would involve added time and expense when they don't even know if the file will prove helpful.

Then, Better Idea says, "Wait a minute, I have a better idea." Better Idea tells Never Quit to wait in the car then goes back to the front door of Mrs. Manner's house and rings the doorbell. When Mrs. Manner answers, Never Quit hears Better Idea begin to ask her about the roses growing next to her porch. Mrs. Manner comes out on the porch to answer the questions and a long conversation follows.

Before long, Never Quit sees Mrs. Manner go back inside the house then return with a quilt. She and Better Idea sit down together in the porch swing and continue talking, apparently about the quilt. After a while Never Quit begins to nod off. The last thing she sees is Better Idea going inside the house with Mrs. Manner.

Sometime later Never Quit is awakened by Better Idea shouting good-byes to Mrs. Manner and opening the car door. As Never Quit sits up, Better Idea hands her a cut rose, a plate full of fresh-baked cookies (I believe they were chocolate chip), and the file of Granny Puttalong, which Better Idea has permission to copy and return to Mrs. Manner. As Better Idea gets in the car he says, "You know, it occurred to me that Mrs. Manner was uptight because she really didn't know us. I thought if I visited with her a little and got to know her she might relax. And what do you know, it worked!"

1. How much time, trouble, and expense have been saved by Better Idea's creative thinking?
2. How important are communication skills (people skills) in investigating?
3. How does this Hypothetical illustrate the importance of a plan of investigation being flexible?
4. Why was Never Quit wise to eliminate her first ideas on how to obtain the Granny Puttalong file?

5. The effective investigator is *perceptive*

Factual investigation is analogous to driving an automobile. We all learn early on that when driving a car you must stay constantly alert, even when driving routes you take every day.

The same type of awareness is required to be an effective investigator. You have to be perceptive, that is, alert and observant. Even if you are tired. Even if you are in a hurry. Even if you have done this a hundred times before. Why? Because if you are not, you are going to miss information you should have noticed. And that information could be critically important to the client's case (not to mention your future).

Another aspect of **perceptiveness** in investigating is **intuition**. Experienced investigators learn to trust their hunches, that is, their feelings or intuitive instincts. They know that the investigator has to be aware—watching, listening, and sensitive to impressions at all times. Such subjective vibes can be just as valuable to the investigator as any learned skill. But you have to consciously flip that invisible switch in your mind to activate those intuitive sensors or you won't be on the receiving end of some important signals.

HYPOTHETICAL 9-3

Assume that Eye Seenit has been identified by Granny Puttalong as an eye witness to the accident between her and Speed Freak. Assume also that Over Worked is assisting the attorney representing Speed Freak and is assigned to interview Seenit. Over Worked contacts Eye Seenit, prepares his questions, arrives at the interview on time, and gets through all his questions in under 15 minutes notwithstanding the witness's irritating habit of leaving the room every few moments.

Following the interview, Over Worked reports back to the supervising attorney that Eye Seenit confirms Granny Puttalong's version of the accident (see Hypothetical 9-1). Disappointed, the attorney concludes that Speed Freak is likely to lose the case on liability and considers settling.

Now assume that instead of Over Worked handling the interview of Eye Seenit that task is assigned to Under Paid (a very good paralegal who is, alas, underpaid). Under Paid contacts Eye Seenit, arranges the interview, prepares her questions, shows up on time, and begins asking her questions.

Maintaining close eye contact with Eye Seenit, she notices that he looks at her directly until she begins to ask about the details of the accident. Then he looks away from her. About five minutes into the interview, Eye Seenit drains the cup he is drinking from at his desk and excuses himself, leaving the room with the cup.

While Eye Seenit is gone from the room, Under Paid looks around and notices a pair of eyeglasses laying on the desk under a pile of papers. Soon Eye Seenit returns with his cup refilled and the interview resumes. Under Paid asks about the glasses and learns that Eye Seenit is near-sighted and was not wearing his glasses or contacts the day he saw the accident. He is pretty sure he saw what happened, though.

Under Paid notices that Eye Seenit sips from the cup frequently and smacks his lips each time. He also wipes his mouth with his hands after each swallow. Soon the cup is empty and again Eye Seenit leaves the room with it. While he is gone Under Paid continues looking around the room. She notices what appears to be a family photo on the wall—a family reunion maybe?

When Eye Seenit returns (with refilled cup in hand), Under Paid asks about the picture and particularly about a little old gray-haired lady in the back. Turns out the little old lady is none other than Granny Puttalong, who is married to Eye Seenit's uncle who is also his business partner.

As Eye Seenit continues to sip from his cup and answer questions, Under Paid notices that his speech is becoming slurred, his voice raised, and his answers slower. He is also a lot more relaxed and friendly than when the interview began. She finds an excuse to lean over Eye Seenit's desk to point at something and gets her nose within a few inches of his cup. Want to bet on what she smelled?

Having finished all other questions, Under Paid finally asks Eye Seenit about the contents of the cup and he admits, albeit somewhat defensively, that he needs a little sip to get him through the day and, yes, he would have been sipping the day of the accident because one day is just like another.

When Under Paid reports back to the supervising attorney, he compliments her, says there is no way they will settle the case now, and adds, "You know, Under Paid, I'm glad we hired you. You're worth every cent of that big salary we pay you!"

1. List everything you can think of that Over Worked failed to do or failed to do well.
2. How would you summarize the differences in how Under Paid and Over Worked handled this interview?
3. Was Under Paid wise to confront Eye Seenit with her suspicions of his drinking? Could that have backfired? What do you think of her decision to wait until all other questions have been asked before addressing that issue?
4. If Eye Seenit had denied that the liquid in the cup was alcohol or that he was a drinker, what other investigation might Under Paid have recommended to pursue this lead?

6. The effective investigator is *skeptical*

By **skeptical** we don't mean cynical. We do mean that the investigator should remember the first and second commandments of legal investigating: **assume nothing** and **verify everything.** It does not matter what the source of our information is—the client, a witness, a document, a government record—we always seek to verify the information given to us. If a lawyer is going to depend on certain facts to advise a client or to take an adversarial position on behalf of the client in civil or criminal litigation, the facts must first be tested in the crucible of investigation.

Specifically, that means that good investigators:

a. *Evaluate the source of information*

We always **evaluate** the source of information that comes to us to determine its reliability. Is the source reliable? Does this person seem believable? Does he seem competent? Does he have any motive to misstate facts or to leave out facts or to exaggerate? Is there any reason to believe he could have been mistaken in what he saw or heard? Or, is the document genuine? Is it complete? Is it the original?

b. *Test information for internal consistency*

We always **test information** given to us to see if it seems consistent, logical, and believable on its own. Does this information seem reliable? Will it hold up as true and credible if an opposing party examines it?

c. *Look for gaps in information*

We always look for holes or gaps in the information given to us— incomplete time lines, incomplete explanations, or implausible stories—and then determine how we can fill in those gaps with reliable information.

d. Compare new information to information already gathered

We always test information given to us by **comparing** it to other information we have to see if there are **contradictions** or **inconsistencies.** If there are, we work diligently to determine why. Why is this witness's story different from that witness's? Why is this document not consistent with what others have told me? Why does the public record say this when my client told me something else? Which one is correct?

e. Seek corroborating information

We always seek **corroborating** (confirming or supporting) information in the form of other witnesses or documents that can back up or confirm the information.

f. Seek explanations and details

We always need to know **who, what, where, why, when,** and **how.** If we come across a thread of new information in an interview or investigation we follow it until the whole ball is unraveled! We stay curious.

g. Seek leads to more information

We always seek **leads** to other sources of information and then follow those leads with the same energy and curiosity.

7. The effective investigator is *flexible*

In this chapter you will learn how to plan an effective investigation. But you will also learn to expect that plan to change, sometimes considerably, as you execute it. That is the nature of factual investigation.

As you will learn in the chapters on interviewing (see Chapters 10 through 13), an interviewer should never make a list of questions and follow it mindlessly in an interview. The investigator must be ready to follow up on answers given or observations made during the interview by asking other or different questions. Similarly, in all investigative activity, we set out with a plan but what we actually find—or don't find—will require us to modify it along the way. That **flexibility** is essential to effective investigating. See Hypotheticals 9-1, 9-2, and 9-4.

HYPOTHETICAL 9-4

Assume that the medical records of Granny Puttalong obtained from Mrs. Manner's attic showed that Dr. Visit had treated Puttalong for chronic back problems for a number of years; that she had undergone surgery on her back twice; and that she had become addicted to the pain medication prescribed for her. She stopped going to Dr. Nohome Visit when he refused to write her additional prescriptions for pain medication. His records indicate the permanent nature of the disability, the addiction, his recommendation of treatment for the addiction, and his warning that she not operate a motor vehicle because of her nervous condition.

1. In light of these discoveries, what new or additional direction(s) would you recommend for this investigation on behalf of Speed Freak?
2. Under the rules of evidence for your state courts, how will the attorney for Speed Freak get the discovered medical records of Dr. Visit for

Granny Puttalong admitted in evidence and how might that affect the investigation Never Quit is doing now?

C. The Importance of Having a Plan of Investigation

No investigation should be undertaken until a written plan has been formulated. Initiating an investigation without a plan is like leaving on a trip without a planned route; you may get there but you probably will be late! And the odds of getting lost will be much greater. Practically speaking, a planned investigation will be:

- more efficient in use of time;
- more efficient economically;
- more likely to be thorough;
- less stressful; and
- more likely to be done effectively.

There will be times when it is tempting to jump into an investigation without doing the planning recommended in this chapter. Time deadlines, busy schedules, the complacency that comes from having done similar tasks many times before, or just pure old laziness may all combine to tempt you. But experienced investigators know that it is always a mistake to shortcut the planning process. For even the briefest or most routine interview or investigation assignment, make a plan before you act, and put it in writing.

D. Formulating a Plan of Investigation

1. Start with what you already know

If I am planning to travel from Nashville, Tennessee (where I have been trying unsuccessfully to break into the country music business as the long-lost love child of Patsy Cline and Buddy Holly), to Los Angeles, California (where I now plan to succeed in the movie business as Cleft Chin, the next great leading man), I would be smart to plan my route starting from Nashville. It would be foolish to plan my trip from Chicago or Baltimore. This sounds obvious but, in reality, many investigations go awry because the investigator fails to carefully take account of the factual and legal basis from which the investigation begins. They fail to consider what they already know before they launch an effort to learn more.

So the first step in planning an investigation is to prepare a summary of all facts that you already have at your disposal. For each fact included in your summary, it is a good idea to note the *source* of that information (i.e., client, witness, document) and an indication of whether the information is deemed *reliable* or *questionable*.

Illustration 9-2 FIRST STEP IN FORMULATING THE PLAN OF INVESTIGATION: SUMMARIZE INFORMATION ALREADY KNOWN

INVESTIGATION PLAN

CLIENT: Granny Puttalong
FILE NO.: YR00-0001
ADVERSE PARTY: Speed Freak
DATE: March 1, YR00

I. SUMMARY OF FACTS KNOWN TO DATE	SOURCE	RELIABLE (Y-N)	STILL TO DO
1. Client is a 70-year-old retired school teacher living with her 2nd husband. . . .	Client	Y	Is age correct? (See accident report.)
6. On December 10, YR-1 client struck a telephone pole head-on while driving her YR-3 Saturn automobile.	Client/Accident report	Y	
7. Saturn purchased in March YR-1 for $16,500. Car totaled in crash. . . .	Client/Invoice/ Accident report	Y	Who owns car?
12. Client has 2 fused discs and surgery upcoming; broken fibula. . . .	City Hospital ER records/Dr. Helen Smith reports	Y	
15. Driver behind client, Speed Freak, tailgating, honking; caused client to panic and lose control. . . .	Client/Accident report inconclusive	N	Need to locate & interview witnesses

Now go over the summary, looking for information that needs to be verified. Look for gaps or inconsistencies in the information. Make a note regarding how you intend to fill in those gaps.

Illustration 9-2 gives you an idea of how this first step might look in an **investigation plan** prepared by a legal professional doing pre-filing investigation on behalf of Granny Puttalong in connection with her potential claim against Speed Freak.

2. Identify the specific goals of your investigation

In other words, determine as precisely as you can where it is you want to go with your investigation—what is it exactly that you want to accomplish? In planning my big career move from Nashville to Los Angeles, I would be unwise to pack up and pull out in traffic before I have specifically identified the location of L.A. on the map. Instead, I'm going to identify *where* I am going and then plan *how* to get there *before* I leave.

It's like that in a factual investigation. Having established what you already know—where you are—now determine what exactly you want to accomplish—where you want to go. Only after these first two steps are completed can we plan the particulars of the investigation—how you're going to get there.

a. Consider the law of the case

Recall the discussion of the relationship between fact and law in Chapter 1. We undertake factual investigation only because the client has a legal problem of some kind and we must locate factual information related to that legal problem. The law defines the context for the investigation. It will point us in the direction we need to go.

In the Granny Puttalong case, we are representing her with a view toward suing any and all parties responsible for the automobile accident in which she was injured. The most obvious legal theory for this contemplated personal injury action is negligence. The most likely target is the other driver, Speed Freak. If Puttalong is going to be able to recover from Speed Freak for negligence she will have to prove that:

- Speed Freak owed her a duty of care in operating his vehicle;
- he breached that duty of care in some way;
- his breach of duty of care was the actual and proximate (foreseeable) cause of injuries sustained by Puttalong; and
- the injuries and other damage Puttalong did in fact sustain were due to the breach of duty by Speed Freak.

That is the law of the case. It will provide the context in which we undertake factual investigation in the Granny Puttalong case. Of course, we know from our study of tort law (and our discussions with the supervising attorney) that in negligence actions there are legal defenses that may be raised—comparative fault, assumption of the risk, third-party intervening causation, and so forth. Sometimes defendants in negligence actions also counterclaim against a plaintiff, alleging that it was the plaintiff who violated a duty of care owed to the defendant and caused damages sustained by defendant. We also know that counterclaims occur with great frequency in automobile accidents where both drivers typically sustain damage to their personal property (the vehicles) and often to their persons. So in our factual investigation for Granny Puttalong we will have to look for facts that might give rise to such defenses or counterclaims on behalf of Speed Freak or other potential defendants. All of these legal considerations define the factual investigation we are planning.

b. Write down the ultimate goals of the investigation

Now that you have summarized what you already know and have considered the legal context of the case, give thought to what else you need to learn. What are the specific goals of your remaining investigation? Write down your goals as you identify them. Putting your plan into words will help you organize it and get it clear in your mind. Illustration 9-3 gives you an idea how this second step might look in the investigation plan prepared by a legal professional doing pre-filing investigation on behalf of Granny Puttalong in connection with her potential claim against Speed Freak.

Illustration 9-3 is by no means an exhaustive list. Each case will raise its own unique questions that must be answered by investigation. See Hypothetical 9-5.

HYPOTHETICAL 9-5

Assume you are working for the attorney defending Speed Freak in the anticipated claim to be made by Granny Puttalong. What might the stated goals of your pre-filing investigation plan look like?

Illustration 9-3   SECOND STEP IN FORMULATING THE PLAN OF INVESTIGATION: IDENTIFY THE GOALS OF THE INVESTIGATION

INVESTIGATION PLAN

CLIENT: Granny Puttalong
FILE NO.: YR00-0001
ADVERSE PARTY: Speed Freak
DATE: March 1, YR00

II. Goals of this investigation

1. Identify all possible plaintiffs.
   - Can the client's husband make a loss of consortium claim?
   - Is he a co-owner of the damaged car?

2. Determine the nature and extent of damages.
   - Value of the damaged car
   - Obtain current medical records on client
   - Ask treating physician for disability rating/future medicals

3. Identifying each possible defendant.
   - Was Speed Freak the owner of the car?
   - Was Speed Freak acting as an agent for another (vicarious liability)?
   - Did Speed Freak have a passenger or was he talking on car phone?
   - Did client's car—brakes, air bag, steering—malfunction in any way?

4. Identify and evaluate all possible legal theories against each potential defendant based on the available facts (e.g., simple negligence, strict liability, breach of warranty, breach of contract, fraud, infliction of emotional distress, etc.).

5. Identify possible defenses (including affirmative defenses) which could defeat client's claim(s) or mitigate damages.
   - Statutes of limitation or repose
   - Comparative fault
   - Assumption of risk
   - Lack of causation
   - Prior existing medical condition(s)
   - Intervening third-party act

6. Identify and evaluate possible personal jurisdiction problems with regard to each possible defendant.

7. Determine the relative financial position of each possible defendant (including the existence of liability insurance and its limits) to evaluate whether pursuing them to judgment will be worthwhile.

8. Determine the options regarding subject matter jurisdiction. Can we file this in federal as well as state court? If we have a choice which would we prefer?

9. Preserve existing evidence.
   - Photo and video scene
   - Photo and video autos
   - Photo and video client injuries
   - Client diary

10. Identify and interview witnesses.
    Eye Seenit

11. Identify and retain accident reconstruction expert.

3. Brainstorm for specifics

Let's see, now. I'm going from Nashville to L.A., so I want to leave Nashville on I-40 West and stay on it through Memphis. Maybe I can get there about noon and try some of those barbeque ribs the city is famous 'for. And maybe I'll have time to take in Graceland; if Elvis is alive, isn't that where he would be? I'll stay on I-40 all the way to Little Rock. There I'll pick up I-30 and go on to Dallas. H'm, if I travel on a weekend I wonder if I could catch the Cowboys at home. And from Dallas . . .

Once the traveler knows where he is leaving from and where he is going to he can then plan the specifics of the trip. Similarly, once the investigator has determined what he knows so far and what he still needs to accomplish, then—and only then—is he ready to plan the specifics of the investigation.

A good way to begin identifying the specific things to be done to accomplish the identified goals of the investigation is to **brainstorm.** Make a list of all the things you need to do to answer every question or achieve every purpose on the list you compiled in step two of the plan. At this stage, don't bother to put the things you think of down in a particular order, just get them out of your head and on paper (or computer file). Here are some tips for the brainstorming step:

- Use the supervising attorney, the client, notes and memoranda in the file, documents gathered to date, and anyone else in the office working on the case as sources for ideas.
- Utilize the old tried and true: who, what, where, why, when, and how.
- Don't confine yourself to the obvious—wonder about things.

There will always be basic things you need to do in an investigation and those will typically come to your mind first (e.g., get the accident report, get the medicals, interview the witnesses, etc.). Be sure to list those. But at that point you have only begun to plan. Let your mind wonder. (Not *wander* off the subject, but *wonder!*) With regard to each thing you know about the case, let yourself wonder about what you don't know. Did Speed Freak tailgate Granny Puttalong and honk at her for going slow? I wonder why he did that. Could he have had an emergency? Was he late to work? Is he just a road rage jerk? Does he do this all the time? I wonder where he had been immediately before this accident or earlier in the day. I wonder why he was in such a hurry. I wonder who might have seen him before he came up on Granny's car. Was anything wrong with his car? I wonder what was on his mind to preoccupy him. I wonder if he could have been angry or upset and why. Was he on a business errand at the time and, if so, for whom?

I wonder, I wonder, I wonder. If you take the time to do this, the creative juices will begin to flow and you might be amazed at what you think of to look into. Of such creative thinking winning cases are made.

Illustration 9-4 shows you how this third brainstorming step might look as applied to stated goal number 2, "Determine the nature and extent of damages" from Illustration 9-3.

Illustration 9-4 THIRD STEP IN FORMULATING THE PLAN OF INVESTIGATION: BRAINSTORM FOR SPECIFICS

INVESTIGATION PLAN

CLIENT: Granny Puttalong
FILE NO.: YR00-0001
ADVERSE PARTY: Speed Freak
DATE: March 1, YR00

III. BRAINSTORMING FOR SPECIFICS . . .

2. Determine the nature and extent of damages.
   - Get all hospital records for client admission, surgery, discharge.
   - Get updated medicals from Dr. H. Smith and ask when disability determination will be made. Will she give us a preliminary determination in writing for possible settlement effort?
   - Get final bills from hospital, ambulance service, towing service, storage facility. Will city charge client for damage to telephone pole? (Should we call city about that or wait and see—don't want to give them the idea—or do we? Ask attorney.)
   - Get updated bill from Dr. Smith. Ask about future medicals. (Can she go ahead and estimate for settlement effort? In writing?)
   - Get value of car from NADA book. Was there any personalty lost in car?
   - Interview Granny's husband re loss of consortium theory.
   - Any photos or videos of injuries, scene or vehicles? Suggest they take photo/video of injuries, disabilities.
   - Suggest client start daily diary to supplement pain and suffering, loss of enjoyment of life claims.
   - Insurance policies? Locate. Notification yet? Verify. Coverage questions?
   - Disability insurance on Granny? Social Security claim?
   - Verify she's not working—workers' comp?
   - Ask about pre-existing condition on back stuff. Other doctors seen? Chiropractors? Get old medicals on her— how far? Ask attorney.
   - Any plans to go back to work in the future? Possible now?
   - Other medical problems that will be worsened by accident? Arthritis exacerbated? Ask Dr. Smith.
   - Who to use for accident reconstruction if needed?
   - Who to use to calculate present value numbers—economist, banker?

4. Identify all possible sources of information

As you create your brainstorming list, or after you have done so, identify and write down all **sources** from which you will attempt to obtain each item of information. Be specific. What person, government office, private business, document, or other source will be likely to provide you with what you need? In general, all information comes from one of eight sources:

1. the client
2. the opposing party
3. eyewitnesses
4. non-eyewitness information sources
5. the scene, site, or thing involved in the incident
6. public documents
7. private documents
8. consulting experts

5. Organize your plan into a logical format and chart it

There is no single format for a final **plan of investigation**. In this section we will discuss four different formats for final plans of investigation: (1) a **chronological to-do list format**; (2) a **topical format**; (3) a **sources format**; and (4) a **litigation or cause of action format**.

These formats are suggestive only. As the legal professional gains experience in investigation she will develop her own customized format for a plan of investigation. However, it will always be important for the investigating legal professional to go through steps 1 to 4 before formatting the final plan of investigation. And it will also be important, no matter what format you use, to **chart** your plan of investigation. That is, put it in some form of writing that makes it easy to read and review, to locate needed information quickly, and to update as you proceed with the investigation. Samples of charted investigation plans are presented with each of the formats discussed in this chapter. (See Illustrations 9-5, 9-6, 9-7, and 9-8.)

If possible, the investigator should keep the charted investigation plan on computer. That generally makes the plan easier to access than a hard (paper) copy sitting in the file folder. (Now where is that darn file? I thought I left it right here on the desk.) It also makes it easier to change and to update the status of the investigation. If you need a hard copy of the investigation plan chart, you can always print it out.

a. The chronological to-do list format

Useful primarily for shorter, less complicated investigations, the to-do list format is simply a list of things to do placed in chronological order. For that reason it is sometimes referred to as a *time line* format. Beside each item on the list a place should be provided to indicate (1) the date when work on that item was initiated, (2) the status of the work on that item at any given time, and (3) the date work on that item is completed.

If the legal professional assisting the attorney representing Granny Puttalong is instructed by the attorney to obtain the client's medicals for the past ten years; get the accident report; and interview the investigating officer, Puttalong's husband, and Eye Seenit, a chronological to-do list format for the investigation plan might look like Illustration 9-5.

b. The topical format

Using this format, the plan of investigation is organized by topic or subject matter. If, for example, the legal professional assisting the attorney representing Granny Puttalong is instructed by the attorney to obtain information on the client's injuries and expenses, a topical format for the plan of investigation might look something like Illustration 9-6.

c. The sources format

This format organizes the final plan of investigation around the various sources from which information will be sought. Sources in any given case might include the parties, fact witnesses, expert witnesses, and documentary proof. Illustration 9-7 shows how the sources format for a

Illustration 9-5   PLAN OF INVESTIGATION USING A TO-DO LIST FORMAT

INVESTIGATION PLAN

CLIENT: Granny Puttalong
FILE NO.: YR00-0001
ADVERSE PARTY: Speed Freak
DATE: March 1, YR00

V. INVESTIGATION TO BE DONE

ASSIGNMENT	DATE INITIATED	STATUS	DATE COMPLETED
1. Contact police dept. for accident rept. records			
2. Photo/video scene			
3. Photo/video car at Moore's Garage			
4. Prepare medical records authorization for client			
5. Interview client re medical providers last ten years			
6. Have client sign med. auth.			
7. Interview husband			
8. Interview investigating officer			
9. Interview Eye Seenit			

plan of investigation prepared by a legal professional assisting the attorney representing Granny Puttalong might look.

d. The cause of action format

The litigation or cause of action format organizes a final plan of investigation around the specific elements of each cause of action or defense to be pled in the case. Each such element is charted allowing the legal professional to identify (1) information needed; (2) sources for that information; (3) the informal investigation you plan to do to gather that information; (4) the formal investigation you recommend be done to gather that information; and (5) a time frame for accomplishing each part of the plan. A **litigation chart** in a negligence case might look something like Illustration 9-8.

Again, it should be kept in mind that the four formats for plans of investigation discussed here are suggestions only. The style of the individual investigator as well as the nature of a particular case may require a customized format.

E.   Limitations on a Plan of Investigation

We cannot always do all the investigation we want or need to do on a particular case. A number of factors determine and limit the scope of the investigation you will be authorized to do. Those factors include:

Illustration 9-6 PLAN OF INVESTIGATION USING A TOPICAL FORMAT

INVESTIGATION PLAN

CLIENT: Granny Puttalong
FILE NO.: YR00-0001
ADVERSE PARTY: Speed Freak
DATE: March 1, YR00

V. INVESTIGATION TO BE DONE

ASSIGNMENT	DATE INITIATED	STATUS	DATE COMPLETED
1. INJURIES			
a. Prepare medical records auth. and have client sign			
b. Obtain hospital records including ER records			
c. Obtain med. records of Dr. Helen Smith			
d. Interview Dr. Smith re injuries/ prognosis/disability			
e. Interview client re injuries/diary			
f. Interview husband re injuries/ disabilities			
2. EXPENSES			
a. Obtain hospital bills from City Hospital			
b. Obtain ambulance bill from Emergency Service, Inc.			
c. Obtain towing/storage bill from Cedar Bluff Towing			
d. Determine book value of car			
e. Obtain invoice on car from client/ husband or dealer (Dodge Dart Cars in city)			
f. Interview client/husband re car value and personal property loss			
g. Interview client re plans for work or other lost income			

1. The amount of work actually required

Engaging in investigation can sometimes require the same type of judgment call that doctors have to make in deciding whether to run more tests on a patient. When is enough enough? At what point have we done all we really need to do and any more would just be running up the bill? It is up to the supervising attorney to decide that question in the exercise of her professional judgment on behalf of the client.

2. The cost of the work to be done

Investigative work can be expensive. In addition to the time of the investigator, there are out-of-pocket expenses frequently incurred, such as long-distance phone calls, postage, copying, mileage, and other traveling expenses. Any time an investigative task is going to require an

Illustration 9-7   PLAN OF INVESTIGATION USING A SOURCES FORMAT

INVESTIGATION PLAN

CLIENT: Granny Puttalong
FILE NO.: YR00-0001
ADVERSE PARTY: Speed Freak
DATE: March 1, YR00

V. INVESTIGATION TO BE DONE

A. FACT WITNESSES

Name	Address/ Phone	Areas of Knowledge	Intervw'd/ Date & By	Follow-up Needed (Y-N)	Documents Provided
1. G. Puttalong					
2. H. Puttalong					
3. S. Freak					
4. E. Seenit					
5. Officer D. Lewis					

B. EXPERT WITNESSES

Name	Address/ Phone	Areas of Knowledge	Intervw'd/ Date & By	Follow-up Needed (Y-N)	Documents Provided
1. Dr. F. Scalion					
2. Officer D. Lewis					

C. DOCUMENTARY EVIDENCE

Description	Source	Location- Originals	Copies in file? (Y-N)	Custodian/ Witness
1. Hospital bills				
2. Doctor bills				
3. Photos (8) of accident scene				

unexpected or significant expense the legal professional should consult with the supervising attorney to obtain advance authority.

3. The value of the case

Small cases do not justify the outlay of significant time or expenses for investigation. It is up to the supervising attorney and the client to decide how much investigation is warranted on a particular case.

4. The resources of the client

The ability of the client to pay for the time and expenses incurred in an investigation must also be considered. Even in a case handled by the law

Illustration 9-8   PLAN OF INVESTIGATION USING A CAUSE OF ACTION FORMAT

INVESTIGATION PLAN

CLIENT: Granny Puttalong
FILE NO.: YR00-0001
ADVERSE PARTY: Speed Freak
DATE: March 1, YR00

V. INVESTIGATION TO BE DONE

Element	Information Needed	Sources for Information	Informal Investigation	Formal Discovery	Date\ Deadline
1. Duty					
2. Breach					
3. Cause in fact					
4. Proximate cause					
5. Damages					

B. DEFENSES TO NEGLIGENCE

Element	Information Needed	Sources for Information	Informal Investigation	Formal Discovery	Date\ Deadline
1. Plaintiff's fault					
2. Assumption of risk					
3. Intervening cause					
4. Statute of repose					

firm on a contingency basis, the client is responsible for the out-of-pocket expenses.

5. The resources of the law office

The resources of the law office may be limited by staffing shortages or by busy schedules, limitations that the supervising attorney should consider in deciding whether to take a case at all. And before taking the case, the attorney should advise the client of the limited resources of the office so the client can make an informed choice.

There are ethical consequences to these decisions and actions. The ethical and professional obligation that the attorney owes the client to represent the client competently and vigorously might be violated by accepting a case that the office does not have the resources to handle. When assisting a lead attorney, your responsibility is to always let that attorney know of any limitations on your time to undertake necessary investigation on a matter.

6. Client authorization

The law office cannot undertake investigative work without the approval of the client. This **authorization** may come at the beginning of the representation and be valid for the duration of the case. Or it may be necessary to obtain authorization for each new investigative task as it arises. The legal professional assisting a lead attorney should always check with that supervising attorney to be sure that the client has expressly or impliedly authorized a task before performing it.

Remember that any plan of investigation must be pre-approved by the supervising attorney before it is undertaken. It is up to the supervising attorney to obtain the client's approval. Likewise, you should keep that attorney advised on suggested changes in the investigation as it progresses and let that attorney know if such changes are going to make a significant difference in costs or time.

F.   Flexibility of a Plan of Investigation

The plan of investigation will be constantly under review and revision. That is as it should be. As you accomplish one investigative task, it may lead to another task that you did not originally anticipate. Always update your investigation plan so you do not forget anything. Check it regularly to be sure you are getting things done on time. And do not forget to keep the supervising attorney advised on a regular basis of the status of your investigation.

G.   The Handling of Documents and Physical Evidence During an Investigation

During the course of the investigation the legal professional may come into the possession of a variety of documentary and physical evidence. Before discussing the proper handling of such material, it will be helpful to define what we mean by *documentary evidence* and *physical evidence*.

1. Distinguishing between documentary and physical evidence

By **documentary evidence** we mean any type of data compilation in paper, electronic format, or other form, and of public, private, or business origin. This is a very broad definition and encompasses all writings, correspondence, memoranda, reports, records, books, publications, sketches, drawings, diagrams, charts, maps, blueprints, photographs, video recordings, movies, slides, audio recordings, microfiche, microfilm, x-ray, MRI or laser imagery, CD-ROM disks, electronically stored information from computers, laptops, personal assistant devices, cell phones, scanners, fax machines, floppy disks, and any similar materials however denominated.

By **physical evidence** we mean any physical or material object that is not documentary in nature, such as machinery, equipment, tools, vehicles, works of art, and all types of consumer and commercial products (food, clothing, cleaning products, etc.).

It is not the purpose of this section to deal with identifying and obtaining documentary and physical evidence. Those subjects are addressed in Chapters 16 through 18. In this section we deal only with the proper handling, storage, and recording of documents and things that come into the possession of the investigator.

2. Creating demonstrative evidence

Although much documentary and physical evidence is collected or gathered by the investigator from various public and private sources, sometimes the law office will itself create or hire a professional to create such evidence.

EXAMPLE

The legal professional may be asked by the supervising attorney to take photographs, video tape, or make sketches of the scene of an accident, the vehicle, or other object involved in the case or to arrange for a professional photographer or commercial artist to do so. Charts or diagrams designed to present financial or other statistical information in a more understandable or striking way may be prepared at the request of the attorney. Computerized simulations may be created by a consulting expert so the jury can more realistically visualize an incident that occurred in the past.

The legal professional may create such documentary or physical evidence herself if it is within the range of her competence. Taking photographs, making a video recording, or generating a simple graph are good examples of tasks frequently assigned to assisting legal professionals.

Or the legal professional may be asked to locate, contact, and make arrangements with an expert (see Chapter 15) to generate the items requested. Sketches, drawings, complex graphs and charts, as well as computerized simulations are all examples of more specialized tasks normally requested of experts. Even when work is turned over to an expert, the assisting legal professional will frequently be the primary contact between the expert and the law office and will be responsible for forwarding needed information to the expert.

3. The role of the rules of evidence in handling documents and things

Whether the documents and things that come into the possession of the legal professional are gathered from witnesses or generated by law office personnel or a retained expert, the legal professional who is responsible for handling and storing those items must be always mindful of relevant rules of evidence. Mishandling evidence could have a severe negative impact on a client's case and may amount to malpractice as well as an ethical violation (remember the duty of competence?).

The most significant evidentiary rules that come into play in the handling and storage of documentary and physical evidence are the rules regarding authentication, chain of custody, privilege, attorney work product, and the best evidence rule. Consequently, the legal professional who comes into custody of documentary or physical evidence should:

- Determine and keep a record of who has the original document or thing.
- Determine and keep a record of who the authenticating witness(es) will be for the document or thing.
- Carefully handle and store documentary or physical evidence, and document its whereabouts at all times.
- Locate the original document or thing and, in the absence of the original, have an authentic copy available and be able to explain why the original is not available.
- Maintain all documents and things in such a way that client confidentiality is not compromised.
- If the document or thing qualifies as work product, label it as such and maintain it in such a way that the privilege is not compromised.

HYPOTHETICAL 9-6

Assume you work for the attorney representing the plaintiff in a products liability case. The plaintiff alleges that a toaster she bought was unreasonably defective because the first time she used it, the toast shot up out of the toaster with such force that it struck her in the left eye even though her face was at least two feet above the toaster at the time. The rocketing toast caused plaintiff severe swelling and permanent partial loss of vision in that eye.

The supervising attorney has instructed you to take possession of the toaster and the receipt showing the plaintiff's purchase of the toaster and to take some pictures of the plaintiff's swollen eye. You visit the plaintiff's house and are surprised to see that the plaintiff is using the toaster to make toast for her family. She asks if you mind if she makes just one more piece of toast before you take the toaster away and you agree. You watch with amazement as the toast, when it is done, shoots out of the toaster at great speed and rises at least five feet in the air. Finally you take the pictures requested and leave with the pictures, toaster, and receipt.

As you leave the plaintiff's house you toss the toaster in the back seat. Since you were on your way home anyway, you take the toaster in, show it to your family, and demonstrate the flying toast. Your family is so entertained that they invite the neighbors over and the toast party goes on all night. Everyone enjoys the pictures of the injured client as well; they are amazed that a simple piece of toast could cause such swelling. Your little sister asks if she can take the toaster and pictures to school the next day for show and tell. Since you dote on her and can't tell her no, you say okay so long as she brings them back home right after school.

Fortunately, the supervising attorney is out of the office the next day so no questions are asked about the toaster and pictures. The receipt you toss in your work file.

The next day you bring the toaster and pictures to work with you. You store the pictures in the work file containing the receipt. Since the toaster is such a conversation piece, you keep it in your office and demonstrate the flying toast to clients, friends, and others in the office.

A month later the supervising attorney comes in your office with an expert he has retained to help in the toaster case. He wants the expert to take a look at the toaster and formulate an opinion regarding the defect. The expert leaves with the toaster. The supervising attorney says he will meet with you and the expert tomorrow to review the case. He tells you to be sure to bring the receipt and pictures to the meeting.

The next day, moments before the meeting, you look in the work file but can't find that darn receipt anywhere. You sit down and type up a receipt that looks as much like the original as you can remember. The pictures are in the file but they were placed facing each other and became stuck together. They rip apart as you separate them, making your client look a lot like the phantom of the opera.

Sheepishly, you go into the conference room for the meeting. The supervising attorney and the expert are studying the toaster, which the expert reports is working just fine.

1. As a result of your work on this file you can consider yourself:
    a. a superstar
    b. promoted
    c. toast
2. Review Chapters 6 and 7 on the rules of evidence and list every evidentiary problem you have created if the toaster, receipt, and pictures are ever offered as evidence at trial.
3. What ethical violations have you committed on this case?

4. Procedures for handling documents and things in your custody

When the legal professional is given custody of documentary or physical evidence, certain procedures should be followed:

a. Label the evidence

The evidence should be labeled or tagged with some identifying number or description. For physical evidence, this may be an adhesive label that can be removed without damaging or defacing the object. If attaching an adhesive is not feasible, then consider tying a tag to the item or placing the item in another larger container and labeling that container. For documentary evidence, labels or tags may be used or the documents may be placed in a labeled folder.

Whenever evidence is labeled or tagged, the label or tag should never be placed over any legible part of the evidence.

b. Secure the evidence

The evidence should be placed in a secure place where no unauthorized person can obtain entry. For documentary evidence and small physical objects, this may mean locking the item away in a fire-proof file cabinet or safe. Larger or more numerous items may require a locked evidence room or a secure storage facility outside the office.

c. Keep an evidence log

Information concerning the evidence should be entered in an **evidence log** or chart. The evidence log should contain certain basic information including:

- a description of the evidence;
- the date it was received in custody;
- the source from whom it was obtained;
- whether the item is the original;
- identity of the custodian or other authenticating witness;
- a record of who has checked the item out and when; and
- when the checked-out item was returned.

An evidence log used in the Granny Puttalong case might follow the form set out in Illustration 9-9.

As with the final plan of investigation, it is advisable to place the evidence log on computer if possible for ease of access and update.

5. Procedures for documents and things not in your custody

Many times it is not possible to take literal possession of evidence. It may be the property of the adverse party or a non-party. It may be something the client needs for his business. In those situations, it is important to obtain exact copies of documents or comprehensive pictures or video recordings of the items as soon as possible. We cannot assume that documents will be preserved or left unchanged, or that things will not be discarded, lost, destroyed, or materially changed.

If, for example, in the toaster case from Hypothetical 9-6, the plaintiff had sold the toaster to another person who would not allow us to take custody of it, we would then try to obtain permission to photograph it, video tape it in use, and have our consulting expert examine it. If by the time of trial it is gone or changed, we will still have admissible proof regarding the defect.

Illustration 9-9   EVIDENCE LOG

CLIENT: Granny Puttalong
FILE NO.: YR00-0001
ADVERSE PARTY: Speed Freak

Document/ Item	Date Rec'd	Source	Original/ Copy	Custodian/Auth. Wit.	Checked Out By	C/O Date	Ret. Date
1.							
2.							
3.							
4.							

Of course, if the person to whom the plaintiff sold the toaster will not allow us access to it for any purpose, our only recourse will be to subpoena the custodian to produce the item for inspection. Locating and obtaining various kinds of information is discussed in more detail in Chapters 16 through 18.

H. The Importance of Diligence and Thoroughness in Executing a Plan of Investigation

1. Diligence

Time is always of the essence in performing a factual investigation. The investigator should always remember that witnesses forget (what were you doing two months ago today?), they lose their initial interest in helping, they move, become ill, and they die. Documents and physical objects get destroyed, discarded, changed, or lost. Accident sites change with the weather and the seasons or with construction.

When a new case is assigned to you for investigation, locate and take possession of all the documentary and physical evidence that you can or to obtain genuine copies, photos, or video as quickly as possible. Identify, locate, and interview all relevant witnesses as soon as possible. The old saying, "the early bird gets the worm" doesn't refer only to early risers.

SLEUTH ON THE LOOSE

Identify a major news story from the past week then access http://news.google.com or http://news.yahoo.com to locate articles written on that story in domestic and foreign papers.

2. Thoroughness

When you are asked to inspect an accident site, physical object, or any other item of evidence, be sure you do it thoroughly. Take pictures from every conceivable angle. Remember some may not turn out well.

Be sure to keep the negatives of pictures taken. You may want to make more copies later and negatives produce new originals far superior in quality to photographed originals. Your supervising attorney may want to have enlarged certain pictures to be used at trial. Having the negatives will guarantee a better quality enlargement. Photos taken with a digital camera that are to be preserved should be uploaded from the camera to a computer file as soon as possible so they are not deleted.

Remember that photographs, videos, sketches, drawings, and diagrams must present a reasonably accurate depiction of the thing shown in order to be admissible at trial. Thus you must be concerned about lighting, angle, and scale when doing such work.

EXAMPLE

Assume you are photographing skid marks on a highway that are about 15 feet in length. If you are using a 35mm camera with an ordinary lens you will have to get several feet away from the skid marks to get them all in one picture. When the picture is developed you probably won't be able to tell if the marks are 15 feet or 15 inches in length! Why? Because your picture is not to scale. Try placing a ruler or yardstick in the picture to help bring it into scale.

> Similarly, if you are photographing or videotaping an object the height of which cannot be determined from the picture, try placing a person in the picture to bring it into scale. Wide angle and zoom lenses can help produce more accurate pictures.

When you are photographing or videotaping the scene of an accident, do so, to the extent possible, at the same time of day and in the same season and weather as the accident.

If you are not proficient with cameras, recommend hiring a professional photographer. And always consider who will be the authenticating witness for the photographs, video tapes, sketches, drawings, and diagrams that you make. For ethical and other reasons, you will generally not want to be the authenticating witness yourself. So be sure you have another person who can authenticate the exhibits you produce or consider taking another person with you who can observe and later testify.

If you are copying documents, do it carefully to be sure all the documents are copied and all the copies are good.

If you are inspecting documents or records, do it thoroughly no matter how lengthy the task or how boring the material. Many leads may be waiting for you in those documents that you will miss if you use too little care.

Chapter Summary and Conclusion

The effective investigator is knowledgeable, skilled, persistent, creative, perceptive, skeptical, and flexible. Having an effective written plan of investigation gives the legal investigator a decided advantage. Developing an effective plan of investigation starts by considering what you know about the case. Then the goals of the investigation must be identified. Brainstorming for specific things to be done can provide the material from which specifics of the plan will emerge. Sources of information must be identified as well. There are a number of different formats for a plan of investigation but the important thing is that a logical format be chosen and charted. There are almost always limitations on the scope of a plan of investigation that must be recognized. Typically, documents and things will be located during an investigation and procedures must be in place for the storing and preservation of such items. Diligence and thoroughness are always essential in executing a plan of investigation.

In Chapter 10, we will begin to focus on how to conduct an interview. We will start with the all-important client interview.

Review Questions

1. Simply put, factual investigation in a law office is the process of _____, _____, and _____ factual information related to the representation of a client.

2. List seven traits of the effective legal investigator.
3. Why it is important to have a plan of investigation? List five reasons.
4. In formulating a plan of investigation, where do you start?
5. What role does brainstorming play in formulating a plan of investigation?
6. List eight different sources of information that a plan of investigation might look to.
7. What are the four alternative formats for a plan of investigation?
8. What is a time line? What role does it play in a plan of investigation?
9. Name six limitations on a plan of investigation.
10. List as many rules as you can for the proper handling of documents and physical evidence that comes into the hands of the legal investigator.

KEY WORDS AND PHRASES TO REMEMBER

assume nothing
brainstorm
chronological to-do list investigation plan
client authorization
compare information
contradictions
creative
documentary evidence
evaluate information
evidence log
flexible
inconsistencies
intuition
investigation chart
investigation plan
knowledgeable
leads

litigation chart
litigation or cause of action investigation plan
perceptive
persistent
physical evidence
plan of investigation
skeptical
skilled
sources investigation plan
sources of information
test information
topical investigation plan
value of the case
verify everything
who, why, what, when, where, and how

LEARN BY DOING

LBD 9-1. Use the Case Studies in Appendix A for the following:

a. Review Case Study No. 1 (The Rowdy Outlaw Case). Assume that Rowdy Outlaw has been charged with first degree murder under the governing statute(s) of your state. Assume further that your law office has been retained to defend Outlaw on that charge. Prepare an initial plan of investigation for the defense of Mr. Outlaw. If your instructor directs, be prepared to present your plan of investigation to the class for discussion and critique.

b. Review Case Study No. 2 (The Red Dog Saloon Case). Assume that your law office is retained to represent Soupspoon Wise in connection with a civil suit to recover his damages in the Red Dog Saloon incident. Prepare an initial plan of investigation for the claims of Mr. Wise. If your instructor directs, be prepared to present your plan of investigation to the class for discussion and critique.

c. Review Case Study No. 3 (The Vidalia Unyon Case). Assume that your law office is retained to represent Mrs. Unyon in her divorce action against Mr. Unyon. Prepare an initial plan of investigation for the representation of Mrs. Unyon. If your instructor directs, be prepared to present your plan of investigation to the class for discussion and critique.

d. Review Case Study No. 4 (The Rocky Road Project). Assume that your law office is retained to assist Rocky Road, Inc., with the legal aspects of its business plans. Prepare an initial plan of investigation for the representation of Rocky Road, Inc. If your instructor directs, be prepared to present your plan of investigation to the class for discussion and critique.

Chapter 10

Preparing for a Client Interview

CHAPTER OBJECTIVES

Arranging and conducting the interview of a client or witness is a basic skill for the legal professional. In this first of four chapters focusing on interviewing you will learn:

- The various kinds of interviews that legal professionals conduct.
- The goals to be accomplished in the initial client interview.
- How to communicate with a potential client to schedule an interview.
- The steps that interviewers go through to prepare for an effective interview.
- The kinds of questions that interviewers use for different purposes.
- The importance of skillfully phrasing questions.
- The importance of seating arrangements in an interview.

A. Introduction to Interviewing

1. Persons to interview

The ability to arrange, plan, and conduct an effective interview is a basic skill of the legal professional and an essential component of investigating. Persons that lawyers and those assisting them routinely interview fall into three general categories:

- clients;
- fact witnesses; or
- other information sources.

a. Clients

By **clients** we mean not only persons whom the attorney has agreed to represent, but any person who contacts the law office seeking legal advice, regardless of whether the attorney takes the case. In this chapter we will consider scheduling and preparing for the client interview. In Chapter 11 we will consider how to conduct the client interview.

b. Fact witnesses

By **fact witness** we mean persons who have or who might have knowledge of facts directly relevant to the matter being handled for the client. In Chapter 12 we will consider arranging and preparing for a witness interview, and in Chapter 13 we will consider how to conduct the interview of a fact witness.

c. Other information sources

By **other information sources** we mean persons who, though not fact witnesses, can provide us with information we need. An example would be the assistant court clerk who helps us locate a recorded document. Contacts with these people are typically brief and less formal than the interview of a client or fact witness. Frequently such contacts are made by phone. But they are important nonetheless. If approached correctly, these people can save us a considerable amount of time. They are also often people that we go back to more than once for help. Remembering the six Bs from Chapter 8 will help you in dealing with these types of information sources.

SLEUTH ON THE LOOSE

Dealing with a client or witness who speaks a language other than English? Need help with translations to or from a different language? Maybe you need an interpreter, but first try www.Translation2paralink.com.

1. Be ready. Know what you are going to ask before you call or see this person.
2. Be brief. Remember everybody's time is important.
3. Be friendly. The sweet draws the flies, not the sour.
4. Be patient. It is almost always rewarded.
5. Be polite. Using "please" and "thank you" will make people like you.
6. Be grateful. And show it—you may need this person again.

2. Different methods and locations for interviews

Interviews may be conducted by phone or in person. They may be conducted in the legal professional's office or outside the office (sometimes referred to as a **field interview**), including a client or witness's home, workplace, automobile, or in a hospital or nursing home. Some interviews are not recorded, some are tape recorded by the interviewer, some are conducted in the presence of a court reporter who records and transcribes it, and some are video taped. Sometimes we obtain a written statement from a witness who is interviewed. On some occasions a supervising attorney will conduct the interview with an associate attorney or paralegal present to assist and sometimes the attorney will ask the associate attorney or paralegal to conduct the interview by himself. As we consider client and witness interviews in this and the next three chapters, we will refer to these differences and how they impact on the planning and execution of client and witness interviews.

B.   Reasons for Conducting Client Interviews

During the course of representation, there will typically be several occasions on which the client is interviewed by the legal professional. Client interviews can generally be categorized according to the various reasons for conducting them.

1. The initial client interview

This is the first meeting that occurs after the client contacts the law office seeking legal advice. It is a critical meeting and in this chapter we will consider in detail scheduling and preparing for the **initial client interview**.

2. Subsequent information-gathering interviews

Once the attorney has agreed to undertake representation of the client, there frequently will be one or more subsequent interviews to gather additional information from the client. Depending on the nature of the case, these information-gathering interviews may continue throughout the representation.

3. The update or status report interview

As we have noted while studying the ethical and professional duties lawyers owe to clients (see Chapter 2), it is critical that the client be kept informed concerning the status of his case. And this is true even if nothing is currently going on in his case. Accordingly, the assisting legal professional may be asked to contact the client regularly for what is usually a brief, informal update regarding the matter being handled.

C.   Goals of the Initial Client Interview

The initial client interview is, in many ways, the most important of all the interviews and contacts you will have with the client. That is because it is in this interview that the foundation for the relationship between the client and the law office is established. In addition, a number of fundamental tasks are usually accomplished during or as an immediate result of the initial interview. Illustration 10-1 sets forth a list of the various goals to be accomplished in the initial client interview.

D.   Scheduling the Initial Client Interview

When you are asked by the supervising attorney to contact a potential new client to schedule the initial interview, keep in mind the goals and purposes of this interview as set forth in Illustration 10-1. You will begin accomplishing those goals with this very first contact, and we all know how important first impressions can be.

Illustration 10-1   GOALS TO BE ACCOMPLISHED IN THE INITIAL CLIENT INTERVIEW

1. Establish a relationship of trust and confidence with the client.
2. Open solid communication channels with the client.
3. Check for potential conflicts of interest.
4. Obtain all relevant information regarding the client's problem.
5. Determine the specific nature of the representation—what is it exactly that the client wants the attorney to do.
6. Establish the fee arrangement and explain billing rates, expenses, and billing procedures.
7. Obtain all needed authorizations from the client.
8. Explain the role of each person involved.
9. Determine a plan of action regarding the agreed-upon representation.
10. Evaluate the client's demeanor, credibility, and reliability.

Interviews are typically scheduled by a phone call to the person to be interviewed. Therefore, when making that phone call, use your communication skills and the phone etiquette we considered in Chapter 8. Here are some guidelines for scheduling the initial client interview.

1. Check all participants' schedules before you call

Before you call the client, check the schedules of any other persons who may be participating in the conference.

2. Have several dates and times in mind before you call

Select several possible dates and times for the interview before you call since the client may have a scheduling conflict with one or more of your suggested times.

3. Allow for plenty of time

Pick a date and time that will allow plenty of time for the interview. Don't try to cram it in before, after, or between other scheduled events.

4. Make sure the interview room is available

If the interview is going to be conducted in a conference room at your office, be sure the room is available for that date and time.

5. Consider what the client needs to bring

Give thought to what you want the client to bring with him to the interview. There are almost always documents that need to be located and brought in for review as soon as possible—court papers that have been served on the client, accident reports, medical records or bills, insurance policies, car titles, contracts, etc. Do not assume that the client will know what to bring, even if it should be obvious. And make your list before you call so you don't leave out anything.

6. Identify yourself when you call

A paralegal contacting a client should always identify himself as a paralegal. As we have learned, this is an ethical requirement and for good reason. Lay persons receiving a call from anyone at a law office may assume they are speaking to an attorney. An assisting attorney contacting a client should always identify herself as an attorney calling on behalf of the supervising attorney.

7. Cover all necessary details in the scheduling call

In the conversation cover all the necessary details including:

- the date and time of the interview;
- directions to the place of the interview; and
- what the client needs to bring to the interview.

8. Take comprehensive notes during the scheduling call

There is no substitute for thorough documentation of all contacts made in the course of a case. Assisting legal professionals will be working on many cases, often simultaneously, and the memory of a particular conversation will fade more quickly than you think.

9. Things to do following the scheduling call

- Confirm the reservation of the conference room for the scheduled date and time
- Notify all participants of the scheduled date and time
- Enter the date and time of the scheduled conference in the docket control system
- Run a conflict of interest check
- Prepare a confirmation letter to the client
- Prepare a **work file** for your own use

HYPOTHETICAL 10-1

Assume that Paul Perfect works as a paralegal for Betty Busy, an attorney in your city. Today Betty Busy drops by Paul's office and hands him a phone call slip. She tells Paul that she received a call from a potential new client, Jay S. DeClient, who has just been sued by his next-door neighbor, Carlotta Falldown. The attorney isn't sure of the details but apparently Jay DeClient gave a neighborhood party at his house about a month ago and some food or beverage was spilled on a hardwood floor. Carlotta Falldown apparently slipped in it and fell on the floor, injuring herself. She apparently wasn't so badly injured that she couldn't sock Jay DeClient in the nose, fracturing it. Now Carlotta Falldown has sued Jay DeClient for negligence. Busy instructs Paul Perfect to contact Jay DeClient and set up an initial conference sometime next week. The attorney explains that she will try to conduct the interview herself but will want Paul there to assist. However, it is possible she may be unable to attend (because she is so *busy*) so he should be prepared to handle the interview himself.

Paul Perfect has been taking notes as the supervising attorney explains this assignment. He now staples the phone call slip to his notes. As he does so, he asks Betty Busy if she has her calendar with her or if he should check with her secretary. She tells him to check with her secretary. He then asks how much time they should schedule for the conference and she replies an hour to an hour and a half should be sufficient.

After the supervising attorney leaves, Paul Perfect checks his own schedule for available times then calls the attorney's secretary to compare. Having found three convenient dates and times that suit both their calendars, he calls the receptionist to check on the availability of the conference room for each date and time.

He enters the name of Carlotta Falldown into the firm's computerized conflict of interest system as a potential adverse party and finds no conflict.

Paul Perfect then makes notes on what he should ask Jay DeClient to bring with him to the interview. The list includes:

- the suit papers;
- any correspondence that Jay DeClient may have received from Carlotta Falldown or her attorney before suit was filed;
- Jay DeClient's homeowner's or lessee's insurance policy, if any, or any umbrella policy he may carry;
- any pictures that might have been taken of the spill or of Carlotta Falldown;
- any medical records he has concerning treatment for his broken nose; and
- medical bills he has incurred from having his nose treated.

Can you think of anything Paul Perfect should add to that list?

Now Paul Perfect places his call to Jay DeClient. Let's listen in to the first part of that conversation:

JD: Hello?

PP: Hello, is this Mr. Jay DeClient?

JD: Yes, it is.

PP: Mr. DeClient, my name is Paul Perfect. I am a paralegal in the office of attorney Betty Busy. Ms. Busy asked me to call you and set up a time for you to come in and meet with us about the suit filed by Carlotta Falldown.

JD: Sure. I was expecting someone to call. When did you want me to come in?

Paul Perfect finds a good time for Jay DeClient to come in, asks him to bring the documents with him, and gives him directions to the office. He also learns that DeClient did have to see a doctor to have his broken nose set. He will have to wear a brace-type device on his face for a month and he missed three days of work because of the injury. He is a salesman who depends on commissions and he feels that having to wear the facial device will result in his losing sales and income. He is seeing Dr. Ken Fixit for his nose and has paid $250 so far in medical bills. He has medical insurance but the co-pay is $500. Now let's listen in again to the end of the conversation.

> **PP:** Okay, I think that's all we need to cover today. We'll see you on October 4 at 2:00 in the afternoon here at our offices. Did you have any other questions?
> **JD:** No, I don't think so. I guess I'll see you next week.
> **PP:** Yes, sir. Take care and we will see you then.
>
> Immediately after hanging up with DeClient, Paul Perfect calls the receptionist and reserves the conference room for the agreed-upon time. He then calls Betty Busy's secretary and asks her to note the conference on the attorney's calendar. Next he enters the date and time of the conference in his own calendar and the firm's tickler system. Now he dictates a memorandum to Betty Busy (see Illustration 10-2) and a confirmation letter to Jay DeClient (see Illustration 10-3). Before signing and sending the letter, he leaves it with Betty Busy's secretary and asks her to have the attorney look it over and tell him if it is okay to send. The next morning, Betty Busy calls Paul Perfect and says, "Paul, the letter looks perfect to me. Go ahead and send it out."

E. ► Preparing for the Initial Client Interview

Once the client interview is scheduled there are a number of things the assisting legal professional will need to do to get ready.

1. Prepare forms

Prepare any forms that the client may need to sign during the initial interview in the event that the attorney agrees to take the case. We will consider two types of forms clients are regularly asked to sign in the initial conference—records authorizations and fee agreements.

a. Records authorizations

Depending on the kind of case and the particular facts, the client may need to sign a **medical records authorization** (see Illustration 10-4), or an **employment records authorization** (see Illustration 10-5), or an **educational records authorization** (see Illustration 10-6) to enable the attorney to inspect and copy those records.

b. Fee agreements

In addition, the client may need to sign the fee agreement at the initial client conference if the attorney agrees at that time to undertake the representation. Remember that because of the prohibition on the paralegal engaging in the unlicensed practice of law, only an attorney can make the decision to undertake representation of the client. When an associate attorney is assisting a senior attorney, the senior attorney will want to make this decision. Accordingly, the supervising attorney should typically be present when the client signs the fee agreement. The role of the assisting legal professional will be to prepare the type of fee agreement the supervising attorney authorizes in a particular case.

Illustration 10-2   MEMORANDUM SUMMARIZING CLIENT CONTACT

MEMORANDUM

TO: Betty Busy, Attorney
FROM: Paul Perfect, Paralegal
DATE: September 27, YR00
RE: Jay S. DeClient
          File Number: YR00-335-L

At your instruction I called and spoke by phone with Mr. Jay S. DeClient today. Mr. DeClient was very personable and cooperative in the conversation. My initial impression of him is that he is friendly and forthright. He gave me no reason to doubt his veracity.

Mr. DeClient confirmed that he received the suit papers filed on behalf of Carlotta Falldown two days ago. The incident itself occurred on August 25 of this year. Mr. DeClient also stated that Carlotta Falldown hit him in the nose as he was trying to help her up after the fall in the kitchen of Mr. DeClient's home on Humphrey Bogart Lane here in the city.

Mr. DeClient has been seeing Dr. Ken Fixit whose offices are next to City Hospital. He has paid $250 so far in medical expenses. He has a medical insurance policy (a group policy through his employer) but the co-pay is $500.

Mr. DeClient has to wear a device he refers to as a nose brace for the next month. He says it is very uncomfortable and interferes with sleeping and eating. In addition, Mr. DeClient advised me that he is a district salesman with Hollywood Sports Equipment and depends on commissions for his income. He missed three days of work because of his broken nose and fears he will lose sales and commissions during the coming month because of the nose brace.

Mr. DeClient is coming in on October 4, at 2 p.m. This time was available on both my calendar and yours. I have scheduled the conference room from 2 p.m. until 3:30 p.m. that day. I have drafted a confirmation letter to Mr. DeClient for your review and approval. As the letter indicates, Mr. DeClient is bringing the suit papers, his homeowner's policy, pictures he took of the spill right after the incident, and his medical bills to date.

It is my understanding that you plan to handle the interview with Mr. DeClient and would like me to be present to assist. I will draft a medical records authorization and an employment records authorization to have available at the conference. Please let me know if you would like me to prepare a legal services agreement to have available at the conference and, if so, what terms we should draft.

I have also run a preliminary conflicts check based on the name of Carlotta Falldown as a potential adverse party and nothing turned up.

Please let me know if there is anything further I need to do at this time.

If that attorney is not present at the initial client interview, the assisting legal professional may later send the fee agreement to the client to sign and return, but only after the supervising attorney has decided to take the case and authorized the one assisting to send the fee agreement to the client.

In general, there are three kinds of fee agreements used by attorneys: (1) an **hourly rate plus expenses agreement;** (2) a **flat fee agreement;** or (3) a **contingency fee agreement.** There are innumerable variations to these agreements and every attorney will develop his own customized form for each kind of agreement. In addition, the legal and ethical requirements for fee agreements vary from state to state, so no one form is going to be suitable for all attorneys in all situations.

Sometimes fee agreements are referred to as **retainer agreements,** meaning that it is the agreement pursuant to which the client retains or

Illustration 10-3 CONFIRMATION LETTER TO CLIENT

Date

Mr. Jay S. DeClient
(Address)

Re: *Conference on Carlotta Falldown lawsuit*

Dear Mr. DeClient:

It was a pleasure to speak with you earlier this week. This will confirm the meeting we have scheduled for October 4, at 2 p.m. here in our offices. Please remember to bring the following with you to the conference:

1. The suit papers served on you.
2. Your homeowner's insurance policy.
3. The pictures you took of the spill the night of the accident with negatives.
4. The medical bills you have incurred to date for treatment of your nose.

We look forward to seeing you next Tuesday. Please feel free to call if you have any questions.

Sincerely yours,
Paul B. Perfect
Paralegal

cc: Betty Busy, attorney
    PBP/ck

Illustration 10-4 MEDICAL RECORDS AUTHORIZATION

To: Doctor's Name and Address

You are hereby authorized to permit my attorney, _____ of the law firm _____, or his designated agent, to inspect and obtain copies of my complete medical records including, without limitation, all patient information sheets, correspondence, notes, memoranda, laboratory reports, and fee statements. This authorization is effective as of the date below and will continue in effect until revoked by me in writing but for no longer than one year from the date below.

My attorney, _____, of the law firm _____, has assured me that he/she will comply with all requirements of the privacy rules promulgated by the U.S. Department of Health and Human Services pursuant to the Health Insurance Portability and Accountability Act of 1996 and found at 45 CFR 160 and 164.

_____   Date: _____

Name of patient
Soc. Sec. No. XXXXXX
DOB 10-1-YR-40

---

employs the attorney or law firm. But the phrase retainer agreement can be confusing since the word **retainer** is also used by attorneys to refer to an advance payment that is required no matter what type of fee agreement is entered into. For example, in Hypothetical 10-1, Betty Busy may require Jay DeClient to pay a $5,000 *retainer* before representation will be undertaken. Better phrases to use for these agreements are **legal services agreement** or fee agreement.

Illustration 10-5   EMPLOYMENT RECORDS AUTHORIZATION

Name of Employer: _____
Address: _____
Name of Employee: _____
Employee ID or Soc. Sec. No. _____

To: Records Custodian or Director of Human Resources:

I hereby authorize and request that you permit attorney _____ of the law firm _____, or his designated agent, to inspect and copy my employment file(s) and provide him or his designated agent with any and all other information that he may request concerning my employment with you.

This authorization shall remain in effect until the _____ day of _____, YR+3 or until revoked in writing by me.

Date: _____   (Signature) _____
                                                      (Name of employee)

Illustration 10-6   EDUCATIONAL RECORDS AUTHORIZATION

Name of School or Institution: _____
Address: _____
Name of student: _____
Maiden or former name (if applicable): _____
Student ID or Soc. Sec. No. _____
Date(s) of enrollment _____
Date of graduation (if applicable) _____

To: Student Records Custodian:

I hereby authorize and request that you permit attorney of the law firm, or his designated agent, to inspect and copy any and all records or information of any kind whatsoever, academic or otherwise, related to my having been a student at and to provide him or his designated agent with any and all other information that he may request concerning my having been a student there.
This authorization shall remain in effect until the _____ day of _____, YR+3 or until revoked in writing by me.

Date: _____   (Signature) _____
                                                      (Name of student)

1. The hourly rate fee agreement. In many cases attorneys will charge the client an agreed-upon hourly rate for their services. If more than one attorney or a paralegal is to be involved in the case, the hourly rates for each may vary. The hourly rate fee agreement may or may not require payment of a retainer. Typically, out-of-pocket expenses incurred by the attorney are billed to the client in addition to the hourly rate charges. See Illustration 10-7.

Illustration 10-7 HOURLY RATE LEGAL SERVICES AGREEMENT

LEGAL SERVICES AGREEMENT

This Legal Services Agreement (the "Agreement") is entered into between _____ ("Client") and _____ ("Attorney"), this _____ day of _____, 20 _____.

1. SCOPE OF REPRESENTATION. Client hereby employs Attorney to represent Client in connection with _____ (the "Matter").

2. ATTORNEY's DUTIES. Attorney shall provide the legal services that, in her independent legal judgment, are reasonably required to effectively represent Client in this Matter and shall make reasonable effort to keep Client informed of the status of the Matter.

3. CLIENT's DUTIES. Client shall cooperate fully with Attorney in connection with the Matter; keep Attorney advised of Client's current address and telephone number and of all developments concerning the Matter; pay all bills received from Attorney on time; and otherwise perform all of Client's obligations under this Agreement in good faith.

4. LEGAL FEES. Client shall pay Attorney for the legal services to be provided by Attorney in connection with this Matter on an hourly basis as follows:

Partners at $250 per hour
Associates at $175 per hour
Paralegals at $90 per hour
Law Clerks and other personnel at $40 per hour

5. RETAINER. Client shall pay the sum of $5,000 to Attorney immediately as an advance against future billings of time and expenses by Attorney. Attorney will deposit the retainer amount in a trust account and it will be used to pay both Attorney fees as agreed to in *Paragraph 4* of this Agreement and expenses as agreed to in *Paragraph 6* of this Agreement. Client hereby authorizes Attorney to withdraw funds from the retainer amount in the trust account to pay bills for time and expenses at the time those bills are mailed to Client. Any unused balance of the retainer amount remaining after payment of the final bill for time and expenses shall be refunded promptly by Attorney to Client.

6. OUT-OF-POCKET EXPENSES. Client also agrees to reimburse Attorney for out-of-pocket expenses incurred by Attorney in connection with the representation including, but not limited to, charges for long-distance phone calls at a minimum rate of $2.00 per call; copy costs at $.20 per page; travel costs including car travel at $.375 per mile; outgoing facsimile charges at $1.00 per page; postage; court filing fees; service of process fees; consultants; experts; court reporters; and similar related expenses.

7. STATEMENTS FOR TIME AND EXPENSES. Attorney will provide Client an itemized statement of time and expenses on a regular basis, usually monthly, and such statement will be payable by the Client within thirty (30) days of receipt.

8. ATTORNEY's LIEN. Client hereby grants Attorney a lien on any and all claims or causes of action related to the Matter which lien will be for any and all sums due from Client to Attorney at the conclusion of Attorney's representation of Client in the Matter. This lien shall attach to any recovery obtained by Client by judgment, settlement, arbitration, or otherwise.

_____
Attorney

_____
Client

2. The flat fee agreement. Sometimes attorneys charge the client a flat fee for the service to be rendered. This way the client knows what the total bill is going to be regardless of the time the attorney spends. The flat fee agreed to may include expenses or the agreement may specify that out-of-pocket expenses are to be paid in addition to the flat fee. Flat fee agreements are generally used for more routine legal services where attorneys, from experience, know almost exactly how much time it will take them to perform the work. Examples include no-fault divorces, simple wills, setting up corporations, and individual bankruptcies. See Illustration 10-8.

3. The contingency fee agreement. In cases where a monetary recovery is sought for a client, and particularly in cases where the client cannot afford an hourly fee arrangement, the contingency fee agreement will be used. In a contingency arrangement, the attorney receives as her fee an-agreed upon percentage, usually one-third of any recovery made. If no recovery is made, the attorney receives no fee. Out-of-pocket expenses are due whether a recovery is made or not. See Illustration 10-9.

HYPOTHETICAL 10-2

Assume that Betty Busy calls Paul Perfect the day before the scheduled interview with Jay DeClient and tells Paul that he will have to conduct the interview because she is too *busy.* Paul swings into action.

He has already drafted a medical records authorization for Jay DeClient to sign, as well as an employment records authorization in the event Jay DeClient has missed work because of the fractured nose. Paul Perfect has also drafted a legal services agreement providing that Betty Busy would

Illustration 10-8   FLAT FEE LEGAL SERVICES AGREEMENT

LEGAL SERVICES AGREEMENT

This Legal Services Agreement (the "Agreement") is entered into between _____ ("Client") and _____ ("Attorney"), this _____ day of _____, 20 _____.

1. Attorney hereby agrees to prepare and file the necessary documents for the incorporation of an entity to be known as Super Sucker, Inc., under the laws of the state of _____.
Specifically, Attorney agrees to prepare the charter, bylaws, and organizational minutes for said corporation and to cause the charter to be properly filed with the Secretary of State of the state of. _____.

2. Client agrees to pay Attorney the sum of one thousand dollars ($1,000) in advance as the full and final fee for the legal services described in *Paragraph 1* of this Agreement.

3. Attorney agrees to pay all out-of-pocket expenses incurred in performing the legal services described in *Paragraph 1* of this Agreement, including copy costs, long-distance phone calls, mailing costs, filing fees, and the cost of one (1) minute book out of the advance payment received from Client as described in *Paragraph 2* of this Agreement.

_____
Attorney

_____
Client

Illustration 10-9   CONTINGENCY FEE LEGAL SERVICES AGREEMENT

LEGAL SERVICES AGREEMENT

This Legal Services Agreement (the "Agreement") is entered into between _____ ("Client") and _____ ("Attorney"), this _____ day of _____, 20 _____.

1. Client hereby employs Attorney to represent Client in connection with any and all civil legal claims for compensation or other damages against _____ and any other person or entity acting with or on the behalf of such person or who may be responsible for the actions of such person in connection with the automobile accident in which Client was involved on the _____ day of _____, 20 _____, in Capital City, Yourstate.

2. Client agrees to pay Attorney, as attorney fees for this representation, a contingency rate of thirty-three percent (33%) of all revenues collected from any source whatsoever in whole or partial satisfaction of any or all of the civil claims that are the subject of this representation, regardless of whether such revenues are collected by compromise, accord, settlement, judgment following suit, collection, or otherwise. In the event a final judgment is entered in a court of law on any or all of the civil claims that are the subject of this representation and in the further event that an appeal shall be instituted from such judgment by either the plaintiff or the defendant(s) in such suit, Client agrees that the contingency rate for attorney fees in this representation shall then be forty percent (40%) of all revenues collected.

3. In addition to the obligation for attorney fees as set forth in Paragraph 2 of this Agreement, Client also agrees to reimburse Attorney for out-of-pocket expenses incurred by Attorney in connection with the representation including, but not limited to, charges for long-distance phone calls at a minimum rate of $2.00 per call; copy costs at $.15 per page; travel costs including car travel at $.315 per mile; outgoing facsimile charges at $1.00 per page; postage; court filing fees; service of process fees; consultants; experts; court reporters; and similar related expenses. Attorney will provide Client an itemized statement for these out-of-pocket expenses on a regular basis, usually monthly, and such statement will be payable by the Client within thirty (30) days of receipt.

4. Client agrees to cooperate fully with Attorney in connection with this representation.

5. Attorney agrees to apply his independent legal judgment in pursuit of the resolution of the claims that are the subject of this representation and in acting on behalf of the Client. Settlement of any and all claims shall require the express consent of the Client.

6. Attorney may terminate this Agreement and withdraw from representing Client in this matter if (a) Attorney determines, in his sole professional judgment, that the claims which are the subject matter of this representation have no merit; (b) a conflict of interest arises; (c) Client fails or refuses to cooperate with Attorney in connection with this representation; (d) Client provides incorrect, incomplete, or deceptive information to Attorney or another person in connection with this representation; (e) Client fails to pay the statements for out-of-pocket expenses in a timely manner; (f) Client otherwise fails to comply with his/her/its obligations under this Agreement; or (g) if the Rules of Professional Conduct or any succeeding code of ethics governing Attorney's representation permits or requires withdrawal of representation.

7. Client may terminate this Agreement upon ten (10) days written notice to Attorney. In the event Client terminates this Agreement, Client agrees to compensate Attorney out of the gross proceeds of any ultimate recovery for the claims that are the subject matter of this representation as follows: as attorney fees, a percentage of the gross proceeds otherwise payable to Attorney as a contingency fee under this Agreement equal to the ratio determined by comparing the number of hours measured in tenths of an hour that Attorney expended on this representation prior to termination with the total number of hours measured in tenths of an hour expended on the matter by Attorney and successive counsel.

8. This Agreement becomes effective when signed by Client and returned to Attorney. By signing this Agreement, Client acknowledges that he/she/it has read and understands all of its terms and agrees to it in full.

9. All amendments or alterations to this Agreement must be in writing and be signed by the parties.

_____
Client

_____
Attorney

represent DeClient on an hourly fee basis in defending the suit by Carlotta Falldown (subject to DeClient's homeowner's policy providing coverage) and on a contingency basis in connection with the anticipated counterclaim DeClient will probably file against her for tortious battery. However, since Betty Busy will not be present during the interview and Paul Perfect knows that only the attorney can decide to accept the case, that decision and finalizing the legal services agreement will have to wait until after the interview.

1. Why did Paul Perfect prepare a medical records authorization for Jay DeClient to sign?
2. Why did Paul Perfect prepare an employment records authorization for Jay DeClient to sign?
3. Why did Paul Perfect prepare two different kinds of fee agreements in this case?

2. Prepare your questions

If the legal professional is assigned by the supervising attorney to conduct the interview himself, preparing questions for the interview is the next important step. Even if the legal professional utilizes an intake sheet or standardized checklist (discussed in the next section), specific questions still should be planned for the initial client interview. Here is a suggested method for preparing your questions for the interview.

a. Review your notes

Review your notes from the assignment conference (or assignment memo from the supervising attorney) closely. Be sure you understand exactly what the supervising attorney has told you concerning the potential client you will be interviewing and what is known about the legal problem that will be presented. The more you know about the potential new client and the legal matter the more thorough preparation you can make. If there are any documents already in possession of the supervising attorney, or any other notes in the file, review those carefully. If you have any questions about the assignment, go back to the supervising attorney for clarification.

b. Consider what you know so far of the legal question involved

In interviewing, always remember that the factual questioning we do is determined by the legal context—what is the legal issue or problem we are dealing with? You may want to review the discussion of factual analysis in Chapter 1 at this time. There we learned that unless the investigator has a basic understanding of the law that is at issue in a client's case, he will be unable to do effective investigation. He won't know what factual information to look for or even recognize relevant information if he stumbles over it. So, as the interviewer plans his questions, thought must be given to what is known so far of the legal problem the client will present.

If the legal professional is instructed by the supervising attorney to meet with a potential new divorce client, the planned questions will relate to residency requirements, grounds for a divorce, possible defenses, property ownership and division, income and debts, child custody and support, spousal support, the need for a domestic protective order, etc.

If the legal professional is instructed by the supervising attorney to meet with a potential new client regarding a business contract dispute, the planned questions will relate to the business, the contract, the nature of the dispute, the elements of an enforceable contract, possible defenses or counterclaims, damages including mitigation efforts, etc.

If the legal professional is instructed by the supervising attorney to meet with a potential new client on defending a criminal charge, the planned questions will relate to the nature of the charges, status of the criminal proceeding (how far along is it), details of the arrest and police interrogation, if any, knowledge of the events surrounding the alleged crime (though not necessarily whether the accused committed the crime—the attorney is more concerned with whether the state can prove the accused committed the crime), possible defenses to the specific crime alleged including alibis, mistake, self- or third-person defense, etc.

If the legal professional is instructed by the supervising attorney to meet with a potential new client regarding a personal injury claim related to a defective product, the planned questions will relate to the details of the event in which the person was injured, including time and place, the nature and extent of the injuries, the purchase and prior use of the product, the maker and distributor(s) of the product, the whereabouts and condition of the product, and possible defenses such as misuse, changed condition, appreciation of the risk, etc.

If the legal professional is instructed by the supervising attorney to meet with a potential new client on a workers' compensation injury, the planned questions will relate to the details of the injury, including nature of the injury, the time and place of the injury, how the injury is work-related, notification of the employer, medical care to date, possible third-party responsibility, etc.

The known legal context controls the questions to be asked.

c. Consider special needs of the client

If you will be interviewing a child, an adult with little education, or anyone whose English is poor, you will want to plan your questions using simple, non-complex words. And you will want to make your questions shorter. With a teenager you may want to deliberately use some recognizable slang or street talk if it will aid communication. Conversely, with an older person you will probably avoid current slang or street talk.

d. Brainstorm a list of topics to be covered

Once you have reviewed the assignment notes and given careful thought to what you know of the legal issues this interview will raise, brainstorm and make a comprehensive list of all topics that need to be covered. Don't worry about organization yet. Just get everything that needs to be covered down on paper in any order that it comes to mind.

e. Organize the topics in a logical fashion

Now organize the topics into the order in which they should be addressed. There is no one right way to organize topics for an interview. Different interviewers have different preferences. With experience in different kinds of cases, you will learn what is effective for you. Some interviewers prefer to address topics chronologically. Some prefer to address them as they relate to the elements of the legal cause of action or defense involved (e.g., in a negligence case by duty, breach, causation, damages, defenses, etc.). And others prefer to approach them by subject matter in some other logical way.

HYPOTHETICAL 10-3

Paul Perfect is preparing his questions for the interview of Jay DeClient. He reviews the file, which consists of his notes from speaking to Betty Busy about the case initially, the notes of his telephone conversation with Jay DeClient, and copies of his memo to Betty Busy (Illustration 10-2) and his letter to Jay DeClient (Illustration 10-3).

Now Paul gives consideration to what he knows of the law involved in the case. He knows from experience and from his discussion with Betty Busy that this is a premises liability case based in negligence. He reviews the law in his jurisdiction regarding the elements of a negligence action in general and defenses to it. Because he knows that this case will involve specific questions about the duty of care that a homeowner owes to his social guests, he researches some case law on that. He finds that the rulings of the state supreme court establish that a homeowner owes a duty of reasonable care to social guests to keep the premises in a reasonably safe condition. That duty of reasonable care has been construed to mean that a homeowner must either remove or warn of hazards that the homeowner knows of (actual knowledge) or should reasonably have discovered (constructive knowledge). However, the state supreme court has distinguished the duty owed by a homeowner to social guests (social invitees) from the duty that the operator of a public business owes to business invitees. Whereas the operator of a public business has a duty to inspect the premises on a regular basis to locate potential hazards, the homeowner owes no such duty to his social guests—only the duty to remove or warn of hazards of which he has actual or constructive knowledge. Among the defenses to premises liability slip-and-fall cases that Paul reads about are assumption of the risk (the plaintiff knew of the hazard herself and still voluntarily encountered it) and comparative fault (the plaintiff failed to exercise reasonable care herself to observe and avoid the hazard). He also reads up on third-party liability as minimizing the defendant's share of the fault or possibly giving rise to an indemnity claim by the defendant.

Betty Busy has advised that there might be a counterclaim by Jay DeClient against Carlotta Falldown. Paul Perfect also reviews the law regarding the torts of assault and battery. He notes that they are intentional torts, but the state courts have held that the intent required to prove the causes of action is not an intent to cause the harm inflicted, only an intent to do the act that caused the harm.

Having reviewed everything in the file carefully, and given thought to what he knows of the law of the case, Paul now brainstorms on the various topics he needs to cover with the client. His list looks like this:

Explain Betty Busy's absence; paralegal limitations

Biographical and background for file, work, and health history—use intake sheet

Previous history as neighbor of Carlotta Falldown; what he knows about her, troublemaker? Other suits?

Details of party

Details of food(?) on floor—how, what, who responsible for it

Did JD know it was there before fall?

How long had it been there?

Location of JD and CF between time (likely time?) of spill and fall

Possible CF saw or should have seen spill?

How large spill area, color, texture?

Details of fall—witnesses—who saw, how CF injured, what said, what happened later, who helped her up

Detail of punch in the nose—how it happened, witnesses, hit anybody else?

Was CF conscious/awake at the time of punch? Say anything to anybody about it then or later?

Punch intentional for JD or just anybody? Could it have been reflex? How hard the blow?

Detail of treatment for CF after fall, ambulance? Witnesses? Anyone go home with her? Ambulatory? Talking?

Detail of treatment for CF. ER? Witnesses?

Get authorizations signed

Prognosis from doctor; next appointment; other treatment possible? Surgery?

Details on income—last three years; how impacted since injury? How to calculate expected loss?

Pain and suffering and loss of enjoyment of life?

Family life? Spouse? Loss of consortium?

Indemnity claim v. whoever responsible for causing spill?

Check homeowner's policy—copy

Review pictures taken—get negatives if available

Copy suit papers

Copy medical bills

1. Is there anything you would add to this list?
2. What topics can you identify from the list that clearly relate to the legal issue of the homeowner's duty of care that Paul Perfect researched?
3. What topics can you identify from the list that clearly relate to the legal issue of intent in the torts of assault and battery?

f. Prepare specific questions within each topic

Now you are ready to prepare the specific questions to be asked within each topic. As you do so, keep in mind that there are different kinds of questions, effective for different purposes. There are:

- open-ended questions
- closed-ended questions
- leading questions
- pressure questions
- hypothetical questions
- multiple-choice questions
- opinion questions
- explanatory questions
- silence as a question

Let's consider examples of each type of question and their usefulness in interviewing.

1. Open-ended questions. These questions encourage the client to provide a narrative of events or a detailed explanation or to otherwise give extended information in the answer. They are overview or summary-type questions used to obtain a broad outline of an event or situation:

What had you been doing during the hours before the accident occurred? Now tell me what happened as you entered the intersection?

Open-ended questions are often used at the beginning of the interview in order to get the person talking:

What can we do for you today?

They are also used to obtain an initial comprehensive under-standing of the facts or an outline of the events before delving into details with more specific questions. Sometimes it might be appropriate to begin the substantive portion of the interview by stating clearly that you intend to ask broad questions first and then to narrow the focus.

EXAMPLE

> **INTERVIEWER:**   Mrs. Brown, let me begin by asking you some general questions so I can get an overview of what happened. Then we will come back to the details. Is that all right?
> **MRS. BROWN:**   Sure. That will be fine.
> **INTERVIEWER:**   Why don't you begin by telling me what happened that day as you remember it?

Think of open-ended questions as asking the person to tell you a story. That is really what you want them to do. Use these questions to get the story told completely and thoroughly—the entire narrative from beginning to end—so you can then go back and examine it more closely for details.

Open-ended questions can also be used to keep a client talking:

What happened next?

or to fill in blanks left by the answer:

What happened when you told him that?

Open-ended questions also provide an excellent opportunity for the interviewer to observe the client and evaluate how well she expresses herself and organizes her thoughts.

2. Closed-ended questions. Questions that call for a specific, narrow answer requiring few words and little or no explanation are closed-ended:

What color was the car that entered the intersection from your right?
What was the man that you saw wearing?

These questions are used to confirm detail in a story:

Did you agree to do as he asked?

or to get the sequence of events straight:

So, it was after the gun came out that you ducked under the counter?

or to pin the person down to a particular version:

What you're saying then is that the blue car came to a complete stop before
it started into the intersection?

Closed-ended questions are most often used after the interviewer has asked a series of open-ended questions to obtain the necessary overview of the events or situation.

3. Leading questions. A specific type of closed-ended question is the **leading question**, which suggests its own answer by calling for a yes or no response:

The first car that you saw enter the intersection was red, is that correct?

Like all forms of closed-ended questions, leading questions are used to confirm detail or pin down a client to a particular version of events. However, it is the unique phrasing of the leading question that distinguishes it from other types of closed-ended questions. In the last example, it is the phrase, "is that correct" that makes it a leading question. That phrase almost demands a yes or no response and that is its purpose.

Leading questions should be used infrequently in interviewing because we want the person to tell us what they know in their own words. (Of course the attorney will use leading questions in cross-examination of witnesses at trial—see Chapter 6.) However, leading questions are legitimately used in an interview to jog the memory of one who is forgetful:

> *I think the speed limit was 50 miles per hour there, wasn't it?*

or one who is being deliberately difficult or vague, or if the interviewer is having a difficult time pinning down details. Leading questions may also be used to lead a wandering client back onto the path of relevant inquiry:

> *Well, that's all quite interesting, Mrs. Brown. But you told me a moment ago that you took a single Valium tablet about 30 minutes before the collision, isn't that right?*

4. Pressure questions. These questions challenge the interviewee directly or indirectly and compel a response involving emotion or feeling as well as fact:

> *As you sat there watching the train approach, you didn't honk your horn or try to do anything to warn the children playing on the track?*

Pressure questions may be used to get a wishy-washy or forgetful person to commit to a particular version of events:

> *If you're not sure if the light was on in the kitchen, how can you be so sure it was Mr. Burnes you saw going out the window?*

or simply to see how a person will likely handle challenging or accusative questions at trial or deposition:

> *If you signed the release and accepted the severance pay on the day they terminated you, why do you say now that they tricked you?*

Pressure questions can be effective but must be used carefully and with forethought. Because they do involve a challenging element, they can offend or anger the person being questioned. To lessen that risk, you probably want to lower your voice and ask such a question softly and with little inflection rather than raising your voice and adopting an accusatory tone.

5. Hypothetical questions. Here the client is asked to assume some set of facts on which to premise an answer:

> *Assume that the blue car was doing no more than 30 miles per hour. Do you think the accident would still have happened?*

Lawyers frequently pose hypothetical questions to expert witnesses to elicit their opinions at trial or deposition. For the interviewer's purposes, hypothetical questions may be used to get some idea how the interviewee's knowledge coincides with other information, or to see how the person will handle a challenge to his testimony from the opposing side, or to jog the witness's memory.

EXAMPLE

> INTERVIEWER: Mr. Crebbs, do you recall how fast the blue car was going?
> MR. CREBBS: No, I really couldn't say.
> INTERVIEWER: You wouldn't hazard a guess as to the speed of that car?
> MR. CREBBS: Not really.
> INTERVIEWER: Well, let me ask you this. Assume that blue car was going no more than, say, 30 miles an hour. Do you think the accident would still have happened?
> MR. CREBBS: Probably. But I'm sure that car was doing more than 30.

6. Multiple-choice questions. Closely related to hypothetical questions, multiple-choice questions invite the person to choose among two or more options offered by the interviewer:

Did the sound you heard seem to come from directly behind you or above you or off to one side?

Multiple-choice questions can be useful to clarify previous answers that were imprecise:

EXAMPLE

> INTERVIEWER: You say you heard a sound just before the gun fired?
> CLIENT: That's right, I did.
> INTERVIEWER: Where did the sound come from in relation to where you were standing at the time?
> CLIENT: Well, it seemed to come from back behind me somewhere.
> INTERVIEWER: Did the sound you heard seem to come from directly behind you or above you or off to one side?

7. Opinion questions. With these questions, the person is simply asked to express an opinion about something or even to speculate:

Why do you think he did that?
What do you believe caused him to say that?
What could have been on his mind to make him go there?

Remember that at trial attorneys generally cannot ask lay witnesses to speculate or offer their opinions about matters. But in interviewing we have no such limitations. Asking a person to speculate or offer an opinion can frequently lead to new and unexpected information or additional lines of inquiry.

> **INTERVIEWER:** When Jesse left the house, did he say where he was going?
>
> **CLIENT:** As I recollect, he said he was going by the bank and then was headed to Lisa's house.
>
> **INTERVIEWER:** He said he was going by the bank first?
>
> **CLIENT:** Yep. That's what I recall.
>
> **INTERVIEWER:** What could have been on his mind to make him go there before he went to his girlfriend's house?
>
> **CLIENT:** Well, I'd say it was to cash that last paycheck since he got laid off earlier that morning.
>
> **INTERVIEWER:** So Jesse got laid off from work the morning before he and Lisa disappeared?

8. Hearsay questions. As we learned in Chapter 7, at trial the lawyer may be unable to introduce hearsay evidence unless some exception can be shown. But there is no such limitation in an interview. The interviewer should not hesitate to ask the person being interviewed what they or others said in the past regarding topics relevant to the interview. Even if what the person repeats would be inadmissible hearsay if offered at trial, it may lead to other valuable information. See the first two questions in the last Example.

9. Explanatory questions. Closely related to the opinion question, the explanatory question asks the person to explain an answer or expound further on it:

What do you mean by that?
Why do you roll your eyes when you say his name?
How did that come about?

10. Silence as a question. We have all heard phrases such as *the sounds of silence* and *the silence was deafening* and *the pregnant pause*. Silence—the meaningful pause—can be used by the interviewer as an effective question in some situations by pausing after an answer is given as if expecting the person to say more. The silent pause certainly should not be overused. But it may prove useful when the interviewer thinks the client has more to say but is reluctant. The interviewer's pause may be an encouragement to speak. Or when the interviewer believes the answer given to a question is obviously false, the pause may be a signal that the interviewer recognizes the falsehood and is giving the person an opportunity to correct the answer.

g. Consider the phrasing of questions

Questions can be phrased to accomplish different purposes or adjust to different kinds of witnesses.

1. Questions phrased as direct questions

Who else was there?
Why did you do that?
What did you see?
When did you first meet him?
Where did you go after that?
How did you get the door open?

2. Questions phrased as an order or directive

Tell me who else was there.
Explain why you did that.

3. Questions phrased as conclusions

And you're sure no one else was there?
So you're telling me you did that just to get him hired?
*What you're saying then is that you came to a complete stop before you
    entered the intersection?*
So, in other words, there wasn't time to honk or shout?
*If I understand what you're saying, the police officer never actually told you
    to stay there?*

4. Questions phrased to challenge

*But if you were looking to your left at the truck how do you know when the
    boy to your right stepped into the street?*
What about the fact that you forgot your glasses that morning?
How do you know he went out the back door?

5. Questions phrased to sound skeptical

Are you sure you came to a complete stop?
If the gun was locked up as you say, how did the boys get hold of it?

Illustration 10-10 PAGE OF INTERVIEWER'S QUESTIONS AND NOTES

QUESTIONS	NOTES

6. Questions phrased as a request for assistance

Can you tell me when you first met Gary?

What I'm trying to figure out is, how could you be in two places at once?

I'm wondering how many times you had seen him swing on the chain before the time it broke?

What we need to know is, did you actually see him fire the gun or did you just hear the shot?

What I need you to show me is about where you were standing at the time in relation to the red car.

As you can tell from these sample questions, we are trying to accomplish something different with each of them. Some people respond better to questions phrased as a request for help. People like to help and many of us are trained to automatically respond to a request for assistance. (Have you ever worked somewhere where they told you that customer service is the most important thing?) Other people respond better to questions phrased as directives or orders—they just need to be led.

Deciding what kinds of questions to use in an interview and how to phrase questions is a true skill. It is in many ways the heart of the interviewing task. The ability to do it well starts with what we are doing here, learning about kinds of questions and phrasing. But in addition to education, you must have experience in preparing questions and asking them in a real-life interview. (See LBD 10-1.)

h. Put questions in a format consistent with any checklist or intake sheet being used

(See discussion of checklists below.)

i. Put questions in a format conducive to taking good notes during the interview

Some interviewers like to use a legal pad with planned questions written on one-half to two-thirds of the left side of the page and leaving the right side of the page blank for notes or spontaneous questions to be written in during the interview. Illustration 10-10 shows how such a page might look.

j. Be flexible—always expect to ask other questions in the interview

No matter how carefully the interviewer plans, many questions will have to be spontaneously formulated during the interview. No interview goes according to a script. For example, going into an initial client interview, the interviewer may have incomplete or inaccurate information about the specific legal problem the new client will present. That potential divorce client may turn out to be a woman already divorced who needs assistance in enforcing a child support decree entered in another state. That business contract dispute may turn out to be a potential trade name infringement matter. That personal injury product liability client may turn out to be an unhappy (but perfectly healthy) consumer with a potential fraud claim. That workers' compensation claim may turn out to be a possible Americans with Disabilities Act claim. The interviewer has to be flexible and able to adjust his questions from one legal context to another with little or no notice.

In addition, something will always require that the interviewer ask unplanned questions—the answers given, the demeanor or personality of the client, or the environment in which the interview is conducted. Expect this—it's a normal part of interviewing. And remember that the careful crafting of well-worded questions comes with hard work and experience. The more you do it, the better you will be at it.

k. Have the supervising attorney review questions and forms

HYPOTHETICAL 10-4

Paul Perfect now puts his brainstorm list in chronological order and drafts specific questions for each topic. These are his questions on the topic of what he finally calls, "Client's prior knowledge of Plaintiff."

1. Client's prior knowledge of plaintiff (CF)

- Where does CF live in relation to your house?
- How long has she lived there?
- Is she married or living with anyone?
- Do you know if she has children?
- Where does she work?
- What does she do there?
- Do you know how long she has worked there?
- How long have you known her?
- How did you two meet?
- Would you say you know her well?
- Do you consider her a good friend?
- How did she come to be invited to the party?
- Did she come with anyone else?
- Is she close friends with anyone else who was at the party?
- Have you ever had any problems of any kind with her before?
- Do you have any reason to believe she doesn't like you?
- Did anything unpleasant or negative occur between the two of you at the party before the fall?
- Do you have any reason to believe she would stage the fall?
- Do you have any reason to believe she would exaggerate her injuries?

Would you add any questions to the list under this topic?

Having prepared his questions, Paul Perfect makes a copy of everything he plans to use in the interview and gives it to Betty Busy's secretary with a note asking the attorney to look it over and let him know if it looks okay to use.

3. Using a checklist or intake sheet

Many law offices have developed written **checklists** or use a new client form called an **intake sheet** to conduct initial client interviews.

Personal injury, divorce, medical malpractice, workers' compensation, bankruptcy, and estate planning are examples of areas of the law lending themselves to such checklists or intake sheets. Illustration 10-11 presents a sample checklist that might be used in the personal injury area.

Checklists can be very useful to the legal professional conducting an interview. They will help you identify the topics you must cover with the client. They can serve as a literal checklist to check off topics as you cover

Illustration 10-11   CHECKLIST FOR PERSONAL INJURY CASE

1. CLIENT BACKGROUND INFORMATION
   Full name
   Nickname/former names
   Current address
   Addresses last ten years
   Phone no. (home/work/cell/pda)
   FAX no.
   E-mail address
   Soc. Sec. no.
   DOB
   Marital status (S/M/D)
   Spouse's name
   Children & D's OB
   Current employer name
   Current employer address
   Current employer phone no.
   Employment duties/title
   Supervisor(s)
   Salary
   Other annual earnings/income
   Former employment last ten years

2. INCIDENT INFORMATION
   Date
   Place
   Summary of incident
   Known witnesses
   Other parties involved in incident
   Third parties who may be responsible
   Incident job related (Y/N)
   Investigating authority
   Investigating officer
   Accident report (Copy Y/N)
   Other physical evidence (photos, etc.)

3. PROPERTY DAMAGE
   Property damaged
   Description of damage (total/partial)
   Owner(s)
   Value and source of estimate

4. PERSONAL INJURY
   Persons injured
   Description of injuries
   Prognosis
   Future disabilities/treatment

   Prior medical history
   Health/medical condition prior to incident
   Medications taking at time of accident
   Treating hospital
   Dates of treatment
   Treating physician
   Dates of visits
   Other physicians
   Description of medical treatment to date
   Medications prescribed
   Physical therapy (Y/N)
   Physical therapy provider
   Medical bills to date (copies Y/N)

5. OTHER DAMAGES
   Lost time from work
   Lost income/how calculated
   Pain and suffering (description)
   Witnesses to pain and suffering
   Loss of consortium claim
   Other loss or damage

6. INSURANCE INFORMATION
   Client's auto insurance carrier/policy no.
   Client's medical insurance carrier/policy no.
   Client's other insurance/policy no.
   Other party's auto insurance carrier
   Other party's other insurance

7. STATUTES OF LIMITATION/REPOSE
   Relevant statutes
   Relevant dates
   Dates entered into docket control (Y/N)

8. OTHER RELEVANT INFORMATION

9. INTERVIEW CONDUCTED BY

10. DATE OF INTERVIEW

11. CONFLICT OF INTEREST CHECK COMPLETED (Y/N)
    Date completed
    Performed by

12. REPRESENTATION UNDERTAKEN (Y/N)
    Date representation undertaken
    File no.

them, and they help ensure you have covered everything and gotten all documents signed before you let the client leave.

Use caution with checklists, however. No matter how comprehensive, no pre-existing list of questions can anticipate all that needs to be asked in a particular interview. Every case is unique in some way. Every client is certainly unique. Therefore, it is important to plan specific questions separately from the checklist. Never become a slave to a checklist. It may stifle creativity and prevent you from following up on leads given in answers.

SLEUTH ON THE LOOSE

Need a quick conversion of foreign money, measurements, distance, time, speed, temperature, etc.? Try www.convert-me.com/en.

4. Prepare the physical environment where the interview is to take place

Whether the interview is conducted in an office or a conference room, there are basic things you want to do.

- Be sure the area is clean and neat
- Put away materials related to other clients
- Be sure enough chairs are available and arranged properly
- Be sure the incidental things are available like note pads, pens, paper clips, etc., and a tape recorder or video camera with extra tapes and batteries

5. Give thought to any special needs of the client

Clients with disabilities affecting *sight, speech, vision,* or *mental comprehension* may require special preparation. If the client is deaf or extremely hard of hearing, consider having a sign interpreter present for the interview. The visually impaired may require a Braille expert.

If you are interviewing a child, remember that the permission and usually the presence of a parent or guardian is required.

Is the client bringing one or more children with her because she has no one to keep them? If possible, arrange for someone else in the office to entertain them while you conduct the interview. Or find some suitable toys or distractions (quiet ones!) for the children.

Is anyone accompanying the client? Any companions will probably need to be excluded from the interview to preserve the attorney-client privilege, so be sure to have a place where they can sit and something for them to read.

6. Plan the seating arrangement

When the legal professional sets up the room where the interview takes place, careful thought should be given to **seating arrangements**. Where the client is seated in the interview room can make a difference:

- in how comfortable they feel;
- in their attention level; and
- in the formal or informal tone of the session.

We will consider seating arrangements in an office with a desk and seating arrangements in an office or conference room around a rectangular or round conference table. Keep in mind that there is no one right seating arrangement. There are alternatives to be considered depending on the physical location of the interview, the person you are interviewing, and the nature of the interview. Each alternative has its advantages and disadvantages.

a. In an office with a desk

In an office there is typically a desk and two or more chairs placed somewhere in front of the desk. In a larger office, you might also have a small, usually round, conference table or couch. In an office with the desk and chairs in front, the interviewer (I) may choose to sit behind the desk with the client (C) in one of the chairs in front of the desk. (See Illustration 10-12(a).) Be aware that this creates a more formal tone for the interview—the position behind the desk is an authoritative one, which may make the client less comfortable.

If the interviewer chooses to come out from behind the desk and sit in one of the chairs across from the client, the tone set is more informal. Since the interviewer has abandoned the authoritative position, the two people are on more of an equal basis and the client may feel more comfortable. (See Illustration 10-12(b).) One disadvantage of this arrangement is that it may make it more difficult for the interviewer to take good notes or to handle necessary documents. A solution may be to seat the person on one side of the desk, diagonally across from the interviewer. (See Illustration 10-12(c).) The desk can still be used for note taking and handling documents but the arrangement is not so authoritative since both people are at the desk.

b. At a rectangular conference table

If the interview is to be conducted at a rectangular conference table, keep in mind that the table will have a recognizable head seat or seat of authority. That is usually the seat at one of the short ends of the table. A guest entering a room with a rectangular table will almost never voluntarily take the head seat. Instead, they will be naturally drawn to one of the seats on a long side of the table. If the interviewer chooses to position herself at the head seat of a rectangular table, a formal tone is set and obvious authority is being asserted. (See Illustration 10-13(a).)

The interviewer may choose to avoid the head seat and select a seat on the side of the rectangular table directly across from the person being interviewed. (See Illustration 10-13(b).) No particular authority is being asserted in this position but some people may feel that sitting directly across from another lends a confrontational tone to the meeting.

Another alternative is for the interviewer to select a seat next to the person on the same side of the table. (See Illustration 10-13(c).) This is non-authoritative and very informal. But it may feel too informal, particularly in a first meeting. Also, any time the interviewer uses this arrangement, she must be careful not to sit too close to the client, which can be perceived as threatening or intrusive. This arrangement also has the disadvantage of making it more difficult to shield notes being taken.

Illustration 10-12   SEATING ARRANGEMENTS IN AN OFFICE

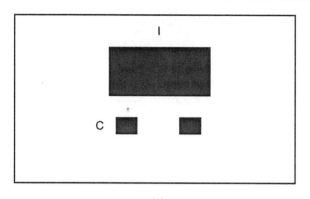

(a)

Creates a formal tone.
The interviewer
sits in a position
of authority.

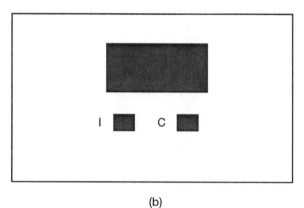

(b)

Less formal. Taking
notes and handling
documents may
be more difficult.

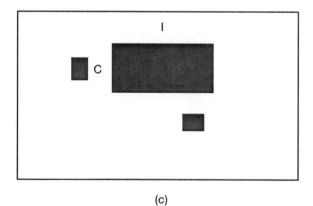

(c)

Still informal. Taking
notes and handling
documents easier.

Illustration 10-13   SEATING ARRANGEMENTS AT A RECTANGULAR CONFERENCE TABLE

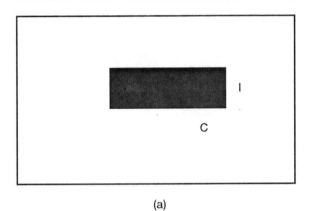

Interviewer is in the
seat of authority.
Formal tone.

(a)

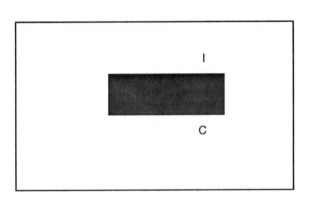

Less authoritative, more
informal tone.

(b)

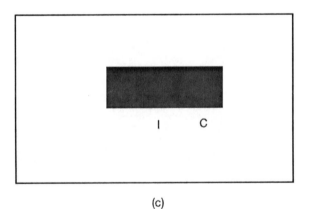

Very informal, but don't
sit too close.

(c)

c. At a rounded conference table

The advantage of a rounded conference table is that it has no head seat. That is why many attorneys and paralegals prefer rounded (circular or oval) conference tables for their offices and conference rooms. It is still possible for the interviewer to sit directly across from the person being interviewed at a rounded table and in some situations that may be viewed as confrontational. Or it may create too great a feeling of distance. (See Illustration 10-14(a).)

Alternatives are to sit diagonally to the person (see Illustration 10-14(b)), or immediately next to them at the table (see Illustration 10-14(c)). The confrontational element is removed from these arrangements, but the closer the interviewer moves to the person being interviewed, the more difficult it is to properly shield notes being taken.

d. Other considerations in seating

No matter what physical arrangement is available for the interview or what seating arrangement is selected, there are several miscellaneous matters to keep in mind:

1. Never sit too close. We all like our space. When another person gets too close to us without our permission it is very uncomfortable and even threatening.

2. Be conscious of the location of doors. In general, you do not want to seat a client with his back to the door leading into the room. It can have the *Wild Bill Hickock effect* on some people, making them uncomfortable in that position. (See Illustration 10-15(a).)

3. Be conscious of the location of windows. Avoid seating a person so that he is looking past the interviewer and out a window, or looking out a window to their side. The view may prove distracting. The interviewer wants the person being interviewed to concentrate on the questions and answers. So, instead, place the person with his back to the window. (See Illustration 10-15(b).)

4. Keep your notes shielded from view. Sit where you can keep your notes shielded from the wandering eyes of the client. Your notes may, and should, contain your impressions of the client and his answers. Only you and the supervising attorney should ever see those notes.

5. No one seating arrangement is always right. Use different seating arrangements in different situations. For example, in some interview situations, the interviewer may want to seat herself in a position of authority relative to the client or witness. Maybe you have been assigned to interview a potential client who is a successful business man. Over the phone he sounded very full of himself and condescending toward you as a paralegal or a mere associate attorney. In that initial interview, you may want to stake out a formal authoritative position for yourself. He may respect that more than a less formal arrangement. If you are interviewing a hostile witness (see Chapter 12), you may deliberately choose a formal or even confrontational arrangement.

7. Avoid interruptions during the interview

If the interview is to take place in your office, switch the phone out so it doesn't ring in your office. Tell the receptionist not to transfer calls

Illustration 10-14   SEATING ARRANGEMENTS AT A ROUNDED CONFERENCE TABLE

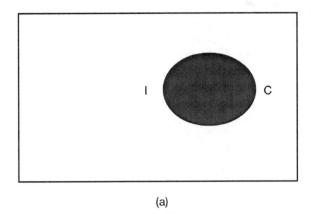

(a)

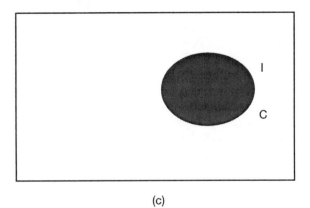

(b)

(c)

Illustration 10-15 DOORS AND WINDOWS IN SEATING ARRANGEMENTS

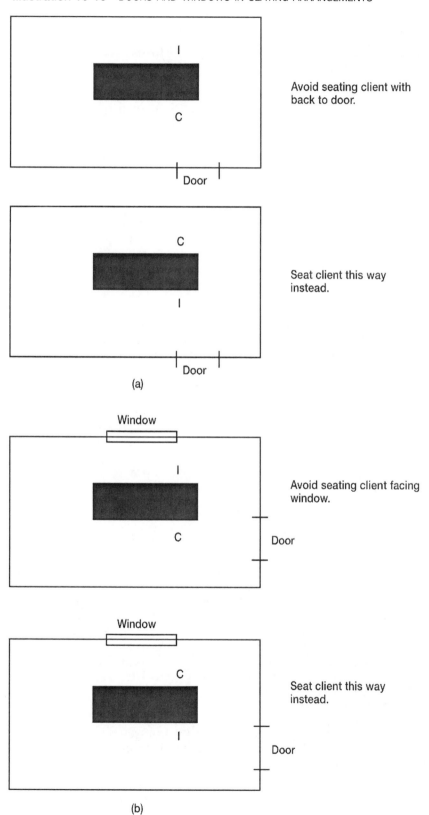

Avoid seating client with back to door.

Seat client this way instead.

(a)

Avoid seating client facing window.

Seat client this way instead.

(b)

while you are in the interview. Tell your secretary that you are not to be disturbed (unless the building is on fire!).

8. Be physically and mentally prepared for the interview

It is also important for the interviewer to prepare himself physically and mentally for interviewing. The act of conducting an interview is taxing. We will do better if we prepare ourselves. That means:

a. Get enough rest the night before the interview

You won't do the job that you should if you're tired.

b. Leave your personal life outside the interview room

Not your *personality*, your personal life. Put aside whatever you are anxious about on a given day and focus 100 percent on this interview. While you worry about cooking for those guests tonight or whatever else is on your mind, you are going to miss a word, a phrasing, a look, or a gesture by the witness that you should have caught.

HYPOTHETICAL 10-5

The evening before the interview with Jay DeClient, Paul Perfect looks over his notes one more time, then prepares for bed at 10 p.m. As he is brushing his teeth, the phone rings. It's his best friend from paralegal school whom he hasn't seen in years. The friend is in town to assist his supervising attorney with a deposition tomorrow morning. He suggests that Paul come down to his hotel and have a drink with him since he has to leave right after the deposition tomorrow. Paul is tempted, but then remembers his interview with Jay DeClient tomorrow afternoon and takes a rain check. He knows that if he stays out late tonight he will be dragging by tomorrow afternoon.

On the way to work in the morning Paul has a flat tire—on the interstate, in the rain, during rush hour. And the tires on his car are almost new! Paul begins thinking about the spleen-venting phone call he is going to make later to the dealer who sold him the tires. He vows to do it as soon as he gets to the office. He rehearses biting and sarcastic remarks to the dealer—was there a typo in that warranty? Was the 60,000 miles supposed to be only 600? He imagines the dealer apologizing and coming down to the office personally to deliver a new tire and offering him a year of free oil changes to make it up to him.

As he enters his office, still soggy, Paul Perfect sees the materials he left for Betty Busy on his desk with a note from her saying she has looked them over and they are fine. He makes his phone call to the tire dealer who (rats!) is out for the week and can't be reached regarding Paul's complaint (probably on a sailboat in the Caribbean, Paul thinks, vacation paid for by yours truly). The person answering the phone does promise to have the assistant manager call as soon as he comes in that morning.

The assistant manager apparently *doesn't* come in that morning because he doesn't call. Before he leaves for lunch at noon, Paul calls the dealership again only to be told that the assistant manager is out to lunch. Paul starts to comment on how true that obviously is but bites his tongue. He asks that the assistant manager call him as soon as he returns and is promised that he will. When Paul returns from lunch there is no message from the assistant manager. Paul groans and starts to dial the dealership number again. Then he looks at the clock and sees that there's barely an hour before his interview with Jay DeClient. He puts the phone down and tells himself to get his act together for the interview.

A little after 1 p.m. Paul checks the conference room where the interview will be held and picks up some papers left over from a previous conference. He politely asks the receptionist to please clean off the top of the table, which has a few cup rings showing from the last use.

Paul looks over the rectangular table with a seat at each end and six chairs on each side. He recalls how friendly and informal Jay DeClient sounded on the phone. He decides that he will sit in one of the chairs on the side of the table—the one facing out the window—and put DeClient directly across from him, looking toward the closed door.

About 30 minutes before Jay DeClient is expected to arrive, Paul calls the receptionist and reminds her that DeClient is coming and to call Paul as soon as he arrives. He tells her where he wants the client to be seated in the conference room. He also reminds her to not put any calls through to the conference room while he is in there. He reminds his secretary of the same thing. Then he reviews the file one last time to be sure everything is ready. Just as he finishes, his phone rings and the receptionist tells him that Mr. Jay DeClient is here to see him.

Chapter Summary and Conclusion

There are three categories of persons that legal professionals interview: clients, fact witnesses, and other information sources. Interviews may be conducted in the legal professional's office or in the field. Legal professionals do not interview a client just once; after the initial interview there are typically numerous subsequent contacts. There are many important goals to be accomplished in the initial client interview and numerous steps to be completed in arranging the initial interview. Client authorizations and fee agreements are important documents often prepared for an initial client interview. In preparing questions for an initial client interview, it is important to start with what you know, consider any special needs of the client, and use brainstorming to create a list of topics to be covered before preparing specific questions within each topic. Many law offices use a checklist or intake sheet for initial client interviews. The interviewer must be prepared to use all different kinds of questions in an interview and to recognize the difference that particular phrasing of a question can make. When the interview is held in the legal professional's office, consideration must be given to the seating arrangement for the interview and to the interviewer's physical and emotional preparedness.

In Chapter 11 we will consider actually conducting a client interview.

Review Questions

1. The ability to _____, _____, and _____ an effective interview is a basic _____ of the legal professional and an essential component of _____.
2. What is the distinction between an in-office interview and a field interview?
3. List as many goals of the initial client interview as you can recall.
4. Why is it important for a paralegal to identify herself as a paralegal when she communicates with someone outside the office?
5. What forms or other documents might need to be prepared for an initial client interview?
6. Distinguish between an open-ended question and a closed-ended question and a hypothetical question and a multiple choice question.
7. What are the different ways that questions can be phrased in an interview?
8. What is a checklist or intake sheet and how is it used in client interviewing?
9. How do you prepare the physical environment where an interview is to take place?
10. List several considerations for the seating arrangement for an interview.

KEY WORDS AND PHRASES TO REMEMBER

clients
closed-ended questions
confirmation letter
contingency fee agreement
educational records authorization
employment records
    authorization
explanatory questions
fact witness
field interview
flat fee agreement
hourly rate plus expenses
    agreements
hypothetical questions
information source
initial client interview

intake sheet
interview checklist
leading questions
legal services agreement
medical records authorization
multiple-choice questions
open-ended questions
opinion questions
phrasing of questions
pressure questions
retainer
retainer agreement
seating arrangement
silence as a question
work file

LEARN BY DOING

LBD 10-1. Schedule and prepare for the client interview in one of the following Case Studies (from Appendix A) as assigned to you by the instructor. Contact the person who will be playing the role of the client. Schedule the interview then prepare: (1) a memo to the instructor summarizing your contact with the client; (2) a confirming letter to the client; and (3) any forms you might need for the interview. Prepare your questions for the interview.

a. Case Study No. 1 (The Rowdy Outlaw Case) Rowdy Outlaw
b. Case Study No. 2 (The Soupspoon Wise Case) Soupspoon Wise
c. Case Study No. 3 (The Vidalia Unyon Case) Vidalia Unyon
d. Case Study No. 4 (The Rocky Road Project) Rocky Road

LBD 10-2. Using one of the four Case Studies included in Appendix A as directed by your instructor, and the information outlined below, draft a fee agreement for the client and a letter to the client (1) transmitting the fee agreement; (2) briefly describing the initial investigation your office has agreed to undertake on behalf of the client; and (3) estimating the cost and time for completing that investigation.

a. Case Study No. 1 (The Rowdy Outlaw Case): The supervising attorney has agreed that Outlaw will pay a $50,000 retainer up front. Monthly billings will show the charges for time and expenses made against the retainer and the remaining balance. The retainer amount will be replenished at the same level ($50,000) within ten days of the receipt by the client of a monthly statement showing the balance of the original retainer to be below $15,000, or two weeks before trial, whichever occurs first. Hourly rates to be charged are $250 per hour for partner attorneys, $175 per hour for associate attorneys, and $100 per hour for paralegals.

b. Case Study No. 2 (The Soupspoon Wise Case): The supervising attorney has agreed that Wise will pay a $10,000 retainer up front to be applied against expenses only, not legal fees. Expenses are to include all out-of-pocket costs incurred by the law office in connection with the representation including, but not limited to, long-distance phone calls, mailing, printing and copy costs, travel expenses (including mileage, food, and lodging), filing fees, court reporter costs, expert fees and expenses, and charges for online research or communications. The legal fee will be a contingency fee of one-third of the gross amount of any recovery by settlement, arbitration, judgment, or otherwise from whatever source and will increase to 40 percent in the event of an appeal by any party. If out-of-pocket expenses exceed the $10,000 retainer amount during the representation, all expenses in excess of $10,000 will be payable out of the balance of the gross recovery after the deduction of the legal fee. If there is no recovery, expenses in excess of the retainer amount will be paid within six months of the dismissal of the case or the termination of the representation, whichever occurs first.

c. Case Study No. 3 (The Vidalia Unyon Case): The supervising attorney has agreed that a motion for temporary support will be filed promptly after the divorce action is commenced, asking that Mr. Unyon be ordered to pay Mrs. Unyon's fees and expenses in connection with the representation or to designate funds in an identifiable account with sufficient balance for that purpose for her discretionary use. In the event that motion is not granted or the court does not order Mr. Unyon to pay or make sufficient funds available to pay the legal fees and expenses of Mrs. Unyon, Mrs. Unyon will pay monthly bills for all excess amounts within ten days of receipt of the statement. Hourly rates will be charged at $190 per hour for the supervising attorney and $95 per hour for paralegals.

d. Case Study No. 4 (The Rocky Road Project): The supervising attorney has agreed that RRI will make no advance payment. There will be monthly billings showing time and expense charges, but only the expenses will be payable, within 30 days of receipt. Accrued attorney fees will be shown on each statement but will not be payable until closing on the optioned ten acres or until the current option expires, whichever occurs sooner. Attorney fees accrued after the closing on the optioned ten acres will be payable as owed at the closing on the additional parcels to be purchased by RRI for the shopping center project or six months from the date of the final bill, whichever occurs sooner. Rocky Road, president of RRI, will sign a personal guaranty securing payment of all corporate fees and expenses owed to the firm now and in the future. Hourly rates will be charged at $250 per hour for partner attorneys, $195 per hour for associate attorneys, and $110 per hour for paralegals.

Chapter 11

Conducting a Client Interview

CHAPTER OBJECTIVES

In Chapter 10 we considered scheduling and preparing for the initial client interview. In this chapter we consider conducting the client interview. You will learn:

- How to greet and make the client feel comfortable and welcome.
- The important things to keep in mind throughout the client interview.
- How to begin a client interview, move to the substantive areas, and conclude the interview.
- How to use active listening skills in a client interview.
- How to evaluate, test, and seek verification of information obtained in a client interview.
- How to work successfully with difficult clients.
- How to prepare an interview summary for the supervising attorney.
- How to prepare follow-up communications to a client.
- The role of the assisting legal professional when the supervising attorney conducts the interview.
- Guidelines for handling subsequent client interviews and contacts.

A. Introduction

This chapter continues our study of preparing for and conducting an initial client interview. When we left Paul Perfect at the end of Chapter 10, the receptionist had just called and told him that the potential new client, Jay S. DeClient, was here to see him. Now let's learn how to actually conduct an effective new client interview.

B. Ten Things to Remember Throughout the Client Interview

1. Be friendly but professional

Don't use the client's first name unless you already know him or he invites you to do so. If appropriate, express empathy for the client's condition or circumstances but never appear *condescending, patronizing,* or *pandering.* Avoid being *judgmental* or appearing *shocked*—you're going to hear it all in this job. Be obvious about *paying close attention* by maintaining *good eye contact.* Never appear *bored* (even if you are bored to tears) or let the client know that this is *routine* (even if it is). Never appear *rushed* or indicate to the client how *busy* or *overworked* you are.

Avoid expressing *personal opinions* in an interview—about the case, the opposing party, or the opposing party's attorney. Don't create *expectations* in the client's mind about the merits of the case one way or another; it is the attorney's responsibility to evaluate the case.

2. Avoid legal or technical jargon except as necessary

Remember that the client is not familiar with legal terms or concepts. He has come with a problem, and may be intimidated just by being in a law office. If the interviewer starts throwing around legal terms and concepts—*res judicata* or *res ipsa loquitur*—it may only increase the client's anxiety, hindering communication rather than advancing it. Some interviewers mistakenly think that using important-sounding legal terms will make them appear more professional in the eyes of a client. Usually it has the opposite effect, making the interviewer appear pompous and self-important. Of course there are times when we must and should use legal terms. With Jay DeClient, Paul Perfect may have to explain that he is asking questions about the punch that Carlotta Falldown threw because Jay DeClient may have (depending on the analysis of the facts by the supervising attorney) a potential counterclaim against her. He will explain as simply as he can what a counterclaim is.

3. The paralegal interviewer and any supervising lawyer must be cognizant of the dangers of the unauthorized practice of law

Even though the paralegal interviewer will have explained to the client at the beginning of the interview that he cannot give legal advice, it will be easy for the client to forget that. The questions raised by the client during the course of the interview about legal rights or remedies may be questions to which the paralegal knows the answer and it would expedite the interview to give an answer and move on. But unless the paralegal interviewer has been specifically authorized by the supervising attorney to communicate that information in response to a specific question, he must not do it, for all the reasons we considered when we talked about

UPL in Chapter 2. And any attorney supervising a paralegal interviewer must remember that the paralegal is acting as an agent of the attorney with all the ramifications of that relationship that we covered in Chapter 1.

4. Take good notes

Good notes are accurate and comprehensive notes. There is an art to good note taking (as most people learn in high school and college). And it is a real challenge to be able to take good notes while you are also observing and actively listening to the witness. But it must be done. We cannot trust ourselves to accurately remember statements made and impressions perceived for longer than a few moments.

Many interviewers develop their own shorthand to make note taking more efficient. Just don't forget your own abbreviations. If the interview is being recorded (see discussion in Chapter 13), the need for notes is lessened, but you will still want to record impressions that the tape recorder will not pick up.

5. Engage in *active listening*

Recall the discussion of **active listening** in Chapter 8. In interviewing, we listen not just to hear words, but to catch *meanings* as well. And watch for that **body language** (facial expressions, eye contact, body position and gestures, nervous signs) that tells us so much about a person.

6. Evaluate the demeanor and behavior of the client

Note traits or characteristics of the client that the supervising attorney will need to know about—relaxed or nervous demeanor, neat or unkempt appearance, appropriate or inappropriate dress, correct or incorrect grammar, normal or abnormal behavior. Evaluate the client's credibility, intelligence, and personality. Make a special note of anything about the client that seems odd or troubles you. For example, is the client egotistical, temperamental, easily manipulated, a political or religious zealot, profane, sexist? Get the idea? Make careful notes of your impressions.

7. The client will not know what to tell you—you have to ask

Because clients are not trained in the law or factual analysis, they do not appreciate, as the interviewer does, the relationship between the law and relevant facts (see Chapter 1). They will typically have no idea which facts are relevant to their problem and which are not. Do not assume that what the client tells you is the problem is everything you need to know. We have to know what to ask. It is up to the interviewer, not the client, to get out all the relevant information.

SLEUTH ON THE LOOSE

In need of a quick map of an area involved in a lawsuit or aerial photographs? Try http://maps.google.com/ and type in the zip code. Need a topographical map or aerial photograph view? Try http://earth.google.com/.

8. Remember the commandments

Recall the two great commandments of interviewing and investigating:

a. Assume nothing

b. Verify everything

And that is why in every interview, we:

- evaluate the source of the information
- test the information for internal consistency
- look for holes or gaps in the information
- compare new information to information already gathered
- seek corroborating information
- seek explanations
- seek details
- seek leads to other information

9. Keep an emotional distance between yourself and the client

It is easy to connect emotionally with clients who have suffered tragedy or who are going through an ordeal of some kind, particularly those who are innocent victims of another's cruelty. We do—and should—feel normal human compassion, express sympathy, and show empathy in those situations.

But there is a danger here for the unwary. None of us can carry all the burdens of the world on our shoulders. We all have the normal load of emotional involvement and resulting stress that comes from our own lives. If you allow yourself to become too personally involved in the problems of the client, you run the risk of losing your objectivity (how objective are you about perceived attacks on family or friends?). Or, you run the risk of emotional burnout from simply taking too much on yourself. We have to develop the ability to feel for clients but at the same time to keep an emotional distance from them in order to protect ourselves and do our jobs. The ability to do that starts with recognizing the danger.

10. Overcome *internal* obstacles to effective interviewing

In any interview we may encounter **internal barriers**—those of our own making—that can interfere with doing an effective job. Four of the greatest internal obstacles that interviewers face are:

a. Concentrating too intently on your next question

A common error of new interviewers is to be so engrossed in wording the next question just right that they miss something in the answer to the last one.

b. Concentrating too hard on taking good notes

It is important to take good notes in an interview. But there is a real art to being able to do that *and* make consistent eye contact with a witness. The ability to do this well comes with experience.

c. Being a slave to the prepared list of questions

Another common error of the beginner is to so slavishly follow the carefully prepared questions that they fail to follow up on leads to new information. Remember, the interviewer must be **flexible**—ready to change directions during the interview at any time based on what you hear. Be ready to test information that seems questionable and ready to follow new leads. If you concentrate solely on that list of questions, you will always miss something important.

d. Letting your own biases affect you

We all have biases, and we're not always conscious of having them. We can identify them, however, because they usually express themselves as either positive or negative feelings toward people. The interviewer has to catch himself when he becomes aware of those negative or positive feelings creeping into the interview to keep them from interfering with his objectivity, his duties to the client, or his commitment to legal ethics and professionalism.

In interviewing, we have to remain objective. We have to recognize and overcome our own prejudices and do the job for the client. How would *you* handle each of the situations described in the Example?

EXAMPLE

> You are interviewing a criminal defendant client who, you discover, has been convicted of child abuse in the past. You have intense feelings of disgust and dislike for the client and think it wouldn't be so bad to see him convicted on the current charge and put away permanently.
>
> You are interviewing a divorce client who admits to having beaten his wife but says it was okay because she beat on him too. He is 6'4" and 250 pounds and the wife is 5'2" and 100 pounds. You realize that you despise this guy.
>
> You are interviewing the wife of the 6'4" 250-pound spouse abuser. She describes in detail the repeated beatings she has suffered and says she would like to kill him. You so closely identify with her that you feel the urge to offer your help!

C. ▶ The Order and Manner of Conducting a Client Interview

1. Greeting the client

Once the potential client arrives for the interview, recall that one of the most important goals we have in connection with the **initial client interview** is to establish a relationship of trust, confidence, and cooperation. That goal is furthered by greeting the client, making him feel welcomed, and seating him comfortably where the interview is to take place.

In some offices the legal professional may leave it to the receptionist to take care of these tasks, but be sure your receptionist knows how to do this effectively. (See Hypothetical 11-1.)

HYPOTHETICAL 11-1

> Assume Paul Perfect tells the receptionist to "go ahead and put Mr. DeClient in the conference room and tell him I'll be right with him."

Here is the dialog that might take place between the receptionist (R) and Jay S. DeClient (JSD):

R: (putting the phone down and smiling): Mr. DeClient, Mr. Perfect will be right with you. He asked me to go ahead and show you to the conference room. If you'll just follow me down the hall this way.

JSD: Sure, that will be fine.

R: (while guiding JSD down the hall): I hope you didn't have any trouble finding our office. (Or, did you find a parking place okay? Or, how were the roads with all that ice and snow? Or, isn't this wonderful weather we're having?)

JSD: No, none at all. Mr. Perfect gave me *perfect* directions. (JSD laughs at his joke.)

R: (laughing politely with JSD at the joke although she has heard a million puns made on Paul Perfect's name): Well, good (motioning into conference room). Here we are. Just have a seat by the window there and Mr. Perfect will be right with you.

JSD: Fine. Thank you very much.

R: May I get you a cup of coffee or a soft drink?

JSD: Coffee sounds good, please.

R: Would you like it black or with cream or sugar?

JSD: Just black, please.

R: Fine. Make yourself comfortable and I'll be right back with that.

Some interviewers prefer to come out to the reception area and greet the potential client themselves, direct them to the conference room, and ask if they would like a refreshment.

HYPOTHETICAL 11-2

If Paul Perfect was to greet Jay DeClient and guide him to the conference room, the dialog might sound something like this:

R: (putting the phone down and smiling): Mr. DeClient, Mr. Perfect will be right with you.

JSD: Okay, that will be fine.

PP: (entering reception area and approaching JSD with hand extended to shake): Hello, Mr. DeClient? I'm Paul Perfect. It's a pleasure to meet you.

JSD: (shaking hands with PP): Hi, I'm pleased to meet you as well. Except for this contraption on my nose (motioning to the nose brace and laughing nervously).

PP: Don't worry about that at all. If it was on my nose people would say it's an improvement. (Everybody laughs, including receptionist.) Let me show you to the conference room. Right this way.

JSD: Fine, thanks.

PP (while guiding JSD down the hall): I hope you didn't have any trouble finding our office. (Or, did you find a parking place okay? Or, how were the roads with all that ice and snow? Or, isn't this wonderful weather we're having?)

JSD: No, none at all. You gave me *perfect* directions. (JSD laughs at his joke.)

PP: (laughing politely with JSD at the joke although he has heard endless puns made on his name): Well, good (motioning into conference room). Here we are. Just have a seat by the window there.

> **JSD:**   Fine. Thank you very much.
> **PP:**   Would you like a cup of coffee or a soft drink before we begin?
> **JSD:**   Coffee sounds good, please.
> **PP**   (picking up phone and dialing receptionist): Would you like it black or with cream or sugar?
> **JSD:**   Just black, please.
> **PP:**   Fine (to receptionist) Janice? Will you bring Mr. DeClient a cup of coffee, black, in the conference room, please? Thanks. No, nothing for me. Thanks again. (To JSD) She'll be right here with that.
>
> Is there anything you would have done differently from Paul Perfect in this situation?

Each scenario will be different, but the goal is to make the potential client feel welcomed and comfortable. A good initial impression has been made and now a solid basis exists to create confidence and trust.

2. Beginning the interview

In addition to the greeting, there are a number of steps to beginning the interview of a client. You will rarely if ever jump right into your questions.

a. If appropriate, express empathy toward the client

Empathy is the capacity to identify with another's feelings. If the client is still ill at ease or upset following the greeting, take additional time to make her feel secure and comfortable. Additional small talk about weather, parking, directions, refreshment choices, etc., may help. For the client who is visibly upset, tell her to take as much time as needed to collect herself, offer tissues for tears, offer to leave them alone for a while, or in the extreme case, to reschedule the interview.

b. Explain the absence of the supervising attorney

This may already have been done when the interview was scheduled but it doesn't hurt to repeat the explanation.

c. Explain your role as a paralegal or associate attorney

The paralegal interviewer must be sure the client understands that he is not an attorney. Make it clear that you cannot answer questions involving legal advice or decide, for example, whether to accept the case or what legal strategies to pursue. Explain that you are there to collect necessary information for the attorney to evaluate and that you or the attorney will then contact her concerning decisions the attorney has made. Ask the client if she understands what you are saying and if she has any questions.

The associate attorney conducting an interview for the supervising attorney should explain her assisting role so the client will not expect the interviewing attorney to make final decisions about how to proceed. Be sure the client knows that all information obtained in the interview will be passed along to the supervising attorney.

d. Explain the attorney-client privilege

The client needs to understand that everything he tells you in the interview is confidential, whether or not the attorney decides to undertake the representation.

e. Briefly review the goals to be accomplished in the interview

An estimation of the time that will be spent is a good idea, too.

f. Explain that you will be taking notes during the interview

Let the client know that note taking is standard procedure in an interview.

g. Ask if the client has any questions

Give the client this opportunity before you begin the substantive portion of the interview. This may prevent questions later that disrupt the flow of the interview.

h. Obtain biographical information for the file

Before getting to your substantive questions—those related to the reason for the client's visit—obtain the biographical data you will need to set up the file on this client if the supervising attorney decides to take the case. This data typically includes full name, nicknames, address, employer's name and address, phone numbers (home, work, cell, and emergency), e-mail addresses, and source of reference to the attorney.

Sometimes the office will have an **intake sheet** (see discussion in Chapter 10) that the new client is asked to fill out while she is waiting to meet with the interviewer. In that case, look over the form as the interview begins to be sure it is complete. Ask any additional questions needed to complete the form.

HYPOTHETICAL 11-3

Assume that Paul Perfect is beginning his interview with Jay DeClient. Let's listen in:

PP: (returning to the table after asking the receptionist to bring JSD coffee and seating himself directly across from JSD at the rectangular conference table): Mr. DeClient, we appreciate your coming in so promptly. Ms. Busy had hoped to be here today, but she had another commitment she couldn't avoid.

JSD: No problem. I know how that happens.

PP: Before we begin, I need to explain to you that I am not an attorney. I am a paralegal, or legal assistant. I work under Ms. Busy's supervision and help her with certain tasks like meeting with you today and getting the information she will need in order to decide whether to take your case and exactly how we should proceed legally. Because I'm not an attorney, I can't make the decision whether to take your case or give you any legal advice at all. Do you understand what I'm saying?

JSD: Yes, I believe I do. But when will I know whether she will agree to take my case?

PP: Well, what will happen is, as soon as we are finished here, I will prepare a written report for her, summarizing all the information I get from you today. She will look it over as soon as she can and either she or

I will call you and let you know. I don't know her schedule over the next few days, but I know she is aware of how important this is to you and will make it a priority. And I will too. I'll remind her that you're anxious to hear back. Is that okay?

JSD: Sure, I understand. That sounds fine.

PP: Now . . . (pausing for the knock at the door). Come in. (The receptionist comes in, smiles, and places the cup of coffee and a coaster in front of JSD.)

JSD: Thank you very much.

PP: (To the receptionist leaving the room): Thank you, Janice. (To JSD) Now, I also want you to understand that everything you tell me today is confidential. You've probably heard of attorney-client confidentiality. (JSD nods his head.) Even though Ms. Busy is not here, that same confidentiality attaches because I'm here as her assistant. And that means no one can compel us to disclose what you tell me today without your consent. And that's true, by the way, whether or not Ms. Busy agrees to take your case. Do you understand that?

JSD: Yes, I do. And I'm glad you mentioned it because I was wondering.

PP: Well, good. (Placing his notes in front of him.) Okay, what we're going to do today is go over this entire situation with Carlotta Falldown pretty thoroughly. I'll be asking you a lot of questions about yourself and about her and the party and the fall and the injuries you both have sustained and just the whole ball of wax. Okay?

JSD: Sure. That's what I expected.

PP: And I'll be taking notes as we go along, which is sort of standard operating procedure in these situations, so don't let that distract you. I may pause sometimes between questions if I'm still writing, but just bear with me. I really scribble pretty fast. Of course, no one can read it but me (smiling).

JSD: (smiling back): Gotcha. I'm ready if you are.

PP: Great. First, let me get some biographical information on you for the file.

3. Conducting the substantive portion of the interview

a. Briefly review any documents the client brought

Take a moment to look over these documents. Doing this at the beginning of the substantive portion of the interview will help you focus more quickly on the facts and give you a better idea of the areas you need to address in your questions.

b. Obtain a broad overview of the client's story

In most interviews it is logical and effective to begin consideration of the substantive portion of the interview by obtaining a **narrative summary** of the problem from the client. It provides the interviewer with an overview of the entire situation and an extended opportunity to observe and evaluate the client. Open-ended questions are ideal for this.

Now, tell me, what we can do for you?

Why don't you tell me how the accident happened first, and then we'll go over the details?

To begin with, tell me how this whole thing happened.

In general, *let the client talk.* Interrupt as little as possible. Make copious notes. Remember, you will have plenty of time later to ask follow-up questions. Try to get the entire story or sequence of events out at this stage. If the client seems to pause or hesitate before getting everything out, encourage them with positive statements such as:

Please go on.
What happened then?
That must have been quite a shock to you.

c. Fill in gaps in the information given

It is critical for the interviewer to get a complete picture of the event or circumstances being described by the client. As the client goes through the narrative explanation, the interviewer should be watching for gaps or incomplete explanations. Now go back and fill those in. Closed-ended, explanatory, and opinion questions are ideal for this purpose.

Now, what happened between the time the light turned green and you began your turn?
Tell me more about what Mr. Brown said when you told him you were quitting.
How many times did you try to call him before you went over there?
What did you mean a few moments ago when you described your neighbor as "nosey"?
Why do you think he refused to talk to you when you called?

d. Ask for definitions of unfamiliar words and phrases

There is no virtue in pretending to know something you don't. Our goal in the interview is to obtain information that we can understand, evaluate, and apply to the client's legal problem. So if the client uses technical, foreign, slang, or other unfamiliar words, ask for a definition.

e. Ask for details

Interviewers have to get the complete factual picture. Clients not only don't always know what we need to know, they don't understand that we need to know *everything.* Never assume the client has told you all she knows until you've made sure of that by asking for details. We need details of *times, places, distances, colors, sounds, smells, events, transactions, people, documents,* and *sequences.* Think *who, why, what, when, where,* and *how.*

Tell me as exactly as you can what time it was when you left home that day.
Try to remember each and every person you saw standing around the wreck area after you came to.
Estimate for me in feet how far away the gunman was from you.
Why did you go back in there when they warned you not to?
Would there be any written record of that agreement and, if so, who would have it?

Be **thorough** in your questioning. Think of interviewing a client as analogous to wringing out a wet rag. Get all the water you can out of it! Squeeze hard. Squeeze repeatedly. Squeeze one way and then another.

You haven't done the job until you are satisfied that you know everything relevant to the matter.

If you need to, be **persistent.** If you think the client or witness is withholding information for any reason, don't drop it. Move on to something else then come back to the subject again. Consider confronting them with your suspicions:

> *If you don't mind, let's go back over the reasons you had for wanting this divorce.*
>
> *Mrs. Brown, I may be mistaken here, but I get the impression you are reluctant to talk about the reasons for your divorce from your ex-husband. Am I right?*

Try to get the client **committed** to as much detail as possible. Obviously, if a person doesn't really know something, then that is the honest answer. We never want to influence people to say something they don't know or believe. But be sure that you find all that they do know, down to the last detail. Use **repetition** and proper phrasing of questions to get the client to commit on details.

> *And you're sure that he said . . .*
> *So what you're telling me is . . .*
> *Now if I understand you correctly, she . . .*

f. Ask for leads to witnesses and documents

Listen closely during the interview for the mention of other persons with knowledge of relevant facts or of documents. If the client doesn't mention it, ask if there are such persons or documents. If the client does mention it, ask if there are others. We are always interested in leads to more helpful information.

g. If helpful, have the client draw a sketch or diagram

Let the client illustrate what happened or what she saw if it will help your understanding of the events. In interviewing we are not limited to words. There is no reason that a client cannot be asked to draw something for us. That drawing or sketch can be helpful to refresh their recollection later and even become an important part of their testimony.

Most people will initially balk at being asked to draw or illustrate something, urging lack of talent for it. The interviewer needs to expect that, explain that talent doesn't matter, and encourage the client to give it a try. (See Hypothetical 11-4.)

The interviewer should ask the client to initial or sign the diagram or sketch to confirm that she did in fact draw it, and to date it. Witnesses may be providing a sketch of the same scene later and that will avoid confusion. In addition, the signature or initials placed on the client's or witness's sketches may help authenticate those sketches later for evidentiary purposes. (See Illustration 11-1.)

Any relevant distances shown on the sketch but not drawn to scale (and they almost never are) should be identified by estimated miles, yards, feet, inches, etc., as appropriate.

HYPOTHETICAL 11-4

Assume that Paul Perfect asks Jay DeClient to draw a sketch of the layout of the kitchen in Jay DeClient's house showing where Carlotta Falldown was found after the fall in relation to the refrigerator and island.

PP: Mr. DeClient, would you mind taking this sheet of paper and just sort of sketching the layout of the kitchen and where you first saw Ms. Falldown on the floor after the fall?

JSD: Whoa, I don't know about that. I'm no artist.

PP: (laughing politely): I understand. I'm not either. But it really doesn't matter how well you can draw. It will help us sort of visualize how things looked so we can all get a better handle on it. (Extending sheet of paper and pen to JSD.) Do you mind giving it a try?

JSD: Well, all right. Just don't enter this into any contest, okay?

PP: (laughing politely again): You got it.

The sketch that Jay DeClient draws for Paul Perfect can be seen in Illustration 11-1.

h. Establish an accurate chronology of events

The easiest way to understand and evaluate a situation is usually to establish the chronology of events. In most interviews this should be a specific goal of the interviewer. Ask specific detailed questions to get the sequence of events as clearly as the client can recall them. Leading questions can be helpful for this purpose (see Hypothetical 11-5).

Illustration 11-1   DIAGRAM OR SKETCH DRAWN IN INTERVIEW

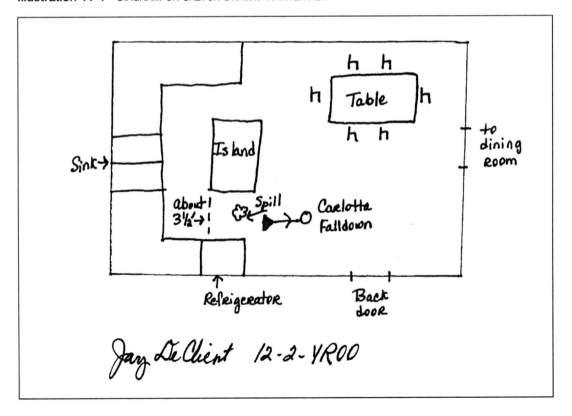

HYPOTHETICAL 11-5

Assume a legal professional (I) is interviewing a client (C) about his work history:

I: Now, let's see if I have this straight. You went to work at Marlin Enterprises on January 5, 2008, right?

C: That's right.

I: And you gave notice there the last day of March, 2008, is that correct?

C: No, it was the last day of May.

I: Okay, so it was the last day of May, 2008, when you gave notice to Marlin Enterprises, is that it?

C: Right, that's it.

I: And it was the last day of March, 2008, that you interviewed for the job at Weaver Company, is that right?

C: That's right. Now you've got it.

I: And you actually started working for Weaver on May 17, 2008, before you gave notice to Marlin Enterprises, is that correct?

C: Yes.

I: And then you were terminated by Weaver on February 3, 2009, is that right?

C: That's right.

It might even be helpful to have the client draw a **time line** for you. A time line that the interviewer might ask the client to draw in Hypothetical 11-5 might look like Illustration 11-2.

i. Clarify errors, inconsistencies, or vagueness in the client's story

Remember the first commandment of interviewing: *assume nothing.* Never simply assume that any person you interview, including the client, is giving you correct, complete, accurate, or even truthful information

Illustration 11-2   TIME LINE DRAWN BY CLIENT

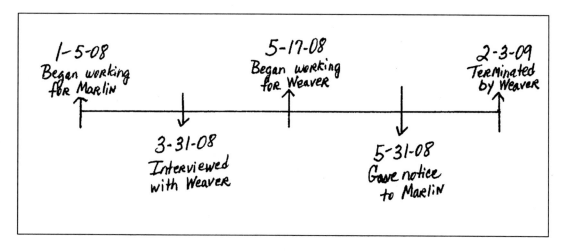

about everything. It may be helpful to review the realities we considered about people in connection with factual analysis in Chapter 1:

- Sometimes people lie.
- Sometimes people tell half-truths.
- Sometimes people are mistaken in what they thought they heard or saw.
- Sometimes people guess but don't tell you they're guessing.
- Sometimes people forget or misremember what they heard or saw in the past.
- Sometimes people make unwarranted assumptions and pass those assumptions off as fact.
- Sometimes people speak in conclusions that are not supported by fact.
- Sometimes people allow their prejudices to color what they "know."
- Sometimes people have only second- or third-hand information rather than first-hand information but leave it to the interviewer to figure that out.
- Sometimes people confuse their opinions with facts.
- Sometimes people are reluctant to tell what they know.
- Sometimes two honest people can hear or see the same event and each describe it differently from the other.
- Sometimes the same types of inaccuracies and falsehoods get included in documents.

So we watch and listen for **inconsistencies** or **contradictions** and try to clear them up. Closed-ended, leading, or sometimes pressure questions are useful for this purpose.

Tell me again where you were at 3 p.m. that afternoon?
But you said that at 3 p.m. you were still at your house, isn't that right?
If you were still at your house at three that afternoon, how could you have seen her leave the office downtown a few moments after three?

j. Verify all information given as best you can

Remember the second commandment: *verify everything.* That means we:

SL**EUTH ON THE LOOSE**

Need statistics and other information on car collisions by make, model, etc.? Try the National Crash Analysis Center at www.ncac.gwu.edu or the Vehicle Research and Test Center at www.nhtsa.dot.gov/portal/site/nhtsa/menuitem.081e92a06f83bfd24ec86e10dba046a0/

- Attempt to determine if the *source* of the information is *competent, honest, reliable,* and *objective.*
- Try to filter out *opinions, guesses, assumptions,* and *statements of prejudice* to get to real provable fact.
- Distinguish between *first-hand information* and *second-* or even *third-hand information.*

We know from our study of the rules of evidence in Chapters 6 and 7 about the importance of a witness who testifies at court speaking from personal knowledge. When a client tells you something, always determine the source of their knowledge—how do they know that? Is it something known to someone else that has been passed on to the client or is it even their guess or opinion?

And remember that people don't always express themselves clearly. A person may say they know something, or even that they "know it for a fact" when they don't know it at all in a factual, legal sense. They've heard it or believe it or assume it. It is the interviewer's job to sort out all the hyperbole and exaggeration.

k. Seek corroborating information

Closely related to the verification task is the need to seek **corroborating information**—information that confirms or supports what the client tells us. Ask about witnesses to the events that the client described. Ask about others who might know if there were other witnesses. Ask who else does or might have knowledge of things the client tells you. Ask about records, correspondence, or other documents that might confirm what the client is saying.

HYPOTHETICAL 11-6

Assume a legal professional (I) is interviewing a client (C) about the job history of a witness. Let's listen in:

C: Well, I can tell you he's never been able to hold down a job in his life.
I: Oh, really?
C: Absolutely.
I: Why do you say that?
C: Well, because I know it for a fact, that's why.
I: What jobs do you know of that he's had and then lost?
C: Why, that job over at the chemical plant for one. He didn't work there more than three months and they let him go.
I: You mean the Vestal Chemical Company plant here in Capital City?
C: That's the one.
I: And when did he work there?
C: Oh, I'm not sure of that. Probably two, three years ago.
I: And do you know for sure how long he worked for Vestal Chemical?
C: No, but I'd say it was no more than three or four months.
I: You're not sure, though.
C: No, I'm not positive on that.
I: And you say Vestal let him go?
C: That's what I heard.
I: Who did you hear that from?
C: Oh, you know, just talk around town.
I: So you can't remember the name of anyone in particular who told you that Vestal let him go?
C: No, not in particular.
I: Did he ever tell you that himself?
C: Him? No, he never told me that himself.
I: Could he have just been laid off in a slow period at the plant or in a reduction in force?
C: Well, I guess it could have been. I know he didn't work there long.
I: Is it possible he quit Vestal himself to go to work somewhere else?
C: I suppose it is.
I: What other jobs do you know of, other than the one at Vestal, that he's had and then lost?
C: Well, none I can call to mind, but I know there have been others.
I: How do you know there have been others?
C: I don't know, it just stands to reason there would have been. And I see him around town all the time and he ain't working.
I: So it's because you see him around town a lot that you think he must not be working?
C: That's right.
I: Or that he gets a job but can't keep it?

C: That's right, exactly.

I: But you don't know of any specific jobs—other than the one at Vestal Chemical—that he had and lost, is that right?

C: That's right, I guess.

I: And you don't know for sure whether he was fired from Vestal or just laid off with others, or quit, is that correct?

C: That's correct, uh-huh.

1. Compare the conviction of this client at the beginning of the interview to the admissions at the conclusion of it.
2. Do you think the client was being dishonest or deliberately misleading at the beginning of the interview or just overstating his knowledge without thinking?
3. If the interviewer had not attempted to pin down the sources of the client's professed knowledge, what misimpression could these statements have created in the mind of the supervising attorney?
4. What, factually, does this client really know about the job history of the person in question?
5. If the interviewer had delved into the motives of the client toward the person in question, what do you think he might have found? How would you ask such questions of this client?

SLEUTH ON THE LOOSE

Need the kind of information you might normally go to an encyclopedia, dictionary, almanac, atlas, or thesaurus for? Try www.infoplease.com/index/html instead.

l. Get the particulars on persons and documents mentioned

When the client mentions the names of others during the interview who might have information, it is not enough simply to get their names. You will need to know as much about them as possible to find them and interview them. Find out their full names, what names they go by, where they live, where they work, their phone numbers, the last time the client saw them, if they are still in town, if they've moved, who would know how to reach them, etc.

It is not enough to be told there might be other documents related to the client's matter. You need to know what documents, how they are titled, who has them now, can the client get them for you, if not who can, who has the originals, etc.

m. Review documents closely and copy or arrange to keep them

You will have briefly reviewed documents brought by the client at the beginning of the interview. But before it is over, take a break and look them over thoroughly. Determine if the documents the client has brought are originals and, if not, who has the originals. Make copies or make arrangements to keep the original documents. Be sure you understand all the information in the documents. If the documents are signed but not acknowledged, see if the client can identify (authenticate) the signatures or handwriting.

n. Determine what the client wants

One of the things that should come out of the initial client interview is a clear understanding of exactly what the client wants the attorney to do. From this will come the scope of the representation. Determining this may not be as easy as it sounds. Clients rarely come to the lawyer's office with a clear understanding of the law or their legal rights. Instead they come with a factual problem and maybe a poorly articulated request for some type of help—maybe not the kind of help that the lawyer can provide.

In addition, some clients relate facts about a number of different legal problems, but they may really only be seeking help with one of them. Or the attorney may only do work in one area in which they need help.

Of course, it is up to the supervising attorney to decide whether to undertake the representation and the scope of it. The job of the paralegal interviewer or the associate attorney interviewer is to get all the facts. If what the client wants the lawyer to do is not made evident, ask the potential client that specifically and communicate the answers to the supervising attorney as best you can.

o. Check off the topics on your question list as you go

This helps ensure that you have covered everything you need.

4. Dealing with special problem clients

a. The reluctant client

People can be reluctant to tell us everything they know for any number of reasons. The interviewer has to recognize the reluctance and find a way to convince the client to open up. There are a number of approaches to consider in getting the **reluctant client** to open up, depending on the cause of the reluctance.

1. A simple case of nerves. If the interviewer senses that it is a simple case of nervousness, the best approach may be to take a little more time to visit with the client. Be open, friendly, patient, and reassuring. Lean slightly closer to the client and maintain close eye contact. Let the client see that smile through your eyes. Try to identify with the client—talk candidly about how nerve-wracking you know it is to come to a lawyer's office.

2. Feelings of guilt, shame, or embarrassment. Sometimes people feel guilt over admitting some wrongdoing. They can also feel shame or embarrassment at having to disclose intimate facts about their circumstances. If the interviewer senses that the client is feeling guilt, shame, or embarrassment, the best approach may be to remind him of the attorney-client privilege. Nothing that is said is going to be repeated outside the office without the client's permission. A lower, quieter voice may be appropriate. Remember that the client would not have come to the lawyer's office if he didn't feel the need for help. Play on that by reminding the client, gently, that the attorney cannot help without full information.

3. Fear of providing harmful information. If the interviewer senses that the client is holding back bad news for fear of hurting his own case or exaggerating the information that might be favorable to the case, the best approach may be to stop and explain to the client that the attorney will need *all* information, good and bad, to be able to help him. Again, appeal to the fact that the client would not have come if he did not feel the need for help.

b. The highly emotional client

Clients can be highly emotional during the initial interview for any number of reasons. They may be deeply saddened by some personal loss, they may be frightened by an uncertain future, or they may be angry at some perceived injustice.

One general rule for dealing with the highly **emotional client** is to let him vent his emotions. The parents who have just lost a child—let them weep. The wife who has just been deserted by her no-good husband leaving her with three children and no money—let her cry and curse him. The businessman who believes he has just been cheated—let him call the wrongdoer colorful names. If the interviewer shows discomfort or disapproval of these displays of emotion, it alienates the client—the opposite of what we want. It also causes the client to internalize the emotions at a time when he needs to vent them so he can begin to think rationally. Give the client the opportunity to vent.

Empathize with the emotional client without getting too personally involved and without offering personal opinions about the matter. Acknowledge the right to be sad, afraid, or angry. After a while, take a break to give the client time to compose himself. Offer some refreshment.

If it becomes clear after a while that the client simply can't get past the emotion to think rationally, it may be appropriate to suggest rescheduling the conference.

c. The self-important or condescending client

Self-important or **condescending clients** may let you know in one way or another that it is beneath them to have to deal with a *mere* paralegal or a *mere* associate lawyer. They may presume that they know more about your business than you do and they—not you—will decide what you need to know about the case. These clients are a real headache, but don't reach for the aspirin just yet. There are ways to handle them.

Don't be intimidated by this client. That is the single biggest mistake you can make. If you are intimidated into not asking the questions you should, the attorney will be disadvantaged in trying to help the client. And you have reinforced the problem for future contacts.

Don't confront or offend this client, tempting though it may be. He is, after all, the *client*, the one the attorney bills and collects from in order to pay, among others, *you*. We can't just insult him and run him off. He may even be a good friend or business associate of the supervising attorney; insulting him could cost you your job.

Unfortunately, we have to stroke the ego of the self-important client—without patronizing—and ignore the condescension. The investigator may want to apologize for having to take the client's time to ask a few more questions. And patiently explain to the client that the attorney may need to know the information the client is objecting to providing in order to advise the client properly.

If none of those approaches work, then go to the supervising attorney, explain the situation to her, and suggest that it might be more appropriate for her to handle this interview.

d. The obviously lying client

As you have learned, we never assume the truth or accuracy of any information we receive, but always test it in various ways in order to verify it. Any time the interviewer senses that the client has told an untruth, first use your closed-ended, leading, or pressure questions to test the apparent misstatement and seek clarification.

But sometimes the interviewer comes across a client who lies and does not care about contradictions or inconsistencies being exposed. That's his story and he's sticking to it. In that situation, **non-hostile confrontation** is generally the next step. Tell the client in a soft but clear voice, with steady eye contact, that the client's case could be severely damaged by the supervising attorney relying on incorrect information. If it is a litigation matter, remind the client that the opposing party at some point will probably be asking the same questions under oath in a deposition or in court and giving incorrect information in those circumstances could have serious consequences.

If non-hostile confrontation does not work, the interviewing legal professional should advise the supervising attorney at the earliest opportunity of her belief that the client is lying and let that attorney decide how to proceed.

5. Concluding the client interview

- Be sure you have covered everything
- Be sure the client signs all authorizations
- Be sure that a plan of action has been discussed
- Give the client an opportunity to ask any other questions
- Advise the client not to discuss the case with others
- Give the client a business card
- Be cordial while walking the client out

HYPOTHETICAL 11-7

Assume that Paul Perfect is concluding his interview with Jay DeClient. Let's listen in one more time.

PP: Well, Mr. DeClient, I believe we are about done. If you will, give me just a moment to look over my notes here.

JSD: (yawning and stretching): Sure.

PP: (after looking over notes carefully): Okay, please sign this medical authorization I mentioned earlier so we can get your medical records from Dr. Fixit. (Hands medical authorization to JSD.) And this employment records authorization in the event we need to get those records. (Hands JSD the employment record authorization and waits for him to sign.) Okay, great. Now, as I've mentioned, I will report promptly to Ms. Busy about what we've discussed here today. She will make the decision on taking your case and then either she or I will be in touch with you. We'll see where we are and go from there. Is that going to be okay?

JSD: Sure, that's fine. I look forward to hearing from you.

PP: Remember not to discuss the case with anyone who may contact you about it. If you are contacted by an insurance company or an attorney for Carlotta Falldown, give them our name and number and tell them to contact us. Okay?

> **JSD:** Sounds good to me.
> **PP:** Do you have any questions about anything?
> **JSD:** No, I can't think of anything.
> **PP:** Well, if you do, don't hesitate to call me or Ms. Busy. (Rises and extends hand to JSD.)
> **JSD:** (rising and shaking hands with PP): I'll do that.
> **PP:** And let me give you one of my business cards so the number will be handy. (Hands business card to JSD.)
> **JSD:** (taking card): Thanks.
> **PP:** (walking to the door with JSD): Do you remember the way back to the reception area?
> **JSD:** I think so. Just to the right and down the hall, right?
> **PP:** That's it. Take care and we'll be in touch shortly.
> **JSD:** I'll wait to hear. Thanks for everything.

6. The role of the supporting legal professional when the supervising attorney conducts the interview

The supervising attorney may choose to conduct the interview herself and ask the paralegal or the associate attorney to assist. If you are the assisting legal professional, you may still be asked to schedule the interview and assist in preparing for it by arranging for the conference room, preparing forms to be signed, and even making suggestions regarding questions.

If you are asked to attend the interview with the supervising attorney, be sure to take good notes. Suggest additional questions to that attorney as appropriate. Point out to that attorney discreetly—usually by written note handed to her—observations you make regarding the client or witness and areas you think might be explored further.

Also assist the supervising attorney by making sure all forms do get signed by the client at the conclusion of the conference and that everyone understands the next steps to be taken.

7. Following the interview

No matter who conducted the interview, the legal professional will typically have a number of responsibilities following the initial client interview.

a. If needed, do another conflict of interest check

During the interview the client may have provided you with additional names of persons whose involvement could give rise to a conflict.

b. Prepare an interview summary

An **interview summary** ought to be clear, organized, and thorough. If an intake sheet or **checklist** was used, the interview summary may be organized around its headings. In any event, the interview summary ought to contain, at a minimum, the following:

- a heading indicating the name of the client interviewed, the date of the interview, the file name and number;

- background information on the client;
- factual information gathered from the client in a logical order. As with the interview, the order may be chronological or topical, whichever is more appropriate for the particular case;
- the interviewer's observations and evaluation of the client in terms of demeanor, credibility, and reliability. Anything unusual or special that the interviewer noted, whether positive or negative, should be pointed out in the interview summary;
- a statement of the next steps agreed to at the conclusion of the interview;
- a listing of all authorizations and other documents signed during the interview and a statement of where the originals are;
- a listing of all documents provided by the client and an indication of where they are;
- the interviewer's conclusions and recommendations regarding what should be done next.

Illustration 11-3 contains some portions of the interview summary prepared by Paul Perfect following the interview of Jay DeClient.

c. Prepare a follow-up letter to the client

The **follow-up letter** should be signed by either the assisting legal professional or the supervising attorney and will summarize the decisions made at or following the interview and enclose any additional documents that need to be signed. As with all correspondence signed by an assisting legal professional, the supervising attorney should review and approve the letter before it is sent. A follow-up letter that Paul Perfect might draft for Betty Busy to send to Jay DeClient following the interview and the decision to take the case is shown in Illustration 11-4.

D. ▶ Subsequent Client Interviews and Contacts

You may have numerous opportunities to work with a client after the initial interview. Many of these contacts will be by phone call and letter. In all verbal and written communication with the client, remember to be polite but professional. (See Illustrations 10-2 and 11-4.)

Remember, too, the importance of maintaining a good working relationship with the client throughout the representation. The matter may continue for weeks, months, or for years. Always assume that a relationship you establish with a client will be long term. Not only does a good working relationship with a client enhance the likelihood of good results in the current representation, it also improves the chances for future representation in other matters. Repeat business from clients brings joy to an attorney's heart. And it is good news for the legal professional who makes it happen, too. The supervising attorney will be more likely to remember you fondly at bonus time and good work tends to increase job security.

As we have noted, assisting legal professionals often have as much or more direct contact with clients than the attorney over the course of a case. That is both a responsibility for you and an opportunity.

Illustration 11-3 MEMORANDUM SUMMARIZING INITIAL CLIENT CONFERENCE

MEMORANDUM

TO: Betty Busy, Attorney
FROM: Paul Perfect, Paralegal
DATE: October 4, YR00
RE: Interview summary for potential client: Jay S. DeClient
Client/File Number: YR00-335-L

1. CLIENT BACKGROUND INFORMATION:

Jay S. DeClient (JSD) was interviewed in our offices on October 4, YR00. JSD is a 38-year-old Caucasian male, DOB 1-2-YR-38. He lives at 111 Humphrey Bogart Lane, Capital City, Yourstate 44444 and has resided there for the past 12 years. He lives by himself since a divorce three years ago. He has no children. JSD works as a district salesman for Hollywood Sports Equipment on Harvest Drive in the city. He has worked for Hollywood for almost ten years and before that worked two years for Oscar's Imports, also as a salesman. Oscar's went bankrupt in YR-10. He is a YR-16 graduate of State University, majoring in Business, and did a four-year tour of duty in the U.S. Army before going to work for Oscar's. Other background data includes:

Home phone: (111) 555-1234
Work phone: (111) 555-4321
Cellular phone: (111) 555-9876

2. FACTS:

A. History leading up to the party on August 25, YR00. The neighborhood in which JSD lives is upper middle class and he advises that the neighbors are unusually friendly with each other. He says that block parties are organized several times a year and when anyone in the neighborhood has a party, everyone is invited. Carlotta Falldown (CF) lives only three houses down the street from JSD at 117 Humphrey Bogart Lane. She is a divorcee who moved there with her two young children (a boy about 10 and a girl about 5) a little over two years ago. She has been active in neighborhood events as has JSD so he has considered her a friend for some time. He denies any prior trouble with CF although he says he has noticed that she is somewhat of a heavy drinker at these neighborhood gatherings. He has heard her joke more than once at such parties that someone needs to drive her home even though she is within walking distance of her house and does walk, not drive, there.

JSD says that CF is a realtor but is unsure of which realty company she is with. He believes her company specializes in commercial property. He describes her as intelligent, fairly attractive, and having a good personality. He thinks she is in her early 40s. He repeatedly stated during the interview that he was surprised when CF hit him in the nose and thinks she only did it because she had too much to drink that night. . . .

B. The August 25, YR00 party. JSD says he planned the party as an end-of-summer fling. Everyone in the neighborhood was invited as usual. About 60 people were there and the party was held in the house and the backyard where he has a nice barbeque grill. The party started at 6 p.m. He doesn't recall exactly when CF arrived and has no idea if she came with anyone. She usually came to neighborhood events by herself he thinks. Pretty much everybody was drinking—beer and wine mostly—but there was some hard liquor there too. He has no idea what or how much CF drank before the fall and assault but she always drank and he believes she would have that night. He cannot recall smelling liquor on her when he tried to pick her up after the fall but says since everyone was drinking—including himself—the smell would have been in the air.

JSD says that CF fell in the kitchen of his house. He has an island in the middle of the kitchen and the beer, wine, and liquor bottles were set out there. The fall occurred at around 9:30 p.m. He was not in the kitchen at the time and did not see it. He was out in the backyard tending the barbeque grill when another neighbor, Esau Itall, told him that CF had fallen and was hurt and he had better come check on her. When he got to the kitchen several people were standing over CF who was laying on her back at the corner of the island nearest the refrigerator. A diagram that JSD drew showing the layout of the kitchen and exactly where he saw CF is attached to this memo.

Illustration 11-3　MEMORANDUM SUMMARIZING INITIAL CLIENT CONFERENCE *(continued)*

JSD really doesn't recall everyone who was standing around CF. He sheepishly admits he had a few too many beers during the evening. He knows that Itall, a golfing buddy of JSD, came to get him. And he remembers another man, Itook Charge, bending over CF and asking her where it hurt. He also recalls hearing the shrill voice of a woman neighbor, Ida Screamer, telling someone to call 911. He thought she would never shut up. JSD located the phone numbers of these three witnesses for me in the phone book. They are:

Esau Itall: Home—555-4356; Work—555-7777
Itook Charge: Work—555-3680
Ida Screamer: Home—555-0098

JSD said that when he got to the kitchen and saw CF on the floor he immediately bent down and took her hand and asked her how she was. He didn't think to look at the floor to see what might have caused her to slip. There were six to eight other people immediately around him and the rest of the kitchen was full of people, too.

It was while he was kneeling down beside CF that she threw the punch that caught him flush in the nose. He was on her left side holding her left hand and had just asked her how she was. He remembers that her eyes were closed when he first knelt beside her. When he spoke to her, her eyes opened and her right hand came out of nowhere to hit him. He knew his nose was broken immediately because he heard the crack. He recalls that it didn't hurt at first and his only impression was surprise that someone so little (CF is about 5'2" and 110 lbs.) could throw such a punch from a prone position. He recalls too that as soon as CF hit him she closed her eyes again and smiled. The room went quiet except for the ever noisy Ida Screamer, who gasped and said, "Did you see that?" . . .

D. Injuries and treatment for JSD. JSD has been seeing Dr. Ken Fixit whose offices are on Oak Avenue next to City Hospital. JSD did not seek treatment for his nose until the next morning (8-26) when he went to the City Hospital emergency room. His friend Esau Itall, who lives on the next block from JSD, drove him there. By that morning he says the nose was three times its normal size and a bright purple color. The nose was x-rayed in the ER and the break confirmed. Dr. Fixit was called in by the ER staff physician whose name JSD does not recall. Dr. Fixit set the nose there in the ER and the brace he is currently wearing was placed on the nose. Dr. Fixit told JSD he will have to wear the brace for 30 days. He has been told that depending on how the break heals he may or may not need surgery later. JSD has seen Fixit twice since the brace was put on his nose. He has received bills for $250 so far from the ER and Fixit and paid them. He brought the original bills and they have been placed in the file. He has a group medical insurance policy at Hollywood Sports but the deductible is $500. After he has met that, his share of the co-pay is 20%.

JSD says the pain and discomfort have been terrific. He cannot breathe through his nose at all. Eating is painful and swallowing difficult. He has to take pain medication regularly (Percodan). Historically a good sleeper, he now has trouble going to sleep and wakes up several times a night.

JSD's biggest concern is his livelihood. At Hollywood Sports he receives a base salary/draw of $2,000 each month and depends on commissions for other income. For the past three years his total income from Hollywood has been $79,000 (YR-3), $82,000 (YR-2), and $72,000 (YR-1). He has made $52,000 through August YR00. He missed three days of work following the assault, which will translate into lost commissions for September. Lower commissions don't reduce his monthly salary/draw unless they drop below the total draw amount for the year ($24,000), in which case he would have to repay the company for the difference. He is in no danger of that since he has had a good year so far, but believes his commissions will be reduced for the rest of the year due to missing time, not feeling well and, frankly, the ridiculous looking brace on his nose which turns customers off. . . .

3. OBSERVATIONS AND EVALUATION:

JSD is of medium height, about 200 pounds, bald-headed with a full beard going gray. He was dressed in a nice-looking sport coat and tie for the interview. He speaks with a distinct nasal sound due undoubtedly to the injury to his nose and the brace. I took several pictures of JSD by Polaroid and those are in the file.

JSD expresses himself well. He smiles easily and has a good sense of humor. He appears very much at ease. His years as a salesman seem to have helped him acquire good skills with people. He is polite and likeable and makes a good impression. He will make a good witness for himself.

Illustration 11-3 MEMORANDUM SUMMARIZING INITIAL CLIENT CONFERENCE *(continued)*

JSD also seemed forthright and credible. The only time in the interview when I sensed a lack of forthrightness was when I questioned him about the witnesses to the fall. When I asked him for detail about Ida Screamer whom he had described as "shrill" and "near hysterical," his mood seemed to shift from pleasant to dark. A small frown creased his forehead, his eye contact diminished, and he became fidgety with his fingers. His answers to my questions about how well he knows Ida Screamer were short and clipped. As summarized above, he denies knowing her well but I wonder if there is some history we need to explore further. . . .

4. DOCUMENTATION:

Currently in the file we have:

Suit papers filed by CF v. JSD in State Superior Court on 9-20-YR00 and served on JSD on 9-21-YR00
Signed medical authorization
Signed employment records medical authorization
Original statements for medical bills to date
Unsigned legal services contract already reviewed and approved
Copy of JSD's homeowner's policy with Extra Safe Insurance Co.
35-mm pictures (3) of the floor where CF fell, taken after she had left and the party was over together with negatives
Polaroid pictures (5) taken by PP of JSD with nose brace

If we undertake representation, JSD is to provide us with:

Canceled checks for the medical bills paid to date
His employment contract with Hollywood Sports

5. RECOMMENDATIONS:

I believe the assault case of JSD v. CF is a viable one. There are several witnesses to CF striking JSD whom we should interview. At this time the only valid defense I can see that CF might raise to a claim of tortious battery is lack of intent if she was unconscious or semiconscious when she acted due to the fall or due to being intoxicated. But the force of her blow to JSD and the smile on her face afterwards should cause her difficulty on such a defense. She appears to be a person of some means against whom a judgment could be collected. We know nothing of insurance for her as yet.

Regarding defense of the negligence suit of CF v. JSD, the homeowner's policy does seem to provide coverage for that defense and the claim made in the suit papers ($100,000) is within the policy coverage limits of $250,000. We should contact, or have JSD contact, the company regarding the claim promptly.

If our firm is retained to defend JSD by the carrier, there are some unknowns. We don't know exactly what the substance on the floor was although there was something there on the floor according to JSD. JSD had not been in his kitchen in over an hour before the fall, so arguably did not create the hazard, whatever it was. The question may be whether he was negligent for NOT checking the kitchen area more frequently. But CF may have difficulty herself proving just what the hazard was which caused her to fall and how long it had been there for JSD to find. Third-party negligence appears to be a valid defense on these facts—some other partygoer probably created the hazard. And comparative fault seems valid here since, at the least, CF was almost certainly somewhat incapacitated by drink herself (and voluntarily so) at the time of the fall.

The amount of damages incurred by JSD is still open. We will need to wait and see what the prognosis is from Dr. Fixit on the nose. And we will need to see how JSD's commission income holds up during the remainder of the year. If you decide to take the case or look at it further, I recommend we proceed to:

interview the three witnesses we know of;
obtain the medical records to date on JSD; and
obtain the additional documents requested from JSD.

Please let me know how you would like to proceed.

Illustration 11-4   FOLLOW-UP LETTER TO CLIENT

Date

Mr. Jay S. DeClient
(Address)

Re: *Carlotta Falldown lawsuit*

Dear Mr. DeClient:

As I indicated to you in our phone conversation earlier today, we will be pleased to represent you in connection with your claim against Carlotta Falldown. I am enclosing a legal services agreement in connection with your contemplated claim against Carlotta Falldown. Please review this agreement and call me with any questions you may have about it. If the agreement looks acceptable, please sign and date it where indicated and return it to us in the enclosed self-addressed stamped envelope. As soon as we receive the signed agreement back from you, we will undertake further investigation in your case.

Regarding the defense of the suit filed by Carlotta Falldown against you, and as you authorized in the telephone conversation this morning, we are sending a letter of notification to Extra Safe Insurance Co. formally notifying that company of the suit and of your request for defense. A copy of that letter is enclosed for your records. The company has the right, under the policy, to choose counsel to represent you in defending the suit. We have advised them in the letter that we will be representing you in your counterclaim against Carlotta Falldown and of your desire that we receive the defense assignment as well. We will advise you of their response. If you should hear from the company yourself please let us know right away.

Keep in mind, as we discussed today, that because the suit papers of Carlotta Falldown were served on you on September 21, YR00, you have only until October 21, YR00, to file an answer or other response with the court. If you fail to do that, a default judgment could be taken against you on her claim. Accordingly, we want to expedite the company's decision regarding your defense.

Please send us copies of your employment contract with Hollywood Sports and the canceled checks for medical bills paid to date.

We look forward to working with you on this matter. If you have any questions, please do not hesitate to call me or Mr. Perfect.

Sincerely,

Betty B. Busy
Attorney at Law

BBB/db

Before you make a follow-up contact with a client by phone or letter, remember that it is just as important to prepare for and plan that contact, however brief, as it was to prepare for the initial contact. Before picking up the phone and calling the client, think carefully about what you want to accomplish in that phone call and how you want to handle that particular client. Make notes for yourself to use in the phone call so you don't forget anything. It is a waste of the client's time and unprofessional to have to make a second call and say, "Oh, there's something else I forgot to ask you."

Do the same planning before you write a letter to a client. What is it you want to say or accomplish with this letter and how can you best communicate with this particular client? And have you covered everything you need to before the letter goes to the supervising attorney for review and out to the client?

Keep in mind the ethical and professional responsibility we have to keep the client reasonably informed regarding the status of the representation. The client is entitled to be advised promptly about every development in the case. Even if nothing is going on in a client's case at the time, it is a good idea to periodically touch base with them by phone or letter to let them know their matter is not being neglected. One of the most frequent ethical complaints made against attorneys is that they do not keep the client adequately informed about the matter. Conversely, one of the nicest things a client can experience is to be contacted by the attorney's office with an update on the case even when he wasn't requesting an update or expecting the contact. When legal professionals do things like that for a client, the client doesn't forget. And that's when the client says good things to the attorney about the assisting legal professional.

Finally, always return a client's call promptly—the same day if at all possible. And remember the importance of meeting deadlines for getting documents organized and drafted or locating information. Meet your deadlines, and work patiently but firmly to help clients meet theirs.

Chapter Summary and Conclusion

There are ten things for the legal professional to remember while conducting a client interview. A client interview starts when the client is greeted. The interviewer should begin with expressions of empathy, if appropriate, and explanations of what is to be accomplished in the interview. Relevant documents should be reviewed, a broad overview of the client's story sought, gaps in information plugged, the chronology clarified, inconsistencies cleared up, and details and leads to other information sources solicited. The interviewing legal professional should know how to deal with special problem clients. There are certain steps to follow in properly concluding an interview. The interviewer should prepare an interview summary for the supervising attorney following the interview, and any appropriate follow-up letter to the client.

While there are similarities, the interview of a witness differs from the interview of a client. We will begin considering the witness interview in Chapter 12.

Review Questions

1. Why is it important to avoid legal jargon during an interview?
2. Name several internal obstacles to effective interviewing.
3. What is empathy and what role does it play in interviewing?
4. Why should documents that the client or witness brings to an interview be reviewed before questions about them are asked?
5. What is a narrative summary? What role does it play in an initial client interview?
6. What is corroborating information? What role does it play in a client interview?

7. What are the possible reasons a client may be reluctant to provide information?
8. How do you handle an overly emotional client in an interview?
9. How do you handle a self-important or condescending client in an interview?
10. How do you handle an obviously lying client in an interview?

KEY WORDS AND PHRASES TO REMEMBER

active listening
body language
committed
condescending client
contradictions
corroborating information
emotional client
empathy
flexible
follow-up letter
inconsistencies
initial client interview
intake sheet
internal barriers

interview checklist
interview summary
lying client
narrative summary
non-hostile confrontation
persistent
reluctant client
repetition
self-important client
thorough
time line

LEARN BY DOING

LBD 11-1. Conduct the interview of the client in one of the following Case Studies from Appendix A assigned to you by the instructor. Then prepare a memorandum to your instructor containing an interview summary and a follow-up letter to the client.

a. Case Study No. 1 (The Rowdy Outlaw Case) Rowdy Outlaw
b. Case Study No. 2 (The Soupspoon Wise Case) Soupspoon Wise
c. Case Study No. 3 (The Vidalia Unyon Case) Vidalia Unyon
d. Case Study No. 4 (The Rocky Road Project) Rocky Road

Chapter 12

Preparing for a Witness Interview

CHAPTER OBJECTIVES

In this third chapter on interviewing we turn our attention to the fact witness. In this chapter we will learn how to prepare for the fact witness interview. You will learn:

- The goals to be accomplished in the witness interview.
- The different kinds of witnesses the legal professional is called upon to interview.
- How to communicate with the witness to schedule an interview.
- The steps that interviewers go through to prepare for an effective witness interview.
- The special considerations that go into preparing for a field interview.
- The importance of using active listening skills and observing the witness's environment.

A. Introduction

As discussed in Chapter 10, a fact witness, as distinguished from a client or a non-witness information source, is a person who has or who might have knowledge of facts directly relevant to the matter being handled for the client. In this chapter we will consider why the investigating legal professional conducts interviews with fact witnesses, the different kinds of witnesses encountered in interviewing, and procedures for scheduling and preparing for the interview of a fact witness.

B. Goals of the Witness Interview

There are a number of goals to be achieved in the interview of a fact witness and several or all of them may need to be achieved in a single interview. Illustration 12-1 summarizes these goals.

C.   Kinds of Witnesses

Witnesses can be categorized in different ways depending on their personalities and their attitudes toward being interviewed. We will consider here a number of different types of witnesses. Different kinds of witnesses call for different approaches and interviewing techniques.

However, categorizing witnesses has its dangers too. Any given witness may fall into more than one of these categories (e.g., they may be friendly but nosey). Also, witnesses may initially impress you as being of one type, but as the interview progresses you realize they are of another (e.g., they start out skeptical but become too helpful). Never be too quick to categorize a person as one type or another. With those caveats in mind, consider the various witness types.

1. The friendly witness

Friendly witnesses are those who, for whatever reasons, look favorably on your client or on you. They will cooperate in scheduling the interview and will be as helpful as they can during it. The friendly witness is therefore the easiest to interview in many ways. But be careful. Don't let his cooperative attitude keep you from asking the tough questions you may need to ask.

And be aware that whatever makes them friendly toward you or your client (e.g., they are friends or relatives of the client) may be used by the opposing side to show bias or interest (e.g., that friendly witness is an employee of the client—and wants to keep his job!). In interviewing the friendly witness try to anticipate a suggestion of bias by the opposing party and give the witness an opportunity to reject that bias as a motive for what they are saying. (See Hypothetical 12-1.)

2. The hostile witness

This is the witness who, for whatever reasons, does not look favorably on your client or you. The **hostile witness** will not want to cooperate in granting an interview or to say anything helpful if they are prevailed upon to grant one.

Illustration 12-1   GOALS TO BE ACHIEVED IN A FACT WITNESS INTERVIEW

1. Find out in detail everything the witness knows about the subject we are interested in.
2. Discover all documents and things the witness may have access to that relate to the subject we are interested in.
3. Discover leads to other witnesses or other documents and things to which the witness may be able to direct us.
4. Observe the witness for purpose of evaluating his strengths and weaknesses, credibility, effectiveness as a witness, cooperativeness, etc.
5. Get the witness committed to a particular version or recollection of the incident.
6. If the witness can damage our client's position, look for information the supervising attorney may use to discredit or impeach that witness including inconsistencies, bias, interest, or unreliability.

How do we convince a hostile witness to even grant us an interview? Here are several suggestions:

a. Be friendly and patient with the witness

The hostile witness may frustrate you by promising to call you back and then not doing so or promising to show and then canceling. But most people feel guilty about acting so rudely, and a little polite persistence may pay off.

b. Try to get the witness to like you

If it is your client whom the witness does not like, try to get the witness to like you. In your conversations with him, not only bowl him over with politeness, but try to find common ground. Use his name frequently to personalize the conversation. He may eventually agree to cooperate because he likes you, even if he still detests your client.

c. Use the witness's natural instinct to help

People have a natural urge to help others; it is ingrained in us. Most people want to help others because it's polite or the right thing to do. Almost everyone today has worked in a service industry where helping the customer was a priority. Use this knowledge to your advantage in working with hostile witnesses. Let them know you need their help and that no one else can provide the information they have. Join that approach with appreciation for the sacrifice of time they are making to do this and an assurance that you will not waste their time.

d. Use subpoena power as a motivator—if you must

As a *last resort*, consider reminding the hostile witness that the supervising attorney can utilize the subpoena to compel his attendance at a formal deposition, which may be set at a much less convenient time and place and involve more time and lawyers, etc.

If the hostility of the witness becomes apparent only during the interview, sometimes the suggestions above can be used then to engender a little cooperation. But sometimes you just have to do the best you can in a difficult situation. Don't be intimidated by the hostile witness into forgoing questions you really need to ask.

HYPOTHETICAL 12-1

Assume that Dee Termined is a new associate attorney in the firm of Quick & Ready which represents N. Big Trouble, a business owner whose business has been sued. The issues in the suit go back to a time when N. Big Trouble owned the business with another man, Dis Gruntled. N. Big Trouble bought out Dis Gruntled's interest in the business last year. The attorney for N. Big Trouble needs information from Dis Gruntled. Unfortunately, N. Big Trouble and Dis Gruntled did not part on good terms. Dee Termined places a call to Dis Gruntled to see if she can schedule a conference with him.

DG: (answering phone): Hello?
DT: Is this Dis Gruntled?
DG: Yes it is.

DT: Mr. Gruntled, my name is Dee Termined. I am an associate attorney with the firm Quick & Ready. We represent N. Big Trouble, a former business partner of yours. I'm calling to see if I could arrange to speak with you briefly about the business you and Trouble owned.

DG: N. Big Trouble? No way I'll help. That guy's a thief as far as I'm concerned. He ran our business into the ground and then forced me to sell out to him for next to nothing.

DT: Yes, sir, Mr. Gruntled. I understand that you and Mr. Trouble had your differences when he bought out your interest.

DT: (raising his voice): Differences! That's an understatement. Ma'am, I'm sorry, but I can't help you. N. Big Trouble in my opinion is a no-good cheat and a lousy businessman.

DT: I understand how you feel, Mr. Gruntled. Anyone would have a right to be upset if they felt they weren't treated right. And I certainly am not trying to change your mind about. . . .

DG: (laughing derisively): Well, that's a good thing, let me tell you, because you couldn't change my mind about that skunk in a million years.

DT: (laughing politely as if DG has said something amusing and without malice): Mr. Gruntled, you sound as hard-headed as me. My daddy always told me that a hard head and thick skin were the two greatest assets you could have in business.

DG: (laughing politely himself and without derision this time): Well, your daddy was a wise man, I'd say.

DT: Well, I always thought so and I appreciate you saying that. Mr. Gruntled, I truly do understand your feelings and I am simply trying to get some information I need about the business while you were still there. If you could accommodate me with just a few moments of your time, I'll promise to be brief and then get out of your hair.

DG: (laughing easily now): Oh, I didn't mean to take all that out on you. Sure, I'll give you a few moments—just don't bring the bum with you!

1. What techniques did Dee Termined use to convince Dis Gruntled to grant her an interview?
2. Identify each point in this conversation when Dee Termined could have given up.
3. Identify the place in this conversation when it first appeared that Dee Termined was going to win over Dis Gruntled.

If the hostile witness has given you information that hurts your client, you will want to bring out the reasons for the hostility. It may be best to do this at the end of the interview. Your supervising attorney may be able to use this information to show bias or interest and thus discredit the witness.

3. The neutral or disinterested witness

This is the witness who doesn't feel strongly one way or the other about the matter you are interested in. If the **neutral witness** will cooperate in giving the interview, he tends to make a credible, reliable witness who will not fabricate or exaggerate.

Assume that Dee Termined is also assigned to interview Reluck Tant, a supplier who has done business with the company owned by N. Big Trouble. The problem is that Reluck Tant is also a customer of the company that is suing N. Big Trouble's company and doesn't want either side to get upset with him. He is, shall we say, reluctant to get involved!

RT: (after listening to DT explain why she is calling): Oh, boy. I was afraid someone would call about that mess. Listen, isn't there someone else you can talk to about this?

DT: Well, Mr. Tant, we are talking to everyone who might know something but, unfortunately, that's just it, we have to talk to everybody.

RT: (sighing): Well, I know what's between the rock and the hard place now. I just don't think I can afford to get involved in this. I don't have a dog in the fight but . . . (lets his voice trail off).

DT: Mr. Tant, I know what a pain it is to get drawn into this. And I understand that you do business with both of these parties. But keep in mind that all we want you to do is tell us what you know and what you recall. I think both sides would want you to do that.

RT: Maybe so, but you just never know who's going to get mad at you and that's grief I don't need, let me tell you.

DT: I understand what you're saying. But I hope you understand that Mr. Trouble really needs your help here. A lot of people know a few things. But frankly, Mr. Tant, no one knows what you do. And what you know could be critical to a full understanding of what went on last year. If that doesn't come out, then Mr. Trouble stands to lose his entire business and could be facing bankruptcy. I know you don't want that to happen to him, or anybody.

RT: I know, I know. It's just . . . (lets voice trail off again).

DT: And I promise not to take any more of your time than is absolutely necessary. I know how busy you are. The sooner all of us can get this behind us the better.

RT: That's for doggone sure. All right, when do you want to do this?

1. What techniques did Dee Termined use to convince Reluck Tant to grant her an interview?
2. Identify each point in this conversation when Dee Termined could have given up.
3. Identify the place in this conversation when it first appeared that Dee Termined might win over Reluck Tant.

4. The skeptical witness

This is the witness who just doesn't want to get involved. The **skeptical witness** may be suspicious of you or your motives or just reluctant to go to the trouble. Consider using the friendly, common-ground, and urge-to-help approaches discussed in connection with the hostile witness. For example, if the law office you work for is representing a person injured in an accident, consider telling the skeptical witness a little about the person's injuries and his or her need for the witness's cooperation (though, of course, nothing confidential or privileged). In other words, play on the witness's sympathies. Shameless maybe, but effective.

5. The nosey witness

Beware of the witness who asks a lot of questions about the case. Some people are intrigued to be involved in a live case. They get excited and want to know details. You may feel pressure to satisfy their desire for details in hopes of obtaining the cooperation. Certainly you want to be friendly toward any cooperating witness, but resist the urge to share details you shouldn't. It's part of being professional.

6. The busy witness

Many witnesses are reluctant to submit to an interview at all because they are busy ("I would like to help but I really don't have time"). Or they grant you an interview but hurry you through it directly ("Are we about done?") or indirectly (looking at their watch every ten seconds). Some witnesses really *are* busy and it really *is* a favor for them to grant us an interview. Many public officials fall into this category. Others just *think* they are that busy. Whichever it may be, we generally gain nothing by suggesting to this witness that they really *do* have time for us.

Instead, treat the **busy witness** much like you would the skeptical witness. To get the busy witness to cooperate, be outspokenly considerate of his time and grateful for his willingness to give you even a little piece of it. You may want to use the urge-to-help/play-on-their-sympathies approach if needed. See Hypothetical 12-2.

When a busy witness does grant you an interview, be respectful of his wish to expedite the matter. Don't engage in more than brief greetings at the beginning, and avoid extended chitchat. Express your appreciation for his cooperation, assure him you will be as brief as you can, and honor that. But always be sure to do a thorough job. Don't let the busy witness hurry you so much that you skip questions that should be asked or neglect to follow up on answers or observations.

7. The too-helpful witness

Every interviewer loves the helpful, cooperative witness. But some witnesses can be too helpful. They try to guess what we want them to say and then they say it. They agree with everything we say. They accept every characterization we make. They make few or no suggestions themselves that would contradict anything they think favors our client. Something may be wrong here.

Frequently, the **too-helpful witness** is a relative or close friend of the client. Instead of being candid and truthful, they are just saying what they think will help the most. It is dangerous to rely on such information or for the attorney to put someone like that forward as a testifying witness.

If you sense during an interview that a witness is being too helpful, don't accuse him of it directly. Instead, politely remind him of your need to obtain candid information about the case or matter, whether it is helpful or hurtful to the client.

8. The show-off witness

These are witnesses who feel the need to impress you. They may be name-droppers. Or they may boast of other cases in which they have testified (and probably won the case singlehandedly). Or they may tell you that they have been urged for years to go to law school or run for president and are just flipping burgers until they decide. What a pain, right?

Tolerance but persistence are the keys to handling **show-off witnesses**. If you don't tolerate them, you will offend them and lose their cooperation. On the other hand, if you encourage them you will never get to what you need to know from them. So, tolerate their boasting with a smile and an occasional "Oh, really" or "Uh-huh," but don't ask follow-up questions about the boasting. Lead them back to the subject you need them to talk about.

9. The big-ego witness

Closely related to the show-off witness is the witness with the big ego. The difference between these two types is that the show-off witness is usually a *wannabe*, whereas the **big-ego witness** has made it at something, and everyone—including you—simply *must* acknowledge it!

What has the big-ego witness made it at? It can be anything—business, politics, sports, a profession (some lawyers and doctors are among the worst offenders). But whatever it is, they will either expect you to know or will let you know quickly. Some will let you know directly ("Hello, I'm Big Shot. That's the Shot in Shot, Snooty, and Proud, you know.") or indirectly (look at all those pictures of famous people on this guy's wall!). Certainly not every successful person has an outsized ego, but when it happens it must be dealt with.

Unfortunately, with the big-ego witness, you're usually going to have to do a little stroking if you want cooperation. So stifle the urge to pop his balloon. Let him feel important and give you the tour of the trophy case. Laugh at his jokes and compliment his achievements. Eventually he will reward you with his attention. At the same time, avoid obvious pandering to this kind of witness. If he catches you doing that, it will turn him off and you will lose his cooperation.

10. The condescending witness

Closely related to the big-ego witness is the **condescending witness**. This is the person who, for whatever reason, looks down on you. It may be a big ego, but more frequently it is something this person perceives or assumes about you that triggers the condescension. It may be that you're young and he assumes you cannot possibly know what you are doing. It may be that you are not a lawyer or not the primary lawyer handling the case and he is offended the primary lawyer isn't there but instead sent the "hired help." The racial- or gender-biased witness you will occasionally encounter falls into this category as well. And often, with this type of witness, the condescension expresses itself with a hostile or too-busy attitude that we have already considered.

The condescending witness is generally best treated by ignoring the condescension and doing your job. If you do that, with many of these people, you will win their respect—and respectful treatment—before you are done. It may be difficult, but remember the number one priority is to get the job done for the client, not to seek redress for your own wounded feelings, or strike a blow for social justice.

11. Special problem witnesses

a. Language barriers

What about the witness who speaks little or no English? If communication in English is possible but difficult, consider speaking slower than usual in the interview. Also use simple words and short sentences. If communication in English really isn't feasible, then locate a reliable interpreter. Today many courts maintain a list of interpreters for use in formal proceedings and your court clerk may be able to help you locate one. High schools and colleges, churches, the local bar organization, as well as social organizations are also good sources to locate interpreters.

b. Physical barriers

What about the witness who is hearing-impaired or deaf? If appropriate, arrange to sit closer to the hearing-impaired witness, speak a little louder, try to speak so that the witness can see your face (many hearing-impaired persons are lip and expression readers), speak slower, and consider using simpler words and shorter sentences. Offer to repeat yourself, and be willing to do so patiently. Watch for tell-tale signs of hearing impairment—a hearing apparatus in or near the ear, a person turning one ear toward you when you speak, a pattern of asking you to repeat a question, or answers that reflect that the witness does not understand.

For the truly deaf witness, inquire without embarrassment about their ability to lip-read. Or a qualified signer may be engaged to assist. The courts, schools, and churches are good sources to locate persons qualified to sign and interpret for the hearing-impaired.

c. Mental barriers

What about the witness who is slow of mind? If the problem appears to be a serious one, there may be a question of minimal competence to understand a question and provide a rational answer. The interviewer must simply do the best she can and report back to the supervising attorney her observations and impressions of the witness. Use simple words and short sentences, speak slowly, and be ready and willing to repeat a question or ask it in a simpler way. Also be sure not to appear condescending or impatient with such a witness.

d. The Romeo (or Juliet!)

Who needs it, right? But it happens. How do you handle the witness who appears interested in, shall we say, more than just your questions? The rule here is to be professional. Be friendly but firm about focusing on the interview. Don't flirt back or lead the witness on in order to secure his cooperation. You will have a bigger problem later and a far less cooperative witness when he realizes what you've done.

But what if you like him too? Remember that the job comes first. Not only are you there to conduct an interview on behalf of a client but personal relationships with witnesses can produce conflict of interest problems for you and the supervising attorney. Better to wait until the case is over, or at least the witness's role in it, before you show an interest in, shall we say, more than just his answers!

Of course, if you have a more serious problem, a groper for example, or someone who is just too aggressive to feel comfortable around, use your sound judgment and protect yourself. If you have reason before the interview to believe the witness will be this way, take someone with you. Or if it happens unexpectedly in your office, ask someone else to come in. But if you're on the witness's turf—home or office—get out of there. Report the situation to the supervising attorney. No interview is worth endangering yourself or tolerating outrageous behavior.

e. The witness for sale

This does not happen often, but it is always a serious matter. You arrive for an interview and the witness either directly or indirectly suggests that some compensation could make a difference in his memory. Do not ever respond to such a suggestion in any way that could be considered positive. Don't go along with him just to see what he has in mind. Tell the person in a friendly way, but very clearly, that you cannot even consider that suggestion for both legal and ethical reasons. Tell him that you certainly want him to tell the complete truth and you are sure that's what he wants to do as well.

Report this event to the supervising attorney immediately and document in the file what was said and done. Do not ever leave yourself open to a later charge that you initiated such an offer, or considered it, or did anything other than reject it.

HYPOTHETICAL 12-3

Assume that attorney Betty Busy has assigned her paralegal, Paul Perfect, to conduct witness interviews with Itook Charge, Esau Itall, and Ida Screamer in the Jay DeClient case. (Review Hypotheticals 10-1 and 10-2 and the sample interview summary in Illustration 11-3.) Paul Perfect has learned from the client that Esau Itall is an insurance agent, and a close friend and regular golfing buddy of the client as well. When Paul contacts Esau Itall by phone to arrange the interview, Itall tells him he will do whatever he can for DeClient and will rearrange his schedule to accommodate Paul Perfect as soon as possible.

1. In which witness category(s) would you suggest that Paul Perfect place Esau Itall as he prepares for this interview?
2. In what ways might the interview with Itall be easy for Paul Perfect?
3. In what ways might the interview with Itall be difficult for Paul Perfect?
4. What recommendations would you make to Paul Perfect as he prepares for this interview?

Paul Perfect has learned from the client that Itook Charge is president and sole owner of Charge Ahead Motors, which operates new and used car dealerships all over the state. Jay DeClient told Perfect he doesn't know Itook Charge well and only met him at the party. Charge doesn't live in Jay DeClient's neighborhood and was attending the party with a friend who does, Bee Mufriends. DeClient has told Paul Perfect that Charge is a self-made multimillionaire who has powerful local, state, and national political connections and possible political aspirations himself. When Perfect calls Charge's office for an appointment, he is unable to get through to Itook Charge himself. Instead, he is transferred to several different people. Finally someone identifying herself as Charge's appointments secretary tells him that Itook Charge can see him for 15 minutes one day next week at 7 a.m. in Charge's office.

1. In which witness category(s) would you suggest that Paul Perfect place Itook Charge as he prepares for this interview?
2. In what ways might the interview with Itook Charge be easy for Paul Perfect?
3. In what ways might the interview with Itook Charge be difficult for Paul Perfect?
4. What recommendations would you make to Paul Perfect as he prepares for this interview?

Paul Perfect has learned from the client that Ida Screamer is an accountant with a local accounting firm, Debit & Credit. When Perfect calls Screamer at the accounting firm to schedule the interview, she hesitates a long time before agreeing to the interview. Even after agreeing to do it, she protests that she really doesn't know anything that could help Jay DeClient, that this is her busiest season at work, that the interview will have to be somewhere other than her office, and that Paul Perfect will have to make it a quick interview.

1. In which category(s) would you suggest that Paul Perfect place Ida Screamer as he prepares for this interview?
2. In what ways might the interview with Ida Screamer be easy for Paul Perfect?
3. In what ways might the interview with Ida Screamer be difficult for Paul Perfect?
4. What recommendations would you make to Paul Perfect as he prepares for this interview?

D. ▶ Scheduling and Preparing for the Witness Interview

The student should review the material regarding scheduling and preparing for the initial client interview covered in Chapter 10. That material is largely applicable here.

1. Scheduling the witness interview

Witness interviews are scheduled much as initial client interviews are, usually by phone call. Let's briefly review those procedures here and then we will look at some special considerations for scheduling the witness interview.

Before calling the witness to schedule the interview, the legal professional should:

- Check all participants' schedules
- Have several dates and times in mind
- Plan for plenty of time to conduct the interview
- If the interview is to be conducted in the legal professional's office, make sure the interview room is available
- Make a list of what the witness needs to bring

When the legal professional calls the witness to schedule the interview, he should:

- Identify himself as a paralegal or assisting attorney
- Cover all the necessary details including time and place of the interview, what to bring, and directions if the witness is traveling to the interview, or directions you need to reach the witness
- Take comprehensive notes

After concluding the scheduling call, the legal professional should:

- Confirm the reservation of the conference room
- Notify other participants of the date and time
- Enter the date and time in the docket control system
- Send a confirmation letter to the witness
- Prepare a memorandum summarizing the call
- Place all notes in the client file

2. Preparing for the witness interview

Preparation for a witness interview is much the same as preparing for a client interview, but because the goals of the witness interview differ from those of the client interview (compare Illustration 10-1 and Illustration 12-1), that will affect preparation. In preparation for a witness interview, the legal professional will:

- Prepare needed authorizations
- Prepare questions by

  - reviewing the file
  - considering the legal issues presented in the case
  - considering any known special needs of the witness
  - brainstorming a list of topics to be covered
  - organizing the topics in a chronological or topical fashion;
  - preparing specific questions
  - putting questions in a format consistent with any checklist being used
  - putting questions in a format conducive to taking good notes
  - being flexible—expect to ask more or different questions during the interview

- Have the supervising attorney review all questions and forms
- Prepare the interview room
- Consider any special needs of the witness

- Plan the seating arrangement
- Make arrangements to avoid interruptions
- Prepare physically and mentally for the interview

3. Special considerations in scheduling and preparing for a witness interview

There are some special considerations that apply to scheduling and preparing for the interview of a fact witness as opposed to a client.

a. Contacting a witness represented by counsel

The assisting legal professional should never contact a witness without the permission of the supervising attorney. And remember that it is unethical and unprofessional to make direct contact with someone who we know is represented by counsel. We are to deal with that person's attorney.

If you are already speaking to a witness when he advises you that he has an attorney, immediately ask for the name and phone number of the attorney. Explain that you did not know he had counsel and that you are obligated to speak to the attorney first. You cannot continue to speak with the person directly *even if he tells you it's okay!*

End the phone call without discussing the substantive matter any further. Then immediately advise the supervising attorney of this development and, if he authorizes, contact the other attorney. Disclose to the other attorney that you did speak to his client but did not know of the representation and that as soon as you learned of it you terminated the conversation. (The supervising attorney may want to make this explanation to the other attorney.)

b. Preserving client confidences and secrets

In dealing with witnesses, we must be careful to avoid disclosing any confidential or secret information or any information related to the attorney's case strategy. This can be a challenge when confronted with a friendly but inquisitive witness, a relative or friend of the client, or the reluctant witness who demands to know exactly why she should cooperate.

The problem can arise when the interview is being scheduled and the witness is asking questions. It can also arise during the interview if the witness asks to see information in the possession of the interviewer or is able to see it because of the seating arrangements.

SLEUTH ON THE LOOSE

There are lots of people search sites on the Internet. A good one is www.zabaserch.com. Use it to try to locate someone you know but haven't heard from in a while.

c. Don't use tricks

Never use deceit or make false promises to a witness to gain his cooperation.

> *I'll take no more than ten minutes of your time, I promise.*
> *If we can talk with you now, you won't be bothered with this matter anymore.*

These tactics do far more harm than good in the long run. When the interview begins, the witness will quickly realize he has been duped. He may become uncooperative or even hostile—then you can forget about getting his help later in the case.

d. The location of the witness interview—the field interview

One significant difference between client and witness interviews is where the interview occurs. The witness interview usually will occur in a place selected by the witness. That may be the office or home of the witness. Or we may have to go to the hospital where the witness is a patient or the nursing home where they are a resident. Certainly clients are sometimes interviewed outside the law office. Sometimes cooperative witnesses will come to our offices. But most witness interviews are **field interviews**—those conducted outside the office of the interviewer.

That means the interviewer has little or no control over the location or environment of the interview. It may be noisy, dirty, busy, cold, hot, crowded, and so on. The significance of this for our preparation is that we must generally be prepared for anything and surprised by nothing! We have to adapt to the circumstances we find and still do our jobs.

The interviewer's lack of control over the environment of field interviews also presents an important opportunity. The interviewer gets to see the witness in his own environment. If we are the careful observers we have been trained to be (see Chapter 8), that can provide us an abundance of helpful information about the witness.

HYPOTHETICAL 12-4

Assume that Paul Perfect is scheduled to interview Itook Charge this afternoon at 3 p.m. At noon he gets a call from the secretary for Charge who tells him that Charge has a business emergency that will require him to leave for Europe immediately. He won't be back for a month so if Paul wants to interview him before that he should come to Charge's office right away. Fortunately, our man Paul Perfect is ready for this interview, so he grabs his coat and races over to Charge's office.

When Paul Perfect arrives in the reception area he sees a small crowd of people walking toward him, surrounding a well-dressed middle-aged man whom he takes to be Itook Charge. As this group of chattering people passes by Paul, a man reaches out and grabs his arm. He says, "Are you the one from the lawyer's office?" Paul says he is, and he is then pulled into the little group going out the office door, down the elevator, and into a waiting limousine.

In the back of the limousine Paul finds himself facing Itook Charge, who is talking on his cell phone. Beside Paul sits a woman looking at papers and thumbing information frantically into a personal digital assistant. Beside Charge sits a younger man who looks at his watch, and tells Paul they will be at the airport in ten minutes and he can ask Charge questions on the way.

When Charge gets off the phone, Paul starts to introduce himself but Charge pays no attention to him and instead gives some orders to the young man next to him who then makes a call on his cell phone. Finally, Charge looks at Paul and says without a trace of a smile, "Did you need to ask me something?"

1. How would you be feeling in Paul Perfect's position? Confident? Ready for that interview?

2. Should Paul Perfect make some light conversation at this point to break the ice?
3. What should Paul Perfect do and say at this point?
4. What should Paul Perfect's demeanor be at this point?

Paul Perfect finds Itook Charge responsive to his questions and quite helpful about the events at the party involving Carlotta Falldown. However, he has to sit with his knees drawn up nearly to his chin to ensure that the woman sitting next to him cannot observe his notes or other documents in the file. Moreover, the limousine arrives at the airport in what seems like two minutes instead of ten. As the limo pulls to a stop in a parking lot near the terminal and the doors fly open, Paul has time to say, "I have a few more questions if I may." Charge and the young man whisper to each other and the young man says to Paul, "You can walk with him to the terminal. We don't have time to wait here."

Paul Perfect finds himself trotting through the parking lot and across the street in front of the terminal beside a briskly moving Charge. He is trying to ask questions, take notes, and watch where he is going all at the same time. Charge answers his questions while giving orders to his two associates about luggage and tickets and business matters. Once inside the terminal Charge dashes into the men's room and tells Paul to stand at the door and keep asking his questions. Paul does so but gets a number of funny looks from other men coming in and out of the restroom.

The group finally makes its way to a long line of people waiting to have their tickets validated and luggage checked. In front of them a mother holds a crying baby. A screaming toddler pulls at her skirt. Behind them two men are arguing in a language Paul does not recognize. Charge doesn't seem fazed. The young man who is Charge's assistant looks at his watch again and says, "It's going to be close." Just then the toddler in front of Paul Perfect deposits his last meal (which happened to be strawberry ice cream) on Paul's new loafers.

1. How would you be doing in Paul's position now? Are we having fun? Glad you chose a career in the legal field?
2. Why was Paul so concerned about the young woman next to him in the limousine being able to see his notes and other materials? Was he overreacting?
3. Should Paul ask the mother to try and keep her children quiet or to clean up his shoes? Should he ask the men behind him to take their argument outside?
4. Should Paul suggest that Itook Charge sit down with him for a few moments to finish the interview?
5. Should Paul give up and tell Itook Charge he will call when Charge returns to the country?
6. What should Paul do at this point?

Having gotten their tickets validated and received their boarding passes, Charge and his two associates are now sprinting toward the security checkpoint. Paul Perfect is struggling to keep up and wishing he was in better shape. (He's also thinking that they didn't cover this in any law course he ever took!) Paul has never heard himself talk while sprinting; he sounds funny to himself.

As they arrive at the security gate, a flight attendant just on the other side opens the door leading out to a departure gate and the noise of the jet engines fills the concourse, along with the smell of jet fuel and a blast of hot air. Now Paul has to shout to be heard. Charge shouts his answers back as he waits in line to for the security check. By the time they reach the metal detector, they are absorbed in the questions and answers. Charge passes through and starts down the concourse toward his gate. Prepared to follow, Paul Perfect feels a hand on his chest and an anxious voice asks, "Do you have a ticket, sir?" Paul realizes he is about to commit a federal offense and stops. He looks up in time to see Charge wave at him as he turns a corner.

Later that evening, back at the office, Betty Busy sticks her head in Paul's office. "How did the interview with Itook Charge go?" she asks.

Paul thinks a moment about how to answer and then says, "Perfect. Just perfect."

e. Telephone interviews and recording or videotaping interviews

Witness interviews are frequently conducted by telephone and frequently **recorded** or **videotaped** than are client interviews. We will consider recording/videotaping interviews and the telephone interview in detail in Chapter 13.

f. Planning multiple witness interviews

The legal professional will frequently be assigned to interview more than one witness in a given case. In that event, consideration should be given to the logical order in which the witnesses should be interviewed. It may be chronological—who was involved first, second, etc. It may be topical—if you need to talk to witness A at length about a particular matter and witness B knows a little about that matter but nothing about anything else, wouldn't it make sense to interview B before A?

If you don't make the effort to plan a logical progression among witnesses, you may have to go back to the first witness you interviewed to ask additional questions. You may find that first witness less than pleased that you are bothering him again or even refusing to talk with you a second time. And you may find yourself in big trouble with the supervising attorney!

HYPOTHETICAL 12-5

Assume that Paul Perfect has been assigned to interview Itook Charge, Ida Screamer, Bee Mufriend, and Esau Itall in the Jay DeClient case.

1. Based on what you know so far, in what order would you recommend he conduct those interviews?
2. Why?

Chapter Summary and Conclusion

Preparation for a witness interview begins with identifying the particular goals of the interview. Witnesses fall into many different categories and preparing for and conducting the interview will be done differently depending upon what category the witness falls into. For the hostile or uncooperative witnesses, threatening a deposition or trial subpoena should be a last alternative to securing cooperation. Whatever challenges a witness presents to the interviewer, the interviewer must remember to stay focused on the job at hand and see it through. Though scheduling and preparing for a witness interview is very similar to what is done in connection with a client interview, there are special considerations when scheduling and preparing for a witness interview, including the prohibition on directly contacting a witness known to be represented by counsel, remembering to preserve client confidences and secrets, and avoiding the use of deception.

In Chapter 13 we will consider conducting the interview of a witness.

Review Questions

1. List as many goals to be achieved in the interview of a fact witness as you can recall.
2. What do we mean by the "friendly witness," and what special challenges does that type of witness pose to the interviewer?
3. What is a witness's "natural instinct to help?" How can the interviewer use that instinct when dealing with a hostile, reluctant, or disinterested witness?
4. At what point should the legal investigator threaten subpoena power to induce a witness to grant an interview?
5. What special dangers are posed by the nosey witness?
6. What special dangers are posed by the too-busy witness?
7. Name as many "special problem" type witnesses as you can recall. How does the effective interviewer handle each?
8. Why is it important to not use tricks or make false promises to induce a witness to grant an interview?
9. What special challenges are presented to the interviewer conducting a field interview?
10. What special challenge is presented when doing multiple interviews?

KEY WORDS AND PHRASES TO REMEMBER

big-ego witness
busy witness

condescending witness
field interview

friendly witness
hostile witness
language barriers
mental barriers
multiple witness interviews
neutral witness
nosey witness
physical barriers

recorded interview
show-off witness
skeptical witness
too-helpful witness
videotaped interview

LEARN BY DOING

LBD 12-1. Schedule and prepare for the interview of one of the witnesses in one of the following Case Studies from Appendix A as assigned to you by the instructor. Contact the person whose name you are given who will be playing the role of this witness. Schedule the interview and then prepare: (1) a memo to the instructor summarizing your contact with the witness; (2) a confirming letter to the witness; and (3) any forms you might need for the interview. Also prepare your questions for the interview.

a. Case Study No. 1 (The Rowdy Outlaw Case)

Candy Carmichael	Detective Willie Parker	Ima Jean Grouse
Outlaw	Dr. Michael Melody	Jack Gates
Connie Cornelius	Georgette B. Good	Charlie Choot

b. Case Study No. 2 (The Soupspoon Wise Case)

Korn Pone	Tanya Trucker	Turtle Shoop

c. Case Study No. 3 (The Vidalia Unyon Case)

Georgia Peach	Hobo Booth	Nosey Nelly

d. Case Study No. 4 (The Rocky Road Project)

Grace Slickspot	Real E. Smart

Chapter 13

Conducting a Witness Interview

CHAPTER OBJECTIVES

In this final chapter on interviewing skills you will learn:

- The important things to keep in mind throughout the witness interview.
- How to begin a witness interview, move to the substantive areas, and conclude the interview.
- How to use active listening and observation skills in a witness interview.
- How to evaluate, test, and seek verification of information obtained in a witness interview.
- How to seek information to impeach the credibility of an unhelpful witness.
- How to prepare a witness interview summary for the supervising attorney.
- How to properly record or video tape an interview.
- How to prepare for and conduct a telephone interview.
- How to prepare a written witness statement.

A. Introduction

This chapter continues our study of preparing for and conducting a fact witness interview. Paul Perfect has pretty much recovered from that wild ride with Itook Charge. But Betty Busy has several more assignments for him in connection with witnesses in the Jay DeClient case. Let's see what Paul Perfect can teach us about actually conducting an effective witness interview.

B. Things to Remember Throughout the Witness Interview

As discussed in detail in Chapter 11 in connection with a client interview, the interviewer should remember these points throughout the witness interview.

- Be friendly but professional.
- Be cognizant of the dangers of UPL.
- Avoid using legal or technical jargon except when necessary.
- Take good notes.
- Engage in active listening.
- Evaluate the demeanor and behavior of the witness.
- Remember the witness does not know what you want or need to know—you have to ask.
- Keep an emotional distance between yourself and the witness.
- Overcome internal obstacles to effective listening and observing:
  - thinking about the next question so intently you don't catch the last answer;
  - concentrating so hard on taking notes that you miss something you should see or hear;
  - being a slave to a prepared list of questions; and
  - being affected by your own biases.

There are some special things the interviewer should remember for the witness interview.

1. Observe and evaluate the witness's environment

One of the opportunities presented to the interviewer in going to the witness for the interview is that we get to see the witness's environment and *listen* to what it tells us. Don't forgo this opportunity. Before, during, and after the interview, while you are in the witness's home or office or conference room:

- Observe the witness's space carefully.
- Evaluate what you see.
- Make note of it.
- Make use of it in the interview.

The observations and evaluations you make of the witness and his space can be used to good advantage before the interview by the careful observer.

EXAMPLE

Use your observations as ice breakers. Is there a putter sitting in the corner? Ask about his golf game. Is there a picture of the witness with Ronald Reagan on the wall? Ask where he met the former president. Is there a crayon drawing taped to the side of the desk? Ask about it. Is the latest best-seller sitting on the desk? Ask how they like the book or author.

Observations of the witness's space can also be used to advantage *during* the interview.

EXAMPLE

Is the witness reluctant to say much about what she saw at the accident site and you sense she is reluctant to get involved with lawyers and all that hassle? You see a family picture on the bookcase showing the witness with her husband and two small kids. Try mentioning to the witness that your client has children whose lives are going to be made more difficult because of this injury to their parent and see if that doesn't help.

HYPOTHETICAL 13-1

Assume that Paul Perfect arrives at the office of Esau Itall to conduct that interview in the Jay DeClient case. Paul identifies himself to the receptionist and tells her he has an appointment to see Itall. The receptionist tells Paul to have a seat in the reception area and he does. Instead of looking over his notes (which he did thoroughly before leaving the office), he spends his time looking around the reception room. Here are some of the things he notes:

- The magazines on the coffee table in the reception area are all sports related: *Sport, Sports Illustrated, Field and Stream*, etc. He also notes some NRA (National Rifle Association) literature on the table. The address labels of all the magazines and literature have Itall's name on them.
- The furniture in the reception area is modern in style and fairly new. What appears to be a quite nice Oriental rug covers the floor.
- A large Impressionist oil painting (an original—Paul knows because he got up and walked over to it) hangs over the couch in the reception area. On two other walls are smaller framed prints that complement the oil painting.
- The fourth wall in the reception area is covered with framed photographs and prints of the State University football team in action. An old team jersey (with No. 12 on it) is also framed and hanging there.
- Paul notes that the receptionist is a well-dressed, middle-aged woman. The phone rings almost constantly while he sits there. He notes that she answers the phone quietly. Although he is no more than 15 feet away from her he can hear her voice but not the words. She smiles as she speaks and seems very efficient. Her desk is neat and orderly. A small picture of a young woman sits in one corner of her desk.

Paul has not yet met Itall. But merely from sitting in the reception room for five minutes Paul believes he knows a few things about Itall.

1. What do you think are Paul's initial impressions concerning:
   a. the success of Itall's insurance business?
   b. Itall's efficiency as a business person?
   c. Itall's education?
   d. Itall's hobbies and interests?
   e. Itall's political leanings?
2. Based on what Paul Perfect has observed so far, should he jump to conclusions with regard to any of these matters?

3. What other initial impressions would you suggest to Paul Perfect about Esau Itall based on what you have seen?
4. What ice-breaking comments or questions might Paul use when he first is introduced to Itall?

2. Overcome *external* obstacles to active listening and observing

We have considered the need to overcome **internal obstacles** in interviewing. But the witness interview is usually conducted away from the interviewer's office. The interview may occur in the home or office of the witness, on a factory floor, in an open field, in a hospital room or, as we saw in Hypothetical 12-4, in a speeding car, an airport terminal, in a long noisy line, or even a restroom!

Any time the interview occurs outside the interviewer's office, she doesn't control the space or environment of the interview. She may not find it as physically convenient or comfortable to conduct the interview in the place chosen by the witness. More distractions and interruptions may occur that she can't do anything about. Phones may ring and be answered by the witness, people may come in and out, the witness may be called away, there may be distracting noises outside, the room may be too hot or too cool.

It is easy to allow these **external obstacles** to interfere with our interview. They can cause us to lose concentration, fail to listen actively, fail to observe things we should, or to get frustrated and let it show. Our job is to overcome these barriers, keep our cool, and do a thorough professional job despite them. A good rule of thumb to keep in mind during any interview is no matter what happens, don't be surprised. Tell yourself, "I thought something like this might happen today and I'm ready for it." Didn't it seem that Paul Perfect did this in Hypothetical 12-4?

3. Avoid disclosing confidential or privileged information

In interviewing a witness, remember that this is not the client. Even if the witness is friendly and helpful or a relative of the client, he is not the client and we must avoid the disclosure of confidential information. It is a breach of our ethical and professional obligation. You should even avoid giving a witness your *opinion* about anything related to the case. Remember you are there to obtain information, not provide it.

Beware the nosey or inquisitive witness who asks questions about the case. Avoid the temptation to tell the reluctant witness more than you should in order to obtain their cooperation.

C.   The Order and Manner of Conducting a Witness Interview

Many of the considerations for conducting the witness interview are similar to those for conducting a client interview, considered in Chapter 11.

That is especially true when the interview of the fact witness is conducted in the interviewer's office or conference room. When interviewing the fact witness, the legal professional will want to consider the following points.

1. Beginning the interview

a. *Greet the witness*

If the interview is conducted in the legal professional's office, make the witness feel welcome (see Hypothetical 11-1). If the interview is conducted in the office or home of the witness or at some neutral location, be friendly and patient with everyone who assists you. Try to make a good impression.

No matter where the witness interview occurs, some greeting and exchange of pleasantries is appropriate. The nature and extent of the greeting will vary with the witness, however. Some people expect to visit for a while before getting down to business and others do not.

There are *geographical* or *regional* distinctions to be made here. Although it is possible to overgeneralize, if you are conducting interviews in a rural area or very small town you might increase your likelihood of success if you slow down and take a little more time to smile and visit with folks before getting down to work. But if you are conducting those interviews in an urban setting you might not gain anything by this except a puzzled look.

The nature and extent of the greeting will vary with the *circumstances* as well.

EXAMPLE

> If you enter an office for an interview and find people sitting around taking it easy, a little visiting may be in order. But if you enter the same office and phones are ringing, and people are typing or running to and fro, it would be inappropriate to do anything but offer a quick greeting and get to the point of your visit.
>
> If you are visiting an elderly person in a nursing home, you might want to take a while to visit before asking your questions. But if you are interviewing that same elderly person when she is very ill in the hospital, your greeting would be brief (so as not to tire the patient) and quiet.
>
> If you are interviewing a couple in their front yard on a Saturday morning while they water the flowers, you will take some time to visit (and admire those flowers, of course). On the other hand, if you are interviewing a police officer getting ready to go on duty (which is when you usually can catch them, by the way), the officer will likely be all business and in no mood for extended visiting.

b. *Express appreciation for the witness's cooperation*

If the legal professional is conducting a witness interview, that means the witness is cooperating in the informal discovery to some extent. (If she wasn't cooperating, she would be subpoenaed to a deposition to be handled by the supervising attorney.) Always express genuine thanks to the witness for that cooperation. You may need that witness again!

If it is appropriate, empathize with the witness as you would a client.

c. Disclose your status as a paralegal or assisting attorney

The witness may assume that a paralegal is an attorney even if the paralegal explained his status in the scheduling phone call. Better safe than sorry—tell the witness again. If an associate attorney is handling the interview she should explain that she is assisting the lead attorney.

d. Briefly state the purpose of your interview

In a client interview, we may go into detail concerning what the interview is intended to accomplish to assist the client. Not so in a witness interview. Again the legal professional must remember that the witness—even the helpful, friendly witness, and even a relative of the client—is not the client. So the interviewer will just briefly state the purpose of the interview:

> Mrs. Brown, I appreciate you seeing me today. As I told you on the phone, I want to ask you some questions about the car accident last week in which you were a passenger in your neighbor's car.

e. Obtain background information on the witness

While this is covered in depth in initial client interviews, generally you won't need the life story of the witness. But having some background information on any witness is helpful for a number of reasons:

- It helps us know the witness better and understand what she tells us.
- It helps us know better what to ask during the interview.
- It helps us investigate the witness further if we need to do that later.
- It helps us locate her later if she moves.

SLEUTH ON THE LOOSE

Identify three companies you would like to know more about then locate their Web site addresses at www.companylink.com.

Therefore, try to obtain some biographical and other background data on the witness: full name, home address and phone, work address and phone, marital status and name of spouse (especially important when the witness is a married woman because phone and other listings may be in the husband's name), employment of spouse, length of time at residence and job, length of time in the community, and familiarity with the client or subject of the interview.

2. Conducting the substantive portion of the witness interview

Again, there are certain similarities between conducting the substantive portion of a witness interview and that of the client interview considered in detail in Chapter 11. But there are some special considerations here too for the witness interview. In handling the substantive portion of the witness interview, the interviewer should:

a. Briefly review any documents the witness has made available

In all likelihood the questions you prepared for the interview did not include questions related to the specifics of documents you had not yet seen. Take time to review the documents and include questions based on them.

b. Obtain a narrative summary of what the witness knows

As we have learned, open-ended questions are ideal for this purpose. And, as with clients, it is generally a good idea to *let the witness talk*. The more the witness talks, the more the interviewer learns about the witness and the incident. It's also an opportunity to observe and evaluate the witness. There is a limit to anything, of course, and if the witness is a runaway talker we eventually have to interrupt (politely) and get back to the subject:

> *That's interesting, Mrs. Brown. But did I hear you say a little while ago that you knew where John had been the night before the robbery?*

But let the witness talk, and act interested even if you are not.

c. Fill in any gaps in the story

Use closed-ended, explanatory, and opinion questions for this purpose:

> *So you had never met Bill Simmons until he went to work at the company?*
> *Tell me why you decided to go home early that day.*
> *Do you think he would have quit if the supervisor hadn't said that to him?*

d. Ask the witness to define unfamiliar terms or concepts

Witnesses often have familiarity with concepts, processes, and systems relating to their life and work that are unfamiliar to the interviewer. And often they do not think to explain or simplify for the benefit of the interviewer. The interviewer must make sure to ask for an explanation or definition as needed. It is foolish to pretend you understand when you do not, and the supervising attorney is going to wonder why you didn't ask.

e. Ask for details

Use those who, what, where, when, why, and how questions. Be *thorough* and *persistent*. And lock in helpful statements. When a witness provides us with statements helpful to our client's position (or that minimize any hurtful information), it is good to lock those statements in by having them repeated. Use repetition and proper phrasing of questions to do this:

> *And you're sure that he said . . .*
> *So what you're telling me is . . .*
> *Now if I understand you correctly, she . . .*

f. Seek leads to other witnesses and documents

Every source can lead to other sources. Remember—wring out that wash rag.

g. If helpful, have the witness draw a sketch or diagram

See Hypothetical 11-4 and Illustration 11-1.

h. Establish the chronology of events known to the witness

If appropriate, have the witness draw a time line. (See Hypothetical 11-5 and Illustration 11-2.)

i. Clarify errors, inconsistencies, or vague points

Remember that we assume nothing in interviewing. So listen for inconsistencies and contradictions and try to clear them up. Closed-ended, leading, or sometimes pressure questions are useful for this purpose:

> *Tell me again what you saw just before the explosion.*
>
> *But you said earlier that you didn't meet Jack until after the graduation, isn't that right?*
>
> *If you were in Vietnam until March 1973, how could you have attended Nixon's second inauguration in January of that year?*

j. Attempt to verify information provided by the witness

Treat information from witnesses as you would information from a client for this purpose (see Hypothetical 11-6):

- Attempt to determine if the *source* of the information is *competent, honest, reliable,* and *objective.*
- Try to filter out *opinions, guesses, assumptions,* and *statements of prejudice* to get to real provable fact.
- Distinguish between *first-hand information* and *second-* or even *third-hand information.*

k. Ask about corroborating sources

Who else would know? Who else might have seen or heard? Does the witness know who else might know? What documents might there be? Who else might know about documents?

l. Get the particulars on all persons and documents mentioned

What is the person's full name? Nickname? Married name? Maiden name? Where do they live? Where do they work? What do they do? Who has that document? Who had it last? Who keeps the records for the company?

m. Make copies of documents produced or arrange to keep them

Before the interview is over, closely review all documents produced during the interview and get permission to take custody of them or make copies.

n. Ask the witness to tell you anything else they remember

Before concluding the interview, always give a witness the opportunity to relate anything else he can remember about the incident or matter that hasn't been mentioned:

> *Okay, I think that's all I had to ask you. Is there anything else you can recall about that night that I haven't asked?*
> *Is there anything else you wanted to tell me?*
> *Is there anything I've left out or skipped?*

Tell him to call you if he thinks of anything after you have left.

o. Ask about other interviews

Remember you may not be the only person who has contacted this witness or who will do so in the future. In a litigation matter, it is quite likely that the office representing the opposing party will contact this witness. Ask about prior interviews. If they have been interviewed, find out by whom and when.

If the witness gave a written statement to the other interviewer, see if there is a copy of the statement and if you can obtain it. Ask the witness to let you know if someone contacts them in the future for an interview and to allow you to have a copy of any written statement given in that interview.

p. Make sure you have covered everything

Check off topics as you cover them in the interview and review your notes before you conclude to be sure you have covered everything.

3. Impeaching a witness

In this section we will consider a matter of special concern in the witness interview: consciously seeking a basis to **impeach** or discredit the witness. You may benefit from reviewing the discussion in Chapter 7 regarding how the state and federal rules of evidence permit a lawyer to impeach a witness at trial.

In interviewing we need to know the facts—the truth as the witness knows or believes it. We need to know those facts whether they are helpful or hurtful to the legal position of our client. However, when a witness says something that is hurtful to the legal position of our client, the legal professional should remember that the supervising attorney will be interested in anything that might discredit either the facts related by the witness or the credibility of the witness himself.

When a witness says something helpful to the interests of our client the legal professional must remember that the opposing party will at some point seek to impeach or discredit what that helpful witness has said. So the supervising attorney needs you to test it for reliability—see if the witness or the information is impeachable.

In either situation, probe for:

a. Inconsistencies or contradictions in the statement

We have already learned to automatically do this in every client or witness interview. However, when a witness makes statements harmful to the client, you want to focus particularly on those harmful statements. Use repetition—come back to the subject again. See if the statement comes out the same way each time and if it is told consistently. Consider the story of the witness as a whole to see if there are any holes in it. Seek details.

b. Unreliability of the witness's information

1. The witness who saw something.   Has the witness told you she *saw* something? To test it, focus your questions on the witness's *capacity* and *opportunity* to see. Regarding the capacity to see, does she wear glasses or contact lenses? Was the witness wearing them at the time she saw what she claims to have seen? Were the glasses or contacts old or new? Was the witness taking any medications or had she consumed any alcohol prior to observing?

Regarding opportunity, how clear was the witness's line of vision at the time? What was the distance and the angle of the witness from what was seen? Any obstacles? Any weather or lighting problems that might make the testimony unreliable?

2. The witness who heard something.   Has the witness told you she *heard* something? Again, focus on the capacity and opportunity to hear. Regarding capacity, how well does she hear? Does she use any hearing aids? When, if ever, has she had her hearing tested? Any hearing problems in the family?

Regarding opportunity, what was her distance from the sound or voice she heard? What were the acoustics? Were there any competing noises?

3. The witness who said something.   Has the witness told you she *said* something? If so, was it recorded? Was it committed to writing? Is she sure of *exactly* what she said? How long ago was it said? Could she be guessing or paraphrasing after the passage of time? Were there any witnesses to it and if so who?

c. Bias of the witness

A witness with harmful testimony may be **biased** for the opposing party or against our client or both. A helpful witness may be biased against the opposing party or for our client or both. The interviewer should determine if this witness might have any reason to favor one party over the other. So we ask, is the witness a relative, friend, neighbor, or co-worker of the party who is helped by his testimony? Does he have common interests or circumstances with that party—religion, politics, age, occupation, etc.? Does the witness have any reason to dislike or disfavor the party who is harmed by his testimony—any past history of problems, business or personal disputes, dislike?

How these questions are asked may vary depending on whether the witness has given helpful or damaging information for our client's case. For the friendly witness, we would never want to sound insulting, accusatory, or disbelieving in the way we phrased a question regarding bias. A question on bias to a helpful witness might be phrased like:

> *If you don't mind me asking, have you ever had any run-ins or problems with Sam Jones?*
>
> *I remember you told me earlier that you had never liked Sam Jones. Is there any possibility that could have unconsciously influenced what you remember that he said?*

Although we certainly do not try to be deliberately rude to a witness because they have given damaging information regarding our client, the interviewer will try to lock in statements from which bias might be implied. The same questions we ask of the helpful witness might be phrased a little more pointedly to the unhelpful witness:

> *Have you ever had any run-ins with Sam Jones? Any problems with him?*
>
> *You have never liked Sam Jones, isn't that what you told me? Couldn't that have an influence on what you remember that he said?*

d. Interest of the witness in the outcome of the case

Interest, or more specifically, *self-interest*, can arise in many contexts. If a witness testifies at trial favorably to his employer, the attorney who offers the employee's testimony will suggest that the employee/witness is being truthful. The attorney for the other party will suggest that the employee just wants to keep his job. Interest in the outcome of a case can impact on the credibility of the witness.

Monetary interest is what we usually look for to discredit a witness, but it can be anything that arguably will advance the personal circumstances of the witness.

It could be the prospect of **advancement** at work:

> *If Mr. Casey's discharge is upheld, could you be promoted to his position?*

Or a possible **inheritance**:

> *If this will is set aside as invalid, you will inherit the entire estate, won't you?*

Or a perceived **romantic advantage**:

> *Is it true you have been dating Mrs. Jones since she separated from her husband?*

Or a perceived **advantage to another**:

> *The ejection of this player from the team could make your boyfriend the starting quarterback, couldn't it?*

As with questions on bias, questions regarding possible self-interest will be worded and phrased differently depending on whether the witness has said something damaging or helpful to our client.

Your tone of voice might be different as well. Using the sample questions above, ask them out loud as you would to a helpful witness and then again to an unhelpful witness. The tone of voice makes a lot of difference, doesn't it? Would you rephrase any of those questions to make them better suited for a helpful or unhelpful witness?

e. *History of the witness affecting credibility*

The history can include:

1. Prior bad acts probative of truthfulness. (See FRE 608(b).)

When you were in college, didn't you write research papers for other students to earn extra money?

2. Reputation for truthfulness. (See FRE 608(a).)

These questions are generally asked of a witness about another witness.

Does Jerry Smith have a reputation for not telling the truth?

3. Prior inconsistent statements. (See FRE 613 and 801(d)(1)(A).)

You say that the first car that entered the intersection was the blue car, but didn't you tell the investigating officer that the red car started first?

4. Prior convictions. (See FRE 609.)

Unless you already have knowledge of a prior conviction, or unless the witness brings it up, it may be offensive to the witness to have this question asked directly. Be sure to obtain the approval of your supervising attorney before doing so. This is something that can usually be located in public records (see Chapters 16 and 17).

4. Concluding the witness interview

At the conclusion of the interview, express gratitude to the witness for agreeing to talk with you. Remember you, or your supervising attorney, may need this witness again—for further information or to testify in the case. Leave the witness with a positive impression of you so that door is open to future contact. If appropriate, leave a business card with the witness, particularly if you have asked him to call you if he thinks of anything else.

5. The interview summary

Following the interview, prepare an **interview summary**. (Or, if the interview was recorded, prepare a transcript. See discussion below.) The interview summary for a witness interview should follow the same basic format of the summary of a client interview (see Illustration 11-3). The witness interview summary ought to be clear, organized, and thorough. It should contain, at a minimum, the following:

- a heading indicating the name of the witness interviewed, the date of the interview, and the file name and number
- background information/personal data on the witness
- factual information gathered from witness and placed in a logical order, usually chronological or topical

- the interviewer's observations and evaluation of the witness's demeanor, credibility, and reliability. Anything unusual or special that the interviewer noted, whether positive or negative, should be pointed out in the interview summary
- a statement of the next steps agreed to at the conclusion of the interview, if any
- a listing of all authorizations and other documents signed during the interview and a statement of where the originals are
- a listing of all documents provided by the witness and an indication of where they are
- the interviewer's conclusions and recommendations regarding what should be done next

Illustration 13-1 shows portions of the interview summary prepared by Paul Perfect following the interview of Itook Charge.

D. Electronically Recording the In-Person Interview

SLEUTH ON THE LOOSE

There are search engines aplenty on the Internet, and there are also a number of good meta search engines that will simultaneously run your search on more than one search engine. See how it works by trying some of these meta search engines: www.dogpile.com, www.metracrawler. com, www.Mamma.com or www.ez2find.com.

Sometimes an interviewer will make a **sound recording** of a witness interview using an old-fashioned **tape recorder** (also called a **cassette recorder** for the tape cassette inserted into the machine) or, more commonly today, a **compact disc recorder,** a **laptop computer,** or a **personal digital assistant** (PDA, such as a smart phone) equipped with **audio interface technology**. The interviewer may also choose to make a **video recording** as well where both the voice and picture of the interviewee are captured electronically. Any of a variety of **video recorders** may be used for video recording face-to-face interviews. For distance interviews, **video conferencing** using satellite downlink systems may be available or **video calling** over the Internet technology such as **Skype** with its **Call Recorder** feature. Another choice would be applications such as the **Tango** app for smart phones, tablets, and PCs or Apple's **FaceTime** app for Mac products. (See LBDs 13-3 and 13-4.) There are some special considerations to keep in mind when making an **electronic recording** of a witness (or client) interview.

1. Obtain the prior consent of the supervising attorney

Before you electronically record any interview, be sure the supervising attorney consents. In general, if a witness is going to provide information hurtful to the legal position of our client, we will not record that interview. Depending on the scope of the work product privilege in your state, a sound or video recording of the witness interview may be discovered by the opposing party. Thus we usually make no physical record of the interview with the unhelpful witness. There are exceptions to that rule, however, and it is always the supervising attorney's call to make.

Illustration 13-1 MEMORANDUM SUMMARIZING WITNESS INTERVIEW

MEMORANDUM

TO: Betty Busy, Attorney
FROM: Paul Perfect, Paralegal
DATE: October 11, YR00
CLIENT: Jay S. DeClient (File Number: YR00-335-L)
RE: Interview with Itook Charge

1. BACKGROUND INFORMATION:

Itook Charge (IC) was interviewed beginning at the offices of Charge Ahead Motors on East Broadway in Capital City on October 11, YR00. The interview moved with the departing IC into his limousine and then into the airport terminal. IC is a 59-year-old Caucasian male, DOB 2-10-YR-48. He lives at 9101 Estate Circle, Capital City, Yourstate 44445, and has resided there for the past 23 years. He is a widower, his wife of 30 years, Barbara, having passed away two years ago from cancer. The couple had three children, all of whom are grown.

IC is the sole owner and president of Charge Ahead Motors, Inc., a Yourstate corporation that owns and operates approximately 25 car dealerships around the state. The car business is the only business IC has ever worked in. He is a high school graduate who went to work washing cars at his uncle's used car lot, took it over when his uncle retired, and has built his company from those roots.

Home phone: (111) 555-5432
Work phone: (111) 555-0087

2. FACTS:

IC did not know Jay DeClient (JSD) before the party on August 25, YR00. He was invited to the party by Bee Mufriend, a woman in her early 30s who previously worked for Charge Ahead Motors. (Home phone: 555-7654) IC has been dating Ms. Mufriend for a couple of months, though he describes her as "just a friend." Bee Mufriend lives in JSD's neighborhood at 123 Gardener Street.

IC and Bee Mufriend arrived at the party a little late, around 8 p.m. as the witness recalls. They did not stay together after the first few moments. There were a number of people that IC knew at the party and he and Bee Mufriend sort of went their own ways. He does recall meeting Carlotta Falldown (CF) at the party before the fall. Bee Mufriend introduced them shortly after they arrived. He did not know her before meeting her at the party.

IC did not see CF fall. He was in the kitchen around 9 p.m. refreshing his drink. He had been in the kitchen about five minutes and was talking with a woman he did already know, Ida Screamer (IS), when the accident happened. He never saw JSD come into the kitchen prior to the fall. He recalls CF coming into the kitchen and saying they needed more ice in the backyard. A man (he doesn't know who but knows it was a man's voice) told her to check the refrigerator freezer compartment and she walked behind IC toward the refrigerator. He says the male voice added loudly, "Be careful over there, it's slippery." Almost at the same time he heard that statement he also heard a gasp behind him and the sound of something hitting the floor. He then remembers that Ida Screamer's hand flew up to her mouth and she . . .

IC says that while he was bent over CF lying there on the floor of the kitchen, he definitely noticed a pool of water or some liquid under her legs and feet. He didn't pay a lot of attention to it but did assume it was what had caused her to slip. He said it could have been water from the ice maker in the refrigerator or liquor that had been spilled. The island containing the liquor bottles was only about two feet away from the refrigerator where CF fell. I have attached to this memo a rough sketch IC prepared (standing in a line and drawing on the back of his assistant's attache case) showing the layout of the kitchen, where CF was after she fell, and where the puddle was that he spotted. . . .

Illustration 13-1 MEMORANDUM SUMMARIZING WITNESS INTERVIEW *(continued)*

IC did not know anyone else in the kitchen at the time of the fall other than Ida Screamer and CF. He does recall that two or three others were there but he did not know them. He says he does not know Esau Itall and does not recall meeting him at the party. . . .

IC does recall CF striking JSD with her right fist. He laughed as he recalled it and shook his head, saying he had never seen a woman throw a punch like that. He said that JSD came into the kitchen about two or three minutes after the fall. Someone apparently had called him though IC doesn't know who. He also has no idea where JSD was at the time of the fall. JSD entered the kitchen and bent down over CF on her left side as she lay on the floor. As JSD knelt, IC says he stood up. JSD said something to CF that IC couldn't make out and CF, without even opening her eyes, swung her right hand and caught JSD flush in the nose. IC said you could distinctly hear the sound of bone. . . .

3. OBSERVATIONS AND EVALUATION:

IC is a short, slim gentleman with silver hair that appears to be colored. He probably has gone gray. He carries himself with confidence, walks and talks quickly and with authority. He does not hesitate to tell you what he knows or doesn't know. He is a no-nonsense type of person. You can tell he is used to giving orders.
Our interview was conducted in a rushed non-private environment. When I arrived at the Charge Ahead Motors offices . . .

Though IC emanates authority and success, I found him very polite (which I frankly had not expected) and considerate. He answered all my questions for as long as he could before boarding the plane and did so candidly and considerately. I found him entirely candid and credible. He did seem a little uncomfortable when speaking of his relationship with Bee Mufriend. He quickly (a little too quickly maybe) volunteered that they are "just friends." She is considerably younger than he and it is probably understandable he should be a little sensitive to disclosing that. On the other hand, he did not hesitate to offer her name or phone number if we wish to contact her.

4. DOCUMENTATION:

IC had no documents relevant to the case other than the attached sketch I had him draw.

5. RECOMMENDATIONS:

I believe we should interview Bee Mufriend just to confirm IC's story to the extent possible. IC will be an important and helpful witness for us and we need to ensure that his credibility is unassailable.

---

2. Consider using a court reporter

You may want to use a court reporter to make a sound or video record of the witness interview. She will do a professional job of recording the witness accurately and, if you request it, will prepare a written transcript of the questions and answers given in the interview. If you plan to use a court reporter to record the interview, make the arrangements well in advance.

Sometimes it is not feasible to utilize a court reporter due to the expense involved, or the attorney may feel the witness may be intimidated by the increased formality of having a court reporter present for the interview, or it may just be impracticable to take a court reporter along. In that event, it is entirely appropriate for the interviewer to record the interview herself.

3. Obtain the witness's consent *before* electronically recording

Consent is needed whether the interview is to be done by phone (discussed below) or in person. Recording a witness without the prior consent of the witness is unethical and even illegal in some jurisdictions.

4. Repeat and record the statement of consent

After you obtain the consent of the witness to record the interview, repeat the statement of consent and record it as you begin the interview.

HYPOTHETICAL 13-2

> Assume that Paul Perfect is going to interview Bee Mufriend and wants to make a sound recording of the interview. He is going to use his smart phone, which is equipped with a high-grade audio interface program. He asks her before he begins recording if she minds him recording it, and she says she doesn't mind at all.
>
> **PP:** (activates audio program on smart phone): Okay, we are now recording. It is October 29, YR00, at 10 a.m. Ms. Mufriend, as you know, my name is Paul Perfect and I am a paralegal for attorney Betty Busy. I have your permission to record this interview regarding a lawsuit filed by Carlotta Falldown against our client, Jay DeClient, involving a slip and fall at the house of Jay DeClient in August of this year, is that correct?
> **BM:** Yes, that is correct.

5. Identify yourself and your position in the recording

You are ethically obligated to make that disclosure and doing so in the recording should negate any later claim by the witness that you deceived her regarding your identity or the purposes of the interview. (See Hypothetical 13-2 above.)

6. State the date and time the interview begins

See Hypothetical 13-2 above.

7. Identify all persons present

Add a statement establishing the connection with the subject matter of each identified person.

HYPOTHETICAL 13-3

> Assume that Paul Perfect is interviewing Bee Mufriend at her home where she is babysitting her nieces.
>
> **PP:** We are here at the home of Bee Mufriend located at 123 Gardener Street in Capital City. Present for this interview are Ms. Mufriend and myself and Ms. Mufriend's two nieces whom she is babysitting this morning. We have, is it Peg?
> **BM:** Yes, Peg Mufriend, who is three.

> PP: Okay, Peg Mufriend aged three. And her sister, Amy, aged . . .
> BM: Amy is four and a half.
> PP: Amy, aged four and a half. And I think it is safe to say that Peg and Amy know absolutely nothing about this incident and are here only to be babysat, is that correct, Ms.Mufriend?
> BM: That is correct.

8. Handling interruptions in the interview

If the recording of the interview is interrupted, always state on the recording that there is going to be a break in the recording, the time the recording device is being turned off, and the time it is resumed.

HYPOTHETICAL 13-4

> Assume that Paul Perfect is 20 minutes into his interview with Bee Mufriend when:
>
> PP: Ms. Mufriend, where were you at the time you first learned that someone had fallen or been hurt at the party?
> BM: Well, I was in the sun room talking with . . .
> PM: (loud and demanding): Aunt Bee, I'm hungry!
> BM: Okay, Peg, it's probably snack time for you guys, isn't it?
> PM and AM: (together): Yea!
> BM: I'm sorry, Mr. Perfect, but I'd better stop and get them something or we'll never have any peace.
> PP: No problem. Take all the time you need. Let me just make a note here for the record. It is now 10:35 a.m. on October 29, YR00. We are going to take a break and stop recording at this time so Ms. Mufriend can get her nieces a snack. We will hopefully resume shortly. (Turns off recording device.)

When the interview resumes after the interruption, record the time of resumption. Try to pick up at the same place you were at in the questioning before the break. We want to avoid any allegation later by the witness or anyone else that part of the interview was erased or edited. Even with interruptions, it should flow smoothly and be a consistent whole.

HYPOTHETICAL 13-5

> PP: (turns recording device back on): It is now 10:52 a.m. on October 29, YR00, and we are resuming the interview with Bee Mufriend. (Smiling.) Are your two charges content for a while, you think?
> BM: For as long as the cookies hold out.
> PP: Okay. Let's see, I believe I had asked you where you were when you first heard that someone had fallen or gotten hurt at the party.
> BM: That's right. As I recall I was in the sun room . . .

9. Avoid "talking over"

Don't "talk over" the witness and encourage the witness to not talk over you. By *talking over*, we mean that someone begins to speak while another person is already speaking. Some people do this without realizing it and certainly without realizing how it sounds on a voice-only recording. Two or more people talking at the same time will produce an unintelligible recording. Even in a video recording, the talk over can cause confusion, so in any recorded interview, if a witness talks over the interviewer, the interviewer should politely point it out and make sure it stops.

10. How to conclude the electronically recorded interview

At the conclusion of the interview, give the witness an opportunity to add anything she wishes, or to change or supplement answers given.

HYPOTHETICAL 13-6

> PP: All right, Ms. Mufriend, I believe that's all the questions I have. Is there anything that you would like to add to what you've told me today?
> BM: (shaking her head): No, I don't think so.
> PP: Is there anything you recall about the night of the incident that I haven't asked or you haven't mentioned?
> BM: No, I think we covered it all.

State the time the interview is concluding, and have the witness reconfirm that the interview has been recorded in its entirety with her permission and that she has given her answers voluntarily and freely.

HYPOTHETICAL 13-7

> PP: Again, Ms. Mufriend, let me thank you for taking the time to talk with me. It is now (looking at watch) 11:15 a.m. on October 29, YR00, and we are concluding this interview with Bee Mufriend. Ms. Mufriend, is it correct that this interview has been recorded with your knowledge and consent?
> BM: Yes, it has.
> PP: And the answers you have given me today have been given voluntarily and freely?
> BM: Yes.
> PP: And the answers you have given me today have been truthful and complete?
> BM: Absolutely.

> As he leaves the interview, Paul uses his smart phone to snap a picture of the front of the house where the interview was conducted. He then e-mails the digital files containing the recorded interview and the picture from his smart phone to Betty Busy's e-mail address so she can download them onto her computer. Driving back to the office from the interview, Paul begins dictating a memorandum to Betty Busy summarizing the interview. He uses his smart phone for that too since it has voice recognition software that actually displays the words that he speaks in text format. As soon as Paul pulls into his parking space, he takes a few seconds to e-mail the dictated text file from his smart phone to his work e-mail address so he can copy it onto the hard drive of the desktop computer in his office and finish it later. He also sends a Tweet: "Having a great day doing the law thing! #lovethelaw."

11. Transcribe the recording or prepare a summary

Ask the supervising attorney if she wishes you to transcribe the recorded interview for the file or to summarize the interview in a memorandum. (See Illustration 13-1.)

12. If appropriate, provide the witness a transcript or digital copy of the interview

Some states require by law or ethical rule that the witness receive a transcript of the interview in written or digital format. Some attorneys do this as a matter of courtesy. The legal professional should be familiar with the laws and ethical rules of his state regarding this procedure and should be aware of the preferences of the supervising attorney. (See LBD 13-2.)

13. Preserve the recorded interview

Preserve the recorded interview in its original form unless the supervising attorney directs otherwise. If the interview was taped or recorded on a designated disc, this will mean preserving the original tape or disc. If other technology was used, the recording should be downloaded to a designated electronic file for preservation. It is important that there be no editing of the recorded interview to be preserved. Mark it and treat it as attorney work product to shield it from discovery by opposing parties, if that is feasible under the laws of your state. (See discussion of privileges in Chapter 6, and LBD 13-2.)

EXAMPLE

If Paul Perfect had videotaped his interview with Bee Mufriend using a video camera, he would preserve the tape or disc on which the interviewed was recorded. If he had used his smart phone to video the interview, he would then e-mail the digital video file to himself and Betty Busy, and they would preserve that file electronically.

E. ▸ The Voice-Only Interview

When the interviewer has a choice between conducting an interview in person or by phone, the in-person interview is to be preferred. This permits the interviewer the opportunity to observe the conduct and demeanor of the witness, which, as we have learned, can tell us so much. Where an in-person interview is not possible, use of video-calling technology such as Skype is a good alternative because it allows both sound and video recording of an essentially live interview. But in the real world, it is not always possible to conduct every interview in person or by distance video. Considerations of location or expense may dictate that witnesses be interviewed by land line telephone, cell phone, or other sound-only technology.

1. Speak and listen carefully

The rules for conducting a **phone interview** are basically similar to conducting any interview. However, since the interviewer cannot observe the conduct and manner of the witness, more emphasis must be placed on listening carefully to the voice of the witness to catch meanings. More care must be taken to speak slowly and carefully so that the witness can understand the questions. This is especially true when a speaker phone (or conference phone) is used. Sometimes the quality of voice transmission is not as high with such equipment. Also, it is easier in a phone interview for the participants to talk over each other, and that must be avoided.

2. Ensure privacy and preserve confidentiality

SL EUTH ON
    THE LOOSE

Have a question involving the law of a foreign nation? One way to get a quick handle on it may be to use the Georgetown University Law Center's Research Guide for Jurisdictions at http://www.ll.georgetown.edu/research/browse_jurisdictions.cfm.

Since the interviewer is unable to see the witness during a phone interview, the interviewer cannot be 100 percent sure that the witness is alone even if the witness says that she is. Again, use of a speaker or conference phone increases the risk that others on the witness's end of the line can overhear questions and answers. The interviewer should do her best to make sure the witness is alone and listen for sounds of others in the background.

3. Using documents or things in a voice-only interview

A special problem for the interviewer in any interview conducted at a distance between the interviewer and interviewee is how to show documents or things to the witness in order to ask questions about them. This is especially challenging in a voice-only phone interview since the participants cannot see each other. But forethought and planning can minimize the complications involved. The interviewer must decide in advance what documents she wants to show the witness and mail, fax, e-mail, or text the documents to the witness beforehand. Or, if it is the witness that is bringing the documents to the interview, arrangements must be made to obtain copies of the documents as far in advance of the interview as possible. The interviewer will want time to review them and prepare questions about them before the interview begins.

Even when both the interviewer and the witness have the same documents, confusion can arise in a distance interview with no video involved as the two parties to the voice-only conversation try to figure out which document the other is referring to. To prevent a guessing game, it is a good idea to number or label the documents in advance so both parties can identify each document quickly. For example, if ten different documents will be referred to during the interview, a list of the documents can be prepared and each one numbered one to ten. The list would then be provided to the witness along with copies of the documents. Now the interviewer can ask the witness to take a look at "the third paragraph of document number three" or "page five of document number ten" and in seconds both parties are, literally, on the same page.

4. Recording the voice-only interview

Interviews conducted by land-line telephone, cell phone, or other communication device, including live interviews, are sometimes recorded, and the earlier discussion of the electronically recorded interview should be kept in mind here. In offices where interviews are regularly conducted by phone and recorded, the phone systems are equipped with a recording capacity.

The rules for recording a voice-only phone interview are substantially the same for recording an in-person interview. Again, consent to record should be obtained *before* the recording begins and then that consent should be repeated and recorded as the taping starts. One difference in the recorded phone interview is that the opening statement made by the interviewer should state clearly that the interview is being conducted by phone.

HYPOTHETICAL 13-8

If Paul Perfect is conducting the interview of Bee Mufriend by phone, it might begin like this:

PP: This is Paul Perfect, a paralegal working for attorney Betty Busy, and I am recording a telephone interview with Ms. Bee Mufriend beginning at 10:00 a.m. on October 29, YR00. Ms. Musfriend is speaking to me from her home at 123 Gardener Street in Capital City, Yourstate. Is that correct, Ms. Mufriend?

BM: Yes, that's correct.

PP: I'm going to be asking Ms. Mufriend some questions regarding a lawsuit filed by Carlotta Falldown against our client, Jay DeClient, involving a slip and fall at the house of Jay DeClient in August of this year. And Ms. Mufriend, I am recording this telephone interview with your knowledge and consent, is that correct?

BM: Yes, that is correct.

PP: Fine. Ms. Mufriend, would you tell me your full name and spell your last name for me?

F.   The Written Witness Statement

It is very common in interviewing to have the witness sign a written statement containing a verbatim account or a summary of the information they have supplied. The decision to have the witness sign a statement is to be made by the supervising attorney, not the assisting legal professional. Depending on the status of the work product privilege in your state (see LBD 13-2), the statement may be discoverable by the opposing party. So always check first with the supervising attorney before having a witness sign a statement.

The **witness statement** may take a number of different forms. The essential things are that (1) the statement be signed by the witness in a manner that clearly adopts the statement as the witness's own; and (2) that the signature of the witness and the statement as a whole be provable (capable of authentication) at trial.

1. The format of a witness statement

The different formats that may be utilized for a witness statement include:

- a copy of the transcript of a recorded interview signed by the witness
- a typed summary signed by the witness
- a handwritten summary signed by the witness
- a questionnaire completed and signed by the witness
- a letter written by the interviewer summarizing the interview and signed by the witness

2. How attorneys use witness statements

To better understand the importance of the witness statement to the supervising attorney, it is helpful to remember the various evidentiary and other uses attorneys can make of properly prepared witness statements. (Review the rules of evidence in Chapters 6 and 7.) Such statements may be used:

- To refresh the witness's memory before testifying
- As part of a settlement effort
- To evaluate the case for the client
- At trial to refresh a witness's recollection (see FRE 612)
- At trial as a prior inconsistent (or consistent) statement (see FRE 613)
- At trial as an admission if the witness is an opposing party (see FRE 801(d)(2))
- At trial for any reason coming within a hearsay exception (see FRE 803 or 804)

3. Preparing the written witness statement

To be useable by attorneys for the various purposes mentioned, the witness statement should comply with the following guidelines.

a. It should identify the witness by name and state the date of the interview

Other identifying information, such as age, address, and social security number, is not essential but may be included.

b. It should be written in the witness's own words

If the witness writes or types up the statement herself, or if the interview is recorded and then transcribed, this is no problem. But it can become a problem when the interviewer prepares the statement based on the interview with the witness.

To the extent possible, the interviewer should use the witness's own words and phrasing when drafting a statement for the witness to sign. Touchy situations can arise, however, concerning the witness's use of poor grammar, incomplete sentences, slang, profanity, and so forth. Do we incorporate those verbatim into the statement? Judgment has to be exercised to achieve the goal of getting an accurate statement without offending the witness. And many people would be offended to see their poor grammar or unconscious use of profanity reduced to paper. If you are in doubt in these situations, go to the supervising attorney for guidance. If you are drafting the witness statement in the field and don't have the time or opportunity to check with the supervising attorney, use your best judgment in the situation.

c. It should state the total number of pages it contains
For example:

> *I have read this statement consisting of 4 pages given this 5th day of Jan., YR00.*

If the statement is only a single page in length, that statement should be drafted as follows:

> *I have read this statement consisting of 1 page given this 5th day of Jan., YR00.*

d. The pages of the statement should be numbered
Each page of a written statement more than one page in length should be numbered consecutively, usually at the bottom, and each page should refer to the total number of pages in the entire statement as in:

> *Page 1 of 3 pages*

This will help avoid a situation in which a witness might later allege that pages were added or deleted to her original statement after she signed it.

e. Every page should be signed or initialed by the witness
If the statement is more than one page long, the witness should be asked to sign her name or initial each page separately in her own hand, usually in a corner of the page. This will help avoid a situation in which the witness later alleges that a page of the original statement has been substituted. If the statement is only one page long, this is not necessary since that one page will be signed by the witness. (See Illustration 13-2.)

f. It should be read and corrected by the witness before it is signed
Before having the witness sign the statement, always give her an opportunity to read and make corrections in the statement. It is, after all, the witness's statement. Each change made by the witness should be initialed by the witness in her own hand. (See Illustration 13-3.)

g. It should be signed by the witness
The statement should be signed by the witness at the end and the signature should appear immediately beneath a sentence giving the date of the statement, affirming that the witness has read the statement, noting the number of pages in the statement, and verifying that the

Illustration 13-2 HANDWRITTEN WITNESS STATEMENT

I, Bee Mufriend, am a 30 year old female. I reside at 123 Gardener Street in Capital City, Yourstate. On August 25, YR00, I attended a party at the home of a neighbor, Jay DeClient, at 111 Humphrey Bogart Lane. I brought a friend, I took Charge, to the party with me. Mr. Charge and I arrived at the party about 8:00 p.m. We stayed together for only a few moments and then separated.

I did not see Mr. Charge from about 8:20 p.m. until a little after 9:00 p.m. At that time, people began to say that a woman had slipped and fallen in the kitchen of Mr. DeClient's house. I did not go to the kitchen. When Mr. Charge came out of the kitchen, he was laughing a little. He said the woman who had slipped and fallen had punched Mr. DeClient in the nose as he bent down and tried to help her. He had been on the other side of the woman at the time and she hit DeClient without even opening her eyes. He said that if she had been up to throwing a combination, she would have hit him too.

Mr. Charge and I left the party shortly after.

I have read this statement consisting of one page given this 29th day of October YR00, and the information contained in this statement is true and correct to the best of my knowledge and belief.

Bee Mufriend
October 29, YR00

Illustration 13-3   TYPED WITNESS STATEMENT

My name is Esau Itall. I reside at 456 Humphrey Bogart Lane in Capital City, Yourstate. I am 42 years old. My social security number is 999-23-1234. I own and operate Itall Insurance Agency in Capital City.

On August 24, YR00 I was a guest at a party in the home of a neighbor, Jay DeClient, at 111 Humphrey Bogart Lane in Capital City. A little before 9 p.m. the evening of the party I entered the kitchen of Mr. DeClient's home hoping to speak with Mr. Itook Charge, a local businessman. I had not met Mr. Charge but knew of him and was hoping to make his acquaintance and possibly be able to obtain some of his personal or company insurance work.

As I entered the kitchen I saw Mr. Charge speaking with Ida Screamer, another neighbor. There were five or six other people in the kitchen at the time. While waiting for Mr. Charge to finish his conversation with Ms. Screamer, I went to the island in the kitchen where the drinks were set out. Stepping around the island I noticed that right in front of the refrigerator there was a puddle of water or other clear liquid on the hardwood floor. The puddle was a rough circle about two inches in diameter. It was fairly visible against the brown oak wood of the floor.

After pouring myself a drink I moved around the kitchen to locate a dishrag to clean up the spill. A few seconds later, another neighbor, Carlotta Falldown, entered the kitchen and said, "We need more ice out in the backyard." I responded to her by saying, "Check the freezer over the refrigerator." Just as I said that I remembered the puddle there in front of the refrigerator and said, in a loud voice, "But watch out for the water over there."

Page 1 of 2 pages

Carlotta Falldown didn't respond to what I said and seconds later she slipped and fell in front of the refrigerator. I don't know if she heard me or not but I spoke loudly enough that I thought she could hear me over the conversations in the room.

A couple of people went to the assistance of Carlotta Falldown on the floor. I left the room to go find Jay DeClient and tell him about the fall. I located him in the backyard at the barbeque grill. He immediately rushed away toward the kitchen.

I did not go back in the kitchen after that because so many people were crowding in there. I learned later from others that Carlotta Falldown punched Jay DeClient in the nose but I did not see that myself.

I have read this statement consisting of two pages given this 20th day of October, YR00, and the information contained in this statement is true and correct to the best of my knowledge and belief.

Esau Itall

Esau Itall

Paul Perfect

Paul Perfect, witness

Page 2 of 2 pages

statement is true and correct to the best of the witness's knowledge and belief:

> *I have read this statement consisting of 4 pages given this 5th day of Jan, YR00, and the information contained in this statement is true and correct to the best of my knowledge and belief.*

Dan Miller

Fact Witness's signature

And you may want to have the witness to the signature sign the statement as such:

> *I have read this statement consisting of 4 pages given this 5th day of Jan, YR00, and the information contained in this statement is true and correct to the best of my knowledge and belief.*

Dan Miller

Fact Witness's signature

Susan Jones

Witness

Having the signature of the fact witness witnessed by another is done for authentication purposes. If the fact witness ever repudiates the statement by alleging the signature is not hers, the one who witnessed her signature can testify that it is in fact the signature of the fact witness. If the witness is willing, you may also have the statement signed in the presence of a notary public who can then certify the signature. Under the FRE and most state rules of evidence a properly notarized signature is self-authenticating.

Illustration 13-2 shows how the handwritten statement of Bee Mufriend might look. Illustration 13-3 shows how the typed statement of Esau Itall might look.

Chapter Summary and Conclusion

Witness interviews are often conducted in the field, providing the opportunity for the interviewer to observe and evaluate the witness's environment, but posing special challenges to overcome external obstacles beyond the interviewer's control. A witness interview should begin with expressions of appreciation and disclosures of status and purpose. Some background information on the witness should be acquired. The substantive portion of the witness interview should follow the track of a client interview by having the witness review relevant documents, obtain a broad overview of the facts before asking for specifics, fill in gaps, clarify inconsistencies, establish chronologies, and seek details and leads to other information sources. The interviewer should always be alert for possible bases on which to impeach a witness, whether that witness is helpful or harmful to the client's case. Recording or taping an interview presents special challenges. The interviewer must be careful to obtain and record consent to the recording, identify all who are present, and document breaks and restarts in the interviewing process. The interviewer may prepare an interview summary or a witness statement following the interview. There are special rules governing the preparation and signing of a witness statement that the legal professional should always be careful to follow.

Before witnesses can be interviewed they must of course be identified and located. Those topics are addressed next, in Chapter 14.

Review Questions

1. What do we mean by "external obstacles" that must be overcome when conducting a field interview? Can you think of examples?
2. What opportunities are presented to an interviewer when the interview is conducted in the witness's home or office?
3. Why is it important to clarify unfamiliar terms or concepts referenced by the witness?
4. What does wringing out a wash rag have to do with interviewing?
5. In interviewing, attempt to determine if the source of the information is competent, _____, _____, and _____. Try to filter out opinions, _____, _____, and statements of prejudice to get to real provable _____. Distinguish between _____ -hand information and _____ -hand or even _____ -hand information.
6. Name the different ways we seek information in an interview that can be used later to impeach that witness.
7. What is the difference between the bias of a witness and the interest of a witness in the outcome of a case? Can you think of examples of each?
8. List as many topics as you can that should be covered in a memorandum summarizing a witness interview.
9. What are some special challenges presented in an electronically recorded interview?
10. What are some special challenges presented in a voice-only interview?

KEY WORDS AND PHRASES TO REMEMBER

advancement
advantage to another
bias
call recorder
cassette recorder
compact disc recorder
electronic recording
external obstacles
FaceTime
ice breaker
impeachment of a witness
inheritance
interest
internal obstacles
interview summary
monetary interest

personal digital equipment (PDA)
prior bad acts
prior convictions
prior inconsistent statements
recorded interview
reputation for truthfulness
romantic advantage
Skype
sound recording
Tango
tape recorder
telephone interview
video conferencing
video recording
witness statement

LEARN BY DOING

LBD 13-1. Conduct the interview of one of the witnesses (as assigned by your instructor) in one of the following Case Studies from Appendix A. Then prepare a draft witness statement for the witness to sign. Do not actually have the person playing the role of the witness sign the statement; instead turn it in to your instructor for review as you would to a supervising attorney.

a. Case Study No. 1 (The Rowdy Outlaw Case)

Candy Carmichael Outlaw	Detective Willie Parker	Ima Jean Grouse
	Dr. Michael Melody	Jack Gates
Connie Cornelius	Georgette B. Good	Charlie Choot

b. Case Study No. 2 (The Soupspoon Wise Case)

Korn Pone	Tanya Trucker	Turtle Shoop

c. Case Study No. 3 (The Vidalia Unyon Case)

Georgia Peach	Hobo Booth	Nosey Nelly

d. Case Study No. 4 (The Rocky Road Project)

Grace Slickspot	Real E. Smart

LBD 13-2. Determine if any statute, court ruling, or ethical rule or guideline in your state requires or encourages attorneys to provide witnesses a transcript of a recorded interview or a copy of any written

statement made by the witness. If there is some requirement to provide the witness with a transcript or copy of their statement, determine if the requirement is conditioned on a verbal or written request from the witness. Prepare a memorandum summarizing your findings. In that memorandum, state whether you agree with the policy of your state on this matter and if not, how you would recommend it be changed.

LBD 13-3. Interview a local attorney or paralegal who is routinely involved with recording client or witness interviews and ask what technology he or she uses for sound and video recording. Why was the equipment they currently use chosen over other available equipment? How big a factor is cost? How important is it for legal professionals assisting in interviewing work to be familiar with current technology in this field?

LBD 13-4. Any technology geeks in the class? Prepare a summary of the current technology available for sound and video recording. Explain how Skype works. What's coming in the future? Consider doing a demonstration for the rest of the class.

LBD 13-5. A study by Professors Marion Eals and Irwin Silverman of York University suggests that women are 60 to 70 percent more proficient than men at remembering details of an event or scene (the "locations of objects in a spatial array"). You can read their article at http://facstaff.uww.edu/eamond/road/216-Research_Methods/Projects/Project_1/Theory%20of%20Spactial%20Sex%20Diffs-Recall.pdf. Assuming these conclusions are scientifically valid, what are the implications for preferring to have a female or male witness to testify from memory regarding an event or scene witnessed? What are the implications for the interviewer of such a witness? Arrange an interview with an experienced trial lawyer or a paralegal who routinely interviews fact witnesses. Do his or her experiences with male and female witnesses confirm the findings of Eals and Silverman?

Chapter 14

Identifying and Locating Fact Witnesses

CHAPTER OUTLINE

A. Introduction
B. Identifying Fact Witnesses
C. Locating Missing Witnesses

CHAPTER OBJECTIVES

The legal professional engaged in investigating work must know how to identify potential witnesses in client cases and how to locate the missing witness. In this chapter you will learn:

- A number of techniques for identifying and locating fact witnesses.
- About a variety of people sources and documentary sources.
- How to use resources that are available to assist the investigator, including the Internet, data base vendors, and tracing companies.

A. Introduction

Nothing is more basic to the investigation process than identifying fact witnesses—persons who have or who might have knowledge of facts directly relevant to the matter being handled for the client—and locating missing fact witness. Be sure to distinguish between the two concepts.

In the first section of this chapter we focus on *identifying* fact witnesses, that is, learning the identity of persons who might have information regarding our client's case. In the second section of this chapter we take up the other concept, *locating* the witness we know about but cannot find. Both sections of this chapter should be read in conjunction with Appendix B, Resources for the Investigator, which contains an abundance of specific sources for use in identifying and locating witnesses.

B. Identifying Fact Witnesses

The need to identify fact witnesses can arise in any type of civil or criminal litigation.

EXAMPLE

> In a car accident case, depending on the specific facts, we may need to determine who might have witnessed the accident, or the course of the vehicles before or after the accident, or the words and behavior of the parties before, during, or after the accident.
>
> In a civil fraud case, depending on the specific facts of the case, we may need to determine who might have witnessed the alleged fraudulent transaction, who might have knowledge of the truth of the matter, or who might have had a similar experience with the alleged perpetrator of the fraud.
>
> In a products liability case, depending on the specific facts, we may need to determine who might have witnessed the injury that occurred due to the alleged defective product; who might have knowledge of the product's alleged defective design, manufacture, or packaging; and who might have knowledge of the plaintiff's awareness of the danger or misuse of the product at the time of the accident.
>
> In an employment dispute case, depending on the specific facts, we may need to determine who might have witnessed the hiring event, heard discussions involving alleged promises made, heard threats made, witnessed the discriminatory events, or been present at the discharge event.
>
> In an armed robbery case, depending on the specific facts, we may need to determine who might have witnessed the crime, or the behavior of the alleged criminal before, during, or after the crime, or who else might have had a motive to commit the crime.

1. People sources

In any given matter, there typically will be a number of people who can help you identify witnesses. Who those people are will depend on the nature and facts of the matter. The following list is only suggestive.

a. The client

Your client is almost always the basic source of information about the matter, including the identity of likely witnesses. Beginning with the initial client interview (see Chapters 10 and 11), you should use this source liberally. Keep in mind that your client may not know how much he knows. In other words, the client will not necessarily appreciate the kinds of information that you need in order to represent his interests and thus will not know what to volunteer to you. You must know to ask and not assume that the client has told you all that he knows.

b. Other witnesses

Witnesses lead to witnesses. When you have located one witness, he may lead you to others. One question that should always be asked of a witness is, "Who else knows or may possibly know something about . . . ?"

c. The investigating officer(s)

In an automobile accident case where a formal investigation was made, the officer who investigated is one of the first people you should interview and is an important source for witnesses. Keep in mind that sometimes, not all witnesses to an accident get reported on the official

accident report prepared by the officer. We have to ask if there were others. Also, although only one officer may be listed on the accident report as the **investigating officer**, other officers may have been present at the accident site and may have unreported knowledge of potential witnesses.

d. Ambulance, rescue squad, and emergency room personnel

In an accident case, consider who may have come to the scene for any reason. Someone had to treat the injured person at the scene, transport him to the hospital, and treat him there. The various documents generated in the case may contain all the names of the persons involved in those tasks.

EXAMPLE

> If you find that the county rescue squad arrived at an accident site you are investigating and retrieved an injured passenger from a mangled car, some report was probably generated by that rescue squad regarding the incident, but it may mention or be signed by only one member of the team. You will need to ask who else participated in the rescue effort and interview all members of the team to be sure you locate all leads. When a person is transported to an emergency room with an injury, make a list of all the different people they are likely to encounter before they are released or admitted to the hospital, then work your way through the list.

e. The scene or neighborhood canvass

Often it is a good idea to simply **canvass** the scene or neighborhood where the incident occurred to determine who might have seen something relevant. Police officers are well acquainted with this investigative procedure when they look for possible witnesses to a crime. If the incident occurred in an office or home, this is simply a matter of contacting persons who were or might have been present and witnessed something. If the incident occurred in a public place, the canvass will be more extensive.

Plan the canvass carefully. How will you present yourself to strangers at their doors or in their shops? At someone's door where you are a stranger, don't stand too close to the door or try to peer inside, as this may be seen as suspicious or threatening. Dress well and have that smile and friendly greeting ready when the door is opened. Remember that you may be being scrutinized through a peep hole or a crack in the curtain before the door is opened.

Exactly what questions will you ask and how will you ask them? Look over the area to be canvassed very carefully to be sure you include all locations where someone could possibly have seen something. If practicable, go at the same time of day that the incident occurred. Be prepared to go back several times if need be to make contact with everyone possible.

f. The neighborhood regulars

Closely related to the neighborhood canvass is the effort to discover persons who regularly pass through a given area where the incident occurred and who may have seen something. The list of possibilities is limited only by your own imagination—delivery people, people on their way to work or school, postal workers, utility workers, etc.

g. The media

If an accident or incident was covered by TV, radio, newspaper, or periodical, consider making contact and identifying the investigating reporter, photographer, and crew. Many media people are fairly cooperative in granting interviews and sharing notes, photos, and video. (Here again, your communication skills become critical—see Chapter 8.)

Remember that sometimes the media does investigate an event but an editorial decision is made not to use the story. So even though an accident or crime was not reported in the media, some reporter may still have information you can use. And remember that if a story carried in the media uses a single photo there may be many more they didn't use. If they used a five-second video clip there may be several more minutes of video that you can obtain if you get to it before it is reused. Or if they showed a ten-second interview there may be many more minutes of recorded interview. You may be seeing or hearing only the tip of a considerable iceberg of information.

h. Advertisements

Sometimes it is appropriate to run an advertisement in the area media asking witnesses to an event to come forward and identify themselves. This may be done where you have good reason to believe that there were witnesses to a matter but other means have failed to identify them. Ads in local newspapers are cost efficient, although other media (the Internet, TV, radio, billboard, or periodicals) may be justifiable depending on the nature of the matter. Newspaper ads can be run in the classifieds or, for additional cost, as a freestanding ad in the paper. The ad should be creative and eye-catching to attract as much attention as possible.

Illustration 14-1 suggests a creative ad that might be used in the Getta Life case from Hypothetical 14-1.

HYPOTHETICAL 14-1

Assume that you are assisting the attorney representing Getta Life who has been accused of murdering his ex-girlfriend, Turnme Loose. The state alleges that Getta Life was angry and distraught after Turnme Loose broke up with him following a six-month romance. Supposedly, Turnme Loose told friends at work on November 8 that she broke up with Getta Life the evening before when he picked her up at her home at 6 p.m. and told her they were going to see *Gone with the Wind* at the local arts theater. She complained that Getta Life had a fetish about *Gone with the Wind*, that they had been to see it together more than a dozen times while they were dating, and that she demanded they go see something else. When he refused, she broke it off. She also told friends at work on November 8 that following the breakup the evening before, she had seen Getta Life driving slowly by her house for several hours.

At 5 p.m. on November 8, Turnme Loose was hit by a car and killed as she was crossing the street in front of her office building on her way to the parking lot on the other side of the street. According to the police accident report prepared by Officer Keepda Peace, a co-worker of Turnme Loose, Omi Gosh, had walked outside with her and witnessed the collision. Omi Gosh told Keepda Peace that a dark-colored car that looked new came around the corner to their left just as she and Turnme Loose came out of their building. The car stopped in the street about 100 feet away. Omi Gosh noticed the car briefly and just thought it was going to let someone out. It had tinted windows so she could not see the occupants. As soon as Turnme Loose stepped into the street the car suddenly accelerated, hit Turnme Loose with the fender of the car on the passenger side, and kept going without ever slowing.

Getta Life has been arrested and charged with first degree murder. According to a story on the incident that appeared in the local paper under the byline of a reporter named Scoop This, the family of Turnme Loose has already retained an attorney to file a civil wrongful death action against Getta Life.

Getta Life confirms that he and Turnme Loose broke up the evening of November 7 but vigorously denies that he was upset by the breakup or that he drove by herself later that evening or that he ran her over the next day. He admits that he has a thing for *Gone with the Wind*. In fact, he says that at the time of the death on November 8 he was at the arts theater watching *Gone with the Wind* for his 1,000th time. After the breakup on November 7 he says he spent the remainder of that evening alone in his apartment watching a DVD of GWTW, although he prefers to see it on the big screen. He also spent some time on the Internet sending e-mail messages to other GWTW fans—apparently there is a club. He does own a new dark blue Ford Fusion automobile but only drove it once on November 8 when he drove to the cinema and then back home.

1. What questions will you ask Getta Life in order to identify potential witnesses helpful to his defense?
2. What witnesses do we know of so far who could lead us to others and what will we ask them?
3. What questions do we want to ask Officer Keepda Peace beyond what appears on the accident report in order to identify other potential witnesses?
4. What scenes or neighborhoods might we want to canvass in this case and for what purposes?
5. If the reporter Scoop This will speak with us, what questions would we like to ask him?
6. See Illustration 14-1 for a newspaper ad that might be utilized in the Getta Life case. Can you think of a different one?

2. Document and record sources

In almost every kind of legal matter there will be documents or other records (e.g., computer files and e-mail messages) that may lead the investigator to potential witnesses. These documents and records should be identified, obtained, and carefully reviewed for potential witnesses. The following list is illustrative rather than comprehensive. The student should consider this section in conjunction with Chapters 16 through 18 in which identifying and obtaining information from all kinds from public and private sources is discussed in greater detail.

a. Medical records

Consider the **medical records** generated by the hit and run involving Turnme Loose in Hypothetical 14-1. An ambulance crew was called,

Illustration 14-1 NEWSPAPER ADVERTISEMENT SEEKING WITNESSES

to call me if you saw or have any information regarding the hit and run accident that occurred on 5th St. in front of the Culpepper Building on November 8, YR00 at approximately 5 p.m. Please call Patty Professional COLLECT at 111-555-2222.

examined Turnme Loose at the scene, began treatment, moved her to the ambulance, and transported her to the hospital emergency room. In the emergency room (ER) a team of nurses and physicians administered trauma care until she underwent surgery. After an hour of surgery she was declared dead. Everyone involved in the treatment of Turnme Loose will generate records that may be a valuable resource for identifying witnesses. The ambulance crew will make detailed records of the call, her condition upon their arrival, the examination, the treatment, the transfer, and her condition upon arrival at the hospital. There will be admissions records at the ER, nurses' notes, physicians' records, lab reports, and pharmacy records. There will be surgical records generated by everyone involved in the procedure including the physicians, the nurses, and the anesthesiologist.

Assume there is a question in the civil wrongful death suit filed by the survivors of Turnme Loose regarding whether she regained consciousness following the accident. This factual question will go to the legal issue of whether the plaintiffs can recover for her pain and suffering. Both sides will be looking for witnesses who can testify one way or another on that factual question. The medical records will be an invaluable source to locate those witnesses.

Or what if the movie Getta Life says he was attending at the time of the hit and run got out at 4:40 p.m. and we have witnesses who saw Getta Life leaving the theater at that moment? Did he have time to leave the theater, drive to Turnme Loose's office building and run her over? The exact moment of the hit and run might be critical on those facts and the medical records could be critical to determining who arrived at the scene, when, and how they documented the time. Medical records often help us identify important witnesses.

b. Employment records

What kinds of records did the employer of Turnme Loose maintain on her? If someone deliberately struck Turnme Loose with a car and it wasn't Getta Life, who was it? The attorney defending Getta Life in both the criminal and civil actions will certainly want to find out. Who else would know where Turnme Loose worked and when she got off work and where she parked? Was she having trouble with a co-worker that she might have reported to another co-worker or superior? If so, it might be documented in her employment records.

In the civil case, on the issue of damages, what was Turnme Loose making at her job? Was she in line for promotions or about to be fired? The employment records may lead us to people who know.

c. Educational records

Was Turnme Loose currently a student at the local college? What about looking at those records for indications of a stalker or hostile fellow student or problems with a professor?

In the wrongful death case, what kind of a student was she? Who were her professors whom we might ask?

d. Personal correspondence and journaling

Everybody has some of this kind of information and many have a lot of it—for example, traditional written correspondence and journaling. That may include notes and letters to family and friends, diary entries, and other personal writings. But we are truly living in the **electronic communication** age. Diaries and journals are more likely to be created on computer software today than on paper.

e. Online correspondence and social networking data

Today we live in a digital world, an **e-cloud**. Worldwide, trillions of **e-mail** and **text messages** are sent every year. Cell phones, smart phones, tablets, and notebooks are ubiquitous. Every day some new **software application (app)** is announced for use with the trendiest mobile device (in 2012 there were more than half a million apps available for Apple's i-products, about 300,000 for Google's Android products). Millions of people and groups have joined the **online social networking (OSN)** craze by creating **Facebook, MySpace,** or **Google+** pages for themselves where they add friends, send and receive messages, and post and update their profiles. As of this writing, Facebook is closing in on a billion users, one-seventh of all humanity and one-half of all Internet users around the world, while the much newer Google+ is already nearing half a billion users. Selective online gathering places like **CafeMom** for mothers only, **Shizzzler** for students and 20-somethings only, or **ibeatyou** and **Zinga** for those who love contests and games are popular. Untold numbers of people operate or contribute to **blogs** dealing with every subject imaginable. More than 3 billion images and videos have been posted on **Flickr**, a popular online community platform. More social networking and mini-blogging occurs today via **Twitter**, where anyone can create a profile page and then "tweet" their every spontaneous thought to "followers." More than 160 million people in more than 170 different businesses and professions now connect and network for career purposes on **LinkedIn**. Millions more participate in general social network sites such as **Bebo, Habbo,** or **BlackPlanet**. Many people post all kinds of videos and images on **YouTube** or **Pinterest** and then interact with viewers. YouTube itself has become a worldwide video sharing arena and boasts 4 billion hits per day. Millions of people search for and communicate with former classmates on **Yearbook.com** and **Classmates.com**. Single people participate in online dating/hookup/chat sites like **Match.com** or **eHarmony**. Both professionals and amateurs are contributing to **collaborative journalism** sites like **WikiNews** and CNN's **iReport**.

Illustration 14-2 lists a few currently popular OSN sites and what they offer.

If defense counsel is looking for someone else with a motive to kill Turnme Loose, think of the valuable resource all her written and electronic communications and the responses to them might be in locating suspects or others who might lead to suspects. (See LBDs 14-6 through 14-9.)

EXAMPLE

If Turnme Loose maintained a Facebook page, would you want to see the messages and photos she posted there, who had friended her, the comments she made on her wall, and the responses to those postings? If she had a business profile on LinkedIn, would you want to see what that profile told you about her happy or unhappy work history, who her connections were, what communications she'd had with them? If she had a G-mail e-mail account or an iPhone, would you want to read the e-mail and text messages received and sent to identify potential enemies?

Illustration 14-2 POPULAR ONLINE SOCIAL NETWORKING SITES

- DailyBooth (http://dailybooth.com/) and Photobucket (http://photobucket.com/): Publish and share pictures of your life.
- Delicious (http://delicious.com/) and Pinterest (http://pinterest.com/): Post and share pictures and thoughts about anything of interest to you from recipes to art, fashion, architecture, trips, animals, vegetation, books, movies, etc.
- Facebook (www.facebook.com/), Google+ (https://plus.google.com/), and MySpace (www.myspace.com/): These are among the premier general sites for creating a personal profile and sharing with friends
- LinkedIn (www.linkedin.com/) and Business Exchange (http://bx.businessweek.com/): These sites are used for business and professional profile sharing and networking.
- Twitter (http://twitter.com/) and Tumbler (www.tumblr.com/): Microblog on these sites for sharing with followers brief messages called "Tweets" or "Tumbledogs," respectively.
- Ibeatyou (www.ibeatyou.com/) and Zinga (https://zynga.com/): These popular sites are for those who like playing games participating in competitions and contests online.
- Reddit (www.reddit.com/) and Trueslant (http://trueslant.com/): Contributors link to articles about any topic of interest to them from politics to poultry.
- Foursquare (http://foursquare.com/) and MeetUp (www.meetup.com/): On sites designed for groups to use, members alert each other to where they are and what they're doing and arrange meetings.
- Yelp (www.yelp.com/) and BuzzUp(http://twitter.com/buzzup): These specialized sites are for sharing, respectively, reviews of restaurants and other businesses and technology hot topics.
- Orkut (www.orkut.com/) and Badoo (http://badoo.com/): multilingual sites are popular in South American and India and in Europe and Latin America, respectively.

f. Business records

Every business activity generates some **records** and correspondence.

EXAMPLE

Consider a single memo generated by the sales force supervisor of a small company involved in selling aluminum siding. Perhaps the memo suggests a change in the pricing structure for some of the company's products. That memo probably didn't happen in a vacuum. There may have been preceding memos or correspondence leading up to it or at least verbal communications among the memo's author and other people inside or outside the company. To whom was the memo sent and who is shown on the memo as receiving copies? Or who may have received copies that isn't shown on the memo? Even the simplest, most routine business record may be a rich source of potential witnesses to be interviewed.

In the Getta Life case, remember he says he spent some time on the Internet the evening of November 7 e-mailing members of the GWTW club? Did you think to ask the client for the identity of those he e-mailed in order to confirm the times? Does this club have any records? Maybe the records from Getta Life's own computer or his Internet service provider can confirm the times of his e-mail messages as well as their content. After all, a man supposedly freaking out over his girlfriend's dumping him arguably wouldn't get too wrapped up in an esoteric debate over whether GWTW, the book, should be required reading in all English literature courses. On the other hand, if Getta Life's e-mail messages on the evening

of November 7 argued that Rhett Butler should have run Scarlet down with a buggy the first time she rejected him, the defense may have a problem!

g. Personal credit, utility, and financial records

Has Getta Life had any repair work done on his car since the accident? How would the prosecution determine that? His checking account records or credit card charges might help. Did Getta Life make any phone calls by land line or cellular to Turnme Loose following the breakup? His phone records and hers might be checked to see. His credit card card bills might show charges for gasoline or other purchases that are consistent with or contradictory of his story of where he was and what he was doing the evening of November 7 and afternoon of November 8.

And identifying others with a motive to kill Turnme Loose? Her credit history and financial records might reveal disputes with persons to whom she owed money or who owed money to her. Or perhaps there are persons she had been paying regularly whose payments stopped without explanation.

h. Public records—local, state, and federal

It is essential for the legal professional engaged in investigating work to be familiar with the various local, state, and federal governmental offices and agencies and the various records available to the public through such offices and agencies. (See Chapters 16 through 18 for a detailed discussion of accessing such records.) Had Turnme Loose been involved in any litigation (like a debt dispute, divorce, custody, or domestic violence problem) with another person recently? The court records will tell us. Did anyone catch all or a part of the license plate number on the car that struck Turnme Loose? The state department of motor vehicles can possibly identify the car and owner or we can at least determine whether it matches the number on Getta Life's car. Had Turnme Loose asserted an involuntary lien against anyone's property recently, been the grantee of a voluntary lien by anyone who owed her money, purchased or sold real property, paid her property taxes, set up a business venture with others, inherited property, filed bankruptcy, made a creditor's claim in a bankruptcy proceeding, etc.? Public records will tell us these things and lead us to people who may know something relevant to her death.

C.   Locating Missing Witnesses

Once we know the identity of witnesses we then have to locate them. If we have a name and a current home and/or work address and phone number, this is easy. But sometimes we know the identity of a witness but not enough information to locate him easily. We may have a physical description without a name ("it was a big guy with a tattoo of an eagle on his right arm") or some vocational information but no name ("a guy driving a Yellow Cab") or just some general description without a name ("an older lady walking an apricot poodle"). Even if we have a name and other information, locating the witness may be difficult. After all, people do move, change jobs, or change names.

How do we find the missing witness? Again, the exercise of common sense and creative thinking are important.

1. Let's play *This Is Your Life*

The key to locating the missing witness is to start with what you already know and then plan what sources to check for more information. We will say more about specific sources to check shortly but first consider a creative technique that can be used to help you identify specific sources to check in a given case. We will call it ***This Is Your Life.***

The premise of this game is that each of us has a history. More specifically, each of us have personal, social, family, religious, educational, vocational, financial, recreational, medical, and community histories. To a large extent our lives can be defined around these areas. If you want to find a person (or just find out as much as you can about a person), give thought to the individuals you might contact and to the public and private sources of documentary information you might check to obtain information in each of the listed categories concerning that person. (See Hypothetical 14-2.) And keep in mind that non-natural persons such as corporations, partnerships, limited liability companies, trusts, and unincorporated associations also have histories that can be outlined and inquired into.

It is not going too far to say that you ought to be able to take one solid piece of information about a person and think of several possible trails to follow to locate them. Everyone has past and present relatives, friends, neighbors, co-workers, supervisors, teachers, fellow students, acquaintances, and business contacts that can tell us something about them. It is in neighborhoods and communities that people are born, go to schools, shop, bank, travel, get jobs, change jobs, go on unemployment, see doctors, choose churches, get married, have children, divorce, buy and sell property, pay taxes, apply for loans, sue each other, vote, get arrested, subscribe to newspapers and magazines, order merchandise by mail, join clubs, have hobbies, join professional associations, belong to unions, get business licenses, file bankruptcy, join the military, drive cars with license plates, rent movies, subscribe to utilities, leave forwarding addresses, write wills, get sick and die, and a lot of other stuff in between! All of these activities leave trails—people trails and paper trails—that can be followed by the enterprising investigator.

HYPOTHETICAL 14-2

Assume that in the Getta Life case you have interviewed Omi Gosh, the co-worker of Turnme Loose who saw her get hit by the car. You have also interviewed Keepda Peace, the investigating officer. You have learned from Omi Gosh that there was another woman on the street at the time of the hit and run who may have gotten a better look at the license plate on the car that hit Turnme Loose. Omi Gosh told you she had never seen this woman before, but that she was a well-dressed older woman (late 60s with short white hair) walking an apricot poodle on a leash and carrying a sack of groceries.

1. How would you go about locating this woman? Before you go driving madly around the streets looking for someone fitting this description, take a moment to play *This Is Your Life*. Start with what you already know about this witness:

a woman	at about 5 p.m.
in her late 60s	on Fifth Street in front of the
short white hair	Culpepper Building
well dressed	carrying a sack of groceries
walking an apricot poodle	

2. If she was walking a poodle doesn't that suggest she lives near where the accident happened? And doesn't the grocery bag also tend to confirm that likelihood? Some door-knocking at apartments in the immediate vicinity might be in order. And where did she buy those groceries? Probably nearby—she was walking. Let's check grocers in the immediate vicinity and ask the managers and clerks. Even if they don't recognize her, maybe they will let us post a notice that this lady will see next time she's in.

3. And what about that poodle? Those dogs usually are groomed pretty regularly at dog parlors. Maybe a check with parlors in the vicinity of the scene might yield some results. And what about veterinarians?

4. Failing all that, we might do a surveillance of the scene and neighborhood at the same time of day as the accident. After all, dog owners usually walk their pets on a pretty routine basis.

5. Can you come up with other ideas to help locate this witness?

6. Assume further that Omi Gosh told you there was a yellow cab parked just down the street from where the hit and run occurred and she remembers the cab pulling out sort of fast right after the collision almost like it was going after the hit and run car. How would you go about locating the cabbie?

7. Assume further that Omi Gosh told you that a big guy wearing jeans and a tank top who had a tattoo of an eagle on his right arm took pictures of the hit and run car driving away. He had a pretty nice-looking camera strapped over his neck and just started clicking away. How would you go about locating this photographer?

8. Assume further that Keepda Peace told you that while he was at the scene, a Hispanic man approached him and told Keepda Peace he saw the whole thing. Keepda Peace told him to wait around but the man didn't. All Keepda Peace can recall is that the man wore a blue work shirt with the name Julio's Plumbing sewn onto a white oval attached to the shirt pocket. How would you go about locating this witness?

2. Sources of information for locating the missing witness

The sources we use to locate the missing witness can be logically divided into people sources, organizational sources, and documentary sources.

a. People sources

As already mentioned, everyone has past and present relatives, friends, neighbors, co-workers, supervisors, teachers, fellow students, former landlords, mail carriers, local merchants, acquaintances, and business contacts that can tell us something about them. When we start with what we know and then play the *This Is Your Life* game, we begin to think of other **people** who might lead us to the person we need to find. We did this with the older lady walking the apricot poodle in Hypothetical 14-2. We considered who might live near where she lives, who might have sold her groceries, who might groom her pet, and what veterinarian might treat her pet. What people sources did you plan to contact to locate the other missing witnesses in Hypothetical 14-2?

b. Organizational sources

At some time during our lives, we are all members of different public and private **organizations**. As a student at the school where you are studying this material, you are part of an organization and will leave a trail of people and records behind you. If you work, you are part of the employer's organization and will leave a people and records trail behind. Just think of all the organizations that people might be part of and that can become sources by which to locate them: schools, employers, clubs, religious organizations, unions, professional and trade associations, sports teams, political parties, the military, homeowners or neighborhood associations, service organizations, charitable groups, etc. Can you add to the list? What organizations did you think to check to locate the witnesses in Hypothetical 14-2?

Many organizations will provide membership information. Many have written membership directories going back years that can be accessed. Today many of them (e.g., school alumni directories) maintain Web sites with membership information on them. (See Appendix B, Resources for the Investigator, for a list of resources available to help identify the numerous clubs and professional associations to which people might belong.)

c. Documentary sources

People not only leave people trails, they leave paper trails or records trails. There are a number of public and private records and private documentary sources that can help us locate people when we have the person's name. The student should consider this section in conjunction with Chapters 16 through 18 in which various sources of information from public (local, state, and federal governments) and private sources, as well as procedures for accessing that information, are discussed in much greater detail. For that reason the following list is a representative sampling only of the many **documentary sources** that may be available for locating missing persons.

1. The telephone book.   Access the book itself or call Directory Assistance, but don't forget this basic resource. Out-of-date phone books can also be useful in locating a person who was once listed but currently is not. The local library will typically have current books for surrounding communities (and maybe many more) but it is a good idea for the law office to keep out-of-date books for later use.

2. City/county directories.   Many counties and municipalities publish **directories** that provide information about individuals and businesses cross-referenced to phone numbers, addresses, and employment information. As with telephone books, it is a good idea for the investigator to keep out-of-date directories. They may be useful to pick up the trail of someone who was once present in the community but has been gone for some time or who has moved or changed jobs within the community. Sometimes, a city/county directory will contain residential phone numbers that are unlisted.

3. Court records.   Not only can the court clerks tell us who has sued whom in the past or who has been charged with a crime, but the court files themselves often prove a treasure trove of information about people. Consider the kind of information that gets put in a court file during a lawsuit—pleadings containing much factual information, sworn answers to interrogatories, transcripts of sworn deposition testimony, briefs and motions containing factual allegations and the affidavits of witnesses, not to mention judgment and lien dockets. (See Chapters 3 through 5.)

4. Property and tax records.   Local and state government offices maintain detailed records regarding the purchase and sale of real property, the pledging of real and personal property as security for loans, and the payment of real and personal property taxes. All this information is recorded or filed with detailed information about the owners, their addresses, etc.

Thanks to the computerization of records, in many communities today just punching in a name or property address can disclose information regarding land transactions or taxes paid that used to take hours to locate by searching through mountains of dusty books.

5. Voter registration records.   These records, usually maintained at the city or county level, may contain basic biographical information such as full name, date of birth, current (and possibly former) residence, etc., and are generally accessible to the investigator.

6. Car registration and driver's license information.   If automobiles have to be registered with the local government there may be a searchable record in the office that maintains those records. If the information is kept by the state government only, check your state rules regarding access to such information. Driver's license and driving record information is usually maintained at the state level and accessibility is determined by state rules (see extended discussion of such records in Chapter 17 on accessing state and local records).

7. Marriage licenses and birth certificates.   In most states, marriage licenses are on file with the county court and are searchable by the public. Birth certificates may be maintained locally and with the state department of vital statistics.

8. The post office.   Forwarding addresses are kept for six months to a year by the post office as standard procedure. For privacy reasons, the post office no longer provides forwarding address information on request as to individuals or families who have moved, except to process servers or pursuant to court order. It will provide such information for businesses or private institutions in response to a written request directed to the appropriate postmaster and payment of a nominal fee, currently $3.

However, during the time that the mail forwarding order is in effect, the investigator may send a letter to the missing person at the old address and allow the post office to forward it. Or, the investigator can send a letter to the old address with instructions on the envelope: "DO NOT FORWARD. ADDRESS CORRECTION REQUESTED," and the postmaster will provide the forwarding address for a nominal fee.

Post office personnel may also be a helpful source of information about people and neighborhoods. Think what your mail tells the person who delivers it about you! (See LBD 14-4.)

Any investigation into post office rules and procedures should begin with a review of the U.S. Postal Service's home page at www.usps.gov.

9. The Social Security Administration (SSA).   The SSA will not disclose the social security number of an individual. Nor will it disclose personal information on another person whose social security number you may have. However, the SSA will forward a letter to the missing person on behalf of the person seeking him if all three of the following conditions are satisfied:

- The missing person would want to know about the contents of the letter.
- The SSA could reasonably be expected to have a valid mailing address.
- All other means of contacting the person have failed.

Of course, the letter is sent without disclosing the address to the sender.

Having the social security number of the person you are seeking can be a valuable tool. Many public and private records that are accessible to the investigator (see Chapters 16 through 18) are keyed to the social security number.

Moreover, when a person really does "disappear," they frequently go back to the state where they were born or where they grew up—which often can be determined by their social security number. The first three digits in everyone's social security number designate the state in which the card was issued. Most persons currently over 20 years of age probably obtained their social security number in the state where they were living when they first went to work, around 14 to 18 years of age. A few years ago, however, the federal tax laws were changed to require that children be assigned a social security number if they are to be claimed as a dependent (and a deduction) on the tax return of a parent or guardian. So most people probably had a social security number assigned to them in the state where they were living as a child.

EXAMPLE

If you are searching for a missing person whom you know to be 45 years old and who has a social security number beginning with the numbers 301, you know that the person was living in the state of Ohio when that number was issued because that is one of the numbers (268–302) assigned to Ohio. You can also consider that the number was probably assigned to him when he was a teenager or young adult going to work for the first time. All of this information can provide you valuable leads to locating the missing person who may have returned to Ohio or left a trail of records there, which can be picked up and traced.

Appendix B, Resources for the Investigator, sets out the three-digit prefix numbers assigned to each state and the District of Columbia by the SSA.

10. Utility company records. People living in a community will need water, electricity, a phone, and, of course, cable TV! Subscribing to these services produces records—a paper trail that can be searched by the investigator.

11. Business license records. It is typically the local government (as opposed to state or federal government) that issues business permits or licenses. These records are generally available for inspection to the public and can reveal a great deal more than biographical data about a person. Sometimes work history, financial data, and even credit information may be available here.

12. State licensing agencies. In every state there are numerous trades and professions that can be practiced only with a license issued by the state. Licensing information is generally available for inspection by the public and must be kept current by the licensed person.

13. The board of education. Records of who was enrolled at a particular school at a particular time, as well as who was employed to teach may be available here.

14. Newspaper indexes. Most newspapers will make back issues available for inspection to the public. Check obituary pages, birth announcements, local sports reports, local interest stories, community activities, organizational news, or employment announcements for the period the person was present in the community. Many public libraries and local colleges also keep back issues of area newspapers.

d. Social networking and search engine Web sites

Have any old friends found you by searching on Facebook or LinkedIn yet? By coming across your tweets? By performing a search on Google, Bing, or Yahoo? It is now possible to perform sophisticated people and business searches via social networking sites and Internet search engines. Most popular search engines such as Google, Yahoo, and Bing provide specific people and business search tools or index sites that do. The Internet also provides telephone and address directories; reverse phone, address, and e-mail directories; and map and directional services once an address has been located. Information regarding the whereabouts of a missing witness may also be accessible on the social networking sites mentioned earlier. (See Appendix B for a comprehensive listing of social networking sites and other resources for performing people and business searches, and see LBDs 14-6 through 14-9.)

e. People search database vendors

There are various commercial **database vendors** that make people search libraries available for subscribers. **Westlaw** and **LexisNexis** are two of the better known and widely used vendors. These vendors compile information from numerous sources, public and private, and make it available to subscribers for searches. For example, the new PeopleMap library on Westlaw allows you to search and cross-reference a network of literally billions of federal, state, and local public records from recorded mortgages, to criminal records, to fishing or hunting licenses, to birth and death certificates. Lexis does much the same with its FINDER:ALLFND and EZFIND databases. An excellent source of people searching tools can be found on the Finding People page of The Virtual Chase (www.virtual chase.com/topics/people_finder_index.shtml). (See Appendix B for a comprehensive listing of database vendors and information on how to contact them.)

f. Determining if someone has died

To see if the person you are searching for is deceased, check the obituaries of relevant newspapers, many of which are available online. Or access the vital records department of your state using the National Center for Health Statistics' Where to Write for Vital Records site at www.cdc.gov/nchs/w2w.htm. Alternatively, you can check the Social Security Death Index at www.ntis.gov/products/ssa-dmf.aspx, also searchable at the popular Ancestory.com site at http://search.ancestry.- com/search/db.aspx?dbid=3693. If you have the social security number of the person, you can run it through the SSN Validator (www.ssnvalida- tor.com/pages/search.aspx), or check Westlaw's OBITPAGE library, or Lexis/Nexis's FINDER:DCEASE or PEOPLE:OBITS libraries.

g. Locating famous people

When searching for the famous or infamous, a simple search using one or more search engines may turn up useful information, though its reliability may be in doubt. Lexis/Nexis has its PEOPLE:GALBIO data- base. Dialog, another database vendor, has a useful BioIndex library. The TV show, biography (www.biography.com) posts brief entries about celebrities. Marquis' Who's Who (http://marquiswhoswho.com/online- database) publishes all kinds of directories of notable persons. Copies of international who's who directories are available from NYPL Express (www.nypl.org/express/). For the wealthy, a search on Forbes (www.for- bes.com/) may prove enlightening.

h. Locating former employees

Business data base companies like Accurint (www.accurint.com) and ZoomInfo (www.zoominfo.com) maintain records regarding the employ- ment history of employees of many companies.

i. *Locating current or former members of the military*

The Defense Manpower Data Center (www.fedstats.gov/key_stats/index.php?id=DMDC) provides data on those currently serving in the military. The investigator can also submit an information request for an **Affidavit of Military Status** from the Department of Defense (see www.militarysearch.org/). To determine if someone has ever served in the military you can use the **Buddy Finder** feature of Military.com (www.military.com) or by filing a form SF-180 request with the National Personnel Records Center (www.archives.gov/st-louis/military-personnel/).

j. *Locating current or former prison inmates*

The National Bureau of Prisons (www.bop.gov/) maintains an Inmate Locator for current prisoners and those released since 1982. Analogous information is normally available from the respective state departments of correction, links to which are available at www.corrections.com/links/show/30. Many states now post **inmate locator information** online (see links at www.corrections.com/links/show?Cat=20). Many more operate **sex offender registries** (see links at www.familywatchdog.us/).

k. *Tracing companies*

There is always the option of utilizing a tracing company to locate the missing witness. These are private businesses, sometimes called **skip-tracing companies**, that will help locate people for a fee. Typically, the company is provided with all the information you have available about the person sought and it then uses its resources, including online computer resources that cater to these companies, to locate the person. See Appendix B for contact information for some of the better-known tracing companies.

l. *Genealogical services*

When locating a relative of the missing person would help or when trying to confirm whether the missing person is still living, a good genealogical service can be of assistance. The National Archives and Records Administration (online at www.archives.gov) maintains genealogical records in Washington and at the 11 National Archives branches around the country (see Appendix B for the location of NARA branch offices).

The ancestory.com site (www.ancestory.com) provides searches using Census, immigration, military, and vital records for subscribers. Some public or college libraries may provide free access to ancestory.com. The Church of Jesus Christ of Latter Day Saints (LDS) has gathered what is probably the best genealogical database in the world through its Family History Library in Salt Lake City, Utah. This data is now being made available by the LDS on the Internet for no charge at www.familysearch.org. LDS also operates numerous computerized Family History Centers around the country, which can provide you assistance in accessing these records. (See Appendix B for information on locating and contacting the LDS Family History Library and the Family History Center nearest you.)

m. Book resources for people searches.

Finally, there are a number of good books devoted to assisting the investigator in locating missing witnesses. Information on several of these is also set forth in Appendix B.

Chapter Summary and Conclusion

There are numerous sources for identifying witnesses to an event, both people sources and documentary or records sources. The legal professional must be knowledgeable and creative in identifying people who may know. Often witnesses that have been identified are missing and must be located. Playing, "This is Your Life," for the missing witness can result in thinking of numerous sources able to assist in locating that witness. Those sources may be people sources, organizational sources, or documentary sources. The Internet now has quite sophisticated people search engines, and there are numerous fee-based people locator services as well.

One type of witness that attorneys routinely work with and against is the expert witness. In Chapter 15 we will consider that special witness.

Review Questions

1. List eight "people sources" for identifying fact witnesses in a case.
2. List eight "documentary sources" for identifying fact witnesses in a case.
3. What does *This is Your Life* have to do with legal investigation?
4. Name as many "people sources" as you can think of that might be consulted to locate a missing witness.
5. Name as many "organizational sources" as you can think of that might be consulted to locate a missing witness.
6. Name as many "documentary sources" as you can think of that might be consulted to locate a missing witness.
7. What kind of information do city/county directories provide?
8. What is a "data base vendor"? How many can you name?
9. What is a "tracing company" and how can they assist in a legal investigation?
10. What do genealogical services have to do with a legal investigation?

KEY WORDS AND PHRASES TO REMEMBER

accident report
Affidavit of Military Status
Bebo
BlackPlanet
Blog

Buddy Finder
business records
CafeMom
city/county directory
classmates.com

collaborative journalism
database vendors
documentary sources
educational records
e-harmony
electronic communications
e-mail
employment records
Facebook
Flickr
Google+
Habbo
inmate locator information
investigating officer
ibeatyou
iReport
LexisNexis
Match.com
medical records

MySpace
neighborhood canvass
online social networking
organizational sources
people sources
personal digital assistant (PDA)
Pinterest
sex offender registries
Shizzler
skip-tracing companies
text messages
This Is Your Life
Twitter
Westlaw
Yearbook.com
YouTube
WikiNews
Zinga

LEARN BY DOING

LBD 14-1. Using one of the four Case Studies included in Appendix A and the information outlined below, outline a detailed plan to identify currently unknown witnesses in each case. In your plan, designate each people source and each documentary/records source you intend to check.

   a. Case Study No. 1 (The Rowdy Outlaw Case). We need to identify any witnesses who saw Rowdy Outlaw the night of the murder.

   b. Case Study No. 2 (The Soupspoon Wise Case). We need to identify all witnesses who may have been present at the Red Dog Saloon at the time of the accident.

   c. Case Study No. 3 (The Vidalia Unyon Case). We need to identify all of Greene Unyon's golf partners during the last year.

   d. Case Study No. 4 (The Rocky Road Project). We need to identify all owners and operators of the gas station that sits on one of the parcels our client is interested in.

LBD 14-2. Prepare an advertisement to run in the local paper seeking the witnesses described in LBD 14-1 and asking them to contact you.

LBD 14-3. We have been unable to locate the following witnesses and would like to interview them. Based on what we currently know, prepare a memorandum summarizing how you would suggest we go about locating these persons.

   a. Georgette B. Good in the Rowdy Outlaw Case (Case Study No. 1).

   b. Tanya Trucker in the Red Dog Saloon Case (Case Study No. 2).

    c. The anonymous caller in the Vidalia Unyon Case (Case Study No. 3).

    d. The heirs of farmer Edward Dig Deep in the Rocky Road Project (Case Study No. 4).

LBD 14-4. How might someone in another part of the country go about finding you if they had only your name and the name of the community you lived in 15 years ago? Play *This Is Your Life* for yourself. Make a list of all the sources—people sources, organizational sources, and documentary or records sources—that might be utilized by an investigator to locate you.

LBD 14-5. Think of someone you haven't seen since childhood but would enjoy visiting with again. Using the people locating resources set out in this chapter and in Appendix B, see if you can locate that person. Keep a record of what resources you use to accomplish this task.

LBDs 14-6 through 14-9 are accessible on the Author Updates link to the text Web site at www.aspenparalegaled.com/books/parsons_investigating/default.asp.

Chapter 15
Working with Expert Witnesses

CHAPTER OBJECTIVES

In this chapter we will consider in detail the expert witness. You will learn:

- Why attorneys use expert witnesses.
- Where to locate qualified experts.
- How to evaluate the resume of an expert.
- How to assist the supervising attorney in preparing to cross examine an opposing expert witness.
- How to work effectively with an expert.

A. Who Experts Are and Why Attorneys Use Them

1. The definition of an expert

Rule 702 of the Federal Rules of Evidence (accessible online at www.law.cornell.edu/rules/fre/) defines an expert witness as:

> a witness who is qualified as an expert by knowledge, skill, experience, training, or education may testify in the form of an opinion or otherwise.

The rule allows an expert witness to testify if:

- the expert's scientific, technical, or other specialized knowledge will help the trier of fact to understand the evidence or to determine a fact in issue;
- the testimony is based on sufficient facts or data;
- the testimony is the product of reliable principles and methods; and the expert has reliably applied the principles and methods to the facts of the case.

2. Distinguishing consulting experts from testifying experts

As we have seen in Chapter 4, for purposes of formal discovery, Rule 26(b)(4) of the Federal Rules of Civil Procedure distinguishes between experts who merely consult with attorneys without testifying at trial (the **consulting expert**), and experts who not only consult but who testify as expert witnesses at trial (the **testifying expert**).

Generally, in a civil case, a party may discover the identity of experts the opposing party intends to offer as witnesses at trial as well as the substance of the facts and opinions to which they are expected to testify. But if an expert is retained by a party only to consult with the attorney and not to testify, the opposing party may not discover either the identity of the consulting expert or the facts known or opinions held by such expert except upon a showing that it is "impracticable" for the party seeking the discovery to obtain the facts and opinions on the same subject by other means.

Once a testifying expert has been disclosed, the opposing party may take the pretrial deposition of that expert. Per FRCP 26(a)(2)(B), the testifying expert who is retained or specially employed to provide expert testimony in the case or whose employment with the party calling him to testify regularly involves giving expert testimony must prepare and provide the opposing side with a written report containing the expert's qualifications to give opinions in the field, list of publications over the past ten years, the opinions to be offered, the basis for each such opinion, the facts and data considered in reaching each such opinion, exhibits to be used to summarize or illustrate each such opinion, cases in which the witness has testified as an expert in the past four years, and compensation. Per new FRCP 26(b)(4)(C), an opposing party cannot obtain through discovery drafts of the report or communications between the expert and the counsel who retained the expert other than communications that relate to the expert's compensation or that identify facts or data that the party's attorney provided and that the expert considered in forming the opinions to be expressed or that identify assumptions that the party's attorney provided and that the expert relied on in forming the opinions to be expressed.

In a criminal case (see Chapter 5), discovery of expert testimony is limited to receiving a written summary of the expected testimony of the testifying witness as well as reports or studies the expert may have conducted in the case (FRCrP 16(a)(1)(D) and (E) and (b)(1)(B) and (C)). There is no provision in the FRCrP for the routine pretrial deposition of the opposing party's experts.

3. How attorneys use experts

The distinction between consulting and testifying experts is important for more reasons than the different discovery rules that relate to them. Often, experts will do both consulting and testifying work. But sometimes an expert will do consulting work only. The expert may be outstanding in their field and able to assist the attorney in understanding the technical subject matter involved in the lawsuit. But that same expert may do poorly at explaining things in lay terms to a jury or may do poorly at holding up under aggressive cross-examination. So that expert, who has rendered a valuable service to the attorney as a consultant, will not testify. Another expert, more experienced and with trial-related skills, will do so instead.

Today, attorneys make regular and frequent use of experts for both consulting and testifying in all kinds of matters. For example, in the Rowdy Outlaw case (Case Study No. 1 in Appendix A), the prosecution may anticipate using:

- an expert in guitars to testify that the guitar string found at the scene of the crime was a string that had been on a guitar owned by Rowdy Outlaw;
- a pathologist to testify as to the cause of death;
- a forensic scientist to testify that the defendant's fingerprints were found on items at the scene of the murder; and
- a jury consultant to develop a juror profile and make recommendations regarding jury selection.

In the Soupspoon Wise case (Case Study No. 2 in Appendix A), the plaintiff may anticipate using:

- an accident reconstruction specialist to testify as to how the accident likely occurred;
- the treating physician to testify regarding the injuries (including causation), treatment, disability, and prognosis for Wise;
- a vocational specialist to testify regarding the available job market for Wise in his permanently disabled state and anticipated income levels;
- an economist or other qualified expert to testify regarding the present value of future medical expenses and lost income to be incurred by Wise; and
- a car salesman to testify regarding the value of the totaled vehicle.

In the Vidalia Unyon case (Case Study No. 3 in Appendix A), the attorney for Mrs. Unyon may anticipate using:

- a DNA expert to prove that Greene Unyon is the biological father of the child born to Georgia Peach;
- an accountant, banker, or financial specialist to trace the bank accounts and financial transactions of Greene Unyon; and
- a real estate appraiser to testify regarding the value of the real property at issue.

In the Rocky Road project (Case Study No. 4 in Appendix A), the attorneys for Rocky Road, Inc., may anticipate using:

- a real estate appraiser to offer an opinion regarding the value of the parcels;
- a surveyor to survey one or more of the parcels to determine their actual size; and
- a water or soil engineer to test the water and soil for contamination.

In many types of civil cases, the use of experts at trial is not just optional, it is necessary in order for the party to establish all the elements of its case.

EXAMPLE

In a personal injury case based on a negligence theory the plaintiff must present proof to establish all four elements of a negligence claim:

1. The defendant owed plaintiff a duty of care.
2. The defendant breached that duty of care by failing to act as a reasonable person would under the circumstances.
3. The breach of duty by defendant was the actual and proximate (foreseeable) cause of the injuries sustained by plaintiff.
4. The plaintiff has sustained such injuries.

In many negligence cases it is necessary to have expert proof to establish the third and fourth elements of the cause of action. Assume the case involves an automobile collision in which the plaintiff suffered permanent loss of use of the right leg. The plaintiff herself can testify about the accident and the problems she has with her leg, but she is not a qualified expert to testify concerning the medical treatment she will need in the future, or that her leg will never get better, or the extent to which she has lost the use of that leg (50 percent or 20 percent, etc.). And that's true even though it's her leg! Her attorney will have to call a qualified expert—probably the treating physician—to testify concerning his professional opinion on these matters to make out the fourth element of the cause of action. And it will probably be that same expert who will offer the necessary opinion that the injuries sustained by the plaintiff were in fact caused (the third element of the cause of action) by the automobile collision.

B.   Locating Qualified Expert Witnesses

The legal professional may be called on by the supervising attorney to help locate an expert to assist in consulting and/or testifying in a case. We need to know where to go to locate qualified experts. Fortunately, there are a number of sources for the legal professional. Consult Appendix B, Resources for the Investigator, which contains comprehensive sources of information for locating experts.

SLEUTH ON THE LOOSE

To learn more about the resources available from Service Corps of Retired Executives, including the availability of such retired workers to serve as consulting experts, access the Small Business Administration Web site at www.sba.gov.

1. Attorneys or paralegals in the office

Attorneys usually keep files on experts they have used successfully in the past or who have been recommended to them by others. Thus the supervising attorney or other attorneys in the office may be able to refer you to someone qualified. Experienced paralegals also maintain files on experts they have worked with. So the first source to turn to may be other people in your office.

2. Other attorneys or paralegals in the area

Consider who you know in your community that you might call for a reference to a good expert: attorneys in town who have worked on the kind of case you have or paralegals with experience. Be sure to get the supervising attorney's okay before you make those calls.

3. Attorneys or paralegals in other parts of the country

If you learn of a case from any part of the country similar to the one you are working on (as you may do in your legal research) in which a favorable outcome was obtained, contact the attorney who worked on that case or a paralegal in that office and ask for the name of the expert they used, and for a recommendation regarding the expert.

4. Lawyer organizations

Many lawyers' groups maintain lists of experts available for consulting and/or testifying work. Two examples of nationwide groups that do so are the American Association for Justice (AAJ), formerly the Association of Trial Lawyers of America), an organization for plaintiffs' attorneys, and the Defense Research Institute (DRI), an organization for defense counsel. Both AAJ and DRI maintain expert witness data banks that may be searched by their members, as well as brief banks, articles, members' forums, and links to state and local organizations that may be utilized to locate potential experts. Many state and local bar associations maintain expert witness lists as well. (See Appendix B for information on how to contact AAJ and DRI and other national organizations maintaining expert witness databases.)

5. Referral companies

There are private businesses that connect attorneys with needed experts. One of the best known is Technical Advisory Service for Attorneys (**TASA**). TASA maintains extensive lists of experts who agree to allow TASA to recommend them to inquiring attorneys. If the attorney retains the expert, the fee for the expert is paid to TASA, which takes its contractual percentage as a fee and passes along the balance to the expert. A leading service for locating medical experts is Technical Assistance Bureau (**TAB**) in Washington, D.C. (See Appendix B for details on how to contact TASA and TAB.)

SL EUTH ON THE LOOSE

Identify a physician you want to learn more about then access the American Medical Association's Physician Select Web site at www.ama-assn.org. Type in the physician's name and see what information you can obtain concerning that physician.

6. Directories

There are numerous directories of experts in different fields. A good example is *Lawyers Desk Reference*, which lists experts by category. The *American Jurisprudence Desk Book* is a helpful source for experts. Martindale-Hubbell maintains a state-by-state consultant service as well. A leading source book for experts used by news media and talk shows is the *Yearbook of Experts, Authorities & Spokespersons*. (See Appendix B for more information on these directories.)

7. Professional, technical, and trade organizations

These organizations frequently provide the service of recommending their members who wish to work as experts to inquiring attorneys. For example, if you have a construction lawsuit and are looking for an expert with experience in commercial construction, contact your local builders' association; if you need a realtor for that lawsuit, contact your local or state realtor's association; if you need an experienced educator, contact the local school board or the National Education Association; or if you need an expert plumber, contact the union that plumbers belong to in your area.

8. Private businesses

Many private companies and firms (accountants, engineers, etc.) have employees who will serve as experts for attorneys. Typically the company or firm receives all or a portion of the fee.

9. Colleges and universities

Colleges and universities are excellent sources for experts. Contact the head of the relevant department within the college or university and ask about faculty (or retired faculty) who serve or who might be interested in serving as an expert. For example, if you are looking for an economist, contact the economics department; if you are looking for an accountant, contact the accounting or business department; or if you are looking for an engineer, contact the school of engineering. A quick look at the current catalog for the college or university will advise you of how the school is organized into various departments. Also, many colleges and universities now maintain Web sites, which provide online faculty biographies.

10. Government agencies

Government agencies or departments, whether federal or state, can sometimes refer you to retired employees who perform consulting/testifying services for attorneys.

11. Literature in the field of expertise

Don't forget to check the current literature in the field of expertise you need. Get the names of authors of notable books or recent articles in the field and contact them. If they do not wish to help you, they likely can refer you to someone who does.

12. Other experts

Other experts can refer us to new experts. If the expert your supervising attorney has been using retires, ask him to refer you to someone. Or if you contact one expert who does not wish to help, ask that expert for references.

Be sure to start and maintain your own file of experts with whom you have worked. Some experts may be used regularly by the supervising attorney but others may be used only on rare occasions. It is efficient and helpful to be able to check your own file and come up with the name of that expert who did so well for a client five or ten years ago.

13. The Internet

There are numerous resources available on the Internet for locating experts in many fields. See Appendix B for a comprehensive listing of Web sites useful for this purpose.

C. ▶ Evaluating the Expert

An expert may look good on paper—the resume—but that doesn't mean he can be effective or successful. Unfortunately, you cannot always trust the information set out in the resume to be completely reliable.

1. Why we evaluate experts

SLEUTH ON THE LOOSE

Identify a physician you want to learn more about then go to the Web site of the Federation of State Medical Boards at www.fsmb.org to see what you can learn concerning the status of the physician's medical license and whether he or she has ever been professionally disciplined.

There are two situations in which we evaluate experts:

- When we are considering using an expert for the first time
- When an expert will testify for the opposing party

2. The expert's resume

The basic tool we use to evaluate an expert is the expert's **resume**, sometimes referred to as a **biography** (or "bio" for short) or as a **curriculum vitae** (or "CV" for short). An example of an expert's resume is set out in Illustration 15-1.

3. How to evaluate an expert

SLEUTH ON THE LOOSE

Pick a medical specialty then access www.guideline.gov to check for practice guidelines for practitioners in that specialty.

There are a number of things we can do to evaluate an expert.

a. Look for education, training, and work experience

Review the resume carefully to determine if the expert has the requisite expertise based on education, training, work experience, and other objective indicators. Although no one factor is ever determinative to a decision about an expert, in general, the more education the expert has the better qualified they are. The same is true with longer and more varied work experience. We also look for other positives such as professional licenses, certifications and affiliations, teaching experience, consulting experience, and authorship—the publication of books and articles in the field.

b. Look at the specific area of expertise

Review the resume carefully to determine if the expert has the requisite expertise in the specific field needed.

EXAMPLE

A physician may be a highly qualified pediatrician, but if the case involves alleged malpractice in heart surgery performed on a baby, we are really looking for a well-qualified pediatric cardiopulmonary surgeon.

Illustration 15-1 EXPERT'S RESUME

RUSS T. NAIL
112 Dunwoody Lane,
Atlanta, Georgia 66332
(919) 444-1290 (H)
(919) 444-1356 (W)
(919) 444-9876 (FAX)
e-mail: rtnail@waxnet.com

EDUCATION:
Ph.D. (Industrial Engineering) Yourstate Institute of Technology, 1984
M.S. (Electrical Engineering) Capital City University, 1982
B.S. (Mechanical Engineering) Capital City University, 1976

EXPERIENCE:
2000–present   Professor, Industrial Engineering, State University (Head of the Department of Industrial Engineering since 2005)
1996–2000   Associate Professor, Industrial and Mechanical Engineering, Western University
1989–1997   Hammer, Saw & Nail, Consulting Engineers, Capital City, Yourstate
1984–1989   Proctor & Proctor Corporation, Assistant Planning Engineer
1976–1981   U.S. Army, Corps of Engineers

REGISTRATIONS:
Registered Professional Engineer in Yourstate since 1984 (License No. 234156)
Licensed Master Electrician

PROFESSIONAL MEMBERSHIPS:
American Society of Safety Engineers (ASSE)
Institute of Industrial Engineers (IIE)
Human Factors Society
American Society of Engineering Education
American Society of Testing and Materials
       (Member, Committee E-32 on Housing Testing Evaluation)
       (Member, Committee E-06 on Construction Materials)
Institute of Electrical and Electronic Engineers (IEEE)

CONSULTING:
Human Factors Analysis of U.S. Soldier Under Stress in Conflict Involving Chemical Weapons, for U.S. Army, 1993–1994
Safety Analysis of Lightweight Plastic Furniture, for American Association of Furniture Manufacturers, 1997
Product Strength Analysis, for Proctor & Proctor, 2000 and 2001
Have worked as case consultant for attorneys in more than 50 cases in 13 different states
Have testified as expert in more than 20 cases

PUBLICATIONS:
Why Geese Fly But Turkeys Can't, Doctoral Dissertation, Yourstate Institute of Technology, May 1984
Stress Experienced by Males in War and Shopping: A Statistical Analysis, International Symposium on Male Problems, Ontario, Canada, September 1992
Fatigue as a Factor in Industrial Accidents, Journal of American Industrial Engineering, Vol. XIII, No. 2, July 2002
The Role of the Computer in Electrical Engineering: A Glimpse into the Future, The Electrical Engineer, Vol. III, No. 1, September 2007
The Basics of Mechanical Engineering, College Technical Publishing, Inc., 2013 (co-authored with Heavy Hammer)

c. Verify information on the resume

1. Why it is important to verify information on the resume. We check the educational history, work experience, and publications references on the resume to ensure that they are accurate and complete. Of course, people do sometimes make honest mistakes on their resume. But it is a sad commentary on our society that some people, even some highly qualified people, fudge their resumes by putting inaccurate, exaggerated, or incomplete information on them. (In doing your own resume, always resist that urge!)

Sometimes the inaccuracy is blatant. There was an actual case where an expert testified at a trial and claimed under oath to have a Ph.D. from a school that it turned out had never had him registered as a student. But usually the errors are minor—the person identifies himself as the sole author of an article that was actually co-written with another. Or the person misstates his job title at a prior place of employment. These may appear to be small errors, but they can be devastating to the credibility of the expert if discovered and exposed by opposing counsel.

Trial attorneys know that one way they can destroy the credibility of the opposing party's expert at trial is to demonstrate that there is some inaccuracy in the resume. Whether honest mistake or dishonesty, it is crushing. So we have to be careful to check the data given on the resume of our own experts the first time we use them and we always check on the expert named by the opposing party.

2. How to verify an expert's credentials. If you are checking on a person's educational background, a phone call or letter to the registrar or other student records custodian of the schools listed is appropriate. Most schools will disclose basic registration and degree information on former students (see Chapter 18). If you are checking on a person's work background, a phone call or letter to the former employer is appropriate, asking only that the dates of employment and job titles be confirmed.

If the expert is licensed to practice his trade or profession, check with the state licensing board or agency (see Chapter 17) to confirm the dates of licensure and to learn of any disciplinary actions. Learn of any malpractice suits filed against the expert by searching the defendant's index in the clerk's offices of the various courts in the expert's state (see Chapters 16 and 17).

Listed publications can be checked by asking the expert to provide a hard copy of the book or article or by locating the publication yourself. Your public library may have a comprehensive catalog of publications. If not, try the library of the nearest college or university. Papers written to fulfill the requirements for masters or doctorate degrees (referred to usually as a **thesis** or **dissertation**) are kept on file by the college or university that granted the degree. You can check with the campus librarian or the head of the department of the expert's field.

d. Check the expert's online presence

Many experts have their own Web sites or the company or university they work for has one. The expert may have a page on Facebook or MySpace, or may operate or contribute to blogs. Compare information these sources provide about the expert with the information on his resume. Clarify any contradictions.

e. Review the expert's publications

Review publications of the expert for consistency of opinion. Many experts list publications on their resume. Others will volunteer a list. For some others, we have to run the publications down through author/publications indexes available in the reference section of the library.

Another trap an expert can fall into is to formulate an opinion for an attorney in a pending case and then have the attorney for the opposing party confront the expert with something contradictory he wrote years earlier in a book or article. For that reason we have to be careful to either check earlier writings of the expert to be sure there is no potential conflict or to have the expert review his own prior writings.

Of course, checking the prior publications of an expert for the opposing party is a standard procedure performed by attorneys who hope to find just such a contradiction. Your supervising attorney may have you check the publications of an expert for the opposing party for that purpose, or may ask his own consulting expert to do so.

This is a time-consuming task, but remember that many technical and scientific publications are available online now. See the Appendix B materials on experts and media sources for resources available to help locate online professional publications.

f. Review publications on which the expert bases his opinions

Any book or article or other publication on which the expert claims to base all or part of his opinion should be reviewed carefully. We want to make sure the publication says what the expert says it does and to determine whether the publication is (or isn't) consistent with the opinion the expert is now expressing. This would include publications by persons other than the expert himself. Experts frequently rely on other experts for their opinions. The attorneys who will be examining the expert on either direct or cross-examination will want to be familiar with those publications.

g. Locate and review prior testimony by the expert

If the expert has testified previously either by deposition, at trial, or by affidavit, locate a copy or transcript of that testimony if possible and review it for consistency with the positions now being taken by the expert. You may locate these in the court file of the prior cases, obtain them from one of the attorneys involved in the prior cases, or ask the expert himself if he has copies or transcripts.

h. Ask for references

Ask the expert to identify other attorneys for whom the expert has consulted or testified and check them. Good experts do not mind giving these references and other attorneys do not mind being asked their opinion of an expert they have previously used. A phone call or a letter to the other attorney will almost always produce a cooperative response. Illustration 15-2 sets out typical questions to be asked of attorney references concerning an expert being investigated.

Illustration 15-2   QUESTIONS TO ASK ATTORNEY REFERENCES CONCERNING AN EXPERT WITNESS

1. Was the expert truly knowledgeable in her field?
2. Was the expert able to communicate effectively with laypersons, including the judge and jury, or did the expert confuse or turn off listeners with too much technical jargon?
3. Was the expert cooperative and easy to work with?
4. Did the expert get things done on time and meet promised deadlines?
5. How well did the expert do in testifying?
6. Did the expert communicate effectively with the jury?
7. Did the jury like/trust/believe the expert?
8. How well did the expert stand up under cross-examination?
9. What result did you obtain from the case and to what extent was the expert responsible for that result?

i. Interview the expert

Interview the expert, in person if possible, but by phone if necessary. The supervising attorney in a case will typically handle this interview, but may want an assisting legal professional to help prepare for it or to participate. In the initial interview, discuss the case only generally without disclosing any details or privileged information. Using your communication skills (see Chapter 8), form an opinion regarding the expert's intelligence, competence, common sense (some highly educated people lack it), attitude for loyalty and cooperation, and credibility. If you handle the expert interview, pass this information along to the supervising attorney.

HYPOTHETICAL 15-1

Assume that you are assisting an attorney who has agreed to handle a products liability case involving an automobile that allegedly self-accelerated. In other words, it unexpectedly accelerated when the driver's foot was not on the gas pedal and crashed, causing the driver serious injuries. The attorney is searching for a mechanical engineer to assist in consulting with him on the case and possibly to testify as well. The resume of Russ T. Nail in Illustration 15-1 is one that you have obtained. Review that resume.

1. Looking at the educational credentials of Russ T. Nail, does he appear to be qualified to consult on this type of case? Are his degrees in the specific areas where expertise is required for this case?
2. Is Russ T. Nail's work experience varied, and do you see that as a strength or weakness?
3. Regarding the professional licenses and affiliations of Russ T. Nail, does he appear qualified to consult on this case?
4. Do the consulting history and publications of Russ T. Nail suggest he has expertise in the specific area involved in this case?
5. What questions might you want to ask Russ T. Nail to get a better idea of his expertise for this assignment?
6. If Russ T. Nail was identified to you as an expert expected to testify for the defendant in this case, what specific steps would you take to do a background check on him?

D.   Working Successfully with Expert Witnesses

The legal professional may have several duties in connection with the expert's work on a client's case. Illustration 15-3 contains a list of typical duties undertaken by the assisting legal professional in connection with expert witnesses.

In many cases the assisting legal professional may become the expert's primary contact in the office and spend more time working with him than anyone else. It is therefore critical for that legal professional to know how to work successfully with experts.

1. Obtain the expert's fee schedule early

Experts typically charge for their services on an hourly basis. Some charge more for deposition or in-court time (e.g., $150 per hour for consulting and $300 per hour for testifying). If so, ask which rate they charge for preparing to testify. Some experts charge for their travel time as well as expenses. Often they will ask for a retainer to be paid in advance. You need to find out how much that will be. Some will bill monthly and expect prompt payment; others will bill at the end of the case. Ask what the expert charges for mileage by car and for copying costs; there is typically a flat rate (e.g., 40 cents a mile for travel by car and 25 cents a page for copying). You should collect all fee-related information early and pass it on to the supervising attorney so an informed decision can be made.

Don't be shy about asking an expert about fees. It is just business and we do not want any misunderstandings or hard feelings to arise later that might interfere with the case.

Illustration 15-3   TYPICAL DUTIES OF THE ASSISTING LEGAL PROFESSIONAL IN CONNECTION WITH EXPERT WITNESSES

1.   Identifying a potential expert to work with on the case as a consulting and/or testifying expert.

2.   Evaluating a potential expert by obtaining and reviewing the expert's resume, interviewing the expert, and by checking the background of experts identified by opposing parties.

3.   Serving as the contact person between the law office and the expert, obtaining and forwarding information for the expert's review.

4.   Inspecting the scene or conducting tests to support the expert's conclusions.

5.   Drafting interrogatory answers involving the expert's opinions and the factual basis for the opinions.

6.   Drafting interrogatory questions designed to elicit information regarding experts to be used by opposing parties.

7.   Arranging the discovery deposition of the expert.

8.   Preparing the expert for deposition or trial testimony.

9.   Summarizing or indexing the deposition testimony of the expert.

10.   Preparing the required expert report under Rule 26(a)(2)(B) of the Federal Rules of Civil Procedure or in reviewing the Rule 26(a)(2)(B) report submitted by the expert for an opposing party.

2. Be sure the expert does not have a conflict of interest

In the initial conversation with the expert tell the expert enough about the case and the parties so you and the expert can determine that there are no conflicts of interest. For example, you want to make sure the expert has not already been contacted by a potential adverse party or isn't working on another matter for the adverse party.

3. Become familiar with technical terms and concepts in the expert's field

The legal professional must learn to speak the expert's language.

How do you acquire this knowledge and information? A trip to the library or bookstore may be in order to check out or purchase books or to review articles that will get you started. A few excursions onto the Internet may enable you to locate helpful information, too. Don't hesitate to ask the expert for help in learning the basics of terminology, concepts, and procedures in the field. But however you do it, it is important to be able to converse with the expert and understand the technical or trade terms the expert uses.

EXAMPLE

If you are going to be working with an electrical engineer in an electrocution case you will need to become familiar with the terminology and concepts that the expert will be using to formulate his opinions—watts, volts, conductivity, arcing, grounding, etc. If you are going to be working with an economist, you will need to become familiar with inflation rates, prime interest rates, points, discounting, capitalization formulas, etc. If you are going to be working with an appraiser in a land dispute case, you will need to become familiar with comparative sales, income flow, distress sale, arms'-length transactions, etc. If you are going to be working with a medical expert in a malpractice case, you will need to become familiar with the medical terminology for the specialty involved, with the body parts and systems affected, with the medications involved, and with the relevant medical procedures involved.

4. Do not identify the expert in discovery until the decision has been made to use him for testimony

Experts are usually retained early on in a case to consult with the attorney. It may be expected that they will eventually testify as well but that decision is typically not finalized until later in the litigation. Interrogatories asking about the identity of experts who will be testifying may be served prior to that final decision being made.

Care must be taken to avoid identifying your expert(s) to the opposing party as anticipated witnesses until that decision has been made. Care must also be taken to supplement your interrogatory answers promptly to provide that information as soon as the decision has been made that the expert will testify. Illustration 15-4 sets forth a typical expert witness interrogatory and appropriate answer prior to the decision of whether a consulting expert will testify.

Illustration 15-4   SAMPLE EXPERT WITNESS INTERROGATORY AND ANSWER

Interrogatory: Identify each and every expert whom you anticipate will testify at trial in this cause and for each one identified state:

a. each and every opinion they will offer at trial;

b. the factual and circumstantial basis for each such opinion; and

c. all information that has been considered by the expert in formulating such opinion.

Answer: The plaintiff (defendant) has not yet made a final decision regarding experts who may be expected to testify at trial of this cause. When that decision has been made, the answer to this interrogatory will be supplemented.

---

5. Do not supply the expert with privileged materials

You should assume that during the course of discovery the opposing party is going to ask your testifying expert witness to produce all the information listed in Illustration 15-5, which tracks new FRCP 26(b)(4)(C) summarized earlier in the chapter. And keep in mind that many state rules of procedure do not yet limit discovery of information related to testifying experts as do the federal rules. In those states, discovery may include copies of preliminary or draft reports prepared by the expert and changed after consultation with counsel, all documents of any kind provided to the expert by counsel in connection with the case, and disclosure of all written or verbal communications between the expert and counsel in any way related to the case. (See LBD 15-5.)

If the expert has been provided materials or information subject to the attorney-client privilege or the attorney work product that fall within the perimeters of discovery permitted by FRCP 26, these privileges may be deemed waived and the opposing party allowed to see and use the materials. Sometimes attorneys will knowingly provide experts with privileged material understanding that the privilege is waived for that material. They will do so because it is necessary for the expert to have the information, and that is a more important concern than preserving the privilege. But that is the decision of the supervising attorney, not the assisting professional. Without the express consent of the supervising attorney, the assisting legal professional should never send an expert any materials or communicate any information containing the attorney's mental impressions concerning the case. Certainly the assisting legal professional should not communicate her own mental impressions concerning the case to the expert. Be sure the supervising attorney reviews *in advance* all of your correspondence to the expert as well as anything you enclose with that correspondence.

This may be a good time to review the trial preparation materials and work product privileges discussed in Section C of Chapter 6, the attorney-client privilege discussed in Section C of Chapter 2, and the dangers of waiver of these privileges discussed in Section F of Chapter 4.

6. Always communicate a neutral picture of the case to the expert

It is critical to the credibility of the expert that the opinions expressed to the trier of fact by the expert appear and, in fact, be objective. Next to having his credentials impeached, the worst thing that can happen to an expert (and the client on whose behalf he has been called to testify) is to have the judge or jury conclude that the expert is biased or that his opinions are for sale.

Remember that anything that is provided to the expert in writing or by recorded (video or sound recording) or electronic communication (e-mail or text) may potentially be discovered and reviewed by the opposing party using the discovery requests set out in Illustration 15-5. Once that information is discovered, the attorney for the opposing party is then going to question your expert in a discovery deposition about all such conversations and materials, hunting for a way to suggest to the jury at trial that your expert is not objective in his opinions, has been led to those opinions by the supervising attorney or any assisting legal professional, and is only selling his opinions for a fat fee.

Consequently, all of your communications to the expert should adopt a neutral tone. We cannot be seen to be urging the expert to formulate a particular helpful opinion. We must be seen as providing the expert with raw data and allowing the expert to formulate his opinions in a fair and objective fashion based on the data. It is usually permissible to indicate to the expert potential theories of the case, but this is better done verbally rather than in writing and is never done in such a way as to influence the expert. (See Hypothetical 15-2.)

Illustration 15-5 INFORMATION TYPICALLY SOUGHT BY ATTORNEYS IN DISCOVERY CONCERNING THE OPPOSING PARTY'S EXPERT WITNESSES

The opposing attorney will use interrogatories and document requests to ask the other party to:

- produce for inspection all information and communications supplied to the expert by retaining counsel that relates to a) the expert's compensation in the case; b) any and all facts or data that counsel has provided to the expert and that the expert considered in forming the opinions to be expressed; and c) any and all facts and data that identify assumptions that counsel provided to the expert and that the expert relied on in forming the opinions to be expressed
- produce for inspection all other documents, records, and communications other than those supplied by retaining counsel and that the expert has considered or relied upon in formulating his opinions
- produce for inspection everything the expert has written or recorded regarding the case, including notes, correspondence, and final report, but excluding preliminary reports and drafts of the final report
- relate the substance and detail of all verbal communications the expert has had with anyone, including the attorney who retained him, the attorney's assistants and staff, and the attorney's client, concerning the case and that refer or relate in any way to the documents, records, and communications produced in response to the other requests

HYPOTHETICAL 15-2

Assume that Dr. Russ T. Nail, whose resume we considered in Illustration 15-1, has been retained as an expert to consult with and testify for the plaintiff in the self-acceleration lawsuit described in Hypothetical 15-1. Assume further that counsel for plaintiff writes Dr. Nail the following letter.

Dear Dr. Nail:

We are pleased you will be working with us on this case. You have been a great asset to this office in obtaining several favorable settlements and judgments over the past years and we look forward to another mutually successful venture in this case.

Once you have examined the automobile in question, we hope to be able to use your expert opinion to support one or both of the following theories:

1. that the car self-accelerated due to a malfunction in or improper design of the regulator of the fuel injection system; or
2. that the car self-accelerated due to improper installation at the factory of the tension rod under the foot pad of the gas pedal. . . .

a. How many problems do you see in the wording and tone of this letter?
b. What kinds of arguments could the opposing attorney make concerning the objectivity of any opinion Russ T. Nail offers in this case based on this letter?
c. Reword this letter to correct the problems you see with it.

7. Provide materials requested by the expert promptly

You do not want to be responsible for any delays in furthering the expert's work. Often experts need considerable time, even after receiving materials concerning the case, to do the necessary review and formulate their opinions. Help them out by getting information to them promptly.

8. Keep a record of all materials sent to or received from the expert

At any given time during a case, you should be able to trace exactly what an expert has received from your office and what has been received from the expert. In addition, if original documents or other physical evidence is sent to an expert, document that in your evidence log for chain-of-custody purposes. (See Chapter 9 and Illustration 9-9.)

9. Do not allow the expert to put preliminary opinions in writing

New FRCP 26(b)(4)(C) now prohibits the discovery of preliminary or draft reports prepared by testifying experts. Nonetheless, the opinions of the expert should generally not be reduced to writing at all until they have been communicated to and discussed with the attorney. Why? Because many state rules of procedure do not limit the discovery of communications containing preliminary findings or draft reports by opposing counsel and because, even in federal cases, no one is yet sure how strictly trial judges will interpret the new rule to limit such discovery. If opposing counsel is able to discover communications or documentation in which the expert has expressed preliminary opinions, potential problems with formulating his opinions that do not appear in the final report, or has repeated statements made to the expert by counsel that could be construed to suggest an attempt to influence the judgment of an expert, opposing counsel will use that information on cross-examination of the expert to challenge the validity or credibility of his final opinions.

EXAMPLE

Dr. Smith, when you wrote this letter containing your preliminary report to Attorney Davis six months ago, you weren't so certain of the conclusions you've expressed to the jury today, were you?

or

Well, Dr. Smith, sometime during the six months since you wrote that preliminary report, Attorney Davis got you to change your opinions to help his client's case a little, didn't he?

10. Be familiar with all rules of evidence and procedure that apply to the expert

The legal professional must not only be familiar with the discovery rules affecting experts (see Chapters 4 and 5), but with the rules of evidence as they relate to expert testimony (see Chapters 6 and 7), and with local rules of court as they may impact on the discovery or required disclosure of expert testimony.

Chapter Summary and Conclusion

FRE 702 defines who may serve as an expert witness. Experts may testify for a party or merely serve as a behind-the-scenes consultant. There are many sources for locating persons qualified to serve as an expert. It is important to evaluate an expert before using her for the first time, and to evaluate any expert used by an opposing party. Evaluation includes verifying the data set forth on the expert's resume or curriculum vitae. The legal professional must not only know how to evaluate an expert, but how to work effectively with the expert as well. That often requires the legal professional to become conversant with the technical language and concepts in the expert's field. The legal professional must also be cautious about sharing with an expert privileged material that may be subject to a discovery request later. It is also important to not attempt to influence the opinion of an expert since that may be used against the expert later to suggest non-objectivity.

In the last three chapters we will consider sources of information for the investigator, both public and private. We begin that next in Chapter 16, with sources of information available from the federal government.

Review Questions

1. What is the difference between a consulting expert and a testifying expert?
2. Name as many lawyer organizations as you can that might be referral sources for experts.
3. Name two leading expert referral services.
4. Why is it important to perform a background check on experts named by an opponent?
5. Why is it important to perform a background check on experts your side plans to use?
6. What is the risk to an expert of having incorrect or misleading information on a resume? What is the risk to you in doing so on your resume?
7. List all the steps you can think of in evaluating an expert.
8. Why is it important for the legal professional to become familiar with concepts and vocabulary in an expert's area of expertise?
9. What is the potential risk in supplying an expert with privileged material?
10. Why is it important to always communicate a neutral picture of the case to an expert?

KEY WORDS AND PHRASES TO REMEMBER

AAJ	expert witness
American Jurisprudence Desk Book	fact witness
background check	*Lawyers Desk Reference*
biography	resume
consulting expert	TAB
curriculum vitae	TASA
dissertation	testifying expert
DRI	thesis

LEARN BY DOING

LBD 15-1. Read and compare *Krisa v. Equitable Life Assur. Soc.*, 196 F.R.D. 254 (M.D. Pa. 2000) with *Regional Airport Authority of Louisville v. LFG, LLC*, 460 F.3d 697 (6th Cir. 2006). Then research the law of your federal circuit to see which approach it takes to the waiver of attorney work product or other privileges by providing such materials to an expert. Research state law to determine which approach your state takes. Do a memorandum summarizing your findings. See also, LBD 4-5.

LBD 15-2. Using the information on locating experts provided in Appendix B, locate one or more expert witnesses in your area whom you would recommend that your supervising attorney consider retaining for consulting and/or testifying purposes in the following Case Studies from Appendix A. If possible, obtain a current resume or CV from each expert. If your instructor consents, it is permissible to contact these experts directly but be sure to explain to them that you are engaged in a learning exercise and not an actual case from which they could expect a fee.

a. Case Study No. 1 (The Rowdy Outlaw Case): a fingerprint expert
b. Case Study No. 2 (The Soupspoon Wise Case): a vocational expert
c. Case Study No. 3 (The Vidalia Unyon Case): a DNA expert
d. Case Study No. 4 (The Rocky Road Project): a soil contamination and reclamation expert

LBD 15-3. Arrange and conduct an interview with someone in your area who has worked as a consulting and testifying expert for attorneys. Your questions should focus on the kinds of cases on which she has worked as an expert, what credentials she believes are most impressive to a judge or jury, what methods or techniques she utilizes to be most effective (believable) with a judge or jury, the importance of appearing objective to a judge or jury, and how she prepares for cross-examination. Ask how well she thinks attorneys do at cross-examination of experts, and what are the positive and the negative aspects of working with attorneys. Prepare a memorandum summarizing your interview for your instructor.

LBD 15-4. Read the cases of *Kumho Tire Co. v. Carmichael*, 526 U.S. 137 (1999) and *Daubert v. Merrell Dow Pharmaceuticals*, 509 U.S. 579 (1993). Prepare a memorandum summarizing the procedure and factors to be considered by a trial judge in deciding whether to admit expert testimony. Research the case law in your state or federal circuit since *Daubert* to see how those courts are applying these rulings of the Supreme Court. Include a summary of those findings in your memorandum. (Note: Do not use this LBD if LBD 7-2 was used.)

LBD 15-5 is accessible on the Author Updates link to the text Web site at www.aspenparalegaled.com/books/parsons_investigating/default.asp.

Chapter 16

Public Sources of Information—Federal

CHAPTER OUTLINE

A. Introduction
B. Public Records in General
C. The Importance of Knowing How Government Works
D. Structure of the Federal Government
E. Determining What a Federal Agency or Department Does and the Records It Maintains
F. How to Access Information from the Federal Government

CHAPTER OBJECTIVES

In this chapter you will come to appreciate the vast amount of information that is available to the investigator from the various agencies and departments in the federal government. You will learn:

- What we mean by public records as they are maintained by different government sources.
- How the U.S. government is structured around the three branches.
- Sources, including Internet sources, that enable the investigator to determine what records and information a particular federal agency or department maintains.
- Practical procedures for obtaining information from federal agencies and departments, including the Freedom of Information Act and the Privacy Act.

A. Introduction

Simply put, locating information is at the heart of the investigative task. In addition to interviewing clients and witnesses, locating missing witnesses, and working with experts, the legal professional engaged in investigation must be skilled at locating pertinent, helpful information in a proper useable form.

This chapter will deal with accessing public information from federal government sources. Chapter 17 will deal with accessing public information from state and local government sources, and Chapter 18 will deal with locating information from private (non-governmental) sources.

By **public records** or **public sources** we mean information compiled and maintained by government agencies and offices at the **federal, state,** and **local** (i.e., city and county) levels. By **private records** or **private sources** we mean information in the custody of private individuals, businesses, educational institutions, or any other non-governmental custodian.

There are two distinct skills to be learned in connection with accessing public and private information as part of your investigation: (1) being able to identify the various sources of public and private information; and (2) knowing how to obtain the information from that source. In other words, knowing *where* to go for information and *how* to obtain it when you get there. And, as always in fact investigating, there are no substitutes for creative thinking and vigorous pursuit of information.

In Chapters 16 through 18 we will be making frequent references to sources of public and private information available on the **Internet**. As you read these chapters, consult the materials in Appendix B, Resources for the Investigator, for details on contacting and accessing information from federal, state, and local government sources.

B.   Public Records in General

The amount of information gathered and maintained by government at its various levels (federal, state, and local) is truly staggering. But for the investigator, public records can present a veritable gold mine of relevant information. Not all of it is accessible in every case or by just anyone, but much of it is truly public—accessible at any time by anyone. Also, much information maintained by the government that is not truly public can be obtained in particular ways or by particular persons.

C.   The Importance of Knowing How Government Works

The more the legal professional knows about how government works at its various levels and the many offices and agencies maintained by the federal, state, and local governments, the more effective and efficient she will be at this investigating task. Here are some specific suggestions for those who wish to be highly skilled at locating public information:

- You should have a basic knowledge of how the federal government and your state and local governments are organized and operate.
- You should familiarize yourself with the various governmental agencies at both the federal and state levels and understand what each of them does.
- If you have not had a course in **administrative law** in your formal course of study, go to your school, public library, or a bookstore and obtain a current administrative law text and educate yourself.
- You should keep within arm's reach a source that gives you the addresses and phone numbers of the central, regional, and/or local governmental offices and agencies.

- You should also keep written notes on the names and disposition of individuals you deal with by phone or in person in government offices and cultivate those contacts for future use. (See Chapter 8 on Communication Skills.)

D. ▶ Structure of the Federal Government

SLEUTH ON THE LOOSE

Identify a company that makes a widely distributed product, then access the Web site of the Consumer Product Safety Commission at www.cpsc.gov to see if that company has had a product recalled.

The starting point to knowing what records are available from the various branches, departments, and agencies of the federal government is understanding how the government is organized, becoming familiar with the various departments and agencies in each branch of the federal government, and knowing generally what each does. Illustration 16-1 sets forth in diagram form the basic structure of the federal government.

Note that although we are using the terms **departments** and **agencies,** a number of federal entities are denominated as **boards, commissions, bureaus, services, authorities,** or **offices.** A comprehensive listing of all such federal entities is not feasible here but Illustrations 16-2 and 16-5 list a few of the numerous federal agencies with which legal professionals have frequent contact.

E. ▶ Determining What a Federal Agency or Department Does and the Records It Maintains

The names of the departments and agencies in Illustrations 16-1, 16-2, and 16-5 must become more than just names on a page to the investigating legal professional. You should have a general understanding of what each federal department or agency is responsible for doing. That will provide you with knowledge, or at least an educated guess, as to the kinds of information or records the department or agency is likely to compile and maintain.

You should also know the location of the national, regional, and/or local offices of the federal agencies with which you most frequently work. Keep handy an up-to-date source from which you can quickly locate the address and phone number for these government agencies and offices.

There are a number of sources the legal professional can utilize to obtain information on federal departments and agencies:

1. Experienced people in the office

The experienced attorneys and paralegals in your office will be primary sources to help you determine which federal agencies might be a source for what kinds of records or at least to direct you to someone who should know. As the legal professional gains experience in working with different federal departments and agencies, she will become the office expert on what is available where. However, experienced people in the office cannot always provide complete direction and the inexperienced legal professional must rely on her own knowledge, initiative, and common sense to track down and obtain available information from government sources. Fortunately, there are a number of helpful sources of information available to you.

Illustration 16-1   STRUCTURE OF THE FEDERAL GOVERNMENT

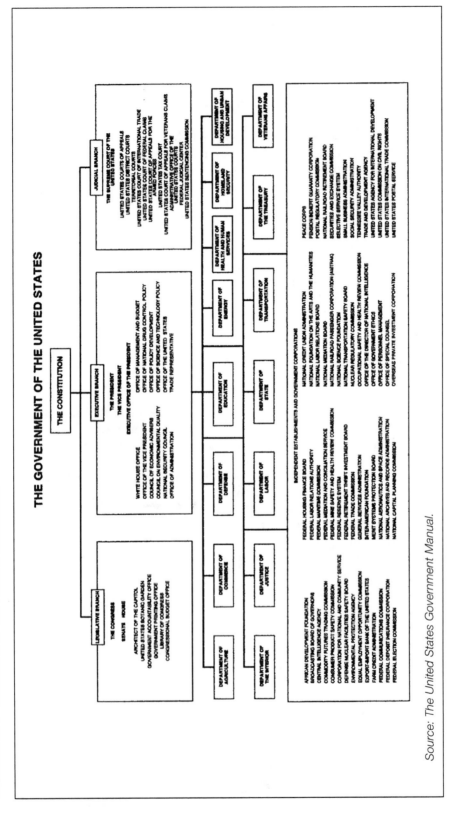

Source: The United States Government Manual.

2. Government publications

The government prints several helpful publications available in the reference section of many schools or public libraries or from the United States Government Printing Office (GPO). These include the *United States Government Manual* (accessible online through **GPO Access** at www.gpo access.gov/gmanual/index.html and the *Congressional Directory* (accessible online at www.gpoaccess.gov/cdirectory/index.html). These publications not only provide information on the scope of responsibilities of the various federal departments and agencies with addresses, phone, fax, and e-mail numbers for Washington and regional and/or local offices, they also contain current Web site addresses for the agencies.

There are numerous other more specific publications that can be obtained from the GPO. A few examples include:

- *Where to Write for Vital Records: Births, Deaths, Marriages and Divorces*
- *Fire Investigation Handbook*
- *Crime Scene Search and Physical Evidence Handbook*
- *Forensics: When Science Bears Witness*

A catalog of U.S. government publications can be obtained without cost from the Superintendent of Documents, U.S. Government Printing Office, Washington, DC 20402 or viewed and ordered at GPO Access (www.gpoaccess.gov).

A number of federal agencies also publish their own brochures summarizing the various publications available through that agency. A phone call to the agency will be sufficient to obtain the guide, usually at no cost.

There are also 1,400 federal depository libraries across the country, which contain comprehensive collections of substantially all publications of the federal government. To locate the depository library nearest you, visit www.gpoaccess.gov/libraries.html. See Appendix B for a comprehensive listing of resources for locating and contacting the various federal departments and agencies.

3. Data.Gov and Agency Web sites

Pursuant to the **E-Government Act of 2002**, 44 U.S.C. §§3601 et seq., the federal government is now committed to making more records and information available online (see LBD 16-8). In 2009 the government established **Data.Gov** (www.data.gov/), an **open data site** (a Web site where data is posted for anyone to access, use, and share without restriction) dedicated to "democratizing the public sector and driving innovation." Mountains of information are posted on the site originating from numerous government agencies and departments; data thought to be of particular concern or interest to large numbers of Americans. Thirty nations have established such open data sites with varying amounts of information available on them (see the list at and see LBD 16-11). Many private organizations have created such sites as well.

In addition to Data.Gov, individual federal departments and agencies have their own Web sites providing a wealth of information on the activities of the agency, information available from it, and, frequently,

Illustration 16-2
WEB SITE
ADDRESSES
FOR FREQUENTLY
CONTACTED
FEDERAL AGENCIES

Social Security Administration	www.ssa.gov
Securities Exchange Commission	www.sec.gov
Federal Election Commission	www.fec.gov
Internal Revenue Service	www.irs.gov
Consumer Product Safety Commission	www.cpsc.gov
Consumer Financial Protection Bureau	www.consumerfinance.gov
Small Business Administration	www.sbaonline.sba.gov
Government Printing Office	www.gpo.gov
Postal Service	www.usps.com
Environmental Protection Agency	www.epa.gov
Federal Trade Commission	www.ftc.gov
Department of Commerce	www.commerce.gov
Food and Drug Administration	www.fda.gov
Department of Agriculture	www.usda.gov

instructions on how to access that information. (See Hypothetical 16-1.) Illustration 16-2 lists the Web site addresses for a number of frequently contacted federal agencies.

Comprehensive listings of Web site addresses for all federal agencies are available in the government publications mentioned above and from numerous online sources including:

1. www.usa.gov The best single-source site to access federal government information
2. www.fedworld.gov Known as FedWorld, this site is an indispensable gateway to all things federal. Operated by the U.S. Department of Commerce.
3. www.whitehouse.gov The White House Web site includes links to practically all federal departments and agencies.

Appendix B contains a comprehensive listing of online and other resources for locating and contacting federal agencies and departments.

4. State and local bar directories and handbooks

Many state and local bar associations publish directories or handbooks containing information on the various federal agencies, including how to contact regional and local offices. (See LBD 16-2.)

5. The phone book

In many locations the phone book has a separate section for government offices. Sometimes referred to as the **blue** (or red, green, etc.) **pages**, for their distinctive color coding, this section of the phone book is a quick source for addresses and phone numbers of regional or local offices of federal agencies.

6. Publications

There are numerous publications available in many school and public libraries containing lists of the various federal departments and agencies, descriptions of their responsibilities and functions, as well as information on how to contact them. These resources include *American Jurisprudence 2d Desk Book* and Philo's *Lawyer's Desk Reference*.

The leading commercial publisher of information on the federal government is probably CQ Press, a division of Congressional Quarterly, Inc. (online at www.cqpress.com/gethome.asp), which publishes more than 300 titles related to government activity, including the comprehensive *Washington Information Directory*, the *Federal Staff Directory*, the *Federal Regulatory Directory*, and *How to Access the Federal Government on the Internet*. (See Appendix B for details on these and other publications.)

7. Enabling statutes and regulations

To get a better understanding of the responsibilities of a particular government department or agency and the kinds of records it maintains, it is frequently helpful to review its **enabling legislation,** that is, the federal statute that created the particular agency or department. The particular **federal regulations** governing that agency or department should be reviewed as well. The **Code of Federal Regulations** (CFR) (searchable online at www.gpoaccess.gov/cfr/index.htm l) contains the current federal regulations for each federal agency and department. The **Federal Register** (www.gpoaccess.gov/fr/index.htm l), published daily by the U.S. government, provides information regarding the status of proposed new or amended regulations.

HYPOTHETICAL 16-1

Assume that you are assisting the attorney representing Rocky Road Developers, Inc. (see Case Study No. 4 in Appendix A). The supervising attorney is concerned that the two acres lying alongside the creek on which a gas station was located for years may cause his client some environmental pollution problems if it is purchased. He specifically mentions the Clean Water Act, 33 U.S.C. §§1251 et seq. He wants you to determine whether the federal agency responsible for enforcing the Clean Water Act has ever inspected this property or acted on it in any way. Do the following:

a. Determine which federal agency is responsible for administering the Clean Water Act.
b. Locate the enabling legislation and current federal regulations for that agency.
c. Locate the address, phone number, e-mail address, and Web site address, if any, for the Washington, D.C., and local offices of that agency.

SLEUTH ON THE LOOSE

Do you think the various government agencies and departments shown in Illustration 16-1 from the U.S. Government Manual is an exhaustive list? Not by a long shot. Check out the A-Z Index of U.S. Government Departments and Agencies at www. usa.gov/ Agencies/ Federal/All_ Agencies/ index.shtml. A good Web site to bookmark.

Mastering the organization of the many federal agencies is challenging not only because of their number but because the control of many agencies with related functions is hardly centralized. For example, there are numerous federal law enforcement agencies but their administration is spread among several different departments. The Department of Justice has administrative control over the Federal Bureau of Investigation, the Drug Enforcement Administration, and the U.S. Marshall's Service. But the Treasury Department controls the Bureau of Alcohol, Tobacco, and Firearms, the Internal Revenue Service, and the Customs Service while the Department of the Interior oversees the National Park Service and the Fish and Wildlife Service. The Transportation Department administers the U.S. Coast Guard while the Defense Department directs the Army, Navy, and Air Force.

Moreover, nearly identical responsibilities often are spread among more than one federal agency. In early 2002, for example, there was publicity over the fact that, in the area of food safety, the Food and Drug Administration (FDA) is responsible for the safety of cheese pizza while the Department of Agriculture (AG) is responsible for pepperoni pizza! AG is responsible for the safety of open-faced sandwiches, the FDA for closed-face sandwiches!

And, of course, Congress occasionally exercises its power to create new agencies or merge existing ones. For example, the Department of Homeland Security created by the Homeland Security Act of 2002 merged 170,000 federal employees from 22 existing agencies and assumed a portion of the responsibilities of 8 other cabinet departments. (See LBD 16-6.)

The more you know about the organization of the federal government, the more efficient you will be at knowing where to go to obtain what you need.

F. ▶ How to Access Information from the Federal Government

Pursuant to the U.S. Constitution, the federal government is divided into three branches—the **judicial,** the **executive,** and the **legislative.** In light of the different kinds of information obtainable from each branch and the different methods of obtaining such information, we will address how to access information from each branch separately.

1. The judicial branch—court records

SLEUTH ON THE LOOSE

To learn more about government sources of information available on the Internet subscribe to the Government Sources listserv accessible at http:// listserv.access. gpo.gov.

a. *Kinds of information available in federal court records*

A brief review of the adversarial process and, in particular, the rules of pleading and discovery covered in Chapters 3 through 5 should help the student appreciate the wealth of information that may be available in federal court records. Sworn answers to interrogatories; deposition transcripts; affidavits; positions taken in prior litigation; detail concerning an individual's personal, financial, and business affairs; or a company's history, finances, and activities may be among these public records available for a copying fee to the investigator who knows where and how to look.

b. *How to conduct searches in federal court records*

Records of proceedings in the federal courts, unless placed under seal by order of the court, are public records accessible by anyone. The standard way to obtain copies of court files is to visit the office of the clerk of the court in which the case was heard, ask for the file by assigned docket number, and pay the going rate for any copies made (usually 50 cents to a dollar per page). Requests for copies of files can also be accomplished by phone call or letter to the **clerk's office,** though there may be a delay in processing such requests and some court clerks may request payment in advance for copy and mailing costs.

After a federal court file has been closed, it will eventually be sent to a regional branch of the National Archives (online at www.archives.gov). To locate a file there, you must obtain the case locator number for the file, which is available from the clerk of the originating court. Details on this process are available in *The Sourcebook of Federal Courts.* (See Appendix B for the addresses of the branch offices of the National Archives.)

Though case files in the clerk's offices will be maintained there by assigned docket number, the investigator who does not have a docket number can still locate files in which a particular person was a litigant. That is because federal court clerks maintain detailed **party indexes** of all civil and criminal cases that come before the court, regardless of their disposition. Increasingly, those index systems have been computerized and the investigator will be expected to conduct the search at a computer terminal. If you are unfamiliar with the computerized index system used in the clerk's office, just ask for help.

In other clerk's offices, the party index system may consist of bound computer printout sheets, or be kept on microfilm or microfiche, or even be recorded in a card file or ledger book. Needless to say, if the index system is nonelectronic, searches can be tedious and time consuming.

However they are kept, the indexes are maintained alphabetically by the names of the litigants. In criminal cases, this means cases are indexed by the defendant's name. In addition to the name, the criminal index will typically state the charge, the disposition, and the docket number. In civil cases, the cases are indexed by the names of the parties, either plaintiffs or defendants. In bankruptcy and U.S. tax court proceedings, the cases are indexed by the name of the petitioner(s). The civil index will typically provide the name of the case, the disposition, and the docket number.

In some clerk's offices, separate indexes are maintained for corporations that are litigants. Some index systems may contain separate plaintiff and defendant indexes though, increasingly, most systems merge both into a "party index." In older index systems, multi-party cases may be indexed only under the first-listed plaintiff and/or the first-listed defendant. But in modern systems, cases are cross-indexed under the names of all the parties.

c. *Computerized resources for searching federal court records*

1. Computerized database vendors.   A number of resources exist to enable the investigator to search federal court files and dockets by computer modem. The two leading computerized **database vendors, Westlaw,** now owned by Thomson Reuters, and **LexisNexis,** a division of Reed Elsevier, Inc., are available by paid subscription only. Both provide docket search libraries that enable the investigator to perform online searches covering cases decided in all the federal appellate courts, increasing numbers of U.S. district courts, the U.S. bankruptcy courts, U.S. tax courts, and other specialized federal courts. Access to both Westlaw and LexisNexis is now available to subscribers through the Internet, eliminating the need for specialized software and phone numbers. Easy-to-use graphic and point-and-click tools have replaced search queries. The LexisNexis research system can be previewed at www.lexisnexis.com/. And Westlaw's system can be previewed at www.westlaw.com.

2. PACER. The court indexes and dockets of most civil, criminal, bankruptcy, and appellate cases filed in the federal courts throughout the country are now searchable using the Public Access to Court Electronic Records (**PACER**) system. Created and administered by the Administrative Office of the U.S. Courts, this service allows any subscriber to dial in by modem to a particular federal district or bankruptcy court clerk's office and quickly retrieve case information and dockets for a modest fee. Information can be downloaded and copied by the user. The U.S. Party/Case Index feature of PACER allows subscribers to search regionally or nationwide by name or social security number in the bankruptcy index, by name and nature of suit in the civil case index, by defendant in the criminal index, and by party name in the appellate court index. An overview of PACER resources is available at www.pacer.gov.

3. The Internet. Increasing amounts of information on the judicial branch of the federal government are available on the Internet. A comprehensive list of such sources is available in Appendix B, but a few noteworthy sites are as follows:

- www.supremecourtus.gov This is the official site of the U.S. Supreme Court. It offers access to court slip opinions, term orders, argument calendar, court rules, etc.
- www.uscourts.gov This is the Federal Judiciary **home page**. It offers information on the structure of the judiciary, statistics on caseloads, judicial vacancies, answers to FAQs, lists of publications and links to other Web sites.
- www.oyez.org/ This site provides access to digital audio recordings of oral arguments before the Supreme Court as well as a multimedia guide to the Court.
- www.abiworld.org This site provides quick access to decisions of the U.S. bankruptcy courts as well as bankruptcy news and information.
- www.law.cornell.edu This is the site for Cornell University's Legal Information Institute, also a comprehensive legal resource.

FindLaw's LawCrawler (http://lawcrawler.findlaw.com) is a powerful search tool for locating court decisions and other law-related material on the Internet.

HYPOTHETICAL 16-2

Assume that the attorney for whom you work has asked you to do some research on a corporation that does business in your area. (For purposes of this Hypothetical, choose an actual corporation doing business in your area—a large retailer, for example.) Specifically, the supervising attorney has asked you to find information on every federal lawsuit this corporation has been a party to in the last five years. That would include being a plaintiff or defendant in a civil suit or a defendant in a federal criminal action.

Write out a plan of investigation covering the sources you intend to search to access this information for your supervising attorney. In your plan, list the sources in the order you plan to access them. (To perform further work using this Hypothetical, see LBD 16-1.)

2. The legislative branch—Congress

Congressional records are, for the most part, readily available to the public. Sessions of Congress are normally open to the public and televised. Most congressional committee hearings are likewise open to the public. The Congressional Record (accessible online at http://thomas.loc.gov and available through Westlaw and LexisNexis) is the official record of Congress and contains floor debate as well as the text of proposed bills and amendments. All committee reports (except those containing classified information) and most committee hearings are published by the government. The *United States Code Congressional and Administrative News* is a valuable source for selected committee reports as well.

In addition, copies of the numerous publications authorized by Congress are available at federal depository libraries throughout the country or through the GPO. (See discussion above and Appendix B.) Furthermore, all members of Congress retain staff members who are typically responsive to requests for information regarding the status of legislation, congressional investigations, or other official matters—at least to their constituents.

SLEUTH ON THE LOOSE

Identify some piece of federal legislation currently being considered by Congress then go to http://thomas.loc.gov and see if you can locate the text of committee debate on the legislation or other information regarding its status.

a. Congress on the Internet

Information from and about Congress is increasingly available on the Internet. A comprehensive listing of Web sites for congressional information is provided in Appendix B. Here are the Internet addresses for a few significant Web sites that may prove important to the legal investigator:

- www.gpoaccess.gov GPO Access provides access to the CFR, Federal Register, U.S. Code, Congressional Directory, U.S. Government Manual, Government Administrative Office (GAO) reports, and the monthly catalog of U.S. government publications.
- http://thomas.loc.gov Operated by the Library of Congress, Thomas provides information on congressional procedures, legislation pending in Congress, and select committee reports.
- www.senate.gov This is the home page of the U.S. Senate.
- www.house.gov This is the home page of the U.S. House of Representatives.
- www.loc.gov/index.html This is the home page of the Library of Congress.
- www.govtrack.us/congress/ GovTrack is a private project for tracking legislation and voting records of individual members.

b. Accessing Congress through database vendors

Westlaw and LexisNexis both provide online legislative research capabilities. Both access the Congressional Record. LexisNexis's Congressional and Congressional Research Digital libraries provide access to legislation, congressional hearings, public issues, more than 200 years of congressional history, as well as legal research. Westlaw's Congressional Information, Bill Tracking, and Legislative History databases provide the full text of all bills pending in Congress, track pending legislation, and provide access to committee reports.

Other computerized databases provide congressional information as well. The Tax Research Network subscription service offered by Commerce

Clearing House (www.cch.com) allows access to current legislative materials dealing with tax, finance, and estate planning. **Dialog** (www.dialog.com), now owned by Thomson Corporation, provides comprehensive research into legislative and other governmental reports. (See LBD 16-2.)

3. The executive branch

a. Executive orders

According to the National Archives, President Kennedy signed 214 executive orders between 1961 and 1963; Johnson, 324 (1963 to 1969); Nixon, 346 (1969 to 1974); Ford, 169 (1974 to 1977); Carter, 320 (1977 to 1981); Reagan, 381 (1981 to 1989); G. H. W. Bush, 166 (1989 to 1993); Clinton, 363 (1993 to 2001), G. W. Bush, 290 (2001 to 2009), and Barack Obama, 135 (2009-September 2012). Executive order tables can be viewed online at www.archives.gov/federal-register/executive-orders.

b. Obtaining information from the White House

The home page of the White House is www.whitehouse.gov. The GPO's **Federal Bulletin Board** also provides access to numerous White House documents at http://fedbbs.access.gpo.gov.

SLEUTH ON THE LOOSE

To learn more about making a Freedom of Information Act request to a federal agency, including forms and information on the FOIA officers for a particular agency, access www.sba.gov/aboutsba/sbaprograms/ foia/index.html.

c. Obtaining information from executive agencies

As Illustration 16-1 suggests, most federal agencies and departments are under the authority of the executive branch. The executive branch of the federal government includes the cabinet departments, the branches of the military, various regulatory agencies such as the Environmental Protection Agency, the Food and Drug Administration, and the Securities Exchange Commission, government corporations, and various law enforcement agencies.

1. The Freedom of Information Act.   The primary means of accessing information from agencies and departments of the executive branch of government is the Freedom of Information Act **(FOIA)**, 5 U.S.C. §552 (accessible online at www.law.cornell.edu/uscode/text). The FOIA was enacted by Congress in 1966 and establishes a presumption that records in the possession of agencies and departments of the executive branch of the federal government are accessible by the public. The scope of the FOIA is broad. It includes the agencies, offices, and departments of the executive branch of the federal government such as the Department of Defense, the Office of Management and Budget, and the National Security Council. It also includes independent federal regulatory agencies such as the Federal Trade Commission, the Environmental Protection Agency, the Securities Exchange Commission, and the Federal Communications Commission. Included too are federal government-controlled corporations such as the Post Office, the Tennessee Valley Authority, the Smithsonian Institution, and Amtrak.

The FOIA does not apply to Congress, the federal courts, or the Executive Office staff such as the White House Chief of Staff or others whose function is to advise and assist the president. It also does not cover state and local government agencies (although, as we will see in Chapter 17, every state has laws guaranteeing citizens access to some records of state agencies), private businesses, private organizations, schools, or individuals.

In general, the kind of information that can be obtained from federal agencies under the FOIA is information concerning how the agency operates, what actions it has been taking, how it has spent money, and what statistics or information it has collected in the course of its operation. Of course, many federal agencies regulate corporations and other private businesses whose reports and other records will be in the possession of the regulating agency.

EXAMPLE

The Food and Drug Administration is authorized to regulate pharmaceutical companies seeking to market new drugs to the consuming public. There is a complex and lengthy testing and application process for a company seeking FDA approval for a new drug, and the company will supply all of its drug development research, testing, animal and human trials, and market information to the FDA as part of the process. All of the information supplied by the company to the FDA may be obtained via a FOIA request, unless it is deemed exempt under the Act.

SLEUTH ON THE LOOSE

Do you think the various government agencies and departments shown in Illustration 16-1 from the U.S. Government Manual is an exhaustive list? Not by a long shot. Check out the A-Z Index of U.S. Government Departments and Agencies at www. usa.gov/ Agencies/ Federal/All_ Agencies/ index.shtml. A good Web site to bookmark.

All agency records are accessible through the FOIA except those falling into one of nine designated **exemption** categories as follows:

- information related to foreign policy or national security if it has been properly classified;
- records related solely to the internal personnel rules and practices of the agency;
- information declared exempt under other federal laws—known as the "catch-all" exception;
- trade secret and other commercial/financial information deemed confidential;
- interagency or intraagency correspondence and policy memoranda;
- information about an individual in personnel, medical, or similar files, the disclosure of which would constitute an unwarranted invasion of that individual's privacy (applies only to living natural persons);
- records or information compiled for law enforcement purposes if disclosure might reasonably violate a right to personal privacy (see LBD 16-12);
- records of financial institutions; and
- certain geological information and data, including maps, regarding oil and gas wells.

The burden is on the agency receiving the request to demonstrate that information requested falls into one of the exempt categories; otherwise it must be produced. If part of a record falls within an exemption and part does not, the part that does not must be produced. Moreover, other than the "catch-all" exemption, the government agency can exercise its discretion to release records that might fall within one of the other exemptions if the requester can convince the agency it is "in the public interest" to do so. The Openness Promotes Effectiveness in our National Government Act of 2007 (called the **Open Government Act of 2007**) amended the FOIA to authorize courts to award attorney's fees and costs to those who are forced to file suit to compel compliance with a FOIA request and who then prevail, either by court judgment or voluntary compliance. When a lawsuit is filed to compel disclosure, a manufacturer or other third party with an interest in preventing disclosure of the information sought may intervene in the lawsuit to assert the appropriate privilege, usually the trade secret or other confidential information privilege. See, e.g., *Appleton v. Food & Drug Admin.*, 451 F. Supp.2d 129 (D.D.C. 2006) (four pharmaceutical companies allowed to intervene in a FOIA compliance suit seeking information regarding the drug levothryoxine sodium).

There is no central government office which handles FOIA requests. Each agency is required to designate an officer to handle requests submitted to that agency. The statute requires that an agency respond to a citizen's request for records within ten working days, though the agency may request an extension. The agency may also charge a nominal fee for locating, reviewing, and copying documents. It is prudent to request the fee schedule from an agency before making the request. Some agencies may require prepayment of fees. Sometimes agencies will waive the fee.

The current name, address, and phone number of the FOIA officer designated by a particular agency can be located in the regulations for that agency. Regulations for the various federal agencies are collected in the Code of Federal Regulations (CFR) (searchable online at www.gpoaccess.gov/cfr/index.html.). Or, the investigator can simply call or write the particular federal agency to obtain that information. *The Congressional Directory*, the *U.S. Government Manual* (searchable online at www.gpoaccess.gov/gmanual/index.html), and other written resources contain comprehensive lists of FOIA officers. The Office of Information and Privacy (OIP) within the Department of Justice (DOJ) is the principal contact point within the executive branch for advice and policy guidance on matters pertaining to the FOIA. The OIP maintains a FOIA Counselor Service that may be reached at (202) 514-3642 (202-514-FOIA). The OIP also maintains an excellent Web site with links to FOIA officers for the various federal agencies and to agency FOIA sites at www.justice.gov/oip/index.html, and the DOG itself has created a quite user-friendly FOIA site at www.foia.gov/.

Two excellent guides that are available to assist you in successfully completing a FOIA request are *How to Use the Federal FOI Act* and *A Citizen's Guide on How to Use the Freedom of Information Act and The Privacy Act of 1974 to Request Government Records*.

FOIA requests must be made in writing, directed to the specific agency from which the records are sought, and must specify the records sought. Illustration 16-3 shows a typical FOIA request letter.

2. The Privacy Act.   Another federal statute that is available for accessing records from executive agencies and departments of the federal government is the **Privacy Act**, 5 U.S.C. §552a (accessible online at www.law.cornell.edu/uscode/text). Passed in 1974 as an amendment to

Illustration 16-3   FOIA REQUEST LETTER

Date

FOIA Officer (or Agency Head)
Name of Federal Agency
City, State and Zip Code

Re: Freedom of Information Act Request

Dear _____:

Pursuant to the provisions of the Freedom of Information Act, 5 U.S.C. §552, I request a copy of the following documents: (list and describe in detail the specific records sought).
In order to determine my status as to fees, you should be aware that I am (insert an appropriate requester description from the five that follow):

- a representative of the news media and this request is for news gathering and not for commercial use
- a representative of a public interest organization and this request is for news gathering and not for commercial use
- affiliated with an educational or non-commercial scientific institution and this request is made for scholarly or scientific purpose and not for commercial use
- an individual seeking information for personal use and not for commercial use
- affiliated with a private corporation and seeking information for use in the company's business

I will reimburse you for fees up to the amount of $ _____. If you determine that the costs will exceed that amount, please advise me of the anticipated total cost before making the copies.

(or)

I am requesting a waiver or reduction in fees for complying with this request because the requested release of information is primarily benefiting the public and not for commercial use.

Thank you for your consideration of this request.

Sincerely,

Name
Address
Phone No.

SLEUTH ON THE LOOSE

Visit the Web site of the Center for Democracy and Technology at www.cdt.org and see what privacy issues are currently being discussed there.

the FOIA, the Privacy Act allows an individual to access personal information held by an agency about herself and to seek the amendment of incorrect information. The executive departments and agencies subject to the FOIA are also subject to the Privacy Act.

Generally speaking, an individual may succeed in accessing more information about himself under the Privacy Act than he could about another person under the FOIA. However, the Privacy Act also recognizes exemptions that an agency may rely on to withhold information. Those exemptions include:

- information classified in the interests of national defense or foreign policy;
- information related to law enforcement activities;
- information developed in connection with Secret Service protection;

- information related to the identity of confidential sources in connection with making decisions regarding federal employment, military service, federal contracts or classification; and
- information related to testing or examination for promotion in federal service or the armed services.

Illustration 16-4 shows a typical Privacy Act request letter.

Since the Privacy Act is limited to an individual's right to request information about himself, its usefulness to the investigator is primarily in assisting a client or cooperative witness to make such a request to obtain relevant information the government may have.

Illustration 16-5 lists several of the agencies mentioned in Illustrations 16-1 and 16-2 together with a brief summary of the kinds of records they maintain and that you will find that you can—or can't—access.

The examples given in Illustration 16-5 are just a drop in the bucket compared to all of the information accessible from federal agencies. The investigating legal professional should be constantly expanding her knowledge of what the different agencies do, the records they maintain, what records are accessible and how.

3. Agency Web sites. The various federal agencies are placing increasing amounts of information on their Web sites. Take note of the numerous agency Web site addresses set out in Illustrations 16-2 and 16-5 and the resources provided for locating all such sites in Section E.3 of this chapter and in Appendix B. The legal professional should maintain her own updated list of such sites and when performing an investigation try assessing the information on those sites before undertaking a FOIA request.

HYPOTHETICAL 16-3

Assume that you are assisting the attorney defending Rowdy Outlaw on charges he murdered Bobbette Bouvier (see Case Study No. 1 in Appendix A). The supervising attorney says that she wants you to obtain Rowdy Outlaw's military service records and those of Jack Gates. She is particularly interested in accessing information regarding the circumstances of Gates's discharge from the military.

a. What government sources will you contact to obtain this information and how will you make contact with them?

b. If you think it advisable or necessary to prepare one or more FOIA or Privacy Act requests, draft those for your instructor's review in as final a form as possible.

c. What additional information would it be helpful to have to complete this assignment?

4. Online database vendors. Much information concerning the actions taken by executive federal agencies is now accessible through online database vendors. For example, both Westlaw and LexisNexis provide access to the Code of Federal Regulations, the Federal Register, track the history of proposed federal regulations, and provide information on sanctions and other oversight actions taken by a myriad of federal

Illustration 16-4 PRIVACY ACT REQUEST LETTER

Date

Privacy Act Officer (or System of Records Manager)
Name of Federal Agency
City, State and Zip Code

Re: Privacy Act Request

Dear _____:

Pursuant to the provisions of the Privacy Act of 1974, 5 U.S.C. §522a, I request a copy of (or access to) any and all records (or list and describe in detail specific records sought) concerning me maintained by your agency. This request is also made under the Freedom of Information Act, 5 U.S.C. §552.

I will reimburse you for copying costs up to the amount of $ _____. If you determine that the costs will exceed that amount, please advise me of the anticipated total cost before making the copies.

Enclosed is a notarized signature page (or other identifying document) that will verify my identity.

Thank you for your cooperation.

Sincerely,

Name
Address
Phone No.

Illustration 16-5 SELECTED FEDERAL AGENCIES AND THEIR RECORDS

---

1. Social Security Administration (SSA) (www.ssa.gov). The SSA maintains extensive records of employment and earnings for virtually all Americans living or dead as well as millions of foreigners who work or once worked in this country. In addition, the SSA maintains records concerning income, indebtedness, marital status, medical history, and household arrangements for anyone who has ever applied for Social Security benefits including SSI, Medicare, Medicaid, or AFDC. SSA records are confidential and generally not available for public or even law enforcement review. However, any individual can access their own SSA records. (See, e.g., the Request for Social Security Earnings Information in Illustration 16-6.) The SSA will consider forwarding requested mail contact "for humanitarian purposes" to a person on whom it maintains records. Also, the social security number of a person itself, although not obtainable directly from the SSA, can provide the investigator with valuable clues regarding the person's whereabouts and can be used to access other information about the individual in the private domain (see Chapter 14 and the Social Security Index of Assigned Numbers in Appendix B).

2. Bureau of the Census (www.census.gov). The Census Bureau collects and maintains substantial data on U.S. residents every ten years, including names, ages, addresses, gender, race, ethnic origin, employment, income, and marital status. The records of the bureau are confidential but can be accessed by the individual concerned, the parent or guardian of a minor, or the surviving spouse or executor of a deceased person.

3. Bureau of Labor Statistics (BLS) (www.bls.gov). The BLS gathers and processes a substantial amount of statistics related to the American work force. Its annual *Area Wage Survey* and monthly *Employment and Earnings Report* are recognized as authoritative guides in this area. But in addition to its publications, the BLS, through its Public Affairs Office, can make available other and more specific statistical breakdowns.

4. Securities and Exchange Commission (SEC) (www.sec.gov). The SEC gathers and maintains records on over 1,100 corporations whose stock is publicly traded, over 1,200 broker-dealers, and over 5,000 investment companies. A company seeking permission to make a public stock offering must file a registration statement (Form S-1),

Illustration 16-5   SELECTED FEDERAL AGENCIES AND THEIR RECORDS *(continued)*

including a prospectus, with the SEC. Those documents, along with the required annual reports (Form 10-K), quarterly reports (Form 10-Q), and proxy statements, are open to public inspection and contain enormous amounts of data not only on the company itself but on the affairs of its officers, directors, insider owners, and beneficial owners of five percent or more of its shares. Whether a regulated company or any of its principals is the target of an investigation by the SEC is determinable by consulting the *Securities Violations Bulletin*, issued quarterly by the SEC. Further, if a civil suit or criminal prosecution has been brought against a company or any of its principals, that litigation file will be open to public inspection in the forum court.

The SEC can provide a wealth of information to the investigator on any company it regulates. This information is easily accessible. All documents on file for regulated corporations may be located, searched, and downloaded from a Web site maintained by the SEC called EDGAR (Electronic Data Gathering Analysis and Retrieval System) at www.sec.gov/edgar.shtml. There is no charge and exhibits are included. The search may be made by company name, type of record sought (e.g., 10-K, proxy statement, etc.), or date of filing. Records are generally accessible on EDGAR within one business day of their filing. SEC filings can also be obtained on Westlaw or LexisNexis, both of which maintain a securities search database.

Other federal agencies that require periodic filings of companies within the scope of their regulatory activities and that are accessible to the public include the Interstate Commerce Commission, the Federal Communications Commission, the Environmental Protection Agency, the Food and Drug Administration, and the Bureau of Alcohol, Tobacco and Firearms.

5. Federal Housing Authority (FHA) (www.fha.gov). The FHA maintains records on all persons who have applied for federal housing assistance. Most of those records are accessible by means of a proper FOIA request.

6. Internal Revenue Service (IRS) (www.irs.gov). The IRS administers the federal tax laws and maintains records on the age, gender, and marital status of taxpayers and their dependents as well as all sources of income. The records of the IRS are confidential, but a taxpayer or his authorized representative can request copies of his tax returns or audit report forms. (See Request for Copy or Transcript of Tax Form set out in Illustration 16-7.) Moreover, the annual reports of charities and tax-exempt corporations and foundations (Form 990) are accessible. These may contain information about the officers of the organization. If the IRS has settled a dispute with a taxpayer for less than the amount originally owed, an IRS Form 7249-M will be filed at the regional IRS office for one year and thereafter in Washington. Furthermore, if the dispute between a taxpayer and the IRS has made its way into the U.S. tax court or the U.S. district court, those case files will be open to public inspection.

7. Federal Election Commission (FEC) (www.fec.gov). The FEC requires candidates for federal public office to file campaign finance reports containing information on donors, consultants, and vendors used by the candidate. These reports are accessible.

8. General Services Administration (GSA) (www.gsa.gov). The GSA maintains records on a wide range of government activity, including its real and personal property, operating costs, construction projects, and personnel. For example, the Civilian Personnel Records Correspondence Section of the GSA is a primary source for information on non-active military personnel, as well as job title, grade, salary, and duty station of all former federal employees. The Office of Personnel Management (www.opm.gov) also maintains records on retired military and civilian employees. Some information on a veteran's military record can be obtained from National Personnel Records Center, Military Personnel Records, 9700 Page Blvd., St. Louis, MO 63132-5100.

To obtain available information on current federal employees, contact the employing agency directly or contact the Office of Personnel Management (www.opm.gov). For information on current military personnel, contact the particular branch of the military in which they serve. Each branch operates a locator service, the address of which is available in the U.S. Government Manual (reviewable online at www.gpoaccess.gov/gmanual/browse-gm-05.html).

9. The National Archives (www.archives.gov). The National Archives makes available a wealth of information on individuals. It provides access to family histories and allows a genealogy search; it maintains veteran's records; and from its Web site it provides access to numbers of government documents including the U.S. Constitution, the CFR, the Federal Register, and the U.S. Government Manual.

10. The Consumer Product Safety Commission (www.cpsc.gov). In August 2008 Congress passed the Consumer Product Safety Improvement Act of 2008, Title II, Section 212 adding new Section 6A to follow 15 U.S.C. §2055, pursuant to which the agency will make publicly available and searchable from its web site all "reports of harm" received by the CPSC involving consumer products and other products and substances it regulates. Included will be reports received from local, state, and federal agencies as well as child services providers, public safety entities, and the public. (See LBD 16-9.)

Illustration 16-6   REQUEST FOR SOCIAL SECURITY EARNINGS INFORMATION

Social Security Administration

Form Approved
OMB No. 0960-0525

REQUEST FOR SOCIAL SECURITY EARNINGS INFORMATION

*Use This Form If You Need

1. Certified/Non-Certified Detailed Earnings Information

Includes periods of employment or self-employment and the names and addresses of employers.

OR

2. Certified Yearly Totals of Earnings

Includes total earnings for each year but does not include the names and addresses of employers.

DO NOT USE THIS FORM FOR:

Non-certified yearly totals of earnings

This service is free to the public.

These totals can be obtained by calling 1-800-772-1213 to receive Form SSA-7004, Request for Social Security Statement

---

PRIVACY ACT NOTICE: We are authorized to collect this information under section 205 of the Social Security Act, and the Federal Records Act of 1950 (64 Stat. 583). It is needed so we can identify your records and prepare the statement you request. You do not have to furnish the information, but failure to do so may prevent your request from being processed.

Paperwork Reduction Act Statement - This information collection meets the requirements of 44 U.S.C. § 3507, as amended by section 2 of the Paperwork Reduction Act of 1995. You do not need to answer these questions unless we display a valid Office of Management and Budget control number. We estimate that it will take about 11 minutes to read the instructions, gather the facts, and answer the questions. *Send only comments relating to our time estimate above to:* SSA, 6401 Security Blvd, Baltimore, MD 21235-6401.

INFORMATION ABOUT YOUR REQUEST

- **How Do I Get This Information?**

  You need to complete the attached form to tell us what information you want.

- **Can I Get This Information For Someone Else?**

  Yes, if you have their written permission. For more information, see page 3.

- **Who Can Sign On Behalf Of The Individual?**

  The parent of a minor child, or the legal guardian of an individual who has been declared legally incompetent, may sign if he/she is acting on behalf of the individual.

- **Is There A Fee For This Information?**

  1. Certified/Non-Certified Detailed Earnings Information

  Yes, we usually charge a fee for detailed information. In most cases, this information is used for purposes NOT directly related to Social Security such as for a private pension plan or personal injury suit. The fee chart on page 3 gives the amount of the charge.

  Sometimes, there is no charge for detailed information. If you have reason to believe your earnings are not correct (for example, you have previously received earnings information from us

and it does not agree with your records), we will supply you with more detail for the period in question. Occasionally, earnings amounts are wrong because an employer did not correctly report earnings or earnings are credited to the wrong person. In situations like these, we will send you detailed information, at no charge, so we can correct your record.

Be sure to show the year(s) involved on the request form and explain why you need the information. If you do not tell us why you need the information, we will charge a fee.

We will certify the detailed earnings information for an additional fee of $15.00. Certification is usually not necessary unless you plan to use the information in court.

2. Certified Yearly Totals of Earnings

Yes, there is a fee of $15 to certify yearly totals of earnings. Certification is usually not necessary unless you plan to use the information in court.

3. Method of Payment

Enclose a check or money order for the entire fee required. Payment can also be made by credit card. To do so, complete page 4 of this form and return it with your request form.

Form **SSA-7050-F4** (07-2010) EF (07-2010)
Destroy prior editions

Illustration 16-6   REQUEST FOR SOCIAL SECURITY EARNINGS INFORMATION *(Continued)*

REQUEST FOR SOCIAL SECURITY EARNINGS INFORMATION

1. From whose record do you need the earnings information?

   Print the Name, Social Security Number (SSN), and date of birth below.

   Name _____   Social Security
                                        Number _____

   Other Name(s) Used   Date of Birth
   (Include Maiden Name) _____   (Mo/Day/Yr) _____

2. What kind of information do you need?

   ☐ **Detailed Earnings Information**   For the period(s)/year(s): _____
      (If you check this block, tell us below
      why you need this information.)

      ....

   ☐ **Certified Yearly Totals of Earnings**   For the year(s): _____
      (Check this box only if you want the information
      certified. Otherwise, call 1-800-772-1213 to
      request Form SSA-7004, Request for Social
      Security Statement)

3. If you owe us a fee for this detailed earnings information, enter the amount due
   using the chart on page 3 . . . .   A. $ _____

   Do you want us to certify the information?   ☐ Yes   ☐ No

   If yes, enter $15.00 . . . .   B. $ _____

   ADD the amounts on lines A and B, and
   enter the TOTAL amount . . . .   C. $ _____

   - You can pay by CREDIT CARD by completing and returning the form on page 4, or
   - Send your CHECK or MONEY ORDER for the amount on line C with the request and
     make check or money order payable to "Social Security Administration"
   - DO NOT SEND CASH.

4. I am the individual to whom the record pertains (or a person who is authorized to sign on behalf of that
   individual). I understand that any false representation to knowingly and willfully obtain information from
   Social Security records is punishable by a fine of not more than $5,000 or one year in prison.

   SIGN your name here
        (Do not print) > _____   Date _____

   Daytime Phone Number   _____ _____
                          (Area Code) (Telephone Number)

5. Tell us where you want the information sent. (Please print)

   Name _____   Address _____

   City, State & Zip Code _____

6. Mail Completed Form(s) To: **Exception:** If using private contractor (e.g., FedEx) to mail form(s), use:

   Social Security Administration   Social Security Administration
   Division of Earnings Record Operations   Division of Earnings Record Operations
   P.O. Box 33003   300 N. Greene St.
   Baltimore, Maryland 21290-3003   Baltimore, Maryland 21290-0300

   Form SSA-7050-F4 (07-2010) EF (07-2010)   2
   Destroy Prior Editions

Illustration 16-7 REQUEST FOR COPY OR TRANSCRIPT OF TAX FORM

Form **4506**	**Request for Copy of Tax Return**
(Rev. January 2012)	OMB No. 1545-0429
Department of the Treasury Internal Revenue Service	► **Request may be rejected if the form is incomplete or illegible.**

Tip. You may be able to get your tax return or return information from other sources. If you had your tax return completed by a paid preparer, they should be able to provide you a copy of the return. The IRS can provide a **Tax Return Transcript** for many returns free of charge. The transcript provides most of the line entries from the original tax return and usually contains the information that a third party (such as a mortgage company) requires. See **Form 4506-T, Request for Transcript of Tax Return,** or you can quickly request transcripts by using our automated self-help service tools. Please visit us at IRS.gov and click on "Order a Transcript" or call 1-800-908-9946.

1a Name shown on tax return. If a joint return, enter the name shown first.	**1b** First social security number on tax return, individual taxpayer identification number, or employer identification number (see instructions)
2a If a joint return, enter spouse's name shown on tax return.	**2b** Second social security number or individual taxpayer identification number if joint tax return

3 Current name, address (including apt., room, or suite no.), city, state, and ZIP code (see instructions)

4 Previous address shown on the last return filed if different from line 3 (see instructions)

5 If the tax return is to be mailed to a third party (such as a mortgage company), enter the third party's name, address, and telephone number.

Caution. *If the tax return is being mailed to a third party, ensure that you have filled in lines 6 and 7 before signing. Sign and date the form once you have filled in these lines. Completing these steps helps to protect your privacy. Once the IRS discloses your IRS return to the third party listed on line 5, the IRS has no control over what the third party does with the information. If you would like to limit the third party's authority to disclose your return information, you can specify this limitation in your written agreement with the third party.*

6 **Tax return requested.** Form 1040, 1120, 941, etc. and all attachments as originally submitted to the IRS, including Form(s) W-2, schedules, or amended returns. Copies of Forms 1040, 1040A, and 1040EZ are generally available for 7 years from filing before they are destroyed by law. Other returns may be available for a longer period of time. Enter only one return number. If you need more than one type of return, you must complete another Form 4506. ►

    Note. *If the copies must be certified for court or administrative proceedings, check here* . . . . ☐

7 **Year or period requested.** Enter the ending date of the year or period, using the mm/dd/yyyy format. If you are requesting more than eight years or periods, you must attach another Form 4506.

_____	_____	_____	_____
_____	_____	_____	_____

8 **Fee.** There is a $57 fee for each return requested. **Full payment must be included with your request or it will be rejected. Make your check or money order payable to "United States Treasury." Enter your SSN or EIN and "Form 4506 request" on your check or money order.**

a	Cost for each return	$ **$57.00**
b	Number of returns requested on line 7	
c	Total cost. Multiply line 8a by line 8b	$

9 If we cannot find the tax return, we will refund the fee. If the refund should go to the third party listed on line 5, check here . . . . . ☐

Caution. Do not sign this form unless all applicable lines have been completed.

Signature of taxpayer(s). I declare that I am either the taxpayer whose name is shown on line 1a or 2a, or a person authorized to obtain the tax return requested. If the request applies to a joint return, **either** husband or wife must sign. If signed by a corporate officer, partner, guardian, tax matters partner, executor, receiver, administrator, trustee, or party other than the taxpayer, I certify that I have the authority to execute Form 4506 on behalf of the taxpayer. **Note.** *For tax returns being sent to a third party, this form must be received within 120 days of the signature date.*

Phone number of taxpayer on line 1a or 2a

Sign Here	► Signature (see instructions)	Date
	► Title (if line 1a above is a corporation, partnership, estate, or trust)	
	► Spouse's signature	Date

For Privacy Act and Paperwork Reduction Act Notice, see page 2.   Cat. No. 41721E   Form **4506** (Rev. 1-2012)

agencies including the Securities Exchange Commission, Food and Drug Administration, and the Department of Justice fraud task force. There are also search companies that, for a fee, will perform electronic searches for public record information available from federal agencies. See Appendix B for a comprehensive list of search companies.

Chapter Summary and Conclusion

The federal government is structured by the Constitution into three separate branches—the legislative, executive, and judicial—and each branch has its own procedures for acquiring the information held there. In order to maximize the opportunities for acquiring information, the legal professional must be well versed in how the federal government is organized and functions. Most information held by the federal government is accessible through one of the many federal agencies Congress has created and given authority to act. Agency information may be accessible from the agency Web site, from any of the numerous publications available containing such information, or the investigator can utilize a Freedom of Information Act request.

In Chapter 17 we will consider acquiring information from state and local governments.

Review Questions

1. By _____ records or _____ sources we mean information compiled and maintained by government _____ and offices at the federal, _____, and _____ levels.
2. What are the two distinct skills involved in accessing public and private records?
3. List seven sources the legal professional can consult to learn more about information available from federal departments and agencies. How is that information accessed?
4. What is the GPO? What is GPO Access?
5. What do we mean by "enabling legislation" as to a governmental agency or department, and how can consulting it assist the investigator?
6. Summarize how judicial records are kept and how they can be accessed.
7. Why does every legal investigator need to know Thomas? What can it do for us?
8. What is the Freedom of Information Act and how do we access governmental information using it?
9. List nine categories of information that are exempt from a FOIA request.
10. What is the Privacy Act? What kinds of information can be accessed using it?

KEY WORDS AND PHRASES TO REMEMBER

administrative agency

administrative law

agencies

authorities

blue pages

boards

browser

bureaus

party/case index

clerk's office

Code of Federal Regulations

commissions

database vendor

Data.gov

departments

Dialog

E-Government Act of 2002

ELISS

enabling legislation

executive branch

exemption

Federal Bulletin Board

federal government

Federal Register

federal regulation

FOIA

GPO Access

home page

Internet

ISP

judicial branch

legislative branch

LexisNexis

local government

offices

open data site

Open Government Act of 2007

PACER

Privacy Act

private records

public records

search engine

services

state government

URL

Web site

Westlaw

LEARN BY DOING

LBD 16-1. For the actual corporation you selected for Hypothetical 16-2, use the federal judiciary information sources set out in Appendix B to determine every federal lawsuit to which this corporation has been a party in the last five years. That includes being a plaintiff or defendant in a civil suit or a defendant in a federal criminal action. Prepare a memorandum summarizing each case you locate by name, court, docket number, date of filing, and a brief summary of the disposition of the case. Also summarize the different resources you utilized to locate this information.

LBD 16-2. Determine whether your state or local bar associations have a handbook or other material listing the national, regional, and/or local offices of federal departments and agencies. Determine who publishes the source you locate, its cost, and how frequently it is updated. Also visit your local library and determine what resources are there to assist you in learning about the various federal departments and agencies, what they do, and how to contact them. As part of your visit, see which of the printed federal government resources listed in Appendix B are available in your local library.

LBD 16-3. Arrange a visit to the local or regional office of a federal agency to tour the office, learn what the agency does, and its procedures, especially its procedures for handling requests for information. Your instructor may want to arrange a group visit for the entire class. Prepare questions to ask while you are there.

LBD 16-4. Select a federal agency and prepare and submit an actual Privacy Act request for yourself. Think of records or information that may be maintained by a federal agency that you would like to see and prepare an actual FOIA request to the appropriate agency.

LBD 16-5. Review today's or a recent newspaper to locate an article discussing legislation currently moving through Congress. Then use the online congressional information sources set out in Appendix B to locate all the information you can on that legislation, including congressional committee reports in both houses.

LBDs 16-6 through 16-12 are accessible on the Author Updates link to the text Web site at www.aspenparalegaled.com/books/parsons_investigating/default.asp.

Chapter 17

Public Sources of Information—State and Local

CHAPTER OBJECTIVES

In this chapter you will learn how to access information from state and local government sources. We will consider:

- The way that state and local governments are organized
- The kinds of records they maintain
- Various resources for accessing those records, including state open records acts and various Internet resources

A. The Structure of State and Local Governments

All 50 states pattern their governments on the federal model. That is, they each have a legislative, executive, and judicial branch, together with numerous administrative agencies, departments, boards and bureaus, as in the federal system. However, within that broad three-branch model, the specific organization of state governments varies greatly, as do the rules for accessing their records.

Pursuant to its fundamental responsibility to provide for the health, safety, and welfare of its citizens (referred to generally as **police powers**), each state regulates a wide range of personal and business activities and accordingly generates substantial numbers of **public records**. Some public records are created by the regulating governmental agency (e.g., restaurant inspection reports generated by inspectors for a state or local department of health; a business license issued by a city of a county department of licensure), whereas others are created by regulated persons or businesses who file, record, or register certain required records with the regulating agency (e.g., deeds transferring title to real property recorded in a city or county register of deeds office; a financing statement documenting a creditor's security interest in personal property filed with a state secretary of state's office).

In addition, though **state government** offices and records are centralized to a large extent in the state capital, all states have **political subdivisions**—counties and incorporated cities and townships (local governments) authorized by the state to provide local government services to their citizens—that collect and maintain their own records. And, some "state" records are primarily or even exclusively accessible at offices on the local level (e.g., civil and criminal case files of the *state* courts accessible in the *county* courthouses). Consequently, it is best to learn about the kinds of state and local records that exist and how to access them by dividing the topic into state and local sources rather than focusing on the three branches of government as we did in considering federal records.

The more familiar the legal professional engaged in investigation is with the organization of the state and local governments of his state, the more effective he will be at accessing the available records. Most state and many local governments publish handbooks or manuals containing names, addresses, and phone numbers, e-mail addresses, and, increasingly, Internet addresses, for the various government departments and agencies. In addition, many state and local bar organizations publish guides containing this information. The legal professional should have ready access to these and keep them current. Also, most phone books will contain separate listings for county and city government offices and the local offices of state agencies. (See LBD 17-3.)

B. Records Maintained by State Governments

In this section we will consider various types of records typically maintained by state governments and frequently sought by investigators. A couple of caveats, though. First, this list is intended to be representative not comprehensive. There will be many more types of records maintained by your state. You should be as familiar as possible with the departments and agencies of your state government and the records they maintain. (See LBD 17-3.) You also must think creatively to locate the right agency—sometimes under a lot of pressure (see Hypothetical 17-1).

HYPOTHETICAL 17-1

Assume you are working for Bragg, Boast & Bluster, the silkiest of the silk stocking firms in town. One afternoon you are working quietly at your desk, waiting for 5:00 to roll around, when the phone rings. You answer it and hear the voice of the firm's senior partner, Justa Boorish Bragg, on the line. (He prefers to go by J.B. I wonder why?) This is the first time Mr. Bragg has ever spoken to you. You didn't even know he knew your name. (And, truthfully, you kind of liked it that way!) Without thinking, you stand up, striking your knee on the corner of the desk and knocking over the chocolate milkshake you shouldn't have had at your desk anyway. Grimacing with pain, and trying to mop up the mess with your free hand, you listen to your next assignment.

It seems that Mr. Bragg is, at this moment, in conference with one of the firm's most important clients. This client owns residential property adjoining the largest river flowing through your state. (You don't have to look that up, do you?) The client is upset because the commercial barge traffic using the river has increased lately, and the barges seem to be coming closer to her property than ever before. She has told Mr. Bragg that the barges sometimes come so close that the workers on the barges can be heard whistling and shouting unseemly things at persons using the swimming pool in her backyard.

Mr. Bragg tells you that he is going to call the responsible agency himself to complain on behalf of the client. (Of course, this enables the firm to bill Mr. Bragg's $300 per hour for this work rather than your piddling $75 per hour. But, we digress.) Mr. Bragg laughingly confesses, however, that he does not know which state agency is responsible for supervising barge traffic on the river. He would like for you to check on it and let him know—WITHIN 15 MINUTES! You start to say that you will get right on it but realize that he has already hung up.

Think through how you would go about locating this information for Mr. Bragg:

1. What written or electronic sources could you use to determine this?
2. What people sources around you might be helpful?
3. If you need to call someone for assistance, how would you decide who to call first?
4. If you are going to depend on helpful government employees to assist you with this, how important will your phone communication skills be? (See Chapter 8 on Communication Skills.)

Your instructor may want you to actually locate the agency in your state that would be responsible for the barge traffic on navigable rivers. (See LBD 17-4.)

A second caveat: Some of the state records listed below may be maintained at the local government level rather than the state. Or they may be available at both levels. For example, vital statistics records are often available at both the state and county levels. UCC-1 financing statements are sometimes filed at both the state and county levels. Records that are maintained solely at the state level are usually accessible through departments and agencies located in the capital city of the state.

1. Vital statistics

Vital records statistics include information and certificates for births, deaths, marriages, and divorces. Every state has a centralized vital records bureau of some kind. The U.S. Department of Health and Human Services has issued a pamphlet obtainable through the Government Printing Office (GPO; online at www.gpoaccess.gov) entitled, *Where to Write for Vital Records: Births, Deaths, Marriages and Divorces,* which provides the address of each state vital records office and tells how far back the state records go. Such records are usually accessible by written request or personal visit. An online site helpful for locating information on vital records is Vital Records Resource at www.vitalchek.com. (See Appendix B for a comprehensive listing of resources for locating vital statistics information.)

Marriage and divorce records originate at the county level, as do **birth** and **death certificates** in many states, and may be accessible there as well as through the state vital records bureau. Even if the issuance of birth and death certificates is now handled exclusively by the state, counties or even city health departments may have older records on file, as may your local public library, especially if it maintains a genealogy section.

2. Motor vehicle and driving records

Every state has an agency or bureau responsible for maintaining records regarding vehicle registration, driver's licenses, driving record, and accident reports. Accessibility of those records varies from state to state but has been made more uniform in recent years by provisions of the Driver's Privacy Protection Act (DPPA), 18 U.S.C. §2721, effective September 1997. The Act prohibits state departments of motor vehicles from releasing or anyone from using certain personal information provided to the departments in connection with a motor vehicle record. There are a number of exceptions to the prohibition on releasing information under the DPPA, including information disclosed to a legitimate business for use in a court or administrative proceeding or an investigation in anticipation of litigation. Some states have revised their statutes in recent years to make them even more restrictive than required by the DPPA because of increasing public concern over stalking incidents.

In states where driver's license information can be obtained, the state will furnish an abstract telling you the subject's date of birth, license number, social security number, gender, basic physical characteristics (height, weight, and eye and hair color), and driving restrictions, if any. Some state departments will also perform searches of license plate numbers or vehicle identification numbers (**VIN**). A few states require the subject's permission to perform a search of these records, and at least two states, Massachusetts and Washington, will not supply driver's license information.

3. Corporate and other business records

As you learn when you study business organizations, corporations and other business entities such as limited partnerships and limited liability companies are created under state laws. Every state has a department, usually called the office of the **Secretary of State**, or something similar, responsible for collecting and maintaining public filings made by these entities. Organizational documents such as corporate charters, amended charters, certificates of limited partnership, notices of dissolution, etc., are filed there, and in most states, are accessible to the public upon request. Tremendous amounts of information may be disclosed in these business filings. Access to tax returns and other financial filings may be more strictly limited. (See discussion of state departments of revenue below.)

The Secretary of State's office usually also handles UCC filings relating to the creation and release of security interests in personal property. Most state offices will perform searches of their UCC records (some for a fee, some for free) and provide an abstract of all recorded filings for your subject. Usually a UCC-3: Request for Information or Copies must accompany the request. As discussed above, there are a number of records search companies who will search these and other accessible state records in a timely fashion for a fee. (See Appendix B for a comprehensive listing of public records search companies.)

4. Licensing and registration records

States **license** a great many professions, occupations, trades, and crafts. Illustration 17-1 contains a representative sampling.

A quick review of your state code will probably reveal many more occupations that are regulated by your state and require some licensing process. In some states, there will be one centralized department to handle licenses. In other states, there may be multiple departments or agencies. Since these occupations hold themselves out to the public, most states make license information readily available. There may be some limitations on accessing information regarding complaints or license suspensions, but the investigator should check the state statute and any governing regulations. Many states are members of **CLEAR** (Council on Licensure, Enforcement, and Regulation, homepage at www.clearhq.org), a national clearinghouse in Lexington, Kentucky, for the reporting of disciplinary actions taken against licensed persons in all professions and trades. (See LBD 17-6.)

Illustration 17-1   TYPICAL PROFESSIONS AND OCCUPATIONS LICENSED BY STATES

accountants	contractors	pharmacist's aides
actuaries	dental hygienists	physician assistants
acupuncturists	dentists	physicians
aircraft mechanics	dieticians	private investigators
aircraft pilots	electricians	psychologists
appraisers	embalmers	realtors
arbitrators	financial management	securities brokers
architects	consultant	security guards
attorneys	nurse consultants	surveyors
auctioneers	nurses	teachers
bankers	nurse's aides	therapists
barbers	pawnbrokers	travel agents
brokers	pest controllers	veterinarians
carpenters	pet groomers	vocational experts
chiropractors	pharmacists	

5. Regulatory commission records

States typically have entire departments or commissions dedicated to the regulation of certain industrial, business, or consumer activities. Examples include departments responsible for regulating hospitals and nursing homes; home health care services; funeral homes; cemeteries; insurance companies; banks, credit unions, and other financial services companies; oil and gas producers and distributors; public utilities; fish and game activities; gambling and gaming activities; and alcohol and beverage control. States differ widely on the accessibility of information from these regulatory commissions, and the investigator should become familiar with the governing statutes and regulations for them.

6. Tax and revenue records

SLEUTH ON THE LOOSE

See if you can find the location of the office in your state that maintains corporate records using the Law Librarian's Society's Legislative Source Book at www.llsdc.org/sourcebook.

Every state has one or more departments responsible for collecting taxes—personal and corporate income taxes, property taxes, sales taxes, use taxes, etc. Some real and personal property assessment values for tax purposes may be accessible, but in general, access to tax returns for individuals and businesses is strictly limited. However, if an individual or business is involved in litigation with the state over a tax levy or in other civil litigation involving the company's finances or if an individual is involved in a divorce action, tax records may be accessible as discovery information located in the court file or as an exhibit at trial.

7. Securities filings

As a counterpoint to the Securities Exchange Commission, states have their own **"blue sky" laws** requiring certain corporations active in trading securities within the state to make regular filings with a designated state securities agency. Access to these filings varies with the states, and the investigator must check governing statutes and regulations of the agency.

8. Social service agencies records

Every state has one or more agencies responsible for overseeing matters related to family support services, child welfare, health care, and unemployment. Many of these agencies work in conjunction with federal agencies, and the accessibility of their records is frequently governed by federal as well as state rules and regulations.

9. Workers' compensation records

Every state has a department or agency charged with overseeing the state's workers' compensation statutes. Accessibility of these records will vary among the states, but is usually restricted. However, in many states, a particular workers' compensation suit or settlement may be processed through the state courts or a special administrative board, the records of which are public and accessible.

10. Law enforcement records

Like the federal government, states typically have various levels of law enforcement: a state police or bureau of investigation to provide security for government officials and to investigate state crimes and the highway patrol, responsible for highway traffic and accidents. Most such records are kept at the state capital and are subject to various restrictions on access. Though records related to ongoing investigations will almost always be inaccessible, some states will allow a criminal background check. Most states allow access to car accident reports, though some restrict this access to the parties involved and their insurance companies.

Assume you are assisting the attorney defending Rowdy Outlaw in connection with the murder charges pending against him in your state (see Case Study No. 1 in Appendix A), the attorney representing Soupspoon Wise in his potential personal injury action (see Case Study No. 2), the attorney representing Vidalia Unyon in her divorce action against Greene Unyon (see Case Study No. 3), and the attorney representing Rocky Road Developers, Inc. (see Case Study No. 4). The supervising attorney has asked you to locate the information outlined below on those cases. For each item of information:

1. Determine which state agency(s) you would contact to obtain the information.
2. Describe the procedure you would follow to obtain the information.
3. Identify any items of information that you think will not be accessible.
4. For each case, are there other kinds of information you would recommend seeking from state public sources?

Note: Because the Case Studies present fictitious cases, you will not be contacting any state office to actually obtain information on the case. You will be determining which state offices you would contact for each type of information and the procedure you would follow to do so.

A. The Rowdy Outlaw case

1. Determine if Jack Gates is in fact a licensed insurance agent and the status of that license. Do the same for Candy Carmichael's hairdresser license and Perry Peter's security guard license.
2. Determine if Dr. Michael Melody is an employee of the state in any capacity including, possibly, a faculty member of a state educational institution.

B. The Red Dog Saloon case

1. Determine whether the Red Dog Saloon or its manager, Turtle Shoop, have a valid liquor license and, if so, the status of that license.
2. Locate a copy of the accident report.
3. Determine whether the Red Dog Saloon is incorporated or some other registered business entity and, if so, who owns it and the name and address of its registered agent for service of process.
4. Determine the status of Tanya Trucker's masseuse license.

C. The Vidalia Unyon case

1. Check the status of Greene Unyon's veterinarian's license, including how long he has been licensed, whether his license is currently in good standing, whether his license has ever been suspended or revoked, and whether any ethical or other complaints have been filed against him with the licensing agency.
2. Find out how the three vehicles are titled and whether any liens exist against them.
3. Determine whether Mr. Unyon's veterinary practice is set up as a professional corporation, professional limited liability company, or other entity and, if so, the status of that entity with the state.

D. The Rocky Road Project

1. Locate records of any environmental reports or investigations by the state on the old gas station property or the stream next to it.
2. Determine if Rocky Road, Inc., is in good standing with the state as a corporation. Obtain a copy of its charter and any amendments.

C. ▶ Records Maintained by Local Government

By **local records** we mean records maintained at the county and city level. Illustration 17-2 provides a summary of the kinds of records typically maintained by local governments and accessed at the county courthouse, town hall, city municipal building, public utilities offices, sheriff's office, police station, election commission, draft board, school board office, and other local offices.

Following is a summary of frequently contacted sources of local records. The legal professional engaged in investigation must be familiar with the local court house, town hall, and other public places where records are kept. He also needs to be familiar with the kinds of records maintained in each of those offices.

1. Records of civil and criminal cases in court clerk's offices

The clerks of the civil and criminal state courts as well as county and municipal courts will maintain indexes of pending and closed files that may be searched and copied unless sealed by court order. The civil indexes will be keyed to the names of the parties and will disclose the names of the parties, the nature of the suit, its disposition if closed, and the docket number assigned to the case with which you can obtain the file itself. The criminal case index is keyed to the name of the defendant and will disclose the charge, the disposition, and the docket number.

In addition, the **judgment docket** (sometimes called the **abstract of judgment index**) along with the wage assignment, garnishment, or **execution index** maintained by the civil court clerk will disclose judgments taken against named defendants, the amount of the judgment, whether it has been satisfied, and possibly how.

As discussed earlier in connection with records of federal judicial proceedings, case files can be rich sources of information on parties and witnesses because they contain pleadings that set out the parties' formal allegations, discovery, and motion material. As in the federal system, these local records are increasingly computerized.

2. Permits and licenses

Local governments **license** or **permit** just about every public activity that occurs in their jurisdictions: vehicle permits, animal licenses, vendor licenses, building projects, parades and marches, signs, fictitious businesses name registration, etc. Individuals and business acquiring these licenses and permits are required to disclose substantial amounts of information and it is usually accessible.

3. Real property transfer records in register/ recorder of deeds office

In most counties, land transaction records are centralized in one office. Warranty deeds, quitclaim deeds, easements, mortgages, option contracts, rights of first refusal, leases, releases, judgment liens, tax liens, **liens** *lis pendens*—all that stuff you learned about in your real property course is here, and it is freely accessible.

Somewhere in your county courthouse (frequently maintained in the register's office along with land transaction records) are records of local UCC filings—UCC-1 financing statements and releases of personal property liens—also available for public inspection.

Illustration 17-2
EXAMPLES OF
LOCAL
GOVERNMENT
RECORDS

birth and death certificates	liens and releases
building permits	marriage records
business licenses and permits	mortgages
civil cases pending	pet licenses
civil judgments	probate records
contracts	property appraisals
criminal cases pending	property tax records
criminal convictions	school records
deeds of conveyance	tax liens
divorce records	UCC filings
easements—public and private	voter registration records
library records	zoning regulations

4. Tax records in assessor's offices

Assessments of the value of real and personal property for tax purposes are available here, together with records of tax payments and delinquencies.

5. Probate court records

Wills offered for **probate** are accessible by the public, as is information in the probate file regarding the collection and distribution of the estate. If a will is contested, the litigation file will typically be open to public inspection. The probate file may also contain information on guardianships, conservatorships, and trusts.

6. Vital statistics

As discussed in connection with state records, local offices may also maintain current or older records on births and deaths. The county coroner's office may be the place to go for death certificate information. Marriage licenses are issued by the local county clerk, legal separations and divorces are granted by local courts, and all those records are accessible.

7. Voting records in election commission offices

Information that may be obtainable from the election commission includes name, current and prior addresses, occupation, political party, place and date of birth, and possibly Social Security number.

SLEUTH ON THE LOOSE

8. Public utilities records

Gas, electric, water, sewer, and phone records can disclose much information about a person. In most states, this locally maintained information is accessible.

Access the Web site for the New York Public Library at www.nypl.org and see what holdings of the library are accessible online. (Or try the Internet Public Library at www.ipl.org; the Carnegie Library at www.clpgh.org; or the Library of Congress at www.loc.gov.)

9. Law enforcement records in police and sheriff's departments

Local law enforcement records are usually restricted in certain ways and the investigator must check applicable statutes, regulations, and rules. However, in many localities, traffic accident reports and some arrest and jail records are accessible.

10. Public school records

Access to records of public schools is generally limited to the student or, if the student is a minor, his parents or legal guardian. The school district office may, however, be helpful in providing information about the school system and in locating a current or former teacher or student.

11. The public library

The local library can be a rich source of information about people and businesses in the community and about the community itself. Genealogy records, current and out-of-date phone books, current and out-of-date city and county directories, current city and county ordinances, census information, and information on local business and industry are just some examples of the kinds of information available in the local library. Another asset valuable to the investigator is the reference librarian, who is typically knowledgeable and helpful not only about the library resources, but about people in the community as well. Often the library staff can refer you to someone likely to have the information you are seeking. The library's ability to obtain information from other libraries by interlibrary loan may be helpful also.

HYPOTHETICAL 17-3

Assume you are assisting the attorney defending Rowdy Outlaw in connection with the murder charges pending against him in your state (see Case Study No. 1 in Appendix A), the attorney representing Soupspoon Wise in his potential personal injury action (see Case Study No. 2), the attorney representing Vidalia Unyon in her divorce action against Greene Unyon (see Case Study No. 3), and the attorney representing Rocky Road Developers, Inc. (see Case Study No. 4). The supervising attorneys has asked you to locate the information outlined below on those cases. For each item of information:

1. Determine which local government office(s) you would contact to obtain the information.
2. Describe the procedure you would follow to obtain the information.
3. Identify any items of information that you think will not be accessible.
4. For each case, are there other kinds of information you would recommend seeking from local government sources?

Note: Because the Case Studies present fictitious cases, you will not be contacting any local government office to actually obtain information on the case. You will be determining which local government offices you would contact for each type of information and the procedure you would follow to do so.

A. The Rowdy Outlaw case

1. Confirm Bobbette Bouvier's ownership of the Palace Towers condominium and any outstanding indebtedness on it.
2. Determine if Bobbette Bouvier, Candy Outlaw, or Rowdy Outlaw has been a party to any civil litigation in the past three years.
3. Determine if Rowdy Outlaw has any prior arrests or criminal convictions.
4. Check on any existing probate proceeding for Bobbette Bouvier.
5. Locate the marriage license for Rowdy Outlaw and Candy Outlaw. If it shows any prior marriages for either, locate the divorce/annulment records.
6. Obtain a copy of the death certificate for Bobbette Bouvier.

B. The Red Dog Saloon case

1. Obtain a copy of all business permits, liquor license, etc., for the Red Dog Saloon.
2. Obtain a copy of the accident report.
3. See if the Red Dog Saloon or its owner has been a defendant in any civil suits in the last ten years.

C. The Vidalia Unyon case

1. Locate the mortgage in favor of First City Bank on the residence of the parties. Determine the date it was executed, the amount of indebtedness secured and the payment terms. Check for any release or renewal of that mortgage and for other recorded indebtedness on the house.
2. Determine the current assessed value of the residence for tax purposes, the date of the most current assessment, and whether the taxes are paid up.
3. Determine if Mr. Unyon has owned or conveyed any realty in the last ten years other than the residence or whether he has pledged any personal property as collateral for any indebtedness during that time.
4. Locate all civil suits in which Mr. Unyon or his veterinary practice has been named as a party, summarize the claims made in each such suit, the disposition of each if not still pending, and, if any judgments were rendered, whether they have been satisfied.

D. The Rocky Road Project

1. Make sure the option agreement on the ten acres is properly recorded.
2. Determine if a probate proceeding has been filed for Edward Dig Deep and, if so, locate any existing will.
3. Determine the titled owner of the old gas station property; confirm that Edward Dig Deep was the sole owner of the five-acre tract and that the city has clear title to the three-acre tract. Check for outstanding or potential liens on any of the parcels (including liens *lis pendens*), and check the status of property taxes on each.

D. State Public Records Acts and Other Statutes and Rules Controlling Accessibility

SLEUTH ON THE LOOSE

Go to www.govspot.com and see what information you can access there concerning your state government or the local government of your state capital or the local government of a nearby large city.

In the United States we have a strong **public policy** in favor of the accessibility of public records by members of the public. As the U.S. Supreme Court said in *National Archives and Records Administration v. Favish*, 541 U.S. 157, 171-72 (2004), "providing access to public records promotes governmental accountability by enabling citizens to keep track of what the government is up to." By *accessibility* we mean that such records should be open for inspection and copying, either electronically or in paper format.

To implement this public policy favoring openness and accessibility of government records, all 50 states have enacted what are usually referred to as **public records acts (PRA)** or **open records acts (ORA)**. Some, like Michigan, Delaware, and Virginia, refer to their laws as **freedom of information acts** (M.C.L.A. §15.231(1). However denominated, PRAs define what is and is not a public record and provide a procedure for

Illustration 17-3 STATEMENT OF PURPOSE FROM PUBLIC RECORDS ACT OF THE STATE OF WASHINGTON

"The people of this state do not yield their sovereignty to the agencies that serve them. The people, in delegating authority, do not give their public servants the right to decide what is good for the people to know and what is not good for them to know. The people insist on remaining informed so that they may maintain control over the instruments that they have created."

Source: Washington Public Records Act, RCW §42.17.251

accessing those records from the state and local government agencies and departments that are the custodians of the records. PRAs also provide a procedure for petitioning a court to compel disclosure of a public record when the governmental entity fails or refuses to disclose it. Illustration 17-3 sets out the statement of purpose codified in the PRA of the state of Washington.

In this section we will consider generally what records PRAs cover and the procedures they set out for accessing public records. But these statutes vary widely from state to state, both in scope of coverage and procedure, and it is imperative that the legal professional be familiar with the PRA or ORA of his own state (see LBD 17-1).

1. What is an accessible "public record" under a state PRA?

Most state PRAs include a very broad definition of what constitutes a public record. Illustration 17-4 contains the statutory definition of public records from the Tennessee PRA, a very typical statute (see LBD 17-1).

What about **metadata** (data that describes other data including formatting information and edited content) containing information once included in an electronically produced document that was later edited

Illustration 17-4 DEFINITION OF "PUBLIC RECORDS" FROM THE TENNESSEE PUBLIC RECORDS ACT

"Public record or records" or "state record or records" means all documents, papers, letters, maps, books, photographs, microfilms, electronic data processing files and output, films, sound recordings, or other material, regardless of physical form or characteristics made or received pursuant to law or ordinance or in connection with the transaction of official business by any governmental agency.

All state, county and municipal records shall, at all times during business hours. . . be open for personal inspection by any citizen of this state, and those in charge of the records shall not refuse such right of inspection to any citizen, unless otherwise provided by state law.

SOURCE: Tenn. Code Ann. §10-7-503(a)(1)(A) and 2(A).

out but can still be traced and recovered? In *Lake v. City of Phoenix*, 218 P.3d 1004 (Ariz. 2009), the Arizona Supreme Court held that metadata buried in electronically edited documents is part of the public record and was subject to disclosure along with the finalized document under the state public records act (involving notes written by public employees supervisor and later edited to justify action taken against employee).

In many states the scope of public records may be construed to include the records of privately owned businesses if those businesses are so intertwined with a government department or agency that the private entity is the **functional equivalent** of that agency (e.g., a corporation administering state-subsidized child care program or a corporation operating a correctional facility under contract with the state) (see LBD 17-9).

Though PRAs typically contain a very broad definition of what constitutes public records and mandate that all records falling within the definition should be available for inspection by the public, note the important qualifying phrase, "unless otherwise provided by state law," in Illustration 17-4. In fact every state PRA will exempt some public

Illustration 17-5   TYPICAL PUBLIC RECORDS EXEMPTED FROM DISCLOSURE UNDER STATE PRAs

—Information of a personal nature if public disclosure would constitute a clearly unwarranted invasion of an individual's privacy

—Law enforcement investigation records if disclosure would interfere with law enforcement proceedings

—Information that would prejudice a public body's ability to maintain the physical security of custodial or penal institutions

—Trade secrets or commercial or financial information voluntarily provided to an agency for use in developing governmental policy

—Information or records subject to the attorney-client, attorney work product, physician-patient, psychologist-patient, priest-penitent, or other privilege recognized by statute or court rule

—A bid or proposal by a person to enter into a contract or agreement, until the time for the public opening of bids or proposals

—Test questions and answers, scoring keys, and other examination instruments or data used to administer a license, public employment, or academic examination

—Medical, counseling, or psychological records of an identifiable individual

—Communications and notes within a public body or between public bodies of an advisory nature to the extent that they cover other than purely factual materials and are preliminary to a final agency determination of policy or action but only if the public interest in encouraging frank communication between officials and employees of public bodies clearly outweighs the public interest in disclosure

—Records of law enforcement communication codes, or plans for deployment of law enforcement personnel, that if disclosed would prejudice a public body's ability to protect the public safety

—Academic records except for the student or his designated agent or custodian

—Records of a law enforcement agency that would identify an informant or undercover officer

—Records of a public body's security measures

—Records or information relating to a civil action in which the requesting party and the public body are parties

—The Social Security number of an individual

records from inspection for reasons having to do with confidentiality. Illustration 17-5 sets out a list of public records typically declared exempt from disclosure under a state PRA. The list in Illustration 17-5 is based loosely on Michigan's statute, M.C.L.A. §15.243.

HYPOTHETICAL 17-4

Look through the list of records exempt from disclosure in Illustration 17-5. Do you see the potential for dispute? What is a "clearly unwarranted" invasion of an individual's privacy? What constitutes a trade secret? When is a communication subject to the attorney-client or other referenced privilege? In addition, many of the exempted categories of records are not exempt if the public interest in disclosure outweighs the public interest in nondisclosure in a particular instance. Just imagine the legal battles over that standard when parents concerned about the low test scores of their children ask to see questions and scoring keys for state administered exams. At what point does the public interest in disclosure outweigh the policy behind declaring such records exempt? This is why, in every state, you will find substantial case law dealing with contests over the disclosure of public records that the state or local governmental entity contend are exempt.

Though the kinds of records listed in Illustration 17-5 are typical of exempted records under all state PRAs, there is in fact wide diversity among the states regarding what information held by state agencies is accessible.

EXAMPLE

In some states you can find out how much money special interest lobbyists have spent courting state legislators and in some you can't. In some states you can find out which funeral homes have been cited for using bait and switch practices to convince families of a deceased to purchase a higher-priced coffin and in some you can't. In some states you can find out which slaughterhouses have been warned about processing contaminated meat and in some you can't.

Whatever the particular exemptions listed in any state PRA, the investigator must be aware that there are hundreds of state and federal statutes, administrative rules, and court decisions that declare other records held by governmental agencies and departments confidential and not automatically subject to public disclosure (e.g., income tax returns per 26 U.S.C §6103; medical records per the Privacy Rule of the U.S. Department of Health and Human Services, 45 C.F.R. §§160-164, promulgated under the federal Health Insurance Portability and Accountability act of 1996 (HIPAA) statute; student educational records per the federal Family Education Rights and Privacy Act (FERPA) statute; juvenile offense records per state law; reports of child abuse and investigation records per state law).

2. Who can access a public record using a state PRA?

Most PRAs allow any member of the public the right to access public records. Some states, like Michigan (M.C.L.A. §15.232(c)), restrict the right of persons serving a sentence in a state or federal penal facility from using the PRA (a "no incarcerated person" restriction). Some states, like Virginia, restrict the use of the PRA to those who are citizens of the state (a "citizens only" restriction) and newspapers, magazines, and radio and television stations that circulate or broadcast into the state.

HYPOTHETICAL 17-5

As suggested in LBD 17-1, see if your state PRA restricts who can access records using the statute. Do you see the problems that a "citizens only" restriction might cause a legal professional who is a resident of one state seeking to access public records in another state? What is the policy behind a citizen's only or a no incarcerated person policy in a PRA, and do you agree with either or both? Such restrictions can give rise to constitutional challenges. For example, citizen's only restrictions have been challenged under the **Privileges and Immunities Clause** of the Fourteenth Amendment to the United States Constitution with varying results. Compare, for example, *Lee v. Minner*, 458 F. 3d 194 (3d. Cir. 2006) with *McBurney v Young*, 667 F.3d 459 (4th Cir. 2012) (Petition for Certiorari granted October 5, 2012, *McBurney v Young*, __ S.Ct. __, 2012 WL 2804998 (Mem) U.S. 2012). Which court do you think gets this question right? (See LBD 17-11.)

3. Procedure for accessing public records under a state PRA

In general, PRAs direct state and local departments and agencies that are the custodians of accessible records to make them available for inspection and/or copying during regular business hours. In many instances the records sought can be inspected simply by personally visiting the department or agency during its visiting hours and asking to see a particular record (e.g., asking a court clerk to see a case file that is not sealed by court order or accessing a deed book in the register of deeds office and asking for or making a copy of a particular entry). If for any reason the records cannot be provided at the time of the personal visit or copies requested cannot be made at the time of the visit (e.g., all personnel are busy or the records have to be obtained from storage), the custodial agency or department is required to comply within a reasonable time (often defined in the PRA to not exceed a certain number of calendar or business days, usually 7 or 10) unless the requestor is notified in writing that additional time will be needed.

Though no charge can be made by the records custodian for simply allowing records to be inspected, the custodian is authorized to charge a nominal per page copying fee and may be authorized to charge a service fee for extra time it may take office personnel to comply with a production request. If **certified copies** of any records are sought, there may be an extra charge for that service. If copies are to be made by the custodial agency or department, the requestor may be required to complete a records request form, discussed below (see Illustration 17-6). Typically, copying fees are to be paid at the time the copies are made. If the copies are to be mailed to the requestor, those costs often must be paid in advance, along with postage costs. In states where there are restrictions on who can access public records, the custodian may properly request to see a photo ID of the requestor bearing an address in order to confirm citizenship.

With more and more public records being made available online at Web sites operated by custodial departments and agencies, a personal visit is no longer needed to access those records. The record may be accessible for inspection and printing at the Web site of the custodial department or agency (e.g., the articles of incorporation for a corporation being investigated may be available on the secretary of state's Web site; lists of registered sex offenders may be accessible on the Web site of the state bureau of investigations or other custodial department). Of course, if the researcher needs certified copies of public records, that can't be accomplished by downloading online and printing. A request will have to be made to the custodial agency or department to make the certified copy, and the copy will have to be mailed to the requestor or picked up at the department or agency office.

Remember that state PRAs do not require custodial departments or agencies to create records for the requestor or summaries of records, only to make available records that they have. Nor can requests for public records go to future records (i.e., those not yet in existence); the request will have to be renewed after the records come into existence.

HYPOTHETICAL 17-6

Assume your supervising attorney asks you to locate all records regarding 1) real and personal property owned by a corporation in your state; 2) all civil lawsuits to which the corporation has been a party in your state in the past 10 years; and 3) all criminal actions that may have been instigated against the corporation in your state in the past ten years. You are going to be seeking records from several different state and local departments to comply with this request. To find records of real property ownership you will need to check with the county tax assessors' offices in all the counties where real property may have been owned during the ten-year period and/or the county register of deeds' offices in those counties to determine conveyances into and out from the corporation during that time. To find records of personal property ownership you will need to check with the state department that maintains financing statement (UCC-1) filings and possibly with county offices that do the same in the various counties where a secured creditor of the corporation may have filed the financing statements to perfect a security interest in the personal property listed in the statement. To find the record of civil suits you will need to check with the county clerk's offices for the various civil courts in each county in which such action might have been filed. And you will need to do the same to learn about the history of any criminal actions filed, except you'll be checking with the clerks of the various criminal courts of your states in the counties where such actions might have been filed. Oops, don't forget to check the U.S. District Court records for the federal districts in your state where civil actions might have been brought in federal court or federal criminal prosecutions might have brought against the corporation. Don't you hope some of these records are searchable online? If not, you have some footwork ahead of you and maybe some travel around the state. Of course, you might want to hire someone in other locations in the state to do the checking for you and save the time and expense of travel. But assume you locate a nest of records of criminal prosecutions in a certain county. You want certified copies of the charging documents and verdicts in each case, but the custodian says it will take several days to locate all those files and make the copies. Should you demand immediate service? Probably not, since your state PRA will allow the custodial department or agency the statutory time to comply. If you have an emergency need for the documents, you should consider using those communication skills you learned about in Chapter 8: Explain the jam you are in, ask nicely, and be reasonable. Offer to pay an appropriate service fee for the expedited work. And don't forget copying fees and service fees when you seek copies. You should always be prepared to pay the statutory rate per page for copying and a service fee where appropriate. The researcher should know these fees and sufficient funds on hand to pay them on a personal visit.

Many public records are not available for inspection by a personal office visit or online. Instead they must be requested in writing from the custodial office or agency (e.g., adoption records, access to which is strictly limited by states or food or workplace safety inspections conducted by state regulatory agencies). Some state have a formal **records request form** while others require a less formal **records request letter**. Illustration 17-6 shows the recommended records request letter for use in connection with the Massachusetts PRA (M.G.L. Chapter 66 Section 10).

The state PRA will require the custodial department or agency to respond to a written request "promptly" or "within a reasonable time" which is not to exceed a designated period of time, typically 7 to 10 calendar or business days. If the records request cannot be complied with in full within the statutory period, the custodial department or agency is required to provide the requestor with a **records request response letter** that will provide an alternative deadline by which the records search will be completed and the records provided. Illustration 17-7 shows a sample response letter recommended for use under the Indiana PRA (Ind. Code §5-14-1.5)

If the custodial agency or department will be unable to provide the records as requested (e.g., they've been destroyed or cannot be located) or

Illustration 17-6   MASSACHUSETTS PRA RECORDS REQUEST LETTER

Date request mailed

Agency Head or Keeper of the Records
Name of Agency
Address of Agency
City, State, Zip Code

Re: Massachusetts Public Records Request

Dear _____:
This is a request under the Massachusetts Public Records Law (M. G. L. Chapter 66, Section 10).

I am requesting that I be provided a copy of the following records:

[Please include a detailed description of the information you are seeking.]

[Optional: I recognize that you may charge reasonable costs for copies, as well as for personnel time needed to comply with this request. If you expect costs to exceed $10.00, please provide a detailed fee estimate.]

As you may be aware, the Public Records Law requires you to provide me with a written response within ten calendar days. If you cannot comply with my request, you are statutorily required to provide an explanation in writing.

Sincerely,

Your Name
Your Address
City, State, Zip Code
Telephone Number [Optional]

---

refuses to provide the records on the grounds that they are exempt, the response letter will advise the requestor of the reason the department is unable to comply or the basis for the claimed exemption Illustration 17-8 shows a sample response letter formulated by the Georgia First Amendment Foundation for use under the Georgia PRA (O.C.G.A. §50-18-70) advising that requested records will be provided but that some information in those records will be redacted (hidden or not provided) on the basis that it is exempt from disclosure.

Of course, the requestor of the records may not agree with the determination that some or all records sought are exempt from disclosure. State PRAs therefore allow a dissenting requestor to file a **petition for access to public records** in a designated state court. The court system will then determine whether the exemption claim is well founded and either compel disclosure or affirm the exemption claim. If the court orders access and finds that the agency or department refused access in bad faith, some states allow the recovery of attorney's fees by the petitioning requestor.

Illustration 17-7   INDIANA RECORDS REQUEST RESPONSE LETTER

May 28, 2008

Jane Doe
123 Main Street
Any Town, Indiana 46000

Dear Ms. Doe:

As required by Ind. Code §5-14-3-9, this letter is a response to your request for access to public records, which was received by this office on May 23, 2008. You specifically request the following: "a copy of the complaint files associated with formal complaints numbered 08-FC-04, 08-FC-09, and 08-FC-2007."

The office is compiling and reviewing the records and anticipates having the entire packet ready (or an update of the progress of compiling and reviewing the records if it will take longer) by June 11, 2008. The copy cost will be $0.10 per page. We will notify you of the copy cost and will send you the records upon receipt of payment. If you prefer to pick up the records from the office, you may submit payment at that time.

Please do not hesitate to contact us if we can be of further assistance.

Best regards,

John Smith

Any Town Public Agency

The legal professional must have a working familiarity with the PRA of his state (see LBD 17-1). A listing of citations to the PRAs for all 50 states and the District of Columbia is available in Appendix B.

E. Other Sources for Accessing State and Local Government Records

1. State and local government sponsored "open data" sites

Following the example of the federal government's Data.Gov site discussed in Chapter 16, 34 states and a number of major cities have established their own **open data sites** where substantial amounts of records and other information is posted for anyone to access. (See LBD 17-10)

2. Non-governmental Web sites

Aside from Web sites operated by state and local government agencies and departments, a number of academic and scientific Web sites contain public records information at no charge. The Yahoo search engine at http://dir.yahoo.com/Government/Law is an excellent tool to use to locate Web sites containing state and local records, as is FindLaw's LawCrawler search engine at http://lawcrawler.findlaw.com. A comprehensive listing

Illustration 17-8   GEORGIA RECORDS REQUEST RESPONSE LETTER CLAIMING EXEMPTION

[Agency's letterhead]

January 1, 2007
John Q. Public
123 Main St.
Any town, Ga. 30001

RE: Game contracts with schools and officials

Dear Mr. Public:

The following is in response to your Open Records request, received by the Uptown School District on January 2, 2007, regarding the above referenced item.

A search for the requested information was made and 22 athletic contracts have been identified and are available for review. In addition, the agency expects to exempt the following information from dissemination if found in the documents:

> Home address, home telephone number, Social Security number, and insurance or medical information of public employees, teachers and employees of a public school *See O.C.G.A. §50-18-72(a)(13.1)*

Please contact [Specify name] at [Phone number] to make arrangements to review the records. If you wish to retain copies of the documents, you will be charged 25 cents per page. There are 177 pages total, and therefore the estimated total cost responsive to your request should not exceed $44.25 (plus postage, if applicable).

Sincerely,

[Respondent's name]
[Title]
SOURCE: Georgia First Amendment Foundation

of Internet resources for locating state and local records is provided in Appendix B.

3. Online database vendors

The leading online commercial vendors for accessing state and local records are **Westlaw** and **LexisNexis**. Both provide their subscribers with online libraries accessing numerous state and local public records sources. Illustrations 17-9 and 17-10 give a representative sampling of the kinds of public records information available from these two vendors.

4. Public records search companies

There are a number of document search companies that, for a fee, will conduct the search of state and local (as well as federal) records for you. Some of these search companies are only statewide or regional and you should look to your local advertising services (e.g., the yellow pages or state and local bar publications) to locate them. Others are national. Some of the leading national document search companies are:

- KnowX (now owned by Lexis/Nexis) (www.knowX.com)
- Government-Records.com (www.global-locate.com)
- NETROnline (http://publicrecords.netronline.com)
- Washington Document Service (now owned by Lexis/Nexis) (www.wdsdocs.com/)
- CT Corporation (http://ctadmin.ctadvantage.com)
- Parasec (www.parasec.com/)
- GovSearch (http://govsearchrecords.com/)
- Corporation Service Company (www.cscglobal.com)

For a fee, these companies will do research nationwide on real and personal property assets, licensing indexes, tax lien filings, court dockets and judgments, judgment liens, UCC filings, motor vehicle records, and much more. A good source to learn about all public records search companies is *The Sourcebook of Public Records Providers* (see Appendix B for details).

Illustration 17-9   SUMMARY OF STATE AND LOCAL RECORDS ACCESSIBLE THROUGH WESTLAW

1. Asset Records: Searches state and local public records to identify real property, motor vehicle, boat, aircraft, and stock holdings of businesses and individuals.
2. Public Records: Searches people-locator databases, asset and adverse filing records, professional licenses, and company filings.
3. Corporate and Limited Partnership Records: Provides abstracts of corporate, limited partnership, and limited liability company filings in 45 states.
4. Adverse Filing Records: Provides abstracts of UCC filings, deeds, liens, judgments, execution dockets, criminal records, dockets, and jury verdict summaries.
5. Bill Tracker: Provides data for tracking pending state legislation.
6. People Finder: Offers databases that search for individuals by name, residence, phone number, public records, employment, etc.
7. State Civil Actions: Provides information on civil actions against state and local government; its divisions, agencies, and officers.
8. Local Government Law: Locate the laws of numerous municipal and county governments.

Illustration 17-10   SUMMARY OF STATE AND LOCAL RECORDS ACCESSIBLE THROUGH LEXISNEXIS

1. Public Filings: Searches and retrieves UCC filings in all 50 states.
2. Docket: Searches court indexes and dockets in selected state and municipal courts.
3. Corporate and DBA: Provides information on incorporation, corporate status, corporate offices, and registered agents in all states as well as "doing business as" records from state and local filings.
4. Judgments and Liens: Searches the judgment dockets of most states for judgment and tax liens.
5. Asset Checker: Accesses real estate and personal property records for individuals and businesses.
6. Verdicts and Settlements: Provides information on verdicts and settlements in state litigation.
7. Bankruptcy: Provides information on business and personal bankruptcy filings on a state-by-state basis.
8. State Capital Updates: Provides access to bills, laws, constitutions, regulations, legislature membership, and news from all 50 state capitals.

5. CD-ROM resources

There are also a number of CD-ROM databases that can be purchased, containing various kinds of state and local records. Examples include The County Locator (LOCUS) and the Public Record Research System by BRB Publications (see Appendix B for a comprehensive listing of CD-ROM products and information on how to contact the vendors). CD-ROM products are typically updated every quarter.

Chapter Summary and Conclusion

There are numerous different types of records maintained by state and local governments. The legal professional must be familiar with them as well as the procedures for accessing that information. At the state level, the state open records act must be consulted to determine what records the state allows access to in the first instance. Many state and local records are accessible by personal visit or written request. Like federal government agencies, many state and local agencies maintain excellent web sites where information may be accessed. There are also online database vendors and public records search companies which, for a fee, can access information for the investigator.

In the final chapter we will consider accessing information from private, non-public sources.

Review Questions

1. Name two political subdivisions of states.
2. What is a state "public records act," and why is it important to the legal investigator?
3. List five ways to access records from state and local governments.
4. Name two leading online database vendors.
5. List as many kinds of records maintained by state governments as you can recall.
6. What is CLEAR?
7. What is the DPPA? How does it limit access and use of vehicle and driving records?
8. What kinds of records are maintained by the secretary of state's office?
9. List as many kinds of records maintained by local governments as you can recall.
10. What is a "judgment docket" and of what assistance is it to legal investigators?

KEY WORDS AND PHRASES TO REMEMBER

abstract of judgment index
birth certificate

"blue sky" laws
business license

certified copies
CLEAR
death certificate
execution index
freedom of information acts
judgment docket
LexisNexis
license
lien *lis pendens*
local records
metadata
open data sites
open records acts (OPA)
permit
petition for access to public records
police powers
political subdivision
Privileges and Immunities Clause

probate
probate court
professional license
public records
public records act (PRA)
records request form
records request letter
records request response letter
register/recorder of deeds
Secretary of State
state government
tax assessor
VIN
vital records statistics
Westlaw

LEARN BY DOING

LBD 17-1. Locate the PRA or ORA adopted in your state (see Appendix B). What does your state call its PRA? Does your PRA contain a statement of purpose similar to that of the State of Washington seen in Illustration 17-3? Does it have a broad definition of what constitutes a public record? What kinds of records are exempt from production under your PRA? Are there any restrictions on who can access records? How many days does your PRA give a records custodian to comply with a proper request to inspect or copy records? What kind of copying or service fees can be charged by the custodian? How does your state's record request form compare with that seen in Illustration 17-6? How many days does your PRA give a department or agency to comply with a request? If a petition for access is filed following denial, can the court award the requestor attorney's fees, and if so, on what basis? Prepare a memorandum summarizing your findings.

LBD 17-2. Locate the adoption records statute or regulations for your state. Prepare a memorandum summarizing the scope and procedure set forth in the statute for accessing the birth and placement records of an adoptee.

LBD 17-3. Determine whether your state or local bar association(s) have a handbook or other material listing central and local offices of state departments and agencies. Determine who publishes the sources you locate, its cost, and how frequently it is updated. Also visit your local library and determine what resources are there to assist you in learning about the various state departments and agencies, what they do, and how to contact them. As part of your visit, see which of the resources listed in Appendix B are available in your local library.

LBD 17-4. Review Hypothetical 17-1. Determine the state agency in your state responsible for supervising commercial barge traffic on your state's navigable rivers. Keep a record of all sources you consult to determine this and in what order, the names of any and all persons you spoke with by phone or in person, and how long it took you to find this information. Here are some suggestions for other state agency questions you may want to use for this exercise; you may think of others as well:

- the agency responsible for regulating billboards on the state highways;
- the agency responsible for air traffic over government buildings;
- the agency responsible for trash/litter pick-up along state roads;
- the agency responsible for regulating the raising of wild animals on private property;
- the agency responsible for regulating the size of trailer trucks;
- the agency responsible for monitoring the size and explosive force of firecrackers sold in the state; and
- the agency responsible for changing burned-out light bulbs in public buildings.

LBD 17-5. Through your instructor, plan and conduct a visit to the central or local office of a state agency to tour the office, get an idea of what the agency does, and its procedures, especially its procedures for handling requests for information. Your instructor may want to arrange a group visit for the entire class. Prepare questions to ask while you are there.

LBDs 17-6 through 17-11 are accessible on the Author Updates link to the text web site at www.aspenparalegaled.com/books/parsons_ investigating/default.asp.

Chapter 18

Private Sources of Information

CHAPTER OBJECTIVES

In this chapter you will learn how to access many different types of information from private sources (as opposed to public or governmental sources) including:

- Medical, employment, and educational records.
- Telephone numbers and phone call records.
- Credit records on individuals and credit information on businesses.
- Financial information on individuals and businesses.

You will also learn about Internet resources for locating information, online database vendors, and search companies. And finally you will learn how to locate and work successfully with a reliable private investigator.

A. An Overview of Private Sources of Information

By **private records or sources** we mean information of any kind that is in the possession of private individuals, businesses, educational institutions, or any other non-governmental custodian. Frequently, information that is maintained by one or more governmental agencies is simultaneously in the possession of a private source. For the investigator, this means that there may be more than one means of accessing this information.

HYPOTHETICAL 18-1

Assume that Soupspoon Wise (see Case Study No. 2 in Appendix A) makes a social security disability claim based on the injuries he received in the car accident in the parking lot of the Red Dog Saloon. As part of that claim he has his medical records submitted to the SSA. Now his medical records are part of a file maintained by a government agency, but they are simultaneously maintained by his private physicians. The medical records are the same in either place, but attempting to access them through the SSA would constitute seeking a public record, whereas attempting to access them through his physicians would constitute seeking a private record—information held by Soupspoon's private physicians and the hospitals where he received treatment.

We will learn how to access information from private sources in this chapter. But, for now, assume you are assisting the attorney representing the Red Dog Saloon and the supervising attorney is anticipating that Soupspoon might file a civil suit for personal injury against her client in the future. She learns of his social security filing and would like to access that file to see his medicals. Based on what you learned in Chapter 16, are you going to be able to get that information for her at this time?

If Soupspoon is denied social security benefits and loses his appeal of this decision through the administrative process, he may initiate a civil action in the U.S. district court to establish his right to the benefits. His medical records will likely be exhibits to his pleadings or to motions made in the civil case or be produced in response to formal discovery requests made in the case. How accessible will those records be now?

SLEUTH ON THE LOOSE

To more fully appreciate the growing problem of identity theft and invasion of privacy in the information age access the Federal Trade Commission site on identity theft at www.consumer.gov/idtheft.

This chapter will summarize various private sources for accessing information commonly sought by attorneys. There is overlap between this topic and the related topic of locating the missing witness, as covered in Chapter 14. The student may want to review the materials in Chapter 14 regarding resources for locating a missing witness. Consider how those resources would also be valuable in obtaining information regarding a person or business whose background or activities you are investigating. However, neither that section of Chapter 14 nor the discussion that follows purports to be a complete and final listing of private sources of information; no list could be. The fact is that the means of accessing privately held information in a legal and ethical fashion (see Ethical Note below) are limited only by the imagination and creativity of the investigator. In an investigation we always ask, "Who might have this information?" and "How might I get it?" And never, ever underestimate the effectiveness of simply *asking* for what you want.

HYPOTHETICAL 18-2

Assume that you are assisting the attorney representing Vidalia Unyon in a possible divorce action against her husband, Greene Unyon (see Case Study No. 3 in Appendix A). In the initial conference with you and the supervising attorney, Mrs. Unyon shows you two ticket stubs to the Sly Dog concert that took place in your city last month and a book of matches bearing the logo of the Ooh La La Motel in your city. She tells you that she found these in her husband's coat pocket and she suspects he took a girlfriend to the concert because he certainly didn't take her. She also says she has never been to the Ooh La La Motel and can only assume her husband has rented a room there at some time with a lover. The supervising attorney slides the ticket stubs and book of matches over to you and tells you, "Check it out."

You sit in your office for an hour trying to decide how you can determine whether Greene Unyon purchased two tickets to the Sly Dog concert or rented a room at the Ooh La La Motel. Finally, in frustration, you go back to the supervising attorney and tell him you need some guidance. He peers at you quizzically over his reading glasses for a moment, then clears his throat and says, "Why don't you just call 'em up and ask?"

After slinking out of his office and back into yours, you call the clerk at the Ooh La La Motel, introduce yourself, and ask her if she could tell you whether a Greene Unyon has rented a room there in the last three months or so. She puts you on hold (a Sly Dog tune is playing—what a coincidence!) then gets back on the line and tells you that, yes, a Greene Unyon has rented a room there every Monday for the past two and a half months, which is as far back as the current ledger goes. Now before you hang up the phone and start dancing on your desktop:

1. What else do you want to ask this helpful information source?
2. What documents might you want to ask her to let you see and copy?
3. How quickly should you get down to the motel office and why?

Later you call the ticket office of the arena where the Sly Dog concert was held. In the middle of your first question, the surly voice on the other end says, "We don't give out that kind of information," and slams the phone down. Oh, well, one out of two isn't bad. But what other sources might you check to determine if Greene Unyon in fact purchased tickets to the Sly Dog concert and attended it?

ETHICAL NOTE

Hypotheticals 18-1 and 18-2 demonstrate the importance of making sure you follow the law and comply with ethical and professional standards in investigating. For example, in some states there may be statutes or regulations restricting access to private records such as motel registration information. If so, you need to be aware of such laws. Or there may be court decisions holding that it is a tortious invasion of an individual's privacy for such information to be disclosed. These are matters you need to be familiar with and cover with your supervising attorney before seeking to access privately held records.

Similarly, ethical and professional standards always come into play in seeking information. For example, what consequences might there be if you had called the Ooh La La Motel, represented yourself as Greene Unyon's executive secretary, and said that you needed the requested information for his tax records?

Or what if the supervising attorney in the Red Dog Saloon case told you to go ahead and contact the local SSA office handling Soupspoon Wise's disability claim and ask to see his file even though it would violate SSA regulations? "After all," he tells you, "weren't you taught that it never hurts to ask?" It hurts

in that situation, doesn't it?

Or what if you told a licensed private investigator helping you on the Red Dog Saloon case about your difficulties in accessing Soupspoon Wise's social security file and he says, "Don't worry, I know how to get hold of stuff like that. I'll do it for $200, just don't ever ask me how." Can you agree to let him do this?

This last example of the private investigator illustrates an important point to remember in investigating. The vast majority of licensed private investigators and information brokers (discussed in more detail later in this chapter) are scrupulously honest and ethical. However, there are

some who are willing and quite able to skirt or bend the rules to access information for a paying client. No matter how tempting it might be in a particular case to use someone like this to obtain otherwise inaccessible information, RESIST THAT URGE. Ethical attorneys and paralegals do not engage in that kind of activity, do not request others to do it, do not encourage others to do it even passively, and do not knowingly use information obtained in that way. Not only is it unethical and unprofessional (and possibly illegal), it is morally wrong. If we don't all obey the rules, the rules become meaningless and the system fails.

B. ▶ Accessing Private Sources of Information

SLEUTH ON THE LOOSE

Access the Gale Academic OneFile site at http://go.galegroup.com/ ps/dispBasicSearch.do? prodId=AONE&user GroupName=tel_s_tsla. From this site you can access more than 48 million full-text articles on physical sciences, technology, medicine, social sciences, the arts, theology, literature and other subjects. See if you can find an article on some medication you or a loved one is taking; on current membership trends in American Islamic, Buddhist, Catholic, Jewish, or Protestant faiths; the problem of severe head injuries in American football; or some other topic of interest to you.

1. Medical records

Medical records constitute one of the most frequently sought-after kinds of information in the legal field. Lawyers regularly need to obtain the medical records of their own clients, of opposing parties in lawsuits, or of non-party witnesses.

Medical records will always be deemed confidential either by state mandate (see LBD 18-1) or by the private rule of the medical practitioner or facility. Thus, those records are accessible from the practitioner or facility only upon the written **authorization** of the patient, by **court order**, or by **subpoena**.

a. Obtaining medical records by written patient authorization

To obtain the medical records of his own client, the supervising attorney will have you prepare and have the client sign an appropriate authorization to obtain medical records. Illustration 10-4 shows a typical **medical records authorization** directed to a physician. Illustration 18-1 shows a typical medical records authorization directed to a hospital.

b. Drafting the medical records authorization

The medical records authorization should provide the full name of the patient, the patient's social security number and date of birth, and the name of the doctor, hospital, or other health care provider to whom it is directed. It should be dated, state how long it is effective, and name the persons to whom the medical office or hospital are authorized to permit inspection and copying of the records.

Illustration 18-1 MEDICAL RECORDS AUTHORIZATION (HOSPITAL)

To: Hospital's Name and Address

You are hereby authorized to permit my attorney, _____, of the law firm _____, or his designated agent, to inspect and obtain copies of my complete medical records including, without limitation, all patient information sheets, fact sheets, admission summaries, emergency room records, out-patient records, patient consents, patient history and physical data, physician orders and progress notes, consultation reports, nurses' notes, operative reports, anesthesia records, radiology records, medications, pharmacy records, physical therapy records, discharge records [or, if appropriate, death certificate or autopsy records], correspondence, notes, memoranda, laboratory reports, and fee statements. This authorization is effective as of the date below and will continue in effect until revoked by me in writing but for no longer than one year from the date below.

My attorney, _____, of the law firm _____, has assured me that he/she will comply with all requirements of the privacy rules promulgated by the U.S. Department of Health and Human Services pursuant to the Health Insurance Portability and Accountability Act of 1996 and found at 45 CFR 160 and 164.

_____   Date_____
Name of patient
Soc. Sec. No. XXXXX
DOB 10-1-YR-40

The authorization should state in a comprehensive fashion and with specificity what records are to be made available. Doctor's offices and hospitals typically will not provide the investigator with any more documentation than he specifically asks for. The inexperienced legal professional may have no idea of the number and kinds of different medical records that may be found in a doctor's or hospital's patient file.

The authorization should contain language assuring the provider of compliance with the privacy rules found at 45 CFR Parts 160 and 164 that govern access to medical information. The authorization should also be signed by the patient or, in the event the patient is a minor or incompetent, by the parent or guardian of the patient. A person who has executed a valid power of attorney for health care has probably authorized the holder of the power of attorney to obtain or authorize another to obtain the patient's records.

c. Using the medical records authorization

The medical authorization is usually mailed to the doctor's office or the hospital's **records custodian** with a cover letter. Illustration 18-2 shows a cover letter forwarding an authorization to a doctor's office.

Illustration 18-2   COVER LETTER TO DOCTOR'S OFFICE

Date

Name of Physician
Address

Re: John J. Patient
Patient No. (if known) or Soc. Sec. No.
DOB

Dear Dr. _____:

This office represents Mr. Patient with regard to personal injuries he sustained in an automobile accident on February 1, YR00. Please provide us with a copy of Mr. Patient's entire medical file per his signed authorization, a copy of which is enclosed.

If there is a charge for the copies made, please enclose your invoice with the copies and it will be paid promptly.

Also, please provide us with your diagnosis and treatment of Mr. Patient's injuries resulting from the February 1 accident and your prognosis of future medical disabilities and treatment.

The records made available to us will be used only for the resolution, by negotiation or litigation, of the personal injury claim made or to be made on behalf of Mr. Patient arising out of the automobile accident of February 1, YR00 against those deemed to be legally responsible. The records made available to us and all copies thereof made for the stated purpose will be returned to you or destroyed at the end of that process. And we will otherwise comply with all requirements of the privacy rules promulgated by the U.S. Department of Health and Human Services pursuant to the Health Insurance Portability and Accountability Act of 1996 and found at 45 CFR 160 and 164.

Thank you for your assistance. If you have any questions, please do not hesitate to call.

Sincerely,

(Signature)
Legal Assistant

Illustration 18-3   COVER LETTER TO HOSPITAL RECORDS CUSTODIAN

Date

Name of Hospital
Address

Re: John J. Patient
Patient No. (if known) or Soc. Sec. No.
DOB

Dear Records Custodian:

   This office represents Mr. Patient with regard to personal injuries he sustained in an automobile accident on February 1, YR00. Please provide us with a copy of Mr. Patient's entire medical file per his signed authorization, a copy of which is enclosed.

   If there is a charge for the copies made, please enclose your invoice with the copies and it will be paid promptly. Our information is that Mr. Patient was a patient at _____ Hospital from February 1 to February 15, YR00.

   The records made available to us will be used only for the resolution, by negotiation or litigation, of the personal injury claim made or to be made on behalf of Mr. Patient arising out of the automobile accident of February 1, YR00 against those deemed to be legally responsible. The records made available to us and all copies thereof made for the stated purpose will be returned to you or destroyed at the end of that process. And we will otherwise comply with all requirements of the privacy rules promulgated by the U.S. Department of Health and Human Services pursuant to the Health Insurance Portability and Accountability Act of 1996 and found at 45 CFR 160 and 164.

   Thank you for your assistance. If you have any questions, please do not hesitate to call.

Sincerely,

(Signature)
Paralegal

Illustration 18-3 shows a cover letter forwarding an authorization to a hospital. You can determine the name and address of the records custodian with a quick phone call. The letter to the hospital should indicate the dates the patient is believed to have been a patient. This will expedite the location and production of the records needed. The letter to an attending physician from the patient's attorney may also request an update on the patient's prognosis if not previously determined.

   Many doctors' offices and hospitals will not automatically make copies of everything in the patient's file—even if you request it. Therefore, the authorization should be comprehensive and specific and, whenever possible, you should physically take the authorization to the medical office and review the file yourself before having copies made. While you are doing so, ask the file custodian if everything is in the file as it is presented to you. Be sure that no patient records are maintained in a separate file and that no patient records are still being processed. Remember that, with regard to hospital records in particular, the number and volume of records generated is substantial and may be quite expensive to copy.

d. Special medical records authorizations

Psychiatrists, psychologists, and institutions treating mental disorders typically have their own pre-printed authorization form that the patient must sign.

The written medical authorization may also be used to obtain the medical records of an opposing party in a pending suit when it is undisputed that the records are relevant and the attorney for the opposing party has no objection to his client signing the authorization.

e. Obtaining medical records by court order

When seeking the medical records of an opposing party in pending litigation, it is customary in some jurisdictions to utilize an **agreed court order** rather than a written authorization. Illustration 18-4 shows an agreed court order allowing one party access to the medical records of the opposing party.

Illustration 18-4   AGREED ORDER ALLOWING INSPECTION OF MEDICAL RECORDS

```
                      IN THE UNITED STATES DISTRICT COURT
                      FOR THE EASTERN DISTRICT OF YOURSTATE
                               NORTHERN DIVISION
BEN RUNOVER WISE,                          )
          Plaintiff                        )
      v.                                   )        DOCKET NO. YR00-00005
THE RED DOG SALOON, INC.                   )
          Defendant                        )

        AGREED ORDER ALLOWING INSPECTION AND COPYING OF MEDICAL RECORDS
```

On motion of defendant, The Red Dog Saloon, and plaintiff having no objection, it is hereby,
ORDERED, that defendant Red Dog Saloon, by and through its attorneys, Dip, Duck & Dodge, is hereby authorized to inspect and copy at its own expense any and all medical records of plaintiff Soupspoon Wise including, without limitation. . . . And it is further,

ORDERED, that defendant shall provide plaintiff's attorneys with copies of all such records copied by or on behalf of defendant within five (5) business days of defendant's copying of such records.

ENTER.

_____
U.S. District Judge

APPROVED FOR ENTRY:

_____
Mellow Fellow
Attorney for Plaintiff Soupspoon Wise
(Address)

_____
Hard Case, Esq.
Attorney for Defendant The Red Dog Saloon, Inc.
(Address)

The agreed order should be as specific about the medical records to be reviewed and copied as the authorization.

f. Obtaining medical records by Rule 45 subpoena

When a civil suit is pending and the attorney needs to obtain the medical records of a non-party witness who refuses to give a written authorization or from an uncooperative opposing party, it may be necessary to use a Rule 45 **subpoena** *duces tecum.* The subpoena will be served on each custodian of such records and will, in the case of a trial subpoena, direct the custodian(s) to appear with the records at the time and place of trial. In the case of a deposition subpoena, it will direct the custodian(s) to appear at the time and place of the Rule 30 deposition. See FRCP 34(c) and 45(a)(2). Illustration 18-5 shows a deposition subpoena *duces tecum* seeking the production of medical records.

Whenever a subpoena is served seeking the medical records of a party or non-party who doesn't want them produced, there may be a motion to quash the subpoena filed with the court that issued it. The issue in such a motion will typically turn on the relevance of the records sought. As previously indicated, your state may have special rules and procedures for accessing medical records by subpoena with which you should become familiar. (See LBD 18-1.)

Illustration 18-5   DEPOSITION SUBPOENA DUCES TECUM SEEKING PRODUCTION OF MEDICAL RECORDS

IN THE UNITED STATES DISTRICT COURT
FOR THE EASTERN DISTRICT OF YOURSTATE
NORTHERN DIVISION

BEN RUNOVER WISE,
     Plaintiff
   v.
THE RED DOG SALOON, INC.
     Defendant

DOCKET NO. YR00-00005

SUBPOENA DUCES TECUM

To: Records Custodian
Capital City Hospital
(Address)

YOU ARE HEREBY COMMANDED to appear and give testimony under oath at the law office of Mellow Fellow, Shake, Rattle & Roll, 100 South Main St., Capital City, Yourstate on the ___ day of ___, YR00 at 1:30 p.m. You are also commanded to bring the following:

All medical records of Soupspoon Wise, Soc. Sec. No. XXX-XX-XXXX including, without limitation, all patient information sheets, fact sheets, admission summaries, emergency room records, out-patient records, patient consents, patient history and physical data, physician orders and progress notes, consultation reports, nurses' notes, operative reports, anesthesia records, radiology records, medications, pharmacy records, physical therapy records, discharge records, correspondence, notes, memoranda, laboratory reports, and fee statements.

DATED:_____

_____
Clerk, U.S. District   Judge

2. Employment records

Like medical records, **employment records** will always be deemed confidential either by state mandate (see LBD 18-1) or by the private policy of the employer. In recent years, many state legislatures have passed laws giving added protection to employment records and courts have expanded the concept of protected privacy rights to include such records. Thus the investigator should use caution in attempting to access these records without the consent of the employee.

When accessing the employment records of a current or former government employee, the employing agency may have its own special regulations and procedures with which the investigator should be careful to comply. In the case of a state or local government employee, reference should be made to the state's open records act.

As with medical records, employment records are typically accessible from the employer only upon the written authorization of the employee, by court order, or by subpoena. Illustration 10-5 shows a written authorization to be signed by the employee allowing an attorney access to his employment records.

3. Educational records

Access to **educational records** from a public school or college may be controlled by a state's open records act or by separate statute. (See LBD 18-1.) Private institutions may be regulated by state rules as well or may have their own internal rules regarding accessibility of records.

Most schools will confirm whether a person ever attended and what degree, if any, was granted and when. Otherwise, the student herself or, in the case of a minor, her parents or legal guardian, have the right to access academic records from either a public or private institution. As with medical and employment records, anyone else seeking to access such records must do so by written authorization, court order, or subpoena. Also as with medical and employment records, if access cannot be agreed upon, a showing of relevance will have to be made to the court which is asked to order access or uphold the validity of a subpoena.

Illustration 10-6 shows an authorization permitting access to educational records.

4. Other sources of academic information

Though access to academic records is limited without the student's consent, investigators should not overlook other sources of information available concerning a student's academic career. Student directories, high school and college yearbooks, faculty directories, campus newspapers and periodicals, master's theses and doctoral dissertations are generally available to anyone from the school library or other school offices.

5. Address and phone records

a. Finding address and phone numbers

Locating the address and telephone number of a person or business may be as simple as checking the phone book or calling Directory

Assistance. As discussed in Chapter 14 under the topic of resources for locating the missing witness, it's a good idea to keep out-of-date phone books to pick up the trail of a missing person, or make sure your local library has them. Most large public libraries also keep telephone directories for a number of other cities around the state and country as well.

1. **City/county directories.** Many cities and counties have **criss-cross** or **reverse directories.** A reverse directory will list residences and businesses first by street name and number. It then lists telephone numbers numerically. Thus you can find an address even if all you have is a phone number and a phone number when all you have is an address. Many such directories also provide the names of all persons living in the household and places of employment. The city/county directories may be purchased from the phone company or found in the local library. Keeping old issues of the city/county directory is a good idea for the investigator.

2. **CD-ROM products.** There are **CD-ROM products** that can be purchased containing phone and address directories and criss-cross directories. Cole's Directory is a popular criss-cross directory and is available in CD-ROM format. CD-ROM products are typically updated on a quarterly basis and thus are more current than paper directories, which appear annually. (See Appendix B for details on Cole's Directory and other CD-ROM products.)

3. **The Internet.** Most popular search engines such as Google, Yahoo, and Bing provide people search services or index sites that will provide addresses and/or phone numbers. The Internet also has free telephone and address directories, reverse phone, address, and e-mail directories, and map and directional services once an address has been located. (See Appendix B for a comprehensive listing of free online resources available for performing people searches.)

b. Accessing unlisted phone numbers

A person can request that the phone company not list their phone number, in which case the number will not appear in the phone book or city/county directory and should not appear in any of the Internet or CD-ROM services—though it might slip in. There is no legal or ethical way for the investigator to obtain unlisted numbers from the phone company without consent or court order and she shouldn't allow a private investigator to do so either. (See Ethical Note above.)

However, people frequently give out their phone numbers, even when unlisted, to friends, employers, creditors, credit card companies, advertisers, merchants, service providers, and phone solicitors. If the investigator locates the number through one of those sources, no law is broken and no ethical violation occurs. Phone numbers, listed and unlisted, are the kind of header information that compilers of marketing mailing lists obtain from these sources, place in their data banks, and sell or make available for a fee to online database vendors and search companies. (See extended discussion below.)

c. Phone call records and wiretapping

The phone company will not voluntarily release a customer's land-line phone call records, nor will cell phone companies or personal digital assistant (PDA) providers. But all such communications are traceable through the **call log** maintained by the company providing the phone service. Of course, the subscriber may consent to the release of that information. If a civil or criminal lawsuit is pending and the information in the phone records is relevant, it may be obtained through formal discovery request, by court order, or by subpoena.

The federal **wiretapping** law, 18 U.S.C. §2510, prohibits the non-consensual monitoring or recording of electronic communications to which you are not a party subject to certain exceptions. States also have their own wiretapping laws, which may be more restrictive than the federal law, and with which the legal investigator should be familiar. (See LBD 18-2.)

6. Credit records on individuals

There are currently 30-some-odd true **credit reporting agencies (CRAs)** in the United States—companies that collect and disseminate information on the credit history and creditworthiness of individuals. (See Appendix B for a more comprehensive list, and see LBD 18-15). Of these, the big three are Equifax, Trans Union, and Experian.

The files of these agencies will contain data on a person's loan repayment history, including car payments, credit card payments, lines of credit, and other secured and unsecured debt. They will also contain much public record information (that you can access in other ways, as you now know), including tax lien information, judgments, and bankruptcy filings. Residence information, employment information, and arrest records are sometimes included in the data. The files of credit reporting agencies will reflect not only the consumer's payment history, but a record of credit inquiries (who has asked about the consumer's creditworthiness) and a credit scoring record as well (how creditworthy the agency deems the consumer based on the data collected). Thus, these records can be a gold mine of information about the financial affairs of an individual.

Credit reporting agencies obtain their data not only from public records but also from subscribing lenders, individual creditors, and businesses that extend credit to consumers. These subscribers will both provide data to the credit reporting agency and purchase a credit report on a consumer from the agency when that consumer applies for credit.

However, not just anyone can legally access the records of a credit reporting agency. These agencies, and access to the very sensitive information they maintain, are governed by the **Fair Credit Reporting Act**, 15 U.S.C. §§1681 et seq. (FCRA) as amended by the **Fair and Accurate Credit Transactions Act** of 2003 (FACTA). At the federal level, CRAs are regulated by the **Federal Trade Commission** (www.ftc.gov/). Effective September 1, 2012, the new **Consumer Financial Protection Bureau (CFPB)** (www.consumerfinance.gov/), created by the Dodd-Frank Wall Street Reform Act of 2010, is empowered to regulate CRAs having more than $7 million in annual receipts, which includes more than 90 percent of them (see LBD 18-14). Some states have their own laws in this area. For example, in Vermont, permission of the consumer is required to access credit information, and in Rhode Island, the consumer must be notified when information is requested. Currently six states,

Oregon, Washington, Hawaii, Illinois, Connecticut, and Maryland, strictly limit the use of credit reports for job screening. (See LBDs 18-10 and 18-11.)

Under the FCRA, an individual can request to see most information in her own file, including the substance of information maintained there, the sources of the information, and the names of those to whom information has been supplied within the past six months or ten months if the information was supplied for employment purposes. There is also a procedure in place for correcting errors.

Access to credit reports by persons other than the consumer herself is limited by the FCRA to persons seeking the information:

- for decisions regarding extension of credit;
- for underwriting insurance;
- for employment evaluation;
- pursuant to court order;
- for granting a government license;
- pursuant to a written authorization by the consumer; or
- for other legitimate business purposes.

It is this last ground for accessing information, the **legitimate business purpose,** that is the most controversial. Banks, department stores, insurance companies, credit card issuers, employers, and landlords can show a legitimate business interest and typically obtain a written consent anyway. But it is well known (and controversial) that some credit reporting agencies are less than diligent in confirming the purported "business purpose" of someone seeking information. And some licensed private investigators seem able to obtain a credit report on request. (See Ethical Note above.) (See LBD 18-3.)

For the legal professional who does not have the consent of the individual being investigated, the only other way to access this information is to locate an existing credit report in the files of an obliging creditor that has previously obtained the report. In general, once a creditor has obtained a report from a credit reporting agency, the creditor is not expressly restricted from showing it to others. Every circumstance is different, however, and care should be taken to ensure that it is legal and ethical for the source to provide the report to the investigator under the existing circumstances.

HYPOTHETICAL 18-3

Assume that in the course of investigating Greene Unyon (see Case Study No. 3 in Appendix A), you learn that until six months ago he leased the offices of his veterinary practice from a man named Leaky Faucet. You know from searching the court house records that Leaky Faucet sued Greene Unyon for unpaid rent, claiming that Greene Unyon abandoned the leased premises before the lease term expired. You interview Leaky Faucet and, being no fan of Greene Unyon, he tells you that he obtained a credit report on Greene Unyon a year ago when Unyon first leased the premises and you can see it if you want.

1. Is this credit report on Greene Unyon information you would like to see? How could it help your supervising attorney in representing Vidalia Unyon?
2. Under the FCRA (or any applicable state law) can you legally accept this credit report from Leaky Faucet?
3. Can you ethically accept this credit report from Leaky Faucet?

7. Credit information on businesses

There are a number of business credit reporting agencies that collect credit information on corporations and other businesses. The big three are Standard & Poor's (www.standardandpoors.com/), Moody's Investors Services (www.moodys.com/), and the Fitch Group (www.fitchratings.com). Dun & Bradstreet (www.dnb.com/) and Experian (www.experian.com), are other examples of companies that collect information on businesses and make it available to subscribers. (See LBD 18-12.)

Most of the credit information compiled by these companies is now accessible over the Internet to direct subscribers or to subscribers of various online database vendors (see full discussion of such vendors below). For example, credit reports compiled by Dun & Bradstreet on more than 9.5 million businesses and by Experian on more than 12 million businesses are accessible to subscribers of Westlaw and LexisNexis. A number of the printed business credit report publications produced by these companies, such as *Dun & Bradstreet Ratings*, are available at public libraries and freely accessible there.

SL EUTH ON THE LOOSE

Pursuant to the Fair and Accurate Credit Transactions Act of 2003, consumers are now entitled to access a summary of their credit information from the three major credit reporting agencies, Experian, Equifax, and TransUnion, every 12 months at no cost. Have you gotten your free summary yet? If not, go to www.annualcreditreport.com and follow the instructions.

8. Bank account, credit card, and general financial information on individuals

In general, bank account, credit card, and other loan information held by a bank or lender is not accessible by anyone other than the customer himself. Of course, when accounts are jointly held by spouses or business partners, either spouse or any partner can access that information—important to remember in domestic cases or disputes between business partners.

The customer may also provide a written consent for a third person to access this information. If the information is relevant to issues in a pending civil or criminal lawsuit, it may be obtained by formal discovery request, court order, or subpoena.

Financial information on individuals is frequently included in public records (see Chapters 16 and 17) by being included in required filings or in testimony in a civil or criminal lawsuit. This information is also included in publicly recorded land transactions, mortgages or personal property lien-filings, bankruptcy proceedings, or federal or state corporate filings. Remember too that general financial information, while not accessible directly from the bank or lender, is often included in other private records that are accessible.

HYPOTHETICAL 18-4

Assume that you are still sitting in the office of Leaky Faucet trying to decide what to do with the credit report on Greene Unyon when Leaky hands you something else. "You might be able to use this, too," he says. He has handed you a rental application form filled out by Greene Unyon which lists his personal and business bank accounts by bank and account number, his outstanding debts by lender name, balance due and monthly payments, and all his sources of income. Best of all, attached to the back of the form is a dated and signed personal balance sheet in which Greene Unyon has listed all of his assets and liabilities and a separate balance sheet for his veterinary practice.

1. How will this information be useful to your supervising attorney in representing Vidalia Unyon?

2. Is there any legal or ethical reason you cannot accept this information from Leaky Faucet?
3. What other private sources might have obtained financial information on Greene Unyon?

Other non-governmental places to look for general financial information on individuals are the newspaper or other local publications, the local library, professional associations, and community organizations. In addition, if the individual you are researching is nationally or regionally prominent or just involved in a particular trade or profession, you might check various directories available in many public libraries and, increasingly, online. The best known of these is probably the *Who's Who In America* series, which includes numerous directories based on criteria such as an individual's wealth, corporate affiliations, profession, or hobby. For example, if you were investigating a person you know to be an art collector you might take a look in *Who's Who In American Art*.

If the individual is involved in a corporation, you might check *Standard & Poor's Register of Corporations, Directors and Executives*, or Thomson-Gale's *Owners and Officers of Private Companies*. If the individual is an attorney, check the *Martindale-Hubbell Law Directory*. If the individual is a physician, check your state's medical directory. The legal investigator should become familiar with the various directories available. (See LBD 18-4.) A good source to check to get an idea of all these directories is Thomson-Gale's *Directories in Print*. (See Appendix B for a comprehensive listing of publishers of business-related directories.)

The best place to locate printed directories is the library. But remember that more and more directories are available online, which can speed up your search and give you access to more sources than your local library may provide.

SLEUTH ON THE LOOSE

Identify a well-known company then access www.hoovers.com for a brief company profile. While you are there, try looking up information on other companies of various sizes, both public and privately held. Note that the site invites you to purchase a full report on the company being searched. If you were doing a pre-filing investigation of that company, your supervising attorney might authorize the expense.

9. Financial and general business data on corporations and other businesses

As we saw in Chapters 16 and 17, corporations—especially publicly traded corporations—and other business entities are closely regulated by the federal and state governments, which often means public filings are made disclosing financial and general business information. Corporations and other businesses also leave a significant paper trail through other accessible public records such as civil suit filings, land and personal property transactions, etc., that disclose much financial information.

Not only is such information concerning corporations and other business entities available in various public records, much of it is collected by attorney organizations and made available to organization members. For example, the American Association for Justice (**AAJ**), formerly the Association of Trial Lawyers of America) and the Defense Research Institute (**DRI**), discussed in Chapter 15 (see Appendix B for information on how to contact AAJ and DRI), maintain and operate brief banks, articles, members' forums, and links to state and local organizations that may be contacted to locate information on businesses with whom other organization members have had prior dealings.

There are many other private sources of financial and business data available on businesses and the individuals involved with them as owners, officers, or directors.

EXAMPLE

> Many companies, large and small, publish sales brochures, annual reports, and other materials, which are available for the asking from their public affairs offices or stockholders, or which may be available in libraries. Such companies may run advertisements in the yellow pages, local newspapers, and regional or national publications. They issue press releases from time to time. Many companies have established their own Internet Web sites accessible to anyone surfing the Net.

SLEUTH ON THE LOOSE

Identify a small publicly held corporation and see if you can locate information on it at www.tripod.lycos.com/smallbiz.

Other good sources of information on businesses include the local Chamber of Commerce and the Better Business Bureau; business periodicals; professional or trade publications; and pamphlets or other information frequently generated by local or statewide business development groups to attract new business, tourists, or residents.

In addition, there are numerous **directories** that collect financial and other data on corporations and other businesses. Dun & Bradstreet, Moody's, Standard & Poors, and other publishers produce literally scores of different business directories. Illustration 18-6 contains a small sampling of such directories.

A good source for the legal professional to learn about the numerous business periodicals available is the *Business Periodical Index*, available in most libraries. Also, most business directories and many business periodicals are now available on the Internet.

Illustration 18-6 EXAMPLES OF BUSINESS DIRECTORIES

1. *S&P's Register of Corporations, Directors and Executives.* A directory of over 55,000 public and private companies along with biographical sketches of executives and directors.
2. *S&P's Corporation Records.* In-depth sketches of over 11,000 publicly held corporations along with general news and financial information (annual reports and interim earnings reports).
3. *D&B's Ratings.* Data on thousands of businesses including credit information, organizational charts, stockbrokers, and wholesale and retail dealers.
4. *MacRae's Blue Book.* Contains information on all manufacturers of industrial equipment, products, and materials. Lists manufacturers alphabetically by company name, product classification, and trade name.
5. *Directory of Corporate Affiliations.* Information on 100,000 companies showing parent/subsidiary relationships and summary business information on each company.
6. *Thomas Register of American Manufacturers.* Directory of over 180,000 companies and 53,000 classes of products and services.
7. *D&B Million Dollar Directory.* Current business information on over 161,000 companies with a net worth of $500,000 or more.
8. *Ward's Business Directory.* Financial and marketing information on more than 150,000 American companies; includes up to ten recent news items on each company gathered from more than 3,000 newspapers and periodicals.
9. *S&P's Stock Reports.* Contains profiles on publicly traded companies.
10. *Moody's Industry Review.* Contains financial and statistical data for several thousand public and private companies.

10. Online database vendors

There are a number of commercial companies that make available online and by subscription vast amounts of information in library or database form. Typically, these companies will charge a base subscription fee plus an additional charge per search.

Westlaw (www.westlaw.com) and **LexisNexis** (www.lexisnexis.com/) are the leading commercial vendors of this kind of information. Both make available libraries or databases containing all kinds of business and financial information; hundreds of daily newspapers, magazines, and newsletters from around the world; business, scientific, and professional journals and periodicals; information summaries; business and financial analyses; national reverse phone/address directories; **people finder** services; whole treatises on every academic and scientific subject imaginable, as well as theses and dissertations; encyclopedias; transcripts of speeches; and much more.

Because these vendors have managed to get legal access to some information sources usually inaccessible to the public (e.g., credit reporting agencies) and because they have the means to locate and compile vast amounts of data from so many sources (from public records nationwide to direct mail marketers' mailing lists), the subscriber is able to access information she could not practically locate otherwise. Illustration 18-7 provides a sampling of the various business and general information databases available to subscribers of Westlaw.

Illustration 18-8 provides a sampling of the various business and general information databases available to subscribers of LexisNexis.

Another large database vendor is **Dialog** (www.dialog.com), now a ProQuest company. Dialog provides its customers access to numerous databases dealing with business, science, engineering, finance, and law. Dialog's DataStar database focuses on worldwide pharmaceutical,

Illustration 18-7   EXAMPLES OF GENERAL BUSINESS INFORMATION AVAILABLE ON WESTLAW

1. Company & Industry Reports; Analysis: Interfacing with Dow Jones News/Retrieval and Dialog, this provides information in the fields of business, medicine, technology, science, social policy, and consumer affairs drawn from thousands of publications and other information sources. It also supplies profiles on thousands of companies including affiliate information, access to SEC filings, and credit history.
2. Company Profiles: Provides detailed financial information on millions of public and private companies.
3. All News and All News Plus Wires: Accesses all the major wire services, hundreds of local, national, and international newspapers, trade journals, and other sources to enable the investigator to track and monitor people, businesses, industries, and current topics.
4. Lawsuit and Litigation Filings: Provides information on filing of civil suits, bankruptcy proceedings, and criminal prosecutions involving individuals and businesses.
5. PeopleMap: Compiles information from the Census Bureau, U.S. Postal Service, voter registration files, telephone directories, professional and trade associations, credit bureau information, city/county tax rolls, publishers mailing lists, vital statistics sources to provide information on more than 150 million individuals, 95 million households, 70 million telephone numbers, 50 million death certificates, and 175 million social security numbers.
6. Public Records: Provides access to more than one billion state and local public records which may contain an abundance of information on businesses and individuals.
7. International/Worldwide Materials: Provides business information, news, and governmental actions from around the world.

Illustration 18-8 EXAMPLES OF GENERAL BUSINESS INFORMATION AVAILABLE ON LEXISNEXIS

1. NEWS: ALLNEWS or NEWS: BUS: Comprehensive news libraries drawn from major wire services, national, and international print and Internet news sources; allows tracking of people, businesses, industries, and current topics.
2. COMPNY: FPDIR: Financial Post Directory of [Corporate] Directors.
3. COMPNY: COMPNY: Profiles of publicly traded companies including SEC filings, stock reports, M & A reports, bankruptcy filings, etc. Covers numerous privately owned companies as well.
4. MEGANW: ALLMGA: Newspaper and magazine articles on individual businesses and whole industries.
5. BUSREF: DCA: Directory of Corporate Affiliations: Provides information regarding parent, affiliate, subsidiary, and division relationships on 180,000 companies worldwide.
6. COMPNY: IND: Comprehensive industry reports.
7. MEGA: MEGA: Comprehensive search of federal and state court records, public filings (e.g., real estate and judgments).
8. Company Dossier: Specialized service providing in-depth profiles on 43 million public and private companies, 1,000 industries, and 58 million executives.

biomedical, biosciences, chemical, computing, engineering, and health-care-related industries.

There are many online database vendors in business today. Some cater primarily to licensed private investigators, but most are available to subscribers. An increasing number of these vendors are headquartered in Europe and specialize in business, scientific, and technical information from around the world. Appendix B contains a comprehensive listing of online database vendors and information on how to contact them. (See LBD 18-5.)

11. Search companies

Mention has already been made of the various public records search companies, which, for a fee, will search federal, state, and local records. A number of those companies will also conduct searches in non-governmental databases and prepare detailed reports, including general business and background information on your subject. An example is History Associates, Incorporated of Rockville, Maryland (www.history associates.com). This firm conducts business and industry research from the National Archives in Washington, Federal Records Centers, presidential libraries, the Library of Congress, state and local governments, private corporations, universities, and professional associations.

Another example is Experian (www.experian.com/business_services), which provides current business information on over ten million businesses around the United States. It also provides new homeowner information; consumer lists totaling nearly 100 million records selectable by income, gender, and dozens of other variables; new movers information; new parents information; and "behavior bank" data on over 25 million consumer households broken down into over 300 data categories. Stock brokerage firms may also be of help in obtaining financial information about companies and their principals. (See Appendix B for a comprehensive listing of search companies and information on how to contact them.)

12. Private investigative firms

A number of private investigative firms specialize in background screenings of potential employees and **due diligence** probes on behalf of corporate clients involved in buyouts, mergers, acquisitions, and divestitures. Other private investigative firms do more routine P.I. work: domestic disputes, including surveillance; criminal defense; and people locating, sometimes called **skip-tracing** (as in so-and-so skipped town and we need to trace his whereabouts). These investigative firms have access to the public records sources and online database vendors we have mentioned—including those that cater to private investigators—and also to their own ever-growing databases.

Most people have little awareness of how much personal information about themselves, including information they thought was private, has been located, compiled, and is sold every day to essentially anyone who wants it. As we have seen, most information on an individual collected by various government agencies is accessible, from vital statistics to marital history, business and professional licenses, property ownership, debt information, charitable contributions, travel reservations, voter registration information, motor vehicle records, civil and criminal court proceedings, and on and on we go.

SLEUTH ON THE LOOSE

Rather than taking photos of a scene or hiring an investigator to do so, consider downloading the scene on Google Earth (www.google.com/ earth/index.html). You'll have to download the software first, but the basic version is free. See if you can locate your school, your home, or a place in another state or country that you've been to. Amazing, no?

But, in addition, any time an individual allows their name, address, and phone number to appear in a phone book, applies for credit with a lender or department store, fills out a credit card application, orders merchandise by mail, sends in a product registration or warranty card, makes a charitable contribution, subscribes to a magazine, answers a consumer questionnaire, places their name on a free mailing list, joins a book club, participates in a polling survey, signs a guest registration book at a tourist attraction, or registers to win a free prize, they have given out free information about themselves, which can be and regularly is sold to **information brokers**. Many banks and other businesses, and even state and local governments, have been found to be selling information about their customers and constituents to information brokers without the knowledge or permission of the persons involved (see LBD 18-7). Internet service companies such as Microsoft and Yahoo gather data from individuals who create e-mail accounts with them and track use made of their "free" online services, a technique called **behavioral targeting**. Some sell the collected data and some simply use it for their own marketing efforts. Issuers of **loyalty cards** such as grocery chains, drugstores, bookstores, and gas companies give you a break on purchases at their stores, but they are often bundling and selling your personal information as well. Catalina Marketing in Florida is the leading processor of personal information generated by loyalty cards. **Data mining software** now exists to enable businesses and the government to sort through massive databases of information, looking for patterns of behavior that enable marketing and other business decisions and provide the government with information.

In the information brokerage trade, all of this private, personal information from consumers is called **header information**, and it is collected and organized in various ways to make it more useable, for example, by geographic region, age, gender, education level, income level, trade, or profession. Merchandising companies seek this information to use for various mailing lists or phone solicitations, trying to sell the consumer something else. But this information is also sold to and used by all kinds of people in the information business, such as the database vendors and search companies already mentioned. It is also acquired and used by private investigative firms or by information warehouses that assemble huge databases and then make them accessible to private investigators for a fee.

With the advent of the Internet, online information brokers have blossomed. For approximately $1,000, these brokers, many of whom are private investigative firms, promise to provide a *profile* of personal and financial information on individuals and businesses. In many cases, they cater to attorneys seeking information on the assets of a potential defendant or seeking assets to seize to enforce a judgment already rendered. This can be a valuable service. But the profiling business is controversial for two reasons. First, many of these information brokers historically have used deceptive and fraudulent methods to obtain financial information on the target. For example, they call a bank with the customer's social security number and pretend to be the customer in order to learn the balances on account, a method known as **pretext calling.** Second, whether ethical procedures are utilized or not, the perceived invasion of privacy involved is troublesome. As a result, the federal government and some state governments recently have enacted legislation that prohibits *pretexting* methods and regulates the providing of customer information to information brokers or other financial institutions (see LBD 18-7).

So long as the private investigative firm is not engaged in illegal or unethical conduct, it is perfectly permissible for the law office to utilize these resources for information searches that, for reasons of time or limited resources, cannot be done by that office. (See Ethical Note above.)

a. Locating a reliable private investigator

There are many private investigators (P.I.'s) around to choose from and they are easy to locate. Many state and local bar organizations publish directories or handbooks listing P.I.'s. State volumes of Martindale-Hubbell carry private investigator listings. Some P.I.'s will advertise their areas of expertise in the yellow pages or in directory listings. The Internet contains a number of sites with directories of P.I.'s. (See Appendix B for a comprehensive listing of resources for locating a private investigator and other related information.)

Regardless of how you locate a P.I., you want to be sure to find someone who is both competent and ethical. Not only because your own standards are high, but because you owe a duty to your client whose work the P.I. will be doing. Seek recommendations from experienced attorneys or paralegals in your area whose judgment and ethics you trust. When you make contact with a P.I., don't hesitate to interview him. Ask about any client complaints to the state licensing agency, any license suspensions or revocations, or lawsuits filed against him. Ask them for references from attorneys or paralegals he has worked with previously and follow up on those.

Depending on what you want the P.I. to do, it may not be necessary or wise to retain someone local. If you want a P.I. to perform a national search for a person or documents, you may want to contact a regional or national P.I. firm. They probably subscribe to all the computer service companies that cater to private investigators. On the other hand, if you only need some surveillance done locally, a local P.I. will be more logical.

b. Working effectively with a private investigator

When you have located a private investigator that seems dependable and qualified, you want to establish a good, responsible working relationship with him. We owe it to our clients to do so. Here are some suggestions.

1. **Fees and expenses.** Always ask in advance about the P.I.'s fee schedule and expenses, and find out about his billing schedule and any required advances. Communicate this information to the client and get the client's approval before formally retaining the P.I.

2. **Scope of the assignment.** Always communicate clearly to the P.I. exactly what the assignment is and any time deadlines you expect him to meet. If there is no time deadline, find out in advance the time frame in which he expects to be able to perform the work and let him know you expect to hear from him within that time frame. Be sure he knows to contact the supervising attorney or you (so *you* can contact the supervising attorney) before undertaking any activities or incurring any expenses outside the scope of the assignment.

3. **P.I. reports.** Let the P.I. know whether you want written reports on his work or verbal reports only. Most P.I.'s will do written reports in memorandum or letter form if you do not specify. Ask the supervising attorney which she prefers and advise the P.I.

4. **Work product.** Mark all your correspondence to the P.I. as work product and ask him to mark his correspondence or written reports to you the same way. It is better if the P.I. directs his written correspondence or reports to the supervising attorney. In states that recognize the work product privilege for P.I. material produced on behalf of an attorney, this will strengthen the argument that the material is not subject to discovery by an opposing party.

5. **Disclosure of status and avoidance of UPL.** If you are a paralegal, make sure the P.I. knows and understands that you are not a licensed attorney. Working with a P.I. is like any other task the paralegal undertakes—it is done under the supervision and authority of an attorney. So be careful not to exercise independent judgment in directing the activities of the P.I. Always run your recommendations by the supervising attorney and communicate her directions.

6. **Confidentiality.** Make sure the P.I. you use understands the importance of attorney-client confidentiality. The P.I. retained by the attorney works as an agent of the attorney and a sub-agent of the client. The P.I. will almost certainly learn confidences and secrets of the client and will need to know to avoid disclosing those. Most P.I.'s are not trained formally in legal ethics and only pick up bits and pieces on the job. Don't let him learn at the expense of your client.

7. **No illegal or unethical conduct.** Make it clear to the P.I. that you do not expect or wish for him to engage in any illegal or unethical conduct in the work he performs on your client's case. Assuming that pretexting methods of compiling personal and financial profiles (or the use of information obtained by those methods) have not yet been prohibited legally (see discussion above and LBD 18-7), the supervising attorney will need to make a decision regarding whether it is ethical to utilize an investigative firm known to use such methods.

8. **Frequent contact.** If the P.I. you use does not stay in regular, frequent contact, you must initiate the contact. Stay in touch with him so that if the supervising attorney should ask you at any time about the status of the P.I.'s work you can give her a fresh report.

9. **Pay your bills.** Try to make sure that the P.I.'s statements for services are paid on time. It's the way we all want to be treated. Taking care of his bills will keep him happy and committed to the client's case.

13. Resources on the Internet

Just as more public records are accessible online today (see Chapters 16 and 17), so too is more personal, business, and professional information. In Section F of Chapter 4 in the context of discovery in a civil case, we considered the modern explosion in **electronically stored information (ESI)**, including electronic communications as well as personal, business, professional, and financial records maintained in electronic format. We noted the presence of metadata in many electronically generated documents and the increasing ability to recover deleted messages and other information that technology provides. In Sections B and C of Chapter 14 we considered the amazing growth of **online social networking (OSN)** via e-mail, text messaging, blogs, and the growing host of OSN sites (see a comprehensive list of OSN sites in Appendix B) as a means of identifying potential witnesses or locating missing witnesses. You may want to reread those sections at this time. Everywhere you look online, people and businesses are voluntarily messaging and creating, preserving, and even posting all kinds of information about themselves, and doing so often from smart phones or other mobile devices. We live in a world that is increasingly online and accessible 24-7, and we are leaving a traceable electronic record behind us.

Much of the information being posted online may be accessible by a simple search of the site involved. Online information to which access is blocked to the uninvited may be accessed by subpoena directed to the individual posting the information, to the online social networking host, or, in the case of e-mail or text messaging, to the Internet or PDA service provider. (See LBD 18-9.) Generally, courts view the Internet as a public forum where there is little or no assumption of privacy. As one judge stated, "A person who places information on the information superhighway clearly subjects said information to being accessed by every conceivable interested person." *U.S. v. Gines-Perez*, 214 F. Supp. 2d 205, 225 (D.P.R. 2005).

A number of colleges and universities have established **Web sites** allowing access to their library holdings, faculty publications, and research efforts. As just one example, the Survey Research Center of

Princeton University (www.princeton.edu/psrc) provides a comprehensive index of polling and survey information on social issues, consumer research, and policy analysis.

Numerous individual businesses and entire industries operate individual Web sites where they will post business summaries, officer and director biographies, shareholder reports, and general financial information. To locate an Internet site operated by a school, industry, or company, utilize a good **search engine** (see Appendix B for a comprehensive listing of search engines) and type in the name to be searched. Or direct your browser to www.[insert the name to be searched or its abbreviation]. (See LBD 18-6.) Thousands of businesses have established Facebook pages and participate in Twitter. LinkedIn is a very popular social networking site designed for business and professional networking. (See LBD 18-4.)

Numerous newspapers from around the world are accessible on the Internet. For example, thousands of newspapers, periodicals, and press releases are organized and sorted by region of the world, country, and state, at DMOZ Open Directory Project (http://dmoz.org/News/Newspapers/Directories). Google News (http://news.google.com) allows you to browse 4,500 news sources at any time and to search for dated stories by topic. All the major television networks have sites where information is available, as do increasing numbers of local television and radio stations.

Hundreds of periodicals are on the Internet too. For example, the Time Warner family of publications (including *Time, Fortune, Life, People,* and *Money* magazines) is available at www.pathfinder.com.

Because of the mass of information available on the Internet and the ever-growing number and changing locations of Web sites, the legal professional needs to keep her own notebook of current sites useable to access different kinds of information. Watch for articles in professional publications advising you of new and updated sites and take note of information made available at seminars. There is also a steady stream of books publishing Web site addresses for all kinds of information but if you're going to invest in one, make sure it is current. Finally, remember that, in general, information located on an Internet Web site may not be as comprehensive or reliable as information accessed through an online commercial vendor or **search company**.

Once civil or criminal litigation is commenced, one party's electronically stored records, their electronic messaging and online postings of information relevant to the dispute and not privileged, can be obtained by the opponent using the formal discovery rules considered in Chapters 4 and 5 and the subpoena power of the courts.

Chapter Summary and Conclusion

Many types of private information are held confidentially, either by informal policy of the information custodian or by law, and are accessible primarily by written authorization of the person whose information it is. The legal professional must be familiar with standard and specialized authorizations. Such information may also be accessible by subpoena or agreed order. Personal information not accessible without a court order, like an unlisted phone number, may be located in other data compilations where the person has voluntarily given out the information. The legal professional must be aware of and comply with legal prohibitions on non-consensual monitoring of electronic communications and accessing credit records of individuals. There are numerous database vendors, search companies, and private investigation firms which, for a fee, can access various compilations of private information.

Review Questions

1. By _____ records or _____ sources we mean information in the custody of private individuals, _____, _____ institutions, or any other non-governmental custodian.
2. What ethical challenges might be presented in seeking private information or records?
3. List two different documents used to access medical records.
4. Why should a medical records authorization have an expiration date?
5. When obtaining medical records from a doctor's office or hospital, why is it better for the investigator to physically inspect the records himself, than to trust a clerk to copy?
6. What is a subpoena *duces tecum*? How can it be used to access private information and records?
7. Summarize the constraints on recording electronic communications imposed by the federal wiretapping statute.
8. List as many suggestions for working with a private investigator as you can recall.
9. List as many online social networking sites as you can think of, and explain their role in legal investigating.
10. What is "skip tracing"? "Data mining"? "Header information"? "Behavioral targeting"?

KEY WORDS AND PHRASES TO REMEMBER

agreed order
AAJ
authorization
behavioral targeting
business directory
call log
CD-ROM product
city/county directory
collaborative journalism
Consumer Financial Protection
    Bureau
court order

credit reporting agency
criss-cross directory
data mining software
Dialog
Dodd-Frank Financial Reform
    Act of 2010
DRI
due diligence
educational records
electronically stored information
    (ESI)
employment records

Fair and Accurate Transactions Act (FACTA)
Fair Credit Reporting Act (FCRA)
header information
information broker
Internet
legitimate business purpose
LexisNexis
loyalty cards
medical records
medical records authorization
online social networking (OSN)
people finder

pretext calling
private sources of information
records custodian
reverse directory
search company
search engine
skip-tracing
subpoena
subpoena *duces tecum*
Web site
Westlaw
wiretapping

LEARN BY DOING

LBD 18-1. Familiarize yourself with the privacy rules for medical records promulgated by the U.S. Department of Health and Human Services (DHHS) pursuant to the Health Insurance Portability and Accountability Act of 1996 (HIPAA), which became effective on April 15, 2003, and which are located at 45 CFR 160 and 164. Check the comprehensive answer guide for the new privacy rules put together by the DHHS Office of Civil Rights at www.hhs.gov/ocr/hipaa. Then prepare a memorandum answering the following questions:

a. Who is a "covered entity" under the HIPAA rules?
b. What patient information is considered "protected health information" under the HIPAA rules?
c. How does an attorney go about obtaining health information for a client or other party under the rules?
d. What are the potential civil and criminal penalties for violating the HIPAA rules?
e. Does the state in which you work have any statute or regulation governing the accessibility of medical records that contains requirements in addition to those set out in the HIPAA rules?

LBD 18-2. Utilizing the current and earlier city/county directories for your city or county, see if you can determine everyone who has lived at your (or any other) current address during the past 5, 10, 15, or 20 years. Determine whether any of those former residents are still in the area and, if so, where.

LBD 18-3. Research the meaning of "legitimate business purpose" under the Federal Credit Reporting Act, 15 U.S.C. §1681, or any analogous state law, and prepare a memorandum summarizing your research as it pertains to the following questions:

a. How have the courts (particularly your state's courts and the federal courts sitting in your state) interpreted that phrase?
b. Do licensed private investigators always have a legitimate business purpose allowing them to access another person's credit records?

c. Do attorneys or those assisting them have a legitimate business purpose allowing them to access another person's credit records simply because they are investigating a matter for a client?

d. What penalties/liability have been imposed on persons or businesses violating the FCRA?

LBD 18-4. Choose a large, local corporation and perform a background investigation of it using the sources of corporate and business information set out in Appendix B. See if you can locate the following information on the company you select and, while doing so, keep a written summary of the information you locate and the research tools you used to locate each item of information.

a. Locate the exact name and all business address(es) of the company.

b. Obtain a detailed description of the business of the company, including its leading products, services, or primary customers.

c. Obtain the names of the officers of the company for the past three years, as well as the name(s) of the chairman of the board of directors and new directors of the company during that time.

d. Determine the profit (or loss) enjoyed (or sustained) by the company for each of the past three years and the average share price at year-end for each of the past three years.

e. Obtain a copy of shareholder reports, advertisements, and press releases issued by the company during the past three years.

f. If the company has a Web page, locate it, then download and print the home page information.

g. Determine if the company or any of its officers utilizes one or more online social or business networking services.

LBD 18-5. If you have access to a commercial information vendor such as Westlaw or LexisNexis, use one or more of these services to locate financial, business, and other information on the company you selected in LBD 18-4. Then use one or more of those services to perform the searches itemized in LBD 18-6.

LBDs 18-6 through 18-15 are accessible on the Author Updates link to the text Web site at www.aspenparalegaled.com/books/parsons_investigating/default.asp.

Case Studies

CASE STUDY #1

THE ROWDY OUTLAW CASE

The law office where you work has been retained by country music star Rowdy Outlaw to defend him on first degree murder charges brought against him by your state (Yourstate). Mr. Outlaw is accused of murdering Bobbette Bouvier, his back-up singer, on September 1, YR-1. The trial has been scheduled for three months from today. Below you will find a summary of the new client memorandum prepared by your supervising attorney from the initial interview with Mr. Outlaw and the police report.

Summary of new client memorandum and police report:

Rowdy Outlaw (real name Herman F. Fripp, DOB 10-1-YR-42) hit the country music big-time two years ago with his record-breaking song, *I'm a Hot Male Looking for a Yahoo Girl.* He and his band, The Holdups, struggled for more than five years before breaking through with the hit song.

During those lean years, Rowdy had an on-going relationship with his female back-up singer, Bobbette Bouvier. But after finding success some two years ago, he surprised everyone by marrying Candy Carmichael, a sometime hair stylist and groupie who had followed the band around the country for years. Outlaw says that, as far as he knows, Bobbette took his marriage to Candy Carmichael in stride. And he heard from one of the members of the band approximately six months ago that she was seeing someone else but he doesn't know who.

Bobbette Bouvier owned a condominium in Palace Towers, a high-rise condo just outside of Capital City, Yourstate, where the band is based. None of the other band members live in Palace Towers.

In the early morning hours of September 1, YR-1 (2:10 a.m., per the police report), a next door neighbor to Bouvier heard a scream and sounds of scuffling. She called police and they arrived around 2:30 a.m. Entering Bouvier's apartment, the police found her body on the floor of her bedroom, in a nightgown, strangled to death with a guitar wire which was still wrapped around her neck. The lock on the door to her condo had been jimmied and the bedroom showed signs of a struggle with lamps and tables knocked over. On the floor near the body police found a black guitar pic with the initials *RO* on it in red. In the living room leading to the bedroom they found a single turkey feather on the floor. Mr. Outlaw is widely known for using only black guitar pics and has all his pics monogrammed in red with his initials. He also wears a black cowboy hat with turkey feathers protruding from the hat band. Police have the guitar pic, string, and turkey feather in their possession.

The neighbor who called the police also told them that after calling them it became quiet next door and she peeked out her door in time to see the back of someone leaving the Bouvier apartment. The person leaving had on a long western style coat, red and black cowboy boots, and a black cowboy hat with turkey feathers sticking out of the band, all of which is the standard stage costume of Mr. Outlaw. According to the police report, the neighbor's name is Georgette B. Good, a part-time legal secretary (working through a temp service) and aspiring country singer whose career hasn't gone anywhere yet. The police report says she has positively identified the man she saw leaving the Bouvier apartment as Rowdy Outlaw.

Acting on the information provided by Good, police obtained a warrant to search Outlaw's house in Capital City. The search was conducted at 6:30 a.m. on September 1, YR-1. Mrs. Outlaw, the former Candy Carmichael, was at home and awakened by the police. Under questioning she said her husband had not been home all evening and she had no idea where he was. In fact, she said he had not been home in weeks and she didn't care whether he ever came home again.

Attached to Outlaw's house is a private recording studio. In the course of searching that studio, the police discovered one of Rowdy's guitars with a string missing. They have taken the guitar into their custody. The police also seized a computer that was in the studio that Mrs. Outlaw said belonged to Rowdy. Mrs. Outlaw also told the police about Rowdy's prior affair with Bobbette and stated that she, "wouldn't be surprised if they were back at it again, 'cause there ain't been nothin' going on around here in a long, long time."

The police obtained a warrant for Rowdy's arrest later that morning and put out an all-points bulletin for his arrest. That afternoon Rowdy turned himself in and the arrest report describes him as looking disheveled, bleary-eyed, and barely coherent. He waived his right to counsel (this was before he called us) and initially told the police he had been home all night. Confronted with the statements of his wife, Rowdy changed his story and told the police he had been out drinking all night with Kato, the drummer for the Holdups.

Police apparently haven't located Kato yet. He doesn't have a permanent residence but, according to Outlaw, just sleeps over at a variety of friends' houses, moving every few weeks when he wears out his welcome.

Outlaw was arrested and processed and that's when he called us. He is still in custody and his preliminary hearing is coming up soon.

Since we were retained, two other witnesses have come to our attention. Jack Gates is an old friend of Outlaw's. They went to high school together in Capital City, joined the Army together shortly after graduating high school, and served together in the first Gulf War in 1991. Outlaw says that he's not sure of the details but knows that Gates got in some trouble over there and was dishonorably discharged. Rumor had it that the discharge had something to do with drugs. Gates changed after that Rowdy says. He is now an insurance agent for Outlaw and handles not only his insurance but most of his financial dealings.

According to newspaper reports, Gates called the police following Outlaw's arrest and volunteered that Rowdy was supposed to have dinner with him the evening before the murder occurred but did not show. They had been scheduled to meet at 8 p.m. at Farley's Fish Shack and then go to Gates' office to review Outlaw's insurance portfolio. Gates supposedly told the police he arrived at Farley's, waited there until it closed at 11 p.m. and then left. He tried to call Outlaw several times while he waited but could not reach him. One call he made was to Outlaw's house and talked with Mrs. Outlaw and was told the same thing she told the police, he wasn't there, hadn't been there in weeks and wouldn't be welcomed if he came back.

According to the newspaper account, the Police were also contacted sometime after the story of the arrest appeared in the media by a Connie Cornelius. Cornelius, according the media, told the police that she was on her way to work at the Capital City Daily News (she operates a press) and passed in front of Palace Towers at about 2:15 a.m. the morning of the murder. She said she saw Rowdy Outlaw coming out of the front doors of Palace Towers, running as if in a hurry. She said she didn't recognize him at first, but her husband, Fred Cornelius, who was driving her to work, recognized him and said, "Hey, look, that's that famous singer, what's his name. I wonder if we could get his autograph."

Yesterday we received a call from a man named Perry Peters who said he had heard about the arrest and read the newspaper accounts and had something we might want to know. He says he was working as the parking lot security guard at the Palace Towers the night of the murder. He said he was in the parking lot of the building from 10 p.m. until 5 a.m. and never saw any sign of Rowdy Outlaw. He told us he did see someone leave the building between 2 and 2:30 a.m. but it was definitely not Rowdy Outlaw. He said it was someone a lot taller and thinner than Outlaw (who is about 5'9" and stocky) and, as he thought about it, the person looked a lot like Mick Jagger.

We have also received a call from a lady who identifies herself as Ima Jean Grouse. She told us she can provide an alibi for Rowdy Outlaw the night of the murder. Rowdy says he does not know this lady but was drinking heavily with Kato all that night and that anything is possible.

The arresting officer with the Capital City P.D. was Detective Willie Parker. Strangely, according to the police report, Parker says Rowdy Outlaw admitted committing the crime to him though he does not have it tape recorded and Outlaw vehemently denies to us that he did so.

We are told by the District Attorney's office that they have an expert, Michael Melody, who will testify that the guitar string found around Bobbette's neck is the same size as the missing string on Rowdy's guitar and will offer the opinion that, at one time, the string in question had in fact been strung on Rowdy's guitar.

CASE STUDY #2

THE RED DOG SALOON CASE

The law office where you work has been retained to represent Soupspoon Wise in connection with potential personal injury and property loss claims arising out of an incident at the Red Dog Saloon. Below you will find a summary of the new client memorandum prepared by your supervising attorney based on her interview with Mr. Wise.

Summary of new client memorandum:

Our client is Soupspoon Wise, a well-known Blues artist reputed to be the best saxophone player living today. He has played concerts all over the world and produced numerous best-selling CDs. He has his own talk show on Sirius Satellite Radio called *All Things Musical.*

One month ago today, Soupspoon was leaving the Red Dog Saloon just outside the city limits with his new girlfriend, Tanya Trucker, a licensed masseuse. Soupspoon and Tanya had just gotten into his one-year-old black Porsche which was parked in the Red Dog parking lot, and put on their seat belts when a white Ford Bronco came racing from behind the Red Dog building and swerved right at them. The Bronco driver hit the brakes of the car but it was too late and it slammed head-on into Soupspoon's YR-1 Porsche.

The air bag on the passenger side of the Porsche deployed on impact and Tanya T. was not hurt. However, Soupspoon says the air bag on his side did not deploy and, even though he was wearing his seat belt, his head was thrown forward and struck the steering wheel.

Soupspoon was knocked unconscious and doesn't remember anything else about the accident. He says that Tanya has told him that the Ford Bronco sped away from the scene. It hasn't been seen since and the occupants are unknown at this time. However, Tanya told the investigating police officer that the Bronco had Michigan plates though she couldn't make out any particular number.

She also told the officer that there were two men in the Bronco, one driving and the other in the back seat. The windows were down in the Bronco and she told the officer that following the collision, she heard the driver say in some kind of foreign accent, "Godfrey Daniel! Where did that car come from? I can't see a bloody thing in this dark parking lot. Why don't they have any torches out here?" She heard the figure in the back say, with no accent, "Just get us out of here. This is your second accident this week. You're going to get sent home and cost me my insurance." That's when the Bronco drove off.

Soupspoon does recall that other Red Dog patrons were coming out into the parking lot while he and Tanya were leaving but he didn't know any of them or what they saw. For some reason he does remember a pickup truck being parked near his car that had KP's Plumbing Service printed by hand on the side of the driver's door.

Tanya T. has broken up with Soupspoon since the accident, gone to Nashville, Tennessee to pursue a singing career and assumed a stage name he can't remember. The manager of The Red Dog Saloon is a man named Turtle Shoop.

Soupspoon bought his Porsche used three months before the accident at Goosie Hoots Hot Cars and the owner, Goosie Hoots, is the salesman that sold him the car.

Damages:

The Porsche was totaled. Soupspoon spent three weeks in Capital City Hospital with several broken facial bones including his jaw as well as a severe concussion. He says his doctor tells him it will take at least six months for the jaw to heal and there is real concern about whether the injury will affect his ability to play the sax. He has had to cancel four appearances scheduled during the last month and fifteen dates he had scheduled over the next six months. Beyond that, we don't know yet.

CASE STUDY #3

THE VIDALIA UNYON CASE

The law office where you work has been retained to represent Mrs. Vidalia Unyon in a possible divorce action. Below you will find a summary of the new client memorandum prepared by your supervising attorney based on her interview with Mrs. Unyon.

Summary of new client memorandum:

Vidalia Unyon is a forty-something year old housewife referred to us by Bill Richards, a local accountant, who is married to Yellow Unyon Richards, the oldest daughter of Vidalia and Greene Unyon.

Mr. and Mrs. Unyon have been married for twenty-seven years. They were married right out of high school and their first child, Yellow, was born a year later. Mrs. Unyon has never worked outside the home and never continued her education after marrying Greene Unyon. Mr. Unyon, however, went on to college at Yourstate University, taking his undergraduate degree and then continuing at Yourstate University School of Veterinarian Medicine. He has been a licensed and practicing veterinarian in this state for 20 years and has what is believed to be a thriving practice here in Capital City, Yourstate.

Mrs. Unyon has never been active in the business and has no financial data on her husband's practice. The couple have two children who are still at home, Greene, Jr., who is sixteen and a daughter, Sweet, who is ten.

Property:

a) Assets: The couple own their residence in the city which they built ten years ago. There is a mortgage on the house the balance of which Mrs. Unyon believes is about $75,000 (held by First City Bank) though she says Mr. Unyon keeps all the financial records for the family as well as his business. She does not have a good estimate of the value of the house but can recall her husband saying recently he thought they could get a half million for it in a good market. There are some certificates of deposit, savings accounts, and checking accounts but, again, her husband keeps up with all that. She does know that they have a joint checking account at First City Bank which she uses but there may be others, she just doesn't know.

She knows her husband uses the Morgan Stanley brokerage firm, but has no idea what investments her husband may have or whether they are in his name only or joint. She also thinks he has a 401K plan through his veterinarian practice but she doesn't know the details.

The couple own three cars, a brand new BMW 325i, a YR-1 Cadillac Seville, and a YR-2 Jeep Grand Cherokee which the 16-year-old son drives. She has no idea how the vehicles are titled.

The couple has collected antiques for the last fifteen years or so. That is Mrs. Unyon's area of specialty, and she says they have some valuable Federal period furniture and French porcelain pieces. Their collection has never been appraised so she cannot put a dollar value on it but would like to keep it all in the divorce.

Mr. Unyon is an avid gun collector. She knows nothing about guns but says he has a room full including some that her husband has said are illegal to purchase now. He can have them as far as she is concerned.

b) Debts: In addition to the mortgage on the house, Mrs. Unyon knows of only a Visa bill and an American Express bill that are owed. She doesn't know the balances but thinks it's a few hundred dollars each. She says that every month lots of mail comes in that looks like bills but her husband always takes care of it.

Property Settlement:

Mrs. Unyon wants to keep all the antiques. She wants to be able to live in the house as long as the children are at home. She has no idea the size of Mr. Unyon's estate or the value of his business since he has always taken care of that but feels she has raised his family and kept his home and should get a fair portion of it. She wants to keep the BMW and the Jeep. Mr. Unyon can keep the Cadillac.

Grounds:

Mrs. Unyon said that her relationship with her husband has not been good for several years. They have grown apart in their interests and attitudes toward life in general. She has always been more family oriented than he, although he is very close to the son. She is a very religious person, and although Mr. Unyon used to go to church with her while the son was young, a few years ago he stopped and would not let her make the son go anymore.

As he has become more successful in his practice she feels Mr. Unyon has stopped loving her. He plays golf all weekend with the son or with his buddies at the Capital City Country Club where they are members and, when he is home, watches sports on TV or works on his laptop computer, which he won't let her see or use. His regular caddy at the country club is someone named Hobo Booth.

The couples' sex life has been non-existent for longer than she can remember and they no longer even have many mutual friends. She also believes he may be having an affair. An anonymous female called her a couple of months ago and told her that Mr. Unyon was having an affair with someone at the office, and that she should "check his e-mails." She isn't sure who the caller was but thought the voice might be that of a woman who worked as Mr. Unyon's receptionist until a few months ago. She never knew this woman's name but her husband always called her Nosey Nelly.

About two weeks ago, she found a little black book in her husband's suit coat pocket that had nothing in it but the names of women with phone numbers along side, all in his handwriting. She confronted her husband with her suspicions at that time, accusing him directly of sleeping with someone else. He didn't deny it but wouldn't talk about it either. When she kept on badgering him about it he finally said, "Well, what if I am."

The final straw came yesterday when her husband was served at home with suit papers from a neighboring state. It seems that a woman named Georgia Peach has filed a paternity suit against him alleging that he is the father of her newborn child and demanding support.

Custody:

Mrs. Unyon wants to have sole custody of both the minor children. She doesn't expect that to be a problem with the ten-year-old daughter but fears her husband will contest her on custody of the sixteen-year-old son and that the son, if allowed to choose, will go with his father. She is concerned about the influence that environment may have on her son who is going through a rebellious stage anyway.

Support:

Mrs. Unyon wants to go back to school. She is interested in the new paralegal program at Yourstate University and feels that if she does well in it, she may even go on to law school. However, she doesn't work, hasn't ever worked and has no marketable skills. She will need her husband to support her while she is in school. She will also want child support for the children through college. The oldest daughter graduated from Yourstate University, being put through college by her parents.

Miscellaneous:

Mrs. Unyon says her husband does not know she is seeing a lawyer. She has not mentioned divorce to him but is fed up with her marriage and wants out. She says they had a big fight about a week ago and he threatened to have her killed if she ever left him. She thinks he means it. He knows how to use all the guns in his collection. He's just not the man she married 27 years ago.

CASE STUDY #4

THE ROCKY ROAD PROJECT

The law office where you work has been retained to represent Rocky Road Developers, Inc., (RRD) in a real estate development project. Below you will find a summary of the new client memorandum prepared by your supervising attorney based on his interview with Mr. Rocky Road, president of RRD.

Summary of new client memorandum:

RRD is a domestic corporation owned solely by Mr. Rocky Road, the president and sole director of the corporation. RRD has done a few real estate development projects in Yourstate and neighboring states and is now working on a deal here in Capital City.

RRD has a one-year option to buy 10 acres of farm land east of Capital City. The option expires three months from today. RRD has hopes of acquiring a total of 20 acres in that location and building a strip shopping center with two anchor tenants and eight to ten other smaller tenants. Rocky Road advised that he thinks the other ten acres may now be available.

Five acres adjoining the ten he has optioned were owned by a farmer by the name of Edward Dig Deep, who Road has learned passed away two weeks ago. Road has no information regarding whether Farmer Deep left a will or not.

Three additional adjoining acres are owned by Capital City and the mayor's office has advised Road that the city has decided not to utilize those acres and may be willing to sell them.

Two other adjoining acres are the site of an old gas station (with a small office and separate garage) that recently closed and has a *For Sale* sign on the window. A shallow stream flows just behind the old gas station site and Rocky Road says it looks like a lot of junk has been thrown in there recently. He wonders if it might be polluted.

He stopped by there several months ago to ask if it might be for sale and talked to a woman named Grace Slickspot, who seemed to be running the place. When Rocky Road asked Slickspot if she was the owner, she answered him, "You're close enough." She didn't express any interest in selling then and Rocky Road left Ms. Slickspot his business card and asked her to call if she changed her mind. Two days ago Rocky Road had a message in his voice mail from Grace Slickspot telling him in a near whisper that the property was now available if he would hurry.

Rocky Road would like for us to advise and assist him in obtaining title to the ten acres he does not yet have optioned and concerning the legal requirements he needs to satisfy to get his project approved.

Regarding tenants, Road advised that he spoke with a Mr. Real E. Smart, a vice president in the real estate department of World Mart, Inc., the world's largest retail discounter about six months ago concerning its interest in locating a new store on the site. Smart expressed great interest on behalf of World Mart in this project, though neither World Mart nor any other tenant has signed a lease commitment with RRD. Rocky Road is also in hopes he can land Super Foods as another anchor tenant and would like for us to help with the negotiations with those two companies.

Appendix B

Resources for the Investigator

TABLE OF CONTENTS TO APPENDIX B

22. Media Resources Online
    A. National Newspapers Online
    B. Directories of Newspapers Online
    C. Periodicals Online
    D. Television Networks Online
23. People Locater Resources
    A. Publications
    B. People Search Free Online Services
    C. People and Business Search Companies
    D. Map and Direction Services Free Online
    E. Popular Online Social Networking Sites
    F. Genealogical Resources—Online
    G. Genealogical Resources—Publications
    H. Veteran's Information
24. Social Security Index of Assigned Numbers
25. Credit Reporting Companies
    A. Individuals
    B. Small and Large Businesses
26. Public Records Search Companies and Resources
27. Online Database Vendors
28. Vital Records
    A. Publications
    B. Online Resources

1. SEARCH ENGINES AND ONLINE DIRECTORIES

A. GENERAL AND META SEARCH ENGINES AND DIRECTORIES

AltaVista (www.altavista.com)
AOL Search (http://search.aol.com)
Ask (www.ask.com)
Axis (www.axis.yahoo.com)
BigHub (www.isleuth.com)
Bing (www.bing.com)
Copernic (www.copernic.com)
Ditto (www.dittosearch.com)
Dogpile (www.dogpile.com)
Euroseek (www.euroseek.net)
Excite (www.excite.com)
Gigablast (www.gigablast.com)
Go From Here (www.gofromhere.com)
Google (www.google.com)
Infomine (http://infomine.ucr.edu)
Kartoo (www.kartoo.com)
Librarians' Internet Index (www.lii.org)
Locate (www.locate.com)
Lycos (www.lycos.com)
Mamma (www.mamma.com)
MetaCrawler (www.metacrawler.com)
MSN.com (www.msn.com)
Refdesk (www.refdesk.com)
SEW (http://searchenginewatch.com)
Snap (www.snap.com)
Virtual Library (http://vlib.org)
Vivisimo (http://vivisimo.com)
WebCrawler (www.webcrawler.com)
Yahoo (www.yahoo.com)

B. LEGAL SEARCH ENGINES, DIRECTORIES, AND NEWS SITES

ABA Media Alerts on Federal Circuit Court Decisions (www2.americanbar.org/SCFJI/Pages/MediaAlertsOnFederalCircuitCourts.aspx)
ABA SCOTUS Preview (www.americanbar.org/publications/preview_home.html)
Alllaw (www.alllaw.com)
Chicago-Kent Guide to Legal Resources (http://library.kentlaw.edu)
Cornell Law School's Legal Information Institute (www.law.cornell.edu)
Emory Electronic Reference Desk (http://library.law.emory.edu/electronic-resources/)

FindLaw (www.findlaw.com)
HG Global Legal Resources (www.hg.org)
Indiana Virtual Law Library (www.law.indiana.edu)
Internet Public Library Consortium (www.ipl.org)
Law.com Legal News (www.law.com/jsp/law/index.jsp)
LawCrawler (http://lawcrawler.findlaw.com)
Law Engine (www.thelawengine.com)
Law Guru (www.lawguru.com/lawlinks)
Law News Network (www.law.com/jsp/law/index.jsp)
Law Research (www.lawresearch.com)
Law Runner (www.ilrg.com)
Law Source (www.lawsource.com)
'Lectric Law Library (www.lectlaw.com)
Legal Ethics (www.legalethics.com)
Purdue's Catalogue of Databases (www.lib.purdue.edu)
Rominger Legal On-Line Research (www.romingerlegal.com)
Search-the-Law (www.search-the-law.com)
University of Chicago D'Angelo Law Library (www1.lib.uchicago.edu/
  e/law)
Villanova Center for Information Law and Policy (ww.vcilp.org)
Vozo (www.vozo.com)
WashLaw (www.washlaw.edu)
Yahoo Law (http://dir.yahoo.com/Government/Law)

2 . LAWYER DIRECTORIES — ONLINE

Attorney Find (www.attorney.find)
Attorney Locate (www.attorney.locate)
FindLaw (http://lawyers.findlaw.com)
Internet Legal Research Group (www.ilrg.com)
Legal Industry Directory (www.lawinfo.com)
LegalOnLine (www.legalonline.com)
Martindale-Hubbell Law Directory (www.martindale.com)

3 . LAW RELATED ORGANIZATIONS

1. American Association for Justice (formerly the Association of Trial
   Lawyers of America), 1050 31st St. NW Washington, DC 20007,
   800-424-2725 (www.justice.org)
2. American Association for Paralegal Education (AAfPE), 19 Mantua
   Road, Mount Royal, NJ 08061, (856) 423-2829 (www.aafpe.org)
3. American Association of Legal Nurse Consultants, 4700 W. Lake
   Ave., Glenview, IL 60025, (877) 402-2562 (www.aalnc.org)
4. American Bankruptcy Institute (ABI) (www.abiworld.org)
5. American Bar Association (ABA), 750 No. Lake Shore Drive,
   Chicago, IL 60611, (312) 988-5000 (www.abanet.org)
6. American Civil Liberties Union, 125 Broad Street, New York, NY
   10004, 1-800-775-ACLU (www.aclu.org)

7. American Law Institute (ALI) (www.ali.org)
8. Defense Research Institute: The Voice of the Defense Bar, 150 North Michigan Avenue, Third Floor, Chicago, IL 60601, (312) 795-1101 (www.dri.org)
9. International Paralegal Management Association, P.O. Box 659, Avondale Estates, GA 30002-0659, (404) 292-4762 (www.paralegal management.org)
10. National Association of Criminal Defense Lawyers, 1025 Connecticut Ave. NW, Washington, DC 20036, (202) 872-8600 (www. criminaljustice.org)
11. National Association of Legal Assistants (NALA), 1516 S. Boston, Suite 200 Tulsa, OK 74119, (918) 587-6828 (www.nala.org)
12. National Association of Legal Secretaries (NALS), 314 East 3d Street, Suite 210, Tulsa, OK 74120, (918) 582-5188 (www.nals.org)
13. National Federation of Paralegal Associations (NFPA), 32 West Bridlespur Terrace, P.O. Box 33108, Kansas City, MO 64114-0108, (816) 941-4000 (www.paralegals.org)
14. Organization of Legal Professionals, 44-489 Town Center Way Ste. D436, Palm Desert, CA 92260-2723, (760) 610-5462 (www. theolp.org/)

4. POPULAR LAWYER BLOGS

1. Above the Law (www.abovethelaw.com)
2. ACLU Blog of Rights (http://blog.aclu.org)
3. Althouse (www.althouse.blogspot.com)
4. American Constitution Society (www.acslaw.org/acsblog)
5. Be Spacific (www.bespacific.com)
6. BLAWG (www.blawg.com)
7. Blawg Review (http://blawgreview.blogspot.com)
8. BLT (the Blog of Legal Times) (http://legaltimes.typepad.com)
9. China Law Blog (www.chinalawblog.com)
10. Concurring Opinions (www.ConcurringOpinions.com)
11. e-Discovery Bytes (http://ediscovery.quarles.com)
12. ForbesLaw (www.forbes.com/law/)
13. Glenn Greenwald at Salon (www.salon.com/opinion/greenwald)
14. Josh Blackman blog (http://joshblackman.com/blog/)
15. Law and More (http://lawandmore.typepad.com/law_and_more)
16. LawProfessorBlogs (www.LawProfessorBlogs.com/)
17. Lawyernomics (www.lawyernomics.awo.com)
18. Legal Current (http://legalcurrent.com)
19. Legal Juice (www.legaljuice.com)
20. Legal Times (http://legaltimes.typepad.com/)
21. Overlawyered (http://overlawyered.com)
22. SCOTUSblog (www.scotusblog.com/)
23. Tax Professor Blog (http://taxprof.typepad.com/taxprof_blog/)
24. WSJ Blog (http://blogs.wsj.com/law/)
25. Young Lawyers Blog (www.younglawyersblog.com)

5. POPULAR PARALEGAL BLOGS

1. Impartial (http://impartialinc.blogspot.com)
2. In Propria Persona (http://selfhelplegal.blogspot.com)
3. New York Paralegal (www.newyorkparalegalblog.com)
4. Paralegal Gateway (http://paralegalgateway.typepad.com/my_weblog)
5. Practical Paralegalism (www.practicalparalegalism.com)
6. Scribe (http://legaldocumentassistant.blogspot.com)
7. The Estrin Report (http://estrinlegaled.typepad.com)

6. RESOURCES FOR ELECTRONIC DISCOVERY

A. ORGANIZATIONS AND WEB-BASED RESOURCES

1. Aderant (www.aderant.com/)
2. AIIM—The Enterprise Content Management Association (www.aiim.org)
3. Applied Discovery (www.applieddiscovery.com/)
4. Conference of Chief Justices' Guidelines for State Trial Courts Regarding Discovery of ESI (www.ncsconline.org/images/EDiscCCJGuidelinesFinal.pdf)
5. DiscoveryResources.org and its discovery blog, SoundEvidence (http://soundevidence.discoveryresources.org)
6. E-discovery blogs (http://ediscovery.quarles.com); or (www.ediscoverylaw.com)
7. E-discovery case database (www.ediscoverylaw.com/articles/ediscovery-case-database)
8. Electronic Discovery Law Web site of the Preston, Gates & Ellis, LLP law firm (www.ediscoverylaw.com); Equivio (www.equivio.com/)
9. Esentio Technologies (www.esentio.com/)
10. Federal Judicial Center Pocket Guide for Judges on Managing Discovery of Electronic Information (www.fjc.gov/public/pdf.nsf/lookup/eldscpkt.pdf/$file/eldscpkt.pdf) and FJC Materials on E-Discovery (www.fjc.gov/public/home.nsf/autoframe?openform&url_l=/public/home.nsf/inavgeneral?openpage&url_r=/public/home.nsf/pages/196)
11. Fios (books, articles, webcasts, and electronic discovery support services) (www.fiosinc.com)
12. Forensics Consulting Solutions (www.aboutfcs.com)
13. InData (http://indatacorp.com/Products/eDiscovery/services.aspx)
14. IntApp (www.intapp.com/)
15. Integreon (www.integreon.com/)
16. International Legal Technology Association (http://iltanet.org/)
17. MindSHIFT Technologies (www.integreon.com/)
18. National Conference of Commissioners of Uniform State Laws Uniform Rules Relating to Discovery of ESI (www.law.upenn.edu/bll/archives/ulc/udoera/2007am_final.pdf)
19. Organization of Legal Professionals (www.theolp.org/)
20. Profiscience Partners (www.profiscience.com/)
21. Recommind (www.recommind.com/)

22. The Sedona Conference publications: *The Sedona Principles: Best Practices Recommendations & Principles for Addressing Electronic Document Production*; Commentary on Ethics and MetaData (March 2012); Database Principles Addressing the Preservation and Production of Databases and Database Information in Civil Litigation (2011); *The Sedona Principles: Second Edition, Best Practices for Recommendations & Principles for Addressing Electronic Document Production* (June 2007); *The Sedona Conference Commentary on Email Management: Guidelines for the Selection of Retention Policy* (April 7, 2007). (Available at https://thesedonaconference.org/publications.)
23. TDC Global Enterprises (www.tdcge.com/Home.html)
24. TechLaw Solutions (www.techlawsolutions.com/index.asp)
25. Traveling Coaches (www.travelingcoaches.com/)

B. PUBLICATIONS

1. ABA Law Practice Management Section: *Electronic Discovery for Small Cases: Managing Digital Evidence and ESI* (Chicago, 2012).
2. Adler, Gary A., et al., *Electronic Discovery Guidance 2008: What Corporate and Outside Counsel Need to Know* (Practicing Law Institute, 2008).
3. Brown, Christopher, *Computer Evidence* (Cengage, 2009).
4. Grenig, Jay, et al., *Electronic Discovery and Records Management Guide: Rules, Checklists and Forms* (West, 2008–2009).
5. Losey, Ralph C., *e-Discovery: Current Trends and Cases* (ABA, 2008).
6. Mack, Mary, et al., *A Process of Illumination: The Practical Guide to Electronic Discovery* (Fios, 2008).
7. Mack, Mary, et al., *Electronic Evidence Management: From Creation Through Litigation*, 2nd ed. (Fios, 2008).
8. Nelson, Sharon D., et al., *The Electronic Evidence and Discovery Handbook: Forms, Checklists and Guidelines* (ABA, 2006).
9. Robertson, Paul M., et al., *Electronic Discovery: A Survey of Relevant Law and Recent Developments*, Committee on Pretrial Practice and Discovery, Vol. 13, No. 1 at 11 (Winter 2005).
10. Scheindlin, Shira A., et al., *Electronic Discovery and Digital Evidence: Cases and Materials* (West, 2008).
11. Schuler, Karen A., *E-discovery: Creating and Managing an Enterprise-wide Program: A Technical Guide to Digital Investigation and Litigation Support* (Syngress, 2008).
12. Volonino, Linda, et al., *Computer Forensics for Dummies* (For Dummies, 2008).

7. EXPERTS

A. ORGANIZATIONS

1. American Association for Justice (AJA, formerly the Association of Trial Lawyers of America), 777 6th St. NW, Ste. 200, Washington, DC 20001, (800) 424-2725 (www.justice.org/)

2. Defense Research Institute, 150 North Michigan Ave., Third Floor, Chicago, IL 60601, (312) 795-1101 (www.dri.org)
3. National Association of Criminal Defense Lawyers, 1025 Connecticut Ave. NW, Washington, DC 20036, (202) 872-8600 (www.criminal justice.org)
4. SCORE Service Corps of Retired Executives, c/o Small Business Administration, 1110 Vermont Ave. NW, Washington, DC 20005, (202) 606-4000 (www.score.org)
5. Technical Advisory Service for Attorneys (TASA), 1166 DeKalb Pike, Blue Bell, PA 19422-1853, (800) 523-2319 (www.tasanet.com)
6. Technical Assistance Bureau (TAB), 13017 Wisteria Drive, Suite 223, P.O. Box 1779, Germantown, MD 20874-1779, (800) 336-0190 (www.tabexperts.com)

B. ONLINE RESOURCES

1. The Collaborative Defense Network for Expert Witness Research (www.idex.com)
2. Expert Pages (http://expertpages.com)
3. Expert Witness Network (www.witness.net)
4. Find/Research Experts (www.llrx.com/features/findingexperts.htm)
5. Internet Expert Sources (www.ibiblio.org/slanews)
6. Kroll Ontrack (www.krollontrack.com)
7. LawInfo (www.lawinfo.com)
8. Legal Concierge (www.mylegalconcierge.com)
9. Marquis Who's Who (http://marquiswhoswho.com/online-database) (biographies of experts/consultants in many areas)
10. PubMed (www.pubmed.gov)
11. Trial Graphix (www.trialgraphix.com)
12. Yahoo (http://dir.yahoo.com/Education/Higher_Education)

C. PUBLICATIONS

1. *American Jurisprudence 2d, Desk Book.* St. Paul, MN: Thomson West, [YEAR].
2. *Martindale-Hubbell Law Directory.* New Providence, NJ: Martindale-Hubbell, [YEAR]. (www.martindale.com).
3. Philo, Harry M., *Lawyer's Desk Reference*, St. Paul, MN: Thomson West, [YEAR].
4. *Who's Who in American Education; Who's Who in American Medicine and Healthcare; Who's Who in American Science and Engineering; Who's Who in American Finance and Business.* New Providence, NJ: Marquis (www.marquiswhoswho.com).
5. *The Yearbook of Experts, Authorities & Spokespersons: An Encyclopedia of Sources*, Washington, DC: Broadcast Interview Source, 2006.

8. PRIVATE INVESTIGATORS

A. PUBLICATIONS—BOOKS

1. Brown, Steven K., *The Complete Idiot's Guide® to Private Investigating*, 2nd ed. NY: Alpha, 2007.
2. Crittenden, Pam, *The Source Book to Public Record Information: The Comprehensive Guide to County, State & Federal Public Record Sources*, 3d ed. Tempe, AZ: BRB Publications, 2001.
3. Dempsey, John S., *An Introduction to Investigations*, 2nd ed. Stamford, CT: Cengage, 2002.
4. *Reporter's Handbook to Documents and Techniques: An Investigator's Guide*, 3d ed. New York: St. Martin's Press, 1995.
5. Sankey, Michael L., *Public Records Online, Fifth Edition: The National Guide to Private & Government Online Sources of Public Records*. Tempe, AZ: Facts on Demand Press, 2004.
6. Travers, Joseph Anthony, *Introduction to Private Investigation: Essential Knowledge and Procedures for the Private Investigator*. Springfield, IL: Charles C. Thomas Publisher, 2005.
7. Wilson, Claire, *Guide to Interviewing Children: Essential Skills for Counselors, Social Workers, Police Lawyers*. NY: Routledge Press, 2001.

B. PUBLICATIONS—PERIODICALS

1. *The Database Files*, 5622 Wood Lane, St. Louis Park, MN 55436.
2. *The IRE Journal*, Investigative Reporters and Editors, Inc., 100 Neff Hall, University of Missouri, Columbia, MO 65211 (bimonthly).
3. *The Legal Investigator*, 3304 Crescent Drive, Des Moines, IA 50312.
4. *Lesko's Info-Power Newsletter*, Information USA, P.O. Box E, Kensington, MD 20895.
5. *P.I. Magazine*, 755 Bronx, Toledo, OH (quarterly).
6. *Privacy Journal*, P.O. Box 28577, Providence, RI 02908.
7. *Private Investigator's Connection*, National Association of Investigative Specialists, Inc., P.O. Box 33244, Austin, TX 78764.
8. *Searcher: The Magazine for Database Professionals*, 143 Old Marlton Pike, Medford, NJ 08055.
9. *Special Libraries*, 1700 18th Street NW, Washington, DC 20009.
10. *Uplink*, National Institute for Computer-Assisted Reporting, 120 Neff Hall, University of Missouri, Columbia, MO 65211.

C. ONLINE RESOURCES FOR LOCATING A PRIVATE INVESTIGATOR

1. Investigative Reporters and Editors (www.ire.org)
2. LawInfo (www.lawinfo.com)
3. National Association of Legal Investigators (www.nalionline.org)
4. Private Investigator Network (www.pimall.com)

5. Security Intelligence Technologies (www.spyzone.com)
6. SuperPages (www.superpages.com)
7. U.S. Department of Labor (www.bls.gov/oco/ocos157.htm)

9. ALTERNATIVE DISPUTE RESOLUTION (ADR)

A. ONLINE RESOURCES

1. American Arbitration Association (www.adr.org). Offers information on ADR including text of AAA rules, AAA forms, and articles on ADR.
2. American College of Civil Trial Mediators (www.acctm.org). This organization offers mediation services throughout North America. The site will assist in locating a qualified mediator in numerous areas of specialty and provides links to helpful articles and publications in the field. ACCTM publishes a newsletter, *The Alternative*.
3. Arbitration Forums, Inc (www.arbfile.org/webapp/).
4. Federal Judicial Center (www.fjc.gov). Provides numerous articles relating to ADR.
5. FINRA (www.finra.org/ArbitrationAndMediation/FINRADisputeResolution/).
6. Interagency Alternative Dispute Resolution Working Group (www.adr.gov).
7. International Institute for Conflict Prevention & Resolution (www.cpradr.org). An organization dedicated to promoting ADR in corporate and law firm practices. Provides training in ADR, assistance in locating qualified mediators, and many excellent publications in the field. The Institute also publishes a newsletter, *Alternatives*.
8. Mediate.com (www.mediate.com).
9. The Mediation Center (www.themediationcenter.org).
10. World Intellectual Property Organization Arbitration Center (www.wipo.int/amc/en).
11. World Services Group, Directory of Arbitrators (www.worldservicesgroup.com/arbitrators-mediators.asp); and (www.hg.org/adr.html).

B. BIBLIOGRAPHY ON ADR

1. Barrett, Jerome T., *History of Alternative Dispute Resolution: The Story of a Political, Social, and Cultural Movement*. San Francisco, CA: Jossey-Bass, 2004.
2. Brunet, E., *Alternative Dispute Resolution: The Advocate's Perspective*, 3rd ed. Dayton, OH: Matthew Bender, 2006.
3. Bush, Robert A., and Folger, Joseph P., *The Promise of Mediation: The Transformative Approach to Conflict*, rev'd ed. San Francisco, CA: Jossey-Bass, 2004.
4. Deutsch, Morton, *The Handbook of Conflict Resolution: Theory and Practice*. San Francisco, CA: Jossey-Bass, 2006.

5. Eaton, Adrienne E., et al., *Employment Dispute Resolution and Worker Rights in the Changing Workplace*. Ithaca, NY: Cornell U. Press, 2000.

6. Folberg, Jay, et al., *Divorce and Family Mediation: Models, Techniques & Applications*. NY: Guilford Press, 2004.

7. Frey, Martin A., *Alternative Methods of Dispute Resolution*. Clifton Park, NY: Delmar Learning, 2002.

8. Furlong, Gary, *Conflict Resolution Toolbox: Models and Maps for Analyzing, Diagnosing, and Resolving Conflict*. Hoboken, NJ: John Wiley & Sons, 2005.

9. Goodman, Allan H., *Basic Skills for the New Mediator*, 2nd ed. Rockville, MD: Solomon Publications, 2004.

10. Greenwood, Mary, *How to Mediate Like a Pro: 42 Rules for Mediating Disputes*. Bloomington, IN: iUniverse, 2008.

11. Lechman, Barbara A., *Conflict and Resolution*, 2nd ed. NY: Aspen Publishers, 2007.

12. Mayer, Bernard, *Beyond Neutrality: Confronting the Crisis in Conflict Resolution*. San Francisco, CA: Jossey-Bass, 2004.

13. Mayer, Bernard, *Staying with Conflict: A Strategic Approach to Ongoing Disputes*. San Francisco, CA: Jossey-Bass, 2009.

14. Moffitt, Michael, L. *The Handbook of Dispute Resolution*. San Francisco, CA: Jossey-Bass, 2005.

15. Moore, Christopher W., *The Mediation Process*, 3d ed. San Francisco, CA: Jossey-Bass, 2003.

16. Nolan-Haley, Jacqueline M., *Alternative Dispute Resolution in a Nutshell*, 3rd ed. St. Paul, MN: Thomson West, 2008.

17. Partridge, Mark, V. B., *Alternative Dispute Resolution: An Essential Competency for Lawyers*. NY: Oxford U. Press, USA, 2009.

18. Patterson, Susan, and Seabolt, Grant, *Essentials of Alternative Dispute Resolution*, 2d ed. Dallas, TX: Pearson Publications Company, 2001.

19. Stulberg, Joseph B., et al., *The Middle Voice: Mediating Conflict Successfully*. Charlotte, NC: Carolina Academic Press, 2008.

20. Ware, Stephen J., *Alternative Dispute Resolution*. St. Paul, MN: West Group, 2001.

21. Westbrook, James E., et al., *Dispute Resolution for Lawyers*, 4th ed. St. Paul, MN: West Group, 2009.

10. COMMUNICATION SKILLS—VERBAL AND NONVERBAL

1. Anderson, Peter, *Complete Idiot's Guide® to Body Language*. NY: Alpha, 2004.

2. Birdwhitsell, R.L, *Introduction to Kinesics*. Lousiville: Louisville Press, 1952.

3. Deaver, Jeffery, *The Sleeping Doll*. NY: Simon & Schuster, 2007.

4. Dictionary of Regional American English (http://dare.wisc.edu/?q=node/1).

5. Dimitrius, Jo-Ellan, *Reading People: How to Understand People and Predict Their Behavior—Anytime, Anyplace*, 2nd ed. NY: Ballentine, 2008.

6. Do You Speak American? (www.pbs.org/speak/).

7. Eckman, Paul, *Emotions Revealed: Recognizing Faces and Feeling to Improve Communication and Emotional Life*, 2nd ed. NY: Holt, 2007.

8. Eckman, Paul, et al., *What the Face Reveals: Basic and Applied Studies of Spontaneous Expression Using the Facial Action Coding System*, 2nd ed. London: Oxford University Press, 2005.

9. Fast, Julius, *Body Language*, Rev'd ed. NY: M. Evans & Co., 2002.

10. Gladwell, Malcom, *Blink: The Power of Thinking without Thinking*. San Francisco: Back Bay Books, 2007.

11. Hogan, Kevin, *The Secret Language of Business: How to Read Anyone in 3 Seconds or Less*. Hoboken, NJ: Wiley, 2008.

12. Medea, Andra, *Working with Emotional Clients: The Virtual Tranquilizer for Lawyers*. Chicago: ABA 2010.

13. Navaro, Joe, et al., *What EveryBODY is Saying: An Ex-FBI Agent's Guide to Speed Reading People*. NY: Collins Living, 2008.

14. Our Nation's Many Voices Online (http://csumc.wisc.edu/American-Languages/).

15. Quilliam, Susan, *Body Language*. Richmond Hill, ON: Firefly Books, 2004.

16. Rosetree, Rose, et al., *The Power of Face Reading*, 2nd ed. Chico, CA: Women's Intuition Worldwide, 2001.

17. Walters, Stan B., *Principles of Kinesic Interview and Investigation*, 3d ed. NY: CRC, 2010.

18. Zulawski, David E., *Practical Aspects of Interview and Interrogation*, 2nd ed. NY: CRC, 2001.

11. Communication Skills — Writing

1. Enquist, Anne, and Oates, Laurel Currie, *Just Writing: Grammar, Punctuation and Style for the Legal Writer*, 3rd ed. NY: Aspen Publishers, 2009.

2. Fowler, H. Ramsey, and Aaron, Jane E., *The Little, Brown Handbook*, 11th ed. NY: Longman, 2009.

3. Garner, Bryan A., *The Redbook: A Manual of Legal Style*, 2d ed. St. Paul, MN: West Group, 2006.

4. Garner, Bryan A. (editor), *Elements of Legal Drafting*. Dayton, OH: Oxford University Press, 2006.

5. Good, Edward C., *A Grammar Book for You and I . . . Oops, Me!: All the Grammar You Need to Succeed in Life*. Sterling, VA: Capital Books, 2002.

6. National Association for Legal Assistants, *NALA Manual for Paralegals and Legal Assistants*, (Chapter 5). Stamford, CT: Delmar Cengage, 2009.

7. Newman, Virginia K., *Certified Paralegal Review Manual: A Practical Guide to CP Exam Preparation (Test Preparation)*, 3d ed. (Chapter 1). Stamford, CT: Delmar Cengage, 2010.

8. Robey, Cora L., et al., *New Handbook of Basic Writing Skills*, 5th ed. St. Paul, MN: Heinle, 2003.

9. Stilman, Anne, *Grammatically Correct: The Writer's Essential Guide to Punctuation, Spelling, Style, Usage and Grammar*. Cincinnati, OH: Writers Digest Books, 2004.

10. Straus, Jane, et al., *The Bluebook of Grammar and Punctuation*, 10th ed. San Francisco, CA: 2007.
11. Strunk, William, Jr., and White, E.B., *The Elements of Style*, 50th Anniversary ed. Upper Saddle River, NJ: Longman, 2008.
12. *The Chicago Manual of Style*, 15th ed. University of Chicago Press Staff, 2003.
13. Wydick, Richard, *Plain English for Lawyers*, 5th ed. Durham, NC: Carolina Academic Press, 2005.
    Online Help
       Elements of style online (www.bartleby.com/141)
    Online Help with Grammar
       EduFind (www.edufind.com)
       Grammar Now (www.grammarnow.com)
       Grammar slammer (http://englishplus.com/grammar)
       Online Writing Lab (OWL) (http://owl.english.purdue.edu/handouts/grammar)
       Plain Language (www.plainlanguage.com)
       Wordsmith (www.wordsmith.org)

12. FREEDOM OF INFORMATION ACT/PRIVACY ACT

A. PUBLICATIONS

1. *A Citizen's Guide on How to Use the Freedom of Information Act and the Privacy Act Requesting Government Documents*, prepared by the United States House of Representatives Committee on Government Operations. Contact: Superintendent of Documents, United States Printing Office, Washington, DC 20402 (www.gpoaccess.gov) (accessible online at www.usdoj.gov/04foia/foi-act.htm).
2. *Freedom of Information and the Right to Know: The Origins and Applications of the FOIA*, Herbert N. Foerstel. Santa Barbara, CA: Greenwood Press, 1999.
3. *How to Use the Federal FOIA Act*, 7th ed. 1994, Rebecca Daughtery, ed., published by the Freedom of Information Service Center. Contact: Freedom of Information Service Center, The FOIA Service Center, 1735 I Street NW, Washington, DC 20006 (online at www.justice.gov/oip/04_2.html).
4. *Using the Freedom of Information Act: A Step-by-Step Guide*, an American Civil Liberties Union Publication. Contact: The American Civil Liberties Union, 125 Broad Street, New York, NY 10004 (800-775-ACLU) (www.aclu.org).

B. OTHER RESOURCES

1. FOIA.gov (www.foia.gov/)
2. OIP (www.justice.gov/oip/index.html)
3. The U.S. DOJ FOIA Library(www.usdoj.gov/oip/04_2.html)

4. Public Citizen, Freedom of Information Clearinghouse (www.citizen.org/litigation/free_info)
5. OpenGovernment.org (http://opengovernment.org)
6. FOIA (www.tncrimlaw.com/foia_indx.html)
7. Reporters Committee for Freedom of the Press (www.rcfp.org/foiact)
8. SBA's Citizen's Guide to Using the FOIA (www.sba.gov/foia/guide.html)
9. FOIA officers for the various federal agencies may be located at this U.S. Department of Justice Web site (www.usdoj.gov/oip/chieffoiaofficers.html) or from FOIA.gov (www.foia.gov/report-makerequest.html) or in the Code of Federal Regulations (www.gpoaccess.gov/cfr) as supplemented by the Federal Register (www.gpoaccess.gov/fr) or in the U.S. Government Manual, searchable at www.gpoaccess.gov/gmanual/browse-gm-09.html.

13. LOCATING AND CONTACTING FEDERAL GOVERNMENT DEPARTMENTS

A. PUBLICATIONS

1. *American Jurisprudence 2d, Desk Book.* St. Paul, MN: Thomson West.
2. *Congressional Directory.* The United States Government Printing Office, searchable online at www.gpoaccess.gov/cdirectory.
3. Philo, Harry M., *Lawyer's Desk Reference*, 9th ed. St. Paul, MN: Thomson West, 2001.
4. *United States Government Manual.* Washington, DC: Office of the Federal Register, National Archives and Records Administration. Available from the GPO (www.gpoaccess.gov) or searchable online (www.gpoaccess.gov/gmanual/browse-gm-09.html).

B. ONLINE RESOURCES

1. SearchGov (www.searchgov.com)
2. GPO Access (www.gpoaccess.gov)
3. Thomas (http://thomas.loc.gov)
4. Federal Bulletin Board (http://fedbbs.access.gpo.gov)
5. U.S. House of Representatives Home Page (www.house.gov)
6. U.S. Senate (www.senate.gov)
7. Library of Congress (www.loc.gov)
8. Internet Law Library (www.lawguru.com/ilawlib/about.htm)
9. FedWorld (www.fedworld.gov)
10. FedStats (www.fedstats.gov)
11. LSU Library Federal Agencies Directory (http://www.lib.lsu.edu/gov)
12. U.S. Depository libraries listed (www.gpoaccess.gov/libraries.html)
13. National Archives (www.archives.gov)
14. The White House (www.whitehouse.gov)

15. All Things Military (www.searchmil.com)
16. Data.gov (www.data.gov)

1 4 . N A T I O N A L A R C H I V E S B R A N C H L O C A T I O N S

1. Atlanta: 1557 St. Joseph St., East Point, GA 30344, (404) 246-7477
2. Boston: 380 Trapelo Road, Waltham, MA 02154, (617) 647-8100
3. Chicago: 7358 South Pulaski Rd., Chicago, IL 60629, (312) 581-7816
4. Denver: P.O. Box 25307, Denver, CO 80225, (303) 236-0817
5. Fort Worth: P.O. Box 6216, Fort Worth, TX 76115, (817) 334-5525
6. Kansas City: 2312 East Bannister Rd., Kansas City, MO 64131, (816) 926-6934
7. Los Angeles: 2400 Avila Rd., First Floor, Laguna Niguel, CA 92677, (714) 643-4241
8. New York: Building 22, Mil. Ocean Ter., Bayonne, NJ 07002, (201) 823-7252
9. Philadelphia: 9th & Market Sts., Room 1350, Philadelphia, PA 19107, (215) 597-3000
10. San Francisco: 1000 Commodore Drive, San Bruno, CA 94066, (415) 876-9009
11. Seattle: 6125 Sand Point Way NE, Seattle, WA 98115, (206) 526-6507

1 5 . U . S . C O N G R E S S I N F O R M A T I O N

1. Code of Federal Regulations (www.gpoaccess.gov/cfr).
2. Congressional Record (www.gpoaccess.gov/crecord or http://thomas.loc.gov).
3. Federal Bulletin Board (http://fedbbs.access.gpo.gov).
4. Federal Register (www.gpoaccess.gov/fr).
5. GovTrack (www.govtrack.us/congress). Allows tracking of legislation and voting records of individual members.
6. Internet Law Library of the U.S. House of Representatives (www.house.gov/house/laws.shtml).
7. Thomas (http://thomas.loc.gov) Provides information on congressional procedures and full texts of all House and Senate bills, the Congressional Record, and many committee reports. Also provides numerous links to the White House, Congress, and all federal agencies.
8. United States Code (searchable at http://uscode.house.gov/search/criteria.shtml; or at http://uscodebeta.house.gov/browse/title1 or at www.gpoaccess.gov/uscode; or at www.law.cornell.edu/uscode).
9. United States Code Congressional and Administrative News (www.house.gov; or http://thomas.loc.gov).
10. United States Code Congressional and Administrative News (available from GPO at www.gpoaccess.gov).

16. Federal Judiciary Information

A. PUBLICATIONS

1. *Sourcebook for Federal Courts.* Available from GPO (www.gpoaccess.gov)
2. *Judicial Staff Directory*, Alexandria, VA: CQ Press (800) 638-1710 (www.cqpress.com/gethome.asp)

B. ONLINE RESOURCES

1. U.S. Supreme Court (www.supremecourtus.gov).
2. Office of the Federal Judiciary (www.uscourts.gov).
3. PACER—Public Access to Court Electronic Records (www.pacer.gov).
4. National Archives (www.archives.gov). The field branches of the NA are the primary source for inactive federal court records.
5. Federal Judiciary Homepage (www.uscourts.gov). Provides information on the structure of the federal judiciary, statistics on caseloads, judicial vacancies, employment opportunities, answers to frequently asked questions, lists of judiciary publications, and links to related Web sites.
6. American Bankruptcy Institute (www.abiworld.org). Provides access to decisions of the U.S. bankruptcy courts as well as bankruptcy news and information.
7. Oyez (www.oyez.org).
8. Cornell Law School's Legal information Institute (www.law.cornell.edu/supct).
9. Federal Rules of Evidence and Federal Rules of Civil Procedure, and all decisions of the United States Supreme Court relating to constitutional issues are available at http://supct.law.cornell.edu/supct.
10. Washburn University Federal Case Finder (www.washlaw.edu).

17. State and Local Government Resources

A. PUBLICATIONS

1. Crittendon, Pam (ed.), *The Sourcebook to Public Record Information*, 9th ed. Tempe, AZ: BRB Publications, 2009.
2. *Directory of State Court Clerks & County Courthouses 2006*. CQ Press 2006 (www.cqpress.com/gethome.asp).
3. McCarthy, David J., and Reynolds, Laurie, *Local Government Law in a Nutshell*, 5th ed. St. Paul, MN: West Group 2003.
4. *Monthly Checklist of State Publications*. Library of Congress (LOC) publication, (202) 707-5522. (www.loc.gov).
5. Reynolds, Osborne, Jr., *Local Government Law*, 2d ed. St. Paul, MN: West Publishing, 2001.
6. Rhyne, Charles S., *The Law of Local Government Operations*. Kingsport, TN: The Kingsport Press, 1980.
7. Sankey, Michael L., et al., *The Sourcebook to Public Record Information: The Comprehensive Guide to County, State & Federal Public Records Sources*, 10th ed. Tempe, AZ, 2009.

8. Stakey, Michael L., *The Directory of Local Court and County Record Retrievers 2004: The Definitive Guide to Searching for Public Record Information at the State Level.* Tempe, AZ: BRB Publications, 2004.

B. ONLINE RESOURCES

1. GovEngine (www.govengine.com).
2. GovSpot (www.govspot.com).
3. State and Local Net (www.statelocalgov.net/index.cfm).
4. State and Local Gov News (www.loc.gov/rr/news/stategov/stategov.html).
5. National Center for State Courts (www.ncsconline.org).
6. National Conference of State Legislatures (www.ncsl.org/index.htm). Outstanding site for tracking legislation around the country and for policy and issue analysis.
7. Council of State Governments (www.csg.org). Provides news, information, legislation, and links.
8. Uniform state laws (www.uniformlaws.org) (Nat'l Conf. of Comm'rs on Uniform State Laws).
9. Cornell Legal Information Institute (www.law.cornell.edu/states).
10. U.S. Department of Justice, Department of Statistics (http://bjs.ojp.usdoj.gov/).
11. Community Information by Zip Code (http://library.csun.edu/GovernmentPublications/ZipStats).
12. State county and city data book (http://quickfacts.census.gov/qfd); or (http://fisher.lib.virginia.edu/collections/stats/ccdb).
13. Law Librarians' Society's Legislative Source Book (www.llsdc.org/sourcebook).
14. National Association of Chief Information Officers of the States (www.nascio.org).
15. University of Michigan Documents Center for local, state, federal, and international law resources (www.lib.umich.edu/govdocs).
16. Internet Law Library (www.lawguru.com/ilawlib/about.htm).
17. Yahoo (http://dir.yahoo.com/Government/Law).
18. Municipal Codes (www.municode.com).
19. Piper State/Local Gov Net (www.statelocalgov.net).

18. CITATIONS TO STATE PUBLIC RECORDS ACTS

Alabama	Ala. Code §36-12-40
Alaska	Alaska Stat. §09.25.110
Arkansas	Ark. Code Ann. §25-19-105
Arizona	Ariz. Rev. Stat. §39-121.01
California	Cal. Govt. Code §6253
Colorado	Colo. Rev. Stat. §24-72-203
Connecticut	Conn. Gen. Stat. §1-210
Delaware	Del. Code Ann. tit. 29 §10003
Florida	Fla. Const. art. 1, §24

Georgia	Ga. Code Ann. §50-18-70
Hawaii	Haw. Rev. Stat. §92-4
Idaho	Idaho Code §9-337
Illinois	5 Ill. Comp. Stat. 160/4
Indiana	Ind. Code §5-14-3-3
Iowa	Iowa Code §22.2
Kansas	Kan. Stat. Ann. §45-215
Kentucky	Ky. Rev. Stat. Ann. §61.872
Louisiana	La. Rev. Stat. Ann. §44:31
Maine	Me. Rev. Stat. Ann. tit. 1 §408
Maryland	Md. Code Ann. §10-612
Massachusetts	Mass. Gen. Laws ch. 66, §10
Michigan	Mich. Comp. Laws §750.492
Minnesota	Minn. Stat. §13.03
Mississippi	Miss. Code Ann. §25-59-27
Missouri	Mo. Stat. Ann. §109.180
Montana	Mont. Code Ann. §2-6-102
Nebraska	Neb. Rev. Stat. §84-712
Nevada	Nev. Rev. Stat. §239.010
New Hampshire	N.H. Rev. Stat. Ann. §91-A:4
New Jersey	N.J. Stat. Ann. §47:1A-2
New Mexico	N.M. Stat. Ann. §14-2-1
New York	N.Y. Pub. Off. Law §88
North Carolina	N.C. Gen. Stat. §132-9
North Dakota	N.D. Cent. Code §44-04-18
Ohio	Ohio Rev. Code Ann. §149.43
Oklahoma	Okla. Stat. tit. 51, §24A
Oregon	Or. Rev. Stat. §192.420
Pennsylvania	65 Pa. Cons. Stat. §66.2
Rhode Island	R.I. Gen. Laws §45-43-7
South Carolina	S.C. Code Ann. §30-4-30
South Dakota	S.D. Codified Laws §1-27-1
Tennessee	Tenn. Code Ann. §10-7-503
Texas	Tex. Govt. Code Ann. §63-2-201
Utah	Utah Code Ann. §63-2-201
Vermont	Vt. Stat. Ann. tit. 1, §316
Virginia	Va. Code Ann. §2.1-342
Washington	Wash. Rev. Code §42.17.260
West Virginia	W. Va. Code §29B-1-3
Wisconsin	Wis. Stat. §19.35
Wyoming	Wyo. Stat. Ann. §16-4-202
Washington, DC	D.C. Code Ann §1-1504

19. Criminal Law—Sources of Information

1. The Federal Bureau of Investigation (www.fbi.gov). Offers information and statistics on domestic and international crime.
2. The National Institute of Justice, the research arm of the U.S. Department of Justice (www.ojp.usdoj.gov/nij). An informative site regarding

research and projects of the NIJ in many areas, including violence against women, drug laws, and community policing.

3. The U.S. Sentencing Guidelines Manuals (www.ussc.gov/guidelines/).
4. Bureau of Justice Statistics (http://bjs.ojp.usdoj.gov/). Provides state and local law enforcement statistics.
5. Federal Bureau of Prisons (www.bop.gov). Provides information on inmate demographics, sentences, and offenses.
6. Internet Crime Complaint Center (www.ic3.gov).
7. ABA Criminal Justice Section (www.americanbar.org/groups/criminal_justice.html).
8. Buffalo Criminal Law Center (http://wings.buffalo.edu/law/bclc).
9. Computer Crime and Intellectual Property Section (www.cybercrime.gov).
10. Florida State University Center for Criminology & Public Policy Research (www.criminologycenter.fsu.edu).
11. Justice Information Center (https://ncjrs.gov/). Provides information and statistics regarding adult and juvenile crime worldwide.
12. MegaLaw Criminal Law Page (www.megalaw.com/top/criminal.php). Links to state criminal laws and attorneys general.
13. National Fraud Information Center (www.fraud.org). A project of the National Consumers League, this site provides a daily report and other information on fraud, as well as the opportunity to report fraud.
14. State Sex Offender Registries (www.familywatchdog.us); and (www.prevent-abuse-now.com/register.htm). Information on sex offenses and links to state registries.
15. National inmate locator (www.corrections.com/links/show?Cat=20).

20. CORPORATE AND BUSINESS INFORMATION

A. PUBLISHERS OF BUSINESS INFORMATION

Gale Cengage (http://www.gale.cengage.com)
Hoovers, Inc. (www.hoovers.com)
H.W. Wilson (www.hwwilson.com)
R.R. Bowker (www.bowker.com)
McGraw-Hill (www.mcgraw-hill.com)
National Register Publishing (www.nationalregisterpub.com)

B. ONLINE RESOURCES

1. Federal government sites:
   Antitrust Division of the U.S. Department of Justice (www.usdoj.gov/atr).
   Business.Gov (www.business.usa.gov/). This federal government program provides access to business-related government information and services.

Consumer Product Safety Commission (www.cpsc.gov). Provides information on regulated products and businesses as well as access to publications.

Department of Commerce (www.commerce.gov).

EDGAR—Electronic Data Gathering Analysis and Retrieval System of the Securities Exchange Commission (www.sec.gov/edgar.shtml). A substantial amount of corporate financial and other information is available in the EDGAR database, including initial public offerings, proxy statements, annual corporate reports, and registration statements. Also, try this private site for a quicker EDGAR search (www.10Kwizard.com).

Environmental Protection Agency (www.epa.gov).

Federal Trade Commission (www.ftc.gov).

Food and Drug Administration (www.fda.gov).

National Labor Relations Board (www.nlrb.gov). Links to sites with NLRB rulings and pending cases.

FTC ID Theft Resource Site (http://www.ftc.gov/bcp/edu/microsites/idtheft).

2. Organizations:

American Bankruptcy Institute (ABI) (www.abiworld.org). Contains a daily and weekly summary of important bankruptcy news affecting American businesses.

American Federation of Labor-Congress of Industrial Organizations (AFL-CIO) (www.aflcio.org). Links to sites with information on ongoing business activities affecting organized labor and employee rights.

Better Business Bureau (www.bbb.org). The BBB also has a new site devoted to information on businesses operations (www.bbbonline.org).

The Center for the Study of Responsive Law (www.csrl.org). This Ralph Nader-inspired public interest center sponsors research and educational projects to encourage political, economic, and social institutions to be more responsive to the needs of consumers. The site provides access to a multitude of reports dealing with companies of all kinds.

Chamber of Commerce (www.uschamber.org).

EnviroLink (www.envirolink.org). Provides information on "socially responsible" businesses, including environmentally conscious firms.

3. Miscellaneous sites:

BizJournal (www.bizjournals.com).

Business News (www.internetnews.com/bus-news).

CEO Express (www.ceoexpress.com). Links to many business sources.

Corporate Information (www.corporateinformation.com).

Corporate Watch (www.corpwatch.org).

Credit reports (www.fool.com or www.thestreet.com).

Directory of sources for business info (www.business.com).

Dun & Bradstreet business rating and company locater (www.dnb.com/).

Executive compensation (www.aflcio.org/corporatewatch/paywatch or www.wageweb.com).

Experian (www.experian.com).

The Fitch Group (www.fitchratings.com).

Gale Academic OneFile (http://go.galegroup.com/ps/dispBasicSearch. do?prodId=AONE&userGroupName=tel_s_tsla). Access more than 48,000,000 full-text articles on physical sciences, technology, medicine, social sciences, the arts, theology, literature and other subjects.

Google business directories (www.google.com/Top/Business).

History Associates (www.historyassociates.com).

Hoover's Online (www.hoovers.com/free). Provides financial, personnel, and business data on more than 1,500 corporations.

International companies (www.jus.uio.no/lm).

Internet Public Library's Business and Economics Page (www.ipl.org/ div/subject/browse/bus82.00.00).

Moody's Investors Services (www.moodys.com). Credit ratings, research, and risk analysis.

NASD brokers information (www.nasdr.com).

Nonprofit information (www.idealist.org/if/idealist/en/Home/default; or www.guidestar.org). See also the Foundation Center (http:// fdncenter.org).

Northern Light Business Search Engine (www.northernlight.com).

Public Register Annual Report Service (www.prars.com). Annual reports on more than 3,000 corporations.

Standard & Poor's (www.standardandpoors.com/).

ThomasNet (www.thomasnet.com). Provides free access to profiles on American and European manufacturers and links to a number of other helpful sites.

The Virtual Chase Company Information Guide (www.virtualchase. com/topics/company_information_index.shtml).

Yahoo's Business and Organizations information (http://yahoo.com/ Business_and_Economy/Organizations/Professional).

Ziggs Business People Search (www.ziggs.com).

21. MEDICAL RESOURCES ONLINE

A. FEDERAL GOVERNMENT SITES

1. Healtcare.gov (www.healthcare.gov/)
2. HHS Health.gov (www.health.gov/)
3. HHS HealthFinder (www.health.gov/)
4. U.S. Center for Disease Control Health Statistics (www.cdc.gov/nchs/ default.htm) and its International Classification of Diseases site (www.cdc.gov/nchs/icd9.htm)
5. National Institutes of Health (http://health.nih.gov/)
6. National Library of Medicine Medline Plus (www.nlm.nih.gov/medline plus/)
7. National Library of Medicine (www.nlm.nih.gov/nlmhome.html)
8. National Guideline Clearinghouse (www.guideline.gov)

B. ORGANIZATIONS

1. American Medical Association (www.ama-assn.org) including its doctor-finder service (www.ama-assn.org/aps/amahg.htm)
2. American Health Care Association (http://www.ahcancal.org/Pages/Default.aspx)
3. American College of Nurse Practitioners (www.acnpweb.org/i4a/pages/index.cfm?pageid=3301)
4. American Council on Science and Health (www.acsh.org)
5. American Board of Medical Specialties (www.abms.org)
6. American Academy of Physicians Assistants (www.aapa.org)
7. American Cancer Society (www.cancer.org)
8. American Physical Therapy Association (www.apta.org)
9. Federation of State Medical Boards (www.fsmb.org)
10. Mayo Clinic (www.mayoclinic.com)
11. National Association for Public Health Statistics and Information Systems (NAPHSIS) (www.naphsis.org)

C. MISCELLANEOUS SITES

1. Doctor's Guide (www.docguide.com)
2. Hospital Locator (www.ahd.com/freesearch.php3)
3. Health Information Organization (http://health-info.org/)
4. Health Hippo (http://hippo.findlaw.com/hippohome.html)
5. Medscape (www.medscape.com)
6. Medical World Search (www.mwsearch.com). Medical information search engine
7. American Society of Health-System Pharmacists (www.safemedication.com)
8. Other pharmaceutical information (www.rxlist.com)
9. The Healing Spectrum (http://www.healthcentral.com)
10. The Baby Center (www.babycenter.com)
11. MyOptumHealth (http://www.myoptumhealth.com/portal)
12. Medem Physician Finder (www.medem.com)
13. Intellihealth (www.intellihealth.com). Searchable health information
14. Physician report (www.physicianreports.com)
15. Rate MDs (www.ratemds.com)
16. Board Certified Docs (www.boardcertifieddocs.com)
17. PDR.Net (www.pdr.net); and PDRHealth (www.pdrhealth.com)
18. Gray's Anatomy of the Human Body online (www.bartleby.com/107)
19. Medical Abbreviations (www.medilexicon.com/medicalabbreviations.php)
20. WebMD (www.webmd.com)

22. MEDIA RESOURCES ONLINE

A. NATIONAL NEWSPAPERS ONLINE

Los Angeles Times (www.latimes.com)
The New York Times (www.nytimes.com)

USA Today (www.usatoday.com)
The Wall Street Journal (http://online.wsj.com)
The Washington Post (www.washingtonpost.com)

B. DIRECTORIES OF NEWSPAPERS ONLINE

1. Business news (http://today.reuters.com/business; www.businessweek. com; www.bloomberg.com; or http://money.cnn.com).
2. Cornell News Site (www.library.cornell.edu/olinuris/ref/refsources. html#news).
3. DMOZ Open Directory Project (www.dmoz.org).
4. Ecola News Directory (www.ecola.com).
5. European Business News (www.eubusiness.com).
6. Google News (http://news.google.com).
7. NewsLink (www.newslink.org).
8. NewsPlace (www3.niu.edu/newsplace). A search engine devoted to locating numerous different news sources on the Internet.
9. NewsVoyager (www.newspaperlinks.com).
10. U.S. News Archives (www.ibiblio.org/slanews/internet/archives.html).
11. Yahoo News Finder (http://news.yahoo.com). Use to locate news stories.

C. PERIODICALS ONLINE

1. The American Lawyer (http://www.law.com/jsp/tal/index.jsp)
2. Corporate Counsel (www.law.com/jsp/cc/index.jsp)
3. CalLaw (www.law.com/jsp/ca/index.jsp)
4. Legal Times (www.law.com/jsp/dc/index.jsp)
5. Lawyers Weekly, Inc. (www.lawyersweekly.com)
6. The National Law Journal (www.law.com/jsp/nlj/index.jsp)
7. Time-Warner Online (www.pathfinder.com). The Time-Warner family of periodicals including *Time, Fortune, Life, People,* and *Money* magazines is accessible here.

D. TELEVISION NETWORKS ONLINE

www.abcnews.go.com
www.cbsnews.com
www.cnn.com
www.c-span.org
www.msnbc.msn.com
www.pbs.org
Local stations (TV and radio) online. Try www.[station's call letters].com

23. PEOPLE LOCATER RESOURCES

A. PUBLICATIONS

1. Barada, Paul W., et al., *Reference Checking for Everyone: How to Find Out Everything You Need to Know About Anyone.* NY: McGraw-Hill, 2004.

2. Johnson, Richard S., et al., *How to Locate Anyone Who Is or Has Been in the Military*, 8th ed. Burlington, NC: MIE Publishing, 1999.
3. King, Dennis, *Get the Facts on Anyone*, 3d ed. NY: McMillan, 1999.
4. Lapin, Lee, *How to Get Anything on Anybody: Book 3*. Lanai City, HI: Intelligence Here, 2003.
5. Nadell, Barry, *Sleuthing 101: Background Checks and the Law*. 2004.
6. Rose, Louis J., *How to Investigate Your Friends and Enemies*, 5th ed. Tampa, FL: Albion Press, 2004.
7. Scott, Robert, *The Investigator's Little Black Book*, 3d ed. Beverly Hills, CA: Crime Time Publishing Company, 2002.
8. Thomas, Ralph D., *How to Find Anyone Anywhere*, 4th ed. Austin, TX: Thomas Investigative Publications, 2001.
9. Tillman, Norma Mott, *How to Find Almost Anyone Anywhere*, rev'd ed. Nashville, TN: Rutledge Hill Press, 1998.

B. PEOPLE SEARCH FREE ONLINE SERVICES

1. About.com (http://websearch.about.com)
2. AnyWho (www.anywho.com)
3. Big Book (www.bigbook.com)
4. FindLaw Reverse Lookup (www.findlaw.com/directories/reverse.html)
5. IAF (www.iaf.net)
6. InfoSpace (www.infospace.com/home/white-pages/email-search)
7. Intelius (www.intelius.com)
8. MyLife (http://creative.mylife.com)
9. PeekYou (www.peekyou.com)
10. People Lookup (www.peoplelookup.com/people-search.html)
11. PeopleSearch (www.peoplesearch.com)
12. Spokeo (www.spokeo.com/)
13. SuperPages (www.superpages.com)
14. Switchboard, USA (www.switchboard.com)
15. The Ultimates (www.theultimates.com)
16. Toll-free directory (http://inter800.com)
17. USPS Zip code directory (http://zip4.usps.com/zip4)
18. Virtual Chase (www.virtualchase.com/topics/people_finder_index.shtml)
19. Virtual Gumshoe (www.virtualgumshoe.com)
20. Wink (http://wink.com)
21. Whitepages.com (www.whitepages.com)
22. Yahoo People Search (http://people.yahoo.com)
23. Yellowpages.com (www.yellowpages.com)
24. Zaba (www.zabasearch.com)

C. PEOPLE AND BUSINESS SEARCH COMPANIES

1. Accurint (www.accurint.com)
2. AnyWho (www.anywho.com)
3. AutoTrackXP (http://atxp.choicepoint.com)
4. Dialog (www.dialog.com)

5. InfoPeople (www.infopeople.org/search/tools.html)
6. Intelius (www.intelius.com/people-search.html)
7. KnowX (www.knowx.com)
8. LexisNexis FINDER:ALLFND and EZFIND (www.lexisnexis.com)
9. Merlin (www.merlindata.com)
10. USInfo.com (www.us-info.com/en/usa)
11. US Search (www.ussearch.com/consumer)
12. USA People Search (www.usa-people-search.com)
13. Webstigate (www.webstigate.com)
14. Westlaw PeopleMap (www.westlaw.com)
15. Zoom (www.zoominfo.com)

D. MAP AND DIRECTION SERVICES FREE ONLINE

1. Bing (www.bing.com/images)
2. Four11 (www.four11.com)
3. Google Earth (http://earth.google.com)
4. Google Maps (http://maps.google.com)
5. MapQuest (www.mapquest.com)
6. WhoWhere (www.whowhere.com)
7. InfoSpace (www.infospace.com)
8. Maps, U.S. (www.mapquest.com or www.mapsonus.com)
9. Maps, international (http://world.maporama.com/idl/maporama; or www.multimap.com)

E. POPULAR ONLINE SOCIAL NETWORKING SITES

General sites

1. Badoo (http://badoo.com/)
2. Bebo (www.bebo.com)
3. Black Planet (www.blackplanet.com)
4. Blippy (http://blippy.com/)
5. Buzzup (http://buzzup.com/us/)
6. CafeMom (www.cafemom.com/)
7. DailyBooth (http://dailybooth.com/)
8. Delicious (http://delicious.com/)
9. DeviantArt (deviantart.com/)
10. Diaspora (www.joindiaspora.com/)
11. DiggIt (www.digg.com/)
12. Facebook (www.facebook.com)
13. Foursquare (http://foursquare.com/)
14. Friendster (www.friendster.com)
15. Flickr (www.flickr.com)
16. Google+ (https://plus.google.com/)
17. Habbo (www.habbo.com)
18. ibeatyou (www.ibeatyou.com)
19. LinkedIn (www.linkedin.com) (for business people and professionals)
20. LiveJournal (www.livejournal.com/)

21. MeetMe (www.meetme.com/)
22. MeetUp (www.meetup.com/)
23. MySpace (www.myspace.com)
24. Ning (www.ning.com/)
25. Orkut (www.orkut.com/)
26. Pandora Share With Friends (http://pandora.com/)
27. Photobucket (http://photobucket.com/)
28. Pinterest (http://pinterest.com/)
29. Reddit (http://www.reddit.com/)
30. Scribd (www.scribd.com/)
31. Shizzler (www.shizzlr.com/)
32. StumbleUpon (www.stumbleupon.com/)
33. Tagged (www.tagged.com/)
34. True/Slant (http://trueslant.com/)
35. Tumblr (www.tumblr.com/about)
36. Twitter (https://twitter.com/)
37. VOX Personal Blogging (www.vox.com/)
38. Where are you now? (www.wayn.com/)
39. Yelp! (www.yelp.com/)
40. Yfrog (http://yfrog.com/)
41. Zinga (https://zynga.com/)

Dating/Hookup sites

1. AdultFriendFinder (http://adultfriendfinder.com)
2. e-Harmony (http://www.eharmony.com)
3. Match.com (www.match.com/matchus)
4. Nerve (www.nerve.com/)
5. OK Cupid (www.okcupid.com/)
6. Plenty of Fish (www.POF.com/)
7. Scientific Match (www.scientificmatch.com/)

Collaborative journalism sites

1. iReport (www.ireport.com)
2. WikiNews (http://en.wikinews.org/wiki/Main_Page)
3. Reddit (www.reddit.com/)

Classmate locating sites

1. Classmates.com (www.classmates.com)
2. Yearbook.com (www.yearbook.com)
3. MyLife (formerly Reunion.com) (www.mylife.com/)

Commercial sites

1. CraigsList (http://craigslist.org)
2. e-Bay (www.ebay.com)

Video broadcasting sites

1. MSN Soapbox Video (http://video.msn.com/video)
2. Yahoo! Video (http://video.yahoo.com)
3. YouTube (www.youtube.com)

F. GENEALOGICAL RESOURCES—ONLINE

1. Ancestory.com (www.ancestry.com)
2. Census Records.net (www.censusrecords.net/?o_xid=2739 . . .)
3. Cyndi's List (www.cyndislist.com/)
4. Genealogy.com (www.genealogy.com/ or http://genealogy.about.com/cs/findpeople)
5. Geni.com (www.geni.com), genealogy related social networking site
6. HeritageQuest (www.heritagequest.com/)
7. LDS Family Search (www.familysearch.org). This site, owned by the Church of Jesus Christ of Latter Day Saints (LDS) (Mormon) and operated by IBM, is billed as "the world's biggest genealogical Web site." It is a free site, providing access to the LDS's massive International Genealogical Index begun after World War II and added to daily.
8. MyFamily.com (www.myfamily.com)
9. National Archives (www.archives.gov)
10. National Genealogical Society (www.ngsgenealogy.org)
11. Rootsweb (www.rootsweb.com/)
12. Search for Ancestors (www.searchforancestors.com/)
13. U.K. GenWeb (www.ukgenweb.com/)
14. U.S. GenWeb (www.usgenweb.com/)
15. WebBiographies.com (www.webbiographies.com)

G. GENEALOGICAL RESOURCES—PUBLICATIONS

1. Carmack, Sharon D., *Your Guide to Cemetery Research*. Palm Coast, FL: Better Way Books, 2002.
2. Helm, Matthew, et al., *Genealogy Online for Dummies*, 5th ed. Hoboken, NJ: For Dummies, 2008.
3. Hendrickson, Nancy, *Finding Your Roots Online*. Palm Coast, FL: Better Way Books, 2003.
4. Porter, Pamela Boyer, *Online Roots: How to Discover Your Family's History and Heritage with the Power of the Internet*. Nashville, TN: Rutledge Hill Press, 2003.
5. Renick, Barbara, *Genealogy 101: How to Trace Your Family's History and Heritage*. Nashville, TN: Rutledge Hill Press, 2003.

H. VETERAN'S INFORMATION

1. Defense Manpower Data Center (www.fedstats.gov/key_stats/index.php?id=DMDC). Provides data on those currently serving in the military.
2. MilitarySearch (www.militarysearch.org).
3. Department of the Defense (www.defenselink.mil). Permits submission of an Affidavit of Military Status.
4. National Personnel Records Center (www.archives.gov/st-louis/military personnel). Permits filing of a form SF-180 request for information.
5. Military.com (www.military.com). Buddy Search Feature.

24. SOCIAL SECURITY INDEX OF ASSIGNED NUMBERS

Alabama 416-424
Alaska 574
Arkansas 429-432
Arizona 526-527
California 545-573
Colorado 521-524
Connecticut 040-049
Delaware 221-222
Florida 261-267
Georgia 252-260
Hawaii 575-576
Idaho 518-519
Illinois 318-336
Indiana 303-317
Iowa 478-483
Kansas 509-515
Kentucky 400-407
Louisiana 433-439
Maine 004-007
Maryland 212-220
Massachusetts 010-034
Michigan 362-386
Minnesota 468-477
Mississippi 425-428
Missouri 486-500
Montana 505-508
Montana 516-517

Nevada 530
New Hampshire 001-003
New Jersey 135-158
New Mexico 525, 585
New York 050-134
North Carolina 237-246
North Dakota 501-502
Ohio 268-302
Oklahoma 440-448
Oregon 540-544
Pennsylvania 159-211
Rhode Island 035-039
South Carolina 247-251
South Dakota 503-504
Tennessee 408-415
Texas 449-467
Utah 528-529
Vermont 008-009
Virginia 223-231
Washington 531-539
Washington, DC 577-579
West Virginia 232-236
Wisconsin 387-399
Wyoming 520
Virgin Islands 580
Puerto Rico, Guam, Samoa, and
Philippine Islands 581-585

25. CREDIT REPORTING COMPANIES

A. INDIVIDUALS

1. Banko (www.banko.com)
2. ChexSystems (www.consumerdebit.com/consumerinfo/us/en/index.htm)
3. CoreLogic (www.corelogic.com/)
4. CoreLogic SafeRent (www.residentscreening.com/index2.php)
5. Equifax (www.equifax.com)
6. Experian (www.experian.com)
7. FidelityInfoServices (http://www.fisglobal.com/)
8. First Data Telecheck (www.firstdata.com/telecheck/index.html)
9. Innovis (www.innovis.com)
10. LexisNexis Personal Reports (https://personalreports.lexisnexis.com/)
11. Medical Information Bureau (www.mib.com/)

12. National Consumer Telecom and Utilities Exchange (www.nctue.com/)
13. National Tenant Network (www.ntnonline.com/)
14. Trans Union (www.transunion.com)

B. SMALL AND LARGE BUSINESSES

1. Dun & Bradstreet business rating and company locater (www.dnb.com/)
2. Experian (www.experian.com/)
3. Fitch Group (www.fitchratings.com)
4. Kroll Ratings (www.krollbondratings.com/)
5. Moody's Investors Services (www.moodys.com)
6. Standard & Poor's (www.standardandpoors.com/)

26. PUBLIC RECORDS SEARCH COMPANIES AND RESOURCES

1. Ameri-Search (www.jigsaw.com)
2. BRB (www.brbpub.com)
3. Capitol Services, Inc. (www.capitolservices.com)
4. CCH SEC Research Service (www.wsb.com)
5. Corporation Service Company (www.incspot.com/global/web/csc/home)
6. CT Corporation (http://ctadmin.ctadvantage.com)
7. Experian (www.experian.com/small_business)
8. Government-Records.com (www.government-records.com)
9. GovSearch (http://govsearchrecords.com)
10. History Associates, Incorporated (www.historyassociates.com)
11. InfoUSA (www.lookupusa.com)
12. KnowX (www.knowx.com)
13. Merrill Corp. (www.merrillcorp.com)
14. NETROnline (http://publicrecords.netronline.com)
15. OneSource (www.onesource.com)
16. Parasec (www.parasec.com)
17. Rominger Legal Online (www.romingerlegal.com)
18. The Company Corporation (www.corporate.com)
19. WebInvestigator (www.webinvestigator.org)
20. Washington Document Service (www.wdsdocs.com)

27. ONLINE DATABASE VENDORS

1. Accurint (www.accurint.com).
2. Commerce Clearing House Information Services (www.cch.com).
3. CT Advantage (http://ctadmin.ctadvantage.com).
4. Database America (www.databaseamerica.com).
5. Dialog, Palo Alto, CA, 800-334-2564 (www.dialog.com).
6. Dialog DataStar (www.datastarweb.com). Provides 350 databases of international business and technical information.
7. Dow Jones (www.dowjones.com).

8. Dun & Bradstreet Information Services (www.dnb.com/us).
9. LexisNexis (www.lexisnexis.com).
10. Loislaw (www.loislaw.com).
11. Moody's Investor Services (www.moodys.com).
12. Online Computer Library Center (OCLC) (www.oclc.org). For library subscribers; provides search and retrieval and document databases from libraries in the U.S. and more than 60 other countries.
13. Questel-Orbit (http://www.questel.com). This European-American company specializes in intellectual property.
14. VersusLaw (www.versuslaw.com).
15. Westlaw (www.westlaw.com).
16. Zoom Info (www.zoominfo.com/Default.aspx).

28. VITAL RECORDS

A. PUBLICATIONS

1. The U.S. Department of Health and Human Services (www.hhs.gov) has issued a pamphlet obtainable through the Government Printing Office (online at www.access.gpo.gov) entitled *Where to Write for Vital Records: Births, Deaths, Marriages and Divorces*, which provides the address of each state's vital records office.
2. *American Jurisprudence 2d, Desk Book*. Rochester, St. Paul, MN: West Group.
3. Philo, Harry M., *Lawyer's Desk Reference*, 9th ed. St. Paul, MN: Thomson West, 2001.

B. ONLINE RESOURCES

1. GovDeathRecords (http://govdeathrecords.com/?tid=dr1).
2. National Association for Public Health Statistics and Information Systems (NAPHSIS) (www.naphsis.org).
3. U.S. Department of Health and Human Services (www.hhs.gov); Center for Disease Control and Prevention (www.cdc.gov); National Center for Health Statistics (www.cdc.gov/nchs/w2w.htm).
4. VitalChek (www.vitalchek.com). Links to state records offices.
5. WorldVitalRecords (www.worldvitalrecords.com/indexinfo.aspx?ix=ssdiall&kbid=1089&sub=DeathRecSocial).

Glossary

Active listening: Listening not just to record the exact words spoken, but to catch meanings as well, by observing body language of the speaker and by noticing things like voice inflection, volume, grammar, enunciation, and accent. See also *Body language*.

Administrative agency: See *Agency*.

Administrative law: The area of law dealing with administrative agencies and their functions. See also *Agency*; *Agency rule or regulation*; and *Enabling legislation*.

Administrative Procedures Act: A statute governing the procedures by which agency action may be challenged or appealed.

Admission by party opponent: Any statement made by or on behalf of a party to the suit, or which has been adopted by the party as true. Is admissible at trial if offered against that party.

Adversarial system of justice: The system that allows disputing parties who are unable to resolve the dispute themselves to present their dispute as adversaries or contestants before a court or tribunal empowered to resolve the dispute for them.

Affidavit: A sworn and signed statement. Also called a *declaration*.

Affirmative defense: A defense raised by a defendant in a civil or criminal action which, if proven, will cause the defendant to prevail over one or all the claims of the plaintiff or prosecution (e.g., statute of limitations, release, or assumption of risk in a civil case; insanity or privilege in a criminal prosecution). The defendant has the burden of proof on the affirmative defense. See also *Burden of proof*.

Agency: A governmental body created by state or federal legislation and charged with administering legislation in specific areas. Governmental agencies are engaged in rule making, investigation, and adjudication. See also *Administrative law*; *Agency rule or regulation*; and *Enabling legislation*.

Agency rule or regulation: A rule or regulation promulgated by a state or federal agency to carry out the administrative responsibility delegated to that agency by the legislative body that created the agency. See also *Agency*.

Agent: See *Principal-agent*.

Alternative dispute resolution (ADR): The process of resolving a legal dispute without pursuing litigation. Most popular forms of ADR are negotiation, mediation, and arbitration. See also *Arbitration*; *Mediation*; and *Negotiation*.

American Association for Justice (AAJ): Prominent private organization for plaintiff's lawyers. See *Defense Research Institute.*

American Bar Association (ABA): The largest and most prominent national organization of lawyers in the United States.

Arbitration: A process in which disputing parties agree to submit their dispute to a disinterested person (or panel of persons) other than a judge or jury. The arbitrator(s) will listen to both sides and then render a decision which may be binding or non-binding depending on the agreement of the parties or a controlling statute. See also *Alternative dispute resolution; Mediation;* and *Negotiation.*

Attorney-client privilege: An evidentiary privilege preventing the disclosure in a court or other formal proceeding, without the client's consent, of confidential communications between the attorney and client related to the matter in which the client is represented by the attorney; also the broader duty of the attorney to not disclose, without the client's consent or for any purpose, the confidences and secrets of the client.

Authentication: Establishing that a document, object, or voice to be offered in evidence at trial is genuine, i.e., it is in fact what it purports to be. See also *Chain of custody.*

Bail: Money or property with a certain monetary value posted with a criminal court clerk to assure the presence of a criminal defendant at trial; forfeited if defendant fails to appear; entitlement to governed by Eighth Amendment to U.S. Constitution.

Bail Reform Act of 1984: Federal statute empowering trial judge in criminal prosecution to deny defendant bail and order pretrial detention if there is good reason to believe defendant will flee or pose a threat to persons in the community.

Bench trial: A trial conducted without a jury. See also *Jury trial.*

Bias: Any reason a witness might have to favor or disfavor one side or another in a dispute; used to impeach a witness. See also *Impeaching a witness; Interest.*

Bill of particulars: A disclosure the prosecution makes in a criminal case, upon request by the defendant and order of the court, the purpose of which is to make general allegations contained in the indictment or information more specific.

Body language: A person's posture, gestures, facial expressions, eye contact, clothes, or environment that communicate information to others.

***Brady* doctrine:** Rule based on Supreme Court case of *Brady v. Maryland* requiring the prosecution in both state and federal proceedings to provide to the defense all exculpatory evidence in its possession, custody, or control.

Burden of proof: The obligation imposed on the party asserting a civil cause of action against another or an affirmative defense to such a cause of action, and on the government in a criminal prosecution and on the criminal defendant asserting an affirmative defense to such criminal prosecution, to prove all of the necessary elements of the cause of action or affirmative defense asserted by the requisite degree of proof. See also *Affirmative defense; Cause of action; Civil law; Criminal law;* and *Degree of proof.*

Business records: Records in written or electronic form of a business's activities that are maintained in the ordinary course of the business's operations; such records are admissible in court over a hearsay objection. See also *Hearsay; Records custodian.*

Canvass: In investigating, the physical inspection of the scene of an incident which normally includes locating and interviewing persons nearby as to their knowledge of the incident.

Cause of action: In the civil law, a recognized theory of liability on which one party may sue another. For example, negligence, breach of contract, etc.

Chain of custody: Establishing the continuous custody of an object to be offered in evidence at trial from the time of a relevant incident until trial; part of the required authentication of some items of evidence. See also *Laying the foundation; Evidence log.*

Chinese wall: See *Invisible wall.*

Circumstantial evidence: Indirect evidence that requires an inference to accept as true.

City-county directory: A publication of many cities and counties setting out individual and business names, addresses, and phone numbers in a reverse directory format. See also *Reverse directory.*

Civil law: The area of the law dealing with the determination and enforcement of all private or public rights, essentially all law that is not a criminal matter. Civil disputes involve claims between persons that one has engaged in conduct injurious to the person, property, or personal rights of the other as, for example, in the areas of torts, contracts, civil and constitutional rights, business associations, and real property. Rules of civil procedure govern the civil process. See also *Criminal law.*

Closed-ended questions: Questions that call for a specific, narrow answer that requires few words and little or no explanation.

Code of Federal Regulations (CFR): Official publication of the U.S. government containing the current federal regulations for each federal agency and department.

Colloquialisms: Words or phrases which are used incorrectly but which have gained widespread use in informal conversation. See also *Idioms*.

Common law: A court decision in a contested case creating a precedent in the jurisdiction. See also *Agency rule or regulation*; *Court rule*; and *Statute*.

Compensatory damages: Money damages sought in a civil lawsuit which *compensate* the plaintiff or make the plaintiff whole. Compensatory damages may be general (compensation for pain and suffering) or specific (out-of-pocket expenses such as medical bills, lost wages, etc.).

Conflict of interest: Anything that compromises or which could reasonably appear to compromise the objectivity or loyalty of the attorney or paralegal to the client.

Congressional Record: Official publication of the U.S. government containing the official proceedings of the Congress.

Consulting expert: See *Expert*.

Consumer Financial Protection Bureau: New federal watchdog agency given broad authority to regulate businesses providing consumers with financial services. See *Dodd-Frank Wall Street Reform Act of 2010*.

Contingency agreement: A type of fee agreement in which the attorney agrees to take a designated percentage, usually a third, of what is recovered for the client as a fee for services.

Court rule: A rule of procedure or practice adopted by a federal or state court. See also *Agency rule or regulation*; *Common law*; and *Statute*.

Credit report: See *Credit reporting agencies*.

Credit reporting agencies: Companies that collect and disseminate information for a fee on the credit history and creditworthiness of individuals; currently the three largest are *Equifax, Trans Union*, and *Experian*. The information is disseminated as a *credit report*.

Criminal law: The area of the law dealing with prosecution by the state or federal government of persons accused of violating societal laws codified in criminal statutes that allow the government to seek punishment by fine or imprisonment or both. Criminal statutes are typically classified as crimes against the person, crimes against property, and crimes against the public. Rules of criminal procedure govern the prosecution process. See also *Civil law*.

Criss-cross directory: See *Reverse directory*.

Cross examination: The questioning of a witness at trial by attorneys who did not call that witness to testify; cross examination follows the direct examination of that witness; leading questions may be used. See also *Direct examination; Leading questions*.

Curriculum vitae: A person's written *resume* or *biography* setting forth his business or professional qualifications and accomplishments.

Database vendors: Commercial businesses that make various libraries of information and search engines available for subscribers. LexisNexis and Westlaw are the two best known. Such vendors accessible to subscribers online are called *online database vendors*.

Data mining: The discovery of metadata within *electronically stored information*.

Daubert hearing: A pretrial hearing conducted by a trial judge acting as gatekeeper to determine the qualifications of a proffered expert witness and the admissibility of his or her opinions in evidence.

Declaration: See *Affidavit*.

Declaratory judgment: A judgment sought from a court that will declare the rights of the parties in some property or situation; a type of equitable relief. See also *Equitable relief; Injunction;* and *Legal remedy*.

Defendant: The party who is sued in a civil lawsuit. The party who is prosecuted by the government in a criminal prosecution. See also *Plaintiff*.

Defense Research Institute (DRI): Prominent private organization for plaintiff's lawyers. See *American Association for Justice*.

Degree of proof: The extent to which a party having the burden of proof in a civil lawsuit or criminal prosecution must convince the finder of fact in order to prevail; the most common are (1) by a preponderance of the evidence; (2) by clear and convincing evidence; and (3) beyond a reasonable doubt.

Demonstrative evidence: Evidence in the form of properly admitted charts, graphs, diagrams, etc. that illustrate something for the court. See also *Documentary evidence; Real evidence;* and *Testimonial evidence*.

Deposition: A type of formal discovery authorized by Federal Rules of Civil Procedure 27–32, and analogous state rules of civil procedure, in which a lawyer asks questions of a party or witness (the deponent) who answers under oath. See also *Interrogatories; Request for production of documents and things;* and *Requests for admissions*.

Deposition summary or **index:** A summary of the transcript of a deposition and arranged by subject matter, selected topic, chronology, or narrative.

Direct examination: Questioning of a witness by the attorney who called the witness to testify; normally leading questions cannot be used. See also *Cross examination; Leading questions*.

Discovery plan: Plan agreed to by attorneys at beginning of a case dealing with deadlines for discovery and other issues related to trial preparation; often incorporated into scheduling order.

Docket control system: A law office system pursuant to which all deadlines are calendared and responsible persons in the office reminded (tickled) as a deadline approaches.

Documentary sources: In investigating, documents that are sources of information whether public records, business records, medical records, educational records, employment records, or personal records.

Document production: See *Request for production of documents and things.*

Documentary evidence: Evidence received from properly admitted documents. See also *Demonstrative evidence; Real evidence;* and *Testimonial evidence.*

Dodd-Frank Wall Street Reform Act of 2010: A federal act reinstating some regulation of Wall Street financial transactions and creating the Consumer Financial Protection Bureau.

Due Process: Mandate for and guarantee of procedural and substantive fairness from government when it acts to deprive any person of life, liberty, or property. Found in Fifth and Fourteenth Amendments to the U.S. Constitution.

EDGAR: The Electronic Data Gathering Analysis and Retrieval system operated by the Securities Exchange Commission allows the accessing and copying of filings by publicly traded companies.

E-discovery: The discovery by formal discovery or informal investigation of information stored electronically, such as e-mail messages or computer files.

E-Government Act of 2002: A federal statute (found at 44 U.S.C. §§3601 et seq.) intended to make more information held by federal agencies available on the Internet.

Electronic filing: A procedure for electronically filing pleadings, discovery, motions, and other documents with a court; paperless filing.

Electronically stored information (ESI): Data that is stored in computer memory or on hard drive or disk.

E-mail: Mail sent electronically by computer.

Empathy: The capacity to participate in another's feelings.

Enabling legislation: In agency law, the statute that created and controls the agency. See also *Agency*; *Agency rule or regulation*; and *Administrative law*.

Equitable relief: A type of remedy sought primarily in civil lawsuits that is based on what is fair and just rather than on what the plaintiff is legally entitled to. Two of the most common forms are injunctive relief and declaratory judgment. See also *Declaratory judgment*; *Injunction*; and *Legal remedy*.

Evidence log: A paper or computerized record of all items of potential evidence accumulated in a case.

Exculpatory evidence: Evidence tending to show that a criminal accused is innocent. See also, *Brady doctrine*.

Exemplary damages: See *Punitive damages*.

Expert: One qualified by knowledge, skill, experience, training, or education to have more knowledge on a topic than one not so qualified. When an expert testifies at trial they become an *expert witness*. An expert who consults with an attorney on a case but does not testify is a *consulting expert*. An expert specially retained to testify in a case is a *retained expert*; one who testifies but is not specially retained to do so is a *non-retained expert*. See also *Lay witness*.

Explanatory question: A question that asks the person to explain an answer or expound further on it.

Factual analysis: A critical thinking skill; the process of taking information, making sure that you understand it, evaluating it in order to determine if it is reliable, and then applying it to determine the impact or difference it makes on your legal question.

Fair Credit Reporting Act: A federal statute, found at 15 U.S.C. §§1681 et seq., which regulates credit reporting agencies and the use of credit reports. See also *Credit reporting agencies*.

Federal Courts Jurisdiction and Venue Clarification Act of 2011: Federal legislation mandating changes to timing and procedure for removal of a case to federal court based on diversity of citizenship. See also *Subject matter jurisdiction*.

Federal Financial Modernization Act: Federal statute commonly known as the Gramm-Leach-Bliley Act found at 15 U.S.C. §§6801 et seq., which regulates the disclosure of non-public information on consumers by financial institutions.

Federal Register: Official daily publication of the U.S. government, containing information regarding the status of proposed new or amended regulations.

Federalism: The division of power between the U.S. government and the various state governments.

Fee agreement: The agreement between an attorney and a client that sets out how the attorney is to be paid. Typical types include the hourly rate plus expenses agreement, the flat fee agreement, and the contingency fee agreement. See also *Contingency agreement.*

Felony: A crime punishable by more than one year in jail. See also *Misdemeanor.*

Fiduciary duty: The high duty of care, competence, trust, loyalty, and confidentiality that the attorney and paralegal owe to the client.

Field interview: An interview conducted outside the interviewer's office.

Finder of fact: In a trial the person(s) charged with deciding contested issues of fact based on the evidence presented at trial. In a jury trial the jury is the finder of fact. In a bench trial it is the trial judge. See also *Bench trial.*

Formal discovery: Discovery governed by rules 26–37 of the rules of the federal or state civil procedure or by applicable rules of federal or state criminal procedure. Such discovery, with very limited exceptions, occurs after a civil lawsuit has been filed or a formal criminal prosecution begun, and requires notice to and the right to participation by all parties to the lawsuit or their legal representatives. See also *Informal investigation.*

Freedom of Information Act (FOIA): Federal statute found at 5 U.S.C. §552 that allows anyone to access certain files, documents, records, and other information in the possession of federal government agencies. See also *Open records acts; Privacy Act.*

Fundamental right: In constitutional law, a right deemed essential to an ordered liberty.

Gramm-Leach-Bliley Act: See *Federal Financial Modernization Act.*

Grand jury: A group usually consisting of 16 to 23 people selected from the community to hear evidence of alleged criminal conduct and having the power to issue an indictment based on a finding of probable cause.

Header information: In the information brokerage trade, personal or financial information about consumers and businesses collected and organized in various ways to make it more usable, e.g., by geographic region, age, gender, education level, income level, trade or profession, then sold to merchandisers wishing to solicit such individuals or businesses. See also *Information broker.*

Hearsay: A statement, other than the one made by the declarant (the one making the statement) while testifying at the trial or hearing (i.e., an out-of-court statement) and offered in evidence to prove the truth of the matter asserted. Hearsay statements are inadmissible at trial unless a recognized exception is found.

Hearsay exceptions: Rules that allow out of court statements to be received in evidence for their truth notwithstanding a hearsay objection. Major exceptions include admission by party opponent, prior inconsistent statement made under oath, prior statement identifying a person after perceiving them, declarations of declarant's state of mind, present sense impressions, business records, dying declarations, excited utterances, former testimony, and statements against declarant's interest.

Homeland Security Act of 2002: A federal statute, found at 6 U.S.C. §§101 et seq., that dramatically consolidates a number of federal agencies and agency functions into a single federal agency.

Hypothetical questions: Questions that ask the client to assume some set of facts on which to premise an answer.

Idioms: A phrase having a meaning different from the literal meaning of the words themselves; established by common usage. See also *Colloquialisms*.

Immunity: Being free of the threat of criminal prosecution; normally granted by the government. Includes *transactional immunity*, which is full immunity from prosecution on all charges related to the witness's testimony, and *use immunity*, which prohibits the government from using the witness's testimony or any evidence derived from it to prosecute the witness but not evidence independently obtained. See also *Privileges; Self-incrimination*.

Impeaching a witness: Attacking the credibility of a witness, usually by showing bias or interest.

Indemnity: A legal doctrine pursuant to which one found to be legally responsible for an obligation is able to place the obligation on another either pursuant to a contract between the parties (contractual indemnity) or to the nature of the relationship between the parties (implied indemnity), e.g., as between principal and agent. See also *Principal-agent*.

Indictment: The formal charge issued by the grand jury in a criminal prosecution.

Informal investigation: Private factual investigation that may be undertaken by an attorney on behalf of a client either before or after a lawsuit is commenced and which need not follow the formal rules set forth in the rules of civil or criminal procedure. See also *Formal discovery*.

Information: The formal charging instrument filed by prosecutors in a criminal prosecution.

Information broker: A company, sometimes called an information wholesaler, in the business of collecting header information on individuals or businesses and selling it to those wishing to solicit those individuals or businesses. See also *Header information*.

Injunction: A court order directing a party to do or refrain from doing something; a type of equitable relief. See also *Declaratory judgment*; *Equitable relief*; and *Legal remedy*.

Intake sheet: A pre-printed checklist of questions used in a new client interview.

Interest: Any self-serving reason a witness might have to not be objective in her testimony; used to discredit a witness. See also *Bias*; *Impeaching a witness*.

Interrogatories: A method of formal discovery pursuant to which written questions are submitted by one party to another which must be answered in writing and under oath by the party being interrogated. See also *Deposition*; *Document request*; and *Request for admissions*.

Interview summary: A written summary of an interview.

Invisible wall: A set of procedures established in a law office to ensure that a designated person in the office, due to a real or potential conflict of interest, will not view files related to a particular legal matter or otherwise become involved in it; sometimes called a *Chinese wall*.

Jencks Act: Federal statute found at 18 U.S.C. §3500 that requires the prosecution to provide the defense, upon request, with prior written or recorded statements of witnesses after they have testified.

Judgment proof: Description of a defendant who has insufficient assets to pay any judgment that may be rendered against him.

Jury trial: A trial conducted in the presence of a trial judge with a jury present to serve as the finder of fact.

Lay witness: A witness who is not an expert. See also *Expert*.

Laying the foundation: Establishing a required factual basis as a prerequisite for the admission of certain evidence; often involving showing a chain of custody or genuineness. See also *Authentication*; *Chain of custody*.

Leading questions: Questions which call for a yes or no response.

Legal assistant: A paralegal. See also *Paralegal.*

Legal malpractice: When an attorney breaches the fiduciary duty owed to a client in a material way. See also *Professional malpractice.*

Legal remedy: The relief that a plaintiff in a civil lawsuit is entitled to by law, usually measured in money damages. See *Compensatory damages; Equitable relief;* and *Punitive damages.*

Legal services agreement: See *Fee agreement.*

Legally relevant: Information that matters, impacts, or makes a difference on the legal issues being considered.

LexisNexis: A leading commercial database vendor. See also *Database vendor; Westlaw.*

Limiting instruction: An instruction given by a trial judge to a jury to consider evidence for one purpose but not another.

Litigation hold: The duty to preserve information and records in any format, including electronic, when it reasonably appears that there may be litigation to which such information and records may be relevant.

Long-arm statute: A state statute that sets forth the factual criteria for determining when a non-resident defendant has sufficient minimum contacts with a forum state to satisfy due process and justify the assertion of personal jurisdiction. See also *Minimum contacts rule; Personal jurisdiction.*

Mediation: The process of attempting to resolve a legal dispute by using a neutral third party (the mediator) who acts as a communicator between the disputing parties, listening to both sides, trying to get both sides to be reasonable and realistic with a goal of helping the parties reach a voluntary settlement that both feel is fair. See also *Alternative dispute resolution; Arbitration;* and *Negotiation.*

Metadata: Data stored on electronic documents that describes other data including formatting information and edited content.

Minimum contacts rule: In civil procedure the requirement that a defendant have sufficient connections with the forum state such that maintenance of the suit does not offend traditional notions of fair play and substantial justice. See also *Long-Arm statute; Personal Jurisdiction.*

Misdemeanor: A crime punishable by up to a year in jail. See also *Felony.*

Motion: An oral or written application made by a party to a lawsuit to the court asking for some kind of relief.

Motion *in limine*: A pretrial motion requesting the court to prior order a party to not question a witness about certain matters or to not allow a witness to mention certain inadmissible things while testifying.

Motion to compel discovery: Motion made by a party seeking an order compelling another party to provide discovery. Compare *Protective order*.

Motion to suppress evidence (sometimes called a **motion to exclude evidence**): A pretrial motion used in a criminal prosecution asking the court to act before trial to disallow the admission of some evidence by the opponent.

Multiple-choice questions: Questions that invite the person to choose among two or more options offered by the interviewer.

National Association of Legal Assistants (NALA): A leading national organization for those working as paralegals or legal assistants.

National Federation of Paralegal Associations (NFPA): A leading national organization for local and state organizations of persons working as paralegals or legal assistants.

Negotiation: The process by which the adverse parties, either before or during the litigation process, meet or talk informally, usually through their attorneys, to try and work out a compromise settlement to resolve the dispute. See also *Alternative dispute resolution*; *Arbitration*; and *Mediation*.

Netiquette: Rules of etiquette for communicating by e-mail.

Nonverbal communication: The impression we convey to others by body language. See also *Body language*.

Nonwaiver agreement: Agreement made by parties to litigation stipulating that privileged information inadvertently produced in discovery will be returned and the privilege not be waived. Also called *clawback* or *quick peek* agreements.

Notice pleading: Old federal standard for adequacy of pleading in a civil case requiring only that pleading be sufficient to put opposing party on notice of the cause of action defense being alleged. Still the standard under most state rules of civil pleading. Compare *Plausibility pleading*.

Online database vendor: See *Database vendors*.

Open data site: A Web site where data are posted for anyone to access and use without restriction.

Open-ended questions: Questions that encourage the witness to provide a narrative of events or a detailed explanation in his or her answer.

Open Government Act of 2007: Federal act amending the FOIA to require agencies to provide more information to support assertion of privilege and authorizing the award of attorney's fees to those prevailing in a compliance suit. See *Freedom of Information Act*

Open records acts: See *Public records acts.*

Opinion questions: Questions that ask the person to express an opinion about something or even to speculate.

Organization of Legal Professionals (OLP): Organization of legal and other professionals involved with electronic discovery.

PACER: The Public Access to Court Electronic Records is a system created and administered by the Administrative Office of the U.S. Courts that allows any subscriber to dial in by modem to a particular federal district or bankruptcy court clerk's office and quickly retrieve case information and dockets.

Paralegal: A person qualified by education, training, or work experience who is employed or retained by a lawyer, law office, corporation, governmental agency, or other entity and who performs specifically delegated substantive legal work for which a lawyer is responsible. Also referred to as *legal assistant.*

Personal jurisdiction (also called *in personam* **jurisdiction**): Legal doctrine dealing with the power of a court to enter an order binding on a particular defendant. See also *Long-arm statute; Subject matter jurisdiction.*

Plaintiff: The party that initiates a civil lawsuit against another. The government in a criminal prosecution. See also *Defendant.*

Plan of investigation: The written plan made by an investigator before undertaking a factual investigation.

Plausibility pleading: New federal standard for adequacy of pleading in a civil case requiring that pleading stating cause of action or defense allege sufficient specific facts to survive motion to dismiss without further discovery. See *Notice pleading.*

Police powers: fundamental responsibility of state and local governments to provide for the health, safety, and welfare of their citizens.

Preservation letter: Formal notification given by one party to a potential legal dispute to other parties that all documents, electronic records, and things relevant to the dispute should be preserved.

Pressure questions: Questions that challenge the interviewee directly or indirectly and compel a response involving emotion or feeling as well as fact.

Pretext calling: An unscrupulous tactic used by some information brokers and private investigators whereby the caller pretends to be someone he or she is not in order to obtain financial or other information on the target.

Principal-agent: Legal doctrine recognizing that one person (agent) may be acting on behalf of another (principal) in such a way that the principal is legally bound by the actions of the agent. See also *Respondeat superior; Vicarious liability.*

Privacy Act: A federal statute found at 5 U.S.C. §552(a) that allows an individual to obtain access to certain information maintained by federal agencies about themselves. See also *Freedom of Information Act; Open records acts.*

Private sources of information: Information of any kind that is in the possession of private individuals, businesses, educational institutions, or any other non-governmental custodian. See also *Public sources of information.*

Privileges: An area of the law that declares that certain information should not be subject to disclosure in informal investigation, formal discovery, or in sworn testimony at trial. Examples include the attorney-client privilege, physician-patient privilege, spousal privilege, the spousal testimonial privilege and the spousal communication privilege. See also *Self-incrimination; Work product.*

Privilege and Immunities Clause: Provision in the Fourteenth Amendment to the U.S. Constitution requiring states to provide their citizens with all the rights they enjoy by virtue of being U.S. citizens.

Probable cause: A more likely than not standard used in preliminary stages of criminal procedure to justify issuance of an arrest or search warrant and for holding a defendant over for trial on the criminal charge.

Procedural law: The law that defines the manner in which substantive legal rights and duties may be enforced. Examples of substantive law include constitutional law, contract law, the law of business associations, tort law, criminal law, real property law, and so on. See also *Substantive law.*

Professional malpractice: When an attorney breaches the fiduciary duty owed to a client in a material way. See also *Legal malpractice.*

Protective order: Order issued by a trial judge protecting a party from abusive or unauthorized discovery. Compare *Motion to compel discovery.*

Public Records Acts: State statutes allowing access to information held by state and local governments. Also called open records acts. See also *Freedom of Information Act; Privacy Act.*

Public sources of information: Information of any kind that is in the possession of a federal, state, or local agency or department. See also *Private sources of information.*

Punitive damages: Damages (sometimes called *exemplary damages*) sought in a civil action which are meant to "punish" the wrongdoer for his conduct rather than to compensate the plaintiff. See also *Compensatory damages; Exemplary damages.*

Real evidence: Evidence (also called *physical evidence*) in the form of properly admitted objects (e.g., the weapon in a murder case). See also *Demonstrative evidence; Documentary evidence;* and *Testimonial evidence.*

Records authorizations: Written authorizations allowing attorneys or others to obtain the medical, educational, or employment records of another.

Records custodian: The person designated as the custodian of records by a business or government agency; the proper person to testify as an authenticating witness for such records. See also *Authentication; Business records.*

Request for admissions: A method of formal discovery in a civil lawsuit pursuant to which one party requests the opposing party to admit the truth of some factual allegation of a document or thing. See also *Deposition; Interrogatories; Request for production of documents and things;* and *Request for physical or mental examination.*

Request for physical or mental examination: A method of formal discovery in a civil lawsuit pursuant to which one party requests that the court order the opposing party or a witness to undergo a physical or mental examination. See also *Deposition; Interrogatories; Request for production of documents and things;* and *Request for admissions.*

Request for production of documents and things: A method of formal discovery pursuant to which a party to a civil lawsuit requests the other party to the lawsuit to produce documents or tangible things for inspection, copying, or testing, and the entry on land or property for inspection and testing. See also *Deposition; Interrogatory; Request for admissions;* and *Request for physical or mental examination.*

Respondeat superior (Latin for "Let the master respond"): When legal responsibility is placed on one party for the acts of another. See also *Vicarious liability.*

Retainer: An advance payment made by a client to an attorney. See also *Fee agreement.*

Reverse directory: A written or electronic directory maintained by many local communities that lists residences and businesses first by street address, then again by telephone numbers numerically.

Rules of appellate procedure: Body of rules that govern the filing and processing of an appeal of a court ruling to a higher court in a civil lawsuit or a criminal prosecution in state or federal court.

Rules of civil procedure: Body of rules that govern the filing and processing of a civil lawsuit in the federal or state courts.

Rules of criminal procedure: Body of rules that govern the filing and processing of a criminal prosecution in the federal or state courts.

Rules of evidence: Body of rules that govern the admission and exclusion of proof before the court in the trial of civil and criminal cases.

Scheduling order: Order entered at beginning of a case by trial judge setting deadlines for discovery and other trial preparation activities. See also *Discovery plan.*

Search company: A company that, for a fee, will search federal, state, and local records.

Self-incrimination: Admitting to criminal activity by one's self. The Fifth Amendment to the U.S. Constitution grants individuals a privilege against being compelled to testify if such testimony would tend to self-incriminate the speaker. See also *Immunity; Privilege.*

Sequestration. The practice of keeping non-party witnesses out of the courtroom until they testify so they cannot hear the testimony of other witnesses.

Simultaneous representation: The legal representation by an attorney of more than one party in a single legal matter; often the origin of a real or potential conflict of interest. See also *Conflict of interest.*

Skip-tracing: The activity of locating a missing person; often performed for a fee by private investigators and other businesses.

Slang: Words or phrases used to mean something other than their standard definition; sometimes referred to as *street talk.*

Spoliation of evidence: The material change or disposal of evidence relevant to a dispute that is being or may be litigated; subject to harsh sanctions such as waiver of claim or defense, payment of attorneys fees, adverse inference jury instruction, or even default judgment.

Statement against interest: A statement made against the speaker's pecuniary (money), proprietary (ownership), or culpability (civil or criminal) interests. Admissible at trial as an exception to the hearsay rule.

Statute: An act of the U.S. Congress or a state legislature. See also *Agency rule or regulation; Common law;* and *Court rule.*

Statute of limitation: A statute stating the time in which a lawsuit must be commenced against a defendant or be forever barred.

Statute of repose: A statute that places an absolute limit on the time in which a lawsuit must be commenced against a defendant without regard to when the cause of action arose.

Subject matter jurisdiction: Legal doctrine dealing with the question of the power of a court to hear a particular kind of case. In federal court limited in civil cases to federal question, diversity of citizenship, supplemental, or removal jurisdiction. See also *Personal jurisdiction.*

Subpoena: A document issued by the court clerk ordering a person to appear at a deposition or trial. A subpoena that compels the production of documents or things at a deposition or trial is called a *subpoena duces tecum.*

Substantive law: The law that defines the rights and duties of persons with respect to each other. See *Procedural law,* which defines the manner in which those rights and duties may be enforced. Examples of substantive law include constitutional law, contract law, the law of business associations, tort law, criminal law, real property law, and so on.

Telephone interview: An interview conducted over the telephone rather than in person.

Testimonial evidence: Evidence received from the sworn testimony of witnesses. See also *Demonstrative evidence; Documentary evidence;* and *Real evidence.*

Time line: A drawing made by a witness showing the chronology of events.

Trust accounts: Bank accounts established by attorneys in which the funds of clients or third parties are deposited.

Unauthorized practice of law: Practicing law without a license.

United States Government Manual: Official publication of the U.S. government containing basic who, what, and where information on the federal government and its agencies.

Venue: A legal doctrine dealing with the most appropriate geographic location (county or federal district) for the case to be heard.

Vicarious liability: Legal doctrine placing legal responsibility on one person for the acts of another. See also *Respondeat superior.*

Vital statistics: Records maintained by local and state governments including information and certificates for births, deaths, marriages, and divorces.

Westlaw: A leading commercial database vendor. See also *Database vendor*; *LexisNexis*.

Witness statement: The written statement of a witness taken or made during or following an interview.

Work product: Material containing the mental impressions, conclusions, opinions, or legal theories of an attorney or other representative of a party concerning the litigation; normally subject to an absolute privilege.

Index

Table of Cases

CPSIA information can be obtained at www.ICGtesting.com
Printed in the USA
BVOW06s2100291113

337557BV00004B/6/P